A Companion to Russian History

BLACKWELL COMPANIONS TO HISTORY

This series provides sophisticated and authoritative overviews of the scholarship that has shaped our current understanding of the past. Defined by theme, period and/or region, each volume comprises between twenty-five and forty concise essays written by individual scholars within their area of specialization. The aim of each contribution is to synthesize the current state of scholarship from a variety of historical perspectives and to provide a statement on where the field is heading. The essays are written in a clear, provocative, and lively manner, designed for an international audience of scholars, students, and general readers.

A COMPANION TO RUSSIAN HISTORY

Edited by

Abbott Gleason

A John Wiley & Sons, Ltd., Publication

This edition first published 2009
© 2009 Blackwell Publishing Ltd

Blackwell Publishing was acquired by John Wiley & Sons in February 2007. Blackwell's publishing program has been merged with Wiley's global Scientific, Technical, and Medical business to form Wiley-Blackwell.

Registered Office
John Wiley & Sons Ltd, The Atrium, Southern Gate, Chichester, West Sussex, PO19 8SQ, United Kingdom

Editorial Offices
350 Main Street, Malden, MA 02148-5020, USA
9600 Garsington Road, Oxford, OX4 2DQ, UK
The Atrium, Southern Gate, Chichester, West Sussex, PO19 8SQ, UK

For details of our global editorial offices, for customer services, and for information about how to apply for permission to reuse the copyright material in this book please see our website at www.wiley.com/wiley-blackwell.

The right of Abbott Gleason to be identified as the author of the editorial material in this work has been asserted in accordance with the Copyright, Designs and Patents Act 1988.

Library of Congress Cataloging-in-Publication Data

A companion to Russian history / edited by Abbott Gleason. – 1st ed.
p.   cm.
Includes bibliographical references and index.
ISBN 978-1-4051-3560-3 (hardcover : alk. paper)   1. Russia–History.   2. Soviet Union–History
3. Russia (Federation)–History.   I. Gleason, Abbott.
  DK40.C66 2009
  947–dc22

                              2008032173

A catalogue record for this book is available from the British Library.

Set in 10/12pt Galliard by SNP Best-set Typesetter Ltd., Hong Kong
Printed in Singapore by Ho Printing Pte Ltd
01   2009

In Memoriam

Daniel Field, Lindsey Hughes, William Odom

Distinguished Colleagues

Contents

Notes on Contributors

Paul Barford is the author of *The Early Slavs: Culture and Society in Early Medieval Eastern Europe*. He lives in Warsaw.

Robert V. Daniels is an Emeritus Professor of History at the University of Vermont.

Ilia A. Dorontchenkov teaches Russian and European art at the European University in St Petersburg, where he is also Dean of the Faculty of Arts.

Christopher Ely is an Associate Professor of History at the Wilkes Honors College of Florida Atlantic University.

David C. Engerman is Associate Professor of History at Brandeis University.

Robert English is an Associate Professor of International Relations at the University of Southern California.

The late **Daniel Field** was a Professor of History Emeritus at Syracuse.

Robert Geraci is an Associate Professor of History at the University of Virginia.

Abbott Gleason is Keeney Professor of History Emeritus at Brown University.

Mark von Hagen is Professor of History and department chair at Arizona State University.

Richard Hellie is the Thomas E. Donnelly Professor of History at the University of Chicago.

The late **Lindsey Hughes** was Professor of Russian History at the School of Slavonic and East European Studies, University College, London.

Nadieszda Kizenko is Associate Professor of History at the State University of New York at Albany.

Nancy Shields Kollmann is the Director of the Center for Russian, East European and Eurasian Studies at Stanford University, where she holds the William H. Bonsal Chair in History.

Nikita Lomagin is an Associate Professor in the Economics Faculty at the University of St Petersburg and Director of its Baltic Research Center.

Louise McReynolds is a Professor of History at the University of North Carolina, Chapel Hill.

George Majeska is Professor Emeritus at the University of Maryland, College Park.

Gary Marker is Professor of History at the State University of New York, Stony Brook.

Janet Martin is Professor of History at the University of Miami.

Gary Saul Morson is the Frances Hooper Professor of Arts and Humanities and Professor Slavic Languages at Northwestern University.

The late **Lieutenant General William E. Odom** (US Army, Ret.) was a Senior Fellow at the Hudson Institute and a Fellow at Berkeley College, Yale University.

Donald Ostrowski is a Faculty Associate at the Davis Center for Russian and Eurasian Studies, Harvard University.

Thomas C. Owen was Katheryn, Lewis and Benjamin Price Professor at Louisiana State University and is now an Associate of the Davis Center for Russian and Eurasian Studies at Harvard University.

Bruce Parrott is Professor and Director of the Russian and Eurasian Studies Program at the Paul H. Nitze School of Advanced International Studies, Johns Hopkins University.

Melissa Stockdale is Associate Professor of History and Coordinator of Russian and East European Studies at the University of Oklahoma.

Lynne Viola is Professor of History at the University of Toronto.

Andrew Wachtel is the Bertha and Max Dressler Professor of the Humanities and the Dean of the Graduate School at Northwestern University.

Elizabeth A. Wood is Professor of History and Director of Women's Studies at the Massachusetts Institute of Technology.

CHAPTER ONE

Russian Historiography after the Fall

Abbott Gleason

These essays are being written and published at a significant moment in Russia's long and difficult history: almost twenty years after the end of the Soviet Union, at the end of the successive presidential terms of the man who has sometimes been called "Tsar Putin."This not very clever moniker nevertheless forms part of the thematic of this period: Russia's attempted recovery of its connection to the imperial past. Another aspect of this historical moment is the Russian leadership's aspiration to recover some portion of the geopolitical (if not ideological) power and influence achieved by the Soviet Union, as we see in the adventure involving Russia and Georgia now (autumn, 2008) unfolding in the Caucasus.

A discussion of the plausibility of the American policy of pushing NATO right up to the Russian border would take us too far afield, but it seems clear that Russia has probably suffered the worst of the inevitable pangs stemming from loss of empire, not to speak of the difficult transition between the decadence of Communism and its replacement by an authoritarian and rather predatory capitalism.[1] Inequality has increased dramatically, but economic productivity is beginning to do the same. Much, but not all, of the old elite managed to hang on to some power during the transition to the new system through a kind of Russian-style insider trading. Remarkably enough, the extremely difficult, indeed chaotic transition was accomplished with an absolute minimum of bloodshed, for which the world will remain grateful to Mikhail Gorbachev far into the future.[2] But, as the late Lieutenant General William Odom (The Hudson Institute and Yale University) points out in the concluding chapter of this volume, Russia today remains – despite the defeat of Communism – very much under the spell of its own deep past.[3]

The end of the cold war and the difficulties that Russia has faced in its post-Soviet incarnation have had a powerful impact on how the course of Russian history is coming to be understood. What is the current status of history writing about Russia, inside and outside the country, and what will it look like going forward? On the one hand, the old and complex sense of Russia's differences from "the West" is likely to remain, if somewhat softened with respect to how central to Russia's identity these differences are judged to be by outsiders. Many insiders will continue to speak of

Russia's special kind of democracy and non-Western identity. But commentators operating in today's global world – politicians, journalists, and academics – are even more likely to treat Russia's differences as failures (as they often have before), as well as to make Russia and Russian history a slightly more provincial and unedifying part of humanity's story, now that the mega-states of the twentieth century are history.

The global world into which the new Russia is now moving is quite different from what it was like during the cold war.[4] Russia's limited economic revival takes place between two economic powerhouses: the European Union and China. Russia, still relatively poor and now bereft of empire, is surely far less of a threat to the neighbors than it was in Soviet times. The Soviet experience will never lose its significance, but for a time now it is likely to be seen more as a gigantic cautionary tale than as a danger to the world. It will be a long time before the possibility of massive violence in the service of *class* (as opposed to religious, confessional or national) conflict re-emerges as a possible instrument of policy in a major state.

The history of the failure of "the Soviet experiment" is surely one of the major themes of the history of the past century, along with the rise and fall of German National Socialism and the emergence – for how long one cannot say – of the global hegemony of the United States.[5] The demise of the Soviet Union diminishes our sense of the possible forms of modernity that can exist in the world today, in a way that is generally welcome. Hypertrophic statism is for now at least not viable in our global world; if anything, the reverse is true. Weak and failed states are almost certainly a greater danger to the world, and Russia in the 1990s changed almost overnight from an apparently extremely strong state into a weak one, a possibility foreseen long ago by George Kennan.[6] But Russia is now engaged in a protracted effort to recover as much as possible of its former authoritarian centralization, only this time around taking account of the market and economic globalization. Does Vladimir Putin dream of donning the mantle of Peter the Great? Whatever he and his successors may accomplish, the change from Soviet to post-Soviet will remain central. Nevertheless, much of Russia's burdensome past still looms large; democracy is still far away and corruption and criminal behavior are apparent to any serious observer.

To take up the stated purpose of this book, the end of the cold war and the collapse of the Soviet Union have made and are continuing to make a very significant difference in the writing of Russian history. This is true in the obvious ways. Imperial Russian history will not in the future be read to anything like the same degree as a run-up to the Russian Revolution and the Soviet Union.[7] There is now an "after" as well as a "before." The Soviet period has less of the quality of the culmination of Russian history and slightly more of the quality of an interruption to it. Although neither description is really apposite, both suggest something about the paradigm shift brought by the end of "the Soviet experiment." The approximately seventy-five-year period of the Soviet Union – if one counts from the actual establishment of the USSR the period is a half a dozen years shorter – may now be cautiously compared with other periods in Russia's history that began with the exhaustion and repudiation of an old world and the creation of new institutions and culture, continuing through a period of expansion, followed by a downturn into decadence and collapse until the cycle recommences. One must, of course, not overstate these similarities.[8] But in this connection we might think of the time between the end of the Riurikovich dynasty and the accession of Boris Godunov in the late seventeenth century, triggering the descent into the "Time of Troubles" (1605–13). This crisis, similar in some ways to the period of war and revolution between 1914 and 1921, was followed by a slow recovery and the movement of state, society, and culture toward the apogee of autocratic centralization (1649). But physical overextension and xenophobic conservatism produced the stagnation ultimately ended by the "revolution" of Peter the Great.

Transition into the post-Soviet cycle upon which Russia is now launched has provided students of that perennially secretive society with considerable information from newly opened (and perhaps now closing) archives dealing with Russia's past. Understandably, the focus of the efforts of non-native historians in particular has been on the Soviet period, especially the period when Stalin was in power, in which arguments about the nature of what the Left sometimes called "Soviet civilization" were most intense. New information from the archives has not essentially changed the larger outlines of Soviet history, but new details abound and the Soviet borderlands have been more dramatically affected than the heartland. The differences between the personality, values, and policies of the Soviet leaders remain, as they have long been, in dispute. The nature of Lenin's and Stalin's policies and, even more, the relationship between them, as argued even today, depends as much on the political values and opinions of the analyst as on any new evidence.[9] Several significant new publications argue passionately, however, that the continuity between Lenin and Stalin has been more closely and deeply established by the opening of the archives.[10] They position themselves in this venerable argument by asserting that Stalin did not so much "betray" as fulfill Lenin's revolution. New information has enabled other significant changes. The British historian and biographer Robert Service has produced new information on Lenin's family and on his medical situation, suggesting that his constitution was a good deal more fragile and his health more precarious than had previously been understood.[11]

To examine another dispute that raged for a long generation, Stalin's personal role in the Soviet terror and purging has been resoundingly affirmed; the attitude of scholars who sought to diminish Stalin's role by revisioning the purges of the 1930s as centrally conditioned by struggles over the makeup of the Communist Party seems misguided.[12] Stalin, however, also appears to be rather more of an intellectual Marxist than earlier scholars believed. On a different but related matter, the number of fatalities from the purges appears to be considerably lower than scholars of an earlier generation like Robert Conquest believed them to be. Nothing that has so far come out of the archives has cast any decisive light on Stalin's responsibility for the murder of the Leningrad Party boss, Sergei Kirov. Unsurprisingly, Lenin and Stalin seem both more complex and a good deal less Olympian than a generation ago, if fully as ruthless and bloodthirsty. Neither the more liberal and Marxisant scholars active in the United States and Europe, nor their conservative opponents, who believed that the Soviet Union was above all a centralized autocracy, have been wholly vindicated by archival disclosures.

Although no truly major surprises have yet emerged, much more of the connective tissue of Soviet history has been made visible by new archive availability.[13] In addition, the accessibility of archives, particularly regional archives, means that Russian history will never again be written so exclusively from the perspective(s) of Moscow and St Petersburg, although the unfettered flow of material from Soviet repositories for which historians hoped for a few years ago was never realized and is unlikely to be any time soon.[14] The end of the Soviet phase of Russian history has improved archival access only up to a point, as the Russian government's ancient suspicion of foreigners has not been banished.

Greater scholarly attention has already begun to be focused on what came before and after the Soviet Union. The sharpness of the divide provided by 1917 is blurring slightly and losing some of its ideological significance. At one and the same time, modern Russian traditions and ties with the longer past are re-emerging in new ways and in some different shapes, while Russia's future in a global age remains baffling. Is real democracy possible there? Can Russia be a successful nation, rather than a failed empire? Can Russia find a place in the current market-driven world? What sort of a place? More than a supplier of raw materials, a "colonial" economy? At the beginning of the 1990s, when the future seemed completely veiled, Russians used to joke about going to the airport and getting on a plane, without knowing where the plane was going to land. Most people hoped for Paris, Berlin, or Washington, but no one was confident. Might the plane be landing in Buenos Aires or Asuncion? Or even Islamabad? The most drastic alternatives seem to have been ruled out at this stage, but the plane's destination is still uncertain.

These dramatic changes, however, have surely changed our sense of pre-Soviet Russia as well as our more speculative sense of Russia's future. Older accounts of Soviet history and society, to take two examples, say relatively little about Soviet crime, save for the submerged "free market" known in the USSR as the "second economy." Crime was scarcely recognized as a problem until near the end of the Soviet period, when it exploded its way into post-Soviet Russia. Its sudden and dramatic emergence into the light of day has clarified some lines of continuity with the criminal world of the late Imperial and early Soviet periods that might with profit be more deeply investigated.[15] It may not be fantastic at least to note that before the eighteenth century Russian merchants were regarded by Europeans as spectacularly corrupt. But the relationship between the end of the Soviet Union, the rise of the Russian Mafia and the expansion of global crime is an important subject.[16]

In earlier discussions, "Russian religion" generally meant the history of the varieties of Orthodox Christianity. But the dissolution of the Soviet Union into a variety of national religious communities, plus the contemporary turmoil in the Middle East, has elevated the importance of Russia's non-Orthodox and borderland populations, especially its Muslim ones, into a much more important subject than in the past. How these populations were acquired and administered must now be adequately accounted for in any new synthesis of Russian history. The chapter by Robert Geraci of the University of Virginia in this volume helps us understand the vital question of minorities and empire.[17] Greater archival access for non-Russian scholars has thus far enabled greater understanding of the specific problems of Russia's extraordinarily diverse religious cultures and politics and the solutions found for them in the nineteenth and twentieth centuries by the Russian authorities.

Our *longue durée* sense of Russian imperial expansion has also altered. The obstacles, dangers, and difficulties of it are clearer to us than they used to be; the dangers for other nations less catastrophically threatening. "Imperial overstretch" helped bring the Soviet Union down, and we may now be disposed to read it back as a chronic problem even further (and more deeply) into Russian history.[18] The recent generation is not the first that has seen the lowering Russian threat suddenly diminish. Something comparable took place a century and a half ago, when Russia's defeat in the Crimean War (1853–6) made Castlereagh's dire warnings at the Congress of Vienna (1815) about the Russian hordes overrunning Europe seem overblown. The "undergovernment" of provincial Tsarist Russia and the extraordinary difficulties attendant upon the government's efforts to colonize Siberia – currently rather understudied – are likely to receive greater emphasis in the wake of Soviet collapse.[19]

The opening (and then partial closing) of Soviet archives is far from the only factor making for synthetic changes in the large canvas of Russian history. Methodologies and viewpoints change over time for many reasons. Some historical problems are strikingly affected by what historians call – with perhaps unintentional condescension – "auxiliary disciplines." For example, the question of how to differentiate the very first manifestations of Slavic from non-Slavic cultures in the early days of the Eurasian world entails an increasingly complex discussion between practitioners of different disciplines and techniques, as Paul Barford's chapter in this volume on "the origins of the Slavs" clearly demonstrates. Philologists, students of material culture, anthropologists, naturalists, and geneticists have different takes as to what we mean when we investigate the question. Should our primary enquiry focus on the language of ancient peoples, their pottery, their place names, and their geographical references, or on what genetics may reveal of them?

The essay of Janet Martin (University of Miami) suggests that the major issues focused upon by recent students of the first East Slavic state, Kiev Rus', do not greatly differ from what they have been for a generation or two. Disagreements on certain of these traditional problems have narrowed, however, thanks to further development of rather traditional tools of enquiry, such as archaeology and the study of coin hoards. The hoary disagreements between Normanists and anti-Normanists over the role of non-Slavs in the creation of the first East Slavic state have become less dramatic and somewhat less tied to the investigator's national point of view than previously. No one now seriously disputes the central role of Scandinavian dynasts in the founding of the Kiev Rus' state.

The significance of Russia's artistic culture, globally and particularly within the Western world, has not been diminished, even if the importance of its political culture has. Both the chapter of George Majeska (University of Maryland) on Kiev's relations with the Byzantine Empire and that of Ilia Dorontchenkov (The European University of St Petersburg) on Russian art suggest the attractive power that East Roman culture exerted on Russian elites, extending from the earliest days of East Slavic contact with Byzantium in the ninth and tenth centuries until well beyond the termination of the Byzantine Empire itself in 1453. Indeed it can be argued, as Dorontchenkov does, that Byzantine culture was the greatest treasure house of Europe at the time when the Eastern Slavs fell under its irresistible influence. Russian visual culture remained "medieval" much longer than the more dynamic culture of Central and Western Europe.

With the notable exception of icons, however, Russian painting over the succeeding centuries has unaccountably failed to impress European and American critics until very recently. The emergence of a group of wealthy "new Russians" since the late 1990s, however, has bid up the price of nineteenth- and twentieth-century Russian painting and increased awareness around the world of the major contribution to both

nineteenth- and twentieth-century European culture made by Russia's long undervalued artists.

Donald Ostrowski of Harvard University takes an exceptionally broad view of one
of the very most significant problems of early Russian history: the fateful and highly
diverse political and cultural interaction of the Eastern Slavs with the Mongols (generally known to the Russians as "Tatars"). His clear and comprehensive account
focuses on the period between the early thirteenth and the sixteenth centuries.[20]
Mongol influences were particularly important in shaping the political culture and
administrative practices of the Eastern Slavs, including taxation, political institutions,
and military methods. Mongol influence played a vital role in helping Rus' become
a dynastic state. But the dominant Russian historiographical tradition – and here the
rise and fall of the Soviet Union has been much less of a factor than Russian nationalism – is to minimize, or altogether deny, this Mongol influence. Mongol culture
scarcely existed, Russian scholars insisted for generations, and could not have had
any significant influence on the "higher" culture of the East Slavs.[21] Scrutinizing and
clarifying this fascinating problem of cultural influence means employing both analytic
skills and imagination in order to penetrate the layers of religious exclusivism and
Russian nationalism in which the historiography is swathed. Precisely who created
the early Slavic sources, and what they left out, may be as important as what their
authors intended to say. Long and painstaking language-learning continues to be a
sine qua non of understanding the culture and politics of the Eurasian steppe between
the thirteenth and the seventeenth centuries. Ostrowski takes advantage less of dramatic new discoveries than of the globalization of historical study, leading slowly but
inexorably to the gradual separation of chauvinistic passion from this particular cultural problem. He looks to the development of a more mature and independent-
minded historiography among "Tatarists, Bulgarists and Mongolian historians" for
further progress in the years ahead.

The predominant methodology of recent investigators of fifteenth- and sixteenth-
century Muscovy has centered on political culture, and their achievements have been
largely the work of non-Russians. Nancy Shields Kollmann (Stanford University),
herself an important contributor, provides us with a brilliant generational narrative
of this scholarly innovation, demonstrating how these scholars forged ideology, political institutions, history, climate, and the way ordinary people lived into a coherent
synthesis that goes far to explain the world of Ivan the Terrible. The work of Harvard
University's Edward Keenan was a crucial catalyst in these collective achievements.

Richard Hellie of the University of Chicago has been the great interpreter of
Russian slavery and serfdom in our generation of historians. He has concluded that
Russian history must treat extensively not only the history of the autocratic institutions that sharply limited the freedom of Russians but equally what he calls "the
history of unfreedom," in which serfdom played a central role. As Nancy Kollmann
observes, the Muscovite state "offered no legal protections or rights to subjects, nor
representative institutions that might share sovereignty." But, in addition, slavery
played a significant role in the social arrangements of early Russia, until it was
squeezed out by later developing and more varied forms of bondage in the seventeenth century. According to Hellie, some 85 percent of the population from the
1590s – when full serfdom may be considered to have come into effect – until the
early twentieth century ought to be considered as unfree. After forced collectivization

began in 1929, Hellie considers that "more than a majority" of Russians were unfree until the Khrushchev-era reforms were under way in 1956. The roller coaster of Russian unfreedom, then, runs from the Mongol–Muscovite period, through the Imperial and the Soviet eras, and, in attenuated form, out the other side. Hellie stresses that the collectivized agriculture of the Soviet Union was experienced by many rural Russians as a "second serfdom."

The remarkable changes wrought upon the body and soul of Russia by Peter the Great are properly understood to constitute a revolution, however anachronistically the term is used here. The late Lindsey Hughes of University College, London, among the great scholars of early modern Russia in our time, suggests that Peter in effect adopted the German philosopher Leibniz's view that Russia was a *tabula rasa* – a blank sheet of paper – upon which a new civilization could be traced by an energetic ruler. But before Peter's unparalleled effort to set Russia on a new course, the power and influence of the Russian Church was badly damaged by a long-lasting church schism that opened the final third of the seventeenth century. It not only divided the Orthodox population of Russia into two irreconcilable flocks, but weakened the Patriarch and made the abolition of his office much easier for Peter to achieve.

However, the eclipse of the work of those Soviet "Westernizers," the Bolsheviks, may subtly diminish the achievement of Peter the Great in the eyes of future historians of Russia, who will surely be less attracted to revolutionary heroics, including the Petrine variety. Nadieszda Kizenko of the State University at Albany integrates the most recent scholarship on the church schism into the groundbreaking work of previous generations.

Gary Marker (State University of New York at Stony Brook) takes up one of the principal legacies of Peter the Great: the now problematized "Westernization" of the Russian elite. He suggests convincingly that the end of the Soviet Union has cast doubt on what he calls "the long-accepted affinities between Westernization, progress and secularization." The existence of an automatic, virtually unilinear opposition between "state and society" in Russia from the Enlightenment until the Russian Revolution, long criticized for over-simplification, received its *coup de grâce* as the official support of the Soviet historical tradition was swept away. The most recent historiography investigates, to take one important example, the degree to which the eighteenth- and early nineteenth-century nobility actually shared most of the government's assumptions about how Russia should be ruled, a rather stark contrast to the work of Soviet historians in particular, who stressed a straightforward development of oppositional forces among the Russian elite, already under way at the accession of Catherine the Great in 1763.

Nor, despite the importance of the Westernization of the upper class, should its extent or numbers of participants be exaggerated. The late Daniel Field (Syracuse University) stressed the small size of the educated elite at the time of the so-called Great Reforms, which, following the Crimean War, sprawled their way across the second half of the nineteenth century. Field, and a variety of Russian, German, and especially American historians, played a central role in rewriting the history of this important period, the centerpiece of which was the emancipation of the serfs. Virtually all of these scholars – Russians and non-Russians alike – were taken under the wing of the greatest student of the reforms, Petr Andreevich Zaionchkovsky, whose politically tactful but inexorably honest influence undermined Soviet orthodoxy on imperial reform long before that orthodoxy was even tacitly opposed on most matters of historical interpretation.

The Russians, of course, invented the idea of an "intelligentsia," a creative minority who embodied the intelligence of the nation in a quasi-Hegelian sense, which also suggested its progressive mission of reform. Conservatives and many liberals had long criticized the enormous influence of the "intelligentsia" in late Imperial Russia. Naturally the Soviet experience made the glorification of the "progressive" intelligentsia more controversial than ever. The closed nature of both politics and culture – and the apparent destruction of the intelligentsia itself – in the Soviet Union seemed to reinforce the conclusion that this gallant, occasionally quixotic, tradition was nevertheless too vulnerable to extreme ideologies. Gary Saul Morson (Northwestern University) invokes the work of the critic and philosopher Mikhail Bakhtin in elucidating the latest stage in the long argument over the extent of the influence of the Russian intelligentsia and the complex blend of positive and negative that its two centuries of existence brought to Russia. Steeped in the work of Tolstoy and especially Dostoevsky, Bakhtin proclaimed that life can never be grasped by any theory. As Morson paraphrases Bakhtin, "there cannot be a social science because . . . contingency reigns" – a modern restatement of what one might say was an age-old point.

The rise and fall of cultural modernism in the Soviet Union are closely linked to the trajectory of the intelligentsia. Most critics have seen Russian modernism as a major phenomenon in the Westernization of the intelligentsia, exploding on to the stage in the first decade of the twentieth century. Russian modernism – in literature, music, art, and film – may have originally been a French import, but the Russians were famously apt pupils. Russian modernism was the only European variant to rival that of the school of Paris in painting and arguably to surpass France in music and certainly dance. Andrew Wachtel of Northwestern University stresses the intolerance of Stalin's Russia for modernism, but he also addresses more recent scholarship that also regards internal cultural evolution as having played at least a subsidiary role in limiting modernist evolution in Russia.

Also linked to the Russian intelligentsia, but in a rather different way, is the so-called "woman question." One of the many paradoxes of Russia's culture of extremes is that within a nation so heavily marked by violence toward women progressive intellectuals should at the same time have put women's emancipation on the front burner in advance of so many other less "backward" societies. Elizabeth A. Wood of the Massachusetts Institute of Technology takes a contemporary look at this fascinating problem, noting that the woman question was also about masculinity and its place in such an autocratic society. Despite its emancipatory valence, the activities of the predominantly male intelligentsia also "perpetuated deeply misogynist notions of women's backwardness." As so often in the Russian story, "les extrêmes se touchent."

The Russian tradition of a critical intelligentsia is today deeply imperiled. But if it cannot be reconstituted in the market-driven Russia of today, there are those who will miss its fierce moralism and humanitarianism.[22] Perhaps the authoritarian rule of Vladimir Putin and his successors will – somewhere down the road – revive the radical alienation of an intelligentsia minority disgusted by the formlessness of Russian culture today and its inability to resist the government's encroachment on free expression.

The crisis of late Soviet society coincided with the increasing use of the concept of "civil society," to suggest developments anterior to and more or less closely related to democratization in Europe. A series of important discussions about Russia ensued. What exactly characterized this kind of society? The rise of "voluntary organizations"? Urbanization? New forms of "sociability"? Aristocratic decline? How closely related to the rise of democracy was the appearance of a civil society? Was the appearance of aspects of a "civil society" after Stalin's death connected to developments under Mikhail Gorbachev that ultimately meant the end of Soviet authoritarianism?

The possibility of understanding the demise of the Soviet Union partially in terms of the belated rise of "civil society" prompted recent investigators to look back to the last phase of Imperial Russia. Was the development of a healthy civil society foreclosed by the vast spaces and overwhelmingly rural character of Russia? Or by hostility of the intelligentsia tradition to market culture? Or by the catastrophe of the First World War? Or by all of the above? By raising such questions, the "civil-society" debate in Russia gradually absorbed and superseded the older discussion of whether Imperial Russia suffered from a "missing bourgeoisie," and, if so, why it was missing. Christopher Ely (Wilkes Honors College, Florida Atlantic University) gives us a searching account of these vital discussions, which bear so centrally on Russia's relationship to the forms of modern life characteristic of Europe.

Whether late Imperial Russia had a civil society or not, it certainly had capitalism – of some kind. But of what kind, exactly? Was it in the end merely a variation on the capitalism of Europe, or something different?[23] Thomas Owen of Harvard University's Davis Center for Russian and Eurasian Studies provides a magisterial survey of the development of Russian capitalism, concluding that early twentieth-century Russia's industrial system – heavily dependent on the state as it was – became strong enough "to generate popular antipathy but remained too weak to defend itself in the political realm . . . and in culture."

Save for political behavior itself, in no area did ideological orthodoxy lay a heavier hand on Soviet life than in popular culture, which the regime was determined to co-opt, shape, and control. As Louise McReynolds of the University of North Carolina, Chapel Hill, brilliantly demonstrates, the end of the Soviet Union freed up scholars to investigate "the personal experiences of lives lived" in twentieth-century Russia and made theoretical and anthropological investigation central. Anthropologists in particular "accepted the relativism inherent in culture" and "endowed quotidian Soviet life with a significance that politics had refused it."

Until recently, the First World War had been dramatically understudied in Russia, overshadowed as it was by the Russian Revolution and the creation of the Soviet Union. Now the "unknown war," as Melissa Stockdale of Oklahoma University calls it, is receiving the full-dress investigation it merits. A crop of distinguished scholars, inside Russia and abroad, are devoting their talents to investigating the dreadful conflagration that was the seedbed of so much that went wrong in the twentieth century and – as Stockdale puts it – was both catalyst and crucible of the revolution.

As the Russian Revolution assumes a slightly more episodic significance for Russian history (its ideological significance for the world of the twentieth century remains undiminished), the importance of the Civil War occasioned by the collapse of Imperial Russia and the Bolshevik seizure of power has also grown greater. As Mark von Hagen of Arizona State University puts the matter, contemporaries did not see 1917 as so definable a "caesura" in the almost decade-long trauma of war and revolution that convulsed Russia between the summer of 1914 and the end of the Civil War. That decade resembles, von Hagen notes perspicaciously, the "time of troubles" that "recalled an earlier period of foreign invasion and internecine violence after the death of Ivan the Terrible."[24]

The great scholar of two generations ago, Barrington Moore, characterized the developments in the Soviet 1930s as constituting "terror and progress."[25] With the decline and fall of the Soviet Union, the progress has become harder to discern, but not the terror. Historians are still bitterly divided over how to understand the "forced modernization" policies of the late 1920s and 1930s in particular. Ought the radical policies of Lenin and Stalin to be understood as essentially the work of the leaders themselves and hence necessitating the coining of "isms" (Leninism, Stalinism)? Or did the roots of the behavior of the Soviet leaders lie in the depths of Russian history? Or in the utopianism of the French Revolution? In the cauldron of the international system between the wars? Lynne Viola of the University of Toronto persuasively argues that what we call Stalinism was "first and foremost a recipe for a non-capitalist modernization (with some decidedly non-modern characteristics)." According to Viola, it was the Russian peasantry that "supported the infrastructure of modernization [and] turned the Stalinist state into an extraction state based on the use of force." She shares Moshe Lewin's view that Stalinism is best described as an "agrarian despotism" but concedes to more traditional scholarship the importance of "certain features of Russian historical development based on a continuation of similar patterns, structures and problems." What we call Stalinism, she concludes, was by and large rooted in a "particular time and country," despite the numerous comparisons that have been made with other mega-states of the twentieth century, often under the rubric of "totalitarianism."

Nothing could dramatize more vividly the historiographical changes of the early twenty-first century than the virtual convergence of Russian and non-Russian scholars on major points of interpretation respecting the Second World War. Western historians have recognized more fully that the war against Nazi Germany was really won on the eastern front and described in more comprehensive ways the enormous devastation that Russia underwent at the hands of National Socialist Germany. Russian scholars are stripping away the mythologizing of the war by their Soviet predecessors, as well as revealing the blunders of the military and political leadership and the desperate straits in which the Soviet Union found itself, as it began its "age of empire" after 1945. Nikita Lomagin of St Petersburg University provides a fluent narrative that takes full account of both Russian and Western historiography.

Do we "now know" all that we can about what drove the cold-war conflict between the West, led by the United States, and the Soviet "East"? There may be some hubris in this coinage, but, with the opening of some Soviet archives, our source base has certainly increased.[26] Along with the interpretation of the Russian Revolution, the cold war was the historical problem that saw the widest divergence between Russian and non-Russian historiography. With the end of the Soviet Union, that abyss too has shrunk dramatically, but it may never be entirely overcome. American triumphalism, even as it diminishes over time, will always be difficult for Russian scholars to accept and for American scholarship to shed entirely. Russians may never wholly eliminate a certain residue of shame at "losing" not only the cold war but also their superpower status and the empire over which its leaders ruled for almost half a century. David Engerman (Brandeis University), a leading member of a new generation of American scholars studying this consuming conflict, has written an account as devoid of triumphalism and as fair-minded as our present historical positioning may allow.

The era of Mikhail Gorbachev and the chaotic sequence of reforms that he initiated inaugurated the last days of the Soviet Union. Scholars defining themselves as "realists" pointed to the growing difficulties of the Soviet economy, "imperial overstretch," and loss of ideological élan as major factors in the reform movement undertaken by Gorbachev and his colleagues. But Robert English of the University of Southern California made a major contribution by analyzing in depth the connection between the reform efforts of intellectuals under Nikita Khrushchev and those that Gorbachev gathered around him. This effort entailed a major commitment to interviewing the living, as well as scrutinizing the careers of the deceased. He summarizes and contextualizes his painstaking work for us here, demonstrating the roots and significance of what, under Gorbachev, came to be described as "new thinking."

No scholar has worked harder or more purposefully to understand the demise of the Soviet Union than Robert V. Daniels of the University of Vermont. He plausibly understands this momentous event as involving "four distinct transformations," all of them quite profound. Not only was the Communist Party and its ideology decisively rejected, but the socialist command economy went with it. The end of the Soviet Empire entailed both surrender of rule over the non-Russian union republics and the release of the nominally independent states of Eastern and Central Europe. As regards the extraordinary complexity of this process, Daniels invokes the philosophy of Leo Tolstoy in observing that "the longer-term movements affecting the country, particularly in economics and in the relationships of international power, will probably [over time] draw greater attention, while the personal ambitions and conflicts among individual leaders fade from prominence." This remarkable development constituted was one of the most important historical moments of the past century.

Since the Soviet Union came to an end, Russia has experienced enormous political and economic turmoil: both the introduction of a peculiar form of capitalism – some would demonize it – and at the same time efforts to restore connections with earlier strands of Russian historical development – some of them pre-capitalist. At the same time, an effort has been made not to lose entirely the centralized institutions and great power influence of the Soviet period, particularly after 1945.

But the cultural chaos is almost certainly even deeper. Who are the Russians? What aspects of the Russian cultural past are available to them? To what can they aspire? Given their dire demographic prospects, what will Russia look like in a quarter century? Our final two contributors, Bruce Parrott of the School of Advanced International Studies, Johns Hopkins University, and the late William Odom, have the difficult privilege of bringing us up to Russia's present and trying to discern, through the mists, what Russia's future may be – an old and oft-played game for previous generations of Russia specialists.

*   *   *

The Blackwell *Companion to Russian History* is intended not as a stand-alone account of Russia's past, but as a stimulating supplement to college course offerings either based on monographs or drawn primarily from a textbook. It can be selectively used for seniors in high school studying Russia in the context of European or even world history. But its primary use will be for professors teaching Russian or European History at the college level. Graduate students too may find it useful as a way of reviewing the shape of the field before their preliminary examinations. And we hope that many of these essays may find favor with that significant, if vaguely defined, entity: the general reader.

Notes

1   Peter Reddaway and Dmitrii Glinski, *The Tragedy of Russia's Reforms*, United States Institute of Peace Press, Washington, 2001.

2   The episodically bloody war in Chechnya constitutes a major exception, which is sometimes overlooked by scholars concerned with post-Soviet Russia's relations with the West. See Anatol Lieven's fundamental *Chechnya: Tombstone of Russian Power*, Yale University Press, New Haven, 1998. More recent developments are discussed in A. V. Malashenko, Dmitrii Trenin, and Anatol Lieven, *Russia's Restless Frontier: The Chechnya Factor in Post-Soviet Foreign Policy*, Carnegie Endowment for International Peace, Washington, 2004. See also Alexander Motyl, Blair A. Ruble, and Lilia Shevtsova, eds., *Russia's Engagement with the West: Transformation and Integration in the Twenty-First Century*, M. E. Sharpe, Armonk, NY, and London, 2005, and Anna Politkovskaia, *A Small Corner of Hell: Dispatches from Chechnya*, Chicago, University of Chicago Press, 2003.

3   For an interesting effort to put a fairly positive spin on this idea, see Marshall Poe, *The Russian Moment in World History*, Princeton University Press, Princeton, 2003. To look at Russia's sense of its trajectory comparatively, see Jan-Werner Müller, ed., *Memory and Power in Post-War Europe*, Cambridge University Press, Cambridge, 2002.

4   See Parag Khanna, *The Second World: Empires and Influence in the New Global Order*, Random House, New York, 2008.

5   Ronald Grigor Suny, *The Soviet Experiment: Russia, the USSR and the Successor States*, Oxford University Press, Oxford, 1998; id., *Structure of Soviet History: Essays and Documents*, Oxford University Press, Oxford and New York, 2003.

6   If "anything were to occur to disrupt the unity and efficacy of the party as a political instrument," wrote Kennan toward the end of Part III of "The Sources of Soviet Conduct," "Soviet Russia might be changed overnight from one of the strongest to one of the weakest and most pitiable of national societies." "X", *Foreign Affairs*, 25 (July 1947), 566–82.

7   Jane Burbank and David Ransel, *Imperial Russia: New Histories of the Empire*, Indiana University Press, Indianapolis, 1998. See also Geoffrey Hosking and Robert Service, *Reinterpreting Russia*, Oxford University Press, Oxford, 1999. Recently founded journals such as *Kritika* and *Ab Imperio* are also partly based on this premiss. See also Thomas Sanders, *Historiography of Imperial Russia*, M. E. Sharpe, Armonk, NY, 1999, and Peter Holquist, Michael David Fox, and Marshall Poe, eds., *After the Fall: Essays on Russian and Soviet Historiography after Communism*, Slavica, Bloomington, IN, 2004.

8   The reasons why Russian history has this peculiar shape to it are provocatively set forth in Tim McDaniel, *The Agony of the Russian Idea*, Princeton University Press, Princeton,

1996. John LeDonne's *The Russian Empire and the World: The Geopolitics of Expansion and Containment*, Oxford University Press, Oxford, 1997, is stimulating.

9 The Harvard historian Terry Martin, however, has argued effectively that both Lenin and Stalin intended to encourage national development within the Soviet republics and did so. See *The Affirmative Action Empire: Nations and Nationalism in the Soviet Union 1923–1929*, Cornell University Press, Ithaca, NY, 2001.

10 Stéphane Courtois, Nicholas Werth, et al., *The Black Book of Communism: Crimes, Terror, Repression*, Harvard University Press, Cambridge, MA, 1999; Dmitri Volkogonov, *Lenin: A New Biography*, Free Press, New York and London, 1994; Richard Pipes, *The Unknown Lenin*, Yale University Press, New Haven, 2003.

11 Robert Service, *Lenin: A Biography*, Harvard University Press, Cambridge, MA, 2000.

12 See Marc Jansen and Nikita Peters, *Stalin's Loyal Executioner: People's Commissar Nikolai Ezhov, 1896–1940*, Hoover Institution Press, Stanford, CA, 2002. The early work of J. Arch Getty on Stalin and the terror (*The Origin of the Great Purges*, Cambridge University Press, Cambridge, 1985) now seems unconvincing. But see also his more nuanced (with Oleg Naumov) *The Road to Terror: Stalin and the Self-Destruction of the Bolsheviks, 1932–1939*, Yale University Press, New Haven, and London, 1999; as well as (edited, with Roberta Manning) *Stalinist Terror: New Perspectives*, Cambridge University Press, Cambridge, 1993.

13 See, e.g., Ethan Pollock, *Stalin and the Soviet Science Wars*, Princeton University Press, Princeton, 2007.

14 For a brief and knowledgeable discussion of what the newly available archives have produced for us, see Sheila Fitzpatrick, "The Soviet Union in the Twentieth Century," *Journal of European Studies*, 37/1 (2007), 51–70. For greater detail, see Soviet Archive Project, www.dac.neu.edu/history/archive/index.html. Two useful collections of assessments by well-regarded scholars may be found in *Jahrbücher für Geschichte Osteuropas*, 51/1 (2003), 36–98; and "Assessing the New Soviet Archival Sources," *Cahiers du monde russe*, 40/1–2 (Jan.–June 1999).

15 Stephen Handelman's *Comrade Criminal: Russia's New Mafiya* (Yale University Press, New Haven, 1995) is aging, but still valuable.

16 See in particular Vadim Volkov, *Violent Entrepreneurs: the use of Force in the Making of Russian Capitalism*, Cornell University Press, Ithaca, New York, 2002 and Frederico Varèse, *The Russian Mafia: Private Protection in the New Market Economy*, Oxford University Press, New York, 2005.

17 See also Robert Geraci and Michael Khodarkovsky, *Of Religion and Empire: Missions, Conversion, and Tolerance in Tsarist Russia*, Cornell University Press, Ithaca, NY, 2001.

18 Dominic Lieven, *Empire: The Russian Empire and its Rivals*, Yale University Press, New Haven, 2002, esp. p. 332. See also Hannes Adomeit, *Imperial Overstretch: Germany in Soviet Policy from Stalin to Gorbachev*, Nomos, Baden-Baden, 1998.

19 S. Frederick Starr, *Decentralization and Self-Government in Russia, 1830–1870*, Princeton University Press, Princeton, 1972; Andrew Gentes, *Exile to Siberia, 1590–1822*, Palgrave-Macmillan, Basingstoke, 2008.

20 Properly speaking, "Tatars" refers not only to the Mongols but to their nomadic neighbors on the steppe: as Ostrowski puts it, to "the amalgamation of Turkic peoples that the Mongols created when took over control of the Western steppe."

21 This tendency is still visible in Nicholas Riasanovsky, *Russian Identities: A Historical Survey*, Oxford University Press, Oxford and New York, 2008.

22 Katerina Clark (Yale University), "The King Is Dead: Long Live the King," Stanford University conference paper, 1998.

23 Lenin himself was a major player in this discussion. See his *The Development of Capitalism in Russia*. A recent printing is available from the University Press of the Pacific, n.p., 2004.

24 For a journalistic early adumbration of this conception, see Abbott Gleason, "The Meaning of 1917," *Atlantic Monthly*, 270/5 (Nov. 1992), 30–4.

25 Barrington Moore, Jr., *Terror and Progress*, Harvard University Press, Cambridge, MA, 1954.

26 John Lewis Gaddis, *We Now Know*, Oxford University Press, New York, 1997. Despite the author's authoritative title, he does concede that knowledge is cumulative. Yet it is striking, as Melvyn Leffler has pointed out ("What Do We Now Know?", *American Historical Review*, 104/2 (Apr. 1999), 501–24), how traditional disputes about what motivated Soviet leaders have continued even after the opening of archives.

PART I

Rus': The Early East Slavic World

CHAPTER TWO

From "Proto-Slavs" to Proto-State

P. M. BARFORD

In one sense the "Russian History" of the title of this collective work begins with the first accounts written in a newly literate Kievan Rus'; in another, it is to be found in the first scant mentions in the works of foreign authors (such as Herodotus) of ethnic groups and events in the areas that were later to be named Russia. A third approach would be to see the historical process as one extending, irrespective of literacy, into the deep past and studied by related disciplines such as archaeology. This chapter aims briefly to set the scene for subsequent ones, concentrating on the two topics mentioned in the title.

The Problem with the Proto-Slavs

The origin of the Slavic-speaking component of the Kievan state is still contentious, a controversy played out between scholars of several nationalities. The problem is more of a linguistic nature than an ethnic or even historical one. The earliest attested forms of an East Slavic language (a regional group of the Slavic language family that now contains Russian, Belarussian, Ukrainian, and Rusyn) are first attested in Kievan Rus'. At some stage Slavic languages had differentiated from other members of the Indo-European group, which had become widespread in Europe and southwest Asia some time in prehistory (disputed current models suggest either the Neolithic or the Bronze Age). Most Slavic languages are not directly attested until quite late in the historic period, though from Kievan Rus' we have a few short pre-twelfth-century inscriptions (for example, graffiti on objects like spindlewhorls and the famous birch bark letters from Novgorod).

Slavic languages were in use by the ninth century over an impressively large region of Eastern and Central Europe, from the Elbe to the Volga, and from the Baltic to the shores of the Black Sea and Adriatic. Furthermore there is evidence that at this time most of them were still relatively poorly differentiated from each other. Scholars have expended great effort to determine when and how these languages became spoken over such a wide area.

Consulting the copious scholarly literature on the origin and early stages of the spread of Slavic-speaking peoples can be confusing. Many different types of evidence are drawn upon by several specialist disciplines (each of which claims to be able to pronounce authoritatively on the issue), and very different interpretations are put on the same evidence. In addition, the problem has become entangled in modern identity politics. Panslavism has at times been seen as the crucial factor uniting various groups (in particular by the Russian states). On the other hand, the demonstration that a certain nation's territory was the ancient homeland of the earliest Slavs has not been just a matter of national pride. It became at times an essential element not only of creating social bonds but also of asserting rights to inhabit a given territory by demonstrating origins there going back almost to the beginnings of history. In such situations, the boundaries between filiopietism and outright chauvinism are fluid and discussions can at times become heated and unscholarly.

These problems are by no means new. The twelfth-century writers of the Russian chronicles (*Povest' vremennykh let (Story of the Olden Time)*, henceforth *PVL*) saw the ethnic situation at the time of the foundation of the Kievan state as a static back projection of that of their own time, thus legitimizing the status quo. The Kievan chroniclers reconstructed the protohistory of their people utilizing the written and other sources that they had available. They wrote that, after Babel, the Slavs had settled on the Danube and, when this area was invaded, migrated to the north and east to settle the area from the Dniepr to Lake Ilmen, and along the Dvina, Desna, Sula, and Seyny. At the time of the various redactions of the *PVL*, the Kievan state had the character of a multi-ethnic, if not multicultural polity linked mainly by a strong dynastic elite, which it was the purpose of the chronicle to bolster. In beginning their text with the origin of the Slavs, the chroniclers ignored the derivation of the other ethnic components of the contemporary Rus' state, a pattern that has repeated itself in later historiography until recently.

For the early medieval Kievan elite, the dominant ethnic group in the northern lands of the state was that of the Slavic tribes of the Viatichi, Kryvichi, and Slovienie. Though the chronicler depicts them as anciently indigenous, these groups were probably late formations in areas that had previously been dominated by Baltic- and Finno-Ugric-speaking communities. The tribes in the south, however (Poliane, Severiane, Derevlane, Volyniane, together with the more marginal Tyvertsy and Ulichi to the southwest), formed in areas that had apparently been dominated by Slavic-speakers for a much longer period. Despite the *PVL* blurring this distinction, these two zones of what was later to become the Kievan state had a separate ethnic, linguistic, and cultural history in the centuries leading up to its creation.

The core of the early medieval state on the middle Dniepr falls at the boundary between two archaeological cultures of the eighth and ninth centuries; the Luka Rajkovetska (forest-steppe area of western Ukraine and Moldova) and the Volyntsevo (much of the left-bank Ukraine, the valleys of the Desna, Seym, Psel, Sula, and Vorskla). Most scholars are agreed that the Luka Rajkovetska material, having affinities with that found in Slavic contexts in Central Europe and on the lower Danube, is the material culture of Slavic-speaking groups. The Volyntsevo material is very similar to it in a number of respects, and its distribution matches very well the location of the Slavic Severjane tribe mentioned in later chronicles. The question of how long Slavic speakers had been established in either area is, however, a matter of controversy.[1]

A few centuries earlier, much of the area of Ukraine had been occupied by the Cherniakhovo Culture,[2] most probably the material correlates of the hegemony over a large area north of the Black Sea by the Goths between the mid-third century and their subsequent migration into the crumbling Western Roman Empire in the face of the Hunnic onslaught in 375. The Huns held sway over much of the area until the 450s, after which there was virtually a power vacuum on the western Pontic steppes and adjacent areas until the rise of a strong polity led by the Avars in the 560s. It was in this intermediate period that the Slavs first appear as raiders on the Danubian frontiers.

"Goths," "Huns," and "Avars" are the names on the colored blobs of our historical atlases, but they obscure the fact that early medieval ethnicities were very fluid; these entities were often little more than a complex web of prestige and tributary relations between an elite (who formed a "kernel of tradition") and often ethnically and culturally diverse subject communities.[3] Very few of them were as ethnically "pure" as the romantic and idealistic nineteenth- and early twentieth-century European historiography portrayed them, and many were probably multicultural and held together by a thin veneer of group identity, either voluntary or imposed. There is reason to think that there were Slav-speakers in the groups we label as "Huns" and "Avars," and probably the Goths as well.

It would, therefore, be mistaken to see the Slavs as an ethnic group. They are a linguistic community. Linguists have proposed that gradual transformation and differentiation led to the creation first of a Proto-Slavic language (sometimes called Common Slavic) and then its various daughter languages. The method of comparative linguistics has been used to reconstruct Proto-Slavic, but there is currently a keen debate on the nature of this language, the form in which it existed, and how (and whether) it can be reconstructed.[4] In particular, there has been debate about how to model the processes of linguistic change over time. The initial model was an evolutionary one where one form mutated into another and gave rise to separate and discrete languages, each deriving from a single "genetic" parent, with the relationships between two languages interpreted as being due to their relationship with a common ancestor. This is exemplified by the family tree (*Stammbaum*) model of August Schleicher, and is the basis of the comparative method of linguistic analysis, and as such is still a model that to some extent dominates the discussion.

This model has been challenged, however, by the wave theory, which proposes that neighboring languages affect and interact with each other, sharing grammatical, phonological, and lexical innovations. Multiple waves of change may overlap within one linguistic area but also cross the boundaries between languages and dialects. Robert Dixon's "Punctuated Equilibrium" model envisages periods of linguistic equilibrium in which these processes operate, but also allows for it to be punctuated by external events that cause the languages to enter a brief period of very rapid change. Such factors may include the movement into the area of new cultures, the expansion into a new area of the people speaking the language, or the introduction of a different, life-changing technology.

These choices of models of linguistic change have further consequences for the study of the past. Consider the so-called Balto-Slavic language, which subsequently played a large part in several disciplines pertaining to the origin of the Slavs. Lexical and morphological similarities suggested to earlier scholars that Proto-Slavic was closely related to the predecessor of modern Baltic languages (represented by Lithuanian and Latvian and the extinct Eastern Baltic and Prussian languages). The application of the *Stammbaum* model implied an evolutionary stage in the development of the Indo-European languages when the two languages came from a common ancestor. Another approach, now gaining more ground, is that some at least of the convergences come from a much later period, when there were close historical contacts between Old Prussian/Lithuanian and Polish/Belorussian, but the dispute about the existence of the Balto-Slavic language is far from over.[5]

More recent work in linguistic anthropology and sociolinguistics has cast doubt on models that presuppose single homogeneous and firmly bounded linguistic entities in the past. Interpretations based mainly in a model of genetic descent fail to recognize that languages (especially preliterate ones in areas of low population density and less-developed social organization) are not bounded and impermeable entities, but mutable, mutually interrelated, and diffuse. Any Proto-Slavic language will, in reality, have included in its area of use and been surrounded by a number of similar dialects, pidgin languages, and transitional forms (such as creoles), as well as other separate languages that were related to it and could have interacted with it in various ways down through the centuries and most of which did not survive. Traditional retrogressive analyses can produce only a vast oversimplification of what must have been an incredibly complex picture.

The supporters of the *Stammbaum* model could only envisage the initial similarities across the wide area where Slavic was spoken as being due to it having been taken there in "finished" form from a much smaller core area. For them, the spread of the relatively homogeneous language over such a wide area meant that it was taken there by migration of Slav-speaking populations. Thus the Slavic *Völkerwanderung* became the subject of research, together with the search for "the *Urheimat* of the Slavic nations," from which this exceptional population explosion would have begun. Various methods and types of evidence have been used to reconstruct these processes; we will examine some briefly below.

In an effort to find the *Urheimat*, attempts have been made to identify Slavic-sounding ethnonyms and other words (like river names) mentioned in written sources created in the literate classical world. For example, a number of the groups inhabiting the area north of the Black Sea (like the Neuroi or Boudinoi) mentioned by Herodotus have been proposed as the ancestors of the Slavs, and a Slavic etymology sought for the ethnonyms used to refer to them. The pages of later classical writers such as the geographer Ptolemy have also been scoured for Slavic-sounding names.[6] These attempts exhibit much ingenuity but are not very reliable as a source of information. By the time the area to the north and east of the Mediterranean world became better known to literate societies (between the sixth and tenth centuries AD), the Slavs were already inhabiting most of the area they did in the medieval period, but we know little about how this situation came about.

There is, of course, no real reason why the ancient written sources should mention the ancestors of the Slavs at all. Before the sixth century AD they could well have been living beyond the zone of Barbaricum immediately visible to the Mediterranean world, with no reason for the classical scholar to take any especial notice of them.

We should recognize that (like many "peoples without a history" of the ancient world) it is entirely possible that they simply failed to register in the world picture of the writers of classical Athens or Rome. Any attempt to wring information out of a few names reported at second hand is futile.

By the early decades of the sixth century, however, Slavic groups were making their presence sorely felt on the northern frontiers of the world of Late Antiquity. From the beginning of Justinian's reign these people (like the Bulgars and later the Avars) had been raiding East Roman territory from the northeastern part of the Danubian Plain and the western Pontic steppes. They had not been there earlier; the Roman frontier had been on the Danube for several centuries and in the period 98–273 the Roman province of Dacia had extended into Transylvania, giving the Romans a reason for interest in and good insight into the ethnic makeup of the surrounding area.

This is the context of the earliest direct reference to Slavic-speaking communities, which appears in the accounts of two historians in Constantinople in the middle of the century. Procopius in his *Wars* refers to the Sclavenes and Antes living then "on the Danube at no great distance from the bank," but says little about how and whence they came there.[7] Jordanes locates their territory in a "boundless area" along the flanks of the Carpathian mountains from "the source of Vistula" to the lower Danube, extending along the Pontic coast to the Dniepr. He was interested in their origins and he equated them with the Venedi, a group known from older literary sources. Many scholars have taken this account at face value, and the Venedi have become implicated in modern historiography with the search for Slavic *Urheimat*. Nevertheless, in the context of *Getica* it is clear that Jordanes was transposing his knowledge of where the Sclavenes and Antes now lived on what he found in his old books; there is absolutely no evidence that he had any first-hand knowledge of the ethnic trans-formations that were taking place beyond the long-abandoned Dacia and by the source of the Vistula. Despite the weight that has been given it in modern histori-ography, in reality Jordanes' account has little value in discussions of the origin of the Slavs. The earliest written records are, therefore, ambiguous and cannot be treated as independent sources of information about the ethnic history of the regions and period that interest us.

Since the nineteenth century, various linguistic methods have been applied to the search for Slavic origins. Nineteenth- and early twentieth-century linguists attempted to use various methods to identify where the *Urheimat* of the Proto-Slavic-speaking peoples had been before their postulated migration. One of them studied loan words that had been borrowed by Proto-Slavic from other languages to indicate where the language had developed by identifying which languages had been its neighbors. The mutual relationships between Proto-Slavic and the Germanic, Baltic, Iranian, Thracian, and Illyrian languages suggest that the Slavic *Urheimat* was somewhere between the areas where these language groups themselves had their origin. The Polish linguist Witold Mańczak uses statistics of lexical similarities to demonstrate the "nearness" of languages and then fix that in geographical terms. On this basis he concludes that the homeland of the Slavs was in the Oder–Vistula watershed, though his methods have been challenged by other linguists.[8]

Another variant of the loan-words method was linguistic research on the terminol-ogy of plants with limited geographical extent. In the 1880s, the Polish botanist and humanist Józef Rostafiński concluded that the *Urheimat* of the Slavs must have been a region devoid of beech, larch, and yew. This is because all Slavic languages have words of Germanic origin for these trees. Proto-Slavic had, therefore, been spoken outside the range of such trees but in a zone where hornbeam grew, since there was an old Slavic word for hornbeam. Rostafiński concluded on the basis of the distribution of these species that the homeland of the Slavs was the marshes along the Pripet River, near the present-day Ukrainian–Belarus border.[9] Many later scholars have also found this "beech argument" enticing. The *Urheimat* in the Pripet marshes was also endorsed by a number of scholars, among them Max Vasmer, the Russian-born German linguist.[10]

Inference based on this type of model assumes that loans and lexical similarities are automatically carried from one language to another by genetic descent. The wave-model approaches challenge this rather simplistic interpretation. It is impossible to date their acceptance, which renders impossible their use in comparison with other types of evidence (such as, for example, the changes over the past few millennia of the distribution of species like beech).

Another linguistic method that has been used to trace the origins of the Slavs is the study of toponyms (place names) and hydronyms (names of bodies of water, such as rivers). The latter have been regarded as particularly useful, because their names seem to be retained even when population changes are demonstrable. Identifying Slavic river names that seem to be derived from archaic roots would mean that they were named by local people speaking that archaic form of Slavic, and thus enable the identification of a region where the most archaic river names appear as the *Urheimat*. Aleksander Pogodin concluded that the two regions with the oldest river names of Slavic origin were Podolia and parts of Volhynia, while Jürgen Udolph's employment of the same type of evidence located the Slavic *Urheimat* in Galicia. Some Polish linguists, however, tried to show that the earliest Slavic-derived hydronyms were in the area of modern Poland. Oleg N. Trubachev used a number of linguistic arguments, including river names, to postulate that the Slavic homeland had been in Pannonia. So different criteria have been used by different scholars to identify the "earliest" Slavic hydronyms, but again mostly deriving from the comparative method based in the *Stammbaum* model.[11]

There has thus been a lack of agreement on the methods to be used in a linguistic search for the Proto-Slavic homeland and which phenomena were or were not suitable for use as evidence in the investigations. Summing up the many decades of using linguistic methodology to determine the *Urheimat* and early history of the Slavs, the Polish linguist Hanna Popowska-Taborska noted the number of mutually contradictory theories and interpretations based on the same evidence. She concludes her survey in a very despairing tone: "Can the matter of the study of ethnogenesis really be so hopeless?"[12]

Advances in sociolinguistics have drawn attention to the reasons why languages change, and why some forms replace others, but these models have yet to be fully applied to the question of the origin of the Slavs. Perhaps when they are, we will be able to break out of the somewhat circular arguments that have plagued the subject. The main problem seems to be that much of the work done so far has been based in nineteenth-century diffusionist and evolutionary paradigms, including migrationist hypotheses, with too little consideration of other linguistic processes. It may well be, however, that a search for a compact Slavic *Urheimat* is futile. The wave model prompts us to think more in terms of linguistic convergence than divergence. The language that gave rise to medieval Slavic languages would then have been in the nature of a hybrid, incorporating linguistic features from a wider range of sources over a wider area. It is tempting as a working hypothesis to suggest that the extent of the several groups of river names that various authors have suggested as earliest in fact represent different parts of that hybridization process. Taken together they may mark the approximate area where an archaic form or forms of Slavic and entities closely related to them were spoken).

One problem that has always been raised with regard to the Slavic migration hypothesis is the source of the tremendous demographic growth that would be required to fill almost half of Europe with this new population in the space of a few centuries. This seems biologically impossible, which forces us to realize that the "Early Slavs" must represent groups of mixed origins who at some stage for some reason began to use the Slavic language (perhaps as a lingua franca). The application of genetics to the study of past populations may help us assess the ability of the migrationist model to explain the spread of Proto-Slavic. For example, the Y-chromosome haplogroup R1a1 (M17) is spread across Eurasia, but with the highest frequencies in Eastern Europe, particularly in Poland and Ukraine; it is also reported as common in Slavic populations in the Balkans but is less common in Western Europe. Its initial spread – probably from the Balkans – was probably due to events occurring some 10,000 years ago, reinforced by later prehistoric population movements. The distribution of this haplotype tells us nothing about these later population movements, but the study of rapidly evolving Y-chromosomal short tandem repeat loci (Y-STRs) may be capable of resolving male genealogies to an unparalleled degree. They can thus provide a useful means to study local population structure and recent demographic history. This rapidly growing area of study is still in its infancy. We may confidently expect it to advance considerably our understanding of ancient population processes in the region in the future.[13]

Archaeological evidence has also been used in the search for Slav origins and invoked no less controversy and debate than some of the other evidence reviewed above. At first sight there may seem to be something preposterous about the idea that by studying material traces like pottery or holes in the ground one might determine the language spoken by those who made them. Material culture, however, can relate to identity in a variety of ways, as can language, so identity may link the two, though probably not as directly as archaeologists once thought. The search for a single "emblematic" artifact that occurs across the whole area where Slavic was spoken is futile; the material culture of the early Slavic-speakers is not open to simplistic interpretation. Dixon's punctuated-equilibrium model, however, implies that linguistic change relates to other changes that may be traceable archaeologically. Language is a social phenomenon, and modern archaeology aims to study societies through material traces, which seems to offer some hope that, while the languages themselves may not be traceable, the social and other processes with which they are linked may.

Medieval Slavic pottery had been identified by the end of the nineteenth century, but the identification of a "Prague Type" pottery in Bohemia[14] which could be assigned to the Slavs of the sixth and seventh centuries AD, was followed by the gradual

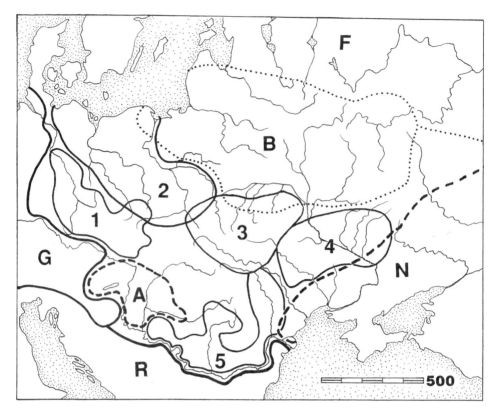

Figure 2.1   Central and Eastern Europe in the late sixth–seventh centuries
key
1. Prague-Type Culture; 2. West Slav groups (Sukow, etc.); 3. Korchak Culture; 4. Penkovka Culture; 5. Southern groups (Prut-Dniestr, Danubian Plain).
A – Avars; G – Germanic groups; R – Roman Empire (Justinian); N – Nomads.
In the northern forest zone, the dotted lines delimit the areas of Baltic (B) and Finno-Ugric (F) hydronyms.
Scale in kilometers.

recognition of a range of material culture traits that were found in fairly similar form across wide zones of Central and Eastern Europe and generally held to be character-istic of the "Early Slavs." Originally the search was for material traces of the "Slav migrations"; archaeologists were looking for the region where the earliest material of Early Slav type could be found, pinpointing the starting place of the migrations.

This approach, however, also opened the way for the use of archaeology in identity politics. Borkovsky had tried to show that the Slavs had developed in Bohemia, because the material he identified resembled prehistoric pottery from the same region. The same arguments, however, were later used by other archaeologists, including Polish and Ukrainian ones, to make the same claims for their own homelands. In the 1930s the study of Russia's Slavic past became part of the Stalinist policies of creation of identities, just as was to happen between 1945 and 1948 in the Central European states under Soviet hegemony. This gave the impetus to broader investigations into the Slavic past of these countries. From the 1950s there were a number of major research projects by a younger generation of archaeologists all over Eastern Europe that produced a new quality of information.

There was, for example, a major program of research into the Early Slav settlements and cemeteries of Ukraine, with excavations carried out on a large scale, including the total excavation of sixth-to-seventh-century villages. These produced a huge amount of information about daily life and the material culture of the Early Slavs of the region. The villages of the so-called Korchak type were composed of several individual home-steads containing small buildings, the excavated structures of which were sunken-floored timber huts with stone ovens in the corner. In the fills of these and other features around them were a number of objects, the most frequent being fragments of handmade pottery vessels of a distinctive form. Also found were fragments of round ceramic baking plates related to some specific culinary method. Fortified settlements are unknown. There are, however, few burials; the method used to dispose of the dead left no archaeological traces.[15]

On the left bank of the Dniepr and extending along the southern edge of the forest steppe to the middle Dniestr, another archaeological complex was identified, known as the Penkovka group, that has many features in common with the Korchak assemblages, with similar settlement form (though the internal arrangement of the houses differs on either side of the Dniepr).[16] Small flat cremation cemeteries with urned and unurned burial are also the rule, although they are mainly concentrated in the Dniepr valley. The main features distinguishing the Penkovka group from the Korchak material are the slightly different and more varied form of the pottery vessels and round ceramic baking plates.

In work carried out since the 1950s in various regions of Central and Eastern Europe occupied in the early Middle Ages by Slavic-speakers, broadly similar material has been found. It is inevitable that over such a wide area there was some variation in things such as pottery form, house type, and burial rite, as well as percentages of different species of domestic animals kept and crops raised. Nevertheless the material tells a similar story across the whole region.

The archaeological material left by the Early Slavs is very modest when compared with, for example, contemporary Germanic groups of northwestern Europe. To some extent this is due to an extensive use of organic materials such as wood, which has not generally survived. Metal was rarely thrown away, but reused. The predominant burial rite was of a type that does not leave archaeological traces (the few small cemeteries that have been found contain urned and unurned cremations with few or no grave goods). Settlements seem to have been largely self-sufficient in most things, with little evidence of imported goods, let alone luxury items. There were few signs of social dif-ferentiation; these societies would seem to have been egalitarian. The archaeological material that is preserved gives the impression of functional, no-nonsense simplicity, without any expression of opulence. Even the pottery (Prague, Korchak, Penkovka types) is minimalist in both the style and effort required to produce it.

A particularly telling example of this tendency is the noticeable lack of personal orna-ment in Early Slav contexts. There is a group of radiate-headed "Slawische Bugelfibeln" found in a zone from Pannonia and the Balkans to the Dniepr but centered on the Carpathians. They have been found in Slavic contexts, such as the exceptionally large cemetery at Sarata Monteoru in southeast Romania. Although they really were used as an emblematic artifact by the Early Slavs, their overall distribution is puzzling. While a few occur in the area of the Penkovka Culture, they are almost totally absent from the Korchak zone and Slavic assemblages north of the Carpathians. They do, however, occur further north in a series of West Baltic cemeteries near Olsztyn, and recent typological work by Florin Curta has shown that they come from the same workshops as the ones on the Danube. This suggests that these objects traveled through Slavic communities, but none was retained for use by them, almost as if they were rejecting the whole idea of the "Fibula tracht" (costume), almost ubiquitous in the Roman period and still surviving further west.[17]

There have been a number of suggestions as to where the Korchak and Penkovka cultures had their origin. In the late 1970s Valentin V. Sedov regarded the Przeworsk Culture of the Roman Period of Central Europe as representing the Venedi mentioned by Jordanes and Tacitus. He suggested that this culture had moved into the Dniepr region, assimilating pre-existing populations (Zarubinets and Kiev cultures), giving rise to the Slavs.[18] In 1970 Petr Tret'iakov linked the Prague type to the Iron Age Zarubinets Culture itself, proposing it was here on the middle Dniepr that the Slavs had had their origin, an idea that was to be particularly persistent and a model that was to play a large part in Polish "allochthonous" models (see below).[19]

Volodymyr D. Baran proposed that the Slavs had emerged as an independent political force from the Cherniakhovo Culture by the end of the fifth century, after the end of Hunnic rule. On the basis of associations of Early Slav material with metalwork in the late Roman Period tradition, he proposes that the earliest Slavic sites lie in Podolia (upper Dniestr valley) on the northeast flanks of the Carpathians (in the general region where Udolph located his earliest Slavic hydronyms).[20] This view has been contested by Mark Shchukin, whose analysis of metal finds dated from the third to fifth century has shown that in the area Baran identifies as the Slavic *Urheimat* there is a chronological gap between the latest Cherniakhovo and earliest Early Slav assemblages. Shchukin locates the *Urheimat* of the Slavs in the Pripet basin, in a region devoid of datable personal ornaments on his maps of datable finds.[21]

In Poland, archaeologists had long been claiming that Slavic origins lay in the Bronze and Iron Age Lusatian (Lausitz) Culture in the valleys of the Oder and Vistula, because of the apparent similarity of material culture (but also engendered by national pride and a desire to oppose German anti-Slav propaganda). The famous fortified site at Biskupin excavated from the 1930s onward was seen as a "Proto-Slavic town." This model, the most vociferous proponents of which were Józef Kostrzewski and Konrad Jażdżewski, proposed that Slavs had been autochthonous in Poland since late prehistory at least.

The development in the 1970s by the Cracow scholar Każimierz Godłowski of the first chronological system for the late Roman and migration periods of Central Europe forced a re-examination of this view. Godłowski pointed to a considerable chronological gap and substantial differences between the Early Slavic culture and its predecessors. He suggested that an ethnic indicator of the Early Slavs was a combination of artifact types, not only pottery, but also sunken huts and cremation burials. These elements appeared together in areas of Eastern and Central Europe that had been abandoned by Germanic tribes only at the end of the *Völkerwanderungszeit*. The archaeological evidence led him to the conclusion that, rather than developing in Poland since the Bronze Age, it was only after *c.* 500 that the Slavs came into existence as a cultural and ethnic group. This idea he published in 1979 in his "little yellow book," which proposed his "allochthonous" model, according to which, in the second half of the sixth century and the early seventh century, the Slavs had migrated into southern Poland from Ukraine, where they had originated. Thus began an extremely heated dispute between the two Polish schools, which has gone on until today. Godłowski's ideas on Slavic origins have been developed by his student, Michał Parczewski.[22]

Social Consolidation

The Luka Rajkovetska Culture developed from its predecessors by the eighth century. In material terms there were few changes from pre-existing cultures; many features

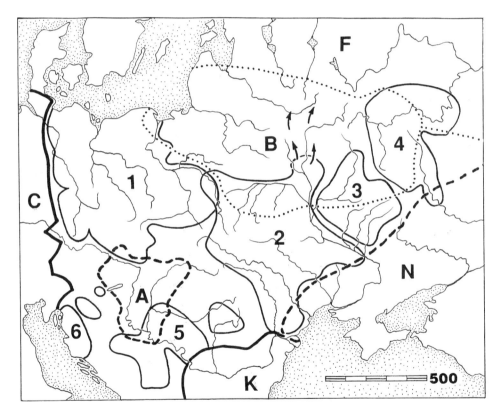

Figure 2.2 Central and Eastern Europe in the eighth and ninth centuries
key
1. West Slav cultural groups (Fedberg, Tornow, Raciborz-Chodlik, Devinska Nova Ves, etc.);
2. Luka Rajkovetska Culture; 3. Volyntsevo Culture; 4. Borshevo Culture; 5–6. Southern groups (Dalmatia, Pannonia, Morava valley, etc.).
C – Carolingian Empire; A – Avars, K – Bulgars and Slavs; N – Nomads.
In the northern forest zone, the dotted lines delimit the areas of Baltic (B) and Finno-Ugric (F) hydronyms.
Scale in kilometers.

were retained, such as village and house form (sunken-floored huts), and burial rite. Many more iron objects have been found in feature fills and hoards; presumably, however, increased production meant that iron was no longer an especially rare material. There seems to have been an increase in population density, together with social and economic consolidation. A new feature is an increase in numbers of strongholds being constructed on steep promontories or in boggy places and surrounded by earthen ramparts and ditches. These communal earthworks indicate a degree of social consolidation and pooling of resources needed to create sizable work teams. They also indicate a need for such constructions to act as public places for the display of the prestige generated by increased wealth and social differentiation as well as defenses.[23] Among these sites are several early strongholds in the Kiev area, including one on the high hill over the river crossing at Kiev itself, dated by associated pottery to the eighth and ninth centuries.

On the left bank of the Dniepr between the upper Oka and Don in the eastern Ukraine (and extending north into what appears to have been Baltic territory) is the contemporary Volyntsevo Culture, which also retains many traits of the previous Penkovka culture. Signs of increased wealth and social differentiation are visible here too. Some of the cemeteries were also large, and contain relatively rich grave goods, such as glass beads, metal ornaments, and iron objects. Volyntsevo material includes a relatively large quantity of Islamic silver coins, which had flowed into the area from Khazaria or from the lands of the Bulgars on the Volga and Kama. These occur, sometimes as loose finds, more often as hoards. Settlements and graves in the area also produce silver jewelery (rings, bracelets) more frequently than other areas of the East Slav lands at this time.[24] There are eighth-to-tenth-century strongholds here too (formerly called Romny-type sites). These were densely built-up settlements having the appearance of fortified villages. The extent of these sites along the Desna, Sejm, Psel, Sula, and Vorksla rivers matches quite closely the area assigned to the Severjane by the *PVL*.[25]

Possibly related to this settlement process are the Borshevo group of eighth-to-tenth-century strongholds on the upper Don and Oka in the former Baltic zone of the northern forest zone and extending into the Finno-Ugric area to the northeast. The involvement of the Slavs in the process leading to the formation of this cultural group is less clear (their distribution, however, matches the area that much later emerges in the written records as the territory of the Viatichi tribe).

Despite the large enclosures on the hills above the Dniepr at Kiev and the efforts of the *PVL* chronicler to give the prehistory of the area some substance, the territory that was later to become the domain of the Poliane seems to have had only limited importance throughout most of the ninth century. There was, for example, only a comparatively limited flow of Islamic silver into this area.

It would seem likely that the origin of the Volyntsevo and Borshevo sites is linked to the consolidation of Khazar power on the adjacent Don steppe and hegemony over the neighboring areas. It may be no coincidence that the Russian Primary Chronicle tells us that the Severjane and Vjatichi paid a tribute to the Khazars in "silver coin and squirrel furs." The construction of strongholds may either reflect the need for defense against nomad raiders and would-be tribute collectors, or may perhaps be part of the mechanism whereby local leaders extracted tribute from their dependants on behalf of Khazar overlords. The archaeological evidence suggests that these groups in proximity to the Khazar state in the eighth and ninth centuries had achieved some form of wealth and perhaps organization, maybe involving the generation of wealth and prestige by controlling tribute networks and some form of long-distance exchange through their territory. The nature of the organization of these polities is unclear; they seem not to have become centralized as states. It was only at the end of the ninth century that the importance of the Volyntsevo and Borshevo polities was to be eclipsed by the growing influence of the Poliane (at least that is what later chronicles name them) under their leaders operating from Kiev.

The Northern Forests

So far we have principally been discussing evidence relating mainly to the area to the south of the Pripet and Seym. The early medieval history of the area of modern Belarussia and southwestern parts of the modern Russian Republic was somewhat different. This is a zone dominated by ancient Baltic (and further north Ugro-Finnic) hydronyms; discussion therefore is about when and how Slavic-speaking populations became established here. As with the situation in Poland, two main models have been proposed. Either Slavic-speaking communities were established here following the breakup of the hypothetical Balto-Slavic linguistic community (the "transition" model), or they developed here because of influences and population movements from the south (the "hybridization" model).

Attempts have occasionally been made to suggest that the archaeological cultures of the area were left by Proto-Slavs already present in the Iron Age.[26] One suspects modern identities were at stake in such assertions. Moscow, the center of the Soviet state, was in this northern zone but endeavored to portray itself as the inheritor of the glorious past of Kievan Rus'; in more recent years independent states have wished to do the same. Thus local early medieval cultures like the Kolochin, the Tushemla-Bancherovska, and Moshchiny have at times been proposed as Proto-Slavic, based partly on apparent similarities of the material culture with later archaeological remains associated with the Slavs, and partly on retrogression from models of a wider spread of Slavs in the early medieval period. Some archaeologists have even detected Slav elements in the Long Barrows and Sopki cultures existing from the sixth or seventh century AD in areas of Finno-Ugric hydronymy even further north.[27] There are, however, no hydronyms that have been seriously considered as archaic or Proto-Slavic in any part of this region. The suggestive similarities in material culture seem more likely to be ascribable to convergence owing to similar lifestyles under similar environmental conditions; there is in reality no convincing evidence that any of these assemblages represent the cultures of Slavic-speaking communities.

The date of penetration of Slavic-speakers into the area to the north of the Pripet and Seym is unclear. At the beginning of the early medieval period, there is a general lack of ethnically specific and closely datable artifacts that can be used to identify the presence of Slavs. While some scholars (such as Sedov) have dated their presence here to the seventh century on linguistic grounds, there is more to incline us towards a later date, nearer the ninth century.[28] In all probability, there would not have been a single massive migration wave but movements of small groups establishing Slav enclaves in the region that in some way eventually consolidated as the tribal groups that are mentioned in the later written sources. The Slavs who settled in the Long

Barrows Culture zone became organized in a tribe later known as the Pskov Kryvichi (centered on the mid-ninth-century stronghold at Pskov). Apparently about the same time various Slav groups were arriving in the areas around Lake Ilmen, finding a home in the areas of Finno-Ugric and Baltic peoples (in the area of the Sopki mounds). Their numbers and importance increased in time, possibly in connection with their involvement in the prestige- and wealth-generating networks of long-distance exchange that were developing at this period. By the tenth and eleventh centuries they became an important ethnic component of the region. They named themselves "Slovene", the Slavs, an obvious ethnonym to choose in alien surroundings.

Recent work using genetic evidence has shown that the populations of the northern forests were of mixed origins, reflecting the intermingling of Slavs and autochthonous Balts and Finns, with a preponderance of the latter. This illustrates the reality behind the so-called Slavic migrations, a process of assimilation, but the emergence of a dominant identity and language that in this case for some reason belonged to the incoming minority. Other work comparing mitochondrial DNA and Y-chromosome analyses appears to indicate that Russian colonization of the north-eastern territories might have been accomplished mainly by males rather than by females.[29]

About the same time, the northern zone attracted another alien group, Scandinavians from Middle Sweden.[30] They were active in the areas around the emporium at Ladoga (*Priladozhe*) from about the middle of the eighth century, coinciding with an increase in the flow of Abbasid silver to the northern forests through Khazar territory. The local Finns, with whom they interacted, apparently named the newcomers Ruotsi (Rus') (meaning "oarsmen"), a name they were soon to adopt for themselves. From their "colonies" in Finnic territory, these adventurers plied the riverways to collect forest products such as wax, skins, and furs as well as slaves, which were the staple of an exchange with the south, initially to and through Khazar territory, a trade that archaeological evidence shows included "Viking" swords and other decorative metalwork. These goods flowed south, and Islamic silver flowed north in exchange.

By the middle of the ninth century the successes of these enterprises were attracting more entrepreneurs from Sweden, among them now groups of warriors with leaders who participated in the taking of tributes, and the military aspects of Scandinavian penetration of the area became more visible. The economic stimulation generated by the development of these long-distance exchange networks were probably among the factors attracting more Slavs into the area to settle around the centers where Scandinavian activity is also attested.

The Viking impact on the area has at times been seen as the result of one-sided acts of a superior immigrant elite, laying the foundations for the creation of the Rus' state. Such an interpretation is highly questionable. The process was presumably much more complex and involved interaction, cooperation, and synthesis. Although the Scandinavian elite is highly visible in the archaeological and written records, without the support of the local elites it would have been almost impossible for it to impose its will over what is today northwestern Russia, with its potentially hostile tribes that would have greatly outnumbered the newcomers. Local Finnic and Slavic populations of northwestern Russia most probably incorporated Scandinavian warriors in the organization of the emerging polities in order to provide military backing and to enforce the rule of local elite, in return for which they were probably paid in commodities such as furs and/or silver.

By the end of the ninth century, Scandinavians were involved in the establishment of economic and political control over the forest communities in the territory between the upper Volga and Oka rivers. They also settled on the upper Dniepr, which seems to be related to the increased development of a route that led, not to Khazaria, but to another powerful neighbor to the south, Byzantium. This development was connected to the strengthening of a power base and tribute-gathering network among the Slavs on the middle Dniepr, a process in which Scandinavian warrior bands operating from Kiev and other centers took part. Kiev increased in importance and became a pivotal point in the prestige-generating long-distance exchange route from the Lake Ladoga region to Constantinople. It was only a matter of time before a group of the Scandinavians, instead of providing military support for a local elite, seems to have decided to take power on their own account, thus founding the Rurikid dynasty of Kievan Rus'. They soon set about extending the influence of their power to the adjacent territories, a process that was aided by their having themselves become consolidated over the previous century and a half. The foundations were thus laid for the creation of a sizable centralized state.

Notes

1 P. M. Barford, *The Early Slavs: Culture and Society*, British Museum Press, London, and Cornell University Press, Ithaca, NY, 2001.

2 Ibid. 24–5; Pavel Dolukhanov, *The Early Slavs*, Longman, London, 1996, 151–60.

3 W. Pohl, "Conceptions of Ethnicity in Early Medieval Studies," *Archaeologia Polona*, 29 (1990–1), 39–49. Repr. in L. K. Little and B. Rosenwein, eds., *Debating the Middle Ages: Issues and Readings*, Blackwell, Oxford, 1998, 15–24; A. Gillet (ed.), *On Barbarian Identity: Critical Approaches to Ethnicity in the Early Middle Ages*, Studies in the Early Middle Ages 4, University of York, York, and Brepols, Turnhout, 2002.

4 H. Birnbaum, *Common Slavic: Progress and Problems in its Reconstruction*, Slavica Publishers, Columbus, OH, 1975; A. M. Schenker, *The Dawn of Slavic: An Introduction to Slavic Philology*, Yale University Press, New Haven and London, 1995.

5 Wave Theory: A. Fox, *Linguistic Reconstruction: An Introduction to Theory and Method*, Oxford University Press, New York, 1995, 129; Punctuated Equilibrium model: R. M. W. Dixon, *The Rise and Fall of Languages*, Cambridge University Press, Cambridge, 1997; Balto-Slavic: O. Szemerenyi, (1957) "The Problem of Balto-Slavic Unity: A Critical Survey," *Kratylos*, 2 (1957), 97–122, and Schenker, *The Dawn of Slavic*.

6 L. Tyszkiewicz, *Słowianie w Historiografii Antycznej do Połowy VI Wieku*, Wydawnictwo Uniwersytetu Wrocławskiego, Wrocław, 1990; id., *Słowianie w Historiografii Wczesnego Średniowiecza od Połowy VI do Połowy VII Wieku*. Wydawnictwo Uniwersytetu Wrocławskiego, Wrocław, 1994.

7 Procopius, *Wars*, V 27, 1–2; Jordanes, *Getica*, 34.

8 M. Gimbutas, *The Slavs*, Thames and Hudson, London, 1971, 23–4; T. Milewski, "Die Differenzierung der Indoeuropäischen Sprachen," *Lingua Posnaniensis*, 12/13 (1968), 37–54; Critique of Mańczak: K. Steinke, "Aktualna dyskusja o praojczyźnie Słowian," in W. Boryś, J. Rusek, and L. Bednarczuk, eds., *Dzieje Słowian w Świetle Leksyki, Pamięci Profesora Franciszka Sławskiego*. Wydawnictwo Uniwersytetu Jagiellońskiego, Cracow, 2002, 199–204.

9   J. Rostafiński, *O pierwotnych siedzibach i gospodarstwie Słowian w przedhistorycznych czasach*, M. Arcta, Cracow, 1908.

10 H. Popowska-Taborska, *Wczesne Dzieje Słowian w Świetle ich Języka*, Warsaw, 1993, 36–48; T. Wojciechowski, *Chrobacja: Rozbiór Starożytności Słowiańskich*, Akademia Umiętności, Cracow, 1873; A. L. Pogodin, *Iz Istorii Slavianskikh Peredvizhenii*, A. P. Lopukhina, St Petersburg, 1901, 85–111; K. Moszyński, *Pierwotny Zasięg Języka Prasłowiańskiego*, Wrocław, 1957, 23–66; J. Udolph, *Studien zu Slavischen Gewässernamen und Gewässerbezeichnungen: Ein Beitrag zur Frage der Urheimat der Slaven*, C. Winter, Heidelberg, 1979, 619–20; id., "Kritisches und Antikritisches zur Bedeutung slavischer Gewässernamen für die Ethnogenese der Slawen," *Zeitschrift für slawische Philologie*, 45 (1985), 33–57; T. Lehr Spławinski, "Rozmieszczenie geograficzne prasłowiańskich nazw wodnych," *Rocznik Slawistyczny*, 21/1 (1960/1), 5–22; id., "Początki ekspansji Słowiań ku wschodowi," *Slavia Antiqua* 9 (1962), 1–7; Z. Babik, *Najstarsza Warstwa Nazewnictwa na Ziemiach Polskich w Granicach Wczesnośredniowiecznej Słowiańszczyny*, Wydawnictwo Uniwersytetu Jagiellońskiego, Cracow, 2001. Pannonia: J. Udolf, "Kamen die Slaven aus Pannonien?," in G. Labuda and S. Tabaczyński, eds., *Studia nad Etnogenezą Słowian i Kulturą Europy Wczesnośredniowiecznej*, vol. 1, Ossolineum, Wrocław, 1987, 168–73.

11 H. Popowska-Taborska, *Wczesne Dzieje Słowian w Świetle ich Języka*, Slawistyczny Ośrodek Wydawniczy, Warsaw, 1993, 144; id., (1997) "The Slavs in the Early Middle Ages from the Viewpoint of Modern Linguistics," in P. Urbańczyk, ed., *The Origins of Central Europe*, Instytut Archeologii i Etnologii PAN, Warsaw, 1997, 91–6.

12 O. Semino, G. Passarino, P. J. Oefner, et al., "The Genetic Legacy of Paleolithic Homo sapiens sapiens in Extant Europeans," *Science*, 290 (2000), 1155–9; R. S. Wells, N. Yuldasheva, R. Ruzibakiev, et al., (2001) "The Eurasian Heartland: A Continental Perspective on Y-chromosome Diversity," *Proc. Natl Acad. Sci. U S A.*, 98/18 (2001), 10244–9.

13 I. Borkovský, *Staroslovanska keramika ve střední Evrop.* [Nákladem vlastním], Prague, 1940.

14 e.g. I. P. Rusanova and B. O. Timoschuk, *Kodyn, Slavianskie Poseleniia V–VIII vv. na r. Prut.* Nauka, Moscow, 1984; V. D. Baran, *Prazhskaia Kul tura Podnestrov'ia po Materialam Poselenii u s. Rashkov.* Naukova Dumka, Kiev, 1988.

15 V. V. Sedov, *Vostochnye Slaviane v VI–XIII vv* [Archeologija SSSR XIV]. Nauka, Moscow, 1982, 10–87; M. Kazanski, *Les Slaves: Les Origines Ier–VIIe siècle après J.-C*, Éditions errance, Paris, 1999, "96–120; O. M. Prikhodniuk, "Anty i penkovskaia kultura," in P. P. Tolochko, ed., *Drevnie slaviane i Kievskaia Rus*, Naukova Dumka, Kiev, 1989.

16 J. Werner, "Slawische Bugelfibeln des 7. Jahrhunderts," in G. Behrens and J. Werner, eds., *Reinecke Festschrift zum 75. Geburtstag von Paul Reinecke am 25. September 1947*, E. Schneider, Mainz, 1950, 150–72; F. Curta, *Making of the Slavs: History and Archaeology of the Lower Danube Region*, c. 500–700, Cambridge University Press, Cambridge, 2001, 247–75; id., "Female Dress and 'Slavic' Bow Fibulae in Greece," *Hesperia*, 74 (2005), 101–46.

17 V. V. Sedov, *Proiskhozhdenie i ranniaia istoriia Slavian*, Nauka, Moscow, 1979; id., *Slaviane v drevnosti*, Nauka, Moscow, 1994; id., "Sovremennoe sostoianie problemy etnogeneza slavian," *Slavia Antiqua*, 37 (1996), 21–40.

18 P. N. Tret'iakov, *U istokov drevnorusskoi narodnosti*, Leningrad, 1970.

19 V. D. Baran, *Prazhskaia Kultura Podnestrov'ia po Materialam Poselenii u s. Rashkov*, Naukova Dumka, Kiev, 1988; see also I. P. Rusanova, "O rannei date pamiatnikov prazhskogo tipa," in T. V. Nikolaeva, ed., *Drevniaia Rus i slaviane*, Nauka, Moscow, 1978, 138–43.

20 M. Shchukin, "The Balto-Slavic Forest Direction in the Archaeological Study of the Ethnogenesis of the Slavs," *Wiadomości Archeologiczne*, 51 (1986–90), 3–30.

21 K. Godlowski, *Z badan nad zagadnieniem rozprzestrzenia Słowian w V–VII w. n.e.*, Wydawnictwo Uniwersytetu Jagiellońskiego, Cracow, 1979; id., (1983) "Zur Frage der Slawensitze vor der grossen Slawenwanderung im 6. Jahrhundert," in *Gli Slavi occidentali e meridionali nell alto Medioevo*, vol. 1, Presso la Sede del Centro, Spoleto, 1983, 257–302; M. Parczewski, *Początki Kultury Wczesnosłowiańskiej w Polsce. Krytyka i Datowanie Źródeł Archeologicznych*, Zakład Narodowy im. Ossolińskich, Wrocław/Warsaw/Cracow, 1988; id., "Origins of Early Slav Culture in Poland," *Antiquity*, 65 (1991), 676–83; id., *Die Anfänge der frühslawischen Kultur in Polen*, Österreichische Gesellschaft für Ur- und Frühgeschichte, Vienna, 1993.

22 Barford, *Early Slavs*, 96–7; Sedov, *Vostochnye slavjane*, 10–87.

23 Barford, *Early Slavs*, 86–8.

24 Ibid. 96–8; Gimbutas, *The Slavs*, 90–1; Sedov, *Vostochnye slavjane*, 10–87.

25 Gimbutas, *The Slavs*, 90–1; Sedov, *Vostochnye slavjane*, 10–87.

26 Barford, *Early Slavs*, 101–2.

27 Sedov, *Vostochnye slaviane*, 10–87; see also Kazanski, *Les Slaves*, 33–7, 120–9. These cultures are also briefly summarized by Dolukhanov, *The Early Slavs*, 167–70. For them as Slavs: V. V. Sedov, "Origine de la branche du Nord des Slaves orientaux," in G. Labuda and S. Tabaczyński, eds., *Studia nad Etnogenezą Słowian*, vol. 1, Ossolineum, Warsaw, 1987, 161–5.

28 Barford *Early Slavs*, 101–3; C. Goehrke, *Frühzeit des Ostslawentums* (Erträge der Forschung, 277), Darmstadt, 1992.

29 V. Orekhov, P. Ivanov, L.Zhivotovksy, et al., "MtDNA Sequence Diversity in Three Neighbouring Ethnic Groups of Three Language Families from the European Part of Russia," in C. Renfrew and K. Boyle, eds., *Archaeogenetics: DNA and the Population Prehistory of Europe*, McDonald Institute, Cambridge, 2000, 245–8; B. Malyarchuk and M. Derenko, "Mitochondrial DNA Variability in Eastern Slavs," in ibid. 249–54; B. Malyarchuk, M. Derenko, T. Grzybowski, et al., "Differentiation of Mitochondrial DNA and Y Chromosomes in Russian Populations," *Human Biology*, 76/6 (Dec. 2004), 877–900.

30 W. Duczko, *Viking Rus: Studies on the Presence of Scandinavians in Eastern Europe*. Brill, Leiden-Boston, 2004; T. S. Noonan, "The Vikings and Russia: Some New Directions and Approaches to an Old Problem," in R. Samson, ed., Social Approaches to Viking Studies, Cruithne Press, Glasgow, 1991, 201–6.

Further Reading

Barford P. M. (2001). *The Early Slavs: Culture and. Society*. British Museum Press, London, and Cornell University Press, Ithaca, NY.

Cross, S. H., and Sherbowitz-Wetzor, O. P. (1953). *The Russian Primary Chronicle*. Mediaeval Academy. Cambridge.

Dolukhanov, P.M. (1996). *The Early Slavs: Eastern Europe from the Initial Settlement to the Kievan Rus*. Longman, London and New York.

Gimbutas, M. (1971). *The Slavs*. Thames and Hudson, London.

Kazanski, M. (1999). *Les Slaves, Les Origines Ier–VIIe siècle après J.-C.* Éditions errance, Paris.

Renfrew, C., and Boyle, K. (eds.) (2000). *Archaeogenetics: DNA and the Population Prehistory of Europe*. McDonald Institute, Cambridge.

Sedov, V. V. (1982). *Vostochnye Slaviane v VI–XIII vv* [Archeologija SSSR XIV]. Nauka, Moscow.

CHAPTER THREE

The First East Slavic State

JANET MARTIN

The first attested East Slavic state has come to be known as Kievan (Kyivan) Rus'. In broad outline its history may be simply stated. Established by the ninth century, it was centered at Kiev and ruled by the Riurikid dynasty, which acquired exclusive authority over its East Slavic and Finnic inhabitants from the tenth century. Over the next two and a half centuries the state expanded into a composite of multiple principalities. At its peak Kievan Rus' stretched from the shores of the Gulf of Finland eastward to the Volga–Oka region, northward toward the White Sea, southward to the mid-Dnieper (Dnipro) region and beyond the steppe to include Tmutorokan', and southwestward to encompass Galicia and Volhynia on the borders of Poland. After the Mongol invasion of 1238–40, Kievan Rus' ceased to exist. This overview, however, does not address some fundamental problems relating to the history of Kievan Rus': the origins of the state, the character of that state; and the factors that drove its development and led to its collapse.

These problems have not been easy to solve. Kievan Rus' was a complex state and society. The Riurikids, its ruling dynasty, were originally from Sweden; early rulers used the title *khagan*, borrowed from the neighboring Khazar Empire; they wielded political authority over a largely East Slavic and Finnic population; their dynastic organization resembled the model of their nomadic Turkic neighbors; their religion came from Byzantium; and they intermarried not only with members of the Byzantine imperial family, but with the royalty of Europe and the leading families of the Turkic nomads of the steppe.

Scholars who have attempted to unravel the tangle of these multiple influences include experts on early Russian history, Ukrainian history, the Viking age, the Byzantine Empire, steppe nomads, and even on the Islamic world. Approaching the problems from different perspectives, employing different theoretical assumptions and methodologies, they have reached startlingly different conclusions, which have generated long-lasting debates and challenged scholars repeatedly to revisit these problems using fresh approaches. Their resulting contributions, based on such a wide range of perspectives, have been constructive, but the complexity of Kievan Rus', its cultural contacts, and the influences under which it developed have made it very

Figure 3.1 Kiev Rus' in the Early Twelfth Century
Source: Jesse Clarkson, *A History of Russia* (second edition) (Macmillan, 1969)

difficult to reach consensus on even the basic themes noted above. The following discussion will review the above-mentioned problems related to the first East Slavic state and the debates surrounding them. The problems are not unrelated. The solutions scholars have favored in relation to one have influenced their insights into the others.

Origins of the First East Slavic State

In the year 839, according to an entry in the *Annales Bertiniani* (Annales of St Bertin), a Byzantine embassy arrived at the court of Emperor Louis the Pious. Accompanying the ambassadors were some individuals who identified themselves as Rhos (Rus') and explained that they had been sent by their *khagan* on a mission to the Byzantine emperor. Because hostile populations blocked their route home, they had been sent to Louis in the hope he would assist them on their return journey. Louis, however, was suspicious. He detained the Rhos envoys and determined they were Swedes, whom he regarded as enemies. Only after receiving further assurances from Byzantium did he release them (Golden 1982: 81; Duczko 2004: 10–59; Shepard 2006: 49, 51).

The mysterious Rus' or Rhos caught the attention of Islamic observers as well. They included comments on Rus' along with Slavic peoples in their geographies and other texts produced in the ninth and tenth centuries (Golden 1982: 82–3; Martin 1986: 173–4, 195–7; Franklin and Shepard 1996: 40–1, 108–9; Gorskii 2004: 62–5). The main written source for Kievan Rus', the Primary Chronicle or Tale of Bygone Years, also contains an entry reporting that the Rus' arrived in the lands of Finnic and East Slavs about 862 (Cross and Sherbowitz-Wetzor 1953: 59).

The repeated references to Rus' in unrelated European, Islamic, and Russian sources make a convincing case that in the ninth century some people, known as the Rus', were present in the part of Eastern Europe that later became Russia. But all of those sources were composed by persons who were far removed from the Rus' state and the events surrounding its formation either by great distances or by lengthy time periods. Their reports are so vague and varied in their details that they have left later investigators just as puzzled about the Rus' as Emperor Louis was when he first encountered them. Scholars have thus been probing for centuries into the questions of who were the Rus' and what role they played in the formation of the first East Slavic state. To compensate for the scarcity of reliable, unambiguous written sources, historians have used linguistic, anthropological, and archeological evidence as well. That evidence has provided significant insights, but it too has been interpreted in widely varying ways and, has, therefore, not provided definitive solutions to the problems posed. Although the precise issues within it have been modified, the debate over the origins of Kievan Rus', known as the "Normanist Controversy," has continued for almost three centuries.

The account of the origins of the first East Slavic state that appeared in the Primary Chronicle stated that, in the year 859, a group known as Varangians arrived "from beyond the sea [and] imposed tribute upon [the Finnic and Slavic tribes called] the Chuds, the Slavs [Slovenes], the Merians, the Ves', and the Krivichians." In 860–2, however, "the tributaries of the Varangians drove them beyond the sea and, refusing them further tribute, set out to govern themselves." Their effort failed and, after engaging in wars among themselves, they appealed to the "Varangian Russes" and invited a prince to rule them "according to the Law." Three brothers, Riurik, Sineus, and Truvor, responded to the invitation, migrated with their kinsfolk, and settled in Novgorod, Beloozero, and Izborsk, respectively. After two years, Sineus and his brother Truvor died, and Riurik assumed the sole authority over a range of northern towns, territories and peoples (Cross and Sherbowitz-Wetzor 1953: 59–60).

Within a short time two members of Riurik's band, Askold and Dir, requested permission to go to Tsar'grad (Constantinople) and sailed with their families down the Dnieper River. On their way south they came upon the "small city" of Kiev, which was a tributary of the Khazars. "Askold and Dir remained in the city, and after gathering together many Varangians, they established their dominion over the country of the Polyanians," who lived in the vicinity of Kiev. The chronicler continues his tale with an account of transfer of Kiev to Oleg, a kinsman of Riurik to whom he had entrusted his realm and the safety of his young son Igor'. In 880–2 Oleg, accompanied by a military force, arrived at Kiev, killed Askold and Dir, established himself as prince of Kiev, and imposed tribute on the surrounding East Slavic tribes as well as on Novgorod (Cross and Sherbowitz-Wetzor 1953: 60–1).

These chronicle entries associate the foundation of the first East Slavic state with the arrival of the Rus', identified as Varangians or Scandinavians, in the northern Volkhov-Ladoga-Il'men region and, later, in the southern mid-Dnieper region. Riurik became not only the prince of the northern tribes who invited him to rule them, but also the progenitor of the Riurikid dynasty that subordinated all the East Slav tribes and their territories to create the new state of Kievan Rus'.

Beginning in the eighteenth century, scholars composed narratives of the early history of Kievan Rus' that essentially followed the sequence of events set forth in the chronicle entries. Because they privileged the role of the Scandinavian Rus' in the foundation of the state, their accounts have been labeled the "Normanist theory." Although later Normanists would acknowledge an earlier date for the arrival of Norsemen, their theory credits Riurik and his clansmen, not the East Slavs themselves, with providing political organization to the East Slavic, Finnic, and Baltic tribes dwelling in the region that became northwestern Russia and, later, those of the mid-Dnieper, which became the center of the state of Kievan Rus'. Scandinavians, not Slavs, were responsible for creating the state. An extension of this theory, perpetuated by Sergei Solov'ev (1820–79) and Vasilii Kliuchevsky (1841–1911), regarded Kievan Rus' as the first stage in a continuum that spanned the history of Russia from the Kievan Rus' era through the periods dominated by the principalities of Vladimir-Suzdal' and then Moscow to the Russian Empire.

This representation of the founding of Kievan Rus' prompted the formulation of an opposing view. Its proponents, known as "anti-Normanists" or "nativists," disputed virtually all their opponents' conclusions. They have disagreed on the timing of the formation of the first East Slavic state, on its location, and on its composition. Their basic disagreement, however, revolved around the relative roles of Scandinavians and East Slavs in its formation. The "anti-Normanists" adopted the position that the East Slavs, not Scandinavians, were responsible for creating the state.

Some of them found support for their views in the same Primary Chronicle that gave rise to the "Normanist" theory. But they highlighted entries that described the Poliane, the East Slavic tribe that dwelled in and around Kiev, and the political structures they had fashioned before the arrival of Riurik's kinsmen and Oleg (Cross and Sherbowitz-Wetzor 1953: 54–5). They surmised from these chronicle entries that, just as the tribes of the northern lands had attempted to form their own political organization before calling Riurik and his brothers to rule them, so the Poliane as well as other tribes in the south had more successfully organized their own political structures well before Riurik established himself in the north and Askold and Dir ventured down the Dnieper and assumed control over Kiev. Although other "anti-Normanists" were more skeptical of the Primary Chronicle because it had been compiled so long after the purported events, they nevertheless reached similar conclusions. They all agreed that the first East Slavic state had developed before the arrival of Riurik in 862; it had been located on the mid-Dnieper (Dnipro) River and centered at Kiev; and it had been created by East Slavs, most particularly by the tribe of Poliane. The Rus' were, correspondingly, not Swedes or any other Norsemen, but Slavs who had dwelled in the mid-Dnieper area long before any Scandinavians appeared to their north. When Varangians did arrive in the Rus' lands, they came in response to invitations from East Slavic princes to defend existing states, the most sophisticated of which was centered around Kiev and dominated by the Poliane. Because of their close association with the East Slavic Rus', the term Rus', which had originated in the Kievan region, was eventually applied to the Scandinavians as well. Although anti-Normanists acknowledged that the Varangians strengthened the state, they assess their political contributions as superficial. Even the establishment of Riurikid political authority amounted to the superimposition of a ruling dynasty on a pre-existing state structure. The "anti-Normanists" thus emphasized the role of East Slavic tribes, particularly the Poliane, in the formation of the first East Slavic state. The role of the non-Slavs in this activity, in their view, was minimal (Hrushevsky 1997: 472–92).

Amplifying and substantiating many of the arguments of the anti-Normanists, Mykhailo Hrushevsky (1866–1934) also added another dimension to the debate. He approached his study by examining a people and a territory, not a state and its rulers. The formation of the first East Slavic state, which he located on the mid-Dnieper River, became an early stage in the history of the Ukrainian nation, a stage distinguished as a period when Ukrainians created and lived within their own state. By emphasizing the continuity of population and location, Hrushevsky departed from Russian historians, who dominated scholarly circles of his period and who had defined the era Kievan Rus' as a stage in Russian history (Hrushevsky 1997; Sysyn 1997: pp. xxii–xxiii, xxxiv–xxxv). During the twentieth century Soviet historians employed ethnographic studies to demonstrate that the East Slavs had remained undifferentiated during the Kievan Rus' era and had divided into Great Russian, Ukrainian, and Belarus' populations only after the Mongol invasion. They thus attempted to refute Hrushevsky's thesis and disallow any special Ukrainian claim to the legacy of Kievan Rus'.

Over the centuries participants on both sides of the Normanist controversy have sought to bolster their arguments by using evidence drawn from other scholarly disciplines and also comparative history to investigate various aspects of the broader problem. They have, thus, explored not only who were the Rus', but also the derivation of the term "Rus'"; not only when Scandinavian Vikings arrived, but also whether Riurik was an actual person or a mythological figure; not only where Varangians were said to have settled, but where they left traces in the archeological records. While these sources, like the written records, have been subject to similarly wide-ranging and equally inconclusive interpretations, they have also led to the production of revised, better-substantiated theories about the formation of the first East Slavic state.

On the basis of his analysis of archeological evidence, most particularly hoards of silver coins, Thomas S. Noonan proposed that Scandinavian Rus' or Vikings were attracted to the Volkhov-Il'men region in search of commercial products at least a century before the alleged arrival of Riurik and his kinsmen. They progressed from engaging in sporadic trading ventures and raids on local populations to acquire goods, for example, fur and slaves, for further commercial exchange to becoming residents at Staraia Lodoga by the mid-eighth century to establishing trade contact with Khazaria where by the end of the eighth century they were exchanging their goods for Islamic silver coins. As their trade system developed, these Rus' commercial adventurers became more aggressive in their efforts to obtain the goods they exchanged for silver coin. By the early tenth century they had transformed their irregular methods of obtaining goods through trading and looting to the more reliable method of tribute collection. In return, they curtailed their raids and offered protection from competing bands of Norsemen. The commercial interests of the Rus' thus led to their establishment of a political order in the region (Noonan 1997).

Noonan's analysis of archeological evidence added substance to the argument that Scandinavian Rus' had reached the Volkhov-Il'men region before the alleged arrival of Riurik in 862 and that they had been responsible for fashioning a political order over the local Finnic and East Slavic tribes in the region. The early trade patterns he described, however, bypassed the Dnieper River and the early political order did not involve the East Slavic tribes dwelling near Kiev, which assumed the proportions of a major town in the late ninth century, just when, according to the Primary Chronicle, Oleg seized control of the town. Noonan's analysis, while highlighting the activities and influence of the Scandinavian Rus', was, nevertheless, not inconsistent with theses concerning an early East Slavic development in the mid-Dnieper region. (Noonan 1997: 147; Golden 1991: 64) It was, however, his view that the band of Scandinavian Rus' known as the Riurikids was responsible for developing Kiev's trade relations with the Byzantine Empire and transforming that town into the center of the state of Kievan Rus'. Other scholars, for example, Jonathan Shepard and Wladyslaw Duczko, although disputing and amplifying some significant points, have broadly followed the contours of Noonan's depiction of the arrival of the bands of Rus' in Eastern Europe, their commercial enterprises, their subjugation of the Finnic and East Slavic tribes, the elevation of the Riurikid band, and its role in the formation in the state of Kievan Rus' (Duczko 2004: 252–8; Shepard 2006: 49–60).

Other scholars have built upon the anti-Normanist side of the debate by comparing the formation of the first East Slavic state with the pattern of development of western and southern Slavic states (Poppe 1997: p. xliii). A. A. Gorskii, also using this method, has merged elements of Noonan's analysis with those of traditional anti-Normanists to offer yet another version of the establishment of the first East Slavic state. He fully accepted the findings that Scandinavians arrived in Eastern Europe by the ninth century, that the East Slavs of the Volkhov-Il'men region had a Viking leader, known as Riurik, by the end of that century, and that the Riurikids formed a dynasty in the ninth and tenth centuries. But he also adopted the notion that the East Slavs, like their cousins to the west, were engaged in the process of state formation independently of the Varangians. In his view, the Riurikids' contribution to the process was the unification of all the East Slavs into a single state. Without the Varangian rulers in Kiev, Gorskii contended, there would have been multiple East Slavic states in the region (Gorskii 2004: 37–49).

Gorskii, however, disputed Noonan's observation that multiple, competing bands of Scandinavian Rus'controlled different East Slavic communities in the tenth century. He proposed that the Riurikids alone ruled the towns and territories along the Dnieper River – that is, the trade route described in the Primary Chronicle "from the Varangians to the Greeks," the importance of which had been previously established by the local Slavic population. Beyond the mid-Dnieper and Kiev, East Slavs had also formed other stable sociopolitical communities in the ninth century. Although they paid tribute to the Riurikids, they survived and continued to function autonomously until the reign of Vladimir (980–1015) (Gorskii 2004: 73–6).

The problems of determining when, where, and by whom the first East Slavic state was founded have defied simple, universally accepted solutions. Using a range of sources and creative approaches, scholars have accumulated a great deal of evidence relating to how the first East Slavic state formed. Their interpretations of that evidence, however, diverge broadly. The conclusions they have drawn on this issue have, furthermore, shaped their approaches to their investigations of the subsequent development of that state.

The State, Dynasty, and Political Development

Although they have not reached consensus on how the first East Slavic state formed, most scholars agree that a state did take shape, and that from the reign of Vladimir (Volodimer) I "the Saint" (d. 1015) the Riurikid dynasty ruled it. But they have had difficulty defining the nature of that state, whose political character changed over time. The Riurikids themselves appear to have had as much difficulty organizing their state and maintaining stable relations among themselves as scholars have had describing the results of their efforts. From the time of Riurik, who reportedly became the sole ruler of his realm after the death of his brothers, the method of exercising power vacillated between a single prince ruling a unified political structure and multiple princes sharing a divided realm. During the reigns of the first generations of Riurikids tensions between the two forms were evident. Sviatoslav divided the realm among his sons, but Vladimir ultimately seized his father's position. Iaroslav gained the Kievan throne by repeating his father's example. Eventually the tendency toward division prevailed over unity. Whereas a "sole ruler" stood at the head of the country in the first half of the eleventh century, by the end of that century it was divided into multiple patrimonies (*otchiny*) (Franklin and Shepard 1996: 245–6).

Over the next two centuries the number of principalities comprising Kievan Rus' grew to over a dozen, most of which were patrimonies of distinct dynastic branches and were further subdivided to create domains for each of the princes of its ruling branch. Although they remained affiliated with Kiev and each other, they became increasingly differentiated and autonomous. The princes of some became powerful and used their resources not only to enhance the economic and cultural status of their own realms, but also to engage in dynastic wars, which became more common during the last century of the Kievan Rus' era. These practices challenged the supremacy of Kiev. They have also challenged scholars to find meaningful ways to describe the political structure of this polycentric state, the position of Kiev within that state, the relationships among its component principalities and their princes, and the dynamics of the development of the state before its ultimate collapse in 1238–40.

One solution to these problems emerged from the theory that Kievan Rus' was a feudal state. The theory that feudal institutions had existed in Russia in the post-Kievan era was proposed in the early twentieth century. Challenging a respected nineteenth-century view that Russia's course of development was unique, it drew upon the notion that Russia's historical evolution paralleled general European patterns of development. This approached received a favorable reception by early Soviet historians, who identified in Russian society certain structural features associated with feudalism, including a fragmentation of political power accompanied by the appearance of large landed properties owned by members of the political elite (princes, their retainers, hierarchs of the Church) who exercised political and economic power over their resident populations and were arranged themselves in a hierarchical order. By the 1930s B. D. Grekov was declaring that the factors denoting feudalism had existed in Kievan Rus'. Grekov's view framed Soviet scholarship for the next twenty years, but during the second half of the century scholars were debating a variety of issues within the context of feudalism. The time of its introduction, the manner in which it developed, the status of laborers, the relative roles of agriculture, and other economic activities such as hunting, fishing, livestock raising, and even craft production, the role and development of towns, and the nature of land ownership were all subjects of extended scholarly discussion. Variations and refinements of the theory, which delved into dynastic relations and discord and proposed concepts such as "collective sovereignty" and "state feudalism," contributed to an extended debate. Despite the competing conclusions they reached on these points, proponents of the feudal theory outlined a course of political development in Kievan Rus', similar to one perceived in European countries, in which the unified, centralized polity divided into numerous principalities whose rulers, like vassals, owed allegiance to a senior or grand prince. The process of feudalization was responsible for the multiplication of principalities within Kievan Rus', the breakdown of unitary authority, and the fatal disintegration of the state (Froianov 1990: 213–318; Tolochko 1992: 13–66; Franklin and Shepard 1996: 369–70; Sverdlov 2003: 5–30).

The many scholars who rejected the feudal model have offered alternative ways to describe the state, its evolution, and the causes of its demise. Using terms such as federation, confederation, and dynastic realm, they have tried to gain an understanding of the changing nature and complexity of Kievan Rus'. Some have approached the problem by examining the component principalities and trying to discern the qualities that distinguished them. Omeljan Pritsak (1995), for example, proposed that, as early as the reign of Vladimir I, Kievan Rus', in addition to Vladimir's own domain, consisted of two types of territories: vassal provinces or common possessions of the dynasty and appanages or heritable principalities.

Most scholars, however, regard Vladimir's son Iaroslav as the ruler who provided the political structure that divided the realm into well-defined principalities. His "Testament," produced sometime before his death and recorded in the Primary

Chronicle, named his eldest son, Iziaslav, as his primary heir with senior status over his brothers; as such, he became prince of Kiev. Iaroslav assigned a share of the realm to each of his other sons as well. Iaroslav issued the testament to keep his realm united, accommodate the interests of his sons, yet also avoid the conflicts that had accompanied succession to the Kievan throne in previous generations. It is less clear whether he intended for each son to hold his share as a patrimonial possession that would be passed down to his own sons or for the territories to remain common dynastic property that would require redistributions as some princes died and others came of age.

S. M. Solov'ev and V. O. Kliuchevsky favored the latter interpretation. They regarded the testament as the basis of a rota, ladder, or staircase system of succession that would bind the component principalities in a single state. Built on principles of seniority and heredity, it introduced a lateral or collateral pattern of succession for the eligible members of the dynasty. The Kievan throne was to pass from brother to brother within the eldest, ruling generation in order of genealogical seniority. When the members of that generation had all died, the next generation would inherit the Kievan throne. Eligibility to reign, however, was to be limited to those princes whose fathers had held the throne. Those whose fathers had died before inheriting the position were called *izgoi* and fell out of the line of succession for Kiev (Vernadsky 1948: 83–4, 90; Stokes 1970: 269–70; Kollmann 1990: 377; Sverdlov 2003: 440–3).

The rota system also assumed a hierarchy among the principalities that comprised Kievan Rus'a. Thus, when the prince of Kiev died and his successor moved from his princely seat to Kiev, the next princes in the line of succession advanced in the hierarchy as well. In this manner, while Iaroslav's son Iziaslav ruled Kiev, his brothers Sviatoslav and Vsevolod sat in Chernigov and Pereiaslavl', respectively. When Sviatoslav died, Vsevolod "rotated" or moved up the ladder to Chernigov. When Iziaslav also died, Vsevolod became prince of Kiev as well. After his reign, Kiev passed to the next generation, first to Iziaslav's son, Sviatopolk (1093–1113), and then to Vsevolod's son, Vladimir Monomakh (1113–25). After Monomakh's death, his sons, Mstislav (1125–32) and Iaropolk (1132–9), held the throne.

This view of the norms of succession corresponds to notions that Kievan Rus' was the shared possession of the dynasty. Princes who were eligible for succession to the Kievan throne did not rule their own patrimonial principalities, but rotated from one principality to the next as succession requirements demanded. In contrast, the domains of *izgoi*, princes who became ineligible for succession to the Kievan throne, became the hereditary possessions of their branches of the dynasty.

Martin Dimnik offered a different interpretation of Iaroslav's testament. In his view, Iaroslav had intended that Kiev exclusively be the object of rotation, to be inherited only by his three eldest sons and their descendants. The other lands of Kievan Rus', which Iaroslav distributed to his sons, were to become their hereditary domains (Dimnik 1994: 24–31, 42–8).

But the details of some successions do not neatly fit into either version of the pattern. Sviatoslav and Vsevolod, for example, evicted Iziaslav from Kiev in 1073. He recovered his throne only three years later. When Vsevolod assumed control of Chernigov after Sviatoslav's death, he retained possession of Pereiaslavl' rather than cede it to the prince following him in the presumed hierarchy. Such violations by the original triumvirs and further disputes among their sons fostered such intense friction by the end of the eleventh century that the Riurikid princes met at Liubech in 1097 to settle their differences. The result was a division of the realm into heritable principalities or patrimonies, which they distributed among themselves. Kiev and, in the opinion of most scholars, Novgorod were the exceptions in that no single branch of the dynasty became their permanent rulers. Dimnik regards this settlement as a return to Iaroslav's original intent. Others regard it as a revision of the system of shared dynastic power that had led to unmanageable friction among the dynasts.

The Congress of Liubech created a federative structure, within which the multiple, hereditary principalities existed but remained bound to Kiev as the center of the state and to each other by dynastic as well as ecclesiastic, cultural, and economic interdependencies. This political structure framed Kievan Rus' for the next century and a half. It was within that framework that some of the principalities developed into strong, semi-independent polities. It was also within this framework that warfare among the princes intensified again by the second half of the twelfth century. Perhaps the best known of the military campaigns was organized by Prince Andrei Bogoliubskii of Vladimir-Suzdal' to remove Prince Mstislav Iziaslavich from the Kievan throne in 1169. It resulted in the sack of Kiev, an event so shocking and devastating that it has come to symbolize for many a turning point in the history of Kievan Rus', the decline of Kiev in favor of Suzdalia. This interpretation of the event reinforces the concept that Kievan Rus' was an early stage in the continuum of Russian history.

The frequency and ferocity of intradynastic warfare has led some scholars to doubt that Iaroslav had introduced any lasting guidelines for succession and to describe the process of selecting Kievan princes as more chaotic than systematic (Presniakov 1966: 34–68; Stokes 1970). Others have argued that the selection process was at best a flawed system and that the outcome of contested successions depended as much on the relative military strength of each contender and the preference of the townsmen as on the dynasty's standards of selection (Franklin 2006: 82).

More commonly scholars have concluded that Iaroslav did introduce a system in the mid-eleventh century, but, despite its revisions by the Liubech conferees at the end of the century, it functioned only through the reigns of Mstislav Vladimirovich (1125–32) and his brother Iaropolk (1132–9) (Vernadsky 1948: 98; Sverdlov 2003: 514). The dynasty that had served as the backbone of the state and bound its components in a unified polity began to fracture. Over the next century dynastic competition for the symbolic center of Kiev intensified, while princes simultaneously focused on the development of their own realms. The state of Kievan Rus' disintegrated.

This view has stimulated investigations to find reasons for the apparent deterioration of the dynastic order. One explanation offered was that the succession system, fashioned in the eleventh century, was ill designed to accommodate the increasing size of the dynasty and the corresponding increasing number of contenders for the Kievan throne who appeared in the twelfth. Concern that they would lose their place in the succession cycle for themselves and their direct heirs repeatedly motivated princes to resort to warfare to gain control of the Kievan throne. According to John Fennell (1983: 5–6, 10, 20, the succession system itself, which did not confer the Kievan throne on a single dynastic branch, created a situation that invited recurrent wars for that throne and destabilized the state. Nancy Kollmann (1990: 279–80) disagreed. She argued that, even though the number of princes in the dynasty rose, the mechanisms that eliminated some branches of the dynasty from the order of succession had the effect of keeping the number of contenders for the throne at manageable levels. Succession struggles, when they did occur, involved only a few competitors and, thus, allowed the system to function.

Rather than seeing a decline in Kievan Rus' through the last century of its existence, other scholars consider the period one of adjustment to changing conditions, such as the size of the dynasty and the complexity of the state. The relative power of Kiev and the other principalities of the state necessarily shifted as some of those principalities, such as Vladimir-Suzdal' in the northeast and Volhynia in the southwest, gained strength. But those changes did not mean that Kiev was losing its political centrality or power, that Kievan Rus' was disintegrating, or that the dynasty no longer served to hold the components together. A. A. Gorskii argued, for example, that, although Suzdalia and Volhynia as well as Chernigov and Smolensk were capable of becoming independent states in the early thirteenth century, the shared, albeit competitive, interests of their princes, who aspired to control Kiev and the other lands that remained dynastic possessions, acted as a centripetal force holding their domains within the Kievan Rus' political framework (Fennell 1983: 6, 20; Noonan 1991: 144–5; Franklin and Shepard 1996: 324, 340–2; Gorskii 1996: 6–27).

From this perspective dynastic wars, such as the 1169 campaign, were not signs of a deteriorating dynasty and decaying state. Mstislav Iziaslavich, who represented a younger generation than Andrei Bogoliubskii's, was not simply a greedy or impatient prince, but a statesman attempting to introduce reform to the dynastic system of succession, to adapt it to changing dynastic and political conditions. His opponent, Andrei Bogoliubskii, on the other hand, becomes a defender of the established system, not its destroyer. Their wars, and others that were similarly fought over succession, were mechanisms used by princes to resolve their disputes in order to preserve Kievan Rus' as it underwent political change.

Economic Development

The problems regarding the political structure of Kievan Rus', the status of Kiev within it, and the relationships among their princes and their domains have also influenced inquiries into the economic development of Kievan Rus'. As previously discussed, competing conclusions on the foundation of the first East Slavic state were based on differing interpretations of economic factors. They have been equally significant in gaining insight into the development of Kievan Rus'.

The economy of Kievan Rus' was broadly divided into two sectors. One, which engaged the vast majority of the population, was rural and agricultural and responsible for the sustenance of the entire society. The other, which employed a much smaller segment of the population, was urban and commercial and was a chief mechanism for generating wealth for the elites of society.

The primary focus of agriculture was the production of grains: wheat, buckwheat rye, millet, and oats as well as non-edible grains, such as flax. But the farming population also raised livestock, including horses, cattle, pigs, sheep, goats, and poultry, and engaged in hunting, fishing, bee-keeping, and gathering berries, mushrooms, and other wild edible products. They constructed carts and wagons to transport their products and also produced other necessary goods, ranging from homes and out-buildings to tools, utensils, and other equipment, to clothing (Golden 1991: 65–6; Kaiser 1991).

Because of the central importance of agriculture and its role, according to the "anti-Normanist" school of thought, in the foundation of the first East Slavic state, some scholars consider the state's further evolution to have been shaped by the development of this sector of the economy. This view found favor particularly with those who regarded Kievan Rus' as a feudal state. The appearance of large landed estates, the resident peasants' loss of their status as free men, the exploitation of their labor, and the appropriation of the products of that labor were all identified as indica-tors of a feudal economy developing in Kievan Rus'. Class conflicts arising from deteriorating conditions for the peasantry were also seen to have contributed to the decline of Kievan Rus' (Blum 1964: 90–2; Froianov 1990: 213–318; Sverdlov 2003: 5–30).

Although the description of the Kievan Rus' economy as feudal was well accepted by Soviet scholars during the twentieth century, Western scholars tended to reject. George Vernadsky (1948: 163–72), for example, while acknowledging the existence of what he called "feudalizing processes" in Kievan Rus', compared the economic structures of Kievan Rus' with those associated with European feudalism and con-cluded that Kievan Rus' was not feudal. In the last decades of the twentieth century some Soviet scholars also challenged the theory that the Kievan Rus' economy was feudal (Froianov 1974: 51, 60, 72, 88, 98–9; 1990: 317–18). Other studies, such as Daniel Kaiser's examination of the Kievan Rus' economy as it was reflected in the law codes, find little reference in the codes to land ownership, regarded as a critical element in the conception of feudalism (Kaiser 1991: 41).

This line of investigation and its results were generated, in part, by the assumption that Kievan Rus' was a European state and its development had much in common with its European counterparts (Sverdlov 2003: 12–14). Disagreement with the conclusions regarding feudalism have led, as a result, to a tendency to reject also examinations of Kievan Rus' in a European frame of reference. Recent studies, such as the work of A. A. Gorskii (2004), whose comparison of the early development of Kievan Rus' with the evolution of contemporary western and southern Slavic states in Europe was noted earlier, suggest that the approach is being undertaken again and with fruitful results.

Alternative views of economic development in Kievan Rus', nevertheless, generally emerge from studies that set Kievan Rus' in non-European contextual frameworks and emphasize influences emanating from other neighboring cultures. Such studies focus primarily not on agriculture, but on the commercial sector of the Kievan Rus' economy and have reached a different set of conclusions about the economic founda-tions of the state and economic influences on its political development.

Vasily Kliuchevsky and Mykhailo Hrushevsky, despite their disagreements on many aspects of the "Normanist Controversy," both associated the development of the first East Slavic state with trade. They each highlighted commerce along the Dnieper river, the route "from the Varangian to the Greeks" and the commercial exchanges between the Rus' and Byzantium. Kiev's prominence was due to its location on this route. Its princes' primacy derived from their ability to secure the route and control the trade conducted along it. But, while Kliuchevsky identified the Varangian Riurikids as the organizers of this trade, Hrushevsky emphasized the role of the East Slavs in the mercantile role. He explained that, to protect the Dnieper route and enforce tribute collection, the Rus' (Polianc) princes had hired Varangian mercenaries, who eventually became identified with the term "Rus'" and also formed a ruling dynasty.

In both versions, however, commercial interaction with Constantinople not only brought wealth to the Rus' princes, who used it to build their military and political might. It also created an avenue by which Christianity and a wide range of cultural attributes, including art and literary language, reached Kievan Rus'. But trade along the route from the Varangians to the Greeks not only contributed substantially to the formation and growth of Kievan Rus'. The subsequent political fortunes of the state were also dependent on the economic operations along this route. From the eleventh century Byzantium's fortunes declined. The appearance of the Seljuk Turks in Asia Minor, the Crusades, and hostile nomads on the steppe all disrupted trade between Constantinople and Kiev. Because Kiev's fortunes were linked to this trade, it economic foundation crumbled. With its center weakened, Kievan Rus' fragmented. Political power became more diffuse; Riurikid princes entered into increasingly destructive conflicts; and the state declined (Kliuchevsky 1960: 69–73; Martin 1986: 44–5; Noonan 1991: 102–3; Hrushevsky 1997: 296–305).

Thomas Noonan, Wladyslaw Duczko, and others, as noted above, also attributed the early development of the first East Slavic state to trade. But they described a more complex and flexible commercial network. Initially, the most significant commerce conducted by the Rus' who arrived in the Volkhov-Il'men region had been with the Islamic world and Khazaria. This trade brought valuable silver into the lands of the Rus'. Kiev's trade with Byzantium began in the early tenth century, later than Kliuchevsky and other earlier historians had asserted. It developed into a sizable exchange only late in the century, at the same time as the city expanded in size and achieved political prominence with the arrival of Oleg.

These scholars also noted changes in the organization of the trade. Initially, the Riurikid princes had led military expeditions to pressure potential trading partners to open their markets and had been directly engaged in forcibly collecting tribute, conveying the goods down the Dnieper to Constantinople, and maintaining security along the route. As they developed a more stable political system, Kiev's princes turned over the task of tax collection to appointed officials; they ceased the practice of accompanying commercial flotillas down the Dnieper and caravans across the steppe, but continued to use their military might to maintain security along the trade routes.

In addition to trade with Byzantium, the princes of Kievan Rus' also oversaw the conduct of regular commercial interaction and irregular exchanges with their nomadic neighbors in the steppe. In addition to using normal methods of trade, the Riurikid princes used looting during military raids, ransoming of captives, exchanging diplomatic gifts, and the provision of dowries in marriages as common, although irregular, methods of acquiring goods. The object of these ventures was mainly the acquisition of horses, cattle, other livestock, and slaves (Golden 1991: 81–3, 95–9; Noonan 1992: 301–27).

The economy developed and diversified in other ways as well. In addition to its prominence as a political, ecclesiastic, and commercial center, Kiev also became a center for the production of crafted goods from the eleventh century. Initially serving the consumer demand of the political and ecclesiastic elites, craftsmen produced goods ranging from jewelery to glassware to glazed pottery. These products joined goods imported from Constantinople in an expanding commercial network among the towns of Kievan Rus'. Not only did domestic trade thus supplement the intercontinental exchange; other towns and principalities developed commercial connections that similarly contributed to their growth and their princes' revenues. Thus, Suzdalia developed commercial ties with Bulgar on the Volga; the southwestern principalities of Galicia and Volhynia benefited from merchants traveling through towns between Central Europe and Kiev; and Novgorod was actively engaged in trade with the merchants of the Baltic Sea region. Their princes did not only use revenues from these economic activities to fund their military forces. They also invested them in the construction of churches, palaces, fortifications, and other grand projects. The architectural embellishments made by Andrei Bogoliubskii transformed his town of Vladmir into a rival of Kiev itself (Noonan 1978: 371–84; 1991: 101–46; Martin 1986: 46–52; 1995: 82, 84, 100).

The broader view of commercial relations taken by Noonan and others yields a very different view of the economic and political development of Kievan Rus' than does the view that focuses more narrowly on trade with Byzantium. By considering trade not only with Byzantium, but also with the Islamic world, Europe, and the populations of the steppe, as well as with domestic partners, these scholars observed a vital, flexible economy that responded to opportunities and crises in ways that continued to provide wealth for the expanding state of Kievan Rus' and revenues for its growing dynasty. In contrast to Kliuchevsky and his followers, who emphasized dependence upon a single trading partner, these scholars saw the early commercial enterprises undertaken by the Varangians develop into a multifaceted economy that involved domestic as well as intercontinental trade, craft production as well as agriculture and trade, and the means to support all the principalities within Kievan Rus' as well as Kiev itself. Rather than an economy that fell into decline in the eleventh century, they observed one that was expanding at that time and that continued to flourish through the entire era of Kievan Rus'.

This view of the economic development of Kievan Rus' has implications for the understanding of its political evolution as well. Kiev did not crumble economically; the notion that it lost its political prominence as a result of an economic decline is, therefore, unfounded. Although its relative status within Kievan Rus' changed as other principalities and towns also gained wealth and power, Kiev remained a significant economic, political, and cultural center. The very fact that it became an object of plunder not only in 1169, but again in 1203 and 1235, suggests a level of economic vitality that enabled it to recover repeatedly from devastating attacks. As Thomas Noonan (1991: 145–6) concluded: "Kiev in the century before the Mongol conquest was a wealthy, prosperous city which was sacked and fiercely contested precisely because it was so rich and flourishing."

This image of Kiev's economic development forms a parallel with the view of Kievan Rus' undergoing dynamic changes in its political structure during the last century of its existence. In contrast to the view that Kievan Rus' was experiencing political and economic decline during this period, it supports the conclusion that Kievan Rus' remained, despite its volatility, a vital, cohesive state until the Mongol invasion in 1238–40.

Conclusions

Scholars have addressed the problems of the foundation of the first East Slavic state, its political structure, its economic development, and its evolution to 1240 for centuries. The paucity and unreliability of sources as well as the gaps contained in them have obliged scholars to seek answers not only in historical sources from Russia, but also from Europe, Byzantium, and the Viking and Islamic worlds. They have also used supplementary evidence drawn from other scholarly disciplines. Yet, definitive solutions to the problems have been elusive.

The problems are not, however, simply esoteric puzzles. The different ways historians have selected, pieced together, and interpreted relevant evidence to solve them are themselves instructive. They reflect not only the investigators' personal biases, but also the intellectual trends of the eras in which they lived and different methods of studying history. Their investigative approaches reflect, furthermore, the diverse, overlapping contexts, in which the foundation and evolution of the first East Slavic state took place. By exploiting the varied sources available from these multiple contexts, scholars have been able to explore the formation and development of Kievan Rus' from a variety of perspectives. In the process they have highlighted the rich range of influences on its development. The insights they have gleaned have led sometimes to competing and sometimes to complementary conclusions. Their efforts, however, have demonstrated the value of taking diverse, creative approaches to explore the problems associated with the history of the first East Slavic state.

References

Blum, J. (1964). *Lord and Peasant in Russia from the Ninth to the Nineteenth Century.* Atheneum, New York.

Cross, S. H., and Sherbowitz-Wetzor, O. P. (eds. and trans.) (1953). *The Russian Primary Chronicle Laurentian Text.* Mediaeval Academy of America, Cambridge, MA.

Dimnik, M. (1994). *The Dynasty of Chernigov, 1054–1146.* Pontifical Institute of Mediaeval Studies, Toronto.

Duczko, W. (2004). *Viking Rus. Studies on the Presence of Scandinavians in Eastern Europe.* Brill, Leiden and Boston.

Fennell, J. (1983). *The Crisis of Medieval Russia.* Longman, London and New York.

Franklin, S. (2006). "Kievan Rus' (1015–1125)," in M. Perrie, ed., *The Cambridge History of Russia.* Vol. I. *From Early Rus' to 1689.* Cambridge University Press, Cambridge, 73–97.

Franklin, S., and Shepard, J. (1996). *The Emergence of Rus 750–1200.* Longman, London and New York.

Froianov, I. Ia. (1974). *Kievskaia Rus': Ocherki sotsial'no-ekonomicheskoi Istorii.* Leningradskii gosudarstvennyi universitet, Leningrad.

Froianov, I. Ia. (1990). *Kievskaia Rus'. Ocherki otechestvennoi istoriografii.* Leningradskii universitet, Leningrad.

Golden, P. B. (1982). "The Question of the Rus' Qağanate," *Archivum Eurasiae Medii Aevi,* 2: 77–97

Golden, P. B. (1991). "Aspects of the Nomadic Factor in the Economic Development of Kievan Rus'," in I. S. Koropeckyj, ed., *Ukrainian Economic History: Interpretive Essays.* Harvard Ukrainian Research Institute, Cambridge, MA, 58–101.

Gorskii, A. A. (1996). *Russkie zemli v XIII–XIV vekakh. Puti politicheskogo razvitiia*. Institut Rossisskoi istorii RAN, Moscow.

Gorskii, A. A. (2004). *Rus'. Ot Slavianskogo Rasseleniia do Moskovskogo Tsarstva*. Iazyki Slavianskoi Kul'tury, Moscow.

Hrushevsky, M. (1997). *History of Ukraine-Rus'*. Vol. 1. *From Prehistory to the Eleventh Century*. Canadian Institute of Ukrainian Studies Press, Edmonton and Toronto.

Kaiser, D. H. (1991). The Economy of Kievan Rus': Evidence from the Pravda Rus'skaia," in I. S. Koropeckyj, ed., *Ukrainian Economic History: Interpretive Essays.*. Harvard Ukrainian Research Institute, Cambridge, MA, 37–57.

Kliuchevsky, V. O. (1960). *A History of Russia*. Vol. 1. Trans. C. J. Hogarth. Russell and Russell, New York.

Kollmann, N. S. (1990). "Collateral Succession in Kievan Rus'," *Harvard Ukrainian Studies*, 14: 377–87.

Martin, J. (1986). *Treasure of the Land of Darkness: The Fur Trade and its Significance for Medieval Russia*. Cambridge University Press, Cambridge.

Martin, J. (1995). *Medieval Russia 980–1584*. Cambridge University Press, Cambridge.

Noonan, T. S. (1978). "Suzdalia's Eastern Rrade in the Century before the Mongol Conquest," *Cahiers du monde russe et soviétique*, 19: 371–84.

Noonan, T. S. (1991). "The Flourishing of Kiev's International and Domestic Trade, ca. 1100–ca. 1240," in I. S. Koropeckyj, ed., *Ukrainian Economic History: Interpretive Essays*. Harvard Ukrainian Research Institute, Cambridge, MA, 101–46.

Noonan, T. S. (1992). "Rus', Pechenegs, and Polovtsi: Economic Interaction along the Steppe Frontier in the Pre-Mongol Era," *Russian History*, 19: 301–26.

Noonan, T. S. (1997). "Scandinavians in European Russia," in P. Sawyer, ed., *The Oxford Illustrated History of the Vikings*. Oxford University Press, Oxford, 134–55.

Poppe, A. (1997). "Introduction to Volume 1," in M. Hrushevsky, *History of Ukraine-Rus'*. Vol. 1. *From Prehistory to the Eleventh Century*. Canadian Institute of Ukrainian Studies Press, Edmonton and Toronto, pp. xliii–liv.

Presniakov, A. E. (1966). *Kniazheskoe pravo v drevnei Rusi: ocherki po istorii X–XII stoletii*. Europe Printing, The Hague.

Pritsak, O. (1995). "The System of Government under Volodimer the Great and his Foreign Policy," *Harvard Ukrainian Studies*, 19: 573–93.

Shepard, J. (2006). "The Origins of Rus' (*c.* 900–1015)," in M. Perrie (ed.), *The Cambridge History of Russia*. Vol. 1. *From Early Rus' to 1689*. Cambridge University Press, Cambridge, 47–72.

Stokes, A. D. (1970). "The System of Succession to the Thrones of Russia, 1054–1113," in R. Auty, R. Lewitter, and A. P. Vlasto, eds., *Gorski Vijenats:. A Garland of Essays Offered to Professor Elizabeth Mary Hill*. Modern Humanities Research Association, Cambridge, 268–75.

Sverdlov, M. B. (2003). *Domongol'skaia Rus'a. Kniaz' i kniazhskaia vlast' na Rusi VI – pervoi treti XIII vv*. Akademicheskii proekt, St Petersburg.

Sysyn, F. (1997). "Introduction to the History of Ukraine-Rus'," in M. Hrushevsky, *History of Ukraine-Rus'*. Vol. 1. *From Prehistory to the Eleventh Century*. Canadian Institute of Ukrainian Studies Press, Edmonton and Toronto, pp. xxii–xlii.

Tolochko, P. P. (1987). *Drevniaia Rus'. Ocherki sotsial'no-politicheskoi istorii*. Naukova Dumka, Kiev.

Tolochko, A. P. (1992). *Kniaz' v Drevnei Rusi: vlast' sobstvennost' ideologiia*. Naukova Dumka, Kiev.

Vernadsky, G. (1948). *A History of Russia*. Vol. II. *Kievan Russia*. Yale University Press, New Haven and London.

Further Reading

Dimnik, M. (2003). *The Dynasty of Chernigov, 1146–1246*. Cambridge University Press, Cambridge.

Dimnik, M. (2006). "The Rus' Principalities (1125–1246)," in M. Perrie, ed., *The Cambridge History of Russia*. Vol. 1. *From Early Rus' to 1689*. Cambridge University Press, Cambridge, 98–126.

Froianov, I. Ia. (1986). "Large-Scale Ownership of Land and the Russian Economy in the Tenth to Twelfth Centuries," *Soviet Studies in History*, 24: 9–81.

Golden, P. (1995). "Rūs," in *Encylopaedia of Islam*, new edn., Brill, Leiden, 8: 618–29.

Ingham, N. W. (1998). "Has a Missing Daughter of Iaroslav Mudryi been Found?" *Russian History*, 25: 231–70.

Martin, J. (2006). "Calculating Seniority and the Contests for Succession in Kievan Rus'," *Russian History*, 33: 267–81.

Noonan, T. S. (1992). "Fluctuations in Islamic Trade with Eastern Europe during the Viking Age," *Harvard Ukrainian Studies*, 16: 237–59.

Noonan, T. S. (1998). *The Islamic World, Russia and the Vikings, 750–900: The Numismatic Evidence*. Variorum/Ashgate, Aldershot.

Raffensperger, C. (2003). "Evpraksia Vsevolodovna between East and West," *Russian History*, 30: 23–34.

Soloviev, S. M. (2002). *History of Russia from Earliest Times*. Vol. 2. *Early Russia, 1054–1157*, ed. and trans. R. Cleminson. Academic International Press, Gulf Breeze, FL.

Soloviev, S. M. (2000). *History of Russia from Earliest Times*. Vol. 3. *The Shift Northward. Kievan Rus, 1154–1228*, ed. G. E. Orchard, trans. Leo J. Sobel. Academic International Press, Gulf Breeze, FL.

CHAPTER FOUR

Rus' and the Byzantine Empire

GEORGE MAJESKA

The Beginnings

Relations between Rus' and the Byzantine Empire centered at Constantinople (modern Istanbul) were not always friendly. Already in the early ninth century, Viking Rus' had apparently pillaged the Byzantine city of Amastris on the Black Sea coast of Asia Minor, and by the 830s the Byzantine government had converted the province of Cherson in the Crimea into a military region. Its apparent goal: to control Rus' predations on the Black Sea, as well as to protect the city of Cherson (Chersonesus, Korsun) itself, an important transshipment port of grain for the Byzantine capital. Perhaps it was to negotiate some sort of peaceful relationship between the Byzantines and the Rus', most likely a trade agreement, that Rus', envoys appeared in Constantinople in 838–9. Whatever the reason for their mission, they could not return home the way they came (via the Black Sea, it would seem, and through the steppe where there was serious nomad military activity) and were dispatched home through Germany.

In 860, for reasons we do not know but probably to pillage, Viking Rus' (the leaders of the early Rus' state were Scandinavian Vikings) attacked Constantinople with two hundred ships. There had been no warning. The emperor was with his army on the Empire's eastern frontier and the navy was also occupied in fighting the Arabs. Only the stout walls of the Byzantine capital kept the invader out of the city itself. According to Photius, Patriarch of Constantinople, who essentially took charge of the besieged city in the emperor's absence, the Rus' attackers pillaged the suburbs mercilessly, killing many, even women and children, before they suddenly withdrew homeward, leaving the area before the emperor returned with his army. Later sources would attribute the Russian retreat to a miracle performed by the Mother of God in order to save the Christian city from the pagan Rus'. The Rus' attack must have been formidable to force the Emperor to leave the eastern frontier.[1] It is unclear from where the Rus' strike force came. Although it is possible that it came from some other Viking Rus' settlement in the north, it is probable that the attack was launched from a Viking Rus' trading colony near the mouth of the river

Don, the most likely point of origin for a flotilla of two hundred ships. The Kievan Rus' state as we normally think of it did not yet exist. The Byzantine response to this new threat of the Rus' was twofold. First, the Byzantines firmed up their alliance with the Turkic Khazars, who dominated the Russian steppe through which Rus' would have to move on their way to Constantinople. Second, Patriarch Photius sent missionaries to convert the Rus' to Byzantine Christianity, a conversion that would supposedly make them more friendly to the Empire. In 867, the same Patriarch Photius announced to his fellow Eastern Patriarchs that the Russians who had attacked Constantinople not too long before had accepted a bishop. Seven years later, we hear of an "Archbishop of the Rus'," although we do not know where his episcopal seat was located.[2]

The first recognizable Kievan Rus' state was formed to protect the by now profitable Rus' trade with Byzantium on the famed "way from the Varangians to the Greeks." Viking traders (the Varangians of Russian and Byzantine sources) unified and fortified the upper and middle Dnieper waterway in the ninth century, replacing the faltering Turkic Khazars, who had earlier guaranteed safety on the trade routes across the steppe. The precious goods of the northern forest lands (furs, slaves, honey) were brought to the stronghold of Kiev on the middle Dnieper River and then transported by flotilla each spring down the river, over the portages, and by boat along the coast of the Black Sea to Constantinople, the capital of the Byzantine Empire. There they were traded for Mediterranean luxury articles (wine, jewelery, fine fabrics), which were brought back to the land of Rus' and beyond, to Scandinavia, and sometimes to the East. The tenth-century Byzantine emperor Constantine VII Porphyrogenitus describes the early Rus' trading expeditions to Byzantium in detail in his ruler's handbook, *de administrando imperio*.[3]

It was to guarantee their trade rights in the Byzantine capital that Rus' again attacked Constantinople. The attack came in the year 907, and this time the Rus' came from the recently created Kiev Rus' state; the Rus' force was led by Prince Oleg. The Russian chronicle description of the campaign is overlain with much legendary detail (boats sailing over land on wheels, attempted poisonings discovered, etc.), and Byzantine sources make no reference to this attack. But the attack must have actually occurred. The text of the treaty that the Byzantines signed in 911 (formalizing the earlier Russo-Byzantine agreement from 907) preserved in Slavic translation in the Russian Primary Chronicle has all the hallmarks of a genuine Byzantine diplomatic document signed under Rus' military pressure. The treaty stipulates the rights of Rus' merchants to trade in Constantinople tax free and to enjoy the benefits of a merchant headquarters in the St. Mamas quarter on the Bosphorus close to the city. It also spells out details on how to settle legal disputes between Rus' people and "Christians." The treaty also guarantees the rights of Rus' who wish to serve in the Byzantine armed forces, and, indeed, a Byzantine source records 700 Rus' serving in the Byzantine navy in 911, offering some confirmation of the genuineness of the treaty from the Greek side.[4]

In June 941 Igor, Oleg's successor, led a new attack on the Byzantine Empire, probably for the same reason: trade rights. The Rus' army approached imperial territory by sea, attacked and pillaged along the Black Sea Coast of Asia Minor, and advanced to the Asiatic shores of the Bosphorus, sacking Chrysopolis located across from Constantinople itself. The leading Byzantine general, John Curcuas, headed

back from the Empire's eastern frontier to lead the successful attack on the Rus'
forces outside Constantinople. As the Rus' were preparing to withdraw, the Byzantine
navy attacked their ships in the Bosphorus with Greek fire, a medieval form of napalm
shot through tubes that could set ships afire. The Rus' fighters who could escape did;
those who had not burned to death were killed by the Byzantine military. Still, the
lure of Constantinople and its trade continued unabated among the Rus', and in just
over two years, the Rus' prince Igor once again assembled a mighty force to attack
Constantinople. This time the Byzantines offered gifts and terms to the Russians,
including essentially reinstating the earlier treaty of 911 negotiated by Oleg, suggesting once again that trade rights were the paramount reason for Igor's campaigns.
Ostensibly at the demand of his retinue, Igor accepted the Byzantine proposals,
and turned back from the river Danube, not even entering Byzantine territory.
He took home with him a new treaty with Byzantium, albeit with somewhat less
favorable terms.[5]

Along with the much desired trade with Byzantium came cultural influences, most
notably the beginnings of Christianity in Kievan Rus'. Already in 944, some of the
Rus' officials swore to the new treaty with the Byzantines in a Church of St Elias in
the city of Kiev, although others followed the pagan Viking rites for ratifying an
agreement. The progress of Christianity in Kievan Rus', probably brought back by
Rus' military men who returned home after serving in the Byzantine military, led to
the baptism of Princess Olga, widow of the murdered Prince Igor and regent for
their young son Sviatoslav, heir apparent to the Kievan throne. This baptism took
place between 954 and 956, and probably in Constantinople. The Russian chronicle
tradition has Olga being baptized, with Emperor Constantine VII acting as her godfather. In honor of the emperor's wife, Olga assumed Helen as her baptismal name
(also recalling the name of the first Christian empress of the Roman Empire).
Although the Byzantine sources are silent about Olga's baptism, they are quite
effusive in describing her official reception at the imperial palace, where she was
richly feted, along with her very significant entourage. She returned home with
appropriately rich gifts, an honorary Byzantine court title, and, one suspects, a
renewed trade treaty.[6]

By the time young Sviatoslav came of age, he had already rejected the Christianity
of his mother (because the members of his military retinue would laugh at him, says
the *Primary Chronicle*); like his father, he was destined to be a military man. Sviatoslav
created a large military force, which he used to conquer several neighboring tribes;
he even defeated the Khazars and took their city of Sarkel (Bela Vezha). Having
proven his military prowess, Sviatoslav was commissioned by the Byzantine emperor
Nicephorus Phocas to put down an impending attack from Bulgaria for a large fee.
Thus, in 968, Sviatoslav appeared on the Danube and quickly overwhelmed the
Bulgarians. He was called back to Kiev, however, by a dangerous siege of his capital
city by the Pechenegs (Patzinaks), perhaps acting in concert with the Byzantines,
who now wanted him out of the Balkans. The Pechenegs had replaced the Khazars
as the dominant power on the steppes of southern Rus'. After relieving the Pecheneg
siege of the city, Sviatoslav announced that he did not want to remain in Kiev, but
would prefer rather to settle in the Bulgarian city of Pereiaslavets on the Danube,
which he now described as the center of his realm. And, indeed, after burying his
mother Olga, Sviatoslav returned to his Balkan conquests and captured and deposed

the Bulgarian tsar Boris II. He also now apparently laid claim to all the European holdings of the Byzantines!

The new Byzantine emperor, the general John Tzimiskes, who had succeeded the assassinated Emperor Nicephorus, had (temporarily) freed himself from military commitments on the Empire's eastern frontier and moved to destroy the Rus' Frankenstein his predecessor had created in the Balkans. He tried to win over the Bulgarian people, who were supporting Sviatoslav against the Byzantines, but also mounted a massive military offensive. In April 971 Tzimiskes' army retook the Bulgarian capital of Preslav, capturing the dethroned Bulgarian king and setting him up again as the ruler. Moving swiftly toward Dristra (Silistria, Dorostolon), the fortified city on the Danube where Sviatoslav had holed up, the Byzantine forces put the fortress under siege, aided by the appearance in the Danube of Byzantine ships capable of launching the dreaded Greek fire. Sviatoslav's Rus' troops fought heroically, but lack of food eventually forced them to come to terms. Sviatoslav was forced to swear to withdraw from the Balkans and never to return, not to attack the Byzantine city of Cherson in the Crimea, and to render military aid to the Byzantines when asked. In return, he and the remnant of his forces were given supplies and allowed to return to the land of Rus'. Under somewhat suspicious circumstances, however, the Rus' force was waylaid on the way home by Pecheneg nomads as it forded rapids on the Dnieper River, and Sviatoslav was killed, his skull being made into a drinking cup for a Pecheneg chief.[7]

The Baptism of Rus'

Given the long tradition of contacts between the Byzantine Empire and Rus', it is not surprising that the Rus' should eventually adopt the Byzantine version of Christianity. The traditional story of the conversion of Rus' is contained in the *Primary Chronicle*, albeit in what can only be described as a mythologized version. Representatives of the major religions come to Vladimir, prince of Kiev, to plead their cases. Vladimir is particularly taken by the presentation of a "Greek scholar" who summarizes the Old and New Testaments and the history of the Christian Church. The scholar caps his presentation by showing the prince an icon of the Last Judgment and suggesting that the prince might prefer to be on the side of the saved rather than on the side of those in torment. After conferring with his boyars, Vladimir sends emissaries to investigate the faiths where they were practiced. Islam is rejected because it forbids the use of alcohol and "Drinking is the joy of the Russian people." Judaism is rejected because God took away the Jews' homeland. Western Christianity is rejected "because there is no glory there." The envoys who went to Constantinople, however, were taken to a solemn service in the great Church of St Sophia, and reported that they knew not whether they were in heaven or on earth, for on earth was not such splendor. "We only know that God dwells there among men . . ." On hearing this report, Vladimir and his boyars agreed to accept baptism from the Byzantine Church. The boyars reminded Vladimir that his grandmother Olga would not have chosen a faith that was evil.

Having decided to align himself with Byzantine Christianity, Vladimir then besieged and captured the Byzantine colony of Cherson in the Crimea, and, according to the chronicler, sent a message to the ruling Byzantine emperors Basil and

Constantine saying: "Behold I have captured your glorious city. I have also heard that you have an unwedded sister. Unless you give her to me to wife, I shall deal with your own city [Constantinople] as I have with Cherson." The rulers of Byzantium would agree to Vladimir's request only if he would be baptized, something he had already determined to do, according to the chronicle. The Greek princess Anna embarked with a retinue, including clergy, and came to Cherson, where Vladimir was baptized, a ritual that cured him of the blindness that he had recently developed. Apparently having put away his five wives and eight hundred concubines, Vladimir married the Byzantine princess. Bringing clergy, sacred relics, and church vessels from Cherson, the princely couple moved on to Kiev, where Vladimir ordered all the populace to gather on the banks of the Dnieper River to be baptized *en masse*.[8]

This was the traditional story. But the faiths examined according to the chronicle were, in fact, already known in tenth-century Rus', and formal presentation of their tenets as recorded in the chronicle are unlikely to have happened. Islam was the religion of the Turkic Bulgars on the upper Volga River; the Khazars of the southern steppe region, defeated by Sviatoslav, practiced Judaism; the Poles to the west were Roman Catholic; and a Byzantine Christian church already existed in Kiev in 944 (see above), not to mention that Princess Olga had been baptized in the Greek rite. Indeed, early in Vladimir's reign, two Christian Varangians who had served in the Byzantine Empire and were living in Kiev were killed by a crowd for refusing to take part in a pagan sacrifice. The "Greek scholar's" presentation is taken from a Bulgarian literary source.[9] Although the chronicle description of the conversion of Vladimir probably contains precious kernels of historical fact, the author or editor of the chronicle has created a pious, mythologized narrative to emphasize divine reasons for the conversion.

The more historical version of Vladimir's conversion reads somewhat differently. Various peoples of Northern and Eastern Europe were adopting Christianity in this period as a means of gaining respect from the older parts of Europe. Vladimir had just taken Kiev from his brother Yaropolk with the help of a significant Viking mercenary force, which was demanding payment that he could not afford. At the same time, 988, the Byzantine emperor Basil II was faced with a rebellion led by one of his generals, Bardas Phocas, who had taken much of Asia Minor and was encamped across the straits from Constantinople itself. The Byzantine ruler, in casting about for military aid, asked Vladimir for soldiers and got from him six thousand Viking warriors who had helped Vladimir to take Kiev and who were now making trouble there. Vladimir's price for this military assistance was the emperor's sister Anna as his wife. The princess Anna, who had born in the purple chamber of the imperial palace and had earlier been refused to the future German emperor Otto II because he was not of sufficient standing, was now to be married to the Russian prince, bringing him high status in the eyes of the world. Of course, to marry the Byzantine princess, Vladimir would have to accept Christian baptism, but this was a slight price to pay in order to raise the prestige of his country on the European scene. Apparently as part of the bargain, Vladimir captured the Byzantine city of Cherson in Crimea from the rebels in the name of his future brother-in-law. Princess Anna arrived in Cherson, Vladimir was baptized (in what order these things happened is unclear), and Vladimir married Anna (called *tsaritsa* in some Russian sources). Shortly thereafter, probably in 989, Eastern Christianity was declared the national religion of the Rus'. Religious devotion combines with political machinations of a high caliber.[10]

Whatever the mix of politics and religion that went into Vladimir's decision to adopt Byzantine Christianity in Kievan Rus', the long-term ramifications were tremendous. First of all, Eastern Christianity became the national religion of the Rus' and eventually of the Russian state in the form of Russian Orthodoxy. Secondly, the conversion brought Rus' into traditional European civilization.

The exact nature of the administrative structure of the new missionary church in Rus' is unclear, except that it was certainly subject to the Patriarch of Constantinople, the head of the Christian Church in the Byzantine Empire. Apparently the actual conversion was overseen by a Greek bishop, Theophylactus (Feofilakt), sent to Vladimir from Constantinople. Although some claim that thereafter the early Rus' Church had a Bulgarian bishop (because Slavic-speaking Bulgarian clergy would have been necessary in Slavic-speaking Rus'), it is more likely that at least at first the new Christian Church of Rus' was ruled by the Archbishop of Tmutorokan' (Tamatarcha), a jurisdiction set up a hundred years earlier that had now become part of the Kievan Rus' state. The first chronicle mention of a metropolitan (that is, a ruling archbishop) in Kiev itself is only from the year 1039. His name was Theopemptus.[11] Although the Kiev metropolitan who headed the Rus' Church was most often a Greek, native Russian clergy in that position are not unknown. Whatever the metropolitan's nationality, however, he served as a conduit not only of the orders of the Patriarch of Constantinople, but also as a spokesman for the Byzantine emperor's interests in Rus' – and, of course, as a conduit of Byzantine culture in Rus'. The Church seems to have spread swiftly, at least in the towns and cities of Rus', and a diocesan structure was quickly set up reflecting the boundaries of the major principalities of the confederation under the leadership of the prince of Kiev. By the year 1240, there were, in fact, fifteen bishoprics on the territory of Rus'. Monastic life also developed quickly, signaled by the foundation of the famous Kiev Caves Monastery by SS Anthony and Theodosius; the monastery became an important center of religious culture and the training ground for many of the young Church's bishops. And, indeed, the generation following Prince Vladimir's conversion of the Rus' people saw the appearance of the first Christian saints of Rus', the brothers Boris and Gleb, sons of Vladimir, who allowed themselves to be murdered rather than embracing "fighting evil with evil" and plunging the land of Rus' into a civil war over a third brother's usurpation of the throne of Kiev. The newly baptized citizens of Kievan Rus' saw the brothers' self-sacrifice as following the example of Christ. The Christian message was obviously taking hold in Rus'.

By the late tenth century, the Byzantine version of Christianity was already in many ways different from the medieval Catholicism of Western Europe. Although both churches accepted the basic dogmas of Christianity, there were noticeable differences in emphasis. The Eastern Church had the feel of a federation of churches compared to the centralized papacy growing up in the West. Thus the new Rus' Church would have considerably more independence than, say, the Catholic Church in Poland. In addition, because the parish clergy in the Eastern Church were normally married and had families, they did not become a separate social group as did clergy in the Western Church and hence remained closer to the people. Eastern Christianity was also more willing to accommodate local cultures and to integrate national traditions into its religious life. The use of the local language in public worship both allowed for the rapid development of a native clergy who did not have to learn a foreign language to become priests and made the teachings of the church more easily accessible to the parishioners. At least in the cities, basic Christianity seems to have caught on quickly. In the countryside, missionary work went much more slowly among the scattered population. Pagan Slavic burials from the late fourteenth century are still being found, reflecting, at a minimum, a continuing tradition of rural *dvoeverie* ("double faith"), where traditional Slavic paganism was overlain with a thin veneer of Christian practices. Still, what came to be called Orthodox Christianity soon became the nationality marker of the people of Rus', distinguishing them both from pagan or Muslim nomads and from Catholic Poles.

The acceptance of Byzantine Christianity in Rus' also brought literacy to Russia. The missionaries brought to Rus' the Cyrillic alphabet, developed for the Slavic-speaking Bulgarians, along with hundreds of pages of Byzantine writings in Slavic translations made earlier in Bulgaria, almost all of it religious material. The possibility of reading and writing in one's own language by just learning the Cyrillic alphabet quickly led not only to widespread literacy, but also to extensive literary production. Kievan Rus' writings followed the Byzantine forms and Byzantine literary models, but were written in Slavic. Not only did the early Rus' writers adopt the Byzantine literary conventions; they also adapted Byzantine literary models to their own environment. The Russian *Primary Chronicle*, which we have cited often, is the most complete source for the early history of Rus', but it is almost slavishly copied from a Byzantine chronicle that came to Rus' in a Slavic translation done in Bulgaria. The Rus' editor simply inserted local material into the Byzantine narrative, sometimes, it would seem, simply inserting material dealing with Rus' in whatever years no Byzantine entries were found.

But this adaptation of the Byzantine Chronicle of George the Monk ("Hamartolus") meant not simply mechanically inserting occasional local entries. Rather, in adapting the Byzantine chronicle to the Rus' situation, in a very Byzantine fashion the Rus' editor integrated the history of the Slavic people into the greater theme of the Greek original – namely, the spread of Christianity and the salvation of the world. The Rus' scribe had absorbed not just Byzantine literary form, but Byzantine thinking. Similarly, Hilarion, the first native Rus' bishop to become metropolitan of Kiev, and thus head of the Rus' Church, displays his competency not only in Byzantine literary form in his famous "Sermon on Law and Grace" (rhetorical balance, use of parallelism, metaphor, apostrophe, and so on), but his Byzantine Christian style of thinking. The latter can be seen in Hilarion's theological juxtaposition of the Old and New Testaments of the Bible, and in describing Prince Vladimir of Kiev as an equal of the apostles in spreading the Gospel to new lands.[12] The acceptance of Byzantine Christianity in Rus' was the acceptance of a whole Byzantine "cultural package" that included new modes of thought as well as of belief, and new mediums and forms of expression in religion and literature as in architecture and painting (see Chapter 8).

As Byzantine Christian culture spread through the land of Rus', particularly during the golden age of Yaroslav the Wise (1019–54), who much patronized Byzantine culture in Rus', large numbers of Rus' Vikings continued to migrate to Byzantium to serve in the Byzantine army, many of them constituting the imperial bodyguard. Still, economic and political issues between the two countries continued. In 1043, for example, a noble Russian trader was killed in an altercation at a market in Constantinople. Using that event as a reason (or as a pretext), Yaroslav of Kiev mounted a major campaign against Constantinople under the leadership of his eldest son, Vladimir. The campaign was possibly planned to join with the revolt of the Byzantine general Maniaces against the Byzantine emperor Constantine Monomachos. A very large Rus' army was dispatched, once again, down the Dnieper and across the Black Sea to attack the imperial city. Once more, Greek fire ended the Russian naval threat to the city, and the Rus' military who survived limped home.[13] This was the last medieval Rus' attack on the Byzantine capital. The fact that there were no more Rus' attempts to pillage Constantinople probably has little to do with warm relations between the two powers, although the Byzantine emperor Constantine IX Monomachus did marry a daughter to one of Grand Prince Yaroslav's sons, Vsevolod, in 1046, probably hoping to guarantee peace with Rus'; their child, Vladimir, eventually took the Kievan throne (1113–25) and proudly used his mother's family name, Monomach, as his sobriquet. Rather, the lack of military encounters between Kievan Rus' and Byzantium has much to do with the appearance of the Polovetsian (Cuman) nomads on the southern Russian steppe. This warlike Turkic people replaced the Pechenegs of an earlier time and created an iron curtain of sorts between Byzantium and Rus' that made major movement of Rus' forces to the Black Sea unlikely.

The Period of Mongol Rule

Between 1240 and 1243, the Polovetsian danger to Rus' gave way to Mongol (Tatar) conquest and rule. Earlier, in 1204, the Byzantine capital of Constantinople had fallen to the Latin crusaders. (Russian chronicles give very detailed descriptions of the event, suggesting close emotional ties with that city.) From this time on, Byzantine contacts with Rus' will be largely ecclesiastical in nature. Trade dwindled, or was taken over by foreigners, military contacts become impossible, and even cultural relations became extremely limited. A Byzantine government in exile regrouped in the Asia Minor city of Nicaea (modern Iznik), and the top hierarchy of the church went with it. It was from here that the last metropolitan of Kiev before the Mongol conquest was appointed in 1237. The metropolitan, whose name was Joseph, is no longer heard of after the Mongol sack of Kiev. He was not replaced until 1250, when a Russian, Cyril II, was consecrated in Nicaea as metropolitan of Kiev. Perhaps no Byzantine candidates were willing to move to the devastated lands of Rus' at this time.

By 1269 the metropolitan of Kiev has an auxiliary, "the bishop of Sarai," whose function seems to have been as a liaison between the Rus' Church and the Mongols, but who also represented Byzantine interests in the Tatar–Mongol capital of Sarai and in the Genoese colony on the Sea of Azov. The liaison role played by the bishop is just one example of the Byzantine Empire taking an important role in Rus' political life through the church. Thus, after 1299, when Metropolitan Maximus of Kiev (1283–1305) moved his seat to the city of Vladimir in Suzdalia, the growing power in northeast Rus', Constantinople off and on allowed the creation of a separate metropolitan ecclesiastical jurisdiction (of "Little Russia") in Volynia and Galicia. These two areas were not in the Suzdal orbit, but were in danger of allying with Catholic Poland, which eventually occupied them and threatened to convert all the Orthodox population to Roman Catholicism by force. Similarly, the Grand Principality of Lithuania, which had occupied most of the western Rus' territories, including eventually Kiev, also claimed and received an independent ecclesiastical province under a local metropolitan, at least temporarily. Only in 1347, after the grand prince of Moscow, now controlling Suzdal and almost all of northeast Russia, had sent a very large sum of money to Constantinople to help rebuild the great Church of St Sophia after the dome had collapsed in an earthquake, were the competing metropolitanates suppressed – and then only temporarily. In principle, however, the Byzantine authorities followed a policy of supporting Moscow in its attempt to unify and lead Rus'. They could have found no stronger a supporter of this position than the metropolitan in Moscow, Alexis (1354–78).

Alexis was the son of an important boyar and had been raised in the grand princely court in Moscow before he took monastic vows. He was first appointed to the bishopric of Vladimir in Suzdalia and then recommended for the post of metropolitan by Grand Prince Simeon (Semen) of Moscow (1341–53) and the aged Metropolitan Theognostus (1328–53), and appointed to that post by Constantinople. Alexis's strongly pro-Moscow stance made it quite unlikely that he would be accepted in the Polish- and Lithuanian-administered Rus' lands, and independent metropolitanates appeared again, apparently despite misgivings by the Byzantine authorities. Alexis occupied himself with advancing Moscow's cause, even guaranteeing a safe conduct to the prince of Tver, Moscow's chief rival in the northeast, and then withdrawing it once the prince was in Moscow. He installed bishops who shared his pro-Muscovite sentiments in many of the dioceses subordinate to him, apparently with the acquiescence of the patriarchate in Constantinople.

Alexis's successor, the Bulgarian Kiprian, had already been appointed by the Byzantine authorities in 1375 as metropolitan of Lithuania and of Little Russia, with the right of succession to Alexis as metropolitan of Kiev and All Rus'. At the news of Alexis's death in 1378, Kiprian left Kiev, where he had been living, and headed for Moscow. There he was arrested by the Muscovite prince Dmitri (1359–89) on suspicion of being pro-Lithuanian, but he escaped and made his way to Constantinople to plead his case. The next several years saw chaos in the Moscow metropolitanate, for the grand prince often had his candidate for the position, and so did the Byzantine emperor and patriarch. Much of the confusion had to do with imperial politics in Constantinople, with alternating emperors appointing their own patriarchs, who favored one candidate for the metropolitan throne of Rus', then another. It was not until 1390 that Kiprian finally replaced the uncanonical Muscovite metropolitan Mityai (Michael) and took up administration of the Muscovite Church while also ruling the Orthodox Church in the Lithuanian state. The rulers of both Muscovite and Lithuanian Rus' apparently now trusted him. He might actually have been the person responsible for arranging a dynastic marriage between the two grand princely families.[14]

The considerable traffic back and forth between the Rus' lands and Byzantium undertaken by metropolitans of Rus' and would-be metropolitans of Rus' that we have seen in the later fourteenth century is, in fact, part of a broader picture of renewed travel between the two countries. Rus' merchants, pilgrims, and monks went south; Balkan merchants, monks, artists and writers moved north. The merchants brought to Rus' Mediterranean luxury articles such as silk, gold jewelry, and wine, and they took south amber, semi-precious stones, and furs. The pilgrims went to Constantinople to pay homage to the many Christian relics preserved there and (with the wandering monks) traveled to the monastic communities of Mount Athos in Greece to pray in its revered monasteries; a Russian monastery had existed on the Holy Mountain since the middle of the twelfth century. In turn, Byzantine monks came to Rus' from the Balkans, Asia Minor, and the Near East to collect alms for their communities, many now subjects of the Turks.[15] In fact, the Turkish incursions into the Balkans seem to have sent a number of members of the cultural elite of Bulgaria and Serbia to seek new homes among their fellow Slavs in the Muscovite and Lithuanian states, which were beginning to prosper in the fourteenth and even more in the fifteenth century.

Byzantine cultural influence on Muscovite life increased dramatically in this period. Metropolitan Kiprian, a Bulgarian, and his Greek successor, Metropolitan Photius (1408–31), were both important literary and cultural figures in Rus' and did much to spread the contemporary mystical theology of hesychasm that was so important on Mount Athos. This religious movement emphasized wordless contemplation of the Divine and prayer "without ceasing." This "second South Slavic influence" was particularly important in literature; it brought the latest Byzantine literary fashions to Muscovy and, as it were, "jump started" Muscovite literature. Epiphanius "the Wise" and Pachomius the Logothete ("the Serb") developed the convoluted style known as word-weaving, supposedly inspired by hesychast tradition. Both are famous for the lives of saints that they wrote.[16] Similar developments came in art, with, for example, Theophanes the Greek bringing the most recent developments in late Byzantine painting to Muscovy. Here, too, hesychasm had a major role (see below, Chapter 8).

The Muscovite state was in the throes of a civil war when Metropolitan Photius died in 1431, and it was some five years before a candidate for the metropolitan throne was chosen by a meeting of Rus' bishops and sent to Constantinople for appointment. The candidate was Archbishop Jonah of Riazan. By the time the Muscovite candidate arrived in the Byzantine capital, however, the Byzantine authorities had already appointed and consecrated a new metropolitan for Kiev and All Rus', Isidore, a Greek from Constantinople. It was agreed that eventually Jonah would succeed Isidore when the latter died or retired, and the two returned together to Moscow in 1437. But Metropolitan Isidore did not stay long in Moscow; he soon set out on a leisurely journey to Ferrara, Italy, to take part in a church council devoted to reuniting the Latin and Greek (that is, Roman Catholic and Eastern Orthodox) churches. The Byzantines hoped that such a reunion with the Western Church would lead to European armies coming to their defense against the Turks. One Russian bishop, Abraham of Suzdal, was in Isidore's retinue. In 1439, the council, which had moved to Florence because of an outbreak of plague, decreed the union of the two churches after much heated debate. The agreement came about after the Orthodox delegation accepted the Catholic position on most doctrinal matters. Isidore was one of the strongest backers of the agreement and was rewarded by the Pope with a cardinal's hat and appointment as a papal legate to Eastern Europe.

Cardinal Isidore spent almost two years on his journey back to Moscow. During his journey, he visited various cities in Eastern Europe, probably arguing the case for union of the two churches. His eventual entrance into Moscow drew incredulous stares. He was preceded by a Latin-style cross with a sculptured body of Christ on it (something unknown in the Eastern Christian world) and a Catholic bishop's staff. Even more shocking to the Muscovites was Isidore's commemoration of the Pope at the liturgy in the great Dormition Cathedral in the Kremlin and the reading of the decree of church union at the service. For generations the Byzantines had warned the Christians of Rus' about the false teachings of the Roman Church and the pretensions of the Roman pope. Now the Byzantine Church had submitted to the Pope and had accepted his false teachings! According to the Muscovite chronicles, Grand Prince Basil II immediately recognized the "madness" of Isidore, declared him defrocked, jailed him in a Kremlin monastery, and then exiled him from Muscovy. The actual events were probably not as dramatic as the chronicles would have it. After all, Russian participants must have long since told the Grand Prince what had happened at the Council of Florence. The basic meaning of Isidore's rejection was that the Byzantine Church had fallen into error. Once Cardinal Isidore had been deposed as metropolitan, his automatic successor was Jonah (1441–61), the original Muscovite candidate for the post proposed by a synod of Rus' bishops earlier. The Muscovite Church was now *de facto* independent of Constantinople, where the pro-Catholic party ruled.[17]

The Byzantine submission to the Papacy had horrified the Orthodox people of Muscovy. Some fourteen years later, on May 29, 1453, the Empire perished when the Ottoman Turks breached the walls of Constantinople (most of the other imperial territories had long since been conquered by the Turks – the much sought after Western military aid had never materialized). The Russians were firmly convinced that the real reason the Byzantine Empire fell to the Turks was the religious treason committed at the Council of Florence, when the Byzantine Church had submitted to the Pope. God had simply withdrawn his support of the Greeks.

Byzantium and Russia after the Fall of the Byzantine Empire

The Byzantine Empire was obviously dead, but its ghost was still powerful. For those who had grown up in the Byzantine cultural orbit (which included Russia), it was almost impossible to conceive of a world without a Christian emperor whose basic function in the great scheme of things was to be the protector of the true, orthodox, Christian Church. But now there was no emperor in Byzantium. Slowly and tentatively, Muscovy asserted its right to the title of Orthodox Christian emperor. Grand Prince Ivan III (1462–1505; "the Great") occasionally used the title of emperor (tsar) in diplomatic correspondence, although he instructed his envoys to defend the title by claiming his descent from St Vladimir, the baptizer of Russia, not by claiming inheritance from the Byzantine imperial line. The title, it seems, was functional rather than hereditary. He also employed the emblem of the Byzantine double-headed eagle on his seals, a symbol reminiscent of Byzantine imperial heraldry. In 1472 Ivan III married a Byzantine princess, Zoe (Sophia) Palaeologos, daughter of the last Byzantine ruler of Morea in southern Greece and niece of the last Byzantine emperor. She brought no hereditary claim to either the title of emperor or to Byzantine territory (her male relatives had already sold those claims in Western Europe), but she and her Greek retainers brought some of the aura of the Byzantine imperial court to the Moscow Kremlin and a familiarity with

Byzantine court ceremonial. New and more pretentious palaces and churches were built in the Kremlin and the daily life of the grand prince became much more formalized in keeping with the Byzantine tradition. Indeed, in 1498, when Ivan decided to change the line of succession to the grand princely throne, he employed the sacred Byzantine ritual for naming an imperial co-ruler and heir apparent. This act should not be construed as a claim to sacred imperial status in the Byzantine sense (that will come in the sixteenth century), but rather as a demonstration of the penetration of Byzantine ideas in Muscovy. Previously, as a vassal of the Mongol khan, the grand prince would have applied to his suzerain to proclaim the change in succession, but, now that he was not subject to a Mongol overlord, he automatically turned to the Byzantine tradition to confirm his decision in this matter.[18]

Still, the idea that the Muscovite ruler might be a successor to the sacred ruler of Byzantium in his position as divinely sanctioned guardian of the Orthodox Church was clearly in the air. Around 1500, for example, Philotheus, a monk from the city of Pskov, wrote to the Russian ruler that the first Rome had fallen because of heresy. He continued: the second Rome, Constantinople, had been conquered by the Turks, but the new, third, Rome of Muscovy shone like the sun, and its ruler was the sole emperor of all the Orthodox Christian faith on all the earth. "For two Romes have fallen, but the third stands, and a fourth shall never be."[19]

The fundamental idea behind the monk's thinking had been carefully spelled out some hundred years earlier in an epistle of Patriarch Anthony of Constantinople to Grand Prince Basil I of Moscow (1389–1425), when the latter had apparently caused the emperor's name to be dropped from liturgical commemoration in the Muscovite realm. The patriarch lectured the prince: "My son, you are wrong in saying, 'We have a church, but not an emperor.' It is not possible for Christians to have a church and not to have an empire. Church and empire have a great unity and community; nor is it possible for them to be separated from one another."[20] The logic is clear: if it is impossible to have the church without an empire and Muscovy has preserved the true church after the Byzantines had accepted the "Latin heresy" and the Byzantine Empire has disappeared, then Muscovy must be the empire because it has the church. It should be noted that the theoretical justification for the empire in Byzantine thinking is protecting the church. If the true church is now in Russia rather than in fallen Byzantium, Russia must be the empire that God has raised up to protect the church, and the Russian ruler must be the emperor (*tsar*, in Russian) divinely appointed to guard the welfare of the church.

Metropolitan Macarius of Moscow (1542–63), the tutor and guardian of the young Ivan IV (1533–84; "the Terrible"), seems to have fashioned this thinking into a coherent political theory of Orthodox autocracy that he taught his youthful charge.[21] Macarius meticulously crafted a Byzantine imperial coronation ceremony for the young Muscovite ruler, even carefully creating equivalencies between Muscovite grand princely accoutrements and Byzantine imperial regalia. In 1547 Metropolitan Macarius crowned Ivan as "emperor (tsar) and autocrat of all Russia." The empire required by the church was reconstituted in Russia; Byzantine political theory as enunciated, for example, by Patriarch Anthony, finally triumphs in Russia. Ivan, in fact, regularly acted as a Byzantine emperor would have in his dealings with the church, appointing bishops, calling church councils, enforcing their decisions, and so on. And in 1589 the Byzantine paradigm of church and state was completed when the metropolitan of Moscow was raised to the rank of patriarch by the patriarchs of the Eastern Church. A truly independent state, particularly an "empire" (tsardom), needs to have an independent church presided over by a patriarch.

Despite its temporary submission to the papacy in 1439, repudiated after the Turkish conquest of Constantinople, the Greek Church in the Ottoman Empire, like its predecessor in the Byzantine Empire, continued to play the role of a standard for Russia. It was assumed that the Greeks had preserved the ancient teachings that should be the standard of the teachings of the Orthodox Church in Russia too. For example, in the late fifteenth century the Muscovite authorities asked for a learned Greek who could correct the Slavic translations of various church books. The patriarch of Constantinople sent the monk Manuel Trivoles, known in Russia as "Maximus the Greek" (active in Russia, 1518–56), who had studied in Renaissance Italy. He came to Moscow from Mount Athos with many Greek books and worked on correcting the Russian books. Similarly, when a major dispute arose between different monastic factions in Russia in the late fifteenth and early sixteenth centuries about the appropriateness of monasteries inhabited by monks who had taken vows of poverty owning estates worked by others, both sides appealed to Byzantine precedents. They searched the writings of the fathers of the church and the traditions preserved in the Greek monasteries to find the correct way of addressing the question. They also sought information on this matter from Maximus the Greek, asking about the current thinking on this subject in the Greek Church. The monastic group that backed monastic land holding did not agree with Maximus' position and when they came into their own with the Muscovite authorities they had him incarcerated in a monastery and deprived of the sacraments. Still, even in his imprisonment, Maximus' counsel and advice on the Greek Orthodox way of doing things was occasionally sought by the Muscovite authorities and used as precedent.[22]

Similarly, in the 1660s, Nikon, the patriarch of Moscow (1652–67), was accused of changing the Orthodox faith by instituting certain liturgical textual reforms to correct errors that had grown up in Russia and also of attempting to usurp the powers of the tsar. A council of representatives of the other patriarchs of the Eastern Church was convened in Moscow in 1666 to consider the charges. The ritual changes were deemed unnecessary, but encroaching on state power was seen as grounds for removing the Russian patriarch. After the foreign clergy had left, Nikon was removed from the patriarchate, but the reforms the council had said were unnecessary were decreed! The Russian Church had matured enough to feel comfortable rejecting the advice of its Byzantine mother church.

The Westernization and secularization of Russia that began with Peter the Great very much diminished Byzantine influence in Russia, particularly in the political sphere. But one cannot but wonder if Catherine the Great's plans to create an independent Greek state and, indeed, the passion on the part of Emperor Nicholas II and of the Provisional Government of 1917 for taking Constantinople (modern Istanbul) does not suggest a nostalgia for Russia's ancient ties to Byzantium.

Notes

1   Photius, Patriarch of Constantinople (1958), 74–110; Vasiliev (1946).
2   Majeska (2004).

 3 Constantine VII Porphyrogenitus (1967), 56–63; (1962), 16–61.
 4 Doubts have occasionally been raised about the historical reality of the Rus' attack on the Byzantine capital in 907, but Vasiliev (1951) has convincingly shown that it happened. The text of the treaty is available in *The Russian Primary Chronicle* (1953), 65–8; on the authenticity of the Rus'–Byzantine treaties, see Sorlin (1961).
 5 *The Russian Primary Chronicle* (1953), 73–7.
 6 Olga's official reception at the Great Palace in Constantinople is described in great detail (as a model for similar ceremonies in the future) in Constantine VII Porphyrogenitus, *De cerimoniis* (1829), 594–8. On the disputed dating of Olga's trip to the Byzantine capital and the place of her baptism, see, most recently, Poppe (1992), which, however, unnecessarily posits two separate visits by Olga to Constantinople.
 7 Runciman (1930), 198–216.
 8 *The Russian Primary Chronicle* (1953), 93–119.
 9 *The Russian Primary Chronicle* (1953), 245–7 (notes).
10 Poppe (1976).
11 See most recently Poppe (1982), which, however, argues for there being a metropolitan of Kiev from 989.
12 See *Russian Primary Chronicle* (1953), 3–50 (Introduction), and Chizhevskii (1960), 20–71.
13 Shepard (1987).
14 On this tangled period of Russo-Byzantine ecclesiastical conflicts, see Meyendorff (1981).
15 Majeska (1996).
16 Chizhevskii (1960), 145–229.
17 Fennell (1995), 170–88.
18 Majeska (1978).
19 The complete text is published in Malinin (1901), Appendix, 49–56.
20 Barker (1957), 195.
21 This is the view of autocracy espoused by the author of the Ivan IV sections of the Ivan IV–Kurbsky exchanges; see *The Correspondence between Prince A. M. Kurbsky and Tsar Ivan IV of Russia* (1963).
22 Haney (1973).

References

Barker, Ernest (ed.) (1957). *Social and Political Thought in Byzantium*. Oxford: Clarendon Press.

Chizhevskii, D. (1960). *History of Russian Literature*. The Hague: Mouton.

Constantine VII Porphyrogenitus (1829). *De cerimoniis aulae byzantinae*, ed. J. Reiske. Bonn: Weber Verlag.

Constantine VII Porphyrogenitus (1962). *De administrando imperio*, ed. Gy. Moravcsik and R. J. H. Jenkins. Vol. 2. London: Athlone Press.

Constantine VII Porphyrogenitus (1967). *De administrando imperio*, ed. and trans. Gy. Moravcsik and R. J. H. Jenkins. Vol. 1. Washington: Dumbarton Oaks.

The Correspondence between Prince A. M. Kurbsky and Tsar Ivan IV of Russia (1963). Ed. and trans. J. L. I. Fennell. Cambridge: Cambridge University Press.

Fennell, J. (1995). *A History of the Russian Church to 1448*. London: Longman.

Haney, J. (1973). *From Italy to Muscovy: The Life and Works of Maxim the Greek*. Munich: Fink Verlag.

Majeska, G. (1978). "The Moscow Coronation of 1498 Reconsidered," *Jahrbücher für Geschichte Osteuropas*, 26: 353–61.

Majeska, G. (1996). "Russo-Byzantine Relations, 1240–1453," *Acts. XVIIIth International Congress of Byzantine Studies, Selected Papers*. Vol. 1: *History*. Shepherdstown, WV: Byzantine Studies Press.

Majeska, G. (2004). "Patriarch Photius and the Conversion of the Rus'," *Russian History/ Histoire Russe*, 31: 413–18.

Malinin, V. (1901). *Starets Eleazarova monastyria Filofei i ego poslaniia*. Kiev: Kievo-Pecherskaia Lavra.

Meyendorff, J. (1981). *Byzantium and the Rise of Russia: A Study of Byzantino-Russo Relations in the Fourteenth Century*. Cambridge: Cambridge University Press.

Photius, Patriarch of Constantinople (1958). *The Homelies of Photius*, trans. and commentary Cyril Mango. Cambridge, MA: Harvard University Press.

Poppe, A. (1976). "The Political Background to the Baptism of Rus: Byzantine–Russian Relations between 986–989," *Dumbarton Oaks Papers*, 30: 197–244.

Poppe, A. (1982). "The Original Status of the Old-Russian Church," No. 3 in his *The Rise of Christian Russia*.

Poppe, A. (1992) "Once again concerning the Baptism of Olga, Archontissa of Rus'," *Dumbarton Oaks Papers*, 46: 271–7.

Runciman, S. (1930). *The First Bulgarian Empire*. London: G. Bell & Sons.

The Russian Primary Chronicle (1953), trans. and ed. Samuel H. Cross and Olgerd Sherbowitz-Wetzor. Cambridge, MA: Mediaeval Academy of America.

Shepard, J. (1987). "Why Did the Russians Attack Byzantium in 1043?" *Byzantinisch-Neugriechische Jahrbücher*, 22: 147–212.

Sorlin, I. (1961). "Les Traités de Byzance avec la Russie au Xe siècle," *Cahiers du monde russe et soviétique*, 2: 313–60, 447–75.

Vasiliev, A. A. (1946). *The Russian Attack on Constantinople in 860*. Cambridge, MA: Medieval Academy of American.

Vasiliev, A. A. (1951). "The Second Russian Attack on Constantinople," *Dumbarton Oaks Papers*, 6, 161–225.

Further Reading

Fennell, J. (1995). *A History of the Russian Church to 1448*. London: Longman.

Levchenko, M. V. (1956). *Ocherki po istorii russko-vizantiiskikh otnoshenii* [Notes on the History of Russo-Byzantine Relations]. Moscow: Akademiia Nauk.

Medlin, W. K. (1952). *Moscow and East Rom: A Political Study of Church and State in Muscovite Russia*. Geneva: Droz.

Meyendorff, J. (1981). *Byzantium and the Rise of Russia: A Study of Byzantino-Russian Relations in the Fourteenth Century*. Cambridge: Cambridge University Press.

Obolensky, D. (1971). *The Byzantine Commonwealth: Eastern Europe, 500–1453*. New York and Washington: Praeger.

Poppe, A. (1982). *The Rise of Christian Russia*. London: Variorum.

Poppe, A. (2006) *Christian Russia in the Making*. Aldershot: Ashgate.

Schaeder, H. (1957). *Moskau das dritte Rom*. Darmstadt: Gentner.

CHAPTER FIVE

The Mongols and Rus':
Eight Paradigms

DONALD OSTROWSKI

The relationship of the Mongols with Rus' is one of those controversial topics that finds no consensus among scholars. On every major point and most of the minor ones, there is ardent and passionate disagreement. Yet, one interpretative framework, for metahistorical reasons, has tended to dominate the historiography. In this chapter, I discuss first what I consider to be the factual background of Mongol–Rus' relations. Other historians with different views would no doubt emphasize different evidence and would dispute the importance of the evidence I present, but it would be incorrect to say that such evidence does not exist. Then I discuss eight main paradigms that I see as having been applied to explaining Mongol–Rus' relations. Finally, I draw some conclusions that are applicable to the present and future of studying those relations. In the process, I hope to provide the reader with an understanding of why such divergent opinions exist in the scholarly literature.

Historical Background

The Mongols first made their appearance in the western Eurasian steppe in 1222. Following the death of the defeated Khwarezmshah Muhammad on an island in the Caspian Sea, the pursuing Mongol expeditionary force continued on around the west coast of the Caspian, through the Caucasus Mountains, and into an area that is also known as the Qipchaq steppe (Desht-i-Qipchaq).

After wintering near the Crimean peninsula, this expeditionary force, which was commanded by Jebe and Sübe'etei (Subudei) (two of the Mongols' leading generals), captured Sudak in the Crimea. In 1223 they encountered and defeated a combined Rus'–Polovtsian army on the Kalka River, north of the Black Sea. Leaving the Qipchaq steppe eastward, they fought a battle against the Volga Bulgars and crossed the Volga River on their way back to their homeland in the eastern steppe.

Following two other campaigns against the Bulgars, one in 1229 (including Saksin and the Polovtsians), the other in 1232, the Mongols returned to the western steppe fourteen years after their first visit. An army commanded by Batu (the grandson of Chinggis Khan) and Sübe'etei during the winter of 1237–8 took Riazan', Moscow,

Vladimir, Suzdal', and a number of other Rus' towns, but turned back before reaching Novgorod, possibly because the Novgorodians agreed to pay tribute. In December 1240 the Mongols conquered Kiev before heading further west, where, in April 1241, they defeated a combined Polish and Teutonic knight army at Liegnitz and a Magyar army at Móhi.

Returning to the area north of the Black Sea, Batu established the Qipchaq Khanate,[1] which lasted until 1502, when the last remnant of it was conquered by the Crimean Tatars. It survived the longest of any of the four original ulus (khanates) distributed by Chinggis Khan to his sons. Among the successors to the Qipchaq Khanate, the Kazan' Khanate lasted until 1552; the Astrakhan', until 1556; the Sibir', until 1587; the Kasimov Khanate until 1681; and the Crimean, until 1783.

The Mongols who accompanied Batu and Sübe'etei in the campaigns of 1237–42 constituted a minority of the forces under their command; the rest of the army was made up of various other steppe peoples, including Qipchaqs, Circassians, Ossetians (Alans and Burtas), and others. To the extent that the khans of the Qipchaq Khanate were Chinggisids (descendants of Chinggis Khan), and that any of the ruling class could trace their ancestry back to the Mongols, they were ethnically Mongol. As a result of intermarriage with local peoples, however, such ethnic distinctions diminished early on and facilitated the generic term "Tatar" being applied in the Rus' sources. Yet, the khan and ruling class continued to see themselves as carrying on the traditions of Chinggis Khan, and in that respect they were culturally and politically Mongol.[2]

From the time of the conquest until 1327, the khan in Sarai administered the Rus' principalities through a system of resident military governors (*basqaqs*; also known as *tammači* [sing. *tamma*] in Mongol sources). Following a revolt in Tver', the Rus' princes took over the role of the military governors in their own principalities. The grand prince of Vladimir was *primus inter pares* among them and was responsible for keeping the others in line. He and the other Rus' princes reported to the khan through the intermediary of a civilian governor (*darugha*) who lived in Sarai. This reporting required, if anything, even more extended sojourns than before on the part of the Rus' princes in the capital of the khanate. A twentieth-century historian remarked that Grand Prince Ivan I (1328–1341) spent half his reign in the process of traveling to and from and staying at Sarai [1]. Much the same can be said for his successors, Semën (1341–53) and Ivan II (1353–9), with envoys (*posoly*) from the khan bringing instructions in the interim. Grand princely visits to Sarai tended to diminish toward the end of the fourteenth century (as the Khanate dissolved into civil war). Sons of the grand princes and other Rus' princes were kept as hostages at the court to ensure loyalty from their fathers, but it also allowed them to learn the administrative practices of the Qipchaq Khanate first hand. When the sons took over as rulers of their respective principalities, they were better able to implement the administrative practices of the Khanate.

From 1327 until 1406, the khan supplied troops on an ad-hoc basis to help the grand prince suppress revolts, maintain order, collect taxes, and defend the area. The last time troops were sent from the Qipchaq Khanate to support the Rus' grand prince was Emir Edigei's supplying of Tatar forces to Vasilii I against Vitovt, Grand Duke of Lithuania [2]. The grand princes, in turn, were expected to supply troops to the khan when needed. The most famous occurrence of the fulfillment of this policy was when Grand Prince Dmitrii Donskoi mobilized Rus' forces to aid Khan Tokhtamysh in his battle against the Emir Mamai in 1380. At the same time, the prince of Riazan' sent troops to aid Mamai.

The khan also determined who would be grand prince of the Rus' principalities and gave the patent (*iarlyk*) directly to that person as well as separate patents to the princes of the other principalities, each of whom had to make the trip to Sarai to receive it. During the fourteenth century, on four occasions the grand princely patent went to someone other than the prince of Moscow (specifically, to the prince of Tver' three times and the prince of Suzdal' once). The last time the khan made a determination of who was to be grand prince was in 1431, when Khan Ulug Mehmed decided in favor of Vasilii II over his uncle Iurii Dmitrievich [3]. By 1449, however, Vasilii II was declaring that he was the only one issuing patents to the other Rus' princes, thus effectively eliminating the role of the Qipchaq khan. From 1462 on, the prince of Moscow ascended to the position of grand prince of Rus' without the patent of the khan, although he still collected the *dan'* (tax for the khan) and supplied the *vykhod* (tribute) to the khan in Sarai (until 1502) and then to the khan of Astrakhan' (until 1556), as well as to the khan of Kazan' (until 1552), the khan of Kasimov (until 1553), and the khan of the Crimea (until 1700) in acknowledgment of their Chinggisid descent and thereby nominal higher status in steppe diplomatic terms.

The Eight Paradigms

The period of conquest and rule by the Mongol/Tatars has been a problematic one to describe in the Russian historiography. Those problems can be seen to derive from the earliest attempts to explain what was happening to the Rus' princes and their land. In all, one can discern eight paradigms (or conceptual frameworks) for trying to explain the Mongol conquest and subsequent Tatar rule, arranged here in approximately chronological order. The following delineation is not intended to be an exhaustive survey of the historiography. Instead, I focus on characterizing each paradigm and describing the most prominent or influential proponents in each case.

1. Punishment for Sins and the Wrath of God

This paradigm was a continuation of the interpretative framework applied by Rus' Churchmen to pre-Mongol western steppe peoples, such as the Pechenegi and Polovtsi. The first mention of the Mongols appears in the Laurentian, Suzdal', and Novgorod I chronicles under the year 1223. The Tatars are described as defeating the Rus' princes "because of our sins":

> That same year, [Novg. I and Suzdal' chronicles add: for our sins, unknown] peoples [*iazytsi*] came, [Suzdal' Chronicle adds: Godless Moabites called Tatars] whom no one knows well, who they are, nor from where they came, nor what their language is, nor of what tribe [*plamene*] they are, nor what their faith is. But they call them Tatars, and others say Taumen, and others Pechenegs, and others say that they are those of whom Methodius, Bishop of Patmos, testifies, that they came out from the Etrian Desert, which is between East and North. [4–5]³

When the Mongols returned home, the chroniclers reported: "we do not know from where they came and to where they went again only God knows [Novg. I adds: whence he fetched them against us for our sins]" [4–5]. Initially the chroniclers used pejorative language about the Mongols couched in biblical terms [6]. In descriptions of the conquests of 1237–40, the Mongols are described as "godless," "lawless," and "accursed," but phrases like "there was no opposing the wrath of God" also appear [4]. Perhaps the fullest expression of this viewpoint appears in the Novgorod I Chronicle's account of the Mongol conquest of Rus':

> Let brothers, fathers, and children, whoever see God's infliction on the entire Rus' land not weep. God loosed the pagans on us because of our sins. God, in his wrath, brought foreigners against the land, and thus crushed by them they [the Rus' people] will remember God . . . God punishes lands that have sinned either with death or famine or an infliction of pagans or drought or heavy rain or other punishment, to see if we will repent and live as God bids us. [5]

But this interpretative paradigm ended in northeastern Rus' within fifteen years of the Mongol conquest.

2. Realpolitik of Rus' Princes and Church Leaders

After 1252, in areas where the Rus' Church was under the Patriarch of Constantinople, we find an absence in the sources of the pejorative terminology that characterized the initial reception. The English historian John Fennell was the first to point out that from the chronicles of this period "one gets the impression that the Tatars were a benevolent rather than an oppressive force" [7]. He goes on to write that the way the Tatar suppression of the revolt in Tver' in 1327 is described "reveals an astonishingly neutral attitude towards the Tatars" [7]. The elimination of pejorative terminology and the neutralizing of the descriptions of the Tatars in northeastern Rus' sources was probably the result of the alliance between Byzantium and the Qipchaq Khanate. It would not have been appropriate for Rus' chroniclers to write critically about an ally of the Byzantine Empire. This alliance, except for brief exceptions, remained in place until the fall of Constantinople to the Ottoman Turks in 1453. In addition, the Church benefited from the patronage of the khan through freedom of worship, being allowed to own land, and exemption from taxation. Rus' Churchmen, in return, prayed for the well-being of the khan and his family. In addition, the Rus' Church in 1261 established an archiepiscopal see in Sarai, the prelate of which attended to the Rus' princes and their entourages when they journeyed there to fulfill their duties to the khan. The archbishop of Sarai also acted as diplomatic liaison with Constantinople. Before Khan Özbeg's conversion to Islam in the early fourteenth century, there may also have been some hope that the archbishop would have a hand in converting the khans and their court to Orthodox Christianity.

The chroniclers and other writers describe the relationship of the Rus' princes and prelates to the rulers of the Qipchaq Khanate in a matter-of-fact way, never going into detail about why the Tatars were ruling Rus'. In the fourteenth century, for example, the chronicles describe many trips of the Rus' princes and grand princes to the capital of the Qipchaq Khanate but rarely provide a reason for those trips. The closest statement of explanation comes from the author of the Galician–Volynian Chronicle, where, *sub anno* 1287, he writes: "for at that time the princes of Rus' were Tatar subjects, having been conquered by God's wrath" [8; 9]. The *Tale about Tsarevich Peter*, the composition of which can be dated to the mid-fourteenth century, also describes matter of factly the adjudication by the Qipchaq khan of a land dispute in Rostov [10–11].

In the grand-princely testaments of the later fourteenth and early fifteenth centuries, there are references to what will happen if the Rus' princes manage to extricate themselves from Tatar suzerainty. In Dmitrii Donskoi's second testament (1389) appears the statement "if God brings about a change regarding the Orda [so that] my children do not have to pay tribute [*vykhod*] to the Orda, then the tax [*dan'*] that each of my sons collects in his appanage [*udel'*] will be his" [12]. This formula is repeated in the three testaments of Vasilii I and the testament of Vasilii II [12]. It shows that the Muscovite grand princes' actions were determined by circumstances of realpolitik and that their concern was for keeping the revenue they collected from the subject population, not for "liberating Russia" or "freeing the Russian people from Tatar oppression." The grand princes wanted to emulate their sovereigns by becoming independent sovereigns themselves and, thus, be able to retain all the expropriated wealth.

This manifestation of a neutral attitude toward the Tatars ended in church sources in 1448, but continued to be represented in state documents. The state view, as in part represented in the *Posol'skii prikaz* (Foreign Office) documents, contain neither anti-Islamic nor anti-Tatar rhetoric. State documents are written in straightforward language as though the state representatives/agents were dealing with co-equals. The principle of realpolitik characterized Muscovite state dealings with the Tatars.

3. Anti-Tatar view of the Russian Orthodox Church

The beginning of the establishment of the anti-Tatar interpretative framework is 1448. At that time, the Rus' bishops and the Muscovite grand prince, Vasilii II, declared the Rus' Church to be administratively autonomous in relation to the patriarchate of Constantinople. The council of bishops nominated one of their own, Iona, the archbishop of Riazan', to be metropolitan, and the grand prince appointed him to that position. As a result, the Rus' Church was no longer constrained by the foreign-policy interests of Byzantium. An anti-Islamic, anti-Tatar ideology developed and was featured in such works as *Skazanie o Mamaevom poboishche* (*Legend of the Battle against Mamai*), *Slovo o pogibeli Russkoi zemli* (*Discourse about the Ruin of the Rus' Land*), and *Povest' o razorenii Riazanii Batyem* (*Tale about the Destruction of Riazan' by Batu*), all of which date to the second half of the fifteenth century. Anti-Tatar remarks were also interpolated into earlier Rus' chronicle accounts. This paradigm, as with paradigm 1, was characterized by calling the Tatars "godless", "sons of Hagar", "Moabites", and so on, but it went much further. While it was admitted that Batu conquered the Rus' land, that is to say "it was God who punished the Rus' for its sins," nonetheless, in the words of the author of *Zadonshchina* (*The Event beyond the Don*), "it will no longer be, as in the early times" [13]. Church writers developed a manichaean-like (Rus'–Tatar) dichotomy. Pelenski discerned seven pairs of binary oppositions in the writings of Metropolitan Makarii (1542–63) in regard to the differences between Muscovites and Tatars: believers versus nonbelievers; religious versus godless; Christian versus pagan; pious versus impious; pure versus unclean; peaceful versus warlike; and good versus bad [14].

After 1448, there were two "discourses" or at least two attitudes. The Church's attitude was that the sons of Hagar were pagan and godless. It was basically an anti-Islamic ideology. So the Tatars themselves were not inherently bad, in the church view of things; they were bad insofar as they were Muslim. Once Tatars converted to Christianity, their Islamic background was forgotten. Those born Tatar who converted to Orthodox Christianity were then accepted as Russians.

A prominent feature of the paradigm was to turn the events in the fall of 1480, in which Ivan III and Khan Ahmed and their armies faced off against each other over the Ugra River for a couple of weeks, into a major historical event. Khan Ahmed had moved his army to the southwestern border of Muscovy in the hope of meeting up with a Polish–Lithuanian army under Kazimierz IV Jagiellończyk, the king of Poland and grand duke of Lithuania, and of proceeding together with it against the Muscovite army. But Kazimierz did not show up, possibly because Ivan had arranged for his own ally, Khan Mengli Girei, to attack with his Crimean Tatar forces the southern reaches of Kazimierz' realm. Eventually, on November 11, according to the chronicle account, Khan Ahmed and his army withdrew. The chronicles of the time depict the Rus' and Tatar armies as disinclined to fight each other.

Vassian Rylo, the archbishop of Rostov and member of the war council, wrote a harsh letter to Ivan III upbraiding him for his indecisiveness. Although the standoff at the Ugra River was not unlike a number of other steppe military encounters, where neither side obtained military superiority, Vassian viewed the events differently. Not much of political, military, or diplomatic significance occurred at the Ugra in November 1480, other than that it was the last encounter between the Muscovite grand prince and the khan of the Qipchaq Khanate. Churchmen, nonetheless, developed their subsequent descriptions of this non-battle into an event of major importance, depicting it as the overthrow of Tatar domination. In the 1550s, an account of the "stand on the Ugra," written by a churchman, presented it as one of the most significant occurrences in the history of the world [15].[4] Another event that was made prominent by this paradigm was the battle on the Don River in 1380. Instead of the Muscovite grand prince's providing Rus' forces in support of Khan Tokhtamysh in a khanate civil war, the battle was depicted as Dmitrii Donskoi's defeat of the Tatars.

Within the period of this paradigm's pre-eminence we also see the period of Tatar rule beginning to be referred to as a "yoke." The phrase "yoke of slavery" (*rabotno igo*) had already appeared in the sixteenth-century *Life of Merkurii of Smolensk* as applied to the period of Chinggisid hegemony in Rus'. By 1575, the imperial ambassador Daniel Prinz reported the concept of a "Tatar Yoke" (*jugo Tatarico*) to apply to the period of Chinggisid hegemony [16]. If we consider it likely that Prinz did not make up this term but that he was simply expressing in Latin a term he had heard in Moscow, then we can conclude the Russian version of this term was being used by the second half of the sixteenth century. Direct evidence of its usage in Russian sources does not appear until the 1660s with an interpolation in one of the copies of the *Skazanie o Mamaevom poboishche*. Subsequently this term appears in the *Synopsis* of Innokentii Gizel' in 1674 [17]. From there it entered the mainstream of Russian nationalist historiography in the late eighteenth century through the multi-volume history of Russia by M. M. Shcherbatov.[5] The term "Tatar yoke" sums up the Church's position about the period of Chinggisid hegemony.

4. Russian Nationalist

The Russian nationalist paradigm represents a secular version, and further develop-ment, of the Russian Orthodox Church view in that it bases itself on a secular con-ceptualization of what a "Russian" is. The proponents of this paradigm, however, divide themselves into those who deny any significant Mongol/Tatar influence and those who see only a negative impact of the Mongol/Tatars.

The Russian nationalist view holds that Russian institutions are all indigenously generated and were established to meet particular Russian needs. The nationalist school does not allow that "outside" influences, especially the Mongols, had any impact. S. M. Solov'ev, professor of Russian history at Moscow University (1844–79), represented the "no-impact" point of view when he wrote: "we have no reason to assume any great influence [of the Mongols] on [Russia's] internal administration as we do not see any traces of it" [18]. He believed that Russian political culture was all indigenously generated and followed its own logic of development free of foreign influences. S. F. Platonov, professor of Russian history at the University of St Petersburg (1889–1916), carried this argument further:

> And how could the Tatar influence on Russian life be considerable when the Tatars lived far off, did not mix with the Russians, and appeared in Russia only to gather tribute or as an army, brought in for the most part by Russian princes for the princes' own purposes? . . . Therefore, we can proceed to consider the internal life of Russian society in the thirteenth century without paying attention to the fact of the Tatar yoke. [19]

In these cases, both Solov'ev and Platonov were referring specifically to the thir-teenth century, but the principle they espoused holds for later centuries in their work as well. B. D. Grekov and A. Iu. Iakubovskii also categorically denied any direct influence of the Mongols on Muscovy, but they did see an indirect result: "The Russian state with Moscow at its head was created not with the assistance of the Tatars but in the process of a hard struggle of the Russian people against the yoke of the Golden Horde" [20]. We can compare this view with N. M. Karamzin's state-ment about the Mongol invasion that "the calamity was a blessing in disguise, for the destruction contained the boon of unity . . . Another hundred years of princely feuds. What would have been the result . . . Moscow, in fact, owes its greatness to the khans" [21]. The proponents of this interpretation, seeing only a negative, destructive impact of the Mongols, credited the positive result of this struggle to the Russians themselves. V. I. Koretskii iterated this negative assessment of the Mongol impact on Russian development: "The Mongol Yoke and its effects were among the main reasons why Russia became a backward country in comparison with several of the countries of western Europe" [22]. In a variant of this interpretation, the impact of the Mongols is seen not only as destructive of Russian society and political culture but also detrimental to the development of the Russian themselves. The military historian Christopher Duffy summed up such views this way:

The princes of Muscovy became the most enthusiastic and shameless of the Mongol surrogates and much that was distinctive and unattractive about the Russian character and Russian institutions has been attributed to this experience. Mongol influence has been held variously responsible for the destruction of the urban classes, the brutalisation of the peasantry, a denial of human dignity, and a distorted sense of values which reserved a special admiration for ferocity, tyrannical ways and slyness. [23]

V. O. Kliuchevskii, who was professor of Russian History at Moscow University (1879–1911), and who many consider to have been the greatest Russian historian, was a prominent proponent of this Russian nationalist paradigm. Scholars have noted two significant absences in his five-volume *Course of Russian History* and other major scholarly writings: his neglect of the Russian Church and his neglect of the Mongols and Tatars [24–28]. The reasons for these two absences may be related. Kliuchevskii biographer Robert F. Byrnes refers to him as "a pious Christian" [27] – Kliuchevskii's father had been a priest, and he himself had studied in a seminar, "attended religious services faithfully, read scriptures every day, and honored all religious obligations," believed in miracles, and kept "icons in every room" [27]. In some of his minor writings, Kliuchevskii discussed aspects of Russian religious life, which he apparently considered important. Byrnes concludes that Kliuchevskii accepted the "scientific obligations" of his time, which among his contemporary scholars meant assigning a minor role to the Church in the historical and cultural formation of Russia. Byrnes points out that, in the first volume of the *Course*, Kliuchevskii announces that it is "an introduction to sociology" and that he is out to uncover "the laws, regularity, and mechanics of historical life," which meant for him as for Solov'ev emphasis on "geography, climate, harsh conditions, and external forces" [27]. Such forces were considered more scientific, and they did not include the Church.

As with the Church, Kliuchevskii displayed a keen interest and knowledge of the Mongols and Tatars in a number of his minor writings, yet they are almost completely absent or mentioned only in passing in his major works. Kliuchevskii grew up in Penza, which had a large Tatar population, so he presumably would have known something about them. Charles J. Halperin, in exploring Kliuchevskii's neglect of the Mongol/Tatars, cited evidence of Kliuchevskii's writing and speaking knowledgeably about Tatars in his minor works and occasional lectures. But in his major works, in addition to the reasons for his avoiding writing about the Church, there seems to have been another dynamic at work. Halperin indicates that Kliuchevskii, like many of his contemporaries, was concerned about Russia's image vis-à-vis Europe. Russian intellectuals were sensitive to how the idea that Russia may have been influenced by the Mongols would appear to Europeans. Kliuchevskii's views on the Tatars were indistinguishable from those of Solov'ev, as Halperin points out. Like Solov'ev, Kliuchevskii eliminated the "Tatar period" from his periodization of Russian history [28]. The decline of Kiev and the rise of the northeast begins for Kliuchevskii in the twelfth century with an imaginary migration of Russians from the area around Kiev to the northeast. Just as Russians tended to treat Tatars as "invisible" in their society, so Kliuchevskii, Solov'ev, and others tended to treat the Mongols and Tatars as invisible in Russian history, although at some level they evidently knew better.

Nicholas V. Riasanovsky, professor of Russian history at the University of California, Berkeley (1957–94), does accept an era of Mongol rule in his periodization of

"Russian" history, but he has been just as adamant in denying any substantial Mongol infuence. In his widely used textbook, Riasanovsky elaborated a negative variant of Karamzin's interpretation:

> It is tempting, thus, to return to the older view and to consider the Mongols as of little significance in Russian history. On the other hand, their destructive impact deserves attention. And they, no doubt, contributed something to the general harshness of the age and to the burdensome and exacting nature of the centralizing Muscovite state which emerged out of this painful background. [29]

In a recently published summation of his views on Russian history, Riasanovsky confirms that he sees *Russia* as an entity stretching back at least to the tenth century: "Russians also fought for their country, Rus, Russia, or the Russian land, which, in the course of centuries, became coterminous with Muscovy. All these elements, family and home, Orthodoxy, motherland, for which one was to live and die, went back at least to 988 or beyond that date" [30].[6] He considers the invasion by the Mongols to have been "utterly devastating" and that the subsequent "Mongol yoke" was "a uniquely catastrophic experience in Russian history . . ." (30: 60). Throughout the struggle with the Mongols, according to Riasanovsky, "Russians also regarded them as defenders of Orthodoxy" and "there was no doubt in the Russian mind who were the defenders and who were the aggressors, even when Russian armies counterattacked deep into the steppe or, for that matter, seized Kazan and Astrakhan" (30: 61). It is clear from Riasanovsky's presentation that he has a low opinion of the Mongols. For example, in characterizing them, he quotes Pushkin in seeing them as "Arabs without Aristotle and algebra" (30: 69). He declares that they "remained nomads in the clan stage of development" and that "their institutions and laws could in no wise be adopted by a much more complex agricultural society" (30: 69).[7] He asserts that the "Mongol states" were not "particularly well organized, efficient, or lasting." Instead, they were "relatively unstable and short-lived" (30: 69) and "rent by dissension and wars and to suffer from arbitrariness, corruption, and misrule in general" (30: 69–70). Furthermore, according to Riasanovsky, they did not "contribute a superior statecraft" and "had to borrow virtually everything, from alphabets to advisers, from the conquered peoples to enable their states to exist" (30: 70). He acknowledges that "cruelty, lawlessness, and at times anarchy, in that period, also characterized the life of many peoples other than the Mongols, the Russians included" (30: 70). Yet "most of these peoples managed eventually to surmount their difficulties and organize effective and lasting states" (30: 70), in contrast to "the Mongols, who, after their sudden and stunning performance on the world scene, receded to the steppe, clan life, and the internecine warfare of Mongolia" (30: 70).

Riasanovsky sees the term *tsar'* as deriving solely from Byzantium and denies that the term has any connection with the Mongols: "Their title was *khan*" (30: 67). He argues that, although the term *tsar'* was used in reference to the Mongol rulers, they were also called "khans or great khans, as the occasion demanded" and it does not "change the basic situation" (30: 67). He declares that "the search for Mongol roots of Mucovite tsars, tsardom, and identity has been essentially illusory" (30: 70). For Riasanovsky, the battle at Kulikovo Field in 1380 was a "successful campaign against the Mongols [and] bore certain marks of a crusade" (30: 61). Furthermore, it resulted in the destruction of the Mongol army (30: 37). Riasanovsky, likewise, accepts that Ivan III "threw off the Mongol yoke in Russia" in 1480 (30: 37) and that he "ended any kind of Russian submission to the Golden Horde" (30: 65). He sees no change or development in Russian-language sources about the Mongols: "As to the Mongols, a single attitude toward them pervades all Russian literature: they were a scourge of God sent upon the Russians as dreadful punishment for their sins" (30: 70).

Riasanovsky does discuss some possible Mongol influences on Russia. He mentions that the Mongol suzerains "granted it [the Church] certain advantages and privileges, notably an exemption from the tribute levied on the conquered Russians" (30: 61). He points out that certain Mongol terms "in the fields of administration and finance have entered the Russian language" and that there were "restricted Mongol influences" on "military forces and tactics," conducting a census, constructing roads, and setting up "a kind of postal service" (30: 67). But even these must be "qualified" in his opinion, since, for example, conducting a census "must have exceeded the resources of the Mongols," so they "probably" allowed "the Russians themselves do the counting and the registering, with the Mongols acting as supervisors and perhaps doing some checking" (30: 69). To the degree that Riasanovsky engages with the evidence, he must be given credit. Yet too often this engagement is accompanied by fallacious arguments and by misrepresenting some and ignoring other evidence that is inconvenient for his purpose of demonstrating Russian superiority.

In the Russian nationalist view, the Muscovite grand princes had dedicated themselves to freeing Russia from the oppression of the Tatar yoke. If there were any alliances between a grand prince and a Tatar khan, they were only ones of expediency in the cause of the larger goal. Thus, the encounter of the Ugra River in the fall of 1480 between the forces of Ivan III and those of Khan Ahmed is seen as a pivotal moment in Russian history, leading soon to the conquest of Kazan' and Astrakhan' and the beginning of the Russian Empire.[8]

The Russian nationalist view has had a stranglehold on the historiography. Its main criterion for historical study of Mongol/Tatar relations with Russia is Russian superiority in ethics, morals, intelligence, battle prowess, inventiveness, and righteousness. To maintain the appearance of this superiority, Russian nationalists have to ignore certain inconvenient pieces of evidence. They will argue, for example, that the Mongols defeated the Rus' princes because of being disunited, yet the chronicles say the Rus' princes would have been defeated anyway. They will argue, for example as the military historian A. N. Kirpichnikov did, that the Rus' armies could not have borrowed anything from the Mongols, because that would not have been in keeping with the "heroic struggle of the Russian people against foreign enemies" [31], while ignoring that certain weapons, armor, tactics, and formations that are the same as those used by the Mongols were not used by the Rus' before the Mongol invasion. They will claim that many of the genealogies of Russian aristocratic families tracing their ancestry back to the Mongols were manufactured, overlooking that the family names were Tatar in origin. In short, the conclusions they reach must advance the glory of a greater Russian nation. In that respect, they bear a striking similarity to the Marxists in subordinating the integrity of historical study to ideological goals.

5. *Marxist*

Two aspects of the theories of Karl Marx affected Soviet Marxist historiography: class struggle and materialism. The first aspect resulted in characterizing stages of historical development as progressive or regressive depending upon whether any particular society was entering a new stage or leaving an old one. The second aspect resulted in focusing on the importance of economic relations. N. A. Rozhkov was among the first historians to attempt a Marxist interpretation of Russian history. Yet Rozhkov hardly mentions the Tatars in his twelve-volume *History of Russia* and sees them as only continuing the processes that had begun in Rus' before the Mongol conquest – of turning southern Rus' into a wasteland [32]. Yet, one should not judge Rozhkov too harshly, as he made a good faith effort to place Russia within the context of world history. B. Ia. Vladimirtsov (d. 1931) formulated the concept of "nomadic feudalism" in applying Marxist historical stages to the steppe [33]. But his basis for applying the concept of "feudalism" to the Mongols necessitated imputing institutions, fiefs, vassalage, serfs, as well as related traits such as oaths of fealty and mutual obligations to evidence that did not support those interpretations.

M. N. Pokrovskii explained Mongol influence in terms of his theory of merchant capital and the role it played in Russian history. He discussed the benefit of Mongol rule to the Russian Church in economic terms – specifically, freedom from taxation. He also pointed to collaboration between the Rus' princes and their boyars with the Tatar khans. In Pokrovskii's view, it was the people who opposed Tatar rule. He saw the Moscow grand princes' benefiting from the support of the Tatar khans against his rivals in the northeast, especially the princes of Tver' [34]. Although Pokrovskii was knowledgeable about the sources for Russian history, he displayed little awareness of the non-Russian sources for Mongol/Tatar history.

With Pokrovskii, what I am calling the "Marxist" interpretative framework toward the Mongol/Tatar impact on Russia ends. As Soviet historians began to adopt a nationalist frame of reference, the framework of Solov'ev and Kliuchevskii re-emerged, although now adorned with Marxist terminology. A seminal essay that marked the beginning of the transition from a Marxist to a nationalist interpretation in Soviet historiography regarding the Mongols and the Rus' principalities was published by A. N. Nasonov in 1940 [35]. Yet, as Halperin pointed out, rather than criticize Pokrovskii's Marxist understanding of Russian history, Nasonov seemed "to adumbrate his own original conclusions and criticize Pokrovskii for not having anticipated them" [36]. One of the ironies of this transition is that no one was more a pure Marxist historian than Pokrovskii. Yet, because he was not nationalist enough and did not always tow the party line, he was accused of being anti-Marxist when the transition to a nationalist interpretation occurred in Soviet historiography. This transition meant a further diminution of the chances for Russian historians to make an accurate assessment of Russia's Mongol/Tatar heritage.

6. *Eurasian and Modified Eurasian*

The Eurasian and Modified Eurasian paradigm posits a dominant role for Russia in the history of Inner Eurasia. The Eurasianists began as a political–cultural position in opposition to the dominant Eurocentric views of the early twentieth century.

Eurasianism's influence on serious scholarship was narrow but deep. Nicholas Trubetskoi claimed "the Russian state" to be "the inheritor, the successor, the continuator of the historical work of Chinggis Khan" [37]. George Vernadsky devoted a volume of his five-volume *History of Russia* to an exploration of the Mongol/Tatar role [38]. Although Vernadsky was influenced by the Eurasian movement, he maintained, for the most part, his own scholarly independence [39–40]. He accepted that the Mongols had many positive influences on Russia and even accepted uncritically some of the claims of the Eurasianists in that regard. Yet he still attributed some negative impact to Mongol rule: "the regimentation of the social classes which started during the Mongol period and was originally based on the Mongol principles of administration, was carried further and completed by the Muscovite government. Autocracy and serfdom were the price the Russian people had to pay for national survival" [38]. Elsewhere in the volume he writes: "inner Russian political life was never stifled but only curbed and deformed by Mongol rule" (38: 344). While acknowledging the destructiveness of the Mongol conquest and negative aspects of Tatar hegemony, Vernadsky discussed a number of positive Mongol influences on administration and the army (38: 344–66).

Previously Vernadsky, echoing Trubetskoi, had written that Russia "in a sense, might be considered an offspring of the Mongol Empire" [41]. Now in *The Mongols and Russia*, Vernadsky considered a number of significant changes in the Rus' principalities (which he called "Russia") of "the Mongol period" to be a result either directly or indirectly of Mongol influence. Vernadsky saw that the "growth of manorial industries was a characteristic feature of the Russian economy of the 14th to 16th centuries" (41: 340–1). In his view, the Mongols had effectively destroyed the free market for the services of crafts by conscripting the majority of craftsmen while many others fled.

Rus' princes used their connections with the khans to increase the size of their estates and recruit returning craftsmen and artisans, both in getting those who fled Rus' initially and those who were able to flee the Mongols after being conscripted. Vernadsky asserted that the "destruction of most of the major cities of East Russia during the Mongol invasion was a crushing blow to the urban democratic institutions which had flourished in the Kievan period all over Russia (and continued to flourish in Novgorod and Pskov during the Mongol period)" (41: 345). According to Vernadsky, the Mongols crushed the opposition of townspeople and eliminated their veches (town assemblies). Vernadsky pointed to the "increase in relative importance of the large landed estates in Russia's political setup" (41: 346). He claimed that "with the decline in cities, agriculture and other branches of exploitation of natural resources of the land and the forests came to the fore" (41: 346).

He saw that "the existence of the supreme Mongol power was . . . a leading" factor that "prevented" the boyars from "clearly defining their political rights" (41: 347). In addition to the personal ambition of the grand princes in attempting to unify the Rus' principalities, Vernadsky figured that "the grim political situation required unity of the nation's effort [for] without it the task of freeing Russia from Mongol rule could not be achieved" (41: 350). Vernadsky accepted Vladimirskii-Budanov's conclusion that both corporal and capital punishment (applicable to more than just slaves) came into Muscovy as a result of the Mongols (41: 355). He attributed the introduction of torture to the Mongols although acknowledging that it "was widely used in the West in this period" (41: 356–7), as was corporeal and capital punishment. According to Vernadsky, the Muscovite "system of taxation and army organization" as "developed in the late 14th to 16th centuries" was based on "Mongol patterns" (41: 358). He pointed out that the grand princely treasury as an institution "was created after the Mongol pattern," evident from the terms for treasure (*kazna*) and treasurer (*kaznachei*) (41: 359). He suggested that the departments of administration known as *puti* may well have been based on "a certain influence of Oriental patterns" (41: 361). Vernadsky also discussed the influence of the Mongols on the army, including organization, weapons, and universal conscription (41: 363–5). One is, thus, justified in designating Vernadsky's views "modified Eurasian."

7. Anti-Russian, Anti-Eurasian

Those who hold an anti-Eurasian, anti-Russian nationalist position do not accept the beneficial role of Russia in regard to the history of Inner Eurasia. They can be divided into three groups: Despotists, Tatarists, and Bulgarists.[9]

The Despotists argue for a negative impact of Mongol influence in contributing to, even creating, the despotism of Russian autocracy. The most prominent non-Marxist use of the concept of *Oriental Despotism* has been by Karl Wittfogel. He asserted that "Tatar rule alone among the three major Oriental influences affecting Russia was decisive . . . in laying the foundations for the despotic state of Muscovite and post-Muscovite Russia" [42]. Wittfogel asserted that the "oriental despotism" the Mongols introduced into Muscovy came from China via the Mongols [42].

Ukrainian nationalist historians have also made use of the concept of "oriental despotism" to account for what they see as Muscovite and Russian despotism. Boleslaw Szczesniak, for example, calls Mongol rule "one of the greatest evils not only for Russia, but for many nations" and refers to "its devious traditions, embodied in the Muscovy state . . . [being] visible even today." He denies that the term "Western Russia" should be applied to Belarus, Lithuania, and Ukraine, asserting that "this fantastic claim cannot be supported since the evil forces created by the Tatar yoke did not reach these countries" [43]. In contrast, Dmytro Doroshenko, moderate in relation to Szczesniak, points to geography, harsh climate, and the fact that "life was excessively primitive" as "peculiar conditions" that influenced the formation of the Russian "national type" – that is, "a strongly developed solidarity, a tendency to support common interests, a readiness to sacrifice the individual to the welfare of the community, and give preponderance to common interests over the individual." He does blame close contact "with the Tatars and centuries of submission to their control that the Russians owe their autocratic form of their own government. From this experience all the Asiatic or Eastern features of their character and philosophy, features that were entirely foreign to the Eastern Slavs, distinguish the Russians from the Ukrainians and from other Slavs" [44]. The Despotists rarely question whether Mongol or Tatar governments were despotic; they simply assumed they were.

Tatarists reject the notion of the Eurasianists and neo-Eurasianists that Russia had a special role in Inner Eurasia [45–46]. According to the Tatarists, the Tatars were the real leaders of the Qipchaq Khanate, which represented the transformation of the western steppe peoples into a Tatar ethnic identity. For the Tatarists, the Qipchaq Khanate was a major empire, in it own right, that had a significant impact on both

Asia and Europe. In the early twentieth century, the Tatarists questioned whether they should accept the name *Tatar* precisely because it was associated with the notion of the "Tatar yoke." One of the ways this group has challenged the Russian nationalist view is through a letter sent in April 2001 from the president of Tatarstan, Mintimer Shaimiev, to the president of Russia, Vladimir Putin, asking him to cancel the annual celebration of the battle of Kulikovo [47].

The Bulgarists, in contrast, accept the idea of a "Tatar yoke" under which the Muslim Volga Bulgars suffered as well as the Christian Russians [48]. The notion that Orientalism (in Edward Said's sense of Europeans' feeling of superiority toward non-Europeans) represents Russian nationalist views is characteristic of Tatar and Bulgar treatments. Neither the Tatarist nor the Bulgarist postion has yet attained the stature of a full-fledged paradigm, but may represent a separate paradigm in the making.

8. Analytical Source-Based Studies of the Mongol Empire and its Relationship to the Rus' Principalities

This group includes to a certain extent those scholars who cannot be subsumed under any of the preceding paradigms. It is, thus, a catchall paradigm, but one that can be characterized by the absence of preconceived notions of the superiority or inferiority of particular ethnic groups, the absence of any particular ideological bent, and the relative absence of present-day political considerations. Within this paradigm, one can distinguish two categories. The first is made up of those who focus on areas of the Mongol Empire other than the Rus' principalities (Mongolists) but whose work touches on those principalities. Most prominent among previous scholars one may include V. V. Bartol'd and Bertold Spuler, while the most prominent present-day scholars include Thomas Allsen, Christopher Atwood, Peter Jackson, and David Morgan. Of those, only Allsen has used Russian-language sources in his work. The rest are dependent on translations of Russian-language sources into Western languages. This dependency limits somewhat, and at times significantly, their access to those sources. As in Russia [49], studies of Mongolists have not had much influence on those of the Russianists in the West.

A second category is made up of those who focus more or less primarily on the Rus' principalities (Russianists) and as a consequence deal with their relationship with the Mongol/Tatars. This group is characterized by a focus on the Russian-language sources and a general inability to use Persian-, Mongol-, and Chinese-language sources in the original. This drawback hinders them from analyzing these sources and doing original, innovative work on them. That problem is mitigated considerably by the excellent translations that the first group has produced and is producing, but there are gaps.

Among earlier Russianists who tried to provide an impartial evaluation of Mongol influence are Alfred Rambaud, Francis Dvornik, and Michael Cherniavsky [50–52]. Among Russianists presently working on this topic are A. A. Gorskii [53], Bulat R. Rakhimzyanov [54], V. V. Trepavlov [55], and I. Zaitsev [56]. Janet Martin, professor of Russian history of the University of Miami, presents an even-handed discussion of the Russian nationalist stand on national liberation in her textbook on early Russian history. As a contrast to that position, she provides the reader with an "alternate interpretation" that sees Muscovite diplomacy during this period within the context of steppe diplomacy [57]. This "alternate interpretation," she acknowledges, owes much to the views expressed by Edward L. Keenan [58–59]. But she also cites the work of other historians, including Halperin, Alexandre Bennigsen, and Chantal Lemercier-Quelquejay as being along the same lines. In her research, Martin has focused on specific aspects of Tatar refugee assimilation into the Muscovite political system.

Halperin has studied this issue across a broad range of topics. He sees Muscovite borrowing of

> a variety of Mongol political and administrative institutions, including the *tamga*, the seal for the customs tax as well as the tax itself; the *kazna*, the treasury; the *iam*, the postal system; *tarkhan*, grants of fiscal or judicial immunity; and *den'ga* for money. Muscovite bureaucratic practices, including the use of *stolbtsy*, scrolls to preserve documents, and perhaps some features of Muscovite bureaucratic jargon, may also derive from the Qipchaq Khanate, as well as selective legal practices such as *pravezh*, beating on the shins. Certainly Muscovite diplomatic norms for dealing with steppe states and peoples were modeled on Tatar ways. Finally, the Muscovites had no choice but to study Tatar military tactics and strategies . . . but the Muscovites also copied Mongol weapons, armaments, horse equippage, and formations. [60–61]

Halperin has questioned, however, the relevance to the Rus' of most of what was being done elsewhere in the lands the Mongols ruled. He has asserted that the Rus' principalities were "not an integral element in the Golden Horde" and that "Russian declamations of fealty to the ulus to which they belonged, the *tsarev ulus*, must be invented fantasies, exercises in bending the truth to suit tendentious political purpose" [62]. As a result, according to Halperin, evidence from sources about other parts of the Mongol Empire have limited value for understanding the Mongol influence on Muscovy.

My own research has led me to be in agreement with Halperin concerning the fundamental influences that he sees. Where we differ is over the extent of those influences and whether they extended to other Muscovite political institutions. I have argued for comparing the administrative practices of the Mongol Empire with those of early Muscovy [63–65]. Mongol/Tatar influence on Muscovy, as I see it, can be divided into two periods. The first period of influence dates to the fourteenth century. Weaponry, such as the recurved composite bow and flail, along with the saddle with short stirrups (for standing in the saddle while shooting), came from the steppe pastoralists of the Qipchaq Khanate as the result of direct contact with the Mongols. Military strategy, tactics, and formations came from direct contact with Mongol-led armies. As a result of their trips to Sarai, as well as being hostages while their fathers were grand prince, the grand princes were able to observe the operations of khanate administration first hand, and introduced a number of innovations into the Muscovite principality. A dual system of administration as practiced in China came by way of the Mongols and was introduced into Muscovite administration by the grand princes. It included overlapping responsibilities for military and civilian governors. Grand princes, also probably as a result of their trips to Sarai, introduced a council of state (known, according to Giles Fletcher, in Muscovy as *Boarstva dumna* (Boyar Duma)) [66], which had the same functions and responsibilities as the divan of qarachi beys among the steppe pastoralists. The grand prince continued the tax system that was practiced in the Mongol Empire and that had been introduced by the Qipchaq khans into the Rus' principalities. Thus, *poshlina* was the Russian name for traditional, non-Mongol taxes that were equivalent to Qipchaq Turkic *qalan* and Mongol *alban*. The *dan'* was the name for Mongol-imposed taxes and tributes that were equivalent to Qipchaq Turkic *yasaq* and Mongol *qubčirin* [65]. The administrative structure of the government as established in the Qipchaq Khanate was introduced by the Muscovite grand princes. The *iam* (or system of post stations) as it functioned in China was introduced by the Qipchaq khans and revived by Ivan III. Shin beating, a punishment that was practiced in China, was imposed by the agents of the Qipchaq khans on Rus' and was continued by the Muscovite grand princes. The *chelom bit'e* (petition) known in China as the *k'ou t'ou* [67] was introduced into Rus' by the Mongols and was continued by the Rus' princes.

Clan ranking within the polity was derived from the steppe pastoralists and was probably introduced by the Muscovite grand princes. Commercial and financial terms, such as *bazar, balagan, bakaleia, barysh, kumach, stakan*, and so forth, derive from the Turkic languages of the Qipchaq Khanate and were introduced by Rus' merchants who traveled to Kaffa, Tana, and Sarai.

The second period of Tatar influence dates to the late fifteenth and sixteenth centuries and resulted from the influx of Tatar refugees into Muscovy. The Chinggisid principle (the notion that only descendants of Chinggis Khan can be rulers) as practiced among the Mongols entered Muscovy probably via the Kazan' Khanate as the result of Turkicized Jochids who entered Muscovite service. *Pomest'e* (or military land grants), as issued in Muscovy from 1482 on, and called *iqta* in the *Dar al-Islam*, was probably made known to the grand prince by refugee Tatars from the disintegrating Qipchaq Khanate. Certain record-keeping methods (such as scrolls) as used initially by the Uighurs were introduced by refugee Tatars from the Qipchaq Khanate. The principle of *beschestie* (dishonor) as practiced by the "courage cultures" of the steppe, was probably introduced by Turkicized Jochids and refugee Tatars from the Kazan' Khanate. The institution of the *zemskii sobor* (Assembly of the Land) known among the Mongols as a *quriltai* was practiced among the steppe pastoralists and probably had its operation described to the Muscovite court by Turkicized Jochids from the Kazan' Khanate [68]. The taking over of the Khanate of Kazan' and then of Astrakhan' would have lacked legitimacy without it, since only a *quriltai* could select a khan/tsar'.

Already in the reign of Ivan III (1462–1505) the administrative practices that characterized the Muscovite principality began to be modified and replaced as Ivan and his successors transformed Muscovy into a dynastic state. Some practices, like *pomest'e*, were transformed. Others, like scroll records, continued to be used through the seventeenth century. The *zemskii sobor*, the last of the Mongol/Tatar institutions to be introduced (1549), ended in the 1680s. The army stopped using the recurved bow as its primary weapon by the early seventeenth century, and Mongol/Tatar military organization began to be replaced with European methods of military organization under Tsar Aleksei (1645–82). Clan politics as practiced in early Muscovy continued to be practiced in much the same way through the eighteenth and into the early nineteenth centuries.

Conclusion

A major difficulty in discussing and analyzing Mongol/Tatar influence on Russia is pre-existing prejudice toward one or another group. Perhaps the main point of the present chapter is that meta-scholarly reasons contribute to the lack of any kind of consensus on Mongol–Rus' relations. The storied British notion that "the wogs begin at Calais" finds an analogue in Russian views, such that *mutatis mutandis* "the wogs begin at the steppe." But cross-paradigmatic attitudes toward the Mongols as "cruel" and "revenge-seeking" have also played a role. Another problem that has characterized a number of these paradigms was and is political relations contemporary to the period when the paradigm flourished.

A major difficulty in the study of Mongol–Rus' relations is the number of languages one is required to master to do specialized research on the sources. Many sources are in Russian, but works such as the chronicles and tales tend to reflect the Russian Orthodox Church position of the post-1448 period. The Posol'skii prikaz documents remain underutilized and, when they are used, this is often done within a Russian nationalist paradigm. Mongolists rarely know Russian well enough to study Russian-language sources in the original. Russianists rarely know sufficient Chinese, Mongolian, Persian, Turkic, or Uighur to study the primary sources about the Mongols or Tatars in those languages. As good as translations into other languages may be, they are no substitute for studying the sources in the language in which they were written.

Differing opinions on the value of specific sources tend to widen the differences in interpretation. And differing interpretative paradigms tend to influence scholars' view of the value of specific sources. One hopes that, in the future, disputes concerning the impact of the Mongols on Rus' can be carried on without resort to prejudices and ideologies, national or political. Ironically, the Tatarists, Bulgarists, and Mongolian historians may assist this development, as they provide a direct counter position to the Russian nationalist paradigm that has dominated the historiography for so long.

Notes

1 Often erroneously called "the Golden Horde." In Rus' sources of the time it is referred to as "Orda" (from the Mongol word *ordo* = camp). For a discussion of the terminological problem, see [69].

2 Thus, in the rest of this chapter, I will use the form "Mongol/Tatar" to indicate the people of this transitional period in the western steppe. When necessary, I will try to maintain a distinction between "Mongols," as designating a specific group of people in the eastern steppe, and "Tatars," as designating the amalgamation of Turkic peoples that the Mongols created when they took over control of the western steppe. The term "Tatar" was initially used as a generic term to apply to pastoral peoples of the eastern steppe as well as to a Mongolian-speaking group who were neighbors of the Mongols. When Chinggis Khan took control of the eastern steppe, he destroyed the Tatars as a political group and discouraged the use of *Tatar* to apply to the pastoralists in general. The term, however, carried over to the western steppe and was accepted by the Turkic-speaking peoples there [70]. The issue of the term's usage arose again in the early twentieth century, as I will discuss below. In Latin sources, the term *Tartar* (with a medial *r*) was used, taking advantage of

the similarity between *Tatar* and *Tartarus*, but as early as 1247 John of Plano Carpini had made the point to Salimbene that the correct spelling is "Tatar" [71].

3 The Galician–Volynian Chronicle also refers to them as "Godless Moabites" for the entry under this year [8].

4 This work, in the form of a letter addressed to Ivan IV, is generally attributed either to Metropolitan Makarii or to the priest Syl'vester.

5 For a description of this process, see [72].

6 Much of what Riasanovsky includes in Russian Identities is a verbatim recapitulation of what he wrote in his textbook, but he does include additional material.

7 Here Riasanovsky does not mention the views of those who attribute to the Mongols the negative impact of reducing the Rus' principalities to agricultural status.

8 Besides the works of the Russian nationalist historians whom I have already mentioned, one may also find this viewpoint represented in [73–77].

9 I am indebted to the work of Marlies Bliz for her analysis of the latter two groups. See her Ph.D. dissertation [78].

References

1. Nasonov, A. N. (1940). *Mongoly i Rus' (Istoriia tatarskoi politiki na Rusi)*. Moscow and Leningrad: Akademiia nauk SSSR.

2. *Polnoe sobranie russkikh letopisei* (1843–2001) (*PSRL*). 41 vols. St Petersburg/Petrograd/ Leningrad and Moscow: Arkheograficheskaia komissiia, Nauka, and Arkheograficheskii tsentr, vol. 15.

3. *PSRL*, vol. 12.

4. *PSRL*, vol. 1.

5. Nasonov, A. N. (ed.) (1950). *Novgorodskaia pervaia letopis'. Starshego i mladshego izvodov*. Moscow and Leningrad: Akademiia nauk SSSR.

6. Chekin, L. (1992). "The Godless Ishmaelites: The Image of the Steppe in Eleventh–Thirteenth-Century Rus'," *Russian History*, 19: 9–28.

7. Fennell, J. L. I. (1970). "The Ideological Role of the Russian Church in the First Half of the Fourteenth Century," in R. Auty et al., eds., *Gorski vijen: A Garland of Essays Offered to Professor Elizabeth Hill*. Cambridge: Cambridge University Press, 105–11.

8. *PSRL*, vol. 2.

9. *The Galician–Volynian Chronicle* (1973). Trans. G. Perfecky, Munich: Wilhelm Fink.

10. Skripil, M. O. (ed.) (1958). *Russkie povesti XV–XVI*. Moscow and Leningrad: Akademiia nauk SSSR.

11. Halperin, C. (1973). "A Chingissid Saint of Russian Orthodox Church: 'The Life of Peter, Tsarevich of the Horde,'" *Canadian–American Slavic Studies*, 9: 324–35.

12. Cherepnin, L. V. (ed.) (1950). *Dukhovnye i dogovornye gramoty velikikh i udel'nykh kniazei XIV–XVI vv*. Moscow and Leningrad: Akademiia nauk SSSR.

13. Jakobson, R., and Worth, D. (eds.) (1963). *Sofonija's Tale of the Russian–Tatar Battle on the Kulikovo Field*. The Hague: Mouton.

14. Pelenski, J. (1974). *Russia and Kazan: Conquest and Imperial Ideology (1438–1560s)*. The Hague: Mouton.

15. Golokhvastov, D. P., and Archimandrite Leonid (1874). "Blagoveshchenskii ierei Sil'vestr i ego poslaniia," *Chteniia v Obshchestve istorii i drevnostei rossiiskikh pri Moskovskom universitete*, bk. 1, pp. 71–2.

16. Prinz [Printz], Daniel (1681). *Moscoviae ortus, et progressus, Gubenae: Christophor Gruber, 1681*. Repr. in *Scriptores Rerum Livonicarum*. 2 vols. Riga and Leipzig: Eduard Franken, 1853, vol. 2.

17. Rothe, Hans (ed.) (1983). *Sinopsis, Kiev 1681: Facsimile mit einer Einleitung.* Cologne and Vienna: Bausteine zur Geschichte der Literatur bei den Slaven, vol. 17.

18. Solov'ev, S. M. (1960–6). *Istoriia Rossii s drevneishikh vremen.* 15 vols. Moscow: Izdatel'stvo Sotsial'no-ekonomicheskoi literatury, vol. 2.

19. Platonov, S. F. (1899). *Lektsii po russkoi istorii.* 3 vols. St Petersburg: Stolichnaia staro-pechatnia, vol. 1.

20. Grekov, B. D., and A. Iu. Iakubovskii (1950). *Zolotaia Orda i ee padenie.* Moscow and Leningrad: Akademiia nauk SSSR.

21. Karamzin, N. M. (1842–3). *Istoriia gosudarstva rossiiskogo.* 5th edn. 12 vols. St Petersburg: Eduard Prats, vol. 5.

22. Koretskii, V. I. (1976–90). "Mongol Yoke in Russia," *in Modern Encyclopedia of Russian and Soviet History,* ed. Joseph L. Wieczynski. 54 vols. Gulf Breeze, FL: Academic International Press, vol. 23.

23. Duffy, C. (1981). *Russia's Military Way to the West: Origins and Nature of Russian Military Power 1700–1800.* London: Routledge and Kegan Paul.

24. Fedotov, G. (1932). "Rossiia Kliuchevskogo," *Sovremennye zapiski,* 50: 353–6.

25. Bushkovitch, P. (1986). "V. O. Kliuchevskii as Historian of Religion and the Church," *Canadian–American Slavic Studies,* 20: 357–66.

26. Freeze, G. (1986). "Russian Orthodoxy in Prerevolutionary Historiography: The Case of V. O. Kliuchevskii," *Canadian–American Slavic Studies,* 20: 399–416.

27. Byrnes, R. (1990). "'Between Two Fires': Kliuchevskii on Religion and the Russian Orthodox Church," *Modern Greek Studies Yearbook,* 6: 157–85.

28. Halperin, C. (2000). "Kliuchevskii and the Tatar Yoke," *Russian History,* 34: 385–408.

29. Riasanovsky, N. (1984). *A History of Russia.* 4th edn. New York: Oxford University Press.

30. Riasanovsky, N. (2005). *Russian Identities: A Historical Survey.* Oxford: Oxford University Press.

31. Kirpichnikov, A. N. (1985). "Fakty, gipotezy i zabluzhdeniia v izuchenii russkoi voennoi istorii XIII–XV vv," in *Drevneishie gosudarstva na territorii SSSR. Materialy i issledova-niia 1984 goda.* Moscow: Nauka.

32. Rozhkov, N. (1919–26). *Russkaia istoriia v sravnitel'no-istoricheskom osveshchenii. Osnovy sotsial'noi dinamiki.* 12 vols. Petrograd and Moscow: Kniga, vol. 2.

33. Vladimirtsev, B. Ia. (1934). *Obshchestvennyi stroi Mongolov. Mongol'skii kochevoi feodal-izm.* Leningrad: Akademiia nauk SSSR.

34. Pokrovskii, M. N. (1933). *Russkaia istoriia s drevneishikh vremen.* 4 vols. Moscow: Gosudarstvennoe sotsial'no-ekonomicheskoe izdatel'stvo, vol. 1.

35. Nasonov, A. N. (1940). "Tatarskoe igo na Rusi v osveshchenii M. N. Pokrovskogo," in B. D. Grekov et al., eds., *Protiv antimarksistkoi istoricheskoi kontseptsii M. N. Pokrovskogo.* 2 vols. Moscow: Akademiia nauk SSSR, vol. 2.

36. Halperin, C. (1982). "Soviet Historiography on Russia and the Mongols," *Russian Review,* 41: 306–22.

37. I. R. [Trubetskoi, N.] (1925). *Nasledie Chingiskhana. Vzgliad na russkuiu istoriiu ne s Zapada, s Vostka.* Berlin: Evraziiskoe izdatel'stvo.

38. Vernadsky, G. (1943–69). *History of Russia.* 5 vols. New Haven: Yale University Press. Vol. 3: *The Mongols and Russia* (1953).

39. Halperin, C. (1985) "Russia and the Steppe: George Vernadsky and Eurasianism," *Forschungen zur osteuropaischen Geschichte,* 36: 55–194.

40. Obolensky, D. (1964). "George Vernadsky as a Historian of Ancient and Medieval Russia," in Alan D. Ferguson and Alfred Levin, eds., *Essays in Russian History: A Collection Dedicated to George Vernadsky.* Hamden, CT: Archon Books.

41. Vernadsky, G. (1938). "The Scope and Content of Chingis Khan's Yasa," *Harvard Journal of Asiatic Studies*, 3: 337–60.

42. Wittfogel, K. (1981). *Oriental Despotism: A Comparative Study of Total Power*. New York: Vintage.

43. Szczesniak, B. (1972). "A Note on the Character of the Tatar Impact upon the Russian State and Church," *Études Slaves et Est-Européens*, 17: 92–7.

44. Doroshenko, D. (1975). *A Survey of Ukrainian History*, ed. and updated by Oleh W. Gerus. Winnipeg: Trident Press.

45. Ischakov, D., and Izmailov, I. (2001). "Etnicheskaia i politicheskaia istoriia tatar," in R. K. Urazmanova and S. V. Chesko, eds., *Tatary*. Moscow: Nauka, 64–100.

46. Ischakov, D. (2001). "Tatarskaia etnicheskaia obshchnost'," in R. K. Urazmanova and S. V. Chesko, eds., *Tatary.*, Moscow: Nauka, 11–25.

47. Bliz, M. (2006). "Deconstructing the Myth of the 'Tatar Yoke,'" unpublished paper.

48. Khamidullin, B. L. (2000). "Osnovnye problemy izucheniia istorii gosudarstvennosti tatarskogo naroda," in A. A. Arslanova, I. K. Zagidullin, and R. S. Khakimov, eds., Aktual'nye problemy istorii gosudarstvennosti tatarskogo naroda. Kazan': Matbugat iorty, 62–7.

49. Halperin, C. (2004). "Omissions of National Memory: Russian Historiography on the Golden Horde as Politics of Inclusion and Exclusion," *Ab Imperio*, 3: 134–44.

50. Rambaud, A. (1893). *Histoire de la Russie*. 4th edn. Paris: Hachette.

51. Cherniavsky, M. (1959). "Khan or Basileus: An Aspect of Russian Mediaeval Political Theory," *Journal of the History of Ideas*, 20: 459–76. Reproduced in M. Cherniavsky, ed., *The Structure of Russian History: Interpretive Essays*. New York: Random House, 1970, 65–79.

52. Dvornik, F. (1962). *The Slavs in European History and Civilization*, New Brunswick, NJ: Rutgers University Press.

53. Gorskii, A. A. (2000). *Moskva i Orda*. Moscow: Nauka.

54. Rakhimzyanov, B. R. (2005). "Nasledie Zolotoi Ordy v formirovanii Rossiiskogo gosudarstva," *Cahiers du monde russe*, 46: 29–38.

55. Trepavlov, V. V. (1994). "Rossiia i kochevye stepi: problema vostochnykh zaimstvovanii v rossiiskoi gosudarstvennosti," *Vostok. Afro-aziatskie obshchestva: istoriia i sovremennost'*, 2: 49–62.

56. Zaitsev, I. (2004). *Mezhdu Moskvoi i Stambulom. Dzhuchidskie gosudarstva, Moskva i Osmanskaia imperiia (nachalo XV–pervaia polovina XVI vv.)*. Moscow: Rudomino.

57. Martin, Janet (1995). *Medieval Russia 980–1584*. Cambridge: Cambridge University Press.

58. Keenan, E. (1965). "Muscovy and Kazan, 1445–1552: A Study in Steppe Politics," Ph.D. dissertation, Harvard University.

59. Keenan, E. (1967). "Muscovy and Kazan: Some Introductory Remarks on the Patterns of Steppe Diplomacy," *Slavic Review*, 26: 548–58.

60. Halperin, C. (2000). "Muscovite Political Institutions in the 14th Century," *Kritika: Explorations in Russian and Eurasian History*, 1: 238–9.

61. Halperin, C. (1985). *Russia and the Golden Horde: The Mongol Impact on Medieval Russian History*. Bloomington, IN: Indiana University Press.

62. Halperin, C. (1982). "Tsarev Ulus: Russia in the Golden Horde," *Cahiers du monde russe et soviétique*, 23: 257–63.

63. Ostrowski, D. (1990). "The Mongol Origins of Muscovite Political Institutions," *Slavic Review*, 49: 525–42.

64. Ostrowski, D. (2000). "Muscovite Adaption of Steppe Political Institutions: A Reply to Halperin's Objections," *Kritika: Explorations in Russian and Eurasian History*, 1: 267–304.

65. Ostrowski, D. (1998). *Muscovy and the Mongols: Cross-Cultural Influences on the Steppe Frontier, 1304–1589.* Cambridge: Cambridge University Press.
66. Fletcher, G. (1591). *Of the Russe Common Wealth, or Maner of Governement by the Russe Emperour (Commonly Called the Emperour of Moskovia) with the Manners, and Fashions of the People of That Country.* London: T. D. for Thomas Charde.
67. Golden, P. (1984). "Turkic Calques in Medieval Eastern Slavic," *Journal of Turkish Studies*, 8: 103–111.
68. Ostrowski, D. (2004). "The Assembly of the Land (Zemskii Sobor) as a Representative Institution," in Jarmo Kotiline and Marshall Poe, eds., *Modernizing Muscovy: Reform and Social Change in Seventeenth-Century Russia.* London: RoutledgeCurzon, 117–42.
69. Ostrowski, D. (2004). "Golden Horde," in *Encyclopedia of Russian History*, 4 vols. New York: Macmillan, vol. 2, pp. 571–3.
70. Atwood, C. (2004). "Tatars," in *Encyclopedia of Mongolia and the Mongol Empire.* New York: Facts on File, 528–30.
71. Salimbene da Parma (1986). *The Chronicle of Salimbene de Adam*, trans. Joseph L. Baird. Binghamton, NY: Medieval and Renaissance Texts and Studies.
72. Halperin, C. (1984). "The Tatar Yoke and Tatar Oppression," *Russia Mediaevalis*, 5: 26–30.
73. Bazilevich, K. V. (1952). *Vneshanaia politika Russkogo tsentralizovannogo gosudarstva.* Moscow: Moskovskii universitet.
74. Cherepnin, L. V. (1960). *Obrazovanie Russkogo tsentralizovannogo gosudarstva v XIV–XV vekah.* Moscow: Sotsial'no-ekonomicheskaia literatura.
75. Huttenbach, H. (1988). "Muscovy's Conquest of Muslim Kazan and Astrakhan, 1552–1556. The Conquest of the Volga: Prelude to Empire," in Michael Rywkin (ed.), *Russian Colonial Expansion to 1917.* London: Mansell, 45–69.
76. Alekseev, Iu. G. (1989). *Osvobozhdenie Rusi ot Ordynskogo iga.* Leningrad: Nauka.
77. Gorskii, A. A. (2000). *Moskva i Orda.* Moscow: Nauka.
78. Bliz, M. (2006). "Tatarstan in der Transformation. Nationaler Diskurs und politische Praxis 1988–1994." Ph.D. dissertation, University of Hamburg.

Further Reading

Atwood, C. (2004). *Encyclopedia of Mongolia and the Mongol Empire.* New York: Facts on File.

Gorskii, A. A. (2000). *Moskva i Orda.* Moscow: Nauka.

Halperin, C. (1985). *Russia and the Golden Horde: The Mongol Impact on Medieval Russian History.* Bloomington, IN: Indiana University Press.

Martin, Janet (1995). *Medieval Russia 980–1584.* Cambridge: Cambridge University Press.

Ostrowski, D. (1998). *Muscovy and the Mongols: Cross-Cultural Influences on the Steppe Frontier, 1304–1589.* Cambridge: Cambridge University Press.

Vernadsky, G. (1943–69). *History of Russia.* 5 vols. New Haven: Yale University Press. Vol. 3: *The Mongols and Russia* (1953).

PART II

To Muscovy and Beyond

CHAPTER SIX

Muscovite Political Culture

NANCY SHIELDS KOLLMANN

The concept of political culture emerged in the 1950s among American political scientists – chief among them Gabriel Almond and Sydney Verba – in their efforts to understand the traumas of Nazism and Stalinism. How, they asked, could European cultures such as Germany and Russia have become totalitarian? What are the factors that predispose societies to democracy or to dictatorship, asked Barrington Moore in his foundational study. Their answers to these questions pushed beyond prescriptive ideas to envision politics in any given setting as a "culture." Lucien Pye's definition is classic:

> Political culture is the set of attitudes, beliefs, and sentiments which give order and meaning to a political process and which provide the underlying assumptions and rules that govern behavior in the political system. It encompasses both the political ideals and the operating norms of a polity. Political culture is thus the manifestation in aggregate form of the psychological and subjective dimensions of politics. . . . it is rooted equally in public events and private experiences.[1]

Through the 1970s political scientists elaborated the concept, exploring how socialization instills political culture, how political cultures legitimize power, and in particular how democratic values are instilled. Almond and Verba's concept of "civic culture" was influential in policy recommendations for the spread of democracy to the developing world. Even while political scientists hoped that the concept would give political science an interdisciplinary richness, Pye himself also acknowledged the critique that the concept is too broad to be pinned down.[2]

In subsequent decades political scientists have struggled with these ambiguities of "political culture," moving from the supposition that political culture "causes" certain outcomes to a greater emphasis on political culture as process. Meanwhile, historians have embraced the concept as a welcome antidote to traditional focuses on ideology, institutions, and top-down power configurations. Writing in 1987, Keith Michael Baker underscores the concept's dynamism.

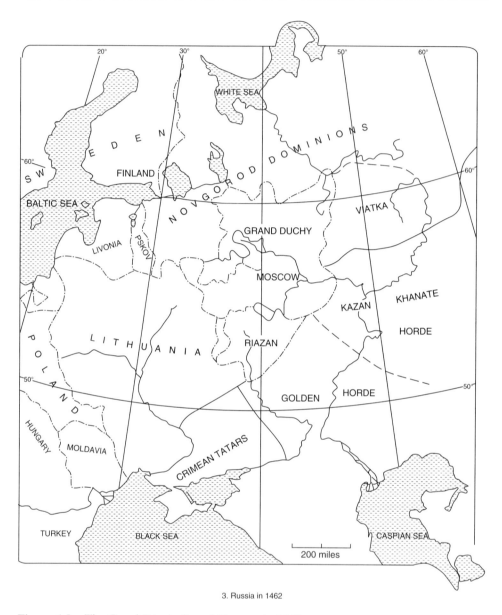

3. Russia in 1462

Figure 6.1   The Grand Principality of Moscow in 1462

If politics, broadly construed, is the activity through which individuals and groups in any society articulate, negotiate, implement, and enforce the competing claims they make one upon another, then political culture may be understood as the set of discourses and practices characterizing that activity in any given community . . . Political culture is a historical creation, subject to constant elaboration and development through the activities of the individuals and groups whose purposes it defines.[3]

Baker's definition highlights what historians like about this concept. It links individuals and groups to institutions, it puts ideas into practice, it presupposes change and conflict. Baker hints at how the concept has grown from its origins to embrace trends streaming into historical studies from other disciplines – discourse analysis of texts, semiotic analysis, anthropologists' concerns with ritual, symbolism, and praxis. Historians have been less interested in assessing political culture as a causative factor and more concerned with using it as an angle to understand "how politics works." Even though Ronald Formisano cautions that historians would do well to be more self-conscious of "the indeterminancy of the political culture concept," consensus is that the concept has enriched historical studies across the board.[4]

Russian historians have embraced the concept of political culture, starting in the 1960s–70s with two scholars at Harvard – Richard Pipes and Edward L. Keenan – who may well have known Barrington Moore and Sydney Verba, active in the Government Department and the Russian Research Center at Harvard in those days. In a monograph that has become classic (delivered as a lecture course at Harvard in the 1972–3 academic year), Richard Pipes advanced a complex model of the Muscovite "political system" (he did not use the term political culture) as shaped around categories advanced by Aristotle and familiar in the modern day as Weberian.[5] He called that system "patrimonial," denoting a state in which all property belonged to the ruler, in which all "public" goods – people, land, trade, natural resources – are the "private" property of the ruler. In depicting Muscovy as an oppressive and coercive state, he replicated a dominant trend of nineteenth-century Russian scholarship about Muscovy, which saw the autocratic state as all powerful and society as passive. Pipes, like these "statist school" predecessors, explicitly contrasted patrimonial control with the freedoms – of person, of property ownership, and of participation of public life – of European states and the institutions that protected them – rule of law, representative bodies. Furthermore, Pipes argued that the political system forged by the Muscovite state endured through the Bolshevik regime.

Pipes's Harvard colleague Edward L. Keenan in 1976 put Muscovite institutions in a very different light. Although it may well have been a response to Pipes, his "Muscovite Political Folkways" essay was not a polemic; the two maintained cordial relations. Keenan exhibited a variety of influences in "Folkways," including not only the concept of political culture but also the system-defining approach of structural linguistics and the "praxis" orientation of social anthropology.[6] Keenan's goal was to define the "rules of the game" at the Kremlin court. Outwardly, in ritual, rhetoric, and symbolism, court politics projected a claim to total power, expressed in the idiom of Orthodox piety. But, Keenan argued, behind that claim, "hardball politics" was shaped by the dogged efforts of powerful boyar clans to maintain equilibrium among themselves and thus stability in the realm at large; that stability was built on the foundation of clan and marriage ties. Keenan, furthermore, argued that the Orthodox Church – whose hierarchs break their ties with natal clans – was not a player in court politics, only the source of its ideological façade.

In some ways Keenan's less negative take on Muscovite court politics replicated another dominant paradigm of nineteenth-century historical scholarship – namely, the Slavophile one. A group of Russian intellectuals influenced both by a neo-hesychast spiritual trend in Orthodoxy in the early nineteenth century and also, as Andrzej Walicki has pointed out, by conservative European romanticism, Slavophiles celebrated what they saw as the spiritual unity of tsar and people in Muscovy, unobstructed by class, bureaucracy, or formal law. The Slavophile ideal of Muscovite political culture as pious and conflict free ignores messy historical reality, but it faithfully reflected the image that official Muscovite sources themselves projected. It is that dualism of the image of Muscovy as sacred kingdom and the reality of a politics shaped by family, marriage, and dependency that Keenan identified as central to Muscovite political culture.

These two works influenced subsequent scholarship on Muscovite politics tremendously, in the United States in particular. They appeared when other heady currents were also flooding in: the Tartu school of semiotics associated with Boris Uspenskii and Iurii Lotman; structuralism; an efflorescence of social anthropologicy, epitomized by the popularity of Clifford Geertz, Victor Turner, and Natalie Zemon Davis. The subsequent decades have seen elaborations and refutations of both approaches – that of Pipes and that of Keenan. One group of historians did not, however, participate in this theoretical elaboration through the 1980s – namely, Soviet historians. There are two reasons for this. First, Marxist ideology in principle objected to the concept's blurring of class interests and rejection of teleological change. French Marxists, for example, did not share historians' general enthusiasm for applying the term to the French Revolution.[7] Secondly, Soviet historians were ill-informed about the work of Western historians, owing to limited knowledge of Western languages and limited access to Western publications. Soviet historians persisted in an approach that interpreted Muscovite history within early modern European terms. Where a political cultural approach would look for relationships and processes, families, and factions, Soviet scholars focused on institutions (the Boyar Duma, the *Zemskii Sobor*), laws, and progressive change. Only in the 1990s did Russian historians begin to engage with these more anthropological and theoretical approaches, as we shall see.

From the late 1970s, studies in Muscovite political culture have persistently explored Muscovite political culture with a consciousness of the deep interconnectedness of ideology and political practice. In addressing ideology, they have introduced innovative new interpretations and dimensions.

Here the grounding work belongs to Daniel Rowland. In many seminal essays Rowland has examined traditional narrative sources – the works of political writers from Joseph Volotskii to Avvakum and, most notably, the historical "tales" concerning the Time of Troubles – as well as representational sources, for their implicit political ideology.[8] He argues that the uniformity of the political vision evidenced in these sources, particularly the *Smuta* tales written by lay and clerical authors alike, suggests that members of Muscovy's political classes shared a common vision of politics. In Rowland's terms, Muscovites portrayed a vision of the realm as "God dependent" – that is, only by presuming the tsar's direct relationship to God can one make sense of public life. The primary role of the tsar, as God's appointee on earth, was to lead his people to salvation, and his power was regarded as complete, since he was assumed to act benevolently. Narrative sources present a vision of politics with a weakly developed concept of resistance: only when the tsar was suborned morally – by the devil, by evil counselors – did an imperative arise for righteous men to give him advice. If he persisted in evil and became a "tsar tormentor," then one writer, Joseph Volotskii, counseled disobedience. Indeed, the strongest opponents of tsars in

Muscovite history did this: for example, to their peril, Metropolitan Filipp and others remonstrated with the tsar. Avvakum and the Old Believers, having exhausted the avenue of righteous critique, resisted by withdrawing from the community. But there was little, if any, support in this political vision for overt opposition.

Rowland explored the relationship of political classes to the tsar by shifting from narrative sources to visual ones.[9] In seminal studies of the "Church Militant" icon and the frescos of the Golden Hall in the Kremlin (a room where boyars would have spent hours daily), Rowland shows that these images insistently depicted the boyar elite as a heavenly army and Muscovy as a "New Jerusalem," a sacred space for the just as they await the End Time. They celebrated the elite's advice-giving role and depicted the ruler as God's ordained representative on earth.

As Rowland's later work suggests, historians of Muscovy have become increasingly sensitive to the importance of the embodied, the enacted, and the visual in a world of limited literacy. In turning to ritual and imagery, they have "brought the church back in," after Keenan had seemingly dismissed its role in politics. Michael Flier has produced an important body of work on court rituals and the built environment of the Muscovite court. Shifting from Rowland's study of the elite, Flier focuses on the tsar. In articles analyzing the central rituals in the Kremlin liturgical cycle – the Blessing of the Waters at the Epiphany and the Palm Sunday Procession – and numerous important objects, Flier explores the tsar's relationship with God, with his boyars, his society, and his kinsmen.[10] He reads the frescos of the Golden Hall Throne room as profoundly Christian and apocalyptic, while he sees that of the Monomakh throne or "Pew" in the Dormition Cathedral as both religious and secular. "In its avoidance of Christian symbolism, the Pew states even more strongly than the Golden Hall the vital nature of the Muscovite tsar as God-chosen, the leader of the latter-day Israelites, the bearer of secular authority in the Muscovite realm, an emperor and his line sustained by God in his house for perpetuity."[11] He reads the dedications of chapels in St Basil's Cathedral as "a direct expression of Ivan's dominance of territorial space and patrilinear time," linking it both with Ivan's imperial conquests and anxiety over his succession.[12] He argues that the tsar's leading the ass in the Palm Sunday ritual demonstrates not his subservience but his control of the political realm, and that Nikon's seventeenth-century modifications on that ritual reveal his nuanced approach to foreign influence in his reforms. Flier's semiotic approach, deeply grounded in the texts, bricks, or paint strokes of the representations he analyzes, demonstrates the apocalyptic and theocratic content of Muscovite political culture.

Many other historians have also explored the ideology of politics implicit in rituals, objects, and other representations. Robert Crummey has analyzed how visual portrayals of the tsar and his men do not depict the tsar as significantly superior to his men; my essay on sixteenth-century pilgrimages explored how tsars traveled about their realm to sanctify newly conquered areas, to define the realm symbolically, and more pragmatically to distribute alms, found spiritual centers, and patronize monasteries, all in fulfillment of their roles as godly rulers. Daniel Rowland and others have demonstrated how Muscovite rulers disseminated Kremlin-based architectural styles to legitimize Moscow as a "symbolic center." Sergei Bogatyrev's essay on the rhetoric of Ivan IV's campaign to Polotsk shows convincingly that sixteenth-century sources across the board – from clerically produced chronicles to prosaic military muster books – "reproduce the same set of quasi-theological ideas associated with the sacred model of the Muscovite state and its policy."[13] Maureen Perrie found that folklore on Ivan the Terrible projects on the whole an image of a good tsar, accessible to his people and just.

Scholars have traced these themes in seventeenth-century political ideology as well. Using mid-seventeenth-century collective petitions, Valerie Kivelson has shown that the presumption of the realm as a godly community and of the tsar as a receiver of advice permeated the sensibilities of gentrymen at the mid-seventeenth century. Gentrymen, for example, appealed to the tsar for local judges who would rule according to local conditions that they knew personally. For them, law was God's justice, not written statute.[14] Biographers of Aleksei Mikhailovich, including Philip Longworth and Michael Cherniavsky, have noted that he, while promoting major cultural and political transformations, projected an image that earned him the sobriquet of "most pious tsar."

Isolde Thyrêt has made a strikingly original demonstration of the interconnections of court political ideology and practice in her study of royal women. Here she demonstrates the endurance of traditional tropes of piety and patrimonialism through Aleksei Mikhailovich's time. Royal women, from the early sixteenth century, cultivated an image of themselves as the "blessed wombs" of the tsars and therefore as privileged intercessors with the ruler for the people. Thyrêt shows that Aleksei Mikhailovich's female relatives, most notably his first wife, Mariia Miloslavskaia, took active political leadership in times of crisis and that Aleksei Mikhailovich depended upon his mother, wife, and sisters for advice and prayers. When away on campaign, he wrote regularly seeking their intercession for him with God. Thyrêt argues that Muscovite political ideology was fulfilled ONLY when the female side of the court played its role of prayerful piety, intercession, and good works.[15]

Ivan IV poses, however, a particular challenge for scholars of Muscovite politics, and works concerning him represent two quite different approaches. On the one hand, the theatricality of his behavior, particularly in the Oprichnina, has lent itself to the semiotic and discursive analysis associated with Bakhtinian theory, the Tartu semiotic school, and deconstructionism. Numerous important essays have illuminated aspects of Ivan's actions and words. B. A. Uspenskii has explored the sacralization of the ruler in the Muscovite era. Several scholars – Uspenskii, Priscilla Hunt, and Andrei Iurganov among them – have explored Ivan the Terrible's symbolic playing at pretenderism or his bizarre punishments in the Oprichnina to his self-perception as God's avenger on the sinful. D. S. Likhachev and A. M. Panchenko explain Ivan IV's alleged empathy for holy fools by arguing that, inasmuch as holy fools act out carnivalesque inversions of conventional morality, they thereby occupy a supra-moral space shared only by rulers. This semiotic and hermeneutic approach to texts and rituals provides a link between the "façade" of court politics and its reality by suggesting that strong-minded tsars, like Ivan, acted out in ways shaped by their understanding of themselves as godly personages.

On the other hand, several recent studies of Ivan the Terrible do not take much notice of the complementary models of court politics as sacred kingdom or as structured by clan and family. There are a variety of reasons for this. Russian scholars often did not have ready access to Western monographs and articles developing these themes. In addition, Soviet paradigms of class struggle and an institutional approach to political structure have endured. Another factor is that many historians have not accepted E. L. Keenan's claim that the correspondence attributed to Ivan IV and Andrei Kurbskii, and the related "History" of Kurbskii, were fabricated gradually over the course of the seventeenth century as a form of political critique and/or literary exercise; thus they take these writings as evidence of the Ivan's psychology and beliefs.[16] So, as scholars struggle to fit all of Ivan – from the energetic reforms of his early years of rule to the excesses of the Oprichnina – into one consistent package, they revert to a tsar-centered, often psychological portrait.

Thus, recent biographies by distinguished scholars – B. N. Floria, D. N Al'shits, V. B. Kobrin, and Isabel de Madariaga – explore Ivan as psychologically complex, but competently pursuing a course of centralization in the face of social resistance of one form or another. The joint biography by Andrei Pavlov and Maureen Perrie admirably fits new scholarship about clan and faction, eschatology and semiotics, into a portrait of an essentially rational tsar.

Given the complexities of sources on Ivan IV, it is not surprising that scholarship here is across the board. As a rule, however, most scholars depict Muscovite political ideology as construing the realm as a sacred kingdom whose ruler was God-appointed and pious, whose political relationships were based on personal obedience, advice-giving, and the ties of family and marriage, and whose theoretical purpose was to attain other-worldly salvation.

Moving on to political practice, recent scholarship does not overturn the image of Muscovy's ruler as autocrat but rather seeks to explain what "autocracy" meant in practice. It argues that the tsar's claim to power was in practice limited by the parameters imposed by ideology – namely, by the expectation of the tsar's personal piety and morality and his traditional obligation of taking advice. Scholars studying Keenan's vaunted "hardball politics" have demonstrated that such an ideology was acted out in practice through the seventeenth century: boyars were expected to give advice and the tsar to welcome it, unanimity and consensus between factions were the goals of political struggle, relationships among members of the political elite were shaped by personal ties – kinship, marriage, and dependence.

Studies of pragmatic politics have moved in many fruitful directions since Pipes's and Keenan's founding works. It is probably the case that the "Folkways" essay represents Keenan's rumination on what Muscovite politics would be like if we took two principled steps. One would be to eliminate the image of a literate, classically educated, and physically able Ivan. (Keenan brought attention to the "tsar's body" – that is, to the autopsy on Ivan IV's skeleton done during Kremlin renovations in the 1960s. It showed that Ivan had suffered fusion of the spine and was likely to have been debilitated by the regular use of mercury as a pain-killer, indicated by mercury deposits on skeletal joints.[17]) Second would be to call attention to the formulaic nature of narrative Muscovite sources. Sources such as chronicles, petitions, and all manner of government documents replicated the ideology of godly community, even when reality was demonstrably different (for example, chronicles and charters depict Ivan IV making policy even when he was less than 10). Sources produced by foreign travelers had different biases yet again. Thus, Keenan's skepticism has inspired a generation of scholars to look beyond prescriptive texts to the workings of politics. We can identify several areas of discussion.

First, disagreement on the normative evaluation of this political system has continued, as evidenced in Richard Pipes's debate with George Weickhardt on the law. Weickhardt argued that *de facto* Muscovite legal culture provided due process, citing the issue of property. Here he argued that, although the tsar in theory had the right to confiscate property at any time, it rarely happened. In practice individuals held and transferred property with dependable and broad property rights. Pipes responded that the fact that the tsar *could* confiscate property proves its fundamentally coercive nature. Richard Hellie has paralleled Richard Pipes normatively in a series of articles that underscore the weakness of the upper classes and the coercive power of the state.

Marshall Poe's book on the trope of despotism and slavery in European travel literature through the seventeenth century stimulated discussion.[18] In demonstrating how persistent the vision of Muscovy as despotic was, it prompted more critical assessments of these tropes. In a key essay on the concept of slavery, Poe argued that the formulae in which Muscovites addressed themselves to the tsar as "slaves" actually expressed a "ceremonial" concept of slavery that both "elevated the status of the tsar" and also provided a means of making claims on the government.[19] Valerie Kivelson extended such analysis, arguing that, for Muscovites, the term "freedom" carried a negative value and that "slavery" envisioned "enfranchised subjecthood" – that is, the fact that these self-proclaimed "slaves" actually possessed a claim on "rights of membership and participation in the plastic political universe" and that the government in practice heeded its subjects' concerns through "listening to their grievances, granting their claims, honoring their entitlements, and conducting its business according to formal, written law." Such "slavery" was not despotism.[20]

Such examination of familiar tropes has transformed historians' normative stance on Muscovy, as a debate between Poe and Kivelson shows. Poe argued, revising his book's argument, that Muscovy, after all, should be considered a "despotism," since the tsar's claim to power was absolute. But he then conceded that "the despot may have a greater opportunity to act capriciously than a monarch or president, but he would be wise not to, for the consequences are grave . . . rulers' actions are impinged upon by a whole host of factors – available resources, technical means, custom, the willingness of subjects and so on and so forth." [21] Kivelson noted in response that this admission negates the negative connotation of "despotism" and brings Poe around to the position of those who see political culture, in Keenanesque terms, as a complex interaction of the state's assertions of complete power and its responsiveness to claims made by groups and individual.[22] Even Poe himself is at pains to deny "despotism" any negative connotation, calling Muscovy a "magnificently successful" state.[23] Thus, scholars are moving beyond any residual cold-war disdain for Russia and trying to assess Muscovite politics in complex, nuanced ways.

Secondly, scholars have dissected the workings of court politics. I demonstrated in *Kinship and Politics* that court political groups were centered around clans which had the hereditary right to put one of their members at the court, and that the supreme prize – marriage to the ruler himself – created an "inner circle" of privileged boyars and a status hierarchy that generally lasted two or three generations. I further argued that political struggles through at least the mid-sixteenth century focused more on primacy among the clans than on policy or class self-interest; that the business of court politics was the process of collective consultation among boyars and tsar, the goal of which was to achieve consensus; and that that consensus gave the state power and internal stability.[24] Subsequent work by M. M. Krom, André Berelowitch, Sergei Bogatyrev, and A. P. Pavlov, among others, has explored court politics as clan politics and has debated the relative importance of kinship and policy interests in Ivan IV's time.

The approach of analyzing court politics as clan-based has been facilitated by fundamental prosopographical studies of the boyar and bureaucratic elite over the last several decades. Eminent Russian medievalists, notably S. B. Veselovskii, A. A. Zimin, R. G. Skrynnikov, V. B. Kobrin, D. N. Al'shits, A. I. Filiushkin, and A. P. Pavlov, among others, have been assiduously cataloguing individuals and clans in politics, generally without theoretizing the data (in theory, clan would have been superseded in political life by feudal relations in the Soviet Marxist model). At the same time that political culture theory was spreading, prosopography was also becoming a vogue among American and European historians as a tool to move beyond an institutional–legal approach to early modern politics to one focusing on family, marriage, clientelage, and patronage. Sir Lewis Namier was the pioneer of this approach in British history. Building on prosopographical data-sets assembled by Soviet historians, as well as on their own work (a team of American and Soviet scholars compiled a database of holders of high court ranks through the seventeenth century, for example[25]), numerous scholars have analyzed court politics as clan politics. Focusing on the fifteenth and sixteenth centuries were Hartmut Russ, Gustave Alef, André Berelowitch, Sergei Bogatyrev, myself, and others.

For the seventeenth century, Robert Crummey subjected the boyar elite to prosopographical analysis. He too found a strong element of heritability in attaining boyar office (although not as systematic as others had found for the preceding two centuries) and of clans in structuring political groups and conflicts. He and Paul Bushkovitch both chronicled how boyar clans acted out the presumptions of political culture through patronage of the Church and manifestations of personal piety.[26] At the same time scholars took prosopography into the eighteenth century and identified the continued significance of clan and personal relations in court politics: Brenda Meehan for Peter the Great's time, John LeDonne for the full eighteenth century, and David Ransel for the factional politics of Catherine II's court.

Russian historians have participated in the articulation of political culture since the collapse of the Soviet Union. Their work has been somewhat hindered by lack of access to the wealth of discussion on this topic published in the 1970s and 1980s in the West, particularly the strong accent on clan and personal relations as an organizing principle in court politics. So, for example, A. I. Filiushkin admirably challenged Russian scholarship on the concept of the "Chosen Council," showing that this concept appeared only in later and tendentious sources. But his attempt to define the "political elite" perpetuated established categories, such as the *Zemskii Sobor* and Boyar Duma (both terms inventions of nineteenth-century historians), and interpreted political struggle as shaped by principled policy differences. In other words, he did not engage fully with new approaches.[27]

Thirdly, historians have explored the practice of autocracy in local politics, advanced by a growing interest in microhistory; M. M. Krom of St Petersburg has, for example, written a textbook introducing Russian scholars to this popular methodology.[28] Microhistorical studies of local politics have shown the fluidity, compromises, and limitations of the tsars' claim to complete power. In studying the provisioning of garrisons on the southern frontier in the seventeenth century, for example, Carol Belkin Stevens found that local governors were forced to tolerate significant variations from central social policies. Here, for example, gentry and runaway serfs alike were recruited into the border guard; here men below the privileged gentry ranks received *pomest'e* land; here governors turned a blind eye to runaway serfs and recruits in their desperate need to protect the frontier. That the state was not a monolith is also the message of the studies of local government by Brian Davies, A. Iu. Zhukov, and G. P. Enin, and of the study of the criminal justice apparatus in Voronezh by B. A. Glazev. All these authors demonstrate how local communities interacted with central appointees to meet their needs, often drawing officials into an informal, reciprocal economy of gift-giving and bribery. Valerie Kivelson's monograph on the Vladimir-Suzdal' provincial gentry in the seventeenth century demonstrates the creation of regional identity by strategies such as endogamous marriage within local families; the clustering of state land grants and private landed property within the region; the monopolizing of local offices, even those that were not supposed to be staffed by locals; and collective petitions to Moscow.[29]

Some works have offered broad, synthetic analysis of the practice of autocracy. Donald Ostrowski has provocatively read as borrowed from Tatar models many of the practices of political structure and interaction described by the patrimonial model discussed here; he furthermore persuasively showed how the Orthodox Church provided the ideological grounding for autocracy in the sixteenth century, displacing real historical memory of Tatar influence.[30] My recent book on honor, using sources of the seventeenth century, identifies three sorts of "strategies of governance" that linked center to periphery according to the principles of political culture discussed here. Coercive strategies, long a focus of historians who label Muscovy a despotic autocracy, cannot be ignored. But in addition the state used co-optation, construing its control of society in ways that gave individuals incentive to submit to authority. Litigations over honor, for example, provided a venue in which people could defend their own personal dignity and often that of their social status; in doing so they in turn affirmed the tsar's legitimacy. Other co-optative strategies can be generalized as the "petitionary order" – that is, the fiction that public life was shaped by the individual's vertical, direct connection with the tsar. The petitionary order included direct appeal through petition and lawsuit, collective petitions by groups, advice-giving by elites in "in consultation" (*v dume*) or by larger assemblies called by modern historians "*Zemskie sobory.*" Finally, a third, very important strategy of governance was ideational, involving the projection of an image of the tsar through word and symbolic form – ritual, art, architecture, as discussed above.[31]

Analysis of Muscovite political culture has also not ignored change over time, for visions and reality of the polity experienced significant pressure in the seventeenth century. Internal stimuli for change are epitomized by the massive 1649 Lawcode and subsequent reforms in the military, judiciary, and bureaucracy that chipped away at the reality and imagery of Muscovy as patrimonial in favor of bureaucratic absolutism. From the outside, Ukrainian clerics at the Kremlin court from mid-century introduced new paradigms of political power.

The late seventeenth century deserves more attention than it has so far received, but some significant work has been done. Robert Crummey's study of the boyar elite of the seventeenth century shows that the number of men in the boyar ranks became so huge (ballooning from around 35 through the mid-1640s to around 145 in the 1680s) as to destroy the fiction that the tsar was personally connected with his men.[32] A. S. Lavrov and P. V. Sedov have examined the growth of the landed class and factional politics in the regency of Sofiia Alekseevna. While the power of inner circles composed of the tsar's in-laws did not subside (note that the major political struggles from the 1680s to 1710s centered around the factions of Aleksei Mikhailovich's two wives – Miloslavskie and Naryshkiny), both scholars demonstrate how the elite became more stratified and political activity became more institutionalized. Bureaucratic "commissions" of boyars and clerks were assigned to specific tasks – compiling the 1649 Lawcode, investigating the abolition of *mestnichestvo* and military reform in 1682, handling judicial appeals. Lavish land distributions during the regency created a quasi-aristocracy at the top. Laws repeatedly tried to curtail individuals' direct presentation of petitions to the tsar, symbolically subverting the image of personal connections between tsar and people. Political structures began to resemble "absolutism" at the same time as old principles – clan and patrimonial relations – persisted.

Ideas and symbolism in court politics also reflected this complex evolution, presenting a fascinating blend of tradition and innovation. Paul Bushkovitch has demonstrated how the sermons and writings of Epifanii Slavinetskii, Semeon Polotskii, and Sylvestr Medvedev at the courts of Aleksei Mikhailovich, Fedor Alekseevich, and Sofiia Alekseevna presented a new morality focused on the inner self and civic consciousness. Endre Sashalmi demonstrates how the monk Avraamii's "Missive" of 1696 is "a mixture of Muscovite traditions and recent Western notions of rulership," particularly shifting the focus from the tsar's religious duties to his role in promoting "an activist idea of the common good."[33] Lindsey Hughes and Isolde Thyrêt have analyzed how regent Sofiia Alekseevna and her ideologues used panegyric and portraiture (a new medium of self-representation) both to praise her in traditional terms – as embodying Divine Wisdom, as intercessor – and also to promote the unprecedented goal of her coronation. Hughes has devoted particular attention to innovations in the visual arts – icon and architecture – under Ukrainian influence, while A. P. Bogdanov explored panegyrics of Sofiia's time; both demonstrate the introduction of new vocabularies of political terminology and symbolism reflecting a more voluntaristic political sphere. Max Okenfuss has chronicled how Latin Humanism, with its late Renaissance tenets of virtue and the "common good," penetrated Kremlin political discourse from Ukraine. The net result was a more energized elite that was beginning to see the political world as oriented toward the common good, as inevitably involving change, and as inviting each individual's voluntaristic contribution.

These fertile ideas of the 1680s and 1690s paved the way for Peter the Great's radical changes in idiom (the rhetoric of German Pietism and European absolutism) and symbolism (classical mythology), as Marc Raeff and Richard Wortman have explored. Nevertheless, Muscovite political culture endured into the eighteenth century in attitudes toward government (personal politics were preferred to legal regulation), in the persistence of clan-based factions at court, and in the continued perception of, and self-presentation by, rulers as pious, merciful, and godly.

The last four decades of study of Muscovite political culture have deepened our understanding of how autocracy worked and how it represented itself. They have shown that the Muscovite state was indeed a powerful one, which offered no legal protections or rights to subjects, nor representative institutions that might share sovereignty. They have also shown that the power of the Muscovite ruler was limited both by the practical constraints of limited manpower, limited resources, and huge empire, and by the expectations that the ruler fulfill his role as godly appointee guiding the moral compass of the realm. They have shown that court politics was structured by clan loyalties and marriage politics focused around the stabilizing center of the grand prince and his marriage, which gave the political system tremendous internal strength. Even when the ruler was a minor, politics remained essentially stable; only when the dynasty died out (and, some would argue, when Ivan IV aggressively attacked the system in the Oprichnina), did things completely fall apart. Recent research shows us the great degree to which this was a symbolic and visual culture, embodying its message in pilgrimages and processions, in icons and frescos, in rituals of consultation from one-on-one to mass assemblies. Most scholars would agree that "despotism" and "tyranny" are insufficient descriptors of this political system, and that terms to encompass it might range from "autocratic" and "patrimonial" to "God-dependent" and "consensus-based." The fact that no one category seems to suffice is a tribute to the many new perspectives that have been opened up on this complex and powerful political system.

Notes

1   Pye, "Political Culture," 218; Moore, *Social Origins.*
2   Pye, "Political Culture," 224.
3   Baker, "Introduction," p. xii.
4   Formisano, "Concept," 393.
5   Pipes, *Russia under the Old Regime.*
6   Keenan, "Folkways."
7   Baker, "Introduction," pp. xi–xii.
8   Rowland's essays using narrative sources include "Problem of Advice," "Did Muscovite Literary Ideology," and "God, Tsar and People."
9   Rowland, "Two Cultures" and "Biblical Military Imagery."
10 Flier, "Iconography," "Iconology," "Breaking the Code," and "Court Ceremony," and "K semioticheskomu analizu."
11 Flier, "Throne of Monomakh," 33.
12 Flier, "Filling in," 121.
13 Bogatyrev, "Battle," 327.
14 Kivelson, "The Devil."
15 Thyrêt, *Between God and Tsar.*
16 Keenan, *Kurbskii-Groznyi.*
17 Keenan, "Vita."
18 Poe, "A People."
19 Poe, "What did Muscovites Mean," 587.
20 Kivelson, "Muscovite 'citizenship'," 488.
21 Poe, "The Truth," 485.
22 Kivelson, "On Words."
23 Poe, "The Truth," 486, and *Russian Moment.*
24 Kollmann, *Kinship and Politics.*

25   Poe et al., *The Russian Elite*.
26   Crummey, *Aristocrats*; Bushkovitch, *Religion*, ch. 2.
27   Filiushkin, *Istoriia*.
28   Krom, *Istoricheskaia antropologiia*.
29   Kivelson, *Autocracy in the Provinces*.
30   Ostrowski, *Muscovy and the Mongols*.
31   Kollmann, *By Honor Bound*.
32   Crummey, *Aristocrats*, 176–7.
33   Bushkovitch, *Religion*, ch. 7; Sashalmi, "Towards a New Ideology," 153.

References

Baker, Keith Michael (1987). "Introduction," in Keith Michael Baker, ed., *The French Revolution and the Creation of Modern Political Culture*. Vol. 1. *The Political Culture of the Old Regime*. Pergamon, Oxford, New York.

Bogatyrev, Sergei (2002). "Battle for Divine Wisdom: The Rhetoric of Ivan IV's Campaign against Polotsk," in Eric Lohr and Marshall Poe, eds., *The Military and Society in Russia, 1450–1917*. Brill, Leiden, Boston, Cologne.

Bushkovitch, Paul (1992). *Religion and Society in Russia: The Sixteenth and Seventeenth Centuries*. Oxford University Press, New York and Oxford.

Crummey, Robert O. (1983). *Aristocrats and Servitors. The Boyar Elite in Russia, 1613–1689*. Princeton University Press, Princeton.

Filiushkin, A. I. (1998). *Istoriia odnoi mistifikatsii. Ivan Groznyi i "Izbrannaia Rada."* VGU, Moscow.

Flier, Michael S. (1992). "The Iconography of Royal Procession: Ivan the Terrible and the Muscovite Palm Sunday Ritual," in Heinz Duchhardt, Richard A. Jackson, and David Sturdy, eds., *European Monarchy*. Franz Steiner Verlag, Stuttgart, 109–25.

Flier, Michael S. (1992). "The Iconology of Royal Ritual in Sixteenth-Century Muscovy," in Speros Vryonis, Jr., ed., *Byzantine Studies: Essays on the Slavic World and the Eleventh Century*. Aristide D. Caratzas, New Rochelle, NY, 53–76.

Flier, Michael S. (1994). "Breaking the Code: The Image of the Tsar in the Muscovite Palm Sunday Ritual," in Michael S. Flier and Daniel Rowland, eds., *Medieval Russian Culture*. Vol. II. University of California Press, Berkeley and Los Angeles, 213–42.

Flier, Michael S. (1995). "Filling in the Blanks: The Church of the Intercession and the Architectonics of Medieval Muscovite Ritual," *Harvard Ukrainian Studies*, 19: 120–37.

Flier, Michael S. (1997). "Court Ceremony in an Age of Reform: Patriarch Nikon and the Palm Sunday Ritual," in Samuel H. Baron and Nancy Shields Kollmann, eds., *Religion and Culture in Early Modern Russia and Ukraine*. Northern Illinois University Press, DeKalb IL, 73–95.

Flier, Michael S. (2003). "K semioticheskomu analizu Zolotoj palaty Moskovskogo Kremlja," in *Drevnerusskoe iskusstvo*. Dmitrij Bulanin, St Petersburg, 178–87.

Flier, Michael S. (2003). "The Throne of Monomakh: Ivan the Terrible and the Architectonics of Destiny," in James Cracraft and Daniel Rowland, eds., *Architectures of Russian Identity. 1500 to the Present*. Cornell University Press, Ithaca, NY, and London, 21–33.

Formisano, Ronald P. (2001). "The Concept of Political Culture," *Journal of Interdisciplinary History*, 31/3: 393–426.

Keenan, Edward L. (1971). *The Kurbskii-Groznyi Apocrypha*. Harvard University Press, Cambridge, MA.

Keenan, Edward L. (1978). "Vita: Ivan Vasil'evich. Terrible Czar: 1530–1584," *Harvard Magazine*, 80/3: 49.

Keenan, Edward L. (1986). "Muscovite Political Folkways," *Russian Review*, 45/2: 115–81.

Kivelson, Valerie A. (1993). "The Devil Stole his Mind: The Tsar and the 1648 Moscow Uprising," *American Historical Review*, 98/3: 733–56.

Kivelson, Valerie A. (1996). *Autocracy in the Provinces: The Muscovite Gentry and Political Culture in the Seventeenth Century*. Stanford University Press, Stanford, CA.

Kivelson, Valerie A. (2002). "Muscovite 'Citizenship': Rights without Freedom," *Journal of Modern History*, 74: 465–89.

Kivelson, Valerie A. (2002). "On Words, Sources, and Historical Method: Which Truth about Muscovy?" *Kritika*, 3/3: 487–99.

Kollmann, Nancy Shields (1987). *Kinship and Politics: The Making of the Muscovite Political System, 1345–1547*. Stanford University Press, Stanford, CA.

Kollmann, Nancy Shields (1999). *By Honor Bound: State and Society in Early Modern Russia*. Cornell University Press, Ithaca, NY.

Krom, M. M. (2002). *Istoricheskaia antropologiia: posobie k lektsionnomu kursu*. Dmitrii Bulanin, St Persburg. Rev. and expanded edn. (2004).

Moore, Barrington (1966). *Social Origins of Dictatorship and Democracy*. Beacon Press, Boston.

Ostrowski, Donald (1998). *Muscovy and the Mongols: Cross-Cultural Influences on the Steppe Frontier, 1304–1589*. Cambridge University Press, Cambridge.

Pipes, Richard (1974). *Russia under the Old Regime*. Scribner, New York.

Poe, Marshall (1998). "What did Muscovites Mean when they Called themselves 'Slaves of the Tsar'?" *Slavic Review*, 57/3: 585–608.

Poe, Marshall (2000). '*A People Born to Slavery'. Russia in Early Modern European Ethnography, 1476–1748*. Cornell University Press, Ithaca, NY, and London.

Poe, Marshall (2002). "The Truth about Muscovy," *Kritika*, 3/3: 473–86.

Poe, Marshall (2003). *The Russian Moment in World History*. Princeton University Press, Princeton and Oxford.

Poe, Marshall, et al. (2004). *The Russian Elite in the Seventeenth Century*. Vol. 2. *A Quantitative Analysis of the "Duma Ranks" 1613–1713*. Annales Academiae Scientiarum Fennicae, Helsinki.

Pye, Lucian W. (1968). "Political Culture," *International Encyclopedia of the Social Sciences*, 12: 218–25.

Rowland, Daniel (1979). "The Problem of Advice in Muscovite Tales about the Time of Troubles," *Russian History*, 6/2: 259–83.

Rowland, Daniel (1990). "Did Muscovite Literary Ideology Place Limits on the Power of the Tsar (1540s–1660s)?" *Russian Review*, 49/2: 125–55.

Rowland, Daniel (1994). "Biblical Military Imagery in the Political Culture of Early Modern Russia: The Blessed Host of the Heavenly Tsar," in Flier and Rowland, eds., *Medieval Russian Culture*, vol. 2, pp. 182–212.

Rowland, Daniel (2003). "Two Cultures, one Throne Room: Secular Courtiers and Orthodox Culture in the Golden Hall of the Moscow Kremlin," in Valerie A. Kivelson and Robert H. Greene, eds., *Orthodox Russia. Belief and Practice under the Tsars*. Pennsylvania State University Press, University Park, PA, 33–57.

Rowland, Daniel (2007). "Muscovy," in Howell A. Lloyd, Glenn Burgess, and Simon Hodson, eds., Yale University Press, New Haven and London), 267–99.

Sashalmi, Endre (2003). "Towards a New Ideology: Muscovite Notions of Rulership and Western Influences in 'Avraamij's Missive'," in Gyula Szvak, ed., *Muscovy: Peculiarities of its Development*, Magyar Ruszisztikai Intezet, Budapest, 143–54.

Thyrêt, Isolde (2001). *Between God and Tsar: Religious Symbolism and the Royal Women of Muscovite Russia*. Northern Illinois University Press, DeKalb, IL.

Further Reading

For the interpretation of Muscovy as a coercive despotism, in addition to Pipes's book cited, see his debate with George Weickhardt: George Weickhardt, "The Pre-Petrine Law of Property," *Slavic Review*, 52/4 (1993), 663–79; Richard Pipes, "Was there Private Property in Muscovite Russia?" *Slavic Review*, 53/2 (1994), 524–30; Weickhardt, "Was there Private Property in Muscovite Russia?" ibid. 531–8. Richard Hellie also argues for the "hypertrophy" of the state and weakness of social groups: "Thoughts on the Absence of Elite Resistance in Muscovy," *Kritika*, 1 (2000), 5–20, and "Why did the Muscovite Elite not Rebel?" *Russian History*, 25 (1998), 155–62.

In addition to Edward L. Keenan's *Apocrypha* book and "Folkways" essay, see his "The Trouble with Muscovy," *Medievalia et Humanistica*, NS 5 (1974), 103–26; "Royal Russian Behavior, Style, and Self-Image," in Edward Allworth, ed., *Ethnic Russia in the USSR*, New York, 1979, 3–16, and "On Certain Mythical Beliefs and Russian Behaviors," in S. Frederick Starr, ed., *The Legacy of History in Russia and the New States of Eurasia*, M. E. Sharpe, Armonk, NY, and London, 1994, 19–40.

On symbolism and ritual at court, in addition to Rowland's and Flier's works cited, see Robert O. Crummey, "Court Spectacles in Seventeenth-Century Russia: Illusion and Reality," in Daniel Clarke Waugh, ed., *Essays in Honor of A. A. Zimin*, Ohio State University Press, Columbus, OH, 1985, 130–58; and my "Pilgrimage, Procession, and Symbolic Space in Sixteenth-Century Russian Politics," in Flier and Rowland, eds., *Medieval Russian Culture*, 1994, vol. 2, pp. 163–81, and "Ritual and Social Drama at the Muscovite Court," *Slavic Review*, 45/3 (1986), 486–502. On the symbolic dissemination of architecture, see Rowland, "Architecture and Dynasty: Boris Godunov's Uses of Architecture, 1584–1606," in Cracraft and Rowland, eds., *Architectures of Russian Identity*, 34–47.

On the "most pious" Aleksei Mikhailovich, see Michael Cherniavsky, *Tsar and People: Studies in Russian Myths*, Yale University Press, New Haven, 1961; and Philip Longworth, *Alexis: Tsar of all the Russias*, Franklin Watts, New York., 1984.

Semiotic interpretations of Ivan IV and his apocalyptic sensibility include B. A. Uspenskii, *Tsar i patriarkh. Kharisma vlasti v Rossii*, Shkola "Iazyki russkoi kul'tury", Moscow, 1998; and "Tsar and Pretender: Samozvanchestvo or Royal Imposture in Russia as a Cultural-Historical Phenomenon," in Ju. M. Lotman and B. A. Uspenskii, *The Semiotics of Russian Culture*, ed. Ann Shukman, Dept. of Slavic Languages and Literatures, University of Michigan, Ann Arbor, 1984, 259–92; Priscilla Hunt, "Ivan IV's Personal Mythology of Kingship," *Slavic Review*, 52/4 (1993), 769–809; A. L. Iurganov, *Kategorii russkoi srednevekovoi kul'tury*, MIROS, Moscow, 1998; and D. S. Likhachev and A. M. Panchenko, *"Smekhovoi mir" drevnei Rusi*. Nauka, Leningrad. See also Maureen Perrie, *The Image of Ivan the Terrible in Russian Folklore*. Cambridge University Press, Cambridge, 1987.

Recent biographies of Ivan include D. N. Al'shits, *Nachalo samoderzhaviia v Rossii*. Nauka, Leningrad, 1988; Isabel de Madariaga, *Ivan the Terrible*, Yale University Press, New Haven and London, 2005; Boris Floria, *Ivan Groznyi*, Molodaia gvardiia, Moscow, 1999; B. Kobrin, *Ivan Groznyi*, Moskovskii rabochii, Moscow, 1989; and Andrei Pavlov and Maureen Perrie, *Ivan the Terrible*. Pearson, Longman, London and New York, 2003.

On court politics and prosopography, see Gustave Alef, "Reflections on the Boyar Duma in the Reign of Ivan III," *Slavonic and East European Review*, 45 (1967), 76–123; A. A. Zimin, *Formirovanie boiarskoi aristokratii v Rossii vo vtoroi polovine XV-pervoi treti XVI v.* Nauka, Moscow, 1988; and Hartmut Russ, *Adel und Adelsoppositionen im Moskauer Staat*. Steiner, Wiesbaden, 1975. See also André Berelowitch, *La Hiérarchie des égaux: La Noblesse russe d'Ancien Régime XVIe–XVIIe siècles*, Éditions du seuil, Paris, 2001; Sergei Bogatyrev, *The Sovereign and his Counsellors Ritualised Consultations in Muscovite Political Culture, 1350s–1570s*, Annales Academiae Scientiarum Fennicae, Helsinki, 2000; M. M. Krom, "Politicheskii krizis 30–40-kh godov XVI veka," *Otechestvennaia istoriia*, 5 (1996), 34–49; and A. P. Pavlov, *Gosudarev dvor i politicheskaia bor'ba pri Borise Godunove (1584–1605 gg.)*. Nauka, St Petersburg, 1992.

On local politics, see Brian L. Davies, *State Power and Community in Early Modern Russia*, Palgrave-Macmillan, Basingstoke and New York, 2004; G. P. Enin, *Voevodskoe kormlenie v Rossii v XVII veke. Rossiiskaia natsional'naia biblioteka*, St Petersburg; V. N. Glaz'ev, *Vlast' i obshchestvo na iuge Rossii v XVII veke*. Izd. Voronezhskogo univ, Voronezh, 2001; A. Iu. Zhukov, *Upravlenie i samoupravlenie v Karelii v XVII v. NovGU im.* Iaroslava Mudrogo, Novgorod, 2003; and Carol Belkin Stevens, *Soldiers on the Steppe: Army Reform and Social Change in Early Modern Russia*, Northern Illinois University Press, DeKalb, IL, 1995.

On late-seventeenth-century court politics, see A. S. Lavrov, *Regentstvo tsarevny Sof'i Alekseevny*, Arkheograficheskii tsentr, Moscow, 1999, and P. V. Sedov, "Sotsial'no-politicheskaia bor'ba v Rossii v 70–80-kh godakh XVII veka i otmena mestnichestva," Candidate dissertation, Leningrad, 1985.

For late-seventeenth-century cultural change, see "The Moscow Armoury and Innovations in Seventeenth-Century Muscovite Art," *Canadian–American Slavic Studies*, 13 (1979), 204–23; *Russia and the West: The Life of a Seventeenth-Century Westernizer, Prince Vasily Vasil'evich Golitsyn (1643–1714)*, Oriental Research Partners, Newtonville, MA, 1984; "Sophia, 'Autocrat of All the Russias': Titles, Ritual, and Eulogy in the regency of Sophia Alekseevna (1682–89)," *Canadian Slavonic Papers* 28/3 (1986), 266–86; and *Sophia, Regent of Russia, 1657–1704*, Yale University Press, New Haven and London, 1990. By A. P. Bogdanov, see *Pamiatniki obshchestvenno-politicheskoi mysli v Rossii kontsa XVII veka: literaturnye panegiriki,*. Institut istorii SSSR AN SSSR, Moscow, 1983, and *Moskovskaia publitsistika poslednei chetverti XVII veka*. Institut rossiiskoi istorii RAN, Moscow, 2001. See also Max J. Okenfuss, *The Rise and Fall of Latin Humanism in Early Modern Russia*, E. J. Brill, Leiden, New York, and Cologne, 1995.

Chapter Seven

Slavery and Serfdom in Russia

Richard Hellie

Slavery and serfdom plus autocracy were the features of Russia that most distinguished it from other polities in the modern era. Autocracy commenced at the beginning of the sixteenth century in the writings of Joseph of Volokolamsk, and the result was what I term "the Agapetos state" from then until 1991, in which the autocrat was assumed to represent God, and then its Soviet replacement, the Marxist historical dialectic. Autocracy combined with slavery and serfdom to create an environment in which almost no one was free in any sense that a person from the West would recognize. Autocracy and Soviet totalitarianism are dealt with in other chapters. The purpose of this chapter is to explain the unfreedom of the vast majority of the population, certainly over 85 percent of the population between the 1590s and 1907, then more than a majority between 1929 and 1956.

Unfreedom in Imperial Russia had many forms, but the two major ones were slavery and serfdom. The rest of the populace were unfree to varying degrees as well, from the townsmen bound to their towns to the servicemen who could not leave their posts in the army and elsewhere, but they are not the subject of this chapter. Slaves and serfs were primarily rural denizens, but not always. Slaves could live in towns, as we shall see, and so occasionally did serfs – but rarely.

The first point that must be made clear is the distinction between a slave and a serf, at least in law. Juridically, the slave typically was the *object* of the law, like a dog or a cow. Although in fact he was a human being, the law treated him as though he were not. This was especially true when it came to responsibility: a slave was not responsible for what he did, rather his owner was. This meant that a slave legally owned nothing in his own name (not even the clothing on his back), could not enter into legal agreements (contracts), and in fact juridically was an extension of his owner. If a slave stole something, his owner answered to the victim and the law, not the slave-thief. A slave's owner could dispose of him in practically any way he chose, such as move him from here to there without his consent, or force him to perform this or that task, and the state was not involved, just as it was not involved with owner–dog relations. Finally, the slave typically did not have to pay taxes.

The serf, on the other hand, was the *subject* of the law. The law did not treat him as an object that could talk, but rather as a human being. He owned not only his own clothing, but typically his agricultural inventory (cattle, tools, seed) as well. The serf had to pay taxes. In theory a serf could enter into contracts. The serf personally was responsible if, for example, he stole something. The law punished him, and he had to compensate the victim, not his lord. As we shall see below, initially the serf's lord could not dispose of his person in any way or move him from here to there and could not tell him what his occupation should be. The serf was bound to a particular piece of land and was obliged to pay rent to the holder of that land, but it was not the concern of the landholder how the serf got the rent. This situation gradually changed for the serf between 1700 and 1861, but initially the serf's legal status was what has been described.

The institution of slavery was present from the dawn of Russian history into the 1720s. Serfdom was created beginning in the 1450s and peaked in 1861, but endured until 1907. Both institutions were revived in the Soviet Union under different names, as will be discussed at the end of this chapter.

One of the generalizations of slavery studies is that a sociological peculiarity of the slave is that typically he is an "outsider," someone of a different race, nationality, or tribal origin from his owner. One of the alleged "truisms" of slavery is that "no society could withstand the tension of enslaving its own people." Throughout history this has generally tended to be true. If the person who is about to be enslaved is in fact an "insider," a fiction is created that makes him into an outsider. Thus Africans resorted to the practice of "exposure" – leaving an unwanted child untended for awhile until someone else came to pick up the child. Thus the person who picked up the unwanted child considered it as an outsider who was suitable for enslavement. This practice also had other consequences. In battle a victorious army could kill the losers or enslave them. But after a while (a number of years, or perhaps as much as three generations), the outsiders became insiders and thus unfit for slavery. They learned the language of the enslavers and their practices, and in most cases it was considered inappropriate to keep such people as slaves.

This was the way slavery began in the ninth century in what became Ukraine/Russia. One East Slavic tribe warred against another tribe and took the losers as captive booty. The East European Plain was inhabited not only by Slavs, who moved into Ukraine in the sixth century, northward to the Baltic in the eighth–ninth centuries, and into the Volga–Oka mesopotamia (Moscow area) in the tenth—thirteenth centuries. The indigenous peoples (Iranians in Ukraine, Balts and Finnic peoples to the north) remained, and were suitable objects for enslavement. Various Turkic, Hungarian, Mongol, and other peoples kept sweeping in from the east across the steppe. The nomads gained much of their livelihoods by enslaving sedentary peoples such as the Slavs, but the East Slavs reciprocally enslaved the nomads when they could. In the Kievan period (loosely, here, between 882 and 1240), there was a booming slave business, and most of the slaves were genuine outsiders. The land–labor ratio was very high, so that initially it was impossible to get anyone to farm for anyone else voluntarily. In that situation landownership was nearly meaningless, because free land had no value. Given the slash/burn system of agriculture, peasants did not remain long farming the same place anyway (typically, after only three years of tillage the fertility of a plot of land was exhausted; it had to lie fallow for another thirty or forty years to regain its fertility), so the government pursued farmers wherever they might be to force them to pay taxes. The concept of "rent" was meaningless. Thus there was no serfdom in the Kievan period. The reality of constant warfare meant, however, that there were always plenty of slaves, and slaves were a major export commodity. This was evident in Novgorod, where archeological digs have uncovered what was present at the intersection of Slave and High Streets for half a millennium, between the tenth and the fifteenth centuries. One may assume that "Slave Street" got its name because the main slave market was there, whence slaves were shipped into the Baltic, to the British Isles, to the European Atlantic coastal region, and into the Mediterranean. Other slaves from the "Slavic slave basin" were sold southward down the Volga into the Caspian Sea and beyond and down the Dnepr into the Black Sea and beyond. Slaves from Rus' were also taken eastward as far as China and westward into the countries of Central and Western Europe. It is not accidental that the word "slave" comes from the word "Slav."

A major point here has to be that the Vikings who traversed the route "from the Varangians to the Greeks" were slave traders, so that, when Oleg "founded the Kievan Russian state" in 882, he was founding a "state" one of whose primary economic pillars was slavery. On their way either south to Byzantium or north into the Baltic, one of the major "forest products" the Vikings were trading was slaves – most of whom they purchased from the sundry peoples along the way – who had been "harvested" by the local indigenous peoples from among their neighbors during their numerous wars.

Not all the slaves were exported. In time groups of them were housed in barracks and forced to farm. Nothing is known about their productivity, but one may assume that it was very low. Most of the slaves were household slaves of the type found almost everywhere in the world who were employed as cleaners, cooks, messengers, and general helpers. Slaves were sufficiently prominent to catch the attention of the lawmakers in the *Russkaia pravda*, which remained the fundamental law of Russia until 1549. In the twelfth century there was even a special section of the *Pravda* devoted to slaves. The articles dealt with such topics as disputes over slave ownership, whether the testimony of slaves could be taken in such cases, the responsibility for slave conduct, and particularly the universally thorny issue of free-slave marriages. In places such as Rus' where there was a perceived population shortage, the issue of slave marriage was especially important. The general solution, in the Russian case, was to convert any person who married a slave into a slave. Of course manumission was part of the institution of slavery, and so an owner always could manumit a slave if he desired to marry her. One may assume that another occupation of slaves was as body servants to their warrior-owners.

In the next period of Russian history, the Mongol period (1240–1480), the importance of slavery changed little from that of the Kievan period. One change stemmed from the fact that Russia turned away from Byzantium and the West toward the east. When the Mongols overran Rus' in 1236–40, they took many slaves and shipped them eastward. This remained the practice while the Mongols were headquartered in Karakorum, Mongolia. The transference of the headquarters of the Golden Horde to Sarai (built in 1254) on the lower Volga undoubtedly diminished the shipment of slaves to Asia, but no numbers are available to prove this. Asiatic

practices had little or no impact on Russian slavery, or on the development of
serfdom, either.

The rise of Moscow, which I believe was "certain" by the 1390s, was one of the
most important developments in East European history. Developments in Moscow
soon had an impact on the institutions of both slavery and serfdom. For the sake of
intellectual coherence, slavery will be discussed until its demise, and then serfdom
will be discussed in some detail, although it is important to bear in mind that serfdom
was developing all the time in the years 1450s–1720s as slavery was also evolving.
For the first half millennium of Russian history slavery was what would later be called
"full slavery": once a person became a slave, by whatever means, he was a slave until
he was manumitted (which almost never happened) or his death. Moreover, his offspring were also slaves. The second half of the fifteenth century witnessed enormous
numbers of social changes in Russia, probably more than any other half-century of
Russian history except 1905–55. As will be discussed below, serfdom took off. The
institution of the Muscovite cavalry also developed greatly: the military "middle-
service class" was created and based on the lands confiscated from Novgorod after
its conquest in 1478. In the sphere of slavery, something called limited-service contract slavery (*kabal'noe kholopstvo*) was created, which was juridically unlike full slavery.
Limited-service contract slavery seems to have been a Muscovite innovation, for the
only other place it existed was Parthia in the second century AD. It worked as follows:
violating the fact that slaves are typically "outsiders," Russians sold themselves into
slavery. When Russians began to sell themselves into slavery is not clear, nor is it clear
how they were able to overcome the moral barrier of enslaving their own people.
(One possibility is that the society was so multi-ethnic that it was not clear who was
an outsider and who was an insider.) Russians had to sell themselves, because charity
was very scarce in Russia; if someone did not want to sell himself, he could starve to
death. Earlier the option had been to sell oneself into full slavery. But limited-service
contract slavery offered (in theory) a variation: the person who was hard up took a
loan for a year and agreed to work for the interest (this was called antechresis in
Parthia). At the end of the year, he either paid off the loan or became a full slave.
How he was to get the money to pay off the loan is not clear, and it is also not clear
that anybody did; what was possible was borrowing money from another person and
using it to pay off the first creditor. Within a century this had become quite "popular,"
and largely replaced full slavery as the first stage of self-sale.

Limited-service contract slavery was *not* debt slavery, which also existed. Limited-
service contract slavery was "totally voluntary," in so far as misfortune or lack of initiative is ever voluntary. Debt slavery, which is outlined in detail in the Law Code of
1649, was not voluntary. In that case, someone defaulted on his debts and then had
to work them off at a specific rate, typically 5 rubles per year. Thus a person who
defaulted on 10 rubles of debt had to work for his creditor for two years to pay off
the debt. By 1649 this was clearly spelled out: a man worked off defaulted debt at
the rate of 5 rubles per year, a woman at the rate of 2.5 rubles per year, and a child
over 10 at the rate of 2 rubles per year.

After the introduction of limited-service contract slavery, slavery remained largely
unchanged until the 1590s. The quarter century before that was one of the periods
of greatest chaos in Russian history. This led to major changes in the institution
of serfdom, which will be detailed below. The consequence was that serfdom was

beginning to look much like slavery, with the difference that the serf had to pay crushing taxes while the slave did not. As a result, a large number of peasants were selling themselves into slavery, dramatically reducing the tax rolls of an already impoverished state. Recognizing that the "loans" were never paid back anyway, the state unilaterally decided to change the nature of limited-service contract slavery. A contract between the owner and slave was still required, but the state changed its terms: the borrower-slave still took the loan, but he could not pay it back. In exchange, he essentially became the full slave of his buyer until the buyer's death, whereupon he had to be manumitted – and presumably put back on the tax rolls. Buyers tried to get around this by setting up multiple purchasers of the same person – for example, a man and his four sons. The hope was that at least one of the owners would outlive the slave and get to exploit the children for awhile, if there were any. The state, however, adamantly insisted that there could be only one buyer.

In the 1620s the state meddled in the institution of limited-service contract slavery some more. The state specified that 2 rubles had to be paid for each slave. In the 1630s this was raised to 3 rubles. Typically the Muscovite state did not intervene in the market and did not set prices, but this was an exception. Before then prices had been agreed upon between the buyer and the person selling himself into slavery. As one would expect, the state's meddling in the market grossly distorted it, for some people desiring to sell themselves were "worth" 2 (or 3) rubles, and others were not. This meant, for example, that a man, wife, and three children in the 1640s could no longer find buyers, because no one would pay 15 rubles for them.

In the Muscovite period after 1500 further opportunities opened up for slaves. The creation of the middle-service class cavalry after the annexation of Novgorod has been mentioned. The cavalrymen wanted to bring at least one body servant to the front with them to wait on them and to guard the baggage train. Then in 1556 the government decreed that all lay-held and owned land had to render service at the rate of one cavalryman per 100 *cheti* (around 250 acres) of cultivated land he held or owned. The serviceman was only one person and could not be split, so he had to get someone to meet the service requirements (or lose his land). The solution was to buy combat slaves, who accompanied their owners on horseback and were in every way combat carbon copies of their owners except that their body armor was usually less expensive. Ordinary slaves at the time cost a ruble or two, but combat slaves were as much as 15 rubles. After 1556 the military muster records list the slave cavalrymen who accompanied their owners to the front; they were in addition to the body servants who waited on their owners and protected the baggage train.

Slaves were used in other spheres as well. As Muscovy expanded in the fourteenth and fifteenth centuries, so did its government. Upper-service class cavalrymen ran the government in the provinces and often had slaves assisting them. Court cases are extant in which a slave tried the case for his owner, and the litigants were slaves representing their owners. Elite merchants also employed slaves, and sent them on their own all over Muscovy on trading missions. Owners of larger lay estates, all of whom after 1556 were cavalrymen and thus in the combat zones during much of the agricultural season, had slaves who managed their estates. All of these uses of elite slaves were not unique to Russia.

Russia experienced the Time of Troubles between 1584 and 1618 – the dates vary among historians. Two of the major uprisings against the government of the time were led by combat slaves, those of Khlopko (1601–3) and Bolotnikov (1606–7). As might well be imagined, this dramatically cooled the enthusiasm for the training and employment of slaves as combat personnel, and after 1613 slaves in combat zones were ordinarily relegated to their historical roles as body servants and guards of the baggage train.

Throughout Russian history slavery was primarily a male-dominated institution. The sex ratio was typically two males for every female. This was typical for slavery in many countries. In cases where females predominated, they were used for lineage expansion and exploited as sex objects, neither of which was a major function of slavery in Muscovy.

As will be shown below, beginning in the 1590s, Russian peasants were converted into serfs who after 1700 took on an increasing slavelike coloration. While Russia remained a labor-short country, serfdom's functions gradually replaced those of slavery, both for the owners and for the owned. Foreign military captives were still enslaved, but, as the polities of Eastern Europe became more organized, one of the features of peace treaties increasingly became the release of foreign military slave captives held in Muscovy. Slavery was so important in Muscovy that it was one of the very few countries on record that had a special central government bureau, the Slavery Chancellery, to record and manage the institution. When the Law Code of 1649 (the *Sobornoe Ulozhenie*) was compiled, slavery was so important that more articles of the code (119 of 962) were included in the special slavery chapter (20 out of 25 chapters) than on any other single topic except the judicial process. Perhaps slavery peaked in importance about that time, but it might be possible to argue that the peak was during the Time of Troubles. In any case, from 5 to 15 percent of the total population was enslaved at that time.

As mentioned earlier, slaves typically paid no taxes, whereas serfs always did. Russia is a poor country, and the government was always seeking additional sources of revenue. A census was taken in 1678, and the count revealed that there were significantly fewer serfs and more slaves than anticipated. It was obvious to the government that many peasants had colluded with their owners to cheat the tax collectors by claiming to be slaves. As a result, in 1679 the government decreed that all slaves engaged in agriculture were to be listed as taxpayers. This effectively abolished the institution of agricultural slavery.

Most slaves worked in their owners' households, and this form of slavery was not touched. But during the reign of Peter the Great another census was taken in 1719. The number of peasants/serfs was less than anticipated, whereas the number of household slaves was higher than expected. The government believed that vast numbers of farming peasants had colluded with their masters to convert themselves into household slaves. The government was not to be outsmarted, and so it put the household slaves on the tax rolls as well in 1724.

This was facilitated by a major alteration in the tax system. Through most of the 1670s agriculture had been taxed on the basis of sown area. The natural peasant response was to reduce the sown area. In the 1678 census, the government changed the basis of taxation to the household. Until that time the nuclear household had been the basic Russian family structure: father, mother, children. The mean household size (m.h.s.) was about 4. In an attempt to outwit the tax collectors after the introduction of the household tax, the peasants created the extended family household and the m.h.s. went up to 10 as surviving grandparents, male children and wives, and their children crowded into one house. Solitaries disappeared, for no single person could possibly meet the tax bill. When Peter was confronted with the results of the 1719 census, he decided to abolish the system of household taxation. In its stead he introduced the notorious poll/"soul" tax, which remained the basis of Russian taxation until 1887. A correct comprehension of the soul tax is needed to understand much of Russian history between 1719 and 1887. It was assumed that all males had souls, so every male (from the baby born one minute ago to the geriatric about to die) was counted when the census taker came around. All the males in a community (a village, for example) had to come up with the total tax burden levied on the community on the basis of males. Coming up with the tax bill became the major function of the peasant commune by the end of the eighteenth century. The initial sum was 70 kopeks, and the sum depended on the government's needs: dividing the budgetary need by the number of souls yielded the tax per soul. The tax burden was collective, so that in reality infants and geriatrics unable to work paid nothing, and each able-bodied male paid about 1.40 rubles. Censuses (called "revisions") were taken about every ten years, and the correct assumption was that, as the demographic pyramid continued to operate, the burden on each able-bodied male remained the same, as the youth became able to produce, and the producers aged and then died off.

Under this taxation regime, it was just as easy to count household males (assumed to be consumption goods who produced nothing on which taxes could be levied) as it was the males in agriculture and other forms of production. Consequently household slaves became house serfs (about 4 percent of the population) and were taxed along with everyone else. Slaves are occasionally mentioned in the 1720s, but slavery was *de facto* abolished by the change in the tax system and the government insistence on collecting taxes on all males.

There was no serfdom in Kievan Rus' The population density was too low and the government and its enforcement mechanisms too weak. This remained the case on the East European plain until the middle of the fifteenth century. Muscovy's first civil war, 1425–53, caused endless chaos and population disruption. As a result of the Black Death in the mid-fourteenth century, monasteries had moved out of the cities and set up operations in the countryside. Agricultural production became a major monastic business, and peasants were lured to monastic estates by tax exemptions. The peasants calculated that their rent burden on the monastery estates was lower than the tax burden if they remained independent farmers, so a number of them opted to migrate to monastery properties. The civil war disrupted those monastery economies. Trying to salvage the situation, a few monasteries in the 1450s petitioned the government to forbid their peasant debtors to move at any time of year except around St George's Day (November 26). This did not violate Russian law or custom exceptionally, because a debtor was not considered a full free human being thanks to the fact that he owed his creditor something. Debtors who defaulted could be converted into slaves. The assumption about peasant debtors, most of whom had borrowed money to tide them over until the next harvest (and may have been lured to monastery estates by the offer of such crop loans), was that they might be trying to avoid repayment if they moved at any time other than St. George's Day, when the crops were harvested and threshed and the ground was slightly frozen – the best time of the year to move in Russia. St George's Day in the pre-Christian, pagan calendar was the end of the agricultural year, something akin to the American Thanksgiving. The government granted these requests, presumably for support in the civil war. Very few monasteries were involved and only a very small fraction of the peasantry were concerned by the beginnings of what was to become the social and economic horror of Russian serfdom.

For reasons that have never been understood, the Law Code (*Sudebnik*) of 1497 applied the St George's Day moving restrictions to all peasants. This was a major step in the enserfment process, for it meant that the state declared that it had the right to limit the geographic mobility of nearly all free people. Henceforth peasants could move only during the period of a week before and a week after November 26. It has been alleged that this was a response after the annexation of Novgorod in 1478 to the creation of the middle-service class provincial cavalry beginning around 1480, but that makes little sense to me. There is no evidence that the cavalry had become of any significant size or had acquired any perceptible political influence between 1480 and 1497, and it is difficult to perceive how limiting the peasants' right to move to those two weeks of the year enhanced the new cavalrymen's ability to render service. It is more likely that the fact that the *Sudebnik* was a copycat move: other polities, such as Pskov, were limiting the right of all peasants to move (St Phillip's Fast Day, September 22), the Polish peasants were enserfed, and so the Muscovites probably just decided that they should have such a limitation as well.

The main point is that, except as a horrible precedent, the universalization of the St George's Day moving restriction for all peasants seems to have made no difference to anyone. At least for Muscovy, the economic times were as good between 1497 and 1558 as they ever got, so there seems to have been no shortage of labor of the type that would have given (or did give) rise to demands for mobility restriction. More importantly, there is no expression of peasant protest on record against the loss of one of their basic freedoms. There are no records of court cases of landlords suing for the return of peasants who moved when it was not the St George's Day period. In fact, peasants seem to have moved whenever they wanted, regardless of the law. One assumes that this was possible because times were relatively good and the competition for labor relatively minimal. The 1497 restriction was repeated in the 1550 *Sudebnik*, with an addition that recognized the good times Muscovy had been having: the three-field system of agriculture was introduced, which indicates that the extensive slash–burn agricultural system was no longer universally used. The *Sudebnik* gave the peasants who had planted their autumn fields the right to return after the crop came up and matured the following year to harvest the fruits of their labor. Another sign that the repeal of the right to move on St George's Day was rather trivial in the life of the peasants was the fact that, after the enserfment had been completed, the peasants referred to a restoration of St George's Day as the restoration of freedom.

The mature Ivan IV Groznyi radically altered these conditions. His quarter-century-long Livonian War (1558–83) sapped Muscovy's strength and the taxpaying peasantry's resources. This was topped off by Ivan's insane Oprichnina (1565–72), a paranoid debauch in which the tsar split the country into two parts, the Oprichnina (his part) and the Zemshchina (for the rest of the country), to save him from imaginary persecutors who wanted to remove him. The Oprichnina had its own army, the oprichniki (which entered the Russian language as a synonym for official persecutor-policemen), who lived off the land. The model was the middle-service class provincial cavalry, but the oprichniki collected as much rent in one year as had formerly been collected in ten. No peasantry can tolerate this, so they deserted the core areas of Muscovy (especially around Moscow and Novgorod) and fled to the newly expanding frontiers: north of the Volga, heretofore inhabited primarily by Finnic peoples; to the newly annexed (1552–6) middle and lower Volga regions, inhabited by Turkic and other peoples, if inhabited at all, and from there into the Urals and Siberia; and to the area south of the Oka, the wild steppe, the prairie lands into which Muscovy was expanding that previously had been traversed only by looting nomads. This initiated the East Slavic colonization of what was becoming the Russian Empire, but the migration flows left many core regions of Muscovy 85 percent depopulated.

A true dilemma was created for the Muscovite government by these population movements. On the one hand, expansion-minded Muscovites wanted the north, the eastern Volga and trans-Volga regions, and the southern trans-Oka/steppe regions settled. Government officials recruited colonists into those areas. But, on the other hand, the middle-service class provincial cavalry, the basis of Muscovy's military strength, was settled on service lands in the Volga–Oka mesopotamia, which extended westward to Novgorod, Pskov, and Smolensk. A cavalryman needed to be in possession of lands farmed by at least five peasant households in order to survive. When those peasants became colonists in the new areas, their landholding cavalrymen from the center could no longer render military service.

In a move that was reminiscent of the situation involving a handful of monasteries owning estates and indebted peasants in the 1450s, in the 1570s and 1580s individual cavalrymen began to petition the government to forbid their peasants to move on St George's Day or at any other time. In other words, the government was requested to bind the peasants permanently to the land. The government found the requests compelling and granted them. Those individual grants were followed by a chorus demanding that all peasants be bound to the land. Mindful of the needs of the provincial cavalry, in 1592 the government repealed the right of all peasants to move on St George's Day – that is, bound them to the plots of land on which they were living. This edict was repeated a number of times in the next two decades, most notably in the 1610 treaty with Poland (the Rzeczpospolita) in which Wladyslaw was invited to become ruler of Muscovy in an attempt to put an end to the Time of Troubles. One of the paragraphs of the long document made special note of the fact that Russian peasants were enserfed and could not move.

With the repeal of the right of peasants to move on St George's Day, the military "lobby" won on the basic issue of the Muscovite labor supply. But there were other "lobbies" that were unwilling to surrender on the issue. The imperial, colonizing "lobby" has been mentioned. The other, major "lobby" was that of the large landowners, members of the upper-service class (mostly cavalrymen) and the monasteries. When peasants moved within the Volga–Oka mesopotamia, they tended to migrate from the small landholdings assigned to members of the middle-service class provincial cavalry to the large hereditary estates of the monasteries and members of the upper-service class elite, because rents were lower on the large estates and higher on the smaller service landholdings.

As a result of what appears to have been a compromise, the 1592 repeal of St George's Day was not a complete triumph for the military lobby. Simultaneously the government imposed a five-year statute of limitations on the initiation of court suits for the recovery of fugitive serfs. There was no statute of limitations on the initiation of suits for fugitive slaves, for example, and one might have expected the situation to be the same for fugitive serfs- – as indeed it was between the 1450s and 1592. Muscovite law knew other statutes of limitations, and one might assume that the 1592 statute on initiating suits to recover fugitive serfs was just part of the process of cleaning up or streamlining the judicial system, which otherwise would become clogged if cases about old grievances could be initiated forever. The subsequent history of the issue indicates otherwise, however, and points to a "compromise" in which the provincial cavalrymen achieved the repeal of St George's Day, and the large estate owners and imperial expansionists limited its effectiveness by imposing the statute of limitations.

Once one understands how the system worked, it is apparent why 1592 was a "compromise." The Agapetos state had almost unlimited pretensions, which was one of the reasons why foreigners called it a "tyranny." But, on the other hand, governmental personnel were few (far fewer comparatively than in Western Europe at the time, where the appetite of governments for funds was responsible for the "seventeenth-century crisis"). Efficiency has never been the hallmark of the Russian state, which by its own admission has always been "backward," and there were many areas that the government simply ignored. The issue of fugitive slaves was one such area. While Muscovy was the only country in the world that had a separate, specialized central bureau that dealt with slavery matters (particularly their sale and registration), the Slavery Chancellery did not get involved in the pursuit of fugitive slaves. The same policy was applied to fugitive serfs. This meant that the legal possessor of a fugitive serf had to find the peasant himself and then file suit to have him returned to where he belonged. Doing this in a gigantic country, such as the expanding Russian Empire, was like looking for a needle in a haystack. The problem was compounded when frontier officials welcomed the fugitive serf-colonists and when large estate owners concealed fugitive serfs on their estates and moved them from one estate to another until the statute of limitations expired.

The centrality of the statute of limitations becomes evident when we note that the history of serfdom between 1592 and 1649 involves that issue. Between 1566 and the early 1650s Muscovy created and lived with a proto-parliamentary, two-chambered institution known at the Assembly of the Land (*Zemskii sobor*), which gave the appearance that some form of civil society that might limit the autocracy was developing. The provincial middle-service class cavalry was a major segment of that developing civil society as well as a major component (along with the townsmen) of the lower house of the Assembly of the Land. In 1637, 1641, and 1645 the middle-service class submitted petitions to the government demanding the abolition of the statute of limitations on the filing of suits for the recovery of fugitive serfs. In response, in 1637 the government lengthened the five years to nine; in 1641, the nine years were extended to fifteen; and in 1645 the government promised to abolish the limitation entirely once a census had been taken. The census was taken in 1646–7, but the limitation was not abolished. In June 1648 there were riots against the government in Moscow and a dozen other towns. One of the rioters' demands was that a new law code be compiled to help to put an end to central governmental corruption. The government appointed a commission headed by N. I. Odoevskii to compile the law and convoked an Assembly of the Land to discuss and approve it. The provincial cavalry delegates to the Assembly of the Land demanded that the 1645 promise be kept. The weakened government was in no position to refuse, and so the Odoevskii Commission compiled chapter 11 of the new law code (the *Sobornoe ulozhenie*) on the peasants. Articles 1 and 2 of chapter 11 repealed the statute of limitations on the filing of suits for the recovery of fugitive serfs. The middle-service class triumphed.

Chapter 11 contains 34 articles. It remained the basis of serfdom until the end of the institution. Fugitives remained a fundamental issue. Ivan's machinations and the Time of Troubles, plus the open frontiers, had reintroduced the issue of labor shortage, which remained until the demographic transition (a fall in the mortality rate while the birth rate remained at natural levels) was well under way in the 1870s and 1880s. This meant that landlords and frontier officials were always willing to receive fugitive serfs. The *Ulozhenie*'s solution was to force the recipient/harborer of the fugitive(s) to surrender them to their rightful lord. This became complicated when marriages and offspring were involved. The Russian Orthodox Church insisted that marriage was inviolable. So, if a lord received a fugitive of either sex who married one of his serfs of either sex, the recipient had to surrender the couple to the rightful possessor of the fugitive. In cases where a marriage of fugitives occurred on "neutral" territory (such as on the frontier), the claimants cast lots; the winner got the couple, and he had to pay the loser for the loss of his serf. For unintelligible reasons, the Russian Orthodox Church did not regard the family as inviolable. Thus, if a fugitive wed another serf and they had children, the receiving lord had to surrender the couple to the fugitive's lord but got to keep the offspring. In addition to chapter 11, at the time of the *Ulozhenie* the government made another huge concession to the middle-service class. It initiated massive dragnet searches for fugitive serfs (and slaves) in violation of tradition. Thousands of fugitives were identified and returned to where they belonged.

In the eighteenth century a major distinction arose between "seignorial serfs" and "state peasants." That distinction did not exist in the *Ulozhenie*, which mentioned only the difference between serfs living on land belonging to private lords, serfs living on land belonging to church institutions, serfs living on land belonging to the state, and finally "taxable" peasants living on land belonging to no one. The first two later became seignorial serfs, the latter two state peasants. The crucial difference was that the first category had human landlords, the second had the state as a landlord.

That distinction first became significant during Ivan the Terrible's Oprichnina. Prior to 1565, when land and the peasants living on it were assigned to a cavalryman, the requirement was that the peasant had to pay the lord the traditional rent. But during the Oprichnina, the obedience formula was changed so that the peasant "had to obey his landlord in everything." This opened the door to the capricious establishment of rents and the massive flight of the peasantry mentioned earlier. It also opened the door to landlord control of the peasant and the ultimate conversion of the serf into a near-slave. The *Ulozhenie* of 1649 made another step in this direction when it permitted landowners to move peasants from one estate to another, essentially without their consent. This did not apply to provincial cavalrymen-landholders, who had to leave the serfs as fixtures on the land where they were when the land was allotted, so that the next servicemen could expect the same rent as their predecessors had got.

The *Ulozhenie* of 1649 finalized the enserfment, as it completed the legal stratification of society in general. (Chapter 19 bound the townsmen to their towns, much as the peasants were bound to the land.) But one might ask whether this was inevitable had the June 1648 urban riots not occurred, had the Assembly of the Land not been convoked, and had the new law code not been promulgated on January 29, 1649. Counterfactual history is an oxymoron, but a couple of major trends are worth considering. The first involves military history. The peasants were enserfed to satisfy the insistent demands of the provincial cavalry, which was based primarily on pre-gunpowder technology: bows and arrows and sabres. They also carried pistols, but the government knew that the traditional Muscovite cavalry was obsolete. Half of the Muscovite army that fought at Smolensk (1632–4) were members of so-called new formation regiments recruited from abroad because the government knew that its traditional cavalry was not up to the requirements of contemporary warfare. After the Smolensk War, which Muscovy largely lost, the new formation regiments were discharged because they were too expensive. But on the eve of the *Ulozhenie* the government began to prepare for another war with the Rzeczpospolita to recapture Smolensk. This war (the Thirteen Years War, 1654–67) witnessed the capture of much of the old Muscovite cavalry and its general replacement by new formation regiments, both cavalry and infantry, both imported mercenaries and trained Russians. A dozen years after the *Ulozhenie* the middle-service class was no longer the powerful pressure group that had engineered the enserfment. Considering the fact that the large landowners and the frontier imperial lobby still wanted a mobile peasantry, in the 1660s would the peasants have been enserfed had it not been for events in 1648–9?

Secondly, the arts in the seventeenth century witnessed what has been termed "individualization." Before that time, few creators signed their works, and works were about rulers and the elite, not "everyman." Enserfment denied the individuality of the peasants and converted them into rent-paying cash machines for the cavalrymen. The pace of elite individualization increased during the Thirteen Years War, as the more Western-oriented regions of Belarus and Ukraine were annexed and their cultural orientation overwhelmed that of Muscovy, especially after Patriarch Nikon had suppressed much of Muscovite culture in the years 1654–8 because it was insufficiently Byzantine. Individualization laid the groundwork for the later opposition to serfdom as members of the elite realized that their free status was incompatible with the slavelike condition of the seignorial peasantry.

The *Ulozhenie* defined Russian society for the next couple of centuries. After 1649 fugitives remained a major issue, and there proved to be insufficient disincentives for landholders/owners to receive them because of the continuing labor shortage. The government tried to come up with a remedy, which initially involved confiscating one of the guilty lord's peasants for each fugitive serf he was harboring. This was ineffective, so the penalty was raised to two for each fugitive. This had little impact, so the government raised the penalty to four, whereupon landlords drove out harbored fugitives en masse. When Peter came to the throne, he decided that the sanctions for receiving fugitives were insufficient and decreed the death penalty for anyone who received a fugitive serf. It is unknown whether the death penalty was ever carried out for this crime.

Peter's reign witnessed a number of events degrading the status of the peasantry. In 1700 both slaves and serfs were freed when enlisting in the army, which equated serfs with slaves. In 1704 church and monastery peasants were forbidden to sign contracts without permission. The ability to sign a contract has always been the mark of a free person.

The major event on the serfdom scene during Peter's reign was the 1724 juridical conversion of all the tax-exempt household slaves into taxpaying house serfs. Also important was the conversion in 1714 of service landholdings into hereditary estates. These events gave the lords more control over the persons of their serfs and advanced the march to proto-slavery. Yet another important step in that direction was Peter's holding lords responsible for the serfs' payment of their taxes. As a result, serf assets came to be at the disposal of their lords as the lords struggled to come up with the poll/soul taxes owed by their peasants.

Peter aimed for military self-sufficiency as a result of the Northern War with Sweden (1700–21). This necessitated moving outside the Volga–Oka mesopotamia, which is almost totally devoid of useful natural resources, into the Urals, where a flourishing metallurgical industry was established. The problem was providing that industry with labor, as the *Ulozhenie* had bound most of the population to where it was situated. To "solve" that problem, in 1721 Peter allowed factory owners to buy serfs – another big step on the road to slavery.

To reinforce the *Ulozhenie* strictures against peasant movement, in 1722 Peter required peasants to have passports to travel, which made it easier to identify fugitive serfs.

The *Ulozhenie* considered all peasants, with and without personal lords, to be serfs, bound to the land and unable to move anywhere else. There may have been some concealed sales of serfs by private lords, with and without land, in the second half of the seventeenth century, but this has never been proved and if there were any, they were few. But the developments of the Petrine era and subsequently made the differences between privately held/owned and other serfs enormous. This became especially important after much of the land belonging to the Church was confiscated by the state, and the serfs living on those lands ceased having personal masters. Ultimately this led to the peasantry being divided into two categories, seignorial serfs and state peasants. The major distinction was that the former had masters, the latter did not. Ultimately, the state peasants demographically multiplied much more rapidly than did the seignorial serfs for reasons that are not understood- – other than the broad generalization that animals in captivity and slaves generally do not multiply, rarely reproduce themselves. There are, of course, major historical exceptions, but Russian serfdom seems to support that generalization.

The story of the rest of the eighteenth century was the further descent of the serfs into slavery. First, there is evidence that serfs were being sold. In 1734 lords were obligated to feed serfs during famines. Such an edict was decreed by Boris Godunov for slaves at the beginning of the seventeenth century and was extended to serfs with the statement that peasants were their owners' chattel. Then in 1760 lords were permitted to banish serfs to Siberia and they got military recruit credits for such serfs. This reinforced serf owners' control over their peasants, and helped to guarantee order in the central parts of the Russian Empire, while simultaneously facilitating the colonization of the land beyond the Urals. A law of 1767 forbade serfs to complain against their masters. In 1775 owners were forbidden to expel aged serfs, which indicated that this abuse had been sufficiently frequent to catch the attention of legislators. Until the removal of the serfdom safety net in 1861, few peasants starved to death, thanks to the laws of 1734 and 1775, plus Paul's orders of the 1790s establishing granaries to feed hungry serfs. Thus it came as a great surprise when a million peasants who no longer had masters to care for them starved to death in 1891 and then died in the ensuing cholera epidemic.

Contributing to the misery of the serfs was the elevation of the status of their owners. In 1762 Peter III abolished the service requirement for landowners that had been instituted in 1556. The serfs believed that their emancipation was a logical consequence, but nothing happened. This helped precipitate the massive Pugachev uprising (1773–4) that encompassed much of the Russian state. That, plus the increasing Westernization of the Russian intelligentsia, led many to believe that serfdom was a wrong that should be abolished. A first important book on this theme was Aleksandr Radishchev's *Journey from Petersburg to Moscow* (1790), which detailed many of the abuses of contemporary serfdom, such as forced marriages, that attempted to maximize population growth. As a result of the extended family created by the household tax of 1679 and the control over the serfs granted by Peter the Great, it was hard to find orphans among the serf population, as the approximately 20 percent of the children without living parents were just assigned to live with other peasants, while single males and females were married off by their owners as soon as possible. All of this may be seen as part of the "serf safety net."

As owners gained increasing control over their peasants and as serfs were freed from service so that they could supervise their own estates, profit-maximizing lords in the Black Soil (southern Russia, Ukraine) regions began to take control over all their land and instituted corvée requirements to force their peasants to farm it. Farming in those regions began to look like slavery in the sugar islands of the Caribbean. As agriculture was relatively poor in the non-Black Soil regions, corvée did not develop there, and lords were more interested in collecting cash rent – which quite frequently had to be derived from non-agricultural work, such as working in the developing towns, in the transportation network, or in the metallurgical and other factories. The abuses of serfdom became so grotesque that Emperor Paul in 1797 forbade corvée labor on Sunday and said that lords could work their peasants only three days of the week.

The year 1796 is regarded as the zenith of serfdom. Every development after that date was directed toward abolition of the institution. After Radishchev's *Journey*, the intelligentsia took up the abolition of serfdom as its cause (along with the abolition of its twin pillar, autocracy). N. M. Karamzin, the creator of the "twin pillar" metaphor in 1811, agreed that something had to be done about both institutions, but said that disturbing either pillar would cause the edifice of the Russian Empire to topple. Emperor Nicholas I, permanently disturbed by the Decembrist uprising that greeted his accession to the throne, throughout his reign (1825–55) wanted to do something about serfdom and appointed nine commissions to study the issue. But he did nothing more.

It took defeat in the Crimean War (1854–5) to convince the government that Russia was backward, that reforms needed to be undertaken, and that serfdom was a priority issue. Emperor Alexander II, noting mounting peasant disturbances, said it was "better to reform serfdom from above than below" – that is, in response to peasant rebellions. There were many issues involved with the abolition of serfdom, but the primary ones were land and finance. On how much land would the freedmen get, how much would the lords retain, was the crux. On compensation, the lords regarded the serfs as assets who could be mortgaged and sold, and the government feared that just freeing the serfs outright would be a lawless expropriation. The problem was that the government had been bankrupted by the Crimean War. Alexander appointed the Nazimov commission to go to Germany to study the emancipation there. It reported back that a landless emancipation was impossible.

The work of Nicholas's nine commissions was brought to bear, and the "Emancipation" of 1861 ended as follows: the seignorial serfs got most of the land, but their owners got to choose what they wanted, usually the pastures and woodlots that the serfs had customarily used free but now had to pay for. The serfs had to pay for the land they got, and probably more than it was worth. Evaluating the land was almost impossible, because there had been almost no market, so calculations were based on rent. This meant that the peasants had not only to pay for the land, but also to buy their own freedom. Payments were to extend for forty-nine years at 5.5 percent interest. Fearing an uncontrolled peasantry in an undergoverned countryside without landlord control, the government turned control over the peasantry to the peasant commune, to which the peasants were bound, primarily to force payment of the redemption fees and to limit rapid urbanization. Essentially, the peasants remained enserfed: landlord (the slave element of later serfdom) control was gone, but the peasants were bound to the land, as they had been in 1592, 1649, and up into the eighteenth century. The state peasants were emancipated separately in 1863.

When the peasants and the intelligentsia learned the terms of the "Emancipation," they were enraged. Peasant disturbances occurred, and the intelligentsia turned into populist revolutionaries trying to undo the injustices of 1861. The autocratic state proved too strong until the Revolution of 1905. On November 3, 1905, the government abolished the redemption payments, and on November 9, 1906, the repartitional commune was broken up, peasants were allowed to separate from the commune, and the peasants were allowed to move freely for the first time since 1497.

That freedom was not to last long. The Soviets between the 1920s and 1953 developed a vast system of concentration camps (GULag) that exploited hundreds of thousands of slave laborers as part of the state plan. Moreover, the Soviets called upon the serfdom experience when they collectivized agriculture beginning in 1929. Not accidentally, the peasants called collectivization "the second enserfment." Soviet agriculturalists were granted passports only in 1957, thus putting an end to half a millennium of serfdom on the East European Plain.

References

Blum, Jerome (1961). *Lord and Peasant in Russia from the Ninth to the Nineteenth Century.* Princeton University Press, Princeton.

Field, Daniel (1976). *The End of Serfdom: Nobility and Bureaucracy in Russia, 1855–1861.* Harvard University Press, Cambridge, MA.

Hellie, Richard (1971). *Enserfment and Military Change in Muscovy.* University of Chicago Press, Chicago.

Hellie, Richard (1983). "Women in Muscovite Slavery," *Russian History*, 10/2: 213–29.

Hellie, Richard (1989). "The Manumission of Russian Slaves," *Slavery and Abolition*, 10/3 (Dec.), 23–39.

Hellie, Richard (1990). "Early Modern Russian Law: Commentary on Chapter 11 (The Judicial Process for Peasants)," *Russian History*, 17/3: 305–39.

Hellie, Richard (1995). "The Great Paradox of the Seventeenth Century: The Stratification of Muscovite Society and the 'Individualization' of its High Culture, Especially Literature," in Simon Karlinsky et al., eds., *O Rus! Studia Litteraria Slavica in Honorem Hugh McLean*. Berkeley Slavic Specialties, Berkeley, 116–28.

Hellie, Richard (1998). *Kholopstvo v Rossii 1450–1725*. Academia, Moscow.

Hellie, Richard (1999). *The Economy and Material Culture of Russia 1600–1725*. University of Chicago Press, Chicago.

Hellie, Richard (2002). "Migration in Early Modern Russia, 1480s–1780s," in David Eltis, ed., *Free and Coerced Migration: Cultural and Economic Determinants and Consequences*, Stanford University Press, Stanford, CA, 292–323, 418–24.

Hellie, Richard (2004). "Interpreting Violence in Late Muscovy from the Perspectives of Modern Neuroscience," in Janusz Duzinkiewicz et al., eds., *States, Societies, Cultures East and West: Essays in Honor of Jaroslaw Pelenski*. Ross Publishing, New York, 295–315.

Hellie, Richard (2006). "Reflections on Muscovite Society in the Second Half of the Fifteenth Century," *Schriften zur Geistesgeschichte des ostlichen Europas*, 30 (Summer), 157–62.

Hoch, Steven L. (1986). *Serfdom and Social Control in Russia*. University of Chicago Press, Chicago.

Macey, David A. J. (1987). *Government and Peasant in Russia, 1861–1906*. Northern Illinois University Press, DeKalb, IL.

Moon, David (2001). *The Abolition of Serfdom in Russia, 1762–1907*, Longman, Harlow.

Pollard, Alan P. (2003). *The Laws on the Russian Peasant Emancipation 19 February 1861*. Charles Schlacks Publisher, Idyllwild, CA.

Swianiewicz, Stanislaw (1965). *Forced Labour and Economic Development*. Oxford University Press, London and Oxford.

Further Reading

Hellie, Richard (1967, 1970). *Muscovite Society*. University of Chicago, Syllabus Division. Contains translations of the major documents on the development of slavery and serfdom in the Muscovite period.

Hellie, Richard (1979). "Muscovite Slavery in Comparative Perspective," *Russian History*, 6/2: 119–75.

Hellie, Richard (1982). *Slavery in Russia, 1450–1725*. University of Chicago Press, Chicago.

Hellie, Richard (1988). *The Ulozhenie (Law Code) of 1649* [translation]. Charles Schlacks Publisher, Irvine, CA.

Hellie, Richard (1989–90). "Patterns of Instability in Russian and Soviet History," *Chicago Review of International Affairs*, 1/3 (Autumn 1989), 3–34; 2/1 (Winter 1990), 15–40.

Hellie, Richard (1992). "Russian Law from Oleg to Peter the Great," in Daniel H. Kaiser (trans. and ed.), *The Laws of Rus'. Tenth to Fifteenth Centuries*. Charles Schlacks Publisher, Salt Lake City, UT, pp. xi–xl.

Kahan, Arcadius (1985). *The Plow, the Hammer, and the Knout: Essays in Eighteenth-Century Russian Economic History*. University of Chicago Press, Chicago.

Robinson, Geroid Tanquary (1967). *Rural Russia under the Old Regime: A History of the Landlord–Peasant World and a Prologue to the Peasant Revolution of 1917*. University of California Press, Berkeley.

CHAPTER EIGHT

Russian Art from the Middle Ages to Modernism

ILIA A. DORONTCHENKOV
(translated by Abbott Gleason)

The history of art in Russia may be said with confidence to have begun with the introduction of Christianity to Rus' in 988. The new era brought religious liturgy with it, which meant architecture, painting, music, and the culture of the book – in the form of illuminated manuscripts. The acceptance of Christianity from Byzantium was occasioned by pragmatic considerations. But the chronicle legend about how Prince Vladimir chose between diverse faiths is nevertheless significant, pointing as it does to the "aesthetic" motive in the decision of Vladimir's messengers. Finding themselves in an Orthodox Church, they allegedly "knew not whether [they] were in heaven or on earth." It was not, evidently, merely a matter of the barbarian simple-heartedness of the Kievans, overcome by the magnificence of Hagia Sophia. The story suggests a particular role for art: the image of beauty that attests the fundamental benevolence of God's world. With only slight exaggeration one might say that art in Russia has preserved this role ever since, even with the loss of religious viewpoint in the eighteenth century. It has continued to be the measure, the standard, rendering powerful judgments on life. The icon was the divine model, the form of a better world. In modern times, art undertook to provide utopias, such as the "New Rome," in Bazhenov's abortive Kremlin Palace; or the romantic Christianity of Alexander Ivanov; or the moral maximalism demonstrated quite differently by the populism of the "Wanderers" (*Peredvizhniki*) in the nineteenth century and the social engineering of the Constructivists in the twentieth.[1]

Kiev Rus' found itself in the political space of Constantinople, and neither any Western state nor Papal Rome could seriously compete. But it is no less important that Rus' took its belief, and its culture, from what was at the time the only European civilization in the full sense of the term. Byzantium was the heir not only of Roman but of Greek culture;[2] Constantinople, the remaining cultural hegemon of Europe, whose radiance nothing could extinguish, naturally drew Kiev, Novgorod, and Vladimir into its orbit.[3] In this sense, Russian art was from the very beginning European. Its autonomy took shape gradually, under the influence of the Mongol invasion and the fall of Byzantium, which turned Moscow into the only remaining

Orthodox polity. At the same time, the West abandoned the medieval understanding of the image for the artistic direction indicated by Giotto.[4]

The first stone temple of Kiev was the Church of Our Lady [Bogoroditsy] (sometimes called the "Church of the Tithe," 990–996), for the building and decoration of which a Byzantine master was sent for. The most ancient stone structure that has been preserved in Rus' is the Spaso-Preobrazhenskii Church (Church of the Transfiguration) in Chernigov, the building of which began a few years before the death of Prince Mstislav in 1036. Already deviations may be seen here from the Byzantine model: closely spaced domes; high gables; a pronounced tendency toward the vertical.

The predominant type of religious structure was already defined in the first churches of the Kievan state, derived from Byzantine models toward the end of the ninth century. Otto Demus has justly compared this exceptionally stable structure – ideally answering to liturgical needs – to the achieved form of the violin. Unlike the basilica churches of the West, the architecture of the cruciform-domed churches embodies the idea of equilibrium. Its space does not draw the visitor in, but situates him in an imagined sphere, above which soar the vaulting and dome. The structure both in its entirety and in its constituent parts makes up a symbolic commentary; the temple becomes an image of the cosmos and embodies the dogmas of belief, not only through decorative elements – the frescoes and icons – but through the body itself (the symbolism of the columns, the vaulting, the domes, the entrance, and so on).

In 1037 Yaroslav the Wise laid the cornerstone in Kiev of the Church of Santa Sofia, not having direct analogies in Byzantine architecture. Its enormous dimensions (five naves), together with its brick masonry, demanded a substantial number of domes for illumination and gave rise to its harmonious if complex inner space. Greek masters created the mosaics for the altar and the domes. Unlike the churches of Constantinople, here the mosaics (the apse, crossing, and dome) and frescoes were considered within the context of a single building. The paintings in the central nave, depicting the family of Yaroslav, were remarkable, as were the hunting scenes on the stairs of the tower (the tower was probably painted during the reign of Vladimir Monomakh in the first quarter of the twelfth century).[5]

Between 1045 and 1052, Santa Sophia in Novgorod was built, differing essentially in its spirit from the picturesque Kievan church, so freely adapted to the space it occupied. The compact domes and the flat walls are reminiscent of contemporary West European architecture. But the similarity with Romanesque churches is not a matter of direct influence, but has to do with the particularities of the vaulting and masonry – stone, not brick, as in the southern regions of Rus'.[6] Constructed in the following years by princely order, the Novgorod churches have preserved a severe appearance; however, the step-by-step disposition of the mass has been replaced by a vaulted roof supported by receding hierarchies of arched gables – a characteristic design for the upper parts of Russian churches; thus the inner space of the church takes on a greater wholeness.

The monumental painting of Kiev developed to a significant degree under the influence of Byzantium. Its grandest complexes were executed by invited masters, as in the case of the figures in the mosaics and frescoes of the St Michael of the Golden Domes Monastery, c. 1108–113. Evidently among the students of the artists who decorated the Assumption (Uspenskii) Church of the Monastery of the Caves in Kiev was Alimpii, the first Rus' artist known by name. The contemporary art of Novgorod was distinguished by a more definite palette, sharper contours, more static figures (the frescoes of the Antoniev Monastery) than the art of Kiev.

It is generally agreed that the painting of Kiev Rus' falls somewhat short of contemporary Byzantine images in psychological delicacy and refinement of form, but represents a directness and expressiveness characteristic of the art of neophytes. From about the middle of the twelfth century, the extent of the forms inherited from Constantinople began to change through flattening and ornamentation; this process was accompanied by the strengthening of narrativity. There was an increase in the number of saints and sacred events depicted.[7]

The churches constructed in the period of fragmentation were as a rule small, with a clear demarcation between the space under the dome and the altar. Novgorod churches of the second half of the twelfth century are distinguished by their concise shape and extreme simplicity of decoration. In this city, as in the other Rus' republic, Pskov, the clientele of the Church included not only princes and bishops, but a broader circle: mayors, merchant corporations, and ordinary parishioners.

The Vladimir princes, striving for the greater glory of their appanage, employed art and architecture more purposefully. The cult of the Mother of God became the fundamental ideology of Vladimir-Suzdal Rus'. The revered Byzantine icon known subsequently as the Vladimir Mother of God was brought from the environs of Kiev to the princely capital; over time it became the palladium of the Russian state. Architecture bore a clear-cut political message. The Church of the Assumption (*Uspenskii sobor*) in Vladimir demonstrated that city's inheritance of the position of Kiev, Chernigov, and Novgorod. For its construction, masters who may have designed churches at Speyer and Mainz were sent by Friedrich Barbarossa in 1160. Builders from among the Western Slavs also worked, in all likelihood, in Vladimir – perhaps from Poland or the Galician principality.[8] The architecture of Vladimir-Suzdal Rus' as a whole (the Church of the Intercession of the Virgin on the Nerl', 1165, the St Dmitrii Cathedral, 1190s) was distinguished by purity of form and harmonious unity with nature.[9] The building, the details of the façades (the perspective of the gates, the ascending rows of arched gables, the belts of small arches in the middle of the façade wall, the singular white stone reliefs carpeting the external flat walls), permit one to look at the architecture of Northeast Rus' in the broad context of European Romanesque architecture.

With the growth of towns at the beginning of the thirteenth century came a greater complexity of regional architectural schools. New centers formed; Smolensk, for example, led the way in stone structures. A new type of structure developed in the Dnieper region: churches emphasizing the vertical, in which the drum was supported by receding ranks of gables and half-gables.[10] This pronounced striving for verticality in a domed-cruciform church distinguishes Old Russian architecture from Byzantine.

The Mongol attack cut short the building of stone structures in the middle of the thirteenth century, even around Novgorod, which was spared the worst. Artels of stonemasons and fresco painters disintegrated, lowering the craft standard of painting. A simplified and expressive artistic language came to prevail, with the repetition of the iconographic schemes of the past. The understanding of forms by volume gave

Figure 8.1   The St Dmitrii Cathedral in Vladimir, Russia
Source: Iakov Filimonov/iStockphoto.com

way to the flat. Color became more intense. Novgorod icons, with their intense red
backgrounds, became exceptionally energetic and formally primitive.

In the last third of the thirteenth century, building in stone revived. At the same
time, Byzantine artifacts returned to Rus', while local schools of icon painting took
shape there, often characterized by particularistic styles and a laconic visual language.
During the Muscovite princely feuds of the 1430s and 1440s the painting of Tver'
continued to flourish. The most fruitful period of Novgorod's artistic development
was bound up with the multifarious commercial and cultural connections with
Northern Europe. Churches of no great size continued to be constructed in the city,
with various and dynamic internal spaces. By the middle of the fourteenth century,
masters from Byzantium and the Balkans were again executing frescoes in Novgorod.
The influence of the Paleologue dynasty could again be seen in a broad spectrum of
artistic phenomena. Visual language became more complex. Multi-figure compositions with complicated foreshortening, deep space, and coloristic reflection became
more widespread. An authoritative simplicity of forms evolved in the direction of
greater emotional variety, gradations of feeling. Among the significant monuments
of the period were the paintings in the Church of the Assumption on Volotovo Field,
created by Greek or Serbian masters in 1363.

At that time, Novgorod and Pskov were more open than other Russian lands to
cultural cooperation with foreigners. In the context of the unsettled spiritual life of

Figure 8.2   The Vladimir *Madonna*
Source: Andrei Rublev, "The Vladimir Madonna and Child", Russian Icon, Moscow School
c. 1370–1430, State Russian Museum, St Petersburg/The Bridgeman Art Library

Novgorod, living through the struggle with heresy, one of the most significant fresco
ensembles of old Rus' deserves particular attention – the paintings in the small Church
of the Transfiguration on Il'in Street, executed by Theophanes the Greek (*Feofan
Grek*) in 1378. This greatest of masters, enjoying the reputation of a "philosopher,"
worked in an expressive style that embodied that rare thing in Russian religious art –
an ardent spiritual asceticism. Feofan's manner was clearly an individual one, as was
his method of work – without a preparatory outline on the wall. Theofanes worked
in Moscow from the 1380s, but the end of the century in Novgorod yielded a series
of fresco ensembles, including the paintings of the Balkan masters in the Church of
the Transfiguration of Savior on Kovalev (1380).

   Under pressure from the increasingly powerful principality of Moscow in the fifteenth century, Novgorod used art and architecture to strengthen its position, through
retrospective invocation of its previous might. Thus, the iconic representation of *The
Battle between the Novgorodians and the Suzdalians* (*c.* 1450), depicting events from
the year 1170, provided a commentary on the contemporary struggle with Muscovite
expansion. In the second half of the fifteenth century, Novgorodian art began to lose
its monumental quality; icon painting began to exert an influence on frescoes.

In the fourteenth and fifteenth centuries, the active development of serfdom and the Church came to the fore in Pskov, where a particular type of religious structure developed: rather low, blending with the landscape or surrounding buildings. Pskov churches were distinguished by eight-sloped roofing, freestanding bell towers, numerous chapels (*pridely*), plastic modeling of the walls; these churches appear to have grown up like mushrooms after a rain, rather than embodying a structural plan. Icon painting of the Pskov school is characterized by a rather melancholy spirituality, stemming from severe and dramatic color effects.

When the Metropolitan seat moved from Vladimir to Moscow in 1325, it increased the influence of the new political center and strengthened the connections of northeast Rus' with Byzantium and the Balkans. Icon painting achieved its highest development in the art of Andrei Rublev, a monk of the Spaso-Andronikov Monastery in Moscow. He brought classical harmony, equilibrium, and spiritual depth to the icon. His masterpiece is the *Old Testament Trinity*, painted around 1411 for the Church of the Trinity in St Sergius Monastery near Moscow. It is the embodiment of the highest spiritual order, in which the physical and spiritual, concrete and abstract, are completely harmonious. In the words of Epiphanius the Wise, "through contemplation of the Holy Trinity the terrible fear of the discords of this world is vanquished." It may be said, however, that these words describe the desired effect – spiritual and psychological – of any icon. The "Trinity" symbolically – and graphically – exhibits the essence of the world, and for that reason has no need to create a visual illusion or an absorbing narrative. Unlike Renaissance art, Rublev's icon does not broaden our knowledge of external reality or appeal to our visual experience, but returns the suppliant to the revealed truth underlying the cosmos. The art of Rublev had a fruitful influence on contemporaries, imparting to the Moscow school for some time models of spirituality and balance, nobility of linear draughtsmanship, and harmony of color.

The number of icon painters in Rus' gradually increased, presumably influenced by the development of the iconostasis, which in the fourteenth and fifteenth centuries became the decorative and symbolic center of the Russian church building. It revealed the image of Heaven, timeless divine hierarchy and harmony, underlying God's world.[11] The low barrier of earlier times grew into a screen with at least three tiers, separating the altar, where the mysteries were consummated, from the remainder of the church, open to all the faithful. In the lowest ("local") row could be found the "royal doors" into the sanctuary, the icons of Christ, the mother of God, and images of the events or saints that had led to the naming of the church. Above were placed – and this could vary locally – the Deisus[12] and the Festival Row (*Prazdnichnyi chin*), depicting events from the lives of Jesus and Mary. Over time the iconostasis grew outward and upward, and by the seventeenth century one might find an additional two tiers, depicting the Prophets and Patriarchs.

In early fifteenth-century Moscow, an architectural school developed that based itself on the tradition of Vladimir. The growing power of the principality under Ivan III, after the period of princely feuding, stimulated construction. Between 1475 and 1479, the Bolognese Aristotle Fioravanti built the five-domed Church of the Assumption (*Uspenskii sobor*) in the Kremlin. The architect's commission was conditional upon modeling the church on its namesake in Vladimir – thus symbolically asserting spiritual and political continuity. Dividing the façade by a belt of small arches, the form of the church's framing "cited" the Vladimir prototype, but combined it with elements of an orderly system unprecedented in Rus'. Producing the external forms of a domed-cruciform church, Fiorovanti deviated from it structurally, for example, by giving a church with three naves five apses and making them flat. He created a contemporary version of a monumental church structure, as mighty as Santa Sophia in Novgorod and as refined as the Church of the Assumption in Vladimir. But, for all this, the majestic interior of the church – with three naves of equal widths, divided by tall, round pillars – gave the impression of a light and simple hall. The medieval white stone walls of the Kremlin were replaced by new red brick ones, erected by the north Italian architects Antonio and Mark Friazin (1485–7) and Pietro Antonio Solari (c. 1516). The new Kremlin became the model for numerous fortifications erected in lands dependent on Moscow, right up to the seventeenth century.

On the whole, however, the period of Ivan III saw a weakening of Western influence in architecture and painting. Painting, given a direction by Rublev, broadened its range of subjects in the fifteenth century. Hagiographical icons developed, depicting saints and their miracles and spiritual exploits. Their storytelling and detail satisfied the taste of broad circles of believers, but might also be looked at in the context of self-perfection, the "strengthening of the soul" as a task for the Christian.

Just as the creativity of Rublev was responsive to the spiritual atmosphere of Rus' in the time of St Sergius of Radonezh, the art of the greatest painter of the fifteenth century, Dionysius, was bound up with the political climate surrounding the establishment of the Muscovite Tsardom. The earthly establishment of the state was understood as the embodiment of a spiritual communion, a reflection of a higher harmony. This gave rise to an art dominated by synthesis and ensemble, where individualism is subordinated to the whole and does not exist outside it. These principles found complete expression in Dionysius' surviving masterpiece, the murals in the church at the Ferapontov Monastery, dedicated to the Mother of God. The philosophical quality in Rublev is transmuted by Dionysius into a clarity that admits of no doubts or internal struggle: "If Rublev revealed the secret life of the human soul, Dionysius presents the spiritual life of humanity as the achievement of an external order."[13]

At the beginning of the sixteenth century, in the time of Vasily III, the external form of buildings and their plans became more complex and façades more decorative. In lands under Muscovite rule the boundaries between regional architectural schools quickly dissolved. The most characteristic expression of the new taste was again the work of an Italian architect – the Church of the Archangel (1505–8), a grand princely tomb in the Kremlin. Aleviz Friazin (Novyi) divided his façades with cornices; his design resembled a collection of Venetian architectural motifs. Thus, the Orthodox Church assumed the worldly look of a palazzo or a *scuola*. Other Russian buildings also gradually took on Renaissance details, but as external decorative elements, not fundamental to architectural logic.

In the first decades of the sixteenth century an essential change took place in the direction of art: rather than presenting an ideal world, it evolved in the direction of rhetoric or exhortation. Artistic composition increasingly turned into detailed illustration of prayers and sacred texts: the sign displaced the form. The analogical phenomenon in literature would be the style called "word weaving." Guild organization began among builders. A number of big churches were built in towns and monasteries, their form based on the Assumption Cathedral in the Kremlin.

In the first third of the sixteenth century appeared the tent-roofed church, the genesis of which has not yet been fully explained. Possible sources include churches with a dome based on several tiers of gables, known since the thirteenth century, and also the bell-tower churches. The Church of the Ascension at Kolomenskoe near Moscow is the oldest surviving tent-roofed church (1532). Almost half of this formally complex white prism, rising up like a candle, resembles a sharpened stone tent, crowned with a miniature dome. The exterior of the church is surrounded by a gallery, an apse unaccented on the outside; the inner space is exceeding small, though very high. It was erected on the occasion of the birth of the heir to the throne, the future Ivan the Terrible.[14] The utilization of these elements in the Kolomenskoe Church indicates a foreign builder, probably the Italian known in Moscow as *Petrok Malyi*.

Tented churches began to be built in tsarist residences, as at Kolomenskoe, but over time these "tents" spread, often replacing onion domes. A series of sixteenth-century buildings constituted a radical break with the domed-cruciform church form. A development of this type of building is the famous Church of the Intercession, better known as St Basil the Blessed, built for Ivan the Terrible in 1555–61 by Barma and Postnik, to commemorate the conquest of Kazan. It united the central tent church with eight surrounding column-like churches of various heights, crowned with onion-like domes of diverse forms.[15] The internal space is extraordinarily small, since the church was built to be experienced from outside rather than within.

In 1551, the so-called Council of a Hundred Chapters, intended to regularize Church life, introduced a strict censorship over the depiction of sacred images. Iconographic codification was a central goal of Ivan the Terrible's normative ordering of life within a state framework. Not surprisingly, Lord God Sabaoth is frequently depicted at this time, creator of order and lawgiver, the heavenly apotheosis of the State. "Art was transformed into an ideal, normative system,"[16] based on the authority of tradition and adherence to the canons.[17]

But, by the 1540s, the didactic and detailed point of view prevailing in the depiction of sacred figures – and the artistic quality of icons – was giving way to the retelling of the events of sacred legends and hagiography. Previously, beauty of line and color had captivated the worshipers, providing them with a convincing image of divine beauty and harmony. Now the icon was becoming a *schema* directed toward the intellect and morality; it did not convince but preached. At the same time, the number of books and prints borrowed from the West was increasing. Western sources may also have provided the motif of "cavalcade" in the enormous icon, overloaded with details, in the Kremlin's Assumption Church: *The Church Militant* (1550–60). It presents the movement of the heavenly host from the burning city of this world (Kazan?) to the heavenly Jerusalem and already seems less a product of sacerdotal art than state propaganda.

After Ivan the Terrible lightness and joy returned. The painting of the late sixteenth, early seventeenth century strove to delight and captivate the viewer. A kind of icon "mannerism" became widespread, combining richness in appearance, an abundance of gold, the mastery of fastidious line, and self-sufficient refinement. So-called Godunov and Stroganov icons were relatively small, made in workshops run by the Stroganov family in Solvychegodsk and other northern towns. Churches of Boris Godunov's time were also distinguished by their coziness and chamber dimensions and by elegant and finely wrought details.

With the onset of the "Time of Troubles" (1605–13), hedonism was resurrected. Decorativeness flourished. Building plans grew more complex. Galleries and porches had to be decorated. Façades became polychrome; bricks took on fantastic designs. "Cold" (summer) and "warm" (winter) churches frequently coexisted in the same building, which complicated church design. These principles also shaped the alterations to the Kremlin, which changed it from a citadel into a decorative ensemble, with the tented Spassky Tower (Christopher Galloway and Bazhen Ogurtsov, 1624–5; tents to other towers were added in the 1670s and 1680s).

Painting revealed its own particular harmonization of religious feeling: it proposed acceptance of reality, love for this world, regular, non-ecstatic belief, bound up with the everyday observation of ritual. To the painting of this epoch one may apply Vasily Rozanov's observation: "Orthodoxy corresponds in the highest degree with the harmonious spirit but in the highest degree does not correspond to the troubled spirit."[18]

In 1653 Patriarch Nikon carried out the Church reform, which affected art directly. Icons were subjected to the censor to ensure that they conformed to the new order of service. A strict architectural style was imposed, based on the traditions of the fifteenth and sixteenth centuries. Five domes became the canon; tent roofs were only for bell towers. The only exception was Nikon's central architectural and ideological project, his residence, the Monastery of the New Jerusalem (*c.* 1658), which was to reproduce the topography and structures of the Holy Land. Gigantic, distinguished by signal luxury, the Church of the Resurrection there was not completed until after the disgrace of Nikon in 1666. It was crowned by a tent roof of enormous size.

The Sovereign's Armory played a significant role in the art of the seventeenth century, uniting the talents of numerous artists, jewelers, engravers, many of whom had been summoned from Europe. Western stylistic innovations also penetrated Russia through new associations with Ukraine. Simon Ushakov was the leading icon painter of this era: a semi-Westernizer of immediate pre-Petrine times. From Western art he derived some ability to model the human form and introduced architectural motifs, mechanically taken from engravings – although he understood neither the principles of anatomy nor the laws of perspective.

Of particular importance are those artifacts that testify to the spread of a certain kind of urban artistic culture beyond the capital, in the prosperous towns of the Volga region, in particular Yaroslavl' and Kostroma. The exteriors of churches founded by merchant benefactors often demonstrate an unprecedented variety and picturesqueness. As many as six or seven tiers of paintings cover the interior walls of these churches, all the way to the vaulting. The contents are drawn from a wide variety of subjects, less from the liturgy than from the lives of saints and prophets, while iconography was often derived from popular Western sources, like the seventeenth-century Dutch Piscator (Fischer) Bible.

Many buildings from the beginning of Peter's reign paradoxically fused Muscovite tradition and Western forms. Such, for example, were the pillar-shaped Church of the Portent at Dubrovitsa, the estate of Prince Golitsyn (1690–1704) near Moscow, and the Church of the Archangel Gabriel, known as the "Menshikov Tower." The latter, designed by Ivan Zarudnyi in 1701–7, was the first Russian church building with a steeple. With the Petrine reforms and in particular with the building of St Petersburg, this period of experimentation went further and further, until Russian architecture was absorbed into the European mainstream.

Various aspects of seventeenth-century Russian architecture have been called baroque (as in the "Naryshkin baroque," associated with Peter's family). We are speaking, however, merely of superficial similarity. The architecture of this period is a hybrid: traditional Russian forms, clothed in externalities deriving from the West. The splendid if fanciful decoration of façades, the turrets, and staircases invites comparison less with Western baroque than with earlier mannerism, or makes us think of the rustification of Western style.[19] Russian architecture thus moved, not toward some new unity, but toward a diverse collection of Western-derived motifs, as if lifted from pattern books. This was "second-hand" architecture, coming to Russia through Ukraine, Belarus, and Holland, whose commercial connections promoted Russian familiarity with Dutch baroque.

Art played an important role in the Petrine reforms. Very often new social institutions entailed a new system of visual symbols – from European "body language" and "dress codes" to genuinely new organization of urban space, laid on top of Muscovite irregularity.

The goals of Petrine art were not primarily artistic. Its utilitarian purpose was to establish a new social reality, new public and private behavior, and to represent a new striving toward empire. The problems posed were new for Russian art, but not to the West: mimesis, the reproduction of reality. But in appropriating the art of the West, Russia also took a step backward, absorbing dated baroque models rather than fashionable French rococo or English neopalladianism. The first Russian museum, the *Kunstkamer*, embodied the already archaic idea of a syncretic collection of *objets d'art* and sports of nature.

St Petersburg itself was a model product of Petrine art: a brand new city, brought to life according to a unified plan realized by architectural decree. Reality constantly found itself in contradiction with the project, and the story of the city unfolded as a conflict between utopia and practice. As with Russian eighteenth-century art in general, the declared programmatic seems to be more important than the flow of concrete events. The physical situation of the new capital – its swampy wastes and enormous river emptying into a vast bay – helped create the new image of the Russian city, which was enhanced by Peter's impact abroad. The regularity of both the plan and its execution suggested less the building of a city than the realization of some set of ideal principles for the creation of a new country, one that could resolve the contradiction between social routine – represented implicitly by Moscow – and true civilization. Its forms represented the ideas of power, order and reason.

The golden spire of the Peter–Paul Church, designed by Domenico Trezzini (1712–32), demonstrated a completely new type of Orthodox church, more like something out of Christopher Wren's London than anything in Russia. Admittedly, however, this type of church did not achieve widespread acceptance on Russian soil. Peterhof, the summer residence on the banks of the Gulf of Finland, also had symbolic significance. It was above all a model – less a place to live than the personification of the political, particularly the naval, ambitions of the new empire. Peter's personal residence was the decidedly modest "Dutch" palace, Mon Plaisir, right on the water at the Gulf of Finland.

Peter's reform of the visual was realized by European masters, among them such gifted architects as Andreas Schlüter, Jean Le Blond, and Nicolas Pineau. Farewell to the hybrid forms of the seventeenth century! Peter imported works of Classical Antiquity, placing a statue of Venus in the Summer Garden, the first representation of a nude woman to be publicly displayed in Russia, and acquiring the first Rembrandt, *David and Jonathan*, now in the Hermitage.

The number of Russian artists receiving European training was at first not large. Among them, Ivan Nikitin studied in Florence, Andrei Matveev in Holland. The latter's *Self Portrait with his Wife* was not only the first known self-portrait in Russian history, but also – unexpectedly – suggests a certain equilibrium if not actual equality between man and woman.

The Petrine reforms played the dominant role in defining the worldliness of eighteenth-century Russian culture – and its unique openness to Western influence. Under Empress Elizabeth, the dominant style became baroque (sometimes defined as rococo), the leading master of which was Bartolomeo Rastrelli (1700–71), the first architect who embodied a genuinely Russian variant of the dominant European style. His buildings are simpler than their European counterparts: long façades, vivid color, and heightened attention to decorative detail. The spectacular palace of Tsarskoe Selo exudes a certain simple-hearted optimism and holiday spirit that distinguished the court culture of Elizabeth's time. The Winter Palace, with façades of variously coordinated colonnades and flat walls and a décor of polychrome detail, is at once self-sufficient and generously open to the surrounding spaces. It defined the scale for the subsequent construction of the capital and, stylistic differences notwithstanding, it forms a unity with the neoclassical ensemble of the center of Petersburg. The return to five-domed church architecture deserves special mention, which under Elizabeth became a symbol of Russian identity. Rastrelli created a series of variations on this theme, from the elegant St Andrew's Church in Kiev to the extensive and varied complex of the Smol'nyi Convent in Petersburg.

The Academy of Fine Arts (1757, 1764) served not only as the avatar of official artistic politics, but as an important instrument of enlightenment. A grandiose classical structure, comparable in scale to the Winter Palace, on the opposite side of the Neva, its plan called for it to be based upon elementary figures – the circle and the square – a kind of "machine" for the production of the ideal artist.

The first obvious result of the new artistic training was the flowering of sculpture, of which Russia had no tradition – Orthodoxy hardly permitted statuary in church. The most important sculptors of the first half of the eighteenth century were foreigners. The monument to Peter the Great by Étienne-Maurice Falconet (erected 1782) suggested the possibilities opened to Europeans in Russia by the Petrine reforms. This masterpiece, a kind of finale to the European tradition of mounted sculpture, also symbolized the transformation of the country and directly affected Russian literature (Alexander Pushkin's *Bronze Horseman* and Andrei Belyi's *Petersburg*). In the last third of the eighteenth century to the early nineteenth century a whole generation of gifted sculptors who had graduated from the Academy of Fine Arts came to the stage, Mikahil Kozlovskii, Fedot Shubin, and Ivan Martos among them.

Figure 8.3   The equestrian statue of Peter I, the Great, by Étienne-Maurice Falconet
Source: Etienne-Maurice Falconet, "Equestrian Statue of Peter I the Great" 1782,
St Petersburg, Lauros/Giraudon/The Bridgeman Art Library

Portraiture was the most interesting and fruitful genre among the Russian arts
of the eighteenth century. Its development was bound up with the formation of a
new kind of individualism born of the Petrine reforms. It developed from an art of
physiognomy and marks of class and status, to one suggestive of psychological states,
to one pointing to the "inner world," as seen in the portraits of Fedor Rokotov.
Eighteenth-century Russian painting achieved its summit in the creativity of Dmitry
Levitsky, the first Russian artist who could legitimately be compared with Europeans.
He was a virtuoso at rendering the material qualities of objects, while at the same
time setting forth a complete rhetorical construction, as in his portrait of Catherine
as Lawgiver (1783).

The enlightened absolutism of Catherine II found adequate visual expression in
neoclassicism, which prolonged itself in the Russian Empire into the 1830s and
became the only important "grand style" that developed broadly on Russian soil
(Giacomo Quarenghi, Adrian Zakharov, Andrei Voronikhin, Carlo Rossi, and others).
Russia had experienced neither Antiquity nor the Renaissance, so the universal
vocabulary of neoclassicism became its way of participating in the general European
heritage of Greece and Rome.

There was a Muscovite classicism too; we may cite the architect Vasily Bazhenov (1737–99). His most important projects, however, remained unrealized (the great Kremlin Palace) for various reasons, or were realized in distorted form (the palace at Tsaritsyno). It is the spatial energy of Petersburg's classicism, however, that at the very least bears comparison with other great examples of the style: Paris, Karlsruhe, Bath, Edinburgh, Washington. The great buildings of St Petersburg were oriented to the broad river intersecting the city, which dictated their scale, clarity of form, and mass. The ensembles of buildings were intoxicating, but overwhelmed the individual, private person; the conflict in Gogol's *Overcoat* was born not only of the imperial bureaucracy but also of the milieu of the city of Petersburg.

The beginning of the nineteenth century was a time of intellectual and moral excitement in Russia, culminating in the Fatherland War of 1812. It stimulated a search for unity among the diverse elements of Russian society, as well as for a national identity, and even a conception of individual responsibility. The emancipation of the personality, launched by Peter's reforms, found its apogee in the gentry intelligentsia of Pushkin's time. The romanticism that developed on Russian soil paid closer attention to the spiritual content of the personality, helped it recognize its own uniqueness. In this sense, Orest Kiprensky's portraits might be considered emblematic of the epoch, emancipated as they often were from both the stereotypes of the genre and the subject's social status, focusing on the subject as a unique model, his or her inner world revealed in a moment of meditative introspection. Kiprensky thus became the first Russian painter to bear witness to the new self-consciousness of the artist – the consciousness less of an engagé professional than of an autonomous creator.

The first half of the nineteenth century saw the evolving complexity of both the artistic infrastructure and the consciousness of the social role of art. At first the number of exhibitions was limited, the audience small, the clientele largely aristocratic. Karl Briullov's *Last Day of Pompeii* (1830–3), however, established that artistic production in Russia could already become a societal event, evoking a variety of echoes beyond the boundaries of the professionally interested. If Briullov's enormous canvas was greeted as a triumph of the national artistic school – and the poet Baratynsky saw Pompeii's "last day" as the "first day for the Russian brush" – then Alexander Ivanov's *Appearance of Christ to the People* had to be, the artist thought, a turning point in the spiritual life of the nation as a whole. Despite Briullov's pretensions, however, the melodrama and superficial effectiveness of his canvas do not allow it to be seriously compared with pictures by Géricault or Delacroix. Briullov's significance is really to be found purely in the Russian context: he brought to Russian soil the traditions of seventeenth-century painting, of which the country had been deprived. He became the first Russian "old master." As such he assumed an air of artistic greatness, even "genius". For a while he became the unquestioned leader of the national school, although the laws of timeless beauty, according to which he operated, were dating rapidly. Not surprisingly, he was bumped off his pedestal in the 1860s by democratic criticism (Vladimir Stasov).

If Briullov brought to Russia the traditions of Italian academicism blended with Rubens and Van Dyck, Ivanov in his "Appearance of Christ to the People" resurrected Poussin, both as the formulator of a picture and as a philosopher. This canvas, the fruit of twenty years work in Rome, is valuable not so much for its achieved result, as for its intentions and the perspectives it opened up. The artist, inspired by new

Figure 8.4 *The Appearance of Christ to the People*, by Alexander Ivanov
Source: Aleksandr Andreevich Ivanov, "The Appearance of Christ to the People" 1837–57,
Tretyakov Gallery, Moscow/The Bridgeman Art Library

interpretations of Christianity, chose for his subject the turning point in the history
of the world: the appearance of the Messiah, after which will follow the transfiguration of humanity. Christ himself remains remote, as if the artist feared the substantial-
ity of the Godhead. But the conventionality of the entire composition goes together
with a profound attempt at historical and visual verisimilitude: an ethnic concreteness
of the populace which will carry conviction visually – as evidenced in the many
detailed preparatory studies.

Ivanov was the first Russian painter to be directly influenced by contemporary
European ideas. His turning to Christianity was affected by the Nazarener movement,
and his understanding of sacred history was influenced by David Strauss's *Life of Jesus*
(1835).[20] Ivanov's friendship with Nikolai Gogol was also significant. In *Selected
Passages from Correspondence with Friends*, Gogol was on the same mission that
engaged Ivanov: the spiritual fulfillment of contemporary humanity.

In addition to creating an art that strove for an ideal – aesthetic or ethical – the
first half of the nineteenth century saw the movement of Russian painting toward
"reality." Despite the fact that a number of eighteenth-century artists depicted peasants (Argunov, Shibanov) or beggars (Ermenev), the first attempt to visualize the
Russian people as a single "body" came via the patriotic visual propaganda of
the Fatherland War of 1812, with the caricatures of Terebenev and others.[21] But
the peasants personifying Russia were not important in themselves – they were

merely foils for the pathetic French, fleeing from Moscow. But still, to picture them meant to recognize their existence. It was the painting of Alexei Venetsianov that proved decisive, however, in making the peasant an object of visual imagination, and lending dignity to his daily round. From time to time Venetsianov's peasants may even be seen sleeping or resting – in a sense sharing the privileges of free people, like pastoral figures from classical Antiquity. Among his gifted followers were a number of serfs.

Pavel Fedotov's paintings were ironical, moral-didactic fables: Hogarth blended with Gogol. Toward the end of Fedotov's life, his narrative inclination weakened, but his palette and compositions exuded an atmosphere of existential emptiness, reminiscent of Dostoevsky's "underground man" (*"Encore*, again *encore"* (1851–2), "Card Players" (1852). These instances of early realism ran parallel to the writings of the "natural school" in the literature of the 1840s and 1850s.

The most significant artistic event arising from the social excitement at the beginning of the 1860s was the "revolt of the fourteen," the first organized statement of Russian artists, testifying to the penetration of liberal ideas into their milieu (1863). Some of those competing for the Academy's gold medal, which conferred support for travel abroad and entry into the academic hierarchy, refused to paint the assigned subject, which they saw as alien to the Russian present: "the Feast of the Gods in Valhalla." They left the St Petersburg Academy without finishing the course and formed a commune of artists, whose task would be the socialization of artistic dissidents and the conquest of economic independence. Their goal was not fully realized, but within ten years the cooperative idea had been embodied in the Society of Traveling Artistic Exhibitions.

The characteristic paintings of the 1860s were about everyday life. These canvases were generally not very large, but they often constituted a social narrative with a clear intent both to mirror "reality" and to criticize social injustice. The Muscovite Vasily Perov became the leader of this generation. At the very beginning of his career, he indicated one of his priorities, while still on his state-supported trip to Paris: "To my mind, rather than devote several years of my life to the study of a foreign country, it would be far more worthwhile to make use of the immeasurably rich subjects from urban and rural life in our own country."[22]

To the storytelling of Fedotov, Perov added a strong inclination to sarcastic didacticism, especially in depicting the habitual drunkenness of the peasants and clergy and the sufferings of the unfortunate. To such canvases as *A Rural Procession on Easter* (1861), however, Perov added some less obvious pictures, in which the tragedy of contemporary life cannot be given some single explanation. Among the best of these is *The Drowned Woman* (1867), in which the psychological reserve and simplicity of the composition allow the spectator space for independent reflection. In *Last Tavern at the Gates* (1868), the external theme of the picture – the drunkenness of the peasantry – yields to the existential cold of Russian life, symbolized by the endless, twilit, frosty expanse beyond the town gates.

In 1871 came the first exhibition of the Society, whose members were popularly known as the *Peredvizhniki* ("Wanderers" or "Itinerants" in English). For many years thereafter, they defined what it was to be "national" in Russian art and organized themselves along democratic lines, putting forward a program both aesthetic and social. They saw their task as the honest depiction of the people's life. The substitution of scenes of peasant life and Russia's own national environment for the abstract, "ideal" forms of academicism was revolutionary in itself.

The Wanderers saw art as an instrument of social influence and the artist as both a judge and a physician. His task consisted in the visualization of the actual problem, but the objectivity of his depiction contained a strand of rhetorical sympathy. The image of the Russian peasant appeared to these educated townsmen to reveal both a pronounced element of humility and also the potential strength of the "simple people." The duty of educated Russian society toward the oppressed and laboring poor was paradigmatically expressed in the *Volga Bargehaulers* of Ilia Repin (1870–3). Those pulling the boat represent the panorama of problems besetting Russia, which can be resolved only by easing the external constraints on the Russian people and liberating their energies.

The Wanderers exhibited not only in the capitals but in major provincial centers as well; and, like the literature of "critical realism," their paintings helped form the taste of the Russian intelligentsia. With help of some wealthy collectors, above all, Paul Tret'yakov, they were able to make their conception of Russian national art central to the canon. Their asceticism led them to aspire to transform their aesthetic language into a neutral vocabulary to reveal content, and to oppose the academic cult of beautiful form, or any kind of aestheticism. The "artistic principle" so central to French painting seemed untimely or out of place or at least of secondary importance in Russian art, raising the real danger of provincialism.

The positive principle sought by Russian artists in this context turned out to consist in a portrait gallery of the Russian intelligentsia – the reason and conscience of the nation. The greatest master of the psychological portrait was Ivan Kramskoi, the intellectual and moral leader of the Wanderers. The *Peredvizhnik* portrait resulted from an implicit agreement: the model gave him or herself up for judgment by society, whose representative was the artist, obliged to speak the truth and nothing but the truth. Quintessential examples: Perov's portrait of Dostoevsky (1872) and Repin's of Modest Mussorgsky just days before the composer's death (1881).

In the 1870s the realists moved from the genre of "unmasking," in which the focus was on victims of injustice, to emphasizing the beauty and dignity of the people. In Kramskoi's famous *Peasant with a Bridle (Mina Moiseev)* (1883) the artist attempts to demonstrate his subject's directness and straightforwardness; the photographic quality of the treatment and the worn, workaday character of Moiseev's costume serve as signs of authenticity. But it is clear that this rhetoric is targeted not at any peasant, but at the educated viewer at the exhibition.

A similar mechanism is at work in Savrasov's well known canvas *The Rooks Have Returned* (1871), which intentionally makes use of an awkward foreshortened glance at some village back yards through spindly birch branches, one of which is broken off. The view is not as a local would see it, but from the perspective of a newcomer, intended to induce the urban spectator to believe in the simplicity, the reality of the depiction and – in the end – sense the humble beauty of the motherland in the prosaic and commonplace. This canvas, seen at the very first *Peredvizhniki* exhibition, achieved enormous popularity. It embodied the mingled lyric and epic qualities of Russian realistic landscape, which taught Russians to value Russian nature in its everydayness, rather than ascribing qualities of ideal beauty to it.[23]

In its more significant productions, the historical paintings of realism depicted events that revealed the archetypes of Russian history. Nikolai Ge's *Peter I Interrogates Tsarevich Aleksei* (1871) is emphatically documentary in its treatment of the heroes and the court setting of the early eighteenth century. But the choice of subject and its treatment broadened the sense of conflict faced by the generation of the 1860s, forcing the recognition that the choice of historical and moral paths to the future was a perennial Russian problem. In the sensational *Ivan the Terrible and his Son Ivan* (1883) Repin seemed to justify the recent murder of the imperial "father" by the "People's Will" terrorist sons by going back to the accursed tsar who had killed his son. Most original both for Russian art and for Europe as a whole were the historical excursions of Vasily Surikov. His depiction of the Peter the Great's execution of the rebellious musketeers (*streltsy*) demonstrates a historical understanding akin to that of Tolstoy's *War and Peace* and the operas of Mussorgsky. Vladimir Stasov called the painting a sort of "choral" work. History is understood here as the suffering of the people, demonstrating dignity and nobility before the figure of death: "in a real tragedy, it is not the hero who perishes; it is the chorus."[24] Peter's soldier helping a condemned man on his way to the gallows, however, forms a kind of bridge between the swarm of musketeers and the ranks of Peter's advisors. Executioner and victims are not enemies, but belong to the same popular body, both carried along in the stream of history/destiny. We see in this canvas a significant characteristic of Surikov's work: people are not in charge of their destinies, but at the mercy of what seem irresistible external forces.

The events of Russian history thus call forth a meditation on the fate of the people, but in some cases religious subjects may also enable reflections on the meaning of contemporary life. Canvases by Kramskoi and the later work of Nikolai Ge suggest something like Tolstoyan Christianity. Some of Ge's preliminary studies for "Crucifixion" bring realist painting to the edge of expressionism. But not all of the outstanding realists were members of the Wanderers. The independent-minded Vasily Vereshchagin provides a unique Russian example of an anti-war painter of battle scenes and anti-colonial orientalist. He painted the Russian conquest of Central Asia and the Balkan War, in which he strove to retain his objectivity, while emphasizing the anti-human character of war itself.

In the 1880s, the creative center of Russian art became the artists' colony of Abramtsevo, on the estate of the entrepreneur Savva Mamontov and his wife Elizaveta, outside Moscow. It was not a formal organization, nor did it have a defined aesthetic program. He differed from Tret′iakov in that he did not collect art but created an atmosphere favorable to its creation. The task of art became not social criticism but the creation of beauty and joy in everyday life. The portrait of Mamontov's daughter by Valentin Serov, *Young Girl with Peaches* (1888), was a signature production of this tendency: light, apparently effortless, and full of *joie de vivre*.

The impact of Abramtsevo on Russian art was profound and various; it included the discovery of the beauty of peasant folk art and the traditions of popular crafts. Elizaveta Mamontova and the artist Elena Polenova organized a studio in which local artisans created objects "in the spirit of the people," but according to the designs of artists. If the generation of the 1870s was inspired by sympathy for the people, the generation of the 1880s strove to steep itself in their spirit. The Abramtsevo circle was concerned about the essence of "Russianness," but substituted a tender lyricism

Figure 8.5 *Young Girl with Peaches*, by Valentin Serov
Source: Valentin Aleksandrovich Serov, "Girl with Peaches" 1887, Tretyakov Gallery, Moscow/The Bridgeman Art Library

for the nationalism of official Russia. Mamontov's private opera company deserves special mention; painters were full collaborators in the creation of the spectacle in a way that anticipated Diaghilev's *Ballets Russes*. Abramtsevo also furthered the revival of interest in icons, begun by the ethnographer Fedor Buslaev and the art historian Nikodim Kondakov in the middle of the nineteenth century.

The Abramtsevo circle was also bound up with the creativity of Mikhail Vrubel. His significance for the Russian art of the last third of the nineteenth century was enormous. He reformed the poetics of painting, reconciling the academic, empirical, and rationalist methods of Russian painting with various currents of world art. Stylistically he gave a contemporary emphasis to the poetics of the classical period of European painting, while introducing an array of European subjects and motifs into Russian painting. He also began to free Russian painting from literal and objective representation and invited the spectator to share in the production of new meanings.

Vrubel brought Russian painting toward symbolism. Another master of this tendency was Victor Borisov-Musatov. Fusing the vocabulary of impressionism and symbolism, he created an artistic utopia in which color – organized like musical harmony – played the decisive role. The estate life of the distant past played a significant role in his work, and we sense an echo of the "peasant idyll" of the almost totally forgotten Venetsianov in the "gentry idyll" of this son of a serf. Musatov's musical and decorative understanding of painting had a direct influence on the young symbolist painters who showed their work in the "Blue Rose" exhibition (1907).

After the exhaustion of neoclassicism in the 1830s, Russian architecture developed along generally European lines, including a phase of neo-medievalism. The most striking appearance in Russian architecture of the late nineteenth century was the Russian version of *art nouveau*, traditionally known as "stil′ modern." It diffused across Russia around 1900. A significant part of what was built in that style consisted of private residences, as well as hotels, railroad stations, and theaters. The style was bound up with the efforts of the new bourgeoisie to express its ambitions in visual terms.[25] The buildings of St Petersburg's modern architecture were distinguished by a refined restraint (Fedor Lidval′) and formal strictness. They employed variations on "northern" or "Scandinavian" motifs and often engaged in a conscious dialogue with the city's neoclassical traditions (Matilda Kshenskaia's residence by Alexander Gogen, 1904–6).

The most obvious master of Russia's "stil′ modern" was a Muscovite, Fedor Shekhtel′. An outstanding example of his buildings was the residence of the millionaire Stepan Riabushinsky (1900–2), in which a deliberately whimsical interior and exterior gave expression to a private utopia in which life was organized along lines of beauty and functionality. Shekhtel's projects after 1910 foreshadowed the functional architecture of the following decade in the distinct expression of the building's structure in the façade, and clarity of spatial organization (House of the Moscow Merchant Society, 1910–11).

Russian art of the 1890s was a complex alloy of *pleinairisme*, variants of impressionism, symbolist tendencies, efforts toward a national style, and first attempts at a *Gesamtkunstwerk* in the theater.[26] Landscape became the fundamental genre of the exhibitions; quick studies became the order of the day, painted outdoors and giving the artist's immediate impression. At the same time, this period saw the flowering of the two greatest masters of realism, Valentin Serov and Isaak Levitan. An intense observer of nature and an acute portraitist, Serov was open to influences ranging from impressionism to the modern (*Ida Rubinstein*, *Rape of Europa*, both 1910).

The 1890s also saw a growing complexity among modernist currents, the totality of which was dubbed "decadence" by its opponents. The "decadents" saw art as independent of the sphere of social interests – liberated both from a privileging of moral duty and a direct imitation of nature. These developments constituted a sharp break with what had come to be regarded as characteristic of Russian art.

The principal modernist organization in Russia became the St Petersburg society known as "The World of Art" (*Mir iskusstva*), which existed between 1898 and 1924. A great deal in its point of view and practice contrasted strikingly with the art of the Wanderers, many of whom were from lower-middle-class and provincial backgrounds. The Petersburgers, by contrast, tended to be members of the cosmopolitan intelligentsia of the capital, to have grown up and attended school together, and to have a distinctly amateur attitude toward art. Their sense of themselves as belonging to European culture was strengthened by interlocking family memories and by the participation of those families in the professional and cultural life of the capital.

Many of the subjects of the World of Art painters were "Western," but of greater importance was their understanding of Russia's past as that of a European country. The generation of the Wanderers and the Abramtsevo had understood Russia's past as pre-Petrine – that is "medieval" – and regarded Peter's reforms mostly as essentially tragic. The painters of the World of Art, on the other hand, centered their vision of the Russian past on the post-Petrine eighteenth and nineteenth centuries, and on the connection of that past with Western Europe.

For Sergei Diaghilev and those who saw the world his way, the definition of Russian art as programmatically European made the rapprochement with contemporary European culture quite harmonious with Russian national identity. Their goal: to be national without being provincial. "I want to tend Russian painting, clean it up and – the main thing – bring it to Europe, glorify it in the West . . .".[27]

The "World of Art" strategy was a double one from the beginning. Inside the country the painters presented themselves as being in the ranks of the international art movement, but outside Russia they tried above all to present themselves as original representatives of the national spirit, to find a language for "Russianness," not repeating the visual language of Europe, but in its spirit. The culmination of their efforts was the so-called Russian seasons in Paris after 1909: ideal expressions of the *Gesamtkunstwerk* and brilliant marketing projects. Russian art was presented as the public expected: it was, above all, irrational, passionate, synthetic.

Around 1910 came a final parting of the ways between the radicals – moving through fauvism to abstraction – and the traditionalists. If the "World of Art" had been the undisputed leader at the turn of the century of the struggle with conservative tendencies, now their successors – having consolidated their ranks around the Petersburg journal *Apollon* (1909–17) – saw themselves as a shaping force, but moderate in nature, accepting responsibility for the national school and began in their turn to fight with the rebellious avant-garde.

Notes

1   Vasily Bazhenov (1737–99): architect of the outsize, grandiose Kremlin Palace, never built because of a lack of resources. Alexander Ivanov (1806–58), who spent the greater part of his career preparing for one revelatory canvas: "The Appearance of Christ to the People." *Peredvizhniki*: artistic partisans of the Russian people, who rejected the sponsorship of the Academy. The Russian Constructivists wished to redesign modern life on a radically democratic basis at the time of the Russian Revolution.

2   In the twentieth century, the "Greek roots" of Russia were often mythologized.

3   Cf. Otto Demus, *Byzantine Art and the West*, New York: New York University Press, 1970.

4   Cf. Hans Belting, *Likeness and Presence: a History of the Image before the Era of Art*, Chicago: University of Chicago Press, 1994.

5   V. N. Lazarev, *Old Russian Mosaics and Frescoes (Drevnerusskie mozaiki i freski)*, Moscow: Iskuustvo, 1973, 26.

6   O. M. Ioannisian, "On the Matter of Elements of Romanesque Architecture in Santa Sophia in Novgorod" (K voprosu ob elementakh romanskoi arkhitektury Sofiiskogo sobora v Nogorode), in V.A. Bulkin, ed., *The Art of Old Russia and its Researchers (Iskusstvo Drevnei Rusi i ego issledovateli)*, St Petersburg: St Petersburg University Press, 2002, 88–213.

7   See, e.g., the frescoes in the Church of the Transfiguration (Spasa Nereditsy), in Novgorod, destroyed during the Second World War.

8   A. I. Komech, "The Architecture of Vladimir, 1150–1180: Artistic Nature and the Genesis of 'Russian Romanesque' (Arkhitektura Vladimira, 1150–1180 gg. Khudozhestvennaia priroda i genezis 'russkoi romaniki'")", in *Old Russian Art. Rus' and the Countries of the Byzantine World (Drevnerusskoe iskusstvo. Rus' i strany Vizantiiskogo mira)*, St Petersburg, 2002, 231–54. O. M. Ioannisian, "Toward a History of Polish–Russian Relations between the End of the Eleventh and the beginning of the Thirteenth Centuries (K istorii pol'sko-russkikh otnosheniakh v kontse XI nachala XIII v.), in ibid. 206–30.

9   One should remember that nineteenth-century restoration, having abandoned the medieval side-chapels and porches, brought these churches toward a contemporary conception of architectural harmony.

10 A surviving example is the Church of St Paraskeva Piatnitsa in Chernigov, dating from the first quarter of the thirteenth century.

11 See Pavel Florensky, *Iconostasis*, Crestwood, NY: St Vladimir's Seminary Press, 1996.

12 A symmetrical composition of Jesus in the center, flanked by those praying to him. These could be as few as two images – Mary and John the Baptist – up to as many as twenty-four.

13 Lev Lifshits, *Russian Art of the 10–17 Centuries (Russkoe iskusstvo X–XVII vekov)*, Moscow, 2000, 117.

14 P. A. Rappoport, *Ancient Russian Architecture (Drevnerusskaia arkhitektura)*, St Petersburg: Stroiizdat, 1993, 167–8.

15 The church received its present colorful appearance in the 1680s.

16 Lifshits, *Russian Art of the 10–17 Centuries*, 125.

17 Michael S. Flier, "Filling in the Blanks: The Church of the Intercession and the Architectonics of Medieval Muscovite Ritual," in Nancy Kollmann et al., eds., *Harvard Ukrainian Studies*, 19/1–4 (1995).

18 Quoted in Wladimir Weidlé, *Russia's Task (Zadacha Rossii)*, New York: Chekhov Publishing House, 1956, 53.

19 B. R. Vipper, *The Architecture of the Russian Baroque (Arkhitektura russkogo barokko)*, Moscow, Nauka, 1978, 9–28. James Cracraft, *The Petrine Revolution in Russian Architecture*, Chicago and London: University of Chicago Press, 1988, 79–109.

20 The "Nazarener": a German movement, based in Rome, that aspired to return to medieval and early Renaissance traditions in painting. They had a considerable influence on the subsequent pre-Raphaelite movement in England.

21 Ivan Petrovich Argunov (1729–1802), considered a rococo painter, was from a serf family belonging to the Sheremetevs. Mikhail Shibanov (fl. 1760–98), a serf of Prince Grigory Potemkin, was known as a portraitist. Ivan Ivanovich Terbenev (1780–1815), a sculptor, produced a famous set of caricatures between 1812 and 1814.

22 Cited in David Jackson, *The Wanderers and Critical Realism in Nineteenth-Century Russian Painting*, Manchester and New York: Manchester University Press, 2006, 32.
23 Among the most important Russian landscape painters were Ivan Shishkin, Aleksei Savrasov, Fedor Vasil'ev, and Isaac Levitan.
24 http://nobelprize.org/nobel_prizes/literature/laureates/11987/brodsky-lecture-e.html
25 Catherine Cook, "Fedor Shekhtel: Architect to Moscow's 'Forgotten Class,'" in *The Twilight of the Tsars: Russian Art at the Turn of the Century*, London: The Centre, 1991, 43–65.
26 "Pleinairisme": the doctrine, originating in France, that landscape painting ought to be done outdoors, rather than in the studio. "Gesamtkunstwerk": the concept that the highest form of art fuses various branches into a single "total work."
27 Letter of May 24, 1897. Cited in Alexander Benois and Sergei Diaghilev, *Correspondence* (*Perepiska*), ed. I. I. Vydrin, n.p., Sad iskusstv, 2003, 32.

References

Anderson, R., and Debreczeny, P. (eds) (1994). *Russian Narrative and Visual Art: Varieties of Seeing*. University Press of Florida, Gainesville.

Averintsev, S. (1992). "Visions of the Invisible," in Roderick Grierson (ed.), *Gates of Mystery: The Art of Holy Russia*, InterCultura, Fort Worth, TX, 11–14.

Bassin, M. (ed.) (2000). "Landscape and Identity in Russian and Soviet Art," *Ecumene*, 7/3.

Benois, A. (1916). *The Russian School of Painting*. Alfred A. Knopf, New York.

Borisova, E., and Sternin, G. (1988). *Russian Art Nouveau*, Rizzoli, New York.

Brumfield, W. C. (1991). *The Origins of Modernism in Russian Architecture*. University of California Press, Berkeley and Los Angeles.

Cooke, C. (1991). *Fedor Shekhtel: Architect to Moscow's "Forgotten Class", The Twilight of the Tsars: Russian Art at the Turn of the Century*. The Centre, London, 43–65.

Cracraft, J. (1988). *The Petrine Revolution in Russian Architecture*. University of Chicago Press, Chicago.

Daniel', S. M. (1999). *Russkaia zhivopis' mezhdu Vostokom i Zapadom*. Aurora, St Petersburg.

Ely, C. (2002). *This Meager Nature: Landscape and National Identity in Imperial Russia*. Northern Illinois University Press, Dekalb, IL.

Evangulova, O. (1987). *Izobrazitel'noe iskusstvo v Rossii pervoi chetverti XVIII века*. Izdatel'stvo Moskovskogo universiteta, Moscow.

Evangulova, O., and Karev, A. (1994). *Portretnaia zhivopis' v Rossii vtoroi poloviny XVIII c.* M. Moscow University Press, Moscow.

Fedorov-Davydov, A. (1929). *Russkoe iskusstvo, promyshlennogo kapitalizma*. Gosudarstvennaia akademiia khudozhestvennikh nauk, Moscow.

Garafola, L., and Baer, N. (1999). *The "Ballets Russes" and its World*. Yale University Press, New Haven.

Gray, R. (2000). *Russian Genre Painting in the Nineteenth Century*. Clarendon Press, Oxford.

Isdebsky-Pritchard, A. (1982). *The Art of Mikhail Vrubel (1856–1910)*. UMI Research Press, Ann Arbor, MI.

Jackson, D. (2006). *The Wanderers and Critical Realism in Nineteenth-Century Russian Painting*. Manchester University Press, Manchester and New York.

Jackson, D., and Wageman, P. (eds) (2003). *Russian Landscape*. BAI, Schoten, Belgium.

Karpova, T. (2000). *Smysl' litsa: russkii portrem vtoroi poloviny XIX века: Opyt samopoznaniia lichnosti.* Aleteia, St Petersburg.

Kennedy, J. (2003). "Pride and Prejudice: Serge Diaghilev, the Ballets Russes, and the French Public," in M. Facos and S. Hirsh (eds), *Art, Culture, and National Identity in Fin-de-Siècle Europe.* Cambridge University Press, Cambridge, 90–118.

Kennedy, J. (1977). *The "Mir iskusstva" Group and Russian Art, 1898–1912.* Garland, New York.

Kirichenko, E. (1991). *Russian Design and the Fine Arts, 1750–1917.* Abrams, New York.

Lang, W. (2003). *Das heilige Russland: Geschichte, Folklore, Religion in der russischen Malerei des 19. Jahrhunderts.* Reimer, Berlin.

Lazarev, V. (1966). *Old Russian Murals & Mosaics: From the 11th to the 16th Century.* Phaidon, London.

Lifshits L. (2000). *Russkoe iskusstvo X–XVII vekov.* Moscow.

Nesterova, Ye. (1996). *The Itinerants: The Masters of Russian Realism: Second Half of the 19th and Early 20th Centuries.* Parkstone, Bournemouth; Aurora, St Petersburg.

Rosenfeld, A. (ed.) (1999). *Defining Russian Graphic Arts: From Diagilev to Stalin. 1898–1934.* Rutgers University Press, New Brunswick, NJ, and London.

Russian Visual Arts: Art Criticism in Context, 1814–909. http://hri.shef.ac.uk/rva/

Riazantsev, I. (2003). *Skul'ptura v Rossii: XVIII – nachalo XIX века.* Zhiraf, Moscow.

Salmond, W. (1996). *Arts and Crafts in Late Imperial Russia: Reviving the Kustar Art Industries, 1870–1917,* Cambridge University Press, Cambridge.

Salmond, W. (2000). "Moscow Modern," in P. Greenhalgh (ed.), *Art Nouveau, 1890–1914.* V&A Press, London.

Sarabianov, D. V. (2003). *Rossiia i zapad: Istoriko-khudozhestvennie sviazi XVIII – nachalo XX века.* Iskusstvo, Moscow.

Sternin, G. (1984). *Russkaia khudozhestvennaia kul'tura vtoroi poloviny XIX – nachala XX века.* Sovetskii khudozhnik, Moscow.

Sternin, G. (1993). "Public and Artist in Russia at the Turn of the Twentieth Century," in A. Efimova and L. Manovich (eds), *Tekstura: Russian Essays on Visual Culture.* University of Chicago Press, Chicago, 89–114.

Uspensky, B. (1976). *The Semiotics of the Russian Icon.* Peter de Ridder Press, Lisse.

Valkenier, E. (1990). *Ilya Repin and the World of Russian Art.* Columbia University Press, New York.

Valkenier, E. (2001). *Valentin Serov: Portraits of Russia's Silver Age.* Northwestern University Press, Evanston, IL.

Vdovin, G. (1999). *Stanovlenie «Ia» v russkoi culture XVIII века i iskusstvo portreta.* Nash dom – L'age d'Homme, Moscow.

Further Reading

Bowlt, J. E. (1982). *The Silver Age: Russian Art of the Early Twentieth Century and the "World of Art" Group.* 2nd edn. Oriental Research Partners, Newtonville, MA.

Brumfield, W. C. (2004). *A History of Russian Architecture.* University of Washington Press, Seattle.

Cracraft, J. (1997). *The Petrine Revolution in Russian Imagery.* University of Chicago Press, Chicago.

Gray, C. (1990). *The Russian Experiment in Art, 1863–1922.* Thames and Hudson, London.

Hilton, A. (1995). *Russian Folk Art.* University of Indiana Press, Bloomington.

Milner, J. (1993). *A Dictionary of Russian and Soviet Artists, 1420–1970.* Antique Collectors' Club, Woodbridge, Suffolk.

Ouspensky, L., and Lossky, V. (1982). *The Meaning of Icons.* St Vladimir's Seminary Press, Crestwood, NY.

Sarabianov, D. V. (1990). *Russian Art: From Neoclassicism to the Avant-Garde, 1800–1917: Painting – Sculpture – Architecture.* H. N. Abrams, New York.

Valkenier, E. (1989). *Russian Realist Art: The State and Society: The Peredvizhniki and Their Tradition.* Columbia University Press, New York.

CHAPTER NINE

The Church Schism and Old Belief

NADIESZDA KIZENKO

Russian history has its share of spectacular turning points. Conversion to Orthodox Christianity at about 988, the invasion of the Mongols and the subsequent rise of Moscow, the reforms of Peter I, the revolutions of 1917, perestroika – all these mark moments that changed the direction of Russian culture and politics. All these, moreover, are generally acknowledged as crucial both by Russians and by outside observers. But one of the most important such ruptures has yet to make it into the "big leagues." Despite over three centuries of furious legislation and polemic, despite over one hundred years of serious scholarship, the seventeenth-century church schism with its consequences has yet to take its place among the pivotal points of Russian history.

And yet the importance of the church schism and Old Belief can hardly be overestimated. In the middle of the seventeenth century, Russian culture underwent a convulsion. After decades of troubles and disorder, Russian authorities – ruler, patriarch, hierarchy, clergy – decided that they could finally start trying to control their fluid and unstable population. Their attempts took both physical and spiritual forms. The law code of 1649, among other things, sought literally to keep people in place: it bound urban taxpayers to their towns and finished the process of enserfing the peasantry. In the religious sphere, the ruler and the patriarch shared several goals. Domestically, they wanted better to educate and control the spiritual lives and the religious practices of their flock; internationally, they wanted to reflect the geopolitical reality that Muscovite Russia was now the only sovereign nation in the Orthodox Christian world. The local goals, they thought, could be met by requiring annual confession and communion. The international goals called for more complex solutions: they concerned different visions of what an Orthodox Christian earthly kingdom ought to be, the balance of power between tsar and patriarch, and the discrepancies in religious ritual and language among Muscovite Russia and other Orthodox nations.

Taken together, these attempts to regularize created the "perfect storm" called the church schism. They galvanized unexpected elements of the population, including elite women and distant monasteries as well as parish priests and common criminals.

The resulting fights led to the deposition of the patriarch, a fundamental restructuring of the relations between Church and State, the torture and persecution of thousands, the subsequent emigration of millions, and the emergence of the first great work of modern Russian literature.

Accounts of the schism and Old Belief were no less charged than the realities they represented. Old Belief has been depicted variously as the knee-jerk refusal of fanatics to accept necessary corrections to liturgical books; a movement subversive both politically and socially; a popular movement of local resistance to central oppression; an authentically Russian, religious, and apocalyptic rejection of the increasingly Westernized, secular, and this-worldly imperial state; and a unique cluster of attitudes towards sexuality and gender.[1] In its blurring of such tidy categories as popular versus official, oppositional practices versus mainstream ones, and finally conservative versus innovative, Old Belief is, among other things, a metaphor for much of the modern Russian experience.

Origins and History

The origins of the church schism go back to the fifteenth century, when Constantinople fell to the Ottoman Turks and Muscovy finally wrested sovereignty from the Mongols and imposed itself over the other Great Russian principalities. It was now the only independent Orthodox Christian kingdom in the world. The question for the Russians was why they, alone of all the Orthodox Christian nations, so enjoyed God's favor. Their church teachings were the same as those of their Greek, Serbian, Bulgarian, Romanian, and fellow Rus-ian (Ruthenian, later known as Belarusian and Ukrainian) brethren. Some monks elaborated the "Third Rome" theory (Rome and the "New Rome," Constantinople, had fallen; Moscow was now the world center of the true faith). Ultimately, Muscovites concluded that, as only ritual and language distinguished them from their less fortunate neighbors, they had to take particular care to preserve those forms. This concern with ritual would manifest itself in numerous church councils, including that of "The Hundred Chapters" (*Stoglav*) in 1550–1. Russia attained full ecclesiastical autonomy in 1589, with the election of the first Patriarch of Moscow.

In the 1630s a group of parish priests who called themselves "Zealots of Piety" went further in seeking to create an ideal Orthodox society. They succeeded in introducing a more solemn celebration of liturgy, better discipline, and more preaching for the clergy; more widespread fasting and participation in the sacraments of confession and communion for the laity; a wider range of religious publications; and the banning of gambling, strong drink, and bawdy *skomorokhi* minstrels. Visiting Orthodox clergy from the Mediterranean were astounded by the results: according to Paul of Aleppo, all of Moscow appeared to be living as one huge monastery, and, with all the hours they spent standing in church, the "Russians must have legs made of stone."[2]

This urge to be a beacon of Orthodoxy took on a new aspect when Nikon, archbishop of Novgorod, was elected Patriarch in 1652. Nikon too believed that Muscovy ought to live like a well-ordered monastery with himself as its abbot. But he took further the idea that Muscovy ought to assume spiritual leadership of the entire Orthodox ecumene. He built a scale version of the Holy Places in his monastery aptly named New Jerusalem and recruited monks of all Orthodox nationalities and languages for its brotherhood.[3] But he also assumed that, if Russians were going to preside over a united Orthodox Christendom, their rites and texts ought to correspond to those used by other Orthodox Christians, particularly those of their ecclesiastical predecessors – the Greeks. And so, between 1654 and 1666, Nikon turned to Greek and Ukrainian liturgical scholars (without summoning a church council or consulting Russian clerics) to bring Russian church practice into line with that used elsewhere. Now the word "Alleluia" was to be said three, not two, times; the sign of the cross was to be made with three fingers crossed on top and two folded below, not the reverse; church processions were to move against the direction of the sun, not towards it; and so on.[4]

To more than a few clerics, all this was disturbing enough. But Nikon alienated Russian clergy not only for his tampering with texts and ritual and for his using suspect authorities to do so, but for the high-handed way with which he went about it. Such priests as Avvakum and Ivan Neronov wrote furious letters in protest. They wanted two things: to maintain the rites and traditions specific to Russian Orthodoxy, and to maintain local autonomy against the encroachment of central control. Nikon retaliated by defrocking, jailing, exiling, or otherwise removing as many of his opponents as he could, though new ones sprang up almost as quickly.

In this early period, between 1654 and 1666, it is not clear just who resisted the new church policies and on just what grounds. Certainly, the people who cared most and who expressed their opinions most forcefully were people who encountered the reforms directly and whose daily routines were most affected by them: nuns, monks, and priests (particularly those who were out of work). Several scholars, including Nikolai Pokrovskii and Robert Crummey, have differentiated between *raskol*, or dissent and schism broadly speaking, and Old Belief as a coherent body of teachings explicitly opposed to Nikon's liturgical reforms.[5] Georg Michels has gone furthest in drawing a line between the two. In the early period, he argues, church schism did not result from the preaching and writing of such prominent Old Believers as Avvakum, but from many unrelated and supremely fragmented local factors. He claims convincingly that the causes of the schism range from

> a serious crisis in the monastic world; the emergence of a significant surplus of unemployed and defrocked priests; the existence of strong anti-church sentiments in isolated villages and towns; the fusion of social banditry and religious radicalism; the quasi-Protestant quests of individual peasants, artisans, and merchants for religious salvation; the disillusionment of women with the church; and a widespread lack of popular knowledge about the basic tenets of the Orthodox faith. These features of seventeenth-century society point to a deep alienation between ordinary Russians and their church. It was this alienation – and not Nikon's reforms or Old Belief teachings – that led to the emergence of the Russian schism.[6]

Whatever the impulses for resistance, however, the council of 1666 marked a clear turning point. Although by then Nikon himself had succeeded in alienating the Tsar, and was confined to his New Jerusalem monastery for life, the 1666 council approved his liturgical reforms. Indeed, the reforms were not only approved, but were also declared to be the only correct ones. Church and state authorities moved quickly to implement the council's decisions. Supporters of the old traditions were excommunicated; in a particularly vicious illustration of how the authorities sought to silence dissenters, some had their tongues cut out. Far from cowing the resisters into submission, however, this only embittered them and led to a full-fledged church schism. The leaders – priests Avvakum, Ivan Neronov, and Lazar, the monk Epifanii, and the deacon Fedor – were exiled to Pustozersk on the Arctic coast, from where they continued to send out increasingly apocalyptic missives. With this official condemnation, and with the clear willingness to impose the revised Orthodoxy by force, the lines became more clearly drawn. With the stakes so high, fellow travelers began to fall by the wayside, while those who opposed the reforms had to explain their position ever more convincingly.

Two scholars have articulated the Old Believer position particularly well. Boris Uspensky noted that the origins of Old Belief were essentially semiotic – that is, cultural and symbolic – rather than dogmatic: as he put it, not only the content of church texts, but also their form, could be understood as a manifestation of divine truth.[7] The mainstream "Nikonian" Orthodox clergy, influenced as they were by Ukrainians who were themselves products of the Polish baroque, took a functional attitude toward the reforms they proposed: for them, the essential thing was to transmit content as effectively as possible. Communication and reception of the message were what mattered. If a gesture or word expressed some notion better than another word, if the Greeks simply used a different one than the Church Slavonic, then the disagreeable word could and should be changed. If most of the Orthodox world said "Alleluia" three times and not two, or bowed twelve times from waist down instead of making full prostrations during the Lenten prayer of St Ephraim the Syrian – if the changes they proposed did not affect dogma, but would lead to greater uniformity in the Orthodox community of nations – why not make the changes? Their position, moreover, was perfectly consistent with the dominant role historically played in the Christian tradition by rulers and patriarchs since Constantine summoned the first council of Nicaea.[8]

The Old Believers, on the other hand, took a symbolic approach: form and content were so intertwined in sacred language and ritual as to be inseparable. Like the Muslims who believe that, because God chose to speak to His followers in Arabic, the Koran cannot be translated, so the Old Believers felt that the forms they defended had an absolute and independent value.

The difference in the Nikonian and Old Believer approaches to sacred signs is particularly striking in the central issue in the conflict – how one held one's fingers to make the sign of the cross. The theological points being illustrated were the duality of Christ's nature (both divine and human) and the Trinity. Like the fingers on one's hand, they were a combination of two and three. At dispute was whether one expressed Christ's dual nature by holding the index and middle fingers up, the three remaining folded together to represent the Trinity (the previous, and still the Old Believer, position), or whether Christ's duality was conveyed by folding down the two smallest fingers and bringing together the thumb, index, and middle fingers (the new, Nikonian position). Both cases expressed exactly the same theological ideas; no one argued that some fingers were more important than others. It was purely a matter of form.[9] For this reason, Nikon's men saw no problem with changing the gesture so that everyone in the Orthodox world could express the same theology in the same way. But Russian saints and Russian church councils and icons had used the previous sign, and won their salvation doing so, the Old Believers argued: why change for the sake of this-worldly convenience? Did one want to maintain unity with one's holy ancestors who had achieved the one thing needful – or the Greeks and Ruthenians who had fallen under the reign, and the influence, of the heretic and the infidel?

Roy Robson explained the Old Believers' religious objections even more forcefully. He observed that, to the Old Believers, rituals did not *represent* heaven on earth, they actually *realized* it.[10] Particularly after St Gregory Palamas's interpretation of the Transfiguration, Orthodox Christians believed that they could and should become like God. Leading a moral, upstanding life was one way. But how one addressed God, and how one acted in His temple – that is, how one encountered God through ritual – was at least as important. Thus, if that language and those rituals were tampered with, salvation itself might be at stake. And salvation was too important to risk.

The Old Believers, then, had reasonable grounds for opposing textual and ritual changes even when those changes did not affect the theological content of the symbol. One can imagine how forcefully they responded to changes that had less legitimacy. And in fact some did not: Nikon's heavy-handed attempt to achieve unity by force backfired also, because it was not at all clear that contemporary Greek practice was more authentic than the traditional Russian one. No tradition is static. Over the centuries, partly because of their contact with Venetians, the Greeks had introduced a number of changes, as had the Ruthenians in the Polish–Lithuanian Commonwealth: paradoxically, Russian texts and practices were closer to early Byzantine ones than were those of contemporary Greeks.[11] But one could hardly expect Greeks and Ukrainians, who had both been influenced by Roman Catholicism and in many cases trained in Catholic seminaries, and who tended to dismiss the Muscovite Russians as uneducated, to consider such niceties. The Old Believer Russians, by contrast, lacked the scholars who could articulate and provide references for what they felt to be true.

Opposition became fierce. The Solovetskii monastery in the White Sea, one of the wealthiest and most powerful in Russia thanks to its monopoly of the local salt trade, became the focus of religious dissent – partly because of the new service books sent there in 1657, but also because Nikon had previously antagonized the Solovki monks by ruling against them in land disputes and removing one of its chief relics, the head of Ivan IV's famous victim, Metropolitan Filipp. In 1666, after the council's condemnation, the Solovki monks' opposition exploded into revolt. The government finally cracked down and besieged the monastery for eight years. Behind their massive walls, the monks grew ever more radical, finally resolving on December 28, 1673, no longer to pray for the tsar. The government could draw the conclusion that the monks – and, by extension, any opponents of the reform – were rebelling not only against church discipline, but against state authority as well. When the monastery fell in 1676, most of the defenders were slaughtered. Those who escaped travelled through northern Russia, recounting and creating a legend of Old Believer purity.[12]

Another celebrated case of dissent was that of Feodosia Morozova. Morozova was a *boiarynia*, a member of the aristocratic elite in the court of Tsar Alexei. As Margaret Ziolkowski has noted, most of the nobility prudently avoided the conflict, to preserve their status and property; Morozova, as a wealthy and independent widow, showed no such caution. Morozova began by offering refuge to other Old Believers; she then attracted unfavorable royal attention by avoiding participation in court ceremonies she now regarded as illegitimate. Even appeals to consider her son did not help. Along with two other companions, Evdokia Urusova and Maria Danilova, she was arrested and tortured in 1672, and died of starvation in an underground pit three years later. Old Believers immediately regarded her as a saint and circulated hagiographic accounts of her life. Centuries later, in 1887, Vasilii Surikov's painting of Morozova making the two-figured sign of the cross would establish her image as an ascetic revolutionary martyr to the cause of freedom of conscience for generations of Russians to come.[13] Morozova's example, which so resembled that of the early Christian martyrs, also strengthened the later scholarly association of Old Belief with other forms of European sectarianism, such as the Anabaptists, who rejected the established church, the sacraments, and the state.

The other prototypical martyr of Old Belief, the archpriest Avvakum, raises the cause's supreme paradox. Avvakum was the spiritual father of Old Belief, because of both his personal charisma and his autobiography. In his *Life*, Avvakum broke with rhetorical literary tradition by using the spoken language of his own time. His splicing of Church Slavonic and the vernacular, vibrant, dead serious, and occasionally hilarious, is the first modern literary work of a Russian for whom theology and ritual are as much a part of daily life as chasing down a lost hen. In its innovative immediacy, its combination of ritual language and the first person, it has much in common with the written confessions that barely literate peasant women would pen at the beginning of the twentieth century.[14] The most conservative group in seventeenth-century Russia had produced the country's most talented and modern writer.[15]

Even more extreme were those who spread the message that Satan had broken the gates of the Church; the Antichrist had come and ruled triumphantly; they, the faithful remnant, were literally living in the last days: faced with this array of disasters, what did any worldly event matter? The best, indeed the only, thing they could do was to save their own souls. When ruled by heathens, the only noble course was martyrdom. The Old Believer groups who actually burned themselves alive in churches rather than submit did just this.

Although self-immolations and the Solovki rebellion worried the government, its associating of Old Believers with rebellion most vividly confirmed itself in the succession crisis of 1682. On July 5 of that year, the *strel'tsy* musketeers, allied with Old Believers, forced the regent Sophia to agree to a public debate of the church reforms. (Perov would depict the confrontation in a painting 200 years later.) Eloquent though the Old Believers were in their theological position, the regent Sophia took to heart the political implications of their argument – her father and brother were heretics, the current bishops were not bishops, all Russian officialdom was illegitimate. She had the ringleader, Nikita "Pustosviat," beheaded for lèse-majesté. Because of this linkage of religious dissent with political subversiveness, and, conversely, of official Orthodox Christianity with political reliability, the Russian authorities would henceforth target the Old Believers for persecution. At the same time, they kept trying to bring them back into the fold.[16] The original mid-seventeenth-century legislation requiring the Orthodox population of Russia to go to confession and communion at least once a year now acquired an additional goal. The object was no longer simply the religious education, discipline, and control of the large and unruly Orthodox flock, but also the identification – and, consequently, punishment – of the Old Believers who refused those sacraments. Confession and communion thus became the markers both of private piety – and of membership in the community of those publicly loyal to Church and State.

The association of the sacraments with good (that is, conservative) citizenship – something remarked upon by sociologists of 1960s France as well as Russian autocrats of the eighteenth century[17] – is all the more potent because the Old Believers and the government agreed on the Church–State linkage. Both believed that Orthodox Christianity was the true faith, and that it was the responsibility of the "secular" Russian state to go after heretics with all its might. The difference, of course, is who got to decide who was truly Orthodox.

Here the written reply of the Old Believer polemicist Andrei Denisov in an important debate on Church and State. The *Pomorskie otvety* is critically important in articulating Old Believer positions (in fact, it would become the cornerstone document of Old Belief). The Old Believers, Denisov argued, had the theological and patristic right to reject the authority of the state Church. In his support he cited St John Chrysostom: "The church is not walls and a roof, but faith and life." (On the other hand, as Father Johannes Chrysostomos later noted, the original text actually read: "The church is not *only* walls and a roof, but faith and life." Thus Denisov was deliberately misquoting to minimize the importance of hierarchy.)[18] With that principle established, Denisov went further. He noted that the reformed service books were internally inconsistent, and that the three-finger sign of cross contradicted the proceedings of Stoglav council. He argued that noetic, or spiritual, communion such as that practiced by St Mary of Egypt could be a substitute for the Eucharist. (On the other hand, he conveniently failed to mention that Mary of Egypt, for all her years of "spiritual communion," nonetheless at the end of her life begged the elder Zosima to bring her the real thing.[19]) In his interpretation, even self-immolation could be another such "communion." But perhaps the most important issue was precisely who was the bearer of Orthodoxy. If the tsar and the state Church were, then the Old Believers were by definition heretics who had no right to oppose true authority. If, on the other hand, one trusted the early saints of Russia and their customs and usages, then the Old Believers who maintained their practices could claim to be considered true heirs to the Orthodox tradition.[20]

The Old Believers thus found themselves in a paradoxical position. On the one hand, they shared many traits of what Ernst Troeltsch has defined as the sect-type as opposed to the church-type. The sect-type insists on a unique possession of truth and rejects the church-type's broader sense of inclusivity and sense of responsibility for the catholicity of the whole church.[21] The Old Believers demonstrated this sectarian quality, keeping their distance from the fallen world to the extent that they refused to eat with (or in some cases even buy food from) the "worldly"; they suspected as foreign innovations such products as potatoes and tea; they tried not to touch any piece of paper bearing the seal of the Antichrist (which included money). Ritual prohibitions like these helped to reinforce a sense of cohesiveness within the Old Believer community and against the world at large.[22] Typically for a persecuted sect, Old Believers also tended to have a greater awareness of the Apocalypse and to believe that the last days were at hand.

But their designation as a "sect" is not really clear-cut. The early Christians also avoided contamination by the outside world; the apostolic canons include prohibitions against eating with heretics as well as praying with them. In this sense the Old Believers were simply being consistent with early tradition. But they also raised the larger issue of what believers are to do if they genuinely believe that the body calling itself the Church has gone astray, and that it is only they, the "faithful remnant," who are now the Church.

For they did not want to be a sect; they wanted to be the Church. Unlike the Protestants, the Old Believers did not believe that every person could judge for himself with scripture as his guide – they staked all on claiming consistency with tradition. But, historically, being part of the Church had meant taking part in its sacraments – particularly those of baptism, or admission, into the community of believers, and the Eucharist. Here the Old Believers foundered.

The Old Believers' most serious and immediate problem after the 1666 council, then, was what to do about the sacraments. No remaining bishops, who were Nikonian to a man, would ordain priests according to the old ritual. As their supply of previously ordained priests began to die without being able to leave any successors, the Old Believers faced a loss of canonically ordained clergy. In a tradition as liturgically based as the Russian Orthodox one, particularly one that claimed to uphold the canons and tradition, this was a disaster.

Different Old Believers came up with different solutions, and split into groups called *soglasiia* (concords) that reflected those differences. The most basic division concerned what to do about priests. The "priestly," or *popovtsy*, argued that priests could still be found; all they had to do was persuade priests from the official church to come over to their side, then bring them back to the old rite by anointing them. This group stood out from the other Old Believers, because, unlike the rest, it accepted the dogmatic canonicity of the post-Nikonian Russian Orthodox Church, even as it rejected its rituals. Because of the gravitation toward having sacraments, particularly the Eucharist, this priestly group predominated in the Old Believer community for over a hundred years. It was particularly strong in central Russia; less so in Siberia and in northern Russia. It is thus not surprising that when in the 1800s the Russian Orthodox Church proposed the nearly equivalent variant of *edinoverie* (unified faith) – people could continue to celebrate according to the old ritual, but under the aegis of the Russian Orthodox Church – many of the "priestly" joined it.

Another "priestly" solution came from the Belokrinitsa group. In 1846, a Bosnian bishop, Amvrosii, agreed to lead an Old Believer diocese in Belaia Krinitsa, Bukovina (in the Austrian Empire). Now that they had their own bishop, in theory the Belokrinitsy could consecrate their own priests and did not need fugitive clergy.

But there were canonical obstacles here as well. Amvrosii took it upon himself to consecrate other bishops himself: this was a clear violation of canon law, which stated that at least two bishops were needed to consecrate a third.[23] Thus some Old Believers preferred to keep taking in fugitive priests rather than risk their souls through this breaking of canonicity. (Of course, Amvrosii's non-Russian background also made him suspect in the eyes of those who relied only on the Russian tradition; and, as Robert Crummey noted, during the Crimean War, the Old Believer presence in two belligerent empires – the Austrian and the Ottoman – stirred even greater government suspicion and persecution.[24]) Nevertheless, thanks partly to the help of the wealthy Rogozhskoe community in Moscow, the Belokrinitsy became the largest single cluster within the Old Believers, and spread quickly throughout the entire empire.

The "priestless," or *bezpopovtsy*, took the principle of apocalyptic gloom to its logical ends. With no consecrated hierarchy who could generate new priests, they were forced to become more inventive in finding ritual solutions that reflected their new realities while maintaining canonicity and fidelity to tradition (to some scholars, their uncompromising stance as regards the official Church, and their assigning greater roles to women, also made them more "authentic" as a sect).[25] "Priestless" Old Believers included the Vyg and Leksa monastic communities, Pomortsy (those along the sea), the radical Filippovtsy and Fedoseevtsy.

In some ways the task was easiest for such Old Believer groups of monks and nuns as the Vyg and Leksa communities. Orthodox monks and nuns had a long tradition of living in remote areas far from regular sacramental life, and of spiritual guidance by a spiritual father or mother. Thus, for the Vyg and the Leksa, ritual life (particularly penance and confession) was not as much of a challenge as it was for those who lived outside monastic communities.

But, as the apostle Paul himself acknowledged, most people could not endure a life of chastity. The issue then was what to do about marriage. Marriage in an Orthodox church meant recognizing the validity of the official Church and its sacraments. Civil marriage – the only form of marriage available to the Christians of the Roman and Byzantine empires for centuries, for marriage became a church sacrament relatively late – might have been a possibility, had it existed in Russia. But even if it had, that might have been out of the question too: radical Old Believers believed that the state was the embodied Antichrist. In the first burst of eschatological fervor, when many Old Believers thought they were living in the last days, it is not surprising that councils like the 1694 Novgorod one enjoined married couples to separate and forbade any new unions from forming. As the years went by, however, it became clear that some form of accommodation with people's physical natures had to be found. Even such pillars of Old Belief as the archpriest Avvakum, himself a husband and father, felt that to avoid sin people should marry in state churches, and to regard this as civil registration. This, however, begged the question of what to do about the promises the state extracted that the children be raised Orthodox in the state Church.[26]

Baptism, by contrast, was relatively simple. Early Christianity, and canon law, allowed any baptized Christian to baptize others. Even contemporary Orthodox Christianity, priest centered though it was, continued to allow this in case of emergency (albeit with the proviso that the baptized person, usually a child, be brought to a priest to regularize and register the baptism once the risk of death or danger had passed).[27] Thus the Old Believers could provide baptism to the community and still hold that they were within the canonical tradition.

Whether priestly or priestless, it took the Old Believers only a generation to create or recast religious practices. In doing so, they diverged ever further from the official Orthodox Church, which in turn became ever more European in its aesthetic forms. Thus, as the Orthodox Church moved toward polyphonic church singing by court composers including Sarti, Galuppi, and Bortniansky, Old Believers stuck to early plainchant written in its own peculiar notation.[28] As the Orthodox Church, particularly among the urban elite, moved towards individual participation in the liturgy – making the sign of the cross, walking around to light candles, and venerating icons as one pleased – it became increasingly important to Old Believers to do these things together, standing still in neat rows so as to make it easier for all to prostrate themselves at the same time without bumping into anyone else. After Peter I, Orthodox churches found themselves decorated with cherubs and spires and Renaissance-perspective religious paintings; Old Believers maintained that icons should remain stylized and truly other-worldly; it was the icon that looked at the viewer, not the other way round.[29]

Icons, of course, were something the Old Believers shared with their fellow Russians who went to the official Orthodox Church. And it was here that the two groups were closest. For, while annual confession and communion had become legal requirements, for most Russian Orthodox Christians religious life continued to revolve not around the sacraments as such, but around such para-liturgical and extra-liturgical practices as blessing eggs, sausages, and *kulichi* and *paskhi* at Easter, apples on Transfiguration, candles on Candlemas (The Meeting of Our Lord in the Temple), and holy water on Theophany; church processions; and blessing everything from crops to carriages. Icons figured prominently in the religious life and religious identity of Russians who called themselves Orthodox Christians, whether mainstream or Old Believer. Icons lined the walls and iconostases of both Orthodox and Old Believer churches; Orthodox Christians of all nationalities celebrated the restoration of icons in worship on the first Sunday of Lent as "The Triumph of Orthodoxy"; Russian peasants often referred to their icons as "God" or "Gods."[30] While the Old Believers maintained icon-painting in the earlier style, and avoided both more naturalistic representations and the use of such modern techniques of reproduction as lithography, functionally, there was little difference in how believers in both traditions venerated icons.[31]

Perhaps the sole difference in the use of icons, one of emphasis, came with the priestless Old Believers. Because (unlike the priestly Old Believers or the Orthodox Christians) they had no Eucharist, for them, of all their rituals, icons became the closest symbolic way to apprehend and to come into physical contact with the Divine world, and thus even more central than they were for Orthodox Christians generally. Similarly, because the priestless Old Believers could not have the Liturgy of the Gifts (where the bread and wine were consecrated), their service had to end with the reading of the gospel: thus, for them, the gospel table took on the symbolic function that approached that of the altar table for Orthodox Christians. This veneration extended both to religious books on which they based their legitimacy – polemical and liturgical texts, including collections of canons – as well as to the Gospels themselves.[32]

On the other hand, there was one point on which the Old Believers most diverged from the Orthodox. And this had to do with praying for the ruler in church. This issue was particularly charged because Orthodox Christianity had a long tradition of praying for the ruler. Praying for secular authorities (even those who persecute Christians), of course, is present in the New Testament itself.[33] From Byzantium onwards, the Christian ruler had special charisma; it was the Orthodox who developed the notion of symphony between sacred and secular powers symbolized by the double-headed eagle. It was Vladimir, prince of Kiev, who baptized Rus' as a state decision; Muscovites continued the tradition of praying for the "most pious Tsar." In other words, praying for the divinely anointed ruler was a normal and utterly characteristic part of Orthodox liturgical practice, much as it was for Roman Catholics and Anglicans (which was perhaps one reason why rulers showed such favor for the state Church).

Russian Orthodox maintained this tradition of praying for the ruler, and even extended it (perhaps partly in response to the Old Believer rejection of the practice). For the Old Believers, by contrast, this was a crucial stumbling-block: some even kept portraits of reigning rulers decked out as the Antichrist (with horns, a tail, and the number 666).[34] But, even when such Old Believer groups as the Vyg decided that some form of prayer for the ruler was acceptable, they still differed sharply from the Orthodox. In the Great Vespers litiia, for example, the Old Believers not only prayed for the health of the tsar and for victory over his enemies (the Orthodox did the same), but they also asked for mercy and remission of his sins; the Orthodox did not. Thus the established Orthodox Church subtly and implicitly raised the ruler above the ranks of ordinary humans; the Old Believers did not. At both Vespers and Divine Liturgy, the Orthodox began to pray, not only for the ruler, but also for his or her extended family (including mother, children, and assorted Grand Princes and Grand Princesses), thus recognizing and deepening their political influence independently of the issue of divine anointment (which only the ruler received). Finally, the Old Believers, unlike the state-sponsored church, did not pray for the "Christ-loving armed forces." Thus, as Roy Robson has convincingly shown, the established Church raised political authority over the community at key moments in services; the old ritual continued to emphasize the relationship between God and the community of the faithful.[35]

Not surprisingly, the Russian state mistrusted those who resisted it, and sought in every way to bring them back into the fold. After Sophia's regency, the imperial administration gradually eased its harsh persecution of Old Believers. Peter I, for example, differentiated between those Old Believers who explicitly opposed his regime, and those who simply wanted to keep old observances. (Of course, it helped that communities like the Vyg were industrious and supported Peter's war machine.) His policies tacitly legitimized the Old Believers, even as they set them apart: he taxed male town-dwellers and visitors who did not shave their beards; he ordered that Old Believers register with government and pay double the amount of poll tax; any Old Believer who did not register was sentenced to hard labor and had to back pay all (double) taxes; any man who kept his beard had also to continue to wear traditional clothing, along with a special medallion. But acknowledgment applied only as long as the Old Believers accepted their label and did not try to "pass": priests who covered for Old Believers by adding their names to the required lists of those who confessed and took communion, were to be defrocked and sent to hard labor.[36]

This combination of limitations and acceptance persisted under the reigns of Empresses Anna and Elizabeth. By contrast, Peter III and Catherine II were beacons of tolerance. Both rulers repealed earlier restrictive laws and allowed Old Believers to flourish. For nearly a hundred years, Old Believers could develop and thrive even in the capital cities; the Preobrazhenskoe and Rogozhskoe communities in Moscow became the financial and administrative centers. In the middle of the nineteenth century, however, Nicholas I, the champion of "Orthodoxy, Autocracy, and Nationality," resumed their persecution with zeal and passion – a policy that would persist in milder form until the Revolution of 1905. Many Old Believers emigrated to the United States, where they established colonies that still flourish in Oregon, Alaska, and Pennsylvania.[37]

This harsh treatment, which was unique to the Old Believers, seems paradoxical. When most people hear about religious persecution in the Russian Empire or the Soviet Union, they assume the discussion concerns Jews or Muslims. And yet the specifically religious hardships these groups faced pale when compared to the groups who most resembled the Orthodox: the Old Believers (and to a lesser extent the Greek Catholic Uniates). This should not surprise us, however. The authorities regarded Old Believers and Uniates as former Orthodox Christians who had fallen away through accident or delusion; it was their spiritual responsibility to bring them back. There was also a pragmatic reason. Virtually no Orthodox Christian in the Russian Empire was going to convert to Judaism or Islam: there was no earthly advantage in doing so, nor, for that matter, any spiritual one either: neither group claimed to be, nor sought to be, the True Church.[38] The Old Believers, on the other hand, personified a potent mix of attractions: they could legitimately claim to be more Orthodox, more Russian, more authentic than the ruling powers or hierarchy. Of all the confessions in the empire, they represented the greatest temptation to fervent Orthodox Christians and the greatest threat to the legitimacy of the state Church. They could represent, in short, both true self and the "other."

Representations

For this reason, the Old Believers came to occupy an increasingly powerful role as symbols of authentic Russian tradition. In the nineteenth century, Russians, like many Europeans, rejected eighteenth-century Enlightenment and classical ideals and became fascinated with Romanticism and the achievements of their respective medieval periods. This led to a revival of interest in Old Believers, who appeared to be living relics. Avvakum's autobiography was published in 1861; the historian Ivan E. Zabelin recounted Morozova's life in his *The Domestic Life of Russian Queens in the 16th and 17th Centuries.* Such writers as Nikolai Leskov and Pavel Mel'nikov-Pecherskii portrayed Old Believers in their stories and novels; Modest Mussorgsky's opera *Khovanshchina* depicted Old Believers leaving this world in a blaze of terrible glory.

Fittingly, given their own role in preserving traditional iconography and other forms of visual culture, Old Believers appeared in contemporary painting.[39] Grigorii G. Miasoedov's depictions of Old Believer heroes included *Self-Immolators* (1882) and *The Immolation of the Archpriest Avvakum*; S. D. Miloradovich's *Black Council* (1885) depicted the 1668–76 uprising at Solovki. Similarly fittingly, given the high proportion of women transmitting Old Belief culture, the most celebrated visual representation of Old Belief was the boiarynia Morozova. While Vasilii Perov, A. D. Litovchenko, and K. V. Lebedev showed different episodes of her trials and torture, the "canonical" representation was that of Vasilii Surikov (1887). In Surikov's painting, Morozova appears being hauled off in a straw-filled sleigh, her gaunt face, piercing eyes, and triumphant two-fingered sign of the cross attracting simultaneous jeers and pity from passers-by. It makes perfect sense that she would inspire such revolutionaries as Sofia Perovskaia and Vera Figner.

In a final paradox, and one that made them all the more attractive to some Orthodox Christians, the Old Believers resolved their ambivalent relation to this world by becoming unusually successful at dealing with it. Like many religious minorities in a hostile context, they quickly learned to rely on themselves and on their own combined strength. A disproportionate number of Old Believers become part of the Russian industrial bourgeoisie – who, for all their success, never forgot how the Russian state had treated them and sought alternatives to existing political culture.[40] Such Old Believers as Savva Morozov and Pavel Riabushinskii became patrons both of the arts and of politics. Riabushinskii's liberal agenda combined Old Believer industrialists' entrepreneurship with the broader Old Believer traditions of self-governance. His was an inventive proposal to the early twentieth-century Russian political crisis, suggesting that innovation could best come from the very groups who had held on to pre-Petrine religious social traditions. Riabushinskii funded his own daily newspaper, *Utro Rossii* (The Morning of Russia), which encouraged its readers to seek a moderate solution, avoiding the extremes of both anarchist revolutionaries and reactionaries who wanted nothing more than the restoration of the old order. The fabulously rich Savva Morozov, by contrast, was more radical and more eclectic: he funded the Russian Social Democrats (that is, the communists), the Moscow Art Theater, and the writer Maxim Gorky. With their long tradition of successful resistance to a hostile state, the Old Believers were better prepared than the Orthodox to resist Bolshevik persecution and practiced their rituals both under Soviet rule and after it, in and outside the former Soviet Union.

The Old Believers continue to adapt traditions to a changing world in inventive ways that echo past attitudes toward both gender and the state. As Douglas Rogers noted, for example, when a town in the Urals recently shifted from priestless to priestly Old Belief, most of its faithful chose to use the priest and the church for baptisms – that is, the official sign of belonging to the community and for legitimacy in this world, just as it was under the tsars – but continued to use old women for funeral rituals.[41] In other words, baptism was still the official, sacramental sign of belonging to the community and practical, this-worldly necessities, and thus entrusted to men empowered to carry it out, while passing into the next life is a non-sacramental act that brings the believer back to his ancestors, and thus continued to be entrusted to the community members who most exemplify the links to tradition and kin.

Scholarship

By the second half of the nineteenth century, the literature on Old Belief fell into two basic groups.[42] Texts by Old Believer apologists and official Orthodox church historians took seriously the religious conflict: they focused on the disputed issues of ritual practice and the implications of those disputes. To church historians, for example, opponents were superstitious, ignorant, and overly literal. These included Bishop Makarii, Elpidifor V. Barsov, and Petr S. Smirnov.[43] By contrast, the populists largely ignored the religious context. Instead, they interpreted Old Belief as a popular movement of political, cultural, social opposition to increasing centralization of the

Russian state, and to Western influence generally. In this reading, the Old Believers were defending "ancient Russian" traditions of self-government, freedom from serfdom, and the local over the central. While Alexander Herzen and Nikolai Ogarev were the first to see Old Belief mostly as a protest against imperial police rule, Afanasii P. Shchapov developed the most consistently democratic and detailed reading of Old Belief.[44] The populist, relatively secular interpretation found a congenial framework in the Soviet period, when Old Belief was presented as a popular, anti-feudal, anti-state movement.[45] Because it could be couched in these terms, Old Belief could be a legitimate area of scholarly enquiry in a way the Orthodox Church, still tainted for its connection to the state, was not. Soviet-era scholars, including Nikolai N. Pokrovskii and Natalia S. Gurianov, led several generations of scholars who contributed a wealth of ethnographic information about contemporary Old Belief.[46]

Theoretical research continued in Europe as well. The works of Pierre Pascal and émigré scholar Serge Zenkovsky provided a foundation for American scholars, including Michael Cherniavsky and Robert O. Crummey. Old Believer communities outside the former Soviet Union, most notably those in the Pacific Northwest of the United States and in Riga, Latvia, have become their own objects of research. In these communities, as with Russian Orthodoxy, the national and ethnic component of tradition is growing less important than maintaining proper ritual observances. Fresh recent perspectives used by Georg Michels, Irina Paert, and Roy Robson include those of gender and comparative analysis. In a final paradoxical coda, after perestroika, the scholarship on Old Belief has become perhaps the most truly international enterprise of all the fields of Russian history.

Notes

1   In a particularly extreme variant, Tadeusz Nasierowski sees Old Belief as the prototypical dissident movement, leading straight to Lenin. See Nasierowski, *Swiat rosyjskiej ducho-wosci*, 263–4.
2   Paul of Aleppo, *The Travels of Macarius*, 170.
3   See the discussion in Lebedev, *Moskva patriarshaia*, 136–55.
4   Rumiantseva, "Patriarkh Nikon," 217–26.
5   For this point and for masterly surveys of the current state of scholarship generally, see Crummey, "Past and Current Interpretations of Old Belief," and Pokrovskii, "Trends in Studying the History of Old Belief by Russian Scholars," unpublished papers I am grateful to Roy Robson for sharing.
6   Michels, *At War with the Church*, 229.
7   Uspensky, "The Schism and Cultural Conflict," 106.
8   Gaspar, "The King of Kings and the Holy Men," 63, 74–88.
9   Uspensky, "The Schism and Cultural Conflict," 107.
10 Robson, *Old Believers in Modern Russia*, 8.
11 Meyendorff, *Russia, Ritual and Reform*.
12 Michels, "The Solovki Uprising," 1–15.
13 Ziolkowski, *Tale of Boiarynia Morozova*.
14 Kizenko, "Written Confessions and the Construction of Sacred Narrative," 93–118.
15 See Mirsky's introduction to: Avvakum, *The Life of the Archpriest Avvakum by Himself.*
16 Michels, "Rescuing the Orthodox," 19–37.

17 Michel Vovelle identified the correlation of right-wing voting in France with those districts with the highest percentage of voters who went to communion at Easter. Vovelle, *Idéologies et mentalités*, 240–4.

18 P. Johannes Chrysostomos, *Die "Pomorskie Otvety" als Denkmal des russischen Altgläubigen gegen Ende des 1 Viertels des XVIII Jahrh.*, quoted in Zenkovsky, *Russkoe staroobriadchestvo*, 464.

19 See the Life of St Mary of Egypt in Talbot, ed., *Holy Women of Byzantium*, 88–90.

20 The distinction between the myth of the Russian nation and the Russian ruler is developed by Cherniavsky, *Tsar and People*.

21 Troeltsch, "Sect-Type and Church-Type Contrasted," in his *The Social Teaching of the Christian Churches*, 331–49.

22 See Robson's stimulating discussion of ritual prohibitions in *Old Believers and Modern Russia*, 96–115.

23 This is the very first apostolic canon. See *Pravila sviatykh apostolov*, 13–15.

24 Crummey, "Interpreting the Fate of Old Believer Communities," in Batalden, ed., *Seeking God*, 158.

25 See the discussion in Paert, *Old Believers*, 30–49.

26 See the discussion in Crummey, *The Old Believers and the World of Antichrist*, 113–22.

27 For a canonical discussion of how laypeople may baptize in case of emergency, see Bulgakov., *Nastol'naia kniga*, 974–77; for a discussion of the various ways in which to receive Old Believers into Orthodoxy, see pp. 1014–17.

28 Ritzarev, *Eighteenth-Century Russian Music*.

29 For examples of how Russian icons diverged, see *Pozdniaia russkaia ikona*.

30 See Vladimir I. Dal', *Tolkovyi slovar'*, 103.

31 For a contemporary discussion of the problems of the mass-produced icon, see Kondakov, *Sovremennoe polozhenie russkoi narodnoi ikonoposi*; for an English-language analysis, see Nichols, "The Icon and the Machine."

32 For a discussion of Old Believer liturgical spaces, see Roy Robson, "An Architecture of Change," in Batalden, ed., *Seeking God*, 160–87.

33 See Romans 13: 1–6, and I Peter 2: 13–17.

34 See illustration 20 in Nasierowski, *Swiat rosyjskiej*, 194.

35 Robson, *Old Believers in Modern Russia*, 41–52.

36 *Polnoe Sobranie Postanovlenii i rasporiazhenii po viedomstvu pravoslavnago ispoviedaniia Rossiiskoi imperii. Tsarstvovaniie Gosudaria tsaria i velikago kniazia Petra Alekseevicha*, 1–251.

37 For the Old Believer experience in the United States, see Colfer, *Morality, Kindred, and Ethnic Boundary: A Study of the Oregon Old Believers*.

38 The issue of Jews or Muslims who converted to Orthodoxy and then wished to return to their ancestral faiths posed a special problem. See Eugene Avrutin, "Returning to Judaism after the 1905 Law on Religious Toleration in Tsarist Russia," *Slavic Review*, 65/1 (Spring 2006):, 90–110, and Firouzeh Mostashari, "Colonial Dilemmas: Russian Policies in the Muslim Caucasus," in Robert P. Geraci and Michael Khodarkovsky, eds., *Of Religion and Empire: Missions, Conversion, and Tolerance in Tsarist Russia* (Ithaca, NY: Cornell University Press, 2001), 229–49. For imperial policies towards Uniates, see Theodore Weeks, "Between Rome and Tsargrad: The Uniate Church in Imperial Russia," in ibid. 70–91.

39 For examples of their work, see the State Historical Museum exhibition catalogue *Neizvestnaia Rossiia*.

40 Blackwell, "The Old Believers," 407–24.

41 Rogers, "Protecting the Young," 1–4.

42   For a contemporary survey of the two schools, see Brockhaus and Efron, *Entsiklopedicheskii slovar'*, t. 26, v. 51, pp. 288–303.
43   Makarii, episkop, *Istoriia russkago raskola izvestnago pod imenem staroobriadchestva* (St Petersburg, 1855); P. S. Smirnov, *Istoriia russkago raskola staroobriadchestva*, 2nd edn. (St Petersburg, 1895); N. I. Subbotin, *Materialy dlia istorii raskola za pervoe vremia ego sushchestvovaniia*, 9 vols. (Moscow, 1874–90).
44   His works include A. P. Shchapov, *Russkii raskol staroobriadchestva, razsmatrivaemyi v sviazi s vnutrennim sostoianiem russkoi tserkvi i grazhdanstvennosti v 17 viekie i v pervoi polovinie 18* (Kazan, 1859).
45   R. G. Pikhoia, *Obshchestvenno-politicheskaia mysl' trudiashchikhsia Urala (konets XVII–XVIII v.* (Sverdlovsk: Sredne-ural'skoe knizhnoe izd., 1987).
46   See, e.g., Natalia S. Gurianova, *Istoriia i chelovek v sochineniiakh staroobriadtsev XVIII veka* (Novosibirsk: Nauka, 1996); Nikolai N. Pokrovskii, *Stavovery-chasovennye na vostoke Rossii v XVIII–XX vv. problemy tvorchestva i obshchestvennogo soznaniia* (Moscow: Pamiatniki istoricheskoi mysli, 2002), and the articles of their research groups.

References

Avvakum (1963). *The Life of the Archpriest Avvakum by Himself*, translated from the Seventeenth Century Russian by Jane Harrison and Hope Mirrlees, with a preface by Prince D. S. Mirsky. Hogarth Press, 1924; repr. Archon Books, Hamden, CT.

Blackwell, W. L. (1965). "The Old Believers and the Rise of Private Industrial Enterprise in Early Nineteenth-Century Moscow," *Slavic Review*, 24/3 (Sept.), 407–24.

Bulgakov, S. V. (1913). *Nastol'naia kniga dlia sviashchenno-tserkovno-sluzhitelei.* 2nd edn., v. 2. Tip. Kievo-Pecherskoi Uspenskoi Lavry, Kiev.

Cherniavsky, M. (1961). *Tsar and People: Studies in Russian Myths.* Yale University Press, New Haven.

Colfer, A. Michael (1985), *Morality, Kindred, and Ethnic Boundary: A Study of the Oregon Old Believers.* AMS Press, New York.

Crummey, R. O. (1970). *The Old Believers and the World of Antichrist: The Vyg Community and the Russian State 1694–1855.* University of Wisconsin Press, Madison.

Crummey, R. O. (1993). "Interpreting the Fate of Old Believer Communities in the Eighteenth and Nineteenth Centuries," in Stephen K. Batalden, ed., *Seeking God: The Recovery of Religious Identity in Orthodox Russia, Ukraine, and Georgia.* Northern Illinois University Press, DeKalb, IL

Dal', V. I. (1956). *Tolkovyi slovar' zhivogo velikorusskago iazyka.* Vol. 1 Gosizdat, Moscow.

Gaspar, C. (2004) "The King of Kings and the Holy Men: Royal Authority and Sacred Power in the Early Byzantine World," in A. Al-Azmeh.and J. M. Bak (eds.), *Monotheistic Kingship: The Medieval Variants. Central European University Press*, Budapest and New York, 63–88.

Kizenko, Nadieszda (2007). "Written Confessions and the Construction of Sacred Narrative," in M. Steinberg and H. Coleman, eds., *Sacred Stories: Religion and Spirituality in Modern Russia.* Indiana University Press, Bloomington, IN, 93–118.

Kondakov, N. P. (1901). *Sovremennoe polozhenie russkoi narodnoi ikonopisi. Tip. I. N.* Skorokhodova, Moscow.

Lebedev, L. (1995) *Moskva patriarshaia.* "Stolitsa/Veche," Moscow.

Makarii, episkop. (1855). *Istoriia russkago raskola izvestnago pod imenem staroobriadchestva.* St Petersburg.

Meyendorff, P. (1991). *Russia, Ritual and Reform: The Liturgical Reforms of Nikon in the 17th Century.* St Vladimir's Seminary Press, Crestwood, NY.

Michels, G. (1999). *At War with the Church: Religious Dissent in Seventeenth-Century Russia.* Stanford University Press, Stanford, CA.

Michels, G. (1992) "The Solovki Uprising: Religion and Revolt in Northern Russia," *Russian Review*, 51: 1–15.

Michels, G. (2001) "Rescuing the Orthodox: The Church Policies of Archbishop Afanasii of Kholmogory, 1682–1702," in R. P. Geraci and M. Khodarkovsky, eds., *Of Religion and Empire: Missions, Conversion, and Tolerance in Tsarist Russia.* Cornell University Press, Ithaca, NY, 19–37.

Nasierowski, T. (2005). *Swiat rosyjskiej duchowosci: Koscioly i ruchy dysydenckie a Cerkiew panujaca.* Wyd. Neriton, Warsaw.

Nichols, R. L. (1991). "The Icon and the Machine in Russia's Religious Renaissance, 1900–1909," in W. Brumfield and M. Velimirovic, eds., *Christianity and the Arts in Russia.* Cambridge University Press, Cambridge.

Paert, I. (2003). *Old Believers, Religious Dissent and Gender in Russia, 1760–1850.* Manchester University Press, Manchester and New York.

Paul of Aleppo, Archdeacon (1936). *The Travels of Macarius, Extracts from the Diary of the Travels of Macarius, Patriarch of Antioch, Written in Arabic by his Son Paul, Archdeacon of Aleppo, in the Years of their Journeying, 1652–1660.* Translated into English and printed for the Oriental translation fund, 1836. Selected and arranged by Lady Laura Riding. Oxford University Press/H. Milford, London.

Pozdniaia russkaia ikona konets XVIII–XIX vek. (1994). Kinotsentr/Limbus Press, St Petersburg.

Pravila sviatykh apostolov, sviatykh soborov, vselenskikh i pomiestnykh, i sviatykh otets s tolkovaniiami (1876). Izd. Moskovskago Ob. liubitelei dukhovnago prosveshcheniia, Moscow.

Ritzarev, Marina (2008), *Eighteenth-Century Russian Music.* Ashgate, Aldershot, England, and Burlington, VT.

Robson, R. R. (1995). *Old Believers in Modern Russia.* Northern Illinois University Press, DeKalb, IL.

Robson, R. R. (2002). *Solovki: The Story of Russia told through its most Remarkable Islands.* Yale University Press, New Haven.

Rogers, D. J. (2003). "Protecting the Young and Sending off the Dead: Old Belief and the Politics of 'Religious Revival' in the Russian Urals," *Anthropology of Eastern Europe Review*, 21/2: 1–4.

Rumiantseva, V. S. (2004). "Patriarkh Nikon i Stefan Vonifat'ev: k postanovke voprosa o tserkovnykh reformakh 50-x godov XVII v.," in E. M. Iukhimenko, *Patriarkh Nikon i ego vremia: sbornik nauchnykh trudov. Gosudarstvennyi Istoricheskii.* Muzei, Moscow, 217–26.

State Historical Museum (1994). *Neizvestnaia Rossiia: k 300-letiiu Vygovskoi staroobriadcheskoi pustyni.* GIM, Moscow.

Talbot, A. M. (ed.) (1996). *Holy Women of Byzantium: Ten Saints' Lives in English Translation.* Dumbarton Oaks, Washington.

Troeltsch, E. (1960). *The Social Teaching of the Christian Churches.* Vol. 1. Harper & Row/Harper Torchbooks, New York.

Uspensky, B. A. (1993). "The Schism and Cultural Conflict in the Seventeenth Century," in S. Batalden, ed., *Seeking God: The Recovery of Religious Identity in Orthodox Russia, Ukraine, and Georgia.* Northern Illinois University Press, DeKalb, IL.

Vovelle, M. (1982). *Idéologies et mentalités.* Prospero, Paris.

Zenkovsky, S. (1970). *Russkoe staroobriadchestvo: dukhovnye dvizheniia semnadtsatogo veka.* Wilhelm Fink Verlag, Munich.

Ziolkowski, M. (comp. and trans.) (2000). *Tale of Boiarynia Morozova: A Seventeenth-Century Religious Life.* Lexington Books, Lanham, MD.

Further Reading

Avvakum (1963). *The Life of the Archpriest Avvakum by Himself*, translated from the Seventeenth Century Russian by Jane Harrison and Hope Mirrlees, with a preface by Prince D. S. Mirsky. Hogarth Press, 1924; repr. Archon Books, Hamden.

Crummey, R. O. (1970). *The Old Believers and the World of Antichrist: The Vyg Community and the Russian State 1694–1855*. University of Wisconsin Press, Madison.

Michels, G. (1999). *At War with the Church: Religious Dissent in Seventeenth-Century Russia*. Stanford University Press, Stanford, CA.

Paert, I. (2003). *Old Believers, Religious Dissent and Gender in Russia, 1760–1850*. Manchester University Press, Manchester and New York.

Pascal, Pierre (1938). *Avvakum et les débuts du Raskol: La Crise religieuse au XVIIe siècle en Russie*. Centre d'Études Russes "Istina", Paris.

Robson, R. (1995). *Old Believers in Modern Russia*. Northern Illinois University Press, DeKalb, IL.

Uspensky, B. A. (1993) "The Schism and Cultural Conflict in the Seventeenth Century," in S. Batalden, ed., *Seeking God: The Recovery of Religious Identity in Orthodox Russia, Ukraine, and Georgia*. Northern Illinois University Press, DeKalb, IL.

Zenkovsky, S. (1970). *Russkoe staroobriadchestvo: dukhovnye dvizheniia semnadtsatogo veka*. Wilhelm Fink Verlag, Munich.

Ziolkowski, M. (comp. and trans.) (2000). *Tale of Boiarynia Morozova: A Seventeenth-Century Religious Life*. Lexington Books, Lanham, MD.

PART III

The Russian Empire

CHAPTER TEN

Petrine Russia

LINDSEY HUGHES

Few reigns have constituted such a watershed in their country's history as that of Peter I, the Great (born 1672, reigned 1682–1725). Contemporaries, using biblical imagery, claimed that he transformed Russia "from non-existence into being". In 1846 the Russian historian Nikolai Pogodin wrote: "The Russia of today, that is, European Russia, diplomatic, political, military, commercial, industrial, scholastic, literary – is a creation of Peter the Great . . . Wherever we look, everywhere we meet this colossal figure, who casts a long shadow over our entire past" [1: 111]. Peter has remained prominently in the public eye in the post-Soviet period, as an inspiration for Gorbachev, Yeltsin, and Putin, voted Russia's "most significant" ruler in a number of opinion polls. Apart from a brief period in the late 1920s–early 1930s when Soviet historians attempted to write personalities out of history, few have disputed the vital significance of Peter's personal impact on his country's history, but disagreement continues about whether his policies were beneficial or detrimental to Russia's development. The Petrine legacy has been viewed in terms of, on the one hand, progress, rationality, and enlightenment, on the other, repression, arbitrariness, and tyranny.

Transformation

The Russia (Muscovy) of 1672 was regarded as "backward" by West European standards, although it showed signs of "modernization" [2]. It was the largest country in the world, but had no outlets to major seas and suffered from a harsh climate and poor communications. Just 4 percent of the estimated population of ten million were registered town-dwellers; over 90 percent were peasants, of whom roughly half were serfs, under a law inscribed in statute as recently as 1649. The long-bearded boyars, Russia's elite, advised the tsar, commanded his armies, headed his chancelleries, lived well off their serf-manned estates, but enjoyed no institutionalized political power and had little formal education or culture independent of the court. The Orthodox Church, headed by its patriarch, ruled the daily lives of all Russians and dominated high culture, but had recently been rent by a schism of "Old Believers" protesting against reforms, as well as suffering state encroachment on its land and courts. Peter's father Alexis was an autocratic monarch, his power unlimited by representative or corporate institutions. He ruled from the Kremlin in Moscow, where his residence, cathedrals, and adjoining spaces provided the backdrop to a constant round of courtly and religious ritual in which the tsar formed the impressive center, surrounded by his boyars, but not by their wives, who lived in seclusion. Alexis's reign saw some modern developments, notably in military reform, but Western influences were experienced mostly behind closed doors (as in the court theatre, founded in 1672) and non-Orthodox West European "heretics" were confined to a walled suburb. Western visitors stressed Russia's "otherness" – the master–slave mentality that permeated all levels of society, the seclusion of women, and the absence of schools and secular culture [3]. Russia was marginal to world affairs.

By Peter's death in 1725 he ruled Russia from the new capital and port of St Petersburg. From 1721 he reigned as emperor, arguably in a more absolute manner than his father. The empire had expanded to the Baltic and along the shores of the Caspian Sea. The Baltic shores were patrolled by Russia's new navy, which frightened even the British. The office of patriarch had been abolished and the Church was harnessed more firmly than ever to the service of the State. Elite men and women mingled socially, clad in Western dress, the men clean-shaven. Foreigners were no longer confined to a ghetto, but played prominent roles as experts. Yet the basis of the Russian economy remained peasant agriculture and the taxes extracted from the peasant population. The "military-fiscal" state had been rationalized and streamlined by edicts and regulations, but it still operated on the principle of autocratic rule. Indeed, Peter's successes were scarcely imaginable without the twin pillars of autocracy and serfdom. Much had changed on the surface, but much remained the same during this "revolutionary" reign. Peter was painfully aware that little could be accomplished without firm direction from above. As he wrote in November 1723: "our people are like children who, out of ignorance, will never get down to learning their alphabet unless the master forces them to do so" [4: vol. 7, no. 4345, pp. 150–1]. Such thinking would inform his successors' policies right down to the early twentieth century.

Formative Experiences

Peter was the son of Tsar Aleksei (Alexis) Mikhailovich (reigned 1645–76) and his second wife, Natalia Naryshkina. At his birth on May 30, 1672, he was only third in line to the throne according to the unwritten custom of male primogeniture, which gave precedence to his two half-brothers, Fedor (born 1661) and Ivan (born 1666). There was little in Peter's early childhood to explain his later radical turn of mind. Russian tutors taught him the basics of literacy and priests inculcated the essentials of religion. Foreigner observers detected liveliness and curiosity, which were given free rein by a peculiar turn of events in 1682. Fedor succeeded his father, but died childless in April 1682. Tradition suggested that Ivan should inherit, but Ivan's disabilities, including visual and speech impairments, gave grounds for intervention by a powerful faction at court headed by Peter's maternal relatives, the Naryshkins and their clients. Peter was declared tsar, but a backlash soon followed from the faction of boyars grouped around the relatives of Tsar Alexis's first wife, the Miloslavskys, who were able to harness the support of Moscow's armed militia, the *strel'tsy*, or musketeers. Following a massacre of Naryshkin supporters in May, a compromise was reached by declaring a joint stardom, with Ivan as senior and Peter as junior tsar under the regency of Ivan's sister Sophia [5]. For much of the regency Peter and his mother resided at Preobrazhenskoe in the Moscow suburbs, while Ivan enjoyed the limelight of courtly and religious ceremonials. This arrangement gave Peter ample scope to develop interests and skills that would prove crucial for his subsequent sole rule. First, he assembled and drilled two play regiments, which, as the Preobrazhenskii and Semenovskii guards, would form the elite corps of a reformed army, commanded by foreign officers and clad in Western-style uniforms. Secondly, he learned to sail using an old English boat, a hobby that would stimulate the founding of the Russian navy [6]. In both activities foreigners were his advisors and companions, a radical break with the practice of his predecessor, who had personally kept "heretics" at arm's length, while taking cautious advantage of their expertise. Peter's reliance on foreigners and their "cunning ways" would stimulate one of many controversies surrounding his methods. As the early nineteenth-century historian Nikolai Karamzin wrote: "We became citizens of the world but ceased in certain respects to be citizens of Russia. The fault is Peter's" [7: 124].

In 1689 Peter's faction ousted Sophia, taking advantage of her regime's failure in two campaigns against the Tatars in 1687 and 1689 under the command of Prince Vasilii Vasil'evich Golitsyn. These were Russia's contribution to the Holy League with Austria and Poland, which it joined in 1686. Although the Sophia–Golitysn government had pursued many policies that Peter himself consolidated, founding an academy in Moscow, signing treaties with Prussia, encouraging foreign expertise and culture, factional struggle went in Peter's favor. He believed that Sophia was plotting to murder him, although the evidence is inconclusive. (Ivan would continue his figurehead role until his death in 1696.)

Foreign Adventures

In the early 1690s Peter's focus was still firmly on southern policy, as determined by Russia's participation in the Holy League. In 1695 he led an abortive campaign against the Turkish fort at Azov at the mouth of the river Don, returning to capture it in 1696 with a fleet constructed further up river at Voronezh. He followed up this victory with a "Grand Embassy" to the West, visiting Livonia, Prussia–Brandenburg, the Dutch Republic, England, Austria, and Poland. The proclaimed purpose was to obtain military and financial aid for the Holy League, but for Peter it was a personal voyage of discovery that confirmed his suspicion that Russia lagged behind the advanced countries of Western Europe. He collected information, artifacts and personnel, studying shipbuilding in Amsterdam and London under the pseudonym Peter Mikhailov. His inseparable companion was a commoner, Alexander Menshikov (1673–1729), who would rise to be the richest and most titled man in Russia.

Peter's pretence that he was a simple shipwright was one of several disguises that he maintained throughout his life. These included his roles as archdeacon Gedeon in the All-Drunken, All-Jesting Assembly, an irreverent gathering of cronies that parodied church rituals, and as the "humble subject" of Prince-Caesar Fedor Romodanovskii, who performed the part of mock tsar in traditional robes, among other things conferring on Peter his promotions in the army and navy. Once dismissed as irrelevant to reform or even too indecent to investigate, these and other examples of mock behavior have recently attracted the attention of serious scholars as ways in which Peter asserted his authority to transform Russia and bonded with his supporters [8, 9]. They owed a debt to foreign examples of the "world turned upside down", as well as to Russian festival culture.

Peter's mock institutions held up for ridicule the old, traditional Russia, on which Peter launched an attack immediately upon his return from the Embassy in August 1698. He forced the boyars to shave their beards [10], compelled them and their womenfolk to wear Western dress [11], adopted the Western practice of numbering years from the birth of Christ (1700), and dealt harshly with the musketeers, whose rebellion had forced him to cut short his travels. The bearded, xenophobic troops were the antithesis of Peter's new reformed guards, clean-shaven, in Western uniforms, and commanded by foreigners.

The Great Northern War and St Petersburg

Army reform would remain at the heart of Peter's program, and became especially critical after 1700, when Russia went to war with Sweden under King Charles XII (reigned 1697–1718), with the aim of regaining "patrimonial" Russian lands on the Baltic. The Great Northern War, as it came to be known, lasted for twenty-one years. It was, in the analysis of the late Tsarist historian Vasilii Kliuchevskii, the driving force behind all Peter's reforms [12]. A key catalyst was Russia's defeat at Narva in November 1700 by a much smaller Swedish army, which provoked a concerted effort to improve recruitment (based on a levy from peasant households), officers, and artillery. By 1702 the Russians were occupying territory on the Baltic (aided by Charles XII's withdrawal to Poland and Saxony to tackle Peter's ally King Augustus II of Poland), and in 1703 they captured the site on the river Neva of the future capital St Petersburg.

St Petersburg, Russia's "window on the West" (the phrase was coined by an Italian traveler in 1739), would grow rapidly from a wooden fortress to become Russia's capital and major port. For Peter it embodied many ideas, both practical and symbolic – it was the new city of St Peter, the tsar's watery "Paradise," the antithesis of Moscow, a microcosm of what he hoped the rest of Russia would eventually become, with Western-style architecture and regulations for everything from street-cleaning to tree-planting. (A Police Department was established in 1718 to supervise public welfare.) Not surprisingly. St Petersburg has provided a debating point for Peter's admirers and opponents, the latter pointing to the unacceptable sacrifice of building a city "on the bones" of conscripted peasant laborers [7], its unsuitable climate and geographical location, and its non-Russian and "artificial" character, in contrast with Moscow, the mother of Russian cities. For Peter the city was his pledge for the future, a fresh beginning. At times of despair during the war he contemplated relinquishing other conquests, but never St Petersburg [13].

In 1705–6 Peter found himself confronting the Swedes in Poland, where Charles XII deposed King Augustus and installed his own puppet ruler Stanislaw Leszczynski. The Swedes moved inexorably toward the Lithuanian–Russian border, where in 1708 they were joined by rebel Cossacks under hetman Ivan Mazepa. Peter bought time with a scorched-earth policy and by destroying Mazepa's base in Ukraine, where in summer 1709 the Russians and Swedes faced each other for the first time in fixed battle under their respective royal commanders at the town of Poltava. The outcome was an "unprecedented" Russian victory, which resulted in the destruction or capture of most of an army previously thought invincible. Russia restored alliances with Denmark and Poland, where Augustus was reinstalled, signed a treaty with Prussia, and in 1710 captured a string of Swedish-held ports on the Baltic, including Riga, Reval (Tallinn), and Vyborg. The war effort shifted to Sweden's remaining possessions in North Germany, where in 1712–13 combined Russian, Danish, and Prussian forces invaded Pomerania, capturing Stettin and other towns. In 1713–14 Russia waged a campaign in Finland, driving the Swedes from their major strongholds and scoring its first major naval success at the battle of Hango in July 1714.

Few have disputed that this period saw Russia emerge as a contender for first-rate-power status in Europe. Permanent Russian embassies sprang up, where previously there had been almost none, and foreign ministers flocked to St Petersburg. For the first time since the sixteenth century Russian royal princes and princesses contracted diplomatic marriages. Yet it also saw a major defeat that could have jeopardized all Russia's advances. In 1710 Turkey, alarmed by Russian military operations in Poland and goaded by Charles XII and his sympathizers, declared war on Russia. In 1711 Peter led an army to the river Pruth in Moldavia, where he found himself surrounded by a superior Turkish force and let down by the Orthodox rulers of Moldavia and Wallachia, with whose help he had hoped to turn the campaign into a crusade on behalf of co-religionists under infidel rule. Luckily for Russia, the Turks were appeased by the return of Azov and anxious to deploy their forces elsewhere. Peter and his army were allowed to return home. The final settlement came with the Treaty of Adrianople in 1713.

During this period Peter had little time to produce a blueprint for changing Russia, something that was not, in any case, a feature of his rather ad-hoc approach; reforms proceeded piecemeal. In 1710 he launched a major building program under foreign architects in St Petersburg. and over the next few years issued a series of decrees – for example, limiting the use of masonry outside the capital and forcing noble families to move there (1714). He reformed the Russian alphabet, creating a plain new "civil" typeface (1708–10) to be used alongside the traditional church script for the publication of increasing numbers of practical manuals on such topics as shipbuilding, navigation, artillery, architecture, and geography, as well as countless government decrees and statutes. There were experiments with schools (the cipher schools, 1714; the Naval Academy, 1715; the Academy of Sciences, 1725), although they mostly proved unpopular. In 1711 Peter created the ten-man Senate to rule in his absence. Its major tasks were to act as a higher court of appeal and to raise money (the "artery of war") and recruits.

In the following years fiscal policy would center on maximizing revenues, with censuses or "revisions" of the taxable population in the 1710s–1720s culminating in the introduction of the poll tax, which replaced assessment by household with a count of individual male "heads." It was collected for the first time in 1724. Debate continues over whether the new tax represented an additional burden on the peasantry, who, serfs and state peasants alike, were subject also to increased demands of recruitment and labor duties. Many formerly "free" categories, such as the sons of priests and smallholders, found themselves subjected to the poll tax, with an associated decline in status. Increased burdens prompted protests, often heavily laced with xenophobic sentiments, notably the Astrakhan (1705) and Bulavin (1707–8) revolts.

In 1716–17 Peter made another major tour of Western Europe, which took him to Germany, Denmark, the Dutch Republic, the Netherlands, and France. In Paris his interests encompassed tapestries, coins and medals, scientific experiments, fountains, and gardens. Versailles would feature as a model for his own country residences that sprung up around St Petersburg in the 1710s–1720s, notably at Peterhof and Strelna. His observation of various administrative systems as well as data gathered by informants abroad resulted in the creation in 1717–18 of nine Colleges or collegiate boards (*kollegii*) – Foreign Affairs; State Revenues; Justice; State Accounting; Military; Admiralty; Commerce; State Expenses; and Mines and Manufacture – to replace the old, overlapping, and often regionally based chancelleries (*prikazy*) inherited from Muscovite times. The system survived until the early nineteenth century. Less successful were Peter's experiments with provincial reform. The creation of provinces (*gubernii*) in 1708 and subsequent revisions in 1715 and 1718–19 failed to bring order to the countryside, where most of the new Swedish-inspired official posts did not take root. Peter's Russia and that of his successors generally suffered from a shortage of reliable officials rather than over-policing. Corrupt local strongmen ruled their own domains.

In August 1721 Russia and Sweden made peace at Nystad in Finland. The Swedes ratified Russia's possession of Livonia, Estonia, Ingria, and part of Karelia in return for financial compensation and the restoration of Finland. At peace celebrations Peter accepted the title of Emperor, "the Great" (the latter with reference to both Alexander and Constantine), and "Father of the Fatherland", an imperial Roman title. The empire expanded further in 1722–3, when Peter led a successful campaign to the Caspian and captured the towns of Baku and Derbent. These provinces were relinquished in the 1730s, evidence of the difficulty of maintaining the fringes of empire.

The Later Reforms

The end of the Northern War unleashed a series of major reforms. In 1720 Peter issued the *General Regulation*, which set out procedures for the Colleges, including instructions on working hours, lines of command, how to keep records, and even the type of tables and clocks to be installed in offices. The introduction set out the principles. Peter created Colleges

> for the sake of the orderly running of . . . state affairs and the correct allocation and calculation of his revenues and the improvement of useful justice (*iustitsiia*) and police (*politsiia*) . . . also for the sake of the utmost preservation of the safety of his loyal subjects and the maintenance of his naval and land forces in good condition as well as commerce, arts and manufacture and the good establishment of his sea and land taxes and for the increase and spread of mining works and other state needs. [4: vol. 6, no. 3534, p. 141]

The *General Regulation* had much in common with both the *Military* (1716) and the *Naval* (1720) *Statutes*, illustrating the degree of regimentation and detail that Peter deemed necessary to maintain a well-regulated military and civil machine.

In 1721 Peter formally ended the patriarchate (the last incumbent had died in 1700 and not been replaced) by announcing the creation of the "governing Holy Synod," where rule by a collegiate board replaced dangerous, as Peter saw it, rule by one man. The *Spiritual Regulation* (1721) and its supplement (1722) covered such topics as education for priests, the Church's educational role, and the running of monasteries. (The tsar's subjects were deterred from shirking their state duties by strict age limits on tonsure as monks and nuns [14].) The Church was now run along the lines of government departments, with a clear program for contributing to public welfare, for example, by establishing almshouses and retired solders' homes. An alarming requirement was that priests should divulge talk of treason confided to them during confession. Arguably the Church had been an arm of the state even before Peter's time. It now surrendered its independence entirely, although Peter stopped short of secularizing church lands. A devout Christian himself, Peter also valued the Church's role as a pillar of autocracy through its provision of ceremonies, loyal sermons, eulogies, and primers. This it would maintain until the fall of tsarism.

In 1722 the Table of Ranks was created, consolidating two decades of decrees on promotion and titles. Four major columns – army, navy, civil service, and court – listed fourteen ranks, each of which contained one or more posts. All the military listings of commissioned ranks conferred hereditary noble status upon men who did not have it already, while non-noble civil servants had to reach rank eight to obtain the same privilege. Sometimes seen as a "meritocratic" measure, the Table still recognized nobles as the natural leaders of society, conferring hereditary nobility on the descendants of those who earned promotion through service. It gave precedence to princes of the blood and aristocrats at social gatherings, but made no concessions to birthright in appointments to actual posts. Service was for life, although this principle was eroded under Peter's successors.

The year 1722 also saw the creation of the post of Procurator-General to oversee the Senate. An Over-Procurator presided over the Holy Synod and lesser procurators over all the Colleges. In a sense these measures were an admission that it was impossible to produce a well-oiled machine of government that ran like clockwork without the intervention of its creator or his representatives. The procurators were known as the tsar's "eyes," bearing witness to the chaos and irregularity that characterized even the Senate, where quarrels often broke out and business was left undone. Peter set great store by consistent laws, which had not been codified since 1649, but, despite his best efforts, the task of codification remained unfinished, and the best that could be done were improvements in court procedures to reduce "red tape" and attempts to elevate crimes against the state above crimes against the person. Too often Peter had to rely on printed exhortation. The following sentiments (from a decree of 1713) appeared in countless documents over the years: "And in order that this our edict be made known to everyone, write it and display it around the towns of [Smolensk guberniia] everywhere, both in churches and on city gates, so that everyone is aware of it and no one makes excuses on the grounds of ignorance" [15: 160]. Frequent repetition of the tsar's edicts suggests that they were often ignored. From breaches of the Western dress code in Siberian towns to refusal by nobles and merchants to send their sons to school, Peter lacked the means to impose his will outside St Petersburg, and such officialdom as existed was riddled with corruption from top to bottom.

Private Life

Peter married twice. His first wife, the Russian noblewoman Evdokia Lopukhina, was chosen for him by his mother in 1689, and bore him two sons, of whom Alexis (1690–1718) survived. On his return from the Grand Embassy, Peter banished Evdokia to a convent and took up again with his German mistress, Anna Mons. In about 1703 Anna was replaced by Martha, an illiterate Livonian peasant woman. She soon bore Peter several children and at an unspecified date was converted to Orthodoxy under the name Ekaterina (Catherine) Alekseevna. In 1711, on the eve of the campaign against the Turks, on which she accompanied him, Peter declared her his legal spouse and "sovereign tsaritsa". In February 1712 he married her. She was his constant companion, sharing his taste for alcohol and bizarre charades. Once barely mentioned in older histories, Catherine has recently been the focus of serious study, not least because she succeeded Peter in 1725 to be Russia's first female monarch. Research has focused on efforts by Peter's publicists to legitimize her, for example, through the cultivation of the cult of St Catherine [16], and also on her court, which she maintained in Western style, whereas Peter himself generally felt more comfortable in the company of dwarfs and shipwrights [17]. She was also the first tsaritsa to live outside the secluded women's quarters of Muscovite times, bringing up her own daughters in Western style.

Catherine bore Peter ten children, but only two girls lived beyond early childhood: Anna (1708–28, mother of the future Emperor Peter III) and Elizabeth (1709–61, ruled as empress 1741–61). Her stepson Alexis was groomed as Peter's heir, but he failed to share his father's enthusiasms, particularly for the navy and St Petersburg; he cultivated friends in religious circles and formed a focus for opposition among certain nobles to the harsh demands of Peter's regime, which tended to impose duties without granting privileges. In 1715 Peter threatened Alexis that he would rather choose a "worthy stranger" to succeed him than his own unworthy son. In 1716 Alexis escaped abroad to the domains of his brother-in-law the Habsburg emperor, where he allegedly fomented a plot to depose Peter and assassinate him [18]. Lured back to Russia with promises of a pardon, he was put on trial and sentenced to death for treason and attempted regicide, dying under suspicious circumstances before execution could be carried out. In 1722, alarmed by the potential of an unsuitable "natural" heir to undo a wise ruler's handiwork and saddened by the death in 1719 of his only remaining son by Catherine, Peter issued a law of succession that required the reigning monarch to nominate his successor on the grounds of suitability. However, Peter died without nominating anyone.

Death and Legacy

Peter died, aged 52, on January 28, 1725, following complications from a recurrent bladder infection. Venereal disease, alcohol, and sheer exhaustion may have contributed to his comparatively early demise. In the words of Archbishop Feofan

Prokopovich's funeral oration, a landmark in the creation of the Petrine myth, Peter had "given birth" to Russia. He was Samson (strong defender of the fatherland), Japhet (creator of the fleet), Moses (law-giver), Solomon (bringer of reason and wisdom), David and Constantine (reformer of the Church) [19]. His admirers grieved that a great life had been cut short with many tasks left unfinished. Others rejoiced that it had been terminated before he could do any more damage. A famous image of "The Mice Bury the Cat," adapted from a traditional folk print subject, suggested "little people" making music and dancing around Peter's coffin.

In the eighteenth century crown and public (that is, the tiny educated, mainly noble minority) were largely united in their positive view of Peter. For Russia's rulers, the Petrine legacy was the guiding light of their policies: The rhetoric of primacy prevailed: Peter the First (his predecessors were known by their given name and patronymic) was regarded as the initiator of imperial expansion and Westernization, the founder of the navy and St Petersburg, who raised Russia in the eyes of the world. To quote a contemporary: "Whatever you look at in Russia, all has its beginnings with him and whatever is done henceforth will also derive its source from that beginning" [20: 424]. (Only in the nineteenth century were the innovations of Peter's predecessors given due recognition.)

Visually, Peter's continuing presence was expressed by the inclusion in royal portraits, engravings, and maps of his bust or statue, or his image in the sky with antique gods and putti, often holding a map or pointing to a globe. In August 1770, to celebrate Catherine II's placing of a captured Turkish naval standard on Peter's tomb, Metropolitan Platon delivered a sermon, which began with the summons: "Arise now, Great Monarch, Father of our Fatherland. Arise and look upon your handiwork; it has not decayed with time and its glory has not dimmed" [21: 253–4]. This and other ideas about Peter's creative genius were concentrated in laconic form in Falconet's equestrian statue (1782), later known as the Bronze Horseman, with its inscription "To Peter I from Catherine II," testifying to his successors' honoring of the Petrine legacy. Paul I's dedication on a re-erected statue by Carlo Bartholomeo Rastrelli – "To the great-grandfather from the great-grandson" (1800) – similarly expressed the motif of dynastic continuity.

All subsequent Russian rulers acknowledged their debt to Peter, Nicholas I most enthusiastically by wearing one of his dressing gowns for inspiration, Alexander I and Nicholas II less so (the last emperor admired Peter's military conquests and work ethic, but deplored his Westernizing ways). Among their subjects, doubts set in from the later eighteenth century and proliferated under the impact of the search for national identity in the early nineteenth. Karamzin was a forerunner of the Slavophile view of Peter, as was Prince Mikhail Shcherbatov (1733–90), who in 1787 wrote an appeal on behalf of the city of Moscow, deploring its eclipse by St Petersburg. In another work Shcherbatov conceded that, without Peter, Russia would have needed another 200 years to reach its current level of development. However, he deplored Peter's cruelty, his subordination of the nobility, his treatment of Alexis and the succession, and his attacks on religion and custom. Shcherbatov's particular target was the "corruption of morals." There was a high price to pay for Westernization, both literally and figuratively [22].

The issue of Peter and Russian national identity was developed more fully in the debate between the Westernizers and the Slavophiles in the 1830s–50s, which was inaugurated by the declaration of Peter Chaadaev (1794–1856) in his first *Philosophical Letter* (published 1836) that once "a great man wanted to civilize us, and in order to give us a foretaste of enlightenment, he threw us the mantle of civilization: we took up the cloak but did not so much as touch civilization." Chaadaev later conceded that, since Peter, Russia's path was irrevocably Western: "In his hand Peter found only a blank sheet of paper, and he wrote on it: Europe and the West" – and acknowledged the advantages of backwardness, which would allow Russia in time to surpass the West; for, "if we have come after others, it is in order to do better than the others" [23: 37, 205].

Some Westernizers, like Vissarion Belinsky (1811–48), adulated Peter – "the greatest phenomenon not only of our history, but also of the history of all mankind; he is the divinity that called us to live, breathing a living soul into the body of the old Russia, colossal but plunged in deathly slumber" – convinced that Peter's work was incomplete and that further radical political and social reform was needed [1: 127]. Slavophiles, on the other hand, emphasized the destructive nature of Peter's reforms, which they deplored as the essentially non-Russian products of Western rationalism, of which St Petersburg was the worst manifestation. They were thankful that the peasants at least had retained their national character, as expressed through their pure Orthodox faith and the peasant commune. In the words of Konstantin Aksakov (1817–60), the government "must understand the spirit of Russia and embrace Russian principles, which have been rejected since Peter's day" [24: 152].

In the latter half of the nineteenth century historians such as S. M. Solov'ev (1820–79) and V. O. Kliuchevskii (1841–1911) exposed the Muscovite roots of many of Peter's reforms, as well as chronicling and analyzing Peter's reign on the basis of primary sources, which tended to reveal the often chaotic and piecemeal nature of his activities [25]. They took a pragmatic, warts and all, view of Peter himself (some of the most famous passages in Kliuchevskii's history described his violent, drunken habits) [12], but they still equated Peter with Progress, allowing the Russian state to achieve its rightful status as a world power. Only toward the end of the tsarist era did historians such as Pavel Miliukov (1859–1943), working on the Petrine economy in particular, emphasize the violence, the arbitrariness, and the sacrifices, "the paucity of the results compared with the magnitude of the wasted resources" [26: 165–6]. Even in Miliukov's work, Peter remained central to debates about Russia's place in the world and its destiny. Only in revolutionary propaganda was Peter dismissed, along with other tsars, as a cruel and crude tyrant whose reign brought no benefit either to Russia or its people.

Petrine Russia was comparatively well served by Soviet historians, not least in the very fact that Peter was one of only two tsars, the other being Ivan the Terrible, about whom it was permissible to publish biographies. Stalin's regime supplemented the exemplary lives of living and recently dead new heroes with the selective revival of key figures from the more distant past. Nevertheless Marxist-Leninist ideology determined that certain aspects of Petrine Russia remained unexplored, notably Peter's private life and the topsy-turvy world of mock assemblies, or were subject to a materialist approach. Approved topics included the history of war and military reform, the peasantry and the poll tax, revolts, and industrial expansion. (The much-quoted expansion of 20 factories at the start of Peter's reign to over 200 by the end heralded the birth of the working class.) It was accepted wisdom that Peter was a secularizer, and, although there was some study of the mechanics of church reform, religious life and culture were virtually ignored.

Mikhail Gorbachev's new openness or glasnost in the 1980s and the collapse of Communism in Russia in 1991 gave rise, among other things, to attempts to fill gaps in the historical record. Although the most spectacular revelations related to twentieth-century Russia, there was also some new thinking about Peter's reign, notably the drawing of certain negative parallels with Communist Russia. The St Petersburg historian Evgenii Anisimov, for example, characterized Peter as "the creator of the administrative-command system and the true ancestor of Stalin", who laid the foundations of the totalitarian state, treating subjects like children with "the pedagogy of the cudgel" to achieve progress in the name of the greater good. He argued that Peter destroyed alternatives ("civil society"), most tragically the Church, and created the "well-regulated police state" with its reliance on spying mechanisms and controls. Referring to the debate about capitalism in Russia, a central issue in the experimental economic climate of the 1980s, Anisimov argued that Peter weakened individual enterprise by increasing the dominant role of the state in the life of society as a whole. What was missing were competition and freedom [27].

In the West in the past decade a number of historians have thrown light on aspects that Soviet historians were unable to explore and Russian historians still have difficulty in pursuing, often for lack of resources. These include the specifics of cultural borrowing and influence. In his monumental three-volume study of Petrine culture [28; 29; 30], James Cracraft works from the premiss that Peter created a "revolution" in Russian life, albeit a top-down "revolution by decree" that was initially narrowly elitist. These generously illustrated works embed Petrine Russia in the European context of Renaissance and Baroque architecture, painting and engraving (Peter is the first Russian ruler of whom we have a reliable likeness) and literary and verbal culture, including foreigners' perceptions of change. The essence of Cracraft's conclusions are distilled in a recent one-volume study [31].

Paul Bushkovitch's research is invaluable for revealing the nuts and bolts of court politics and networks, ultimately reducing, without effacing, Peter's importance by revealing the contribution to decision-making of leading men and the restrictions imposed by the need to maintain a balance in court politics. His is the most detailed analysis available of the dynamics and factional aspects of the Tsarevich Alexis affair. He offers a vital corrective to the idea that Peter experienced little opposition from the elite, bringing to light new archival sources, notably the writings of foreign diplomats and travelers [32: 18].

The world turned upside down discloses some, if not all, its secrets in the research of Ernest Zitser, which goes beyond not only the older "statist" approach to government and politics but also more recent studies of kinship and clientele networks such as Bushkovitch's to look at networks of Peter's own devising, demonstrating how he initiated an inner circle and kept them on board by participation in mocking rituals. This helped them to bond and believe in the transformation of Russia by a "divinely ordained charismatic leader" [8]. Events such as the weddings of the dwarfs (1710) and the Prince-Pope (1715) subverted traditional family values and old hierarchies, allowing the acting-out of opposition to the old order by use of ridicule. Much of this was achieved with the use of Christian rhetoric and the creation of new sacred locations in imitation of existing models, not least the "Paradise" of St Petersburg.

Serious research on other aspects of Petrine religious culture, including sermons and iconography, is only just beginning. One may cite the work of Julia Gerasimova [33] as an example of fresh revelations about the use of Orthodox imagery in the elaboration of the Petrine cult, and, in Russia, Elena Pogosian [34] and Olga Ageeva [35], on the ceremonial and symbolic aspects of Peter's reign, and Viktor Zhivov on the sacred/secular divide [36].

In my own work on Petrine Russia I have attempted, in both broad and more specialized studies, to integrate hitherto neglected aspects such as Peter's family life, his mock institutions and cultural issues such as shaving and dress reform with the aim of providing a more rounded and detailed coverage than most previous military-dominated studies [37; 38]. In particular, I continue to monitor Peter's image in today's Russia, which remains remarkably visible.

In the 2000s the debate about Peter in Russia is as lively as ever. He and other major historical figures provide a convenient hook on which to hang discussions about contemporary Russia, especially with reference to styles of leadership, the relationship between rulers and ruled, and Russia's relations with the West. Vladimir Putin, himself a St Petersburger born at Peterhof, emulated Peter's firm rule from the center, his emphasis on the state and suspicion (or despair) of independent institutions, opening up Russia to the West, while at the same time discouraging foreign interference in Russian domestic affairs, maintaining a post-Soviet "empire" and a strong voice in world affairs. Critics seize upon this perceived Petrine influence as confirmation that Russia is somehow doomed to repeat fatal historical patterns such as reliance on absolutism, reform from above, the development of personality cults, and the subordination of the individual to the State, which prevent it from becoming a modern country

On another level, Peter's portrait or name endorses such products as cigarettes, champagne, and vodka. New, often controversial, statues of him have been erected or restored, for example, a copy of Bernshtam's "Tsar-Carpenter" (1910, demolished by Bolsheviks in 1918) was re-erected c. 2000 not far from its original place in front of the Admiralty. In the entrance hall of St Petersburg's Moscow rail station a large copy of Carlo Rastrelli's bronze bust of Peter (1723; copy c. 1992) replaced a statue of Lenin, a nice example of the unseating of symbols of the old regime by, in this case, an iconic figure from the most distant past. A new interpretation of Peter by the émigré sculptor Mikhail Shemiakin (June 1991, Peter-Paul fortress) was inspired by the same Rastrelli's 1725 wax model of the tsar. It is disliked by many Petersburgers, who are averse to grotesque interpretations of their hero, despite the fact that he was in reality a 6 feet 7 inch giant with a small head, long spindly limbs and a threatening manner.

Moscow's main contribution to Petrine imagery is the Monument to the Tercentenary of the Russian Fleet (Zurab Tsereteli, 1997), on a small island in the Moskva River to the west of the Kremlin. It was sponsored by the mayor of Moscow Yurii Luzhkov. At one point public access was restricted following threats to blow it up by neo-Bolsheviks protesting against monuments to tsars. Peter stands on a galleon, supported by an ornate structure of piled-up prows bearing metal windvanes in the shape of the St Andrews flag. He steers the ship of New Russia, a metaphor for far-sighted leadership from above, looking toward the West, the inspiration for much of new Moscow. The unveiling of the monument stimulated discussions in the press about Russia's place in the modern world, many emphasizing that Russia's independence and its security were impossible without the strengthening of its naval traditions (now in sad decline), initiated three centuries earlier by the young Peter. To critics the statue's gigantic size and ostentation recall the excesses of Soviet monumentalism, waste of public money, and leaders' tendency to impose their own visions upon Russia's cities without much consultation.

A more unexpected development of Peter's image in post-Soviet Russia is that of the pious tsar, a shift away from the emphatic Soviet, and indeed Western emphasis on Peter's secular credentials as terminator of the patriarchate. Peter is unlikely to be canonized as Nicholas II has been, but there are several religious sites associated with him in St Petersburg. These include his first cabin (*domik*), which in the late tsarist period was indeed the destination of pilgrims, the attraction being an allegedly miraculous icon of the Savior in the cabin's chapel. In the Soviet period all indication that there had been a chapel disappeared, but in the 1990s information about it was restored in the guidebook and a copy of the icon was installed. The original image (which was credited with saving Alexander III and his family from a train crash in 1887) is now in the church of the Preobrazhenskii Guards (Peter's own regiment), where Vladimir Putin's mother had him secretly baptized. Religious symbolism has also been restored to Peter's tomb in the Peter–Paul cathedral, which in Soviet times was a departure point for troops going to war. At Lakhta on the Finnish gulf Peter allegedly saved some solders from drowning shortly before his own death, in an "act of Christian heroism." Now a shrine originally dedicated in 1893 and destroyed by the Bolsheviks has been restored and the nearby church of SS Peter and Paul reopened [39]. Peter's self-sacrifice in saving men in peril on the sea is laced with strong Christ-like undertones.

New books continue to appear in Russian, although on closer investigation many turn out to be translations, reprints, or revised extended versions of older histories – for example, the work of the veteran Petrine scholar Nikolai Pavlenko [40]. The tercentenary of St Petersburg in 2003 stimulated funds for a number of new scholarly publications of primary sources – for example, volume 13, part 2, of *Letters and Papers of Emperor Peter the Great*, the first volume of which appeared in 1887 and the most recent of which still only reaches the year 1713 [41: 15]. With more anniversaries coming up – Poltava in 2009, Hango in 2014 – it seems unlikely that we have heard the last word on Petrine Russia.

References

1. "Petr Velikii," quoted in Riasanovsky, N. (1985). *The Image of Peter the Great in Russian History and Thought*. Oxford University Press, New York and Oxford.
2. Kotilane, J., and Poe, M. (eds.) (2004). *Modernizing Muscovy: Reform and Social Change in Seventeenth-Century Russia*, Routledge Curzon, London and New York.
3. Poe, M. (2000). "A People Born to Slavery," in *Russia in Early Modern European Ethnography 1476–1748*. Cornell University Press, Ithaca, NY, and London.
4. *Polnoe Sobranie Zakonov Rossiiskoi Imperii* (1830). First series, 45 vols. His Majesty's Own Chancellery, St Petersburg.
5. Hughes, L. (1990). *Sophia Regent of Russia*. Yale University Press, New Haven and London.

6. Janco, A. P. (2003). "Training in the Amusement of Mars: Peter the Great, War Games and the Science of War," *Russian History*, 30/1–2: 25–112.

7. *Karamzin's Memoir on Ancient and Modern Russia* (1966), ed. Richard Pipes. Athenaeum, New York.

8. Zitser. E. A. (2004). *The Transfigured Kingdom: Sacred Parody and Charismatic Authority at the Court of Peter the Great*. Cornell University Press, Ithaca, NY, and London.

9. Hughes, L. (2000). *Playing Games: The Alternative History of Peter the Great*. School of Slavonic and East European Studies, London.

10. Hughes, L. (2004). "A Beard is an Unnecessary Burden: Peter I's Laws on Shaving and their Roots in Early Russia," in R. Bartlett and L. Hughes, eds., *Russian Society and Culture and the Long Eighteenth Century. Essays in Honour of Anthony G. Cross*. LitVerlag, Munster, 21–34.

11. Hughes, L. (2001). "From Caftans into Corsets: The Sartorial Transformation of Women during the Reign of Peter the Great," in P. Barta, ed., *Gender and Sexuality in Russian Civilization*. Routledge, London, 17–32.

12. Kliuchevskii, V. (1958). *Peter the Great*, trans. L. Archibald. St Martin's Press, London.

13. Lincoln, W. Bruce (2000). *Sunlight at Midnight: St Petersburg and the Rise of Modern Russia*. Basic Books, New York.

14. Muller, V. (1972). *The Spiritual Regulation of Peter the Great*. University of Washington Press, Seattle and London.

15. Preobrazhenskii, A. A., et al. (eds.) (2003). *Pis'ma i bumagi imperatora Petra Velikogo*. Tom 13, vypusk 2. Drevlekhranilishche, Moscow.

16. Marker, G. (2004). "Peter the Great's Female Knights of Liberation: The Order of St Catherine of Alexandria", in R. Bartlett and L. Hughes (eds), *Russian Society and Culture in the Long Eighteenth Century*. Lit Verlag, Munster, 35–47.

17. Hughes, L. (2004). "Catherine I of Russia: Consort to Peter the Great", in C. Campbell Orr, ed., *Queenship in Europe, 1660–1815: The Role of the Consort*. Cambridge University Press, Cambridge, 131–54.

18. Bushkovitch, P. (1997). "Power and the Historian: The Case of Tsarevich Aleksei 1716–1718 and N. G. Ustrialov 1845–1859," *Proceedings of the American Philosophical Society*, 141: 177–212.

19. Prokopovich, Feofan (1725). "Funeral Oration," in L. Jay Oliva, *Peter the Great: Great Lives Observed*, Prentice-Hall, Englewood Cliffs, NJ, 1970, 78–81.

20. "Zapiski Ivana Ivanovicha Nepliueva (1693–1773)", in *Imperiia posle Petra 1725–1726* (1998). Fond Sergeia Dubova, Moscow.

21. Novoselov, S. (1857). *Opisanie kafedral'nogo sobora vo imia sviatykh Pervoverkhovnykh Apostolov Petra i Pavla*. "Ianov Trei," St Petersburg.

22. Lentin, A. (ed.) (1969). *On the Corruption of Morals in Russia*. Oxford University Press, Oxford.

23. McNally, R. T. (ed.) (1969). *The Major Works of Peter Chaadaev*. University of Notre Dame Press, Notre Dame, IN, and London.

24. Aksakov, K. (1855). "On the Present State of Russia," in L. Jay Oliva (1970). *Peter the Great: Great Lives Observed*. Prentice-Hall, Englewood Cliffs, NJ, 1970.

25. Solov'ev, S. M. (1851–79). *Istoriia Rossii s drevneishikh vremen*. 29 vols. St Petersburg.

26. Miliukov, P. (1903). *Ocherki po istorii russkoi kul'tury*. Pt. 3. Skorokhodov, St Petersburg.

27. Anisimov, E. (1993). *The Reforms of Peter the Great: Progress through Coercion in Russia*, trans. J. Alexander. M. E. Sharpe, Armonk, NY.

28. Cracraft, J. (1988). *The Petrine Revolution in Russian Architecture*. University of Chicago Press, Chicago.

29. Cracraft, J. (1997). *The Petrine Revolution in Russian Imagery*, University of Chicago Press, Chicago.
30. Cracraft, J. (2004). *The Petrine Revolution in Russian Cultur*e. Belknap Press of Harvard University Press, Cambridge, MA, and London.
31. Cracraft, J. (2003). *The Revolution of Peter the Great*. Belknap Press of Harvard University Press, Cambridge, MA, and London.
32. Bushkovitch, P. (2001). *Peter the Great. The Struggle for Power, 1671–1725*. Cambridge University Press, Cambridge.
33. Gerasimova, J. (2004). *The Iconostasis of Peter the Great in the Peter and Paul Cathedral in St Petersburg*. Alexandros Press, Leiden.
34. Pogosian, E. (2001). *Petr I – arkhitektor rossiiskoi istorii*. "Iskusstvo SPB", St Petersburg.
35. Ageeva, O. G. (1999). *Velichaishii i slavneishii bolee vsekh gradov v svete" – Grad Sviatogo Petra*. Blits, St Petersburg.
36. Zhivov, V. (2004). *Iz tserkovnoĭ istorii vremen Petra Velikogo: issledovaniia i materially*. Novoe literaturnoe obozrenie, Moscow.
37. Hughes, L. (1998). *Russia in the Age of Peter the Great*. Yale University Press, New Haven, and London.
38. Hughes, L. (2002). *Peter the Great: A Biography*. Yale University Press, New Haven, and London.
39. Hughes, L. (2000). Review of Nikolai Pavlenko, *Vokrug trona*, Moscow, 1999, *Kritika: Explorations in Russian and Eurasian History*, 1/4: 1–6, 783–8.
40. Mikhailov, N. V. (2001). *Lakhta. Piat' vekov istorii 1500–2000*. 'Ves' mir', Moscow–St Petersburg.
41. Hughes, L. (2006). "Documentary Sources about Peter the Great," *Kritika: Explorations in Russian and Eurasian History*, 7: 123–32.

Further Reading

Anisimov, E. (1993). *The Reforms of Peter the Great: Progress through Coercion in Russia*, trans. J. Alexander. M. E. Sharpe, Armonk, NY.
Bushkovitch, P. (2001). *Peter the Great: The Struggle for Power, 1671–1725*. Cambridge University Press, Cambridge.
Cracraft, J. (2003). *The Revolution of Peter the Great*. Belknap Press of Harvard University Press, Cambridge, MA, and London.
Hughes, L. (1998). *Russia in the Age of Peter the Great*. Yale University Press, New Haven and London.
Massie, R. K. (1981). *Peter the Great: His Life and World*. Weidenfeld and Nicolson, London. Tells a vivid tale, but should not be relied upon for details.
Riasanovsky, N. (1985). *The Image of Peter the Great in Russian History and Thought*. Oxford University Press, New York and Oxford.
Zitser, E. A. (2004). *The Transfigured Kingdom. Sacred Parody and Charismatic Authority at the Court of Peter the Great*. Cornell University Press, Ithaca, NY, and London.

CHAPTER ELEVEN

The Westernization of the Elite, 1725–1800

GARY MARKER

Until recently the transformation of the nobility during Russia's long eighteenth century was described as following a straightforward and unitary trajectory, the onward march of the "Age of Reason." By most accounts the story began with the brutal but fundamentally progressive state-imposed and aggressively secularizing reforms of the "Petrine revolution" described in the previous chapter, continued apace through the adaptation of French manners, ideas, and literary trends during the second half of the century, and concluded with a mutual disaffection between the government and educated nobility, culminating in the tragic/heroic Decembrist revolt of 1825. This experience was subsumed under the rubric of the Enlightenment, the pursuit of reason both in statecraft (often referred to as "the well-ordered police state" of the "German" Enlightenment) and in individual improvement (associated most often with Voltaire, Denis Diderot, and the French Encyclopedists in general).

For much of the twentieth century this teleology fell into two competing schools of thought. The first, associated primarily but not exclusively with Soviet scholarship, insisted upon the irreconcilable opposition between state and society, especially from mid-century onward. The enlightenment of the Russian elite generated a social conscience, a dawning awareness of the incompatibility between the high ideals of the European Enlightenment, on the one hand, and the immorality of serfdom and the cruel authoritarianism of the imperial state on the other. In this telling, Enlightenment moved inexorably forward, and the revolt of the elite guards' regiments in 1825 constituted its logical and heroic culmination.

This interpretation came under scrutiny in the 1970s and 1980s, primarily from Western scholars. They challenged – convincingly in the eyes of most specialists today – the state versus society opposition, and showed through detailed exegeses that, for the most part, Russia's intellectual elite supported the government, the main lines of reform, and their rulers. Literati may have satirized certain practices and mocked the unthinking adoption of French and French manners. They may even have expressed some sense of disorientation or psychological dislocation brought on by the withering pace of cultural change. Some scholars, influenced by the work of Marc Raeff, have perceived alienation in their writings, while others, largely linked to Iurii Lotman's

Moscow and Tartu school of semiotics, deemed their Westernization so complete as to make them virtual foreigners in their own country.[1] But with few exceptions, both Raeff and Lotman believed, the nobility shared the outlooks of Russia's major rulers and believed that the state and law could be agencies of institutional reform, legal rationalization, and the pursuit of happiness.

Over the past two decades, coinciding approximately with the demise of the Soviet Union, the field has changed, subtly perhaps, but decisively. The by-now stale competition between these alternative views has given way to a more complex and considerably less optimistic set of interpretations than had typified either variant of Westernization-as-progress. First to fall was the oldest chestnut, the antinomian interpretation of state and society. Recent scholars have begun to probe still deeper, questioning, if not necessarily rejecting, the long-accepted affinities between Westernization, progress, and secularization. Others have pointed out that the very term "Westernization" is pre-eminently a mid-nineteenth-century construct, a product of Romanticism and a modern form of nationalism that rings anachronistically within Russia's age of Enlightenment. Rarely did eighteenth-century Russians speak of "the West," preferring instead "Europe," a term that, upon reflection, implies rather different binarisms than does "the West." So how should one cast an abbreviated synopsis such as this of Russia's eighteenth-century elite in the current atmosphere of historiographic rethinking?

Let us begin with some terminology and chronology – the building blocks with which to give coherence to the time and subject. First, who were Russia's elite? Other chapters explain Russia's mode of social organization and the cumbersome legal, religious, tax-linked, and geographic categories assigned directly or indirectly to all the tsar's subjects, male and female, young and old, Russian and non-Russian. At the top of the social pyramid stood a group of landed serving men (*dvorianstvo* or *pomeshchiki*), their clans and immediate families, who had achieved significant wealth and status either through their own service to the tsar or through the service of an ancestor. None of the available English terms (gentry, nobility, aristocracy) quite captures the collectivity of these clans, but, whatever term one employs, no one questions that this group, constituting perhaps 1 or 2 percent of the empire's population, held a uniquely exalted standing in Russia. In exchange for their land, whether held as hereditary land or in lifelong tenure, they were obliged to serve the sovereign according to his will and appropriate to their station. Such service gave them access to influence, graft, the accumulation of more land, freedom from direct taxation (the so-called soul, or poll tax), specific sumptuary and travel rights, and entrée to the tsar's court. Their privilege, tradition of service, and wealth also exposed them to the winds of cultural change coming from Europe, the Westernization that is this chapter's theme.

This service elite was highly stratified, and when one speaks of access to cultural changes one must be careful to recognize that the experiences of landed nobles were varied. The Russian Empire was enormous, relatively unfertile, and underpopulated when compared to its neighbors to the west. Life in the capital was expensive, and the salaries drawn from the Table of Ranks fell far short of meeting the forbidding costs of St Petersburg society. Without large estates and many serfs from whom to collect dues, big city living was simply prohibitive. Some scholars have estimated that urban living of any sort lay beyond the means of 80 percent of the nobility. True, a price inflation lasting most of the eighteenth century worked to the benefit of the rural population (especially landlords), and noble families had increasingly easy access to loans and credits. Still, only those with truly lavish holdings of several hundred or more serf households, a small elite within the elite, could afford full participation in the political and cultural currents of the new capital.

These changes did not appear all at once, of course. During the second half of the seventeenth century, especially during the regency of Sophia Alekseevna in the 1680s, families close to the Muscovite court witnessed an influx of Baroque art, architecture, and theater, largely because of Polish influence. Without a doubt, though, the reign of Peter the Great (1689–1725) profoundly altered and accelerated the exposure of Russia's service families to outside influence. Forced to move from the familiar confines of Moscow to the far away and utterly new and physically wide open capital of St Petersburg, they simultaneously confronted massive changes within everyday life, all of which bore the unmistakable imprint of Peter's drive to modernize his realm according to the latest standards of the rest of Europe so as to emerge victorious from the Northern War. These have already been detailed, but some of the cultural changes bear repeating, if only to demonstrate their disruptive break from the past and their bridge to the future. Shorn of their beards, long sleeves, and cloaks, and forced to wear uniforms that closely imitated the regimental garb of armies elsewhere in Europe, young noblemen appeared as virtual strangers to their fathers and grandfathers, who had proudly borne the insignias and drums of their clan militias when marching into battle.

Noble households – men and women – participated in an enforced new public sociability at the court of St Petersburg in the form of balls, masquerades, and outdoor spectacles. In 1718 Peter introduced official assemblies that required both men and women to be in attendance, dressed (and occasionally cross-dressed) in contemporary European fashion, endeavoring to learn the unfamiliar movements of ballroom dancing. A good many of the revelers could neither read nor write, and most had never been abroad, but official decrees determined that they look the part of European gentility and go through the proper motions. To assist them in this endeavor Peter's aide Jacob Bruce, a Russified Scotsman whose family had entered Russian service decades earlier, compiled a handbook of etiquette from Western models entitled *A Youth's Honest Mirror, or How to Show Good Manners* (*Iunosti chestnoe zertsalo ili pokazanie k zhiteiskomu obkhozhdeniiu*). From these pages a young nobleman learned not to spit in public, when and when not to bow, how to treat young women, how to minimize using profanity, and so on. Some, especially the parvenus, embraced the new ways of public life – or at least the principles behind them and the advantages that they bestowed, others bore them stoically as necessary to their oaths of loyalty, while an equal number of service families fumed privately and not so privately at the assault on their traditions, established networks, and financial security. Remarkably, though, the Petrine order, in particular its cultural dimensions, endured and even thrived in the decades following Peter's death, as the cultural bedrock of the newly proclaimed empire.

Education, Language, and Print

Between 1725 and the mid-1760s the nobility elite came under several new waves of acculturation to European manners and letters, a process that in many ways made them into refined gentlemen and ladies. Although the sources of gentility were multiple, two institutions stand out as the most vital: secondary education and the printing press. Simply put, education constituted the threshold, literary language framed the laboratory, and print provided the public instrument by which European letters could be learned and then reproduced *à la russe*. Motivated in equal measure by utility and social engineering, the Russian state generated several new schools and attendant publishing houses where next to none had existed earlier. These included Corps of Cadets for the Navy, Land Army, and Engineering Corps, classes at the new Academy of Sciences, and, from 1755, Moscow University (Russia's first) complete with pansions, or secondary schools, one for nobles and one for the non-noble urban estates. Most concentrated their attention on the male offspring of service nobles, and all were granted a privilege to publish.

The history of education constitutes one of the less gripping narratives of Russian history, so we will not linger very long on specifics. But two points need to be made. First, by the 1760s these schools collectively were producing several dozen to a few hundred graduates annually, nearly all of whom entered into state service with a higher degree of education than had their predecessors. By the 1780s these numbers had grown into the hundreds. The education they received also moved them much further in the direction of European gentility than anything that had come before and light years beyond the crude lessons of the *Mirror*. The curricula included modern languages, literature, poetry, and – especially for the cadets – a heavy regimen of formal dancing and fencing, hallmarks of the life of a gentleman. It was from their midst that the first wave of the notorious and much caricatured French-speaking dandies emerged. These young men were raised with the full expectation that their lives would include considerable space for a gilded leisure, irrespective of their choice of service, and that this leisure would be spent in the European manner. They would truly be, rather than merely ape the manners of, a European noblesse.

One important feature of this transformation is the emergence of Russian literati, men who simultaneously pursued profitable careers in service and literary pursuits during their extensive spare time. As self-conscious men of letters, they, much like European literati elsewhere since Petrarch, turned their attention to inventing a modern literary Russian language, or, to put it more accurately, a secular written language appropriate for literature and exposition alike. Motivated by a desire to translate and publish, the leading intellectuals of the middle third of the century imagined that they were presiding over something epochal in its implications, and they struggled among themselves to shape a literary language faithful to its roots but reflective of the newly widened possibilities to render European literature in Russian. This story has been told countless times, and we should note that the furious debates over versification and literary language ultimately had little bearing on the vernacular Russian that over time evolved on the printed page. Still, the three individuals most closely linked to this enterprise – the scholar Mikhail Lomonosov, the poet and translator Vasilii Trediakovskii, and the Moldavian Prince in Russian service Antioch Kantemir – deserve attention and no small measure of respect for understanding the importance of literary Russian in the changed cultural landscape.

Beginning in the mid-1750s – that is, precisely when the number of educated nobles had grown large enough to constitute an audience – Russian journalism came into its own, reflecting much of the form and substance of journalism elsewhere in

Europe. Strictly speaking, printed periodicals had come into existence decades earlier in the form of governmental gazettes, or *Vedomosti*, begun in 1702. These too appropriated templates that Peter had observed in Holland and elsewhere during his Great Embassy in Western Europe of 1697–98. Thus, *Vedomosti* (1702–27) and its successors, *St Peterburgskie vedomosti* (1727–1917) and *Moskovskie vedomosti* (1756–1917), presented official and semi-official accounts of affairs of state, public celebrations, foreign affairs, commercial activity, events abroad, and anything else that officialdom deemed appropriate for a metropolitan readership. Foreign diplomats and merchants in the Russian capital found the format entirely familiar, and, in order to incorporate them into the government's audience, the state produced regular German-language editions.

A smattering of other journals appeared during the second quarter of the century, and they included some literature and poetry. The first ripple of more independent periodicals, however, began in the late 1750s and lasted about a decade, producing several literary and topical periodicals, with titles such as *The Diligent Bee, Holiday Time*, and *Good Intentions*, that suggested a new non-utilitarian view of reading as amusement and evoked an urbaneness and a shared European-ness in which the Muscovite past seemed but a distant memory, at least on the printed pages. True to their titles, these magazines blended original and translated works, and they offered venues for their mostly noble contributors to display their newly minted sophistication. Most of these magazines lasted just a few issues and circulated at most a few hundred copies. But the transplanted model of the European literary magazine had taken root, and by the late 1760s a new and somewhat larger output of periodicals had emerged, the so-called satirical magazines of 1769–74. Over the years many gallons of ink have been devoted to these journals, and those who have perceived signs of a "gentry opposition" to Catherine the Great have situated its literary beginnings here. The basic facts are these. During this five-year period St Petersburg's young literati produced sixteen, mostly short-lived, magazines – *The Painter, The Drone, Bits of This and That, The Babbler*, and so on – not all of which were satirical. Whole sections of these journals reproduced essays from earlier English satirical journals, such as *The Spectator* and The *Tatler*. What drew the rapt attention of readers, however, was the element of counterpoint, the dialogues in which the editors of the journals pilloried the observations of one another. In that sense these journals drew their readers, culturally and socially at one with the editors themselves, into a single textual community.

Part of the excitement arose from the rumor that the Empress herself was a participant in these exchanges, specifically in the pages of *All Sorts of Things*, edited by her private secretary. To this day specialists disagree on whether Catherine was speaking through her secretary, but the mere possibility hinted at something previously unimaginable in Russia: a public debate, mediated through print, in which the ruler crossed swords with her learned and witty subjects on more-or-less even terms. The fact that these interchanges coincided with Catherine's Legislative Commission only added to the sense of portent. Charged by the Empress in her famous Instructions (*Nakaz*) with drawing up a new and long overdue digest of Russia's laws that would reflect the Enlightenment's pursuit of reason, rational government, fairness in the law, and happiness, this Commission convened in one form or another for several years, and it drew representatives from the entire empire and from all free populations (that is, everyone but serfs). Its recording secretaries and leading orators included several leading lights of the service literati and it generated a momentary excitement that Catherine was leading Russia not merely into Europe but into the advance guard of progressive rationalism. In the end the Commission's sessions came to naught, and no new digest emerged from it. But the sense of new possibilities riveted the elites, both positively and negatively, and it helped to shape their understanding of the place of public expression, especially print, in civic life.

During the final three decades of the eighteenth century Russian publishing grew exponentially, as increasing numbers of graduates filled the ranks of literati and audience simultaneously. Emboldened by the experiences of the early 1770s, they took over institutional publishing houses and set the tone for what the secular presses produced until a wave of repressive measures restricted their activities in the 1790s. By the 1770s Russia's secular presses averaged close to 200 titles per year, up from about 50 per year in the late 1750s. Of these, the largest single category was belles-lettres, which constituted 20 percent of all new titles, and well over half of these were translations from other European languages. Clearly, this was a publishing boom by and for the leisure class, consisting overwhelmingly of service nobles. In the 1780s print culture grew still further, aided by a decree of 1783 that permitted private presses to come into operation relatively simply. Literati and entrepreneurs alike took advantage of this new freedom, which functioned for several years with very little a priori censorship. By the late 1780s Russia's presses generated nearly 500 titles per year, while maintaining the overall profile of the previous decade. Following a practice well established in publishing elsewhere, editors and publishers pursued subscription campaigns to generate both funds and loyal followings within the reading public. Such campaigns helped to subvent several journals and a number of translation series. Typically the names and titles of advance subscribers were listed in the publications themselves, thereby inscribing them forever as sponsors and as members of the literary public.

These changes in reading and leisure habits were breathtaking in their rapidity, requiring only a generation or two to effect. On the whole the government and ruler let the changes develop unhindered. Indeed, Catherine the Great was one of their leading champions, at least until the radicalism and regicide of the French Revolution made her rethink the place of the printed word in Russian life. Catherine's admirers – or shameless flatterers, depending upon one's point of view – among European intellectual luminaries, most notably Voltaire, openly praised her as the paragon of an enlightened ruler, comparing her favorably with Louis XVI, Frederick the Great, and Maria Theresa. When at the end of her life Catherine, alarmed by the course of the revolution in France, turned against the very corps of Russian writers whom she had done so much to promote, her admirers abroad mostly turned a blind eye.

Estate Life

Anyone who has read nineteenth-century Russian novels, such as Saltykov-Shchedrin's *The History of a Town*, Goncharov's *Oblomov*, or even Turgenev's *Fathers and Children*, will recall the picture of the somnambulant provincial gentry and stultifying life in backwater towns and remote estates. This image is exquisitely captured in the Russian term *glush* – literally, "realm of silence" but used invariably to mean

something akin to "the sticks." New scholarship has poked some holes in this enduring myth by showing that estate life during the second half of the eighteenth century
and the early nineteenth participated quite actively in the Europeanization of elite
culture. James Cracraft's study of architecture,[2] Priscilla Roosevelt's work on gardens,
palaces, and estate life,[3] and most recently Richard Stites's analysis of the arts in the
era of serfdom,[4] suggest that at least some nobles saw their estates as personal landscapes, arcadias on which they could create an idealized rural splendor of pleasure,
fellowship, and reason. According to a view popular among nineteenth-century
scholars, the rise of provincial sociability coincided with Peter III's decree of 1762,
which emancipated the hereditary nobility from compulsory service. Henceforth,
although nobles remained the service class *par excellence*, the decision whether to
serve rested entirely with them. Freed from the burdens and costs of state service,
nobles, by some accounts, filled the highways heading back to their estates to pursue
a life of leisure and local celebrity away from the heavy guiding hand of imperial
power. Out of this retreat emerged local salons, literary clubs, lodges, all – in this
view – part of a provincial *fronde*, a transposition of noble identity and status away
from the state and toward the province. A closer look reveals that, in fact, only a
small proportion of metropolitan nobles resigned their positions, and most of those
were near retirement or had proven unsuccessful at climbing the ladder of patronage.
A number of those who did depart the capital for good ended up bringing their social
and cultural preferences with them. But by and large the resurgence of provincial
cultural life was led by magnates – that is, landlords of sufficient means in land and
serfs to maintain estates and homes in the capital. They may have spent considerable
time in the countryside, but they were by no means in flight from the capital. Some
of the more prosperous landlords hired landscape gardeners from abroad to design
perfectly manicured landscapes, reminiscent of Versailles or Saint-Souci. As if to
demonstrate their mastery over their domain, nature included, and their supremacy
over the forbiddingly long winter season, Russian magnates, such as Andrei Bolotov
in Bogoroditsk and Prince A. B. Kurakin in Saratov, commissioned elaborate tropical
paradises, replete with warm-weather plants, fountains, and reflecting pools. Others
built Greek temples, classical statuaries, Gothic halls, Italianate palaces, French reception halls, and the like, while greeting their visitors dressed in waistcoats, frocks, and
powdered wigs.

These exercises demonstrate that elite Europeanization had a broad geographic
reach and was not a characteristic of metropolitan nobles alone. Thousands of kilometers east of the Seine, the estates of dozens of Russia's newly Europeanized nobility
announced deafeningly to all who came near that, given enough money, life in the
Russian provinces could be as European as that of any Frenchman. Provincial theaters
and opera houses also were more commonplace and more vibrant than previously
thought. They staged Italian operas and French plays, translated and in original languages, often employing highly trained local peasants performing before invitation-
only audiences of local magnates and their friends. According to some estimates,
provincial Russia had eighty-six manorial theaters employing serf performers. Vladimir
province, roughly 100 kilometers from Moscow, had several local theaters, including
one owned by Count Alexander Vorontsov, which employed almost a hundred performers – male and female, complete with a small orchestra, all from the peasantry.
Audiences there could see plays by Molière, Sheridan, Kotzebue, as well as those of

Russian playwrights. In addition, several provincial towns opened theaters under the patronage of local nobles. These extended as far east as the Siberian town of Tobolsk, whose relatively small nobility maintained a theater, published two literary journals, and operated a school.

A handful of the wealthiest nobles (one recent scholar puts their number at about twenty[5]) carried out elaborate reform projects on their estates, so as to introduce modern farming techniques – "enlightened seigniorialism," as one author put it. Some of them, like the 1751 "Instruction" of I. P. Rumiantsev, described in elaborate detail precisely how work was to be physically organized. Typically the projects began with a series of written instructions to the estate manager, since many of these would-be scientific *latifundistas* were absentee landlords, and they intended to intervene in the pace of work of the peasant communities so as to increase yields and expand the commercial reach of the estate. This was the goal of the super-rich Sheremetevs and Vorontsovs, although their poor grasp of the social realities of peasant communities very much limited their effectiveness. A very few even established schools for their serfs, and thereby furthered the goals of human improvement and enlightenment that were at the heart of these schemes.

We should be careful, though, not to overstate either the size or significance of Westernization in the provinces. Their social and numerical reach remained shallow, so far as one can judge, and the sociability that they engendered was decidedly local. It would be extreme to imagine that these constituted sites of an incipient civil society or centers of regional self-consciousness in opposition to the center. These same provincial grandees famously avoided taking part in the noble assemblies that derived from Catherine the Great's 1775 provincial legislation and 1785 Charter to the Nobility put into place. Wealth, title, privilege all remained closely tied to the court, and those landlords with the ambition to get ahead tended to pursue their careers in St Petersburg. Indeed, there is something not quite right about the endeavor among many nobles to reimagine the landed estate as some kind of earthly paradise, providing identity and a sense of place and belonging.

Let us keep in mind the impact of partible inheritance, the legal requirement of dividing one's property among all of one's heirs – including the widow – rather than passing it down undivided to the oldest son. This practice, fiercely defended by noble families as recently as the succession crisis of 1730, meant that the ties between a specific landlord and a fixed piece of land were unstable and probably of recent vintage. Clans employed sophisticated strategies to keep estates intact, *de facto* if not *de jure*, but this was an endlessly uphill struggle. Heads of noble households, both male and female, bought and sold land quite regularly, internecine law suits were common and difficult to resolve, and the pressure to satisfy all one's heirs was invariably intense. The most successful families adapted to this diffusive pressure by buying land in several locations, often far removed from one another, or by receiving land grants as reward for distinguished service. But such adaptability, by definition, meant a willingness to move away from the land of one's ancestors. Hence this insistence upon asserting a patriarchal, or even primordial, attachment to a specific piece of land was, more often than not, an exercise in creative fiction. But why? What motivated dozens, perhaps hundreds, of well-to-do, Westernized, educated landlords to engage in such make-believe during the latter third of the eighteenth century?

One explanation put forth by Raeff about four decades ago suggests that a sense of dislocation, even alienation, lay at the heart of this behavior. Having lost links with their own past, serving men could not even claim state service as the foundation of their privilege. Disaffected from home, school, and – after 1762 – service, they searched for other bases of a collective self, a journey that sometimes led to literary life (Raeff's primary sources were memoirs and private letters). They generated imaginary family histories (the notorious *rodoslovnye knigi* of the late eighteenth century that claimed, usually erroneously, to trace a family's nobiliary status back through the ages). At other times they led to intrepid assertions of a multigenerational attachment to land, even if it had only recently come into the family's possession, and the intent to transform that land into a visual testament to that affinity.

Some critics doubted this explanation, pointing out for example that most noble memoirs and family albums from this era reflect fondly on childhood, the immediate family, and life in the countryside. But the sense of cultural and social unease that Raeff described, a discomfort amidst privilege, mastery, and pleasure, was surely there, at least to some extent. One recent literary scholar aptly characterized this elusive tone as "the serpent in the garden," and he argued that Bolotov, that most enlightened and self-satisfied of Russia's eighteenth-century diarists (not to mention the most prolix: his manuscript diary ran to over 5,000 pages!) was a quintessential example. In other words, joy at being modern, urbane, and European commingled with a growing anomie, and in the most extreme cases a feeling of utter foreignness, when they reflected on their diminished cultural and physical connection to Russia as they imagined it to have been. Most of the nobility experienced this as something short of a moral crisis. But there were others, like Nikolai Novikov and his friends, who found the contradictions of Russian modernity deeply problematic. Their search led at times to a renewed engagement with Christianity and the Church. Alternatively, it led to an embrace of mystical variants of Freemasonry.

The Clergy and Enlightenment

This chapter has focused most of its attention on the nobility as the most visible estate and the most visibly affected stratum in Russia's adaptation of European manners and identities. We should not imagine, however, that they were the only such group. State-sponsored secondary education recruited representatives of all social strata, including a scattering of non-Russians, and, if we include the handful of private schools, young women as well. Some, such as the Moscow merchants' school and Ivan Betskoi's boarding school for orphaned children, specifically targeted the non-nobility. Several of Russia's foremost intellectuals came from the peasantry, such as the poet, psalmist, and literary translator Vasilii Trediakovskii. The man most often identified as the central figure of the Russian Enlightenment, Mikhail Lomonosov ("the Russian Benjamin Franklin"), was the son of a state peasant, a fisherman by trade. As we have seen, some serfs rose to the status of artistic stars on stage and in the opera, and some of these participated in salon life as well.

But by any measure these were the exceptions, at least among the laity. The old idea of a large and socially engaged eighteenth-century "democratic intelligentsia," once fashionable among Soviet scholars, greatly exaggerated the social heterogeneity of the literary elites. One group for whom education was not exceptional, however, was the clergy, and in purely numerical terms Russia's several dozen Orthodox seminaries (opened between 1737 and the mid-1780s) and the handful of theological academies (seminaries that taught advanced courses in philosophy and theology) produced many more pupils than secular secondary schools did over the course of the eighteenth century. How do their experiences comport with the notions of Westernization or Europeanization? They did, but in a special sense. Adapted from a Jesuit model via Ukraine, seminary education was conducted in Latin and emphasized mastery of Latin above all else. While Latin had minimal practical value for the seminarians who became parish priests, a virtually closed caste at the time, it did mark them as being learned in some palpable sense and linked them, however, faintly, with educational practices that were commonplace in Europe and throughout the Christian world. Typically, seminarians spent at least eight years in the classroom studying Latin and little else, often biding their time until their father's position came free. A few used their Latin as entertainment, such as the priest celebrated by Bolotov, who traded Latin doggerel and lines from Cicero with Bolotov in their idle hours together. Hundreds of others, primarily from among those in the advanced courses, found that a mastery of Latin provided a bridge to non-clerical careers, whether as students in medicine, recruits to the new teaching academy founded in 1782, or as members of the diplomatic corps. Among parish priests, however, a return to the countryside offered few opportunities to use whatever Latin they had managed to retain.

For the monastic clergy, especially those who pursued ecclesiastical careers, the situation was rather different. Their libraries were filled with Latin manuscripts, and quite a few of them achieved a level of learning unmatched by any other Russians outside the University and the Academy of Sciences. Several were active participants in the intellectual life of the capitals, reading the journals and writing for them, and frequenting the literary salons. Leading officials, such as Platon Levshin, the Metropolitan of Moscow during much of the reign of Catherine the Great, and Gavriil Petrov, his counterpart in St Petersburg, were important authors in their own right, and active participants in Russia's Enlightenment. They followed in the footsteps of earlier prelates, such as Feofan Prokopovich and Gavriil Buzhinskii in the early part of the century and Dmitrii Sechenov in the middle, who had studied abroad and who endeavored to reconcile modern rationalism with the primacy of faith. Their instrument of preference was the sermon, orated in a prominent church or cathedral, often in the presence of the ruling family and other dignitaries, and then subsequently published so that it would be available more widely.

Commonplace elsewhere in Christendom, individually authored sermons had come to Russia only in the latter decades of the seventeenth century, once again under the influence of Ukrainian clergy schooled in Western scholasticism and baroque styles, who were invited into Russian service in considerable numbers from the 1670s onward. The first generations of preachers, from Semen Polotskii in the 1660s and 1670s to Prokopovich in the 1720s and 1730s, followed the strictures of scholasticism rigorously, relying almost exclusively upon scriptural exegesis to explicate the virtues of a particular saint, the meaning of a given holiday, or the divine hand guiding the policies of the ruler. By mid-century, however, Russian homiletics – still the exclusive province of a small number of clerical hierarchs – began to reflect literary fashion and, more importantly, to anticipate the moral sensibilities of the elite laity to whom they were addressed. Scripture and the religious calendar continued to provide context, but the narratives of sermons took on the cast of parables, dwelling upon moral issues of everyday life. Preached in a modern and literary Russian, they were intended to hold the attention of the audience, by means of literary allusion, entertaining turns of phrase, and relevance to the increasingly individualized concerns of educated nobles. In order to produce such prose clergy had to be intimate with the cultural and literary world of the lay elites; indeed they had to partake in them in ways that would have appeared alien and even dangerous to their more conservative forebears.

Given this insistence on accessible literary language, tropes, and messages, the zealous insistence on a Latinized clergy, European in its own way, to be sure, but linguistically marked as separate from a Westernizing laity that had scant familiarity with Latin, is rather surprising. Two issues seem to be involved here, both reflecting the cultural politics of language. The first derives from the conviction that Latin was the universal mark of learning and scholarship. There had been a time in the late seventeenth and early eighteenth centuries when much of the black clergy had resisted the influence of the "Latinizers" within the Church, arguing instead for a more nativist or Grecophilic approach to the written word. But the seminary reforms of the 1730s had installed Latin as the gold standard, and, for clerical Enlighteners such as Platon, it constituted a basis for distinguishing clergy as the learned estate within the empire. From a cosmopolitan perspective, knowing Latin implicitly put Russia's lettered priests on an equal footing with Christian clergy everywhere.

The second aspect of this outlook was the affinity between language and social standing overall, in particular within the local parishes. Although state-sponsored reforms had increased the number of primary schools, basic literacy remained the responsibility of the clergy, most commonly through informal gatherings of students and tutors. This understanding had been true for a very long time, and it became legally instituted in Peter the Great's Spiritual Regulations of 1721, which discussed the Church's commitment to education and the role of the clergy as teachers. While the clergy and the higher states could be taught all manner of subjects, local parishioners (that is, the peasants) would learn, at most, their ABCs. More importantly they would learn them in Slavonic script through memorizing prayers, rather than in the modern Russian orthography. This approach continued as church policy throughout the eighteenth century, modified only slightly in the last quarter of the century when Platon consented to allow ABC books to include the modern orthography. Language (or access to it), in short, marked one's station in life, and the Church embraced this sort of linguistic cameralism as a way of demarcating itself (the Latinists), the service and better-off estates (civil Russian), and the peasants (church Russian learned by rote).

Freemasonry

Masonic lodges began appearing in Russia some time during the 1730s or 1740s, imported by travelers and diplomats from German-speaking lands and from France. They soon proved quite popular among the urban nobility, and at freemasonry's height in the 1770s and 1780s there were several dozen lodges in and around the two capitals, enrolling as many as 3,000 members, as well as a scattering of lodges in provincial towns. A number of the century's most distinguished intellectual figures were masons, including the historian Mikhail Shcherbatov, the ambassador Zakhar Chernyshev, the high official Nikita Panin, the poet Ivan Elagin, and many more. Because of their private rituals and penchant for secrecy, Masonic lodges have been, and remain, the object of the most extravagant speculations, nowhere more so than in Russia, where even today one can read about global conspiracies being hatched behind the locked doors of the lodges. What exactly did take place in their inner sancta, especially in the third or fourth (or even seventh) degrees to which only the highest grade masons were privy? Well, we do not exactly know, but, from the moment they took root on Russian soil, other Russians, including officialdom, worried about them. Their connections with secret societies in Germany, some of which were thought to harbor republican sympathies, generated suspicion among police officials, particularly in Moscow, and led to several lodges being closed. On the whole, however, Masonic lodges functioned largely as centers of male sociability, talking, gambling, and the like. Given their well-connected memberships, lodges were sites of political networking and cementing bonds of patronage.

Following the lead of Margaret Jacob,[6] recent specialists, Douglas Smith in particular, have embraced the once-popular idea that the lodges imported not just ritual from the West, but a belief in brotherhood, a kind of equality within that contrasted with the inequality outside. In this view Russia's lodges were incubators of civil society or a more-or-less modern understanding of a public sphere, intervening between state and society at large.[7] Other scholars have downplayed this idea of a nascent public sphere, and have focused instead on the handful of lodges, referred to as Rosicrucians or Martinists, who by all accounts saw themselves as a moralizing and spiritualizing force within Russian educated society. Centered in Moscow, they are most commonly linked to the publishing empire of Nikolai Novikov during the 1780s, and his many enterprises most assuredly loomed large in their existence. Rosicrucianism as a set of spiritual ideals and practices was a direct import from France and Germany, associated in Russia with Johann Georg Schwarz, a German scholar and tutor who had become a professor at Moscow University during the late 1770s. It was there that he made the connection with Novikov and other Moscow masons with links to the University.

What did these affinities mean for the Russians who opted for Rosicrucianism? Scholars are not of one mind on this question. Some see no major difference between Rosicrucians and other lodges, no fundamental tension between their thinking and the precepts of Enlightenment, except perhaps in their flirtation with alchemy.[8] Others are not so sure, and they draw a subtle distinction between the simple importation of ideas from Europe and the adaptation, or re-creation, of those ideas to respond to what they see as Russia's customs and abiding concerns (*sklonenie na nravy Rossii*). In this context Novikov's circles loom large, for their activities embraced simultaneously the optimism of the age regarding human understanding and dismay at the declining regard for native traditions and history as well as the diminishing spirituality of the Enlightened individual.

During Novikov's prime as a print impresario between 1779 and 1789, the presses under his direction accounted for well over a third of new titles. These included a massive number of translated novels and essays, as well as quite a lot of original Russian writing, nearly all of which was written according to styles and genres brought in from elsewhere. Thanks in large measure to his efforts, educated Russians of his generation had access to as wide a range of European letters as did readers elsewhere in Europe. Thanks to the easing of press laws, private publishing firms flourished in the 1780s. The Empress's aggressive patronage of French men of letters enabled Russians to read some works that had fallen under heavy censorship in France itself, more than a few of which came from cooperative ventures between the Empress and Novikov. But Novikov's reservations about modernity reverberated in his publishing profile as well. Several of his more widely circulated periodicals, such as *The Ancient Russian Library*, as well as some other works went to great lengths to celebrate Russia's own heritage, in particular its written heritage of laws, court records, and chronicles. He reminded his readers repeatedly that Russia had good writers before the eighteenth century, whom he celebrated in his 1772 *Historical Dictionary of Russian Writers*. The proto-nationalist message of these compendia was unmistakable: the culture inscribed onto the Russian language was old and meritorious, and those who chose to displace it *in toto* in favor of European modernity risked abandoning their heritage and, by implication, their native identity. Of equal concern was the perceived loss of inner spirituality, which led Moscow's Rosicrucians to read and translate a large body of mystical writings that meditated on godliness, matter, the soul, and supernaturalism. This mystical turn reflected a worry about the separation of the literati from organized religion, and, while there was nothing uniquely Orthodox about the religiosity of Novikov's circle, neither was it simple mimicry of French "Martinism." Instead it constituted a kind of pan-Christianity that implicitly urged the elite public to build their outlook around faith, the Resurrection, and the hope for salvation. Little wonder, then, that clergy constituted some of Novikov's leading supporters, and, in the case of his journal *The Morning Light* (1777–80), the organizers of a subscription campaign on his behalf. Only under the prodding of police officials, such as the Moscow chief of police General A. A. Prozorovskii, did the clerical hierarchy cooperate in suppressing Moscow Freemasonry in the late 1780s. Even then, once masonry had revived in the early nineteenth century, this spiritualist world view reblossomed in St Petersburg in the Masonic circle of Alexander Labzin and his Dying Sphinx lodge, which, before it too was suppressed, worked in partnership with the Orthodox hierarchy and the court to produce the first printed New Testament in vernacular Russian.

Conclusion: Russia, Europe, and the Enlightened Elites

In retrospect, there is little question that the educated elites reacted favorably and optimistically to the changes that went on around them and the reordering of their own lives over the course of the eighteenth century. They looked upon Russia's entry into Europe as a positive and civilizing development. Nearly all of those who ventured an opinion expressed pride in the empire, regard for the rulers, and awe at the accomplishments of the age. Theirs were voices of affirmation, and few of the educated nobility doubted their own European-ness, even if they often viewed their less privileged countrymen in a less optimistic light. Still, some of them found that the closer they got to acting as Europeans the more disconnected they felt themselves to be from that which they had considered native. For a number of them this constituted a genuine crisis of identity to which European rationalism offered stimulation but no ultimate solutions. In a very few instances the moral crisis took on a political coloration, leading them to turn the gaze of rationalism against Russia's own political and social institutions. This was the case with Alexander Radishchev, whose fictitious *Journey from St Petersburg to Moscow* (freely published in 1790) decried the brutalities and unfreedom of serfdom, the venality and corruption of the elites, the hypocritical contrast between the high moral ideals of enlightenment, and the violent debasements of everyday reality. Moreover, the unhappy 1790s, in which Catherine's conservative final years were followed by her son, Paul I's, systematic assault on the printed and spoken word, soured several literati on the good will of the ruler. But all of them, even the doubters, fundamentally embraced almost matter-of-factly the westward-looking orientation. Not until the shock of the Decembrist revolt in 1825 would the core ideals of this orientation come under reconsideration.

Notes

1   Marc Raeff, *The Origins of the Eighteenth-Century Intelligentsia: The Eighteenth-Century Nobility*, New York: Harcourt, Brace and World, 1966, *passim*.

2   James Cracraft, *The Petrine Revolution in Architecture*, Chicago: University of Chicago Press, 1988.

3   Priscilla Roosevelt, *Life on the Russian Country Estate: A Social and Cultural History*, New Haven: Yale University Press, 1995, esp. chs. 1, 2, and 4.

4   Richard Stites, *Serfdom, Society and the Arts in Imperial Russia: The Pleasure and the Power*, New Haven: Yale University Press, 1995, ch. 6: "Playing the Provinces."

5   Edgar Melton, "Enlightened Seigniorialism and its Dilemmas in Serf Russia, 1750–1830," *Journal of Modern History*, 62 (Dec. 1990), 681.

6   Margaret Jacob, *Living the Enlightenment: Freemasonry and Politics in Eighteenth-Century Europe*, New York: Oxford University Press, 1991.

7   Douglas Smith, *Working the Rough Stone: Freemasonry and Society in Eighteenth-Century Russia*, DeKalb, IL: Northern Illinois University press, 1999, esp. ch. 2: "The Russian Public; or, Civil Society in the Eighteenth Century."

8   The standard argument regarding Russia's Rosicrucians follows closely the reasoning in Frances Yates, *The Rosicrucian Enlightenment*, London: Routledge, Keegan, Paul, 1972.

References

Cracraft, James (1988). *The Petrine Revolution in Architecture*. University of Chicago Press, Chicago.

Cross, A. G. (1997). *By the Banks of the Neva: Aspects of the Lives and Careers of the British in Eighteenth-Century Russia*. Cambridge University Press, Cambridge.

De Madariaga, Isabel (1981). *Russia in the Era of Catherine the Great*. Yale University Press, New Haven.

Dixon, Simon (2001). *Catherine the Great*. Longman, London.

Dukes, Paul (ed.) (1977). *Russia under Catherine the Great*. Vol. 2: *Catherine the Great's Instruction (Nakaz) to the Legislative Commission of 1767*. Oriental Research Partners, Newtonville, MA.

Freeze, Gregory (1977). *The Russian Levites: Parish Clergy in the Eighteenth Century*. Harvard University Press, Cambridge, MA.

Jacob, Margaret C. (1991). *Living the Enlightenment: Freemasonry and Politics in Eighteenth-Century Europe*. Oxford University Press, New York.

Jones, W. Gareth (1984). *Nikolay Novikov, Enlightener of Russia*. Cambridge University Press, Cambridge.

Kelly, Catriona "Educating Tat'yana: Manners, Motherhood, and Moral Education (*Vospitanie*), 1760–1840," in Linda Edmondson (ed.), *Gender in Russian History and Culture*. Palgrave, Basingstoke and New York.

Lotman, Iurii (1985). "The Poetics of Everyday Behavior in Eighteenth-Century Russian Culture," in Alexander D. Nakhimovsky and Alice Stone Nakhimovsky (eds.), *The Semiotics of Russian Cultural History*. Cornell University Press, Ithaca, NY.

Marker, Gary (1985). *Publishing, Printing and the Origin of Intellectual Life in Russia, 1700–1800*. Princeton University Press, Princeton.

Marrese, Michelle Lamarche (2002). *A Woman's Kingdom: Noblewomen and the Control of Property in Russia, 1700–1861*. Cornell University Press, Ithaca, NY.

Melton, Edgar (1990). "Enlightened Seigniorialism and its Dilemmas in Serf Russia, 1750–1830," *Journal of Modern History*, 62 (Dec. 1990).

Newlin, Thomas (2001). *The Voice in the Garden: Andrei Bolotov and the Anxieties of Russian Pastoral, 1738–1833*. Northwestern University Press, Evanston, IL.

Papmehl, K. A. (1971). *Freedom of Expression in Eighteenth-Century Russia*. Mouton, The Hague.

Papmehl, K. A. (1983). *Metropolitan Platon of Moscow (Petr Levshin, 1737–1812): The Enlightened Prelate, Scholar, and Educator*. Oriental Research Partners, Newtownville, MA.

Raeff Marc (2003). "The Emergence of the Russian European: Russia as a Full Partner of Europe," in Cynthia Hyla Whittaker (ed.), *Russia Engages the World, 1453–1825*. Harvard University Press, Cambridge, MA, 118–37.

Raeff, Marc (1966). *Origins of the Russian Intelligentsia: The Eighteenth-Century Nobility*. Harcourt, Brace and World, New York.

Raeff, Marc (1983). *The Well-Ordered Police State: Social and Institutional Change through Law in the Germanies and Russia, 1600–1800*. Yale University Press, New Haven.

Riasanovsky, Nicholas V. (1976). *A Parting of Ways: Government and the Educated Public in Russia, 1801–1855*. Oxford University Press, Oxford.

Rogger, Hans (1960). *National Consciousness in Eighteenth-Century Russia*. Harvard University Press, Cambridge, MA.

Roosevelt, Priscilla (1995). *Life on the Russian Country Estate: A Social and Cultural History*. Yale University Press, New Haven.

Segel, Harold B. (1967). *The Literature of Eighteenth-Century Russia: A History and Anthology*. 2 vols. E. P. Dutton, New York.

Smith, Douglas (1999). *Working the Rough Stone: Freemasonry and Society in Eighteenth-Century Russia*. Northern Illinois University Press, DeKalb, IL.

Stites, Richard (2005). *Serfdom, Society, and the Arts in Imperial Russia: The Pleasure and the Power*. Yale University Press, New Haven.

Wirtschafter, Elise Kimerling (2003). *The Play of Ideas in Russian Enlightenment Theater*. Northern Illinois University Press, DeKalb, IL.

Wortman, Richard S. (1995). *Scenarios of Power: Myth and Ceremony in Russian Monarchy*. Vol. 1: *From Peter the Great to the Death of Nicholas I*. Princeton University Press, Princeton.

Yates, Frances, A. (1972). *The Rosicrucian Enlightenment*. London: Routledge, Keegan and Paul.

Further Reading

There is quite an extensive English-language literature on the eighteenth-century nobility and its cultural transformation. Marc Raeff's *Origins of the Russian Intelligentsia* remains the classic statement and is the starting point for any discussion of the subject. For alternative views, see Arcadius Kahan, "The Costs of Westernization in Russia: The Gentry and the Economy in the Eighteenth Century," *Slavic Review*, 25/6 (Mar. 1966), 40–66. See also John LeDonne, *Absolutism and Ruling Class: The Formation of the Russian Political Order, 1700–1825*, and Robert Jones, *The Emancipation of the Russian Nobility, 1762–1785*, both of whom discuss the relationship of the nobility to service, estate, and province. There has been a recent out-pouring of literature on the Western influences on the arts in eighteenth-century Russia. See, in particular, Elise Kimerling Wirtschafter's *The Play of Ideas in Russian Enlightenment Theater*, which provides a thorough analysis of original Russian plays of the era, and Richard Stites's *Serfdom, Society, and the Arts in Imperial Russia*. Priscilla Roosevelt's *Life on the Russian Country Estate* offers a vivid glimpse of estate life, complete with excellent illustrations. There are quite a few informative biographies and memoirs of prominent individuals, including Gareth Jones, *Nikolay Novikov, Enlightener of Russia*, and Jesse V. Clardy, *The Philosophical Idea of Alexander Radishchev* (old but still quite helpful). *The Memoirs of Catherine the Great*, ed. Dominque Maroger, although incomplete, is the most accessible translation. Simon Sebag Montefiore's *Prince of Princes: The Life of Potemkin*, in *The Dictionary of Literary Biography*, vol. 150: *Early Modern Russian Writers*, ed. Marcus Levitt, offers brief discussions of the lives and works of many literati. Biographies of rulers abound, especially those of Peter the Great and Catherine the Great. On Catherine and her reign by far the most helpful books are Isabel de Madariaga, *Russia in the Era of Catherine the Great*, and John Alexander, *Catherine the Great Life and Legend*. There are other reliable studies, but students should steer clear of the many sensationalist biographies that fill the shelves of bookstores and libraries.

CHAPTER TWELVE

The "Great Reforms" of the 1860s

DANIEL FIELD

At the accession of Emperor Alexander II in 1855, more than 80 percent of Russia's population consisted of peasants. Almost half the peasants, some twenty-two million, were serfs; their status was like slavery. The other peasants, mostly "state peasants," were similarly constrained. Outside a few cities, there was almost no functioning local government. The judiciary system was purely bureaucratic and was notorious for secrecy, delays, and corruption. All printed matter was subject to word-by-word precensorship. Conscripts into the army, drawn only from the lower orders, had, by and large, to serve for twenty-five years – in effect, for life.

By 1875, serfdom had been abolished and a similar reform extended to other peasants. Cities, provinces, and districts in European Russia were endowed with elective agencies of self-administration. The regime instituted European-style courts, with lawyers, independent judges, and trial by jury open to the public. Modernization of the armed forces included a new system of conscription to which all males were liable, with terms of service set at between six months and seven years, depending on the conscript's level of education. These are called the "great reforms." One great reform was discussed but never enacted. In 1855 the emperor was an autocrat, accountable to no one, with no formal limits on his authority. There was talk of "crowning the edifice" – that is, establishing an elected nationwide assembly – but the talk came to nothing, and Alexander remained an autocrat.

Before an examination of the reforms, some background considerations are in order. In 1855 (and, at least ostensibly, until 1917), Russia's population was divided into "estates of the realm" – the Russian term is *soslovie*. *Soslovie* was a function of a man's relationship to the state (a woman took the status of her husband or father); each *soslovie* had its own package of obligations and, for some, privileges. Nobles served the state directly and personally, in the military or the bureaucracy; their obligation to serve was abolished in 1762, but most nobles continued to spend at least part of their lives in state service. Originally, nobles were provided with serfs as compensation for their service, and, by the nineteenth century, only nobles could acquire serfs. By 1855, however, a majority of nobles did not hold serfs. Clergy served the state personally; although clerical status, unlike noble status, was not hereditary, most parish priests (who were required to marry) were the sons and grandsons of priests. Merchants also served the state directly, mostly by collecting taxes, and could gain or lose merchant status according to their declared wealth. Townsmen rendered service to the state as communities. So did peasants, the last and by far the largest of the estates; their status was hereditary.

More important than distinctions of *soslovie* was the binary distinction between educated society (*obshchestvo*) and the common people (*narod*) [1: 69–70]. Educated society was a tiny minority composed of bearers of a written, cosmopolitan culture. Like their counterparts in Western and Central Europe, they read newspapers, wrote letters, went to the theater, and played pianos. The common people, which included almost all peasants and some members of other *sosloviia*, was composed of bearers of an oral, traditional culture. If they read at all, they read the lives of the saints; they watched bear-baiting instead of plays, and listened to or performed traditional music. Attachment to one or the other of these two groupings was plainly visible from a person's dress and deportment, but attachment involved much more than culture narrowly considered. The common people held and acted on assumptions and beliefs that were utterly different from the values that prevailed in educated society. From this perspective, the authors of the reforms were like colonial rulers, legislating for people with utterly different standards and values.

We must also consider the issue of underdevelopment. In the seventeenth century, Russia lagged well behind the West in certain technologies; in the eighteenth, rulers and statesmen made energetic efforts to overcome the lag, with mixed results. In 1800 Russia produced more iron than any other country. In the ensuing half-century, its output doubled. During the same interval, British iron output increased twenty-four times over; an iron industry that relied on wood fuel and forced labor could not keep pace. In 1855 the industrial revolution had penetrated Russia only in a few areas. The agricultural revolution, which began in Britain in the mid-eighteenth century, had some admirers in rural Russia, but almost no practitioners. Russia lagged as well according to non-economic indicators, such as literacy rates.

There was a direct connection between economic underdevelopment and the gulf between educated society and the common people. Non-peasants want peasants to produce surpluses. By 1855 agriculture in Western and Central Europe was ever increasingly involved in the market economy; farms and estates were set up to produce commodities to sell. Peasant agriculture in Russia was not, strictly speaking, subsistence agriculture. It was, rather, organized to avert starvation. This organization was appropriate to prevailing conditions: the long, harsh winters, the erratic rainfall in the south, the poor soils of Northern and parts of Central Russia. Peasant villages were periodically afflicted with a *neurozhai* – literally a "non-harvest." Hence plowland was held by the community as a whole, and the village commune (*obshchina*) reallocated it from time to time among households in the village. The criterion of allocation was the number of able-bodied workers in a household, which was a measure of the household's consumption needs and also of its capacity to meet obligations imposed by the serfholder and the state, for which the village was collectively responsible. Peasants generally practiced three-field cultivation, so that one-third of the plowland was left fallow each year. Moreover, plowland was allocated in scattered strips, differing in their soil quality, access to water, and the like. These and other aspects of Russian village agriculture were well calculated to maximize the possibility that everyone would get enough to eat. They were not calculated to produce surpluses. If fortune smiled and there was a surplus, peasants would sell it to get cash to meet their obligations, such as the capitation or "soul tax," but they kept their involvement with the market to a minimum. The system did not encourage enterprise or innovation. Liability to repartition discouraged investment in improving the land. The scattered strips were too small for harvesters and other machines to work, and much labor time was expended in moving from strip to strip. Since the village's cattle were turned out on the stubble after harvest, every household had to plant the same crop in each of the three fields, and innovators were frustrated. The system was sensible, in that every element was calculated to meet a genuine need, but it was not "rational," as economists use the word.

Peasant agriculture was the infirm foundation of manorial agriculture. Consider, by contrast, the slave plantations of the American South. Every aspect of the plantation was deliberately designed and operated to produce a maximum volume of commodities. In Russia, serfdom was simply superimposed on a system of cultivation that only incidentally benefited the master. Serfholders had two basic means of exaction from their serfs. One was *obrok*, or dues in money; the serfs were allocated virtually all the plowland, and from their labor on that land (plus off-farm earnings) they were to pay their dues. The other was *barshchina*, or dues in labor; peasants would work part of the week on their own allotments and part of the week on their master's demesne land, from which the harvest went directly to the squire. In either event, it was the peasants' puny draft animals and their primitive tools that worked the land. Productivity was dismal by Western standards. Some serfholders, to be sure, became very rich, but only by amassing thousands of serfs, meager collections from each of whom combined to make a great sum. The average estate in mid-nineteenth century Russia had 1,000 male serfs; only a handful of American plantations had that many slaves. Gigantism, not innovation, opened the way to wealth.

The Abolition of Serfdom

Of the great reforms, the most important was the abolition of serfdom, because it directly affected the lives of millions of Russians, because serfdom was the defining institution for society, the economy, and almost every other aspect of life, and because, as we shall see, other reforms flowed from the abolition of serfdom.

The cause of the abolition of serfdom has been debated since the reform era. Establishing causality is especially hard because of the nature of the regime. Nicholas I (1825–55) was notoriously conservative, and his son Alexander ascended the throne with his father's belief system. He appointed or confirmed in office his father's ministers, who were hostile to reform. In March of 1856 he told the nobility of Moscow Province: "It is rumored that I want to give liberty to the peasants; this rumor is unjust, and you can say this to everyone;" he did concede that it would be better for reform to "come from above than from below." Despite his reputation, Nicholas had fiddled with the reform of serfdom, to no significant result; his chosen instruments were a series of secret committees, composed of high officials. In January of 1857 Alexander appointed another secret committee; many of its members were veterans of previous committees "on the peasant question." After eight months of deliberation, the new secret committee declared: "it is not presently possible to undertake the general emancipation of the peasants . . . Not only the peasants and the *pomesh-chiki* [serfholders] but even the Government itself are not prepared" for emancipation. Alexander expressed his gratitude for the committee's report.

Three months later, on November 20, 1857, the regime made a public commitment to a reform of serfdom, setting in motion a complex process that would produce the emancipation legislation of February 19, 1861. More important than the policies the government advanced was the fact that it made them public. There could be no turning back.

What produced this turnaround? Many historians [2: 2] point to Russia's defeat in the Crimean War (1853–6), but the defeat left the regime discredited and impoverished, ill-positioned to challenge the serfholding elite. Some Soviet historians emphasized the government's fear of peasant rebellions [3: 9]. The regime, however, had believed and continued to believe that peasant rebellions were more likely as a *result* of reform than from clinging to the status quo, especially since, in much of the countryside, maintaining law and order was the responsibility of the serfholders and their agents. Other Soviet historians emphasized deep-seated problems in the servile economy and attributed the reform to these problems [4: 378–85], but in the 1850s neither the reformers nor their antagonists perceived them. The regime did hope for economic growth if serfdom were abolished, but dreaded the economic disruption that meaningful reform would entail. It understood that serfdom was outmoded, but it seemed to work, and serfholders' revenues were generally steady or rising. Recently, sophisticated historians in Russia, notably M. D. Dolbilov [5] have emphasized the regime's concern for its great-power status and the force of nationalist sentiment in the upper bureaucracy, but they do not attribute causality to these considerations.

Moreover, we must not only explain the commitment to reform in 1857 but the evolution of policy on serfdom in the ensuing thirty-nine months. The reform promulgated in 1861 was far more thoroughgoing than anyone with influence or authority had imagined in 1857.

The explanation of both the initial commitment and the subsequent evolution of policy lies not in the causal considerations that have been advanced but in the weakness of serfdom as an institution. Serfholders overwhelmingly dominated the upper bureaucracy and the officer corps and held most of the nation's private wealth; not one in a hundred – perhaps not one in a thousand – wanted the abolition of serfdom. They were, however, dependent upon the state, to which they had mortgaged two-thirds of their serfs and on which they relied to keep the serfs subordinate. In the face of insubordination or the threat of rebellion, slaveholders in the American South, assisted by other whites, subdued the slaves, but in similar circumstances serfholders called in the army. Serfholders had no political experience, nor any need to develop it, since the regime, of its own accord, lavished favors upon them. The serfholders were strikingly incohesive. Rank-and file serfholders looked to wealthy, titled grandees for leadership. The grandees, as I. A. Khristoforov has pointed out [6: 297, 313], were hoping to extract from the reform process an oligarchic form of rule, through which they would dominate the government. Most of the rank and file cared only for their revenues; the debates of 1859–60 would show that they would – again, unlike their counterparts in the American South – surrender their powers and privileges if only the government would compensate them richly for their losses. Moreover, grandees and lesser nobles alike were in the grip of "monarchist illusions." These illusions are generally attributed to uneducated peasants and epitomized in the peasant saying "The tsar wishes us well but the *boiars* [i.e., self-seeking and conniving officials] resist"; sooner or later the tsar's good wishes would be realized [7: 5]. Recently historians have shown that peasants had no monopoly on monarchist illusions; members of Russia's elite, including even men who met regularly with the emperor, indulged in them [8: 150, 170–5]. Assumptions that followed from these illusions were pervasive and were held by ardent reformers and by opponents of reform. In great part because of these assumptions, ministers and other high officials who opposed the reform legislation that was being drawn up in 1858–60 never rose to the challenge. Alexander II did not, by and large, like reformers; he dismissed the principal authors of the peasant reform within days of its enactment. The reformers' highly placed opponents, however, grumbled and bumbled but never presented Alexander with an enactable alternative to the reformers' drafts. In retrospect, these men seem feckless, but we should remember that the abolition of bondage in the United States required a great civil war; monarchist illusions in Russia kept the political temperature low.

Almost all serfholders, including the grandees and the high officials, shared a culture oriented to Western Europe, where serfdom had disappeared. No articulate voice in Russia could call serfdom good. Nikolai Gogol' came close to doing so in a book published in 1847, and almost everyone took the book for proof that the author was deranged. Thanks to censorship, nothing critical of serfdom, but also nothing supportive of serfdom, appeared in print. Russia had no Garrison, but also no Calhoun. Serfdom had no ideology, and a sociopolitical institution without an ideology is vulnerable.

The breakthrough of November 1857 took the form of a rescript and a directive to the governor-general of three northwestern provinces, where most of the serfholders were Polish. These incoherent and contradictory documents were the by-product of an abandoned initiative, but their publication committed the government to doing something about serfdom. And the directives did contain the germ of a resolution of the key problem. The government believed that a noble's land was inalienable private property; peasants believed the land was theirs because they tilled it. Freedom without land would, from a peasant perspective, be a monstrous injustice. To give privately owned land to the peasants seemed no less monstrous from an elite perspective – the perspective of educated society. The directives emphatically reaffirmed the serfholders' property rights in the land, but provided peasant households with the *use* of allotments of land.

The government's dilemma at the beginning of 1858 – burdened with a commitment to reform without a plan of reform – opened the way to extraordinary political developments. Ostensibly, the serfholding nobility of each province was to participate in drafting the reform. The government learned that there was no flim-flam the nobility would not tolerate. It made a series of promises to the nobility and withdrew or ignored each one. The nobles barely responded. They were confident, because most top positions in government were held by men who were as hostile to reform as they were, that the reformers could not prevail.

The ability to disregard the views of the serfholders, however, did not provide any positive solutions. Solutions began to emerge toward the end of 1858. Alexander II was confused and uncertain on matters of policy but firm in his attitudes toward people. He turned to General Ia. I. Rostovtsev, a personal friend in whom he had boundless trust, to find a way out of his dilemma. Rostovtsev was an elderly courtier with no qualifications on the matter at hand except the emperor's trust and his willingness to take up his task seriously. He looked for people with qualifications and found them – some in the second tier of the bureaucracy, some from the public. These men, notably N. A. Miliutin, Acting Deputy Minister of Internal Affairs, had formed a loose network of reform sympathizers in the 1840s and 1850s. Once they had access to the emperor's confidant, a man who could shield them from their enemies, their reforming zeal redoubled. They assembled in an innocuous-sounding agency called the Editorial Commission, and in this commission they drafted the statues that would abolish serfdom.

The reformers displayed a level of energy and dedication without precedent in the annals of the Russian state. Some of them also displayed considerable guile and political finesse. Through intermediaries, they managed to convince Alexander that those who criticized their drafts and those who tried to get the regime to honor its promises to the nobility were actually challenging his autocratic prerogatives. Moreover, although they are often called "liberals," the authors of the peasant reform made their peace with the principle of autocracy and did not join the chorus of voices in 1861 and after calling for an elected national assembly. There was much in their own handiwork that they saw as flawed, as concessions to the exigencies of the moment or to their conservative critics. They counted on the autocrat to repair these flaws over time. As Larisa Zakharova has observed, their "bet" on the autocrat was "misplaced" [2: 12].

The legislative process was epitomized when the commission's draft came before the Council of State in early 1861. The council was composed of Alexander's friends and confidants. It voted down each section of the draft by large margins. The members were counting on the emperor's sympathy for themselves and his distrust of reformers; they would never have challenged Alexander if they had supposed his commitment to the reformers' plan was firm. These dignitaries could not, however, come up with a coherent alternative. Furthermore, the council was not really a legislature. With each section of the draft except one, the emperor used his prerogative to endorse the minority position, and the Editorial Commission's version became law without significant change. The result was a cautious reform that was nonetheless much more radical and more generous to the peasants than anyone in authority had contemplated.

The terms of the legislation promulgated on February 19, 1861, varied from province to province. The reformers wanted to accommodate the nobility. Hence in the north the allotments of land assigned to the ex-serfs were relatively large but costly; since the land was of little value, the squires would rather have cash. To the south, where land was valuable, the allotments were smaller but not so costly. The complexity of the legislation is compounded by special cases, some involving millions of peasants. The commune was unknown in Ukraine and was not imposed there. About one-twentieth of the serfs were "household people" (*dvorovye liudi*), who performed domestic and other services for their masters; they did not have allotments of land and were not awarded any land by the reform legislation. State peasants would be more generously treated than serfs when the reform was extended to them in 1866; the regime was more willing to sacrifice its own interests than those of serfholders. If we focus on a majority of ethnic Russian serfs, we can grasp main elements of the reform by comparing it to the system of serfdom.

The essence of serfdom was the subjection of the serfs to the arbitrary power of their master or mistress. Serfholders could buy and sell serfs and subject them to physical or sexual abuse. They could relocate serfs on another estate, and their exactions from the serfs were limited only by custom or by their sense of what they could get away with. The laws limiting their powers were vague and rarely enforced. The arbitrary power of the serfholding noble was utterly abolished by the legislation of 1861. The ex-serfs, however, found themselves subject in a new way to the nobles as a class, because they dominated local administration, including the new agencies charged with implementing the peasant reform. And most ex-serfs were dependent, as renters or wage-laborers or sharecroppers, on a noble landowner in the neighborhood.

A second element of serfdom was ascription, or fastening. The reform left peasants ascribed to their home villages, but transferred the power to regulate their comings and goings from the serfholder to the village commune, which now issued the passports that enabled peasants to go off in search of wage work. The government regarded limits on peasants' movement as essential to security.

Paradoxically, it was the economic elements of the reform that most severely restricted the freedom of ex-serfs. Most peasants received (through the commune) an allotment of land and had to meet the obligations that went with the allotment. It was almost impossible to dispose of the allotment. Few peasants who wanted to pull up stakes and start afresh could do so. Servile agriculture had been linked to the repartitional commune. Plowland was held by the commune and subject to periodic repartition among households. The reform legislation, following the practice of serfholders and using the commune as intermediary, imposed a system of mutual responsibility: if one household did not meet its obligations, the others had to make up the difference. It was in the interests of the commune that each household had plowland proportional to its labor power, to maximize its ability to meet its obligations.

Also characteristic of the servile economy was "extraeconomic compulsion." Under serfdom, it was not the market but the serfholders's arbitrary authority that determined the size of the serfs' allotments and the dues they had to render. After the reform, these were determined not by the market, but by the terms of the reform statutes. For each province, the statutes specified a maximum and a minimum size of allotment per male peasant and prescribed corresponding payments (or days of labor service).

These characteristics of the servile economy broke down slowly because, to minimize disruption, the reformers took the economic elements of serfdom as their point of departure. The size of the allotments set by statute derived from the size of allotments under serfdom. In the interests of security, the reformers retained the commune, although they were convinced that it was an archaic institution that impeded agricultural progress and economic development; they nonetheless gave the commune major functions in the post-reform village because the regime did not have the personnel or resources to deal directly with twenty-two million ex-serfs in such areas as conscription and taxation.

The statutes did seek to minimize the economic dependence of ex-serfs on their former masters. They provided that peasants could redeem their allotments over a forty-nine-year period. Redemption entailed an agreement between the squire and his ex-serfs, which was hard to achieve. Until the redemption process began in a village, the ex-serfs were in a state of "temporary obligation," subject to yesterday's serfholder – obligated, within limits set by statute, to render dues in cash or in labor to their former master or mistress.

The abolition of serfdom regulated more than it changed, but regulation represented an enormous change: the arbitrary power of the serfholder had been the essence of serfdom. The reform could not and did not provide an immediate stimulus to economic development. The regime set a higher value on stability, on the prosperity of the nobility, and on the welfare of the peasantry, than on development; it feared chaos more than it wanted progress. So it imposed stability and opened the way for a slow passage out of the structures of serfdom.

The emperor signed the statutes abolishing serfdom on February 19, 1861, but they were not promulgated until early March, at the beginning of Lent. The delay was due to the regime's expectation of disorders or worse, especially now that the authority of the serfholders – the only authority in vast areas of rural Russia – had been renounced from the height of the throne. Orthodox Christians are supposed to abstain from alcohol during Lent, and the regime hoped that sober peasants would take a favorable view of the legislation. In addition, elements of eighty regiments were sent out to provinces where serfs were numerous in the hope that disorders could be nipped in the bud. Finally, the emperor sent out his adjutants, generals, and colonels who worked directly for him and had his monogram on their collars to explain to the peasants that the new statutes were indeed the tsar's true will. None of these measures did any good. To be sure, disorders were few, and blood was shed only because of the nervousness of a few army officers. The history of the regulatory charters (*ustavnye gramoty*), however, attests to the peasants' massive repudiation of the newly promulgated statutes.

A regulatory charter specified the size of the allotments the ex-serfs would get and the dues they would render to their former masters. It was not a contract. The law encouraged free agreements between squires and their former serfs, but, if agreement was not forthcoming, statutory norms were imposed on squire and peasants alike. Representatives of both parties were obliged to sign the charter prior to its implementation, but the *assent* of the parties was not required. When peasants refused to sign a charter, they were not withholding assent but seeking to avoid any involvement in a corrupt process that, they supposed, might impair their rights to the bounty the tsar must have in store for his faithful peasants. As of January 1, 1863, 73,185 charters had been implemented (about two-thirds of the total required), and slightly less than half of these had been signed by the peasants involved. Since the peasants had no valid reason under the law for refusing to sign and were under great pressure to do so, and since any peasant or even a designated outsider could sign for the whole community, these figures are eloquent. They attest to an astonishingly wide spread of fabulous disillusionment and ecstatic hopes. The hopes were pinned on the person of the far-off tsar, while the disillusionment was a function of peasant values.

The Russian common people completely refused to adopt the concept of property in land that prevailed in Russian educated society. From their point of view, to claim ownership of plowland in the sense that one owns a hat or an axe was as absurd as a claim to own sunshine or the Volga. Land *belonged* to the person who tilled it, but it was the *property* of God, of the tsar or (which came to the same thing) of no one. By this reasoning, plowland belonged to the serfs who tilled it. Hence the dues specified in the charters were unjust and could not correspond to the wishes of the tsar, who must share the values of the *narod*. Peter Kolchin has written: "Given the complexity and class bias of the emancipation legislation of 1861 . . . it is in many ways hard to imagine a less promising formula for the transition to freedom than that prescribed for the Russian peasants" [9: 95]. (Recently, Steven Hoch has argued that the "class bias was not so great as almost all historians have maintained" [10: 274]. Nonetheless, given the complete disjunction between the values of the ex-serfs and the values of the reformers, the initial implementation of the reform was astonishingly serene.

Other Reforms

It is argued that the other great reforms followed from the abolition of serfdom, but the peasant reform reordered the Russian village, while most other reforms addressed the opposite end of the social spectrum. For example, the education reform (1863) restored autonomy to Russia's universities, permitting the rector and faculty to run them; the minister of education, however, had broad authority to interfere. It doubled government funding of universities. The reform also provided for technical secondary schools. However, only graduates of the traditional, classical schools could enter the universities; the regime supposed that the study of Greek and Latin would dampen any inclination for radical politics. The reform also gave new authority, but little money, to local agencies to establish primary schools. At first, the results were meager, and most schools in rural areas were informal, "wild" schools, set up and funded by peasants for the education of their children. By 1896, however, the number of schools in Russia had expanded tenfold, and almost four million pupils were enrolled. Still, overall literacy rates were very low; in 1897 they ranged, for example, from 16 percent to 21 percent in the six Central Blacksoil Provinces. Finally, the reform opened some kinds of educational institutions to women, provided that they would get an education "appropriate for the future wife and mother."

The censorship was reformed in 1865. Under the old system, a censor went over every word of a book or magazine, deleting or changing anything subversive. This system had been supportive of serfdom, but useful publications had been impeded, and pre-censorship had not prevented the dissemination of radical ideas. Some historians have portrayed the reform era as a period when the press was relatively open and influential; they speak of glasnost, using a term that would be revived in the 1980s. Boris Mironov has even written: "All the liberal reforms carried out under Alexander II were dictated to the sovereign authority by liberal public opinion through the medium of the press" [11: vol. 1, p. 252]. Editors and writers who wanted to air their views on reforms did not see matters Mironov's way. For a period, the regime did allow a number of new journals to be published, including two devoted specifically to issues involving the abolition of serfdom. By January of 1859, however, the regime imposed stifling restrictions on articles of that kind, and the two specialized journals had to shut down. The emperor himself took a characteristically ambiguous stance. He told a censor: "There are tendencies which do not accord with the views of the government; they must be stopped. But I do not want any restrictive measures. I very much wish that important questions be reviewed and discussed in a scholarly manner" [12: 150–1]. We can say that the censorship reform achieved Alexander's wishes. It eliminated the prepublication censorship of books and most journals, except for those in some non-Russian languages. The number and circulation of journals increased substantially. Editors and publishers were responsible for everything they printed, however, and they were subject to heavy fines, criminal penalties, and the closing of periodicals if they offended the government. The regime appreciated that publishing was increasingly regarded as a business and that publishers dreaded financial loss. The result was self-censorship, more exacting, on the whole, than precensorship.

The Judiciary Reform (1864) was not closely related to the abolition of serfdom, since peasants were not usually subject to the new courts. Instead, unless they were accused of a major felony or were involved in litigation with a non-peasant, they were subject to peasant courts. Judges in these courts had no legal training and were supposed to rule according to customary law. Thus four-fifths of the population had almost no dealings with the regular courts of the empire.

Under the old system, the regular courts had operated in a purely bureaucratic manner. There were no juries, no legal profession, and trials were closed to the public. Most judges had no legal education. Corruption and delay were notorious. For example, commercial loans were available only on short terms and at high interest because the courts could not protect the interests of creditors.

The reform legislation provided for independent judges with life tenure; for trial by jury in criminal cases, and for an organized bar of lawyers to staff the new adversarial system. Trials were oral and open to the public; the courtroom was a unique domain of free speech. Peasants (particularly village officials, who had already been vetted by the authorities) were formally eligible to serve on juries, but property qualifications for jury service excluded all but a few of them. The authors of the legislation explained: "The property qualification for jury service should be fairly high . . . otherwise, poor people, lacking a satisfactory education and inadequately developed to carry out the serious and difficult responsibility of a juror, would serve on juries." Precisely because jury service was indeed a difficult responsibility, prosperous and well-educated Russians contrived to avoid it, and most juries consisted largely of peasants.

The reform of the courts had been under consideration since 1850. Progress was almost nil, in part because the emperor agreed with those officials who were suspicious of lawyers and juries; in 1858 Alexander told the Minister of Justice: "I completely share your opinion that we are still not mature enough for the introduction of public justice and lawyers" [13: 163]. The minister and his kind, however, were unable to produce *any* workable alternative to the chaos they knew; here, as with the reform of serfdom, senior officials could not perform, or get performed, the complex bureaucratic tasks that were required if their views were to be enacted. Indeed, Richard Wortman has argued that the legislative process of 1858–61 helped "create political forces that could convince ruling circles and the tsar himself that only independent courts could provide stability" [13: 260]. He also finds that the path to reform was smoothed by the collapse of Russia's banking system; no credit was available to noble landowners who wanted to revamp their operations in the wake of the reform of 1861. Hence some highly placed conservatives who wished to protect the interests of landowners supported the reform proposals.

So it was that the task of drafting the reform legislation passed to a group of younger men with advanced legal training, usually acquired in an elite law school established by Nicholas I. With the task came powers of decision-making. The reformers acted in the spirit of the cosmopolitan legal ethos they had acquired with their training. They, alone of the drafters of reform statutes, avowedly followed Western models and produced the most thoroughgoing of the reforms. The reform proved too thoroughgoing for the regime. As early as 1867, Alexander II tried to remove a judge (who had helped draft the reform) and he was vexed when the minister of justice, D. N. Zamiatin, explained that he did not have the right to do so. Zamiatin and S. I. Zarudnyi were the principal authors of the reform. Zamiatin was dismissed in 1867, and Zarudnyi soon after. In the decade that followed, the ministers of justice were hostile to the new system and cut into the reform in various ways.

The connection between the abolition of serfdom and the zemstvo, or local government, reform (1864) was obvious. While serfdom had prevailed, local government in serf villages was provided by the squire and his agents; in villages inhabited by state peasants, a tiny number of state officials tried to fulfill these functions. Now the authority of the serfholders was gone. Although Russians liked to complain about intrusive bureaucrats, rural Russia was, in S. F. Starr's term, almost grotesquely "undergoverned" [14]. Hence the zemstvo reform, which was extended to cities in 1870. The term 'zemstvo' appears to derive from a distinction made in medieval Russia between the "affairs of the sovereign" (diplomacy and warfare) and the "affairs of the land" or local notables (all the other functions of government). During the debate over the reform, the central argument paralleled the ancient distinction. Was the zemstvo to be a part of the government as a whole, with corresponding authority, or was it a voluntary agency like, say, a ballet school, with limited authority but also subject to limited control by the state? As the reform was enacted, the zemstvo got the worst of both worlds. For example, a zemstvo had limited taxing powers, but it was up to government officials to collect these taxes, and about half of the money raised went to functions specified by the central government, such has handling the process of conscription. The provincial governor could suspend any decision taken by a zemstvo.

The reform was initially extended to nineteen provinces; by 1875 thirty-five provinces (all overwhelmingly ethnic Russian in population) had zemstvo institutions. The reform provided for elective assemblies at the district and provincial levels; the electorate was divided into three curias: landowners (mostly nobles), peasant communities, and towns. Voting power was proportional to the value of real estate held by each curia, but no curia could have more than half the members.

The zemstvo's jurisdiction included the upkeep of roads, fire insurance, education, gathering statistics, and public health. Squires and their ex-serfs sat together in the assemblies, if not in proportion to their share of the population. Public-spirited squires found a sphere of activity in the boards elected by the assemblies (which met only once a year). These boards, in turn, hired health workers, teachers, and other professionals. The zemstvo provided an arena of public service apart from the state bureaucracy, where liberal landowners and dissidents (such as agronomists and teachers) interacted. After a slow start, the zmestvos elicited genuine enthusiasm, and by the 1890s their accomplishments were remarkable, given their limited resources and the government control over them.

Alexander II's distrust of reformers did not extend to D. A. Miliutin, minister of war from 1861 to 1881 and brother of the architect of the abolition of serfdom. Miliutin initiated a series of reforms, and the emperor supported him at every turn, in the face of withering criticism from conservative officials. Miliutin carried out sweeping reforms in the organization and deployment of the army, the training of soldiers, and the education of officers. He equipped his troops with modern weapons. Finally, in a reform enacted in 1874, he transformed the system of recruitment. Until then, men from the "unprivileged" orders, mostly peasants, were drafted at a rate of one or two per hundred in periodic call-ups. Their term of service had been reduced at the beginning of Alexander II's reign from twenty-five years to fifteen. The old conscription system was intertwined with serfdom. The regime feared that sending a demobilized serf back to his village would threaten security; with his worldly experience and (perhaps) literacy, he might organize his neighbors and incite them to rebellion. This fear was not misplaced. The product of the conscription system was an enormous, costly, and inflexible armed force. Russia had permanently to feed, clothe, and house a standing army large enough to meet whatever threat that might arise. Miliutin's reform set the term of active duty for conscripts at between six months and seven years, depending on the recruit's level of education. After his term of active service, the conscript was to serve a further term in the reserve, subject to recall in the event of war. Thus the active-duty army was relatively small and could be rapidly expanded should the need arise. Other European countries had already adopted such a system. For Russia, the Achilles heel of the system was its economic underdevelopment compared to other European powers. Because of its primitive transportation system, Russia needed a long time to mobilize its reserves, which would prove fateful in 1914. Moreover, despite the regime's devotion to the military, it could not adequately finance the active-duty army. Soldiers in infantry regiments had to spend most of year working to provide themselves with food, clothing, and shelter rather than training [15: 574]. The army's performance in the Balkan War of 1877–8 and the Russo-Japanese War of 1904–5 suffered accordingly. It may be that these conflicts and the First World War would have gone better for Russia if the great reforms had boldly addressed the problem of economic underdevelopment.

The conscription was linked to the other great reforms, because it provided for truly universal liability. There were numerous occasions for exemption or deferment, but every Russian male, from a grandee to a day laborer, was liable to serve. A university graduate served on active duty for only six months, and a conscript with no formal education served for seven years, but estate of the realm was ignored. A peasant who had somehow managed to graduate from a university would serve only six months. Similarly, an ex-serf could sit beside his former master in the first curia of a zemstvo if only he managed to acquire as private property (as opposed to his allotment) enough land to meet the property qualification. The property qualification for sitting on a jury was also set high, but was waived for peasants who served or had served as village officials – village elder, judge on a peasant court, and so on. As a result, in many jurisdictions a majority of jurors were peasants. Distinctions of estate remained on the books, and there were some attempts to revive them in the 1890s. Essentially, however, because of the great reforms, Russia shifted from criteria of estate to criteria of class, following the lead of the governments of Western and Central Europe.

Conclusion

Boris Mironov maintains, almost alone among serious historians, that the great reforms went too far; they "went beyond Russia's level of socio-political development" [11: 227–8]. His view is congruent with his belief that serfdom was not as bad as it is painted and that it had not exhausted its economic potential. Most historians, however, wonder why the regime did not do more and, in particular, why it did not institute an elective national assembly. For P. A. Zaionchkovskii, the greatest historian of the reforms, it was a matter of intense regret that a plan for such an assembly, endorsed by Alexander II on March 1, 1881, was abandoned after his assassination on that very same day [16: 298–9]. The last three emperors did cherish their autocratic powers. Moreover, they realized that genuine constitutional change would favor the rich and the educated, not the peasants; many nobles sought a national zemstvo as compensation for their supposed losses. Most important, to let authority pass to judges, juries, editors, and others not under direct bureaucratic discipline (to say nothing of a national legislature) required a trust in which the regime was deficient. Finally, many senior officials feared that the reforms would come back to haunt the regime. They were right. As they predicted, the bar did become a rallying point for dissidents, the economic and social position of the nobility did decline, and the zemstvos eventually did rise up in protest with demands for representative government. Cautious officials can be good prophets, even if the solutions they offer are ineffective.

References

1. Field, D. (1992). "Sotsial'nye predstavleniia v dorevoliutsionnoi Rossii," in V. S. et al. Diakin, eds., *Reformy ili revoliutsiia? Rossiia 1861–1917. Materialy mezhdunarodnogo kollokviuma istorikov.* Nauka, St Petersburg, 67–79.
2. Zakharova, L. G. (2005). "Velike reformy 1860–1870 gg.: povorotnyi punkt rossiiskoi istorii?" www.polit.ru/research/2006/03/05/zakharova_html
3. Nechkina, M. V. (1960). "Revoliutsionnaia situatsiia v Rossii v iskhode 1850-kh – nachale 1860 gg," in M. S. Nechkina, et al., eds., *Revoliutsionnaia situatsiia v Rossii 1859–1861 gg.* Vol. 1. Nauka, Moscow, 3–14.
4. Koval'chenko, I. D. (1967). *Russkoe krepostnoe krest'ianstvo v pervoi polovine XIX v.* Izdatel'stvo Moskovskogo universiteta, Moscow.
5. Dolbilov, M. D. (2003). "The Emancipation Reform of 1861 in Russia and the Nationalism of the Imperial Bureaucracy," in H. Tadayuki, ed., *The Construction and Deconstruction of National Histories in Slavic Eurasia.* Slavic Research Center, Hokkaido University, Sapporo, 205–35.
6. Khristoforov, I. A. (2002). *Aristokraticheskaia" oppozitsiia Velikam reformam (konets 1850 – seredina 1870-kh gg.).* Russkoe slovo, Moscow.
7. Field, D. (1988). *Rebels in the Name of the Tsar.* Unwin Hymen, Boston.
8. Marasinova, E. A. (1999). "Obraz imperatora v soznanii elity rossiiskogo dvorianstva poslednei treti XVIII veka (po materialam epistoliarnykh istochnikov)," in A. A. Gor'skii et al., eds., *Tsar' i tsarstvo v russkom obshchestvennom soznanii.* Institut rossiiskoi istorii RAN, Moscow, 153–74.

9. Kolchin, P. (1999). "After Serfdom: Russian Emancipation in Comparative Perspective," in S. L. Engerman, ed., *Terms of Labor: Slavery, Serfdom, and Free Labor*. Stanford University Press, Stanford, CA, 87–115, 293–309.

10. Hoch, S. L. (2004). "Did Russia's Emancipated Serfs Really Pay Too Much for Too Little Land? Statistical Anomalies and Long-Tailed Distributions," *Slavic Review*, 63/2: 247–74.

11. Mironov, B. N. (1999). *Sotisal'naia istoriia Rossii perioda imperii*. 2 vols., Dmitrii Bulanin, St Petersburg.

12. Field, D. (1976). *The End of Serfdom: Nobility and Bureaucracy in Russia, 1855–1861*, Harvard University Press, Cambridge, MA.

13. Wortman, R. S. (1976). *The Development of a Russian Legal Consciousness*. University of Chicago Press, Chicago.

14. Starr, S. F. (1972). *Decentralization and Self-government in Russia, 1830–1870*. Princeton University Press, Princeton.

15. Bushnell, John (1980). "Peasants in Uniform: The Tsarist Army as a Peasant Society," *Journal of Social History*, 13: 565–75.

16. Zaionchkovskii, P. A. (1964). *Kriziz samoderzhaviia na rubezhe 1870–1880 godov*. Izdatel'stvo Moskovskogo universiteta, Moscow.

Further Reading

Bushnell, John, Eklof, Ben, and Zakharova, L. G. (eds.) (1994). *Russia's Great Reforms*. Indiana University Press, Bloomington, IN.

Emmons, Terence (1968). *The Russian Landed Gentry and the Peasant Emancipation of 1861*. Cambridge University Press, Cambridge and London.

Gerschenkron, Alexander (1968). *Continuity in History and Other Essays*, Harvard University Press, Cambridge, MA.

Hoch, Steven L. (1991). "The Banking Crisis, Peasant Reform, and Economic Development in Russia," *American Historical Review*, 96/3: 796–820.

Lincoln, W. Bruce (1990). *The Great Reforms: Autocracy, Bureaucracy, and the Politics of Change in Imperial Russia*. Northern Illinois University Press, DeKalb, IL.

Lincoln, W. Bruce (1982). *In the Vanguard of Reform: Russia's Enlightened Bureaucrats, 1825–1861*. Northern Illinois University Press, DeKalb, IL.

Taranovski, Theodore (ed.) (1995). *Reform in Modern Russian History: Progress or Cycle?* Cambridge University Press, New York.

Zakharova, Larisa Georg'evna (1987). "Autocracy and the Abolition of Serfdom in Russia, 1856–1861" [abridged translation of *Samoderzhavie i otmena krepostnogo prava v Rossii, 1856–1861 gg.*], *Soviet Studies in History*, 36/2 (1987).

CHAPTER THIRTEEN

Industrialization and Capitalism

THOMAS C. OWEN

The great drama of industrialization in the past three centuries has transformed agrarian societies by drawing a majority of the working population into mining, metallurgy, manufacturing, transportation, finance, commerce, and the provision of services. This process began in Russia far later than in Britain, where the first technological breakthroughs occurred. Although some inventors and entrepreneurs made important innovations in Russia, the imperial economy tended to import technologies that had first been invented and applied in Europe: large-scale mining and metallurgy, the steam engine, heavy machinery, chemical engineering, petroleum, the electric motor, the internal combustion engine, and aviation.

The debate over the positive and negative consequences of industrialization became a central issue in Russian intellectual history in the early nineteenth century. Under the last three emperors, the notion of an essentially agrarian Russia – whether ruled by an Orthodox Christian autocrat or composed of self-governing peasant communes as an anarchist utopia – came under attack by scholars who considered the spread of the industrial system to be a worldwide phenomenon that had already begun to transform the economy of the Russian Empire. Whether liberal or Marxist, these historians and economists traced the development of corporations in the eighteenth century, banks, railroads, foreign trade, factory labor, and protective tariffs on imported goods. Some successful merchants published self-congratulatory histories of their family businesses as well. Besides laying a foundation for further study, these works enlivened the debate over the political, social, and economic destiny of the empire in the final decades of the tsarist period.

Soviet historians tended to exaggerate the importance of industrial development in the tsarist period so as to legitimize the Bolshevik Revolution, in which the working class, the hero of the Marxist theory of history, allegedly provided the impetus for the overthrow of both the tsarist and liberal governments in 1917. Accordingly, the rise of cartels, monopolies, and huge banks – the hallmarks of an advanced capitalist economy – received much attention from Soviet scholars. The Soviet government published many monographs devoted to the labor movement in the largest factories and plants before the Revolution. This series appeared under the general editorship of Maksim M. Gorkii, whose fictional works portrayed the suffering of the masses under tsarism. During the cold war, Soviet scholars claimed that "socialism" had brought the blessings of industrialization not only to the peoples of the former Russian Empire but also to those of Eastern Europe.

In the decades after the Second World War, European and American historians examined the economic history of the Russian Empire in an effort to place in proper perspective the Soviet claim that "socialist" economic planning in the USSR and its satellites represented a "rational" alternative to capitalism. At first, historians investigated the administrative means by which the tsarist government had sought to overcome economic backwardness in a given period. In the past several decades, they have examined critically the institutions – primarily serfdom – that the tsarist government had maintained for military and fiscal reasons, regardless of their deleterious effects on economic development over the long term, and the irrational and perverse incentives that the autocrats imposed in their haste to foster industrialization by administrative means. To understand the social and political context of economic behavior, historians have also turned their attention to questions that were neglected before 1917, such as the sources of entrepreneurship in Russian society and the extent to which the policy recommendations of business organizations (known as "trade associations" in the United States) influenced the economic policies of the autocratic government. Recent research on specific regions and industrial sectors has revealed a much more complex picture than before.

Definitions

Precise definitions of key terms are essential, especially because of the vague and polemical meanings that they often carry. "Economic backwardness" is the least controversial. Karl Marx and his followers referred to various kinds of political, social, and economic "backwardness." In an influential article entitled "Economic Backwardness in Historical Perspective" (1952), the economic historian Alexander Gerschenkron argued that industrial development occurred in specific historical settings in Europe and Russia from 1750 onward as a result of distinctive institutional catalysts: small-scale commercial banking in England; Saint-Simonian utopianism, which inspired the grand projects of the Crédit Mobilier investment bank in France; large banks and cartels in Germany; and the state itself in Imperial Russia [1: 5–30]. The phrase denotes the relatively small percentage of the population engaged in technologically advanced agriculture, industry, commerce, and finance, coupled with relatively low levels of output. The standards of comparison in the Russian case are the economic institutions of the relatively advanced countries of Europe in a given era, whether Sweden and Poland in the eighteenth century, Britain and France in the nineteenth century, and eventually Germany and the United States in the several decades before the First World War.

Economists refer to "extensive development" to describe the use of increased inputs – whether land, labor, capital, or managerial expertise – to produce a correspondingly increased amount of output. In contrast, "intensive development" occurs when the application of improved technology (including advanced managerial techniques) permits the combination of constant or decreasing inputs in the production of increased amounts of output. Russia's economic backwardness owed much to the

fact that the government tended to pursue its economic objectives by means of extensive development, as ever larger amounts of raw materials were processed in ever greater
numbers of plants and factories by methods of production that became outdated as
time went on. Intensive development proved too delicate and complex a task for the
autocratic state to master, under both the tsarist and Soviet regimes [2: 91, 101].

The term "capitalism" refers to the institutional structure in which economic assets
are allocated predominantly in markets, not by traditional patterns of reciprocity,
barter, or administrative decree. According to the Soviet scheme of Russian history,
"feudalism" prevailed from 1054 to 1861, "capitalism" from 1861 to 1917, and
"socialism" from 1917 thereafter [3: 136, 403, 783]. This terminology, supplemented by the notion of "class struggle" and other concepts drawn from Karl Marx's
stage theory of history, fit the Russian experience imperfectly, however, as it imposed
on Russia a teleological interpretation of history based on the experience of Western
Europe.

More satisfactory for historians of economic development is Max Weber's six-part
definition of "modern capitalism." In a fully capitalist system, according to Weber,
investments of capital are made on the basis of rational calculation, and the funds of
the enterprise are kept separate from the finances of the family of the managers and
investors; advanced technology is employed; individuals are free to enter and exit the
market regardless of social status, religion, ethnicity, or other arbitrarily defined criteria of discrimination; the legal system protects private property and adjudicates disputes on the basis of impersonal norms; hired workers earn wages in a labor market
that is free from the influences of non-market forces, whether slavery, serfdom, legis-
lated wage levels, or contracts negotiated by labor unions; and entrepreneurs and
managers accumulate large amounts of investment capital through the public sale of
shares in enterprises [4: 276–8]. As an "ideal type," Weber's definition is an abstraction that, by definition, has never existed in its pure form anywhere or at any time in
history. The benefit of such a definition lies in its precise specification of behavior that
social scientists can examine empirically so as to determine, in a value-free way, the
degree to which institutions in a given place and time conform to the ideal type.

The Eighteenth Century

For centuries, rulers of the Russian state had contended with geographical realities
that placed the country at a disadvantage in its economic relations with Europe and
Asia: the harsh climate, the difficulty of exploiting mineral deposits and other natural
resources in regions far from populated areas, slow and expensive modes of transportation across vast distances, dependence on foreign entrepreneurs for the introduction
of advanced manufacturing techniques and for commercial relations with the rest of
the world, and the high cost of maintaining military technologies equal to those of
Russia's geopolitical rivals. Under Peter I (ruled 1689–1725) and Catherine II (ruled
1762–96), industrialization in the Russian Empire made remarkable advances, especially in the production of armaments. These successes came at a high cost, however.
The state's preference for promoting industrial development by fiat instead of fostering capitalist institutions led to a familiar paradox: the very market forces that might
have invigorated the Russian economy remained stifled by the impatient tsarist
autocracy.

Peter pursued industrialization primarily to expand the arms industry. A new mining and metallurgical complex arose in the Ural mountains to exploit the rich deposits of iron and copper ore there. The vastly increased production of cannons, muskets, gunpowder, ships, and sail cloth allowed Peter's generals and admirals to challenge the most advanced armies and navies in Europe. After suffering initial defeats, Peter's armed forces triumphed in the long and costly Great Northern War (1700–21) against Sweden and made some territorial gains in the south at the expense of Persia.

Manufacturers and traders did not necessarily benefit from industrialization under Peter, however. On the one hand, the state granted to members of the merchant estate (*kupecheskoe soslovie*) exclusive rights to engage in manufacturing and commerce and transferred some mines, plants, and factories to favored merchants, who received the added benefit of serf labor assigned to enterprises, just as gentry landlords profited from the unpaid labor of serfs bound to the land. On the other hand, merchants who produced textiles, leather goods, and other unsophisticated products for the market had to contend with a labor shortage caused by serfdom. They found it necessary to pay relatively high wages to their hired workers, generally serfs whose wages passed to their landlords in the form of dues paid in cash (*obrok*).

Gerschenkron and Theodore Von Laue considered Emperor Peter I the forerunner of the Soviet dictator Joseph Stalin, because both autocrats acted vigorously to implant industrial facilities by fiat, without the slightest respect for the market [1: 147–9; 5: 34–5]. Shortly after the fall of the Soviet Union, Evgenii V. Anisimov stressed the negative effects of these policies. "The state's very stimulation of industry primarily had the character of bondage." Thus, even as it created "a powerful economic base," it caused "simultaneously the essential arrest of the country's capitalist development" [6: 182, 183].

Peter's military and diplomatic successes inspired Catherine II to renew the expansion of Russian territory. Having absorbed huge territories during the partitions of Poland (1772–93), she ordered the creation of Odessa, a new port city and naval base on the Black Sea. As a defender of the social and economic privileges of the gentry, Catherine deprived the other social estates of the right to own land populated with serfs. Merchants, who hired serfs on leave from their landlords, found it difficult to compete with the gentry, in whose workshops serfs produced coarse woolen cloth and other commodities without receiving wages. The number of merchants remained small and their entrepreneurial spirit extremely limited. Cities in the predominantly agrarian empire served primarily as centers of governmental administration, not commerce and industry. The urban population lacked meaningful self-government until 1870 [7: 207–17; 8: pt. 1].

Arcadius Kahan concluded that, although advanced technology found application in large enterprises, the state supplied most of the investment capital in the form of grants of land and labor and, by purchasing huge amounts of military equipment, enjoyed predominance (monopsony) in the market for industrial goods. The autocratic government remained above the law [9: ch. 3]. The crude and brutal methods by which the tsarist government administered the economy prevented the emergence of several features of capitalism enumerated by Weber: ease of entry and exit for entrepreneurs, firm legal norms, a free market in labor, and the public sale of shares.

From the Napoleonic Wars to the Crimean War

Russia's eventual victory over the armed forces of Napoleon Bonaparte in 1815 appeared to vindicate the tsarist government's strategy of extensive economic development. Emperor Alexander I (ruled 1801–25) showed little interest in modern technology. His son Nicholas I (ruled 1825–55) likewise trusted in the vastness of the western provinces and the numerical superiority of the Russian army to keep the empire secure from invasion [10: 127 n.7]. Alarmed by demands for political and social reform throughout Europe and in the New World after the French Revolution, the tsarist government resisted borrowing European technology and its corollary, the factory system.

Egor F. Kankrin, a Baltic German who served as minister of finance from 1823 to 1844, bore primary responsibility for this cautious policy. Inspired by doctrine of the German nationalist Friedrich List, who denounced the theory of free trade as a justification of Great Britain's industrial primacy, Kankrin reversed the short-lived policy of low import duties on imported goods, which had devastated Russian workshops immediately after the Napoleonic Wars. From 1822 to 1850 Russian industry enjoyed a significant degree of tariff protection. Kankrin favored the tariff as a simple and inexpensive means of supporting domestic industry. Thousands of serfs in the northern provinces of European Russia, where agriculture provided a livelihood only during the short growing season, earned a supplementary income from their labor, primarily in rural workshops. Protectionism had the added benefit of raising revenue for the state in the form of customs duties.

Kankrin opposed rapid industrialization, however, fearing that mass poverty and social unrest would result from the formation of a working class isolated from the village. His hostility to innovation extended even to railroads, which, in his view, offered only one benefit: the rapid transport of troops in time of war. In a report to the emperor in 1838, he minimized the economic benefits of railroads. Most of them, he wrote, were simply objects of "artificial need or luxury" that "fleece the public of excess funds" while fostering "unnecessary travel from place to place, which is entirely typical of our time" [quoted in 11: 15–16]. Canals, not railroads, remained the primary means of transporting grain destined for export. Kankrin's minor reforms included the reorganization of the merchant guilds and the stabilization of the value of the paper currency. In the words of William L. Blackwell, "the conservatism of intellectual and official circles" buttressed the regime's "resistance to change, to innovation, to departure from past procedures, to threats to economic or bureaucratic vested interests, to experimentation or needless risks, and to extravagance in ideas or money matters" [10: 140, 273]. Walter M. Pintner concluded that Kankrin and Nicholas I simply "had no general theory of economic policy" [12: p. viii].

Roger Portal, the leading French historian of the tsarist economy, stressed that the application of steam power in the textile industry in 1830s and 1840s did not constitute a "real revolution." The impressive development of sugar-beet cultivation on gentry estates – totaling 30,000 tons in 1857, four-fifths of it in Ukraine, where the soil and climate were ideal – testified to the benefits of gentry status. So too did the continued production, by serfs, of large amounts of crude woolen cloth, purchased by the state for the production of army uniforms [13: 809]. The persistence of serfdom caused a perennial shortage of hired labor that kept the wages paid to unskilled workers higher than in Europe [14: 17]. As in the eighteenth century, the rate of urbanization remained low and the number of merchants small [8: pt. 2; 15: chs. 1–2]. Foreigners brought crucial contributions of investment capital and managerial expertise, so that shipping, foreign trade, and finance in the major cities remained largely in non-Russian hands [10: ch. 10].

The only comprehensive law to regulate the operations of corporations in Russia reflected Kankrin's aversion to innovation. Alarmed by episodes of speculation in corporate shares (*azhiotazh*, from the French *agiotage*) on the tiny stock market in St Petersburg in the early 1830s, he declared: "it is better to reject [the proposed charters of] ten companies that fall short of perfection than to allow one to bring harm to the public and to the enterprise itself." The law, issued in 1836, formalized the existing system of incorporation by concession, under which all corporate charters took the form of separate laws, each signed by the emperor himself. Because of this restrictive policy, only 136 corporations were founded in the reign of Nicholas I, and only 68 existed in 1847 [11: 18–20].

The refusal of the tsarist government to consider policies that would have quickened the pace of industrial development had serious consequences. In 1800, Russia had led the world in the production of pig iron, but by 1860, despite a steady increase in output, it had slipped to fourth place, and in terms of national income, Russia ranked fifth, behind the United States, Germany, Great Britain, and France [10: 130–48, 423; 13: 808–9; 16: fig. 2.1]. The defeat of Russian land and naval forces in the Crimean War (1853–6) made clear to all the dimensions of the empire's economic backwardness.

The Ambiguous Legacy of the Great Reforms

The humiliation of the Russian armed forces convinced Alexander II (ruled 1855–81) to launch the so-called Great Reforms, including the emancipation of the serfs (1861), the creation of law courts on the European model (1864), the introduction of limited self-government in the countryside (1864) and the cities (1870), and the inauguration of universal military service (1874). As minister of the navy, the emperor's brother, Grand Duke Konstantin Nikolaevich, led the effort to bring Russian military forces up to the European standard [17: 122–32]. New plants, equipped with the latest European machinery, began producing modern cannons, steam-powered naval vessels, and other tools of war.

The immense costs of the so-called Great Reforms and the modernization of the armed forces placed such a strain on the treasury that the government lacked funds for ambitious industrial projects, despite the $7.2 million gained by the sale of Alaska to the United States in 1867. The task of encouraging private investment in industry fell to Mikhail Kh. Reutern, a Baltic German economic expert who, as minister of finance from 1862 to 1878, sought to harness the forces of supply and demand. Having studied railroads in Germany and the United States, Reutern sponsored a major campaign of railroad construction in Russia. Railroads promised enormous economic benefits: the facilitation of travel and shipments of freight among the far-flung regions of the empire; increased exports of grain, which earned currency for the purchase of imported equipment; the stimulation of coal mining; and the production of iron rails, sophisticated transportation equipment, and other industrial goods in Russia. His reforms included the creation of new consultative organs for commerce and industry, the chartering of the first corporate banks in Russia, and the granting of railroad concessions to corporations. These policies earned him the reputation of being an economic "liberal," but this term had no political connotation. His devotion to the principle of autocracy never wavered [18: 8–41].

In the absence of adequate capital in Russia to build the railroad network, the emperor and his advisors turned to European bankers. The most extreme example of this trend was the government's decision in 1857 to create the Russian Railroad Company, with a basic capital of 75 million rubles, the largest corporation chartered in Russia in the entire nineteenth century. The company planned to build 4,000 versts of rail lines linking Moscow to port cities on the Baltic and Black seas and to Nizhnii Novgorod, a major commercial center on the upper Volga River. To assert Russia's claim as a maritime power capable of maintaining its own merchant marine, Grand Duke Konstantin Nikolaevich sponsored the Russian Steamship Company (ROPIT), founded with a basic capital of 6 million rubles in 1856, which inaugurated scheduled service by Russian-owned ships between Odessa and ports in the Mediterranean Sea and on the Indian and Pacific oceans [11: 39–42, 36–7]. (So poorly developed is the field of Russian business history that no monographic analysis of either of these major corporations has yet been written.)

In response to the European trend toward free trade in the mid-nineteenth century, the tsarist government reduced import tariffs somewhat in 1850 and 1857. Reutern's imposition of higher tariffs in 1868 and 1878 signified a return to moderate protectionism. This change helped light industry – especially textile manufacturing – most of all, as the government continued to allow duty-free imports of machinery from abroad because plants and factories in Russia could produce only a small proportion of the rails, locomotives, and rolling stock needed to equip the rapidly expanding railroad network. The value of imported machinery rose dramatically between 1856–60 and 1876–80, from 7.5 to 51 million rubles. As before, the Russian Empire accumulated the currency to pay for these imports by exporting raw materials, primarily grain, and by borrowing heavily from European bankers [19: 84; 13: 814–15].

The tsarist government reformed the estate system slightly by reducing the number of merchant guilds from three to two in 1863. The abolition of serfdom eased the labor shortage in industry. However, peasants who took factory work far from their villages remained responsible for their share of redemption payments and taxes as members of their commune. Most unskilled factory workers retained their peasant outlook and returned to their villages to seek the support of their families when ill, injured, or unemployed. The recruitment of factory labor therefore remained difficult, and the training of skilled labor proceeded slowly [14: 17].

Boom and Bust under Finance Minister Sergei Witte

Industrialization proceeded at an unprecedented pace under the last two emperors. The finance ministers of Alexander III (ruled 1881–94) introduced important policy changes, including tariff protection for heavy industry and legislation to regulate working conditions and the length of the workday in factories, especially for the benefit of women and children [18: 42–103]. However, a comprehensive strategy of state-sponsored industrial development emerged only in the last decade of the century under the energetic leadership of Minister of Finance Sergei Iu. Witte (1892–1903), the most competent official in the government of Nicholas II (ruled 1894–1917).

The "Witte system," as Von Laue called it, consisted of several bold initiatives. These included high protectionist duties on imported metals and machinery, achieved through a tariff war (1892–3) and a trade treaty (1894) with the German Empire; the rapid completion, at state expense, of the longest railroad in the world, the Trans-Siberian (1891–1900), which connected cities in European Russia to Vladivostok, Russia's principal warm-water port and naval base on the Pacific Ocean; and the introduction of the gold standard (1897), which guaranteed to foreign financiers and manufacturers the value of their huge investments in Russian mining, metallurgy, industry, finance, commerce, and transportation [5; 20]. In his memoirs, Witte claimed credit for other achievements as well: attracting at least 3 billion rubles (approximately $1.5 billion) in foreign capital investment, doubling the length of railroad tracks, inaugurating a system of workers' compensation, and improving the lot of the peasantry through the abolition of collective responsibility for tax payments and the relaxation of the passport system, which restricted peasants' mobility in their search for employment outside the village [21: 318–26].

In purely statistical terms, the case for Witte's successful stewardship of the Russian economy appeared convincing. Industrial output in the 1890s increased at an average rate of approximately 8 percent per year [1: 129]. In 1899, the Ukrainian scholar Mikhail I. Tugan-Baranovskii clinched the Marxist argument against agrarianism – in both its reactionary and utopian socialist versions – by demonstrating the importance of factories in transforming the Russian economy during the previous century [22].

It is essential, however, to put the successes of the "Witte system" into perspective. Much to the consternation of ethnic Russian manufacturers in the Moscow region, the greatest successes in industrial development occurred in the periphery of the empire: coal mining and steel production in Ukraine, petroleum drilling and refining in Baku, and heavy and light industry in St Petersburg, Riga, and the Polish provinces, for example. The influx of foreign capital and expertise appeared to put the future of the Russian economy in the hands of European financiers [23]. Cutbacks in the state's purchases of industrial goods intensified the depression that ravaged Russian industry at the turn of the century [13: 828]. The recent monograph by Steven G. Marks on the Trans-Siberian Railroad – the first scholarly study in any language – demonstrated the enormous shortcomings of the tsarist government's greatest construction project, including a single track, light rails, sharp curves, and shoddy construction. As a result, the Trans-Siberian line and its Russian-built extension through Manchuria, the Chinese Eastern Railroad, lacked sufficient capacity to supply the Russian armed forces in the Far East during the war with Japan in 1904–5 [24].

The generally positive assessments of Witte's strategy offered by Gerschenkron and Von Laue in the 1960s and reiterated by Sidney Harcave [25] have given way in recent decades to a systematic criticism in the historical literature. The different interpretations owed much to the sources on which they were based. To document the positive results of state action, Gerschenkron and Von Laue relied mainly on Witte's own policy statements, the works of his supporters and critics, and official statistics of industrial production, foreign investments, and the like. In contrast, other scholars, including Paul R. Gregory and Peter Gatrell, have cited statistical evidence of vigorous entrepreneurial and market-oriented activity on the microeconomic level, even in peasant villages, which did not depend on the state's intervention. In 1982 and 1994, Gregory published a highly detailed table of national income statistics from 1885 to 1913. On the basis of these data, he concluded that Gershenkron had over-estimated the state's purchases of industrial goods and exaggerated the positive effects of protectionist tariffs on domestic industry [16]. This assessment of Russian economic development placed the policies of the tsarist government in a much less positive light than before. To the extent that the state's sponsorship of industry enjoyed less success than claimed by Witte and his admirers, market-based decision-making by foreign and domestic entrepreneurs assumed greater importance in the Russian economy than previously believed.

Even the most precise statistics fail, however, to reveal the complexities of economic development. Entrepreneurs perceived economic risks and opportunities within specific political, legal, and cultural contexts. In her study of the Association of South Russian Coal and Steel Producers, Susan P. McCaffray demonstrated that, despite Witte's public encouragement of heavy industry, manufacturers often encountered ignorance, meddling, and lack of sympathy on the part of tsarist officials [26]. For example, when the association took action to slow the fall of prices of iron and steel during the industrial depression by facilitating the creation of the syndicate Prodameta in 1902 and the coal syndicate, Produgol, two years later, it violated laws against collusion in the marketplace [3: 675–81; 23: 278–86]. The tsarist government granted corporate charters to these and other syndicates, but it refused to abolish the laws against price-fixing [11: 132–7].

Thus, even under Witte, corporate entrepreneurship in the Russian Empire remained constrained by bureaucratic fetters and legal inconsistencies. For example, from 1872 onward, some charters issued to new corporations founded in nine Western provinces contained a clause that limited to 200 desiatinas (approximately 540 acres) the amount of land that the enterprise could own if the managers, staff, or stockholders of the enterprise were Jewish; in 1884 this restriction became mandatory. By this means the government curbed the economic activity of Jews, who established corporations in an effort to go into business where they were banned by law from doing so as individuals. Witte appointed a commission to draft a law allowing the incorporation of new companies by registration, but he quietly abandoned the proposed reform, as Reutern had done earlier [11: chs. 3–6]. The concessionary system of incorporation had been abolished in Britain in 1844, in France in 1867, in the North German Confederation in 1870, in Italy in 1882, in Switzerland in 1883, in Japan in 1892, and even in China in 1904, but it remained in effect in Russia until 1917. Likewise, Witte's reform of the patent law in 1896 did not constitute a major concession to the principle of individual property rights. According to the Finnish scholar Anneli Aer, the autocracy "was at no time prepared to give up the centuries-old principle of minute and close bureaucratic control over the slightest details of business activity" [27: 205].

From Revolution to Cataclysm: The Final Decade

The rapid growth of industrial production resumed after the Revolution of 1905. On the eve of the First World War, the empire's output of iron, coal, petroleum, machinery, textiles, and agricultural products earned it a place among "the world's major economic powers," as its "aggregate output" ranked fourth behind that of the United States, the German Empire, and the United Kingdom [16: 22]. The number of corporations in existence, having more than doubled from 614 in 1894 to 1,354 in 1905, rose at an even faster pace in the next decade, to 2,167 in 1914. Total basic capitalization – the amount of stock and bond capital authorized in the corporate charters – more than doubled, from 3.498 billion rubles in 1905 to 7.225 billion in 1914. The number of corporations chartered in foreign countries and operating in the Russian Empire under special agreements negotiated with the Ministry of Finance, numbered 262 in 1914; their declared capitalization stood at 649.2 million rubles [28: fig. 2.2 and table 3.8].

However, as in centuries past, the Russian Empire owed its position as a major industrial power to extensive, rather than intensive, development. The number of corporations remained extremely low by European standards, especially in per-capita terms. Other statistics revealed the unevenness of capitalist development and its foreign complexion. More than a quarter of the corporations (29.8 percent) in existence in 1914 maintained their headquarters in St Petersburg, and these accounted for almost half (46.3 percent) of the total corporate capital in the empire. Moscow ranked second (with 23.4 percent of the corporations and 30.8 percent of the capital), followed by Warsaw (6.9 and 3.2 percent, respectively). Seven other cities – Kiev, Odessa, Riga, Kharkov, Lodz, Baku, and Rostov-on-Don, in order of the number of corporate headquarters – qualified as major centers, with between 4.8 and 1.6 percent of corporate headquarters each, although none could claim more than 1.9 percent of the total capitalization. Less than a quarter (23.6 percent) of Russian corporations were headquartered outside the ten most important cities, and their small share of the total capital – only 12.5 percent – reflected the limited scale of their operations [28: tables 2.1, 2.3].

The importance of non-Russians among the corporate elite may be seen in the somewhat low percentage of ethnic Russians (37.4 percent) and the relative prominence of ethnic Germans, Jews, Poles, and Armenians (in that order) among corporate managers in 1914 [28: table 3.9]. Entrepreneurs from various ethnic and religious groups as well as foreigners figured prominently in the commercial–industrial elite of all the major cities in the Russian Empire in the early twentieth century [15: ch. 6; 23; 26; 28: ch. 3; 29; 30; 31: chs. 4, 6; 32: chs. 3–4].

Soviet assertions of the triumph of "finance capitalism" – the control of major industrial enterprises by a handful of banks – appeared dubious in light of recent studies in the nascent field of Russian business history. For example, Jonathan Grant found that the huge Putilov Company, once thought to have been controlled by banks, in fact remained "an actor in its own drama," capable of using the banks for its own purposes [32: 101].

Nor did the tsarist government abandon its hostility toward capitalism. The first national business organization in the empire, the Association of Industry and Trade (1905–18), won few successes in its campaign for a reduction of the state's control over the economy and the implementation of reforms favorable to capitalist enterprise [33; 34: 58]. The commercial–industrial elite enjoyed so little popular support that it failed to create a political party capable of defending its interests in the State Duma, which was elected by universal (but unequal) and indirect male suffrage from 1906 onward. Contrary to the assertions of Soviet historians, very few capitalists moved back and forth between industry and the tsarist bureaucracy.

After reviewing the debates among Soviet political leaders and scholars from 1918 to the 1970s over the relationship between capitalists and the tsarist policy-makers, including the controversy over whether a "coalescence" had occurred or whether the "bourgeoisie" had achieved the "subordination" of the tsarist state to its control, a German scholar, Heiko Haumann, concluded that the entire Soviet notion of "state-monopoly capitalism" was "obviously inadequate" [35: 68]. Gatrell wrote unequivocally that "corporate power did not bring about the subordination of the tsarist government to big business." Rather, "the peculiar tsarist combination of ideological antipathy and administrative obstacles towards private enterprise" prevailed in Russia on the eve of the First World War:

> The old regime never came to terms with the needs of a modern industrial economy. Its tariff policy offered little effective protection to the infant machine tool industry. The government had no coherent policy for improving industrialists' access to credit. Its tax policy did not encourage investment. The government was unwilling to consult or consort with industrialists, showing no inclination to establish a regular forum in which business leaders could articulate their views. [36: 290, 326]

McCaffray found the same pattern in the Donets Basin [26: 226–7].

The Russian economy collapsed early in 1917, after two and a half years of war. The railroads, which had failed to transport fuel, grain, and passengers without delays even in peacetime, became hopelessly clogged. Food, fuel, and military supplies no longer reached the major cities and the front in adequate quantities. Ruinous inflation forced some factories to curtail production. Sensing the vacuum of power, peasants seized land and livestock in the villages, workers looted food stores and took control of factories, and soldiers rebelled against their officers. During this spontaneous social revolution, the imperial government fell in February 1917. Eight months later, the Bolshevik Party overthrew the liberal–socialist coalition government in the name of the revolutionary workers, peasants, and soldiers. In the apt words of Timothy McDaniel, the imperial government's resistance to reform had led to disaster by creating "an uneasy combination of capitalism without a suitable political framework and autocracy without the kind of social policy that might have given it legitimacy" [37: 28].

Conclusion

None of the episodes of industrial expansion in imperial Russian history, including the one that occurred in 1890–1914, qualified as a genuine "take-off," as alleged by Walt W. Rostow in 1960 [38: 38]. Gatrell argued convincingly that industrial output increased gradually throughout the last third of the nineteenth century [19] and that the "intermittent bursts" of industrialization under Peter I, Nicholas II, and Stalin did not alter the main pattern of Russian economic history: the failure of the country "to sustain increases in output per capita over the long term" and to overcome "endemic poverty in the long run" [2: 89]. What Rostow called the "take-off" lost momentum both in the depression of 1900–3 and in the disruptions caused by the war with Japan and the Revolution of 1905. Soon thereafter, the war, the revolution, the civil war, and the economic isolation of the young Soviet state proved so destructive that industrial output in the Soviet Union did not reach the level of 1913 until 1928, when per-capita output remained "at least 10 percent below that of 1913" [16: 165].

Our understanding of the economic policies of the tsarist state and their effects on capitalist institutions has undergone significant changes in the past several decades. Von Laue and Gerschenkron argued that Russia would have remained mired in economic backwardness without the state's efforts to implant industry by autocratic fiat. In contrast, Kahan and others have emphasized the deleterious effects of the autocracy's contempt for markets and the rule of law. Most scholars now agree that, although the emperors and their advisors prudently encouraged some elements of capitalist enterprise for the sake of military power, they regarded the free market as too weak to harness the productive forces of the empire. From the Napoleonic Wars onward, they further legitimized their preference for arbitrary administration of the economy with the notion, based on revolutionary events in Europe, that unrestricted industrial development would cause urban overcrowding, social unrest, and demands for constitutional government. Bureaucrats, generals, and landed aristocrats feared the threat to their social and political prerogatives represented by the rise of a bourgeoisie on the European model. As defenders of autocracy, they refused to consider reforms that might have promoted capitalist enterprise by encouraging long-term economic calculations of risk and profit, such as the creation of a state based on the rule of law (*pravovoe gosudarstvo*, from the German *Rechtsstaat*) and the establishment of firm property rights. The debates within the tsarist bureaucracy centered on how best to strike a balance between the competing imperatives of economic development and autocratic control.

If the vicious circle of autocratic arbitrariness and weak entrepreneurship were ever to be broken, the initiative would have had to come from the state. In the absence of reforms by the tsarist bureaucracy to encourage capitalist enterprise, merchants quite rationally avoided risk, pursued short-term profits, and only slowly abandoned the dishonest practices for which they had been famous for centuries.

These political realities had a momentous impact on the attitudes of Russians toward capitalism. Even as Russians advanced a variety of rationales in favor of industrial development [39], the prominence of foreigners and members of minority groups among founders and managers of corporations contributed to the widespread hostility that capitalism encountered in Russian society [28: ch. 5]. The Orthodox Church preached the essential sinfulness of great wealth and distrust of foreigners. Poets, novelists, and playwrights generally portrayed capitalists as unscrupulous and inordinately greedy, although less so in the Kingdom of Poland than in European Russia [11: 49–50; 15: 121–2, 138–9; 31: pt.7; 40: chs. 2–4]. From the era of the Enlightenment to 1917, the relevance of European institutions for economic development in Russia remained a topic of contentious debate. Most intellectuals, even those few who inclined toward liberalism, tended to express sympathy with the long-suffering masses rather than to endorse the free play of market forces as the solution to economic backwardness [41]. Finally, workers resorted to violent demonstrations to denounce what they considered excessively low wages, cruel treatment by foremen, and inhumane living conditions. The industrial system became strong enough in

Russia to generate popular antipathy but remained too weak to defend itself in the political realm – zemstvos, municipal dumas, and the national legislature – and in culture in the early twentieth century.

Much remains to be learned about the process of industrial development in the Russian Empire. New techniques of statistical analysis are available to assess the effectiveness of tsarist fiscal, monetary, and tariff policies; to measure the effects of economic cycles in Europe and North America on Russia; and to pinpoint the structural weaknesses that led to periodic crises and the collapse of the economy during the First World War. Biographical and institutional studies are needed to illuminate the differing motivations for capitalist entrepreneurship among various ethnic and religious groups within Russian society. In cultural history, the condemnations of capitalism that emerged in various social strata, from intellectuals and bureaucrats to workers and peasants, remain a fertile field for future research. The implications of such scholarship go beyond Russia. What cultural and political attitudes account for resistance to, and acceptance of, capitalism in specific times and places in the modern world? Stage theories and other attempts to interpret history in terms of universal patterns risk losing sight of crucial contrasts among historical cases and the manifold ways that cultural traditions have not only been modified by economic institutions but have often exerted their own influence.

References

1. Gerschenkron, A. (1966). *Economic Backwardness in Historical Perspective*. Harvard University Press, Cambridge, MA.
2. Gatrell, P. (1999). "Poor Russia: Environment and Government in the Long-Run Economic History of Russia," in G. Hosking and R. Service, eds., *Russia*. Arnold, London, 89–106.
3. Lyashchenko, P. I. (1949). *History of the National Economy of Russia to the 1917 Revolution*, trans. L. M. Herman. Macmillan, New York.
4. Weber, M. (1927). *General Economic History*, trans. F. H. Knight. Greenberg, New York.
5. Von Laue, T. H. (1963). *Sergei Witte and the Industrialization of Russia*. Columbia University Press, New York.
6. Anisimov, E. V. (1993). *The Reforms of Peter the Great: Progress through Coercion*, trans. J. T. Alexander. M. E. Sharpe, Armonk, NY.
7. Pipes, R. (1974). *Russia under the Old Regime*. Scribner, New York.
8. Hildermeier, M. (1986). *Bürgertum und Stadt in Russland 1760–1870: Rechtliche Lage und soziale Struktur*. Böhlau, Cologne.
9. Kahan, A. (1985). *The Plow, the Hammer, and the Knout: An Economic History of Eighteenth-Century Russia*. University of Chicago Press, Chicago.
10. Blackwell, W. L. (1968). *The Beginnings of Russian Industrialization, 1800–1860*. Princeton University Press, Princeton.
11. Owen, T. C. (1991). *The Corporation under Russian Law, 1800–1917: A Study in Tsarist Economic Policy*. Cambridge University Press, New York.
12. Pintner, W. M. (1967). *Russian Economic Policy under Nicholas I*. Cornell University Press, Ithaca, NY.
13. Portal, R. (1965). "The Industrialization of Russia," in H. J. Habakkuk and M. M. Postan, eds., *The Cambridge Economic History of Europe*, vol. 6, part 2. Cambridge University Press, Cambridge, pp. 801–72.

14. Kahan, A. (1989). *Russian Economic History: The Nineteenth Century*, ed. R. Weiss. University of Chicago Press, Chicago.
15. Rieber, A. J. (1982). *Merchants and Entrepreneurs in Imperial Russia*. University of North Carolina Press, Chapel Hill, NC.
16. Gregory, P. R. (1994). *Before Command: An Economic History of Russia from Emancipation to the First Five-Year Plan*. Princeton University Press, Princeton.
17. Kipp, J. (1994). "The Russian Navy and the Problem of Technological Transfer," in B. Eklof, J. Bushnell, and L. Zakharova, eds., *Russia's Great Reforms, 1855–1881*, Indiana University Press, Bloomington, IN, 115–38.
18. Stepanov, V. L. (1996). "Three Ministers of Finance in Postreform Russia," *Russian Studies in History*, 35: 8–103. [On Mikhail Kh. Reutern, Nikolai Kh. Bunge, and Ivan A. Vyshnegradskii.]
19. Gatrell, P. (1994). "The Meaning of the Great Reforms in Russian Economic History," in B. Eklof, J. Bushnell, and L. Zakharova, eds., *Russia's Great Reforms, 1855–1881*, Indiana University Press, Bloomington, IN, 84–101.
20. Shepelev, L. E. (ed.) (1995). "The Commercial–Industrial Program of the Ministry of Finance, 1893: New Documents from the Imperial Archive," *Russian Studies in History*, 34: 7–39.
21. Witte, S. Iu. (1990). *The Memoirs of Count Witte*, trans. and ed. S. Harcave. M. E. Sharpe, Armonk, NY.
22. Tugan-Baranovsky, M. I. (1970). *The Russian Factory in the Nineteenth Century*, trans. A. Levin, C. Levin, and G. Grossman. R. D. Irwin, Homewood, IL.
23. McKay, J. P. (1970). *Pioneers for Profit: Foreign Entrepreneurship and Russian Industrialization, 1885–1913*. University of Chicago Press, Chicago.
24. Marks, S. G. (1991). *Road to Power: The Trans-Siberian Railroad and the Colonization of Asian Russia, 1850–1917*. Cornell University Press, Ithaca, NY.
25. Harcave, S. (2004). *Count Sergei Witte and the Twilight of Imperial Russia: A Biography*. M. E. Sharpe, Armonk, NY.
26. McCaffray, S. P. (1996). *The Politics of Industrialization in Tsarist Russia: The Association of Southern Coal and Steel Producers, 1874–1914*. Northern Illinois University Press, DeKalb, IL.
27. Aer, A. (1995). *Patents in Imperial Russia*. Suomalainen Tiedeakatemia, Helsinki.
28. Owen, T. C. (1995). *Russian Corporate Capitalism from Peter the Great to Perestroika*. Oxford University Press, New York.
29. Kaser, M. C. (1978). "Russian Entrepreneurship," in P. Mathias and M. M. Postan, eds., *The Cambridge Economic History of Europe*, vol. 7, pt. 2, Cambridge University Press, Cambridge, 416–93.
30. Guroff, G., and Carstensen, F. V. (eds.) (1983). *Entrepreneurship in Imperial Russia and the Soviet Union*. Princeton University Press, Princeton.
31. Clowes, E. W., Kassow, S. D., and West, J. L. (eds.) (1991). *Between Tsar and People: Educated Society and the Quest for Public Identity in Late Imperial Russia*. Princeton University Press, Princeton.
32. Grant, J. A. (1999). *Big Business in Russia: The Putilov Company in Late Imperial Russia, 1868–1917*. University of Pittsburgh Press, Pittsburgh.
33. Roosa, R. A. (1997). *Russian Industrialists in an Era of Revolution: The Association of Industry and Trade, 1906–1917*, ed. T. C. Owen. M. E. Sharpe, Armonk, NY.
34. Hartl, J. H. (1978). *Die Interessenvertretungen der Industriellen in Rußland, 1905–1914*. Böhlau, Vienna.
35. Haumann, H. (1980). *Kapitalismus im zaristischen Staat 1906–1917: Organisationsformen, Machstverhältnisse und Leistungsbilanz im Industrialisierungsprozeß*. Hain, Königstein/Ts.

36. Gatrell, P. (1994). *Government, Industry and Rearmament in Russia. 1900–1914: The Last Argument of Tsarism.* Cambridge University Press, New York.
37. McDaniel, T. (1988). *Autocracy, Capitalism, and Revolution in Russia.* University of California Press, Berkeley.
38. Rostow, W. W. (1960). *The Stages of Economic Growth: A Non-Communist Manifesto.* Cambridge University Press, New York.
39. Gatrell, P., and Anan'ich, B. (2003). "National and Non-National Dimensions of Economic Development in Nineteenth- and Twentieth-Century Russia," in A. Teichova and H. Matis, eds, *Nation, State, and Economy in History,* Cambridge University Press, New York, 219–36.
40. Holmgren, B. (1998). *Rewriting Capitalism: Literature and the Market in Late Imperial Russia and the Kingdom of Poland.* University of Pittsburgh Press, Pittsburgh.
41. Kingston-Mann, E. (1999). *In Search of the True West: Culture, Economics, and Problems of Russian Development.* Princeton University Press, Princeton.

Further Reading

Barnett, Vincent (2006). *A History of Russian Economic Thought.* Routledge, New York.

Brumfield, William Craft, Anan'ich, Boris V., and Petrov, Yuri A. (eds.) (2001). *Commerce in Russian Urban Culture, 1861–1914.* Woodrow Wilson Center Press, Washington. Analyses of banking, commercial architecture, and philanthropy in St Petersburg, Moscow, Nizhnii Novgorod, and Odessa.

Carstensen, Fred V. (1984). *American Enterprise in Foreign Markets: Studies of Singer and International Harvester in Russia.* University of North Carolina Press, Chapel Hill, NC.

Fenin, Aleksandr I. (1990). *Coal and Politics in Late Imperial Russia: Memoirs of a Russian Mining Engineer,* trans. Alexandre Fediaevsky, ed. Susan P. McCaffray. University of Northern Illinois Press, DeKalb, IL.

Gatrell, Peter (1986). *The Tsarist Economy, 1850–1917.* Batsford, London.

Henriksson, Anders (1983). *The Tsar's Loyal Germans: The Riga German Community, Social Change and the Nationality Question.* East European Monographs, Boulder, CO.

Herlihy, Patricia (1986). *Odessa: A History, 1794–1914.* Harvard Ukrainian Research Institute, Cambridge, MA.

Hogan, Heather (1993). Forging Revolution: Metalworkers, Managers, and the State in St. Petersburg, 1890–1914. Indiana University Press, Bloomington.

Owen, Thomas C. (2004). "Recent Developments in Economic History, 1700–1940," in M. David-Fox, P. Holquist, and M. Poe, (eds.), *After the Fall: Essays in Russian and Soviet Historiography.* Slavica, Bloomington, IN, 39–50.

Owen, Thomas C. (2005). *Dilemmas of Russian Capitalism: Fedor Chizhov and Corporate Enterprise in the Railroad Age.* Harvard University Press, Cambridge, MA.

Ruud, Charles A. (1990). *A Russian Entrepreneur: Publisher Ivan Sytin of Moscow, 1851–1934.* McGill-Queen's University Press, Montreal.

Singer, Israel J. (1980). *The Brothers Ashkenazi,* trans. J. Singer. Atheneum, New York. Originally published in Yiddish in 1936, this novel depicts the Jewish business elite of Lodz, a center of textile manufacturing in Russian Poland.

Tolf, Robert W. (1976). *The Russian Rockefellers: The Saga of the Nobel Family and the Russian Oil Industry.* Hoover Institution Press, Stanford, CA.

West, James L., and Petrov, Iurii A. (eds.) (1998). *Merchant Moscow: Images of Russia's Vanished Bourgeoisie.* Princeton University Press, Princeton. Rare photographs with commentary by experts on the Moscow merchants.

CHAPTER FOURTEEN

The Question of Civil Society in Late Imperial Russia

CHRISTOPHER ELY

Despite a wealth of new research in recent years, the topic of civil society in Imperial Russia remains very much unresolved. Although the recent edition of a venerable Russian history text includes an entire section on civil society that had not appeared in earlier versions, few historians are yet willing to refer to civil society in Russia without careful qualification.[1] Some scholars have begun to emphasize "the growth of political pluralism . . . [and] the dramatic increase in the political power of society at the expense of the state," but others still consider that whatever civil society might have come into being during the late-imperial period was insufficient and lacked "a spine."[2] Such questions are hotly contested because a good deal hinges on them. The fact that Russia rejected liberal democratic government and founded a communist state in 1917 is a crucial issue not just in a European context, but globally as well. The reasons we give to account for Russia's special trajectory do not only speak of Russian historical particularities; they continue to be of interest as a precedent, a model, and a warning to societies in transition around the world, as well as to those involved in promoting liberal-democratic systems. The relative power and political maturity of Russian society in the years leading up to the Revolution have great significance in a world in which liberal ideas and democratic government continue to play a consequential role.

That the formation of civil society in late Imperial Russia constitutes an important historical topic is not in question, but almost everything else about the subject is. A large part of the problem results directly from terminological imprecision. Any attempt to apply an abstract idea to a concrete historical situation must begin with a careful delineation of terms, and, with respect to the role of civil society in late Imperial Russia, the need is all the greater. To begin with, the term "civil society" is notoriously soft, used in such a multiplicity of ways as to have prompted the publication of several recent books seeking to pin down its precise meaning. In addition, we are faced with the problem that what we tentatively refer to as civil society does not always resemble manifestations of the phenomenon elsewhere. Not surprisingly, whether or not one is willing to identify a civil society in Russia hinges largely on the way one defines the term. Therefore this chapter will begin with an attempt to offer a general working definition of civil society based on the long, varied, and sometimes contradictory, history of its use. The resulting definition will serve as the basis for an attempt to refine our understanding of the civic structure that took shape under the final three Russian tsars.

The Historical Idea of Civil Society

"Civil society" is one of the most open-ended and contested pieces of political terminology in use today. Because, however, it encompasses a familiar set of assumptions about contemporary societies for which there exists no close approximation, it appears, for the time being at any rate, destined for continued widespread usage. Ernest Gellner has offered a short, preliminary definition that we may borrow as a departure point: "Civil Society is that set of diverse non-governmental institutions which is strong enough to counterbalance the state and, while not preventing the state from fulfilling its role of keeper of the peace and arbitrator between major interests, can nevertheless prevent it from dominating and atomizing the rest of society."[3] This definition points to two crucial features: (1) that the part of society not directly linked to power – the press, voluntary associations, the Church, commercial centers, trade unions, and so on – is important in its own right, and (2) that the part of society separate from power has a political role to play in any sociopolitical formation referred to as civil society. As much as this definition reveals, Gellner himself acknowledges that it cannot do justice to the larger complex of ideas that underlies the notion of civil society. For one thing, by focusing on the separations between the various parts of a society, it overlooks the fact that the term "civil society" may also be used to denote the entire interlocking political and social mechanism of state and society. Further, by stressing particular institutions, Gellner's definition does not account for the fact that civil society often refers less to material phenomena than it describes a set of values or principles regarding the relationship between state and society.

Perhaps the first political theorist to refer to civil society in a way that would be familiar to modern ears was John Locke. Locke's *Second Treatise of Government* (1690) presents civil society as inherently, and necessarily, founded on the peaceful practice of civil interaction within a safe and untroubled society. But for Locke it is precisely the need to keep that society safe and untroubled that necessitates the right (sometimes necessity) of society to involve itself in, and provide the fundamental ethical grounding to, political practice. For Locke, in other words, the good state rests on a well functioning, or civil, society. Since the *raison d'être* of such a society is that it continue to exist, it must at times exercise power in order to do so. Locke's civil society was capable of guaranteeing the freedoms of its members and of securing and maintaining the safety, stability, and political independence it enjoyed. Locke argued that, without civil society, human potential would remain unrealized: "Those who are united into one body and have a common and established law and judicature to appeal to, with authority to decide controversies between them and punish offenders, are in civil society one with another; but those who have no such common appeal . . . are still in the state of nature."[4]

This Lockean view of civil society has long underpinned the essential conception of relations between state and society that came to be called "liberal." But it also helped fix in place an abiding conflation of social interaction and political responsibility that left many questions unanswered. Was civil society essentially an arena of productive sociability that occasionally engaged with power? Or was it in essence a politically active society? How often and to what extent did it need to engage in the exercise of power? Such questions left room for serious reservations about the limits of civil society. In the wake of the French Revolution these took shape most clear in G. W. F. Hegel's *Philosophy of Right*. Hegel understood civil society as a necessary part of the human experience, one avenue by which humanity was led toward the universal good. He conceived of civil society as a complex of civic associations that could provide a bulwark against the domination of any one group or policy, including protection against potential abuses by the state. But he also believed civil society suffered from the fact that it was made up of private interests in competition with one another. Its autonomy necessarily entailed a degree of impunity from external control, and that impunity could be abused by unscrupulous individuals and groups. The existence of civil society meant outsiders and insiders, winners and losers, and thus it could foster no more than a very incomplete realization of the universal interest. Only in conjunction with the oversight of the state, a higher, more universal institution according to Hegel's way of thinking, would civil society function properly. Hegel's version of civil society emphasized the need to keep state and society separate and in balance so that both could make their distinct contributions to the greater good. From this perspective, social limits on government were a less central feature of Hegel's conception of civil society, while the state's assurance of basic satisfactions and creative freedom was essential.

If Hegel's way of thinking can be said to conform only partially with traditional liberalism, Karl Marx would make a complete departure. Marx emphasized the ways in which civil society's apparently apolitical sphere could in fact serve as a political instrument of the ruling class. From Marx's materialist perspective, the primacy of socioeconomic relations put the possessors of capital, the bourgeoisie, firmly in control of society. Marx's influence helped cement a growing identification between civil society and the middle class. For Marx, civil society was tantamount to bourgeois society, and bourgeois society could be trusted only to ensure its own interests. In stark contrast to Hegel, Marx argued that the state was in the hands of the bourgeoisie and could offer no removed, beneficial oversight. Thus civil society for Marx meant little more than a useful cover for bourgeois domination, and change could come only from those excluded from it.

In spite of Marx's repudiation of civil society, one of his followers would later help to revitalize the concept. Beginning from Marx's key insight that bourgeois society was indeed a center of power and moral authority (or hegemony), Antonio Gramsci reaffirmed the importance of civil society. He argued that, if civil society was indeed used effectively for the assertion of "bourgeois hegemony," by the same token it ought to serve as a platform from which to attack that hegemony. Civil society could be understood as a political battlefield on which one waged a "war of position" for influence within society as a whole.[5] Rather than interpret civil society as the emanation and expression of a particular class structure, as had Marx (and less explicitly many others), Gramsci instead stressed communication as the formation of public opinion. Following Gramsci, political theorists such as Hannah Arendt and Jürgen Habermas drew on metaphors of political "space" to convey their understanding of civil society. The free association and relatively unimpeded communication available within a well-functioning polity formed what Habermas called a "public sphere" (a "space of public appearance" for Arendt) within which it was possible to contribute one's voice to issues of collective concern. In this way civil society maintained channels through which the public could influence the development of both state and society.

In short, civil society has been conceived of in a variety of strikingly disparate ways. At the present time, the liberal understanding of civil society remains the most commonly referred to, probably because the concept of civil society matters most within a liberal context. It provides a way of discussing the lines of power and influence that, ideally speaking, lead from the individual, through myriad social groups, to state and society as a whole. In this framework, sometimes civil society emphasizes the importance of social autonomy and individual freedom; at other times it emphasizes the struggle for political influence. The first case portrays civil society as that social realm within which individuals and groups, unencumbered by excessive state-imposed burdens, interact freely and build a satisfying collective existence in mutual association with one another. The second case conceives of society as one part of a complete political whole, in which the social realm takes part in its own government and checks excessive use of power by the governing body. Most importantly, the liberal understanding of civil society implies the existence of a natural and inevitable relationship between social autonomy and political involvement.

The simultaneous existence of these two emphases has created a mountain of confusion with respect to the question of civil society in late Imperial Russia. As the foregoing discussion implies, civil society always involves the relationship between society and political power, but it does not *necessarily* entail a direct trajectory toward liberal-democratic government. Still, we can at least be more precise about the socio-political values that promote the expansion of civic culture. While institutions form the essential material basis of a functioning civil society, even more important is the principle that society, in its very separation from power, is imbued with political significance. By attaining legitimate and lasting autonomy from government, society can claim to be the site of moral authority in that it serves as a justification for the existence and use of political power. Therefore, in considering the position of civil society in late Imperial Russia, we must keep in mind two essential questions: (1) to what extent did Russian society manage to build the network of autonomous social institutions that form the human and material infrastructure of civil society, and (2) did society come to believe in itself as the center of moral authority in Russia?

The Obstacles to a Russian Civil Society

The terminology that evolved in Russian to refer to aspects of civil society suggests that the initial concept had some difficulty taking root. Russian contemporaries rarely used what might be the most direct translation from the key European languages: *grazhdanskoe obshchestvo*. Instead terms appeared in Russia that highlighted the elite and alien nature of this new segment of society. The less common *tsennovoe obshchestvo* (roughly "monied society") designated the wealthy as those who shaped public opinion. But the more typical *obshchestvennost'* is probably the closest Russian equivalent to civil society. It derives from the adjective for the noun *obshchestvo*, meaning "society" in the English sense of "educated society," and it is formed by adding a suffix that re-creates it as a new noun. In the process *obshchestvennost'* becomes an intriguingly flexible term in that it can be translated to mean, at one and the same time, society and public opinion. The best translations of *obshchestvennost'* would be "civil society" or "civic culture," since these terms refer to that part of society with the capacity to contribute to public opinion.

As noted above, it remains in dispute whether or not the concept of civil society can provide a helpful tool for understanding the Russian experience. A theoretical construct created to explain sociopolitical conditions elsewhere, it is often assumed, cannot prove useful as a means of elucidating the unique circumstances of Russian history. While this point has merit as a sensible precaution against the indiscriminate application of theory to history, arguments about whether Russia had a "genuine" civil society, and what that might or might not imply about the direction of Russian history, are not likely to go away. Because the question of Russia's transition to the market and democracy remains a fundamental concern in global politics, discussion of the "ground" for that transition remains thoroughly interwoven into attempts to understand Russia's past and future course.

To try to sidestep the question of civil society in Russian history would be a mistake on two further grounds as well. First, in the general sense, Russia was not so remote from Western Europe that the historical experience and political experiments of the latter could somehow be quarantined from the former. In this sense at least some of the ideas and institutions that constituted civil society in the West also came to form a fundamental part of Russia's political culture. As a rule, one should be careful not to assume civil society is an exclusively "Western" phenomenon. To argue that an authentic civil society has not materialized (and perhaps cannot) in non-Western parts of the world is one way to affirm the West's uniqueness, to validate its moral authority, to justify its global power, and so on, but in order to make such an argument one must ignore developments similar to the rise of civil society that have taken place in other parts of the world, within very different political contexts.[6] From the Western perspective, Russia has a long history of providing just such a ne'er-do-well counterpoint to its brilliantly successful civilizations. The implication, however, that Russia never possessed the capacity to build its own civil society rests on a specious exceptionalism of which we should remain skeptical. The obvious point here is that Russia is best understood as part of a European, or even a global, continuum. Secondly, and more specifically, the Great Reforms under Alexander II can be understood as a cautious attempt to furnish Russia with much of the basic infrastructure of civil society. If, notoriously, the seeds sown by Alexander's reforms did not bear quite the anticipated fruit, they nevertheless helped to reshape Russia as a very different sort of society than it had been before, with elements that strongly conform to the description of civil society given above.

All the same, one must be careful about going in search of similarities only to ignore equal, or more important, differences. Thus we will begin our discussion of Russia's civil society with an account of the substantial obstacles in the path of its development. Although the idea has been challenged effectively from a number of perspectives in recent years, it remains widely accepted that Russia's political and socioeconomic development either powerfully inhibited or entirely prevented the rise of civil society. The mainstream Soviet position held that, because the bourgeoisie was relatively underdeveloped in Russia, it was unable to coerce society into accepting

its dominance, and thus Russia ultimately managed, in place of the bourgeois hegemony prevailing in capitalist societies, to establish the control of the working class
under the auspices of the Soviet state. Gramsci offered a similar diagnosis when he
attributed the success of the Russian Revolution (as opposed to failed socialist revolutions in Western Europe) to the notion that in Russia "the structures of national life
[were] embryonic and loose" by comparison to the well-organized character of civil
society in the West. "In the East," Gramsci wrote, "the state was everything and civil
society was primordial and gelatinous."[7] Gramsci's view of Imperial Russia implies
that the great solidity of the Russian state (relative to the chaotic muddle that was
society) could be replaced by nothing so much as another strong state.

In the West, liberal and conservative explanations of Russia's progress toward
revolution echoed the Marxist understanding of a state/society imbalance. In both
cases Russia was overmastered by its dominant state and thereby predestined to lack
a sufficiently vigorous society. Through this remarkable conjunction of viewpoints,
the absence of civil society became one of the essential guiding ideas in the study of
Russian history. For example, Richard Pipes's *Russia under the Old Regime*, is simultaneously a history of prerevolutionary Russia and a sustained analysis of why Russia
never managed to develop a civil society. Pipes set out to explain, in his words, "why
in Russia – unlike the rest of Europe to which Russia belongs by virtue of her location, race and religion – society has proven unable to impose on political authority
any kind of effective restraint?"[8] In other words, why did Russia fail to bring into
being the kind of civil society Western Europe managed to create? Pipes's answer to
the question identified the roots of this modern problem in Russia's distant past. He
and many other historians have stressed the deep patrimonial roots of the Russian
state and the progressive binding of the various segments of the population in a vertical structure that inhibited the formation of horizontal ties within society. In the
eighteenth century, adjustments in Russia made in the hope of keeping pace with the
West only further encouraged the subordination of society to the state. By the nineteenth century, when it had become abundantly apparent that a basic reason for the
flourishing of Western Europe was societal autonomy, not only did the state continue
jealously to guard its power, but it remained understandably cautious about relinquishing control to a small educated elite that had little experience with public affairs.

In the meanwhile, the social segment that was coming to dominate affairs in
Western Europe consisted of the entrepreneurial and professional middle classes. The
relative absence of this sector from Russian society has long been at the heart of
arguments about Russia's essential difference from Europe. Pipes, for example, based
an entire chapter on the *absence* of a Russian middle class. This characteristic differentiated Russia from parts of Europe where cities and merchants did in places, and
increasingly over time, accumulate significant wealth and power. Russia never possessed the kind of wealthy, influential middle class capable of uniting society around
its particular values and aspirations, and that basic difference from Western Europe
would have a distinct impact on the shape of late Imperial Russian society.

The widespread conception of a basic absence, not only of a bourgeoisie but of
civil society in general, offered such a compelling explanation for Russia's radical and
non-Western historical trajectory that it became something of a self-fulfilling proph-
ecy. In Soviet Russia as in the West, historians looked for and easily found essential
differences, while supposing little need to focus on similarities. For many years, the

assumption of inevitable difference restricted enquiry into the development and nature of Russian society by making the central question of Imperial Russian history "what went wrong"? In this context, the second half of the nineteenth and the beginning of the twentieth centuries came to look particularly debased and chaotic. And in the midst of the big picture of collapse that took shape, those little scenes of progress and order that sometimes appeared tended to seem out of place and unaccountable.

The portrait of late Imperial Russian society that emerged focused not incorrectly on extensive impoverishment, massive social dislocation, ideological extremism, and violent political conflict. Worse still, the only sector capable of addressing such problems, the state, wavered between ineffective and intransigently traditional. It remained unprepared to let society contribute to the search for a solution. While Tsar Alexander II and certain high-ranking officials may have recognized the value of limited societal autonomy, the basic autocratic reflex was to restrict, watch over, or shut down independent activity. Special police forces charged with the surveillance and control of Russian society date back to the early eighteenth century. Konstantin Pobedonostsev, the deeply conservative advisor to two Russia's final two tsars, referred to the rapidly expanding press as "one of the falsest institutions of our time," and Tsar Nicholas II himself characterized his subjects' aspirations for participation in public affairs as "senseless dreams."[9] Even at those times when the state accepted the need for change and ceded to society a degree of autonomy, it had a habit of simultaneously minimizing its concessions. Alexander's lauded reforms operated in this fashion. When municipal government was introduced, few incentives were created to make it appealing; when censorship was reformed, it continued to exist in other guises; when rights of association were granted to educated society, they were not allotted to workers. The state's tremendous confidence in its right and responsibility to control society easily slipped into arrogance. One of Russia's more authoritarian bureaucrats, Count Kleinmichael, demonstrated the contempt in which officials sometimes held society when he was dismissed under Alexander II in the late 1850s. "The Sovereign finds it necessary to have me removed in view of public opinion," he queried, "What does this mean? Doesn't he have his own opinion?"[10]

Civil Society in Late Imperial Russia

In fact, societal autonomy and civic culture did begin to emerge in late Imperial Russia, and evidence of essential change at this time is abundant. The origins of Russian civil society date back to the late eighteenth century. After Tsar Peter III had released the nobility from its obligation to serve the state in 1762, Catherine II sought to instill within Russian society hitherto unknown forms of autonomous activity. She instituted press freedoms, expanded educational opportunities, and encouraged a certain amount of free association. Masonic societies, along with clubs, salons, and the theatre, helped constitute an early, if minute, public sphere in which at least some members of the elite could take part. Catherine envisioned a kind of independent activity on the part of society that would ultimately work in tandem with the aims of the state. But by the 1820s – as exemplified by the Decembrist Revolt – a significant minority within society had already rejected the principle of autocracy and united in an attempt to overthrow the government.

Independent, unsanctioned civic activity remained minimal, however, until the reign of Alexander II (1855–81). In the wake of the disastrous Crimean War, in which European powers defeated Russia on its own territory, it was clear that Russia's greatest untapped potential, its human resource power, had to be unleashed if Russia was to have any chance of keeping up with the expansive and powerful West. Alexander began by abolishing serfdom, the most essential socioeconomic impediment to change. He then proceeded to institute a number of reforms – from local self-government, to the expansion of education and the establishment of an independent judiciary – all largely intended to encourage society to take a role in its own government. These and other reforms were undertaken at a time when increasing urbanization and industrialization were already underway, and these processes did not substantially abate until the Revolution. Thus many factors at this time interacted to initiate an upsurge of extra-governmental activity, from the growth of the market, to rapidly improving communication and transportation networks, to the expansion of urban public space in new places such as shopping arcades, railroad stations, and increasingly crowded streets. As a result, public life during the reign of Alexander II became less the static, state-sanctioned phenomenon it had been under previous tsars and began to take on a momentum of its own.

The spread of independent, voluntary activity on the part of society was facilitated by an increasing sense of national identity within urban society. Over the course of the nineteenth century, educated Russians came in one way or another to conceive of Russia not merely as the domain of the tsar but as a government created by its people and for its people (despite the welter of opinion about what that meant). This indistinct but essential reconceptualization of Russian nationhood may help explain why certain segments of society sought to participate actively in the transformation. As early as 1856, Konstantin Kavelin was able to proclaim that "public opinion had begun to spread its wings."[11] Premature at the time, Kavelin's statement presaged substantial changes that came about in the next several decades. With the autocracy's willingness to foster a limited degree of glasnost (openness) in public affairs, this period witnessed not only the rise and rapid expansion of the daily press, but also the proliferation of legal journals of opinion, illegal political tracts published abroad, and the first mass-culture fiction. Numbers of people receiving at least a rudimentary education went up by more than ten times from the 1850s to the eve of the First World War, and literacy rates climbed to as much as 40 percent (with even higher rates in the cities). Between 1860 and 1914 the number of books published went from 2,085 to 32,338 and the number of periodicals from 170 to 606 in 1900. Newspaper circulations, in the tens of thousands in the 1870s, had risen into the hundreds of thousands by the early 1900s.[12]

At the same time, the era of reforms saw the formation of hundreds of voluntary associations involved in everything from sport and the arts to quasi-political discussion on hot-button topics such as education and economic policy. The formation of a mass-circulation press and its capacity to invest the concept of public opinion with real significance encouraged the development of what Alfred Rieber has termed "political interest groups."[13] Also during the period of reforms, the creation of places and events devoted to the public, such as exhibits and museums, got underway, and successful fund-raising campaigns allowed society to have an impact on poor relief, temperance, and even foreign policy. Association and a sense of belonging to a large community in the city were not restricted to the educated elite but began to take hold among the working classes as well. Among workers in St Petersburg literacy rates eventually climbed over 50 percent, and by the end of the nineteenth century a mass-circulation press had gained a foothold among them. Workers also formed clubs for Sunday outings and self-improvement, and, although the government attempted to repress such developments, unionization and agitation increased dramatically during this period, resulting in massive, ongoing labor unrest by the turn of the century.

With the advent of industrialization, large-scale urbanization followed suit. The population of St Petersburg, around 500,000 at mid-century, had grown to over two million by the time of the Revolution. The expansion of a relatively independent sphere of private enterprise, not to mention the spread and densification of urban space, began fundamentally to transform the cities from around mid-century forward. The rise in Russia of the busy metropolis as a sphere of independent activity created, in some ways for the first time, a tangible community, largely separate from the state, with which people could identify and feel they belonged. Moscow and Petersburg became seats of identity that offered an alternative to the other ethnic, estate, occupational, imperial, and national forms of identity available. By offering a model of community that surmounted or cut across traditional communities in Russia, the Russian city itself served as an important environment for the spread of civic community, as opposed to ingrained, traditional forms of belonging.

In the cities in particular, alongside disillusionment with the slow pace of reform, a spirit of service and participation also emerged. The merchant N.A. Naidenov recalled in his memoirs that "the new social arrangement called the urban population to unheard of new activities, awakening the desire to participate among groups that had never before been touched by social activities."[14] Memoirists have noted a particular change in attitude that took place during the famine relief efforts of 1891–2, when it became obvious to many for the first time that the government could not function effectively without the help of society. Not just the elite but the larger public slowly came to be considered a force for change. An important figure in the world of charities noted in 1912 that fund-raising on the street was more effective than fund-raising at private affairs, because on the street "a public affair is everyone's affair."[15] The rise of associations, public opinion, professional autonomy, and a general sense that civic activity could, under certain circumstances, have an effect in turn helped establish a basis on which political pluralism could eventually emerge.

Another set of reforms that exerted an important impact on Russian society involved the judicial system. The courts became an important center of autonomous social activity, because the government managed for the most part to stand behind the notion that a legal system could not work unless all parties were granted the necessary independence to carry out justice. The judicial reform of 1864 was based on the principle of an independent judiciary. Judges were granted lifelong tenure, trials were opened to the public, and criminal cases were tried by jury. The openness and social importance of these courts can be measured in part by the public and press interest in many trials and the publicity they generated for political causes (even though political trials were intentionally placed within a separate jurisdiction). Another jurisdiction, that of minor crimes and civil conflicts, was presided over by the new office of Justice of the Peace. This too proved successful in its dual mission to mete out justice to the population and to instruct the public about legal norms.[16]

Arguably the most important path toward greater social involvement in public affairs ran through the state-established institution known as the zemstvo. Elected institutions of local self-government, Russia's zemstvos were expected to take charge of such responsibilities as education, medical care, road maintenance, emergency food reserves, and other local matters. Although the zemstvos were generally presided over by gentry elites and possessed only local and limited powers, they served as important organizing nodes of civic participation. As the network of zemstvos developed, larger and larger numbers of technical specialists (known as the Third Element) came to exert an influence over them, and through the zemstvo over Russian society. At the beginning of the twentieth century over 70,000 such specialists worked within the zemstvo network.[17] In a predominantly rural society, the zemstvos brought into the countryside educated professionals, modernizing ideas, and connections to the larger world.

Because of the obvious contrast between their capacity to effect change and the limits under which they were placed, the zemstvos also became rallying points in the move to increase society's role in government. Calls to move toward some form of constitutionalism in Russia were typically founded on the expansion of the zemstvo system. "Crowning the edifice," as it was called, would turn the isolated, local organs of the zemstvo system into a nationally directed body, theoretically capable of becoming the basis for popular government. Not surprisingly, the state discouraged this movement at every turn, but in the run-up to the 1905 Revolution a General Zemstvo Organization was achieved. Until Nicholas II granted political rights to society and thus shifted the focus of power, the zemstvo was slowly becoming an alternative center of government with its roots in society. And, in spite of its new position in national politics, the zemstvo network continued to expand its budget and serve as a center for political activism right up to the collapse of the tsarist regime in 1917.[18]

As important as were the zemstvos, the city was the main center of social autonomy and calls for political participation. In particular, the two large urban metropolises of St Petersburg and Moscow became, in the words of one scholar, "a place of struggle for political influence and social control."[19] It was in the cities as well that the various middle classes began to gain prominence. The combination of public associations within which one could participate, the expansion of private wealth, and the need for specialists and subsequent professionalization essentially meant that no matter what the government did politically the public profile of capable groups and individuals continued to rise. Greater prominence did not necessarily translate into greater political power, but over time society became emboldened and eventually shifted over into political activism. Toward the end of the reform era political culture in the cities had become predominantly "liberal," and "anti-governmental tendencies" had worked their way firmly into municipal government.[20] The public sphere of these urban environments provided a stage on which, at certain junctures, society managed to assert its independence. From the movement to assist the Balkan Slavs in the 1870s, in which funds generated by the Russian public helped field a volunteer army in a foreign war, to famine relief efforts in the early 1890s, which linked city and country in a large, interconnected operation, to the remarkable general strike of

1905 that finally forced the Romanov dynasty to grant political rights to its subjects, urban civil society found ways to demonstrate its steadily increasing power and importance.

From the perspective of a Gramsci or a Pipes, such moments came across as anomalies of Russia's unruly history. But over the past few decades a new cohort of historians has shed light on the changes within late Imperial Russia that made such accomplishments possible. Historians of this period have begun, to borrow Joseph Bradley's helpful phrase, to shift their attention "from what did not happen to what did."[21] Studies of (among other subjects too numerous to name here) urban government, the press, voluntary associations, charity, temperance, leisure activities, civil rights, commercial culture, and professionalization have made it much easier to perceive the remarkable complexity of a late-imperial society that was capable of moving in many directions at once. Clearly a version of civil society emerged toward the end of the nineteenth century in Russia, in particular that version that stresses the importance of a realm within society of autonomous thought and action. If, however, we remain in search of a civil society that provides the essential preconditions for liberal-democratic government, we still run up against Russia's social and ideological disunity. The result was a diffusion of that other ingredient necessary to the formation of a powerful civil society: moral authority.

Society, Intelligentsia and Moral Authority

In 1905 Russian society managed, at least temporarily, to unite in sufficient numbers to assert itself as the center of moral authority in Russia and to stand up to the state as an effective political force. The demonstrations, strikes, and especially the general strike of that year united all classes of urban society (from workers and students to educated professionals) into a remarkably solid block of anti-autocratic opinion. In spite of increasing flexibility on the part of the autocracy as the year wore on, society continued to pressure the government, and eventually brought Russia to a standstill until its demands for limitations on the government were met. In October of 1905 Tsar Nicholas II finally had to concede the formation of a legislative body while granting civil liberties that included "freedom of conscience, speech, assemblies and associations." The Tsar's manifesto was greeted with nearly unanimous jubilation, but the joy was short-lived. Russia never managed to marshall its new rights into a force effective enough to exert a sustained influence on the state. The autocracy soon regained control, and slowed the pace of change under the new prime minister Petr Stolypin. When the tsarist regime finally collapsed for good in 1917, liberal-democratic government once again failed to assert itself and was replaced by an even more commanding state. That a liberal state did not materialize has lent support to the conclusion that Russia's civil society was too weak to follow its natural course to democracy. Hence the oft-repeated argument that Russia's civil society was ultimately insufficient seems to be substantiated by the outcome of the Revolution.

In Western Europe, as in Russia, public opinion broke down into a multiplicity of competing interests and ideologies. One of the most remarkable achievements of modern European history has been the stability its various civil societies have managed to maintain in spite of perpetual differences of opinion and intense, sometimes violent, conflict. Without underestimating the conflicts, difficulties, and lapses that have occurred throughout modern European history, it remains an impressive feat that so many European societies have worked through their differences and achieved sufficient stability to keep a politics of social participation afloat while continuing to thrive economically and culturally. The most common reasons given for the success of these societies involve some version of the rise of the middle class. Whether through bourgeois hegemony and "the manufacture of consent," or by shared values and tolerance, the entrepreneurial and professional middle class has been credited with bestowing the relatively stable center at the heart of European and North American political systems.

By the middle of the nineteenth century, political opinion in Russia was at least as varied and contested as in the Western world. But where public opinion in at least some Western countries managed to consolidate around the center and cling to the status quo, Russian public opinion proved less likely to do so. Where moral authority in Europe and North America came to be vested in the middle class (or at least in the *idea* of the middle class) in Russia moral authority had to be vested elsewhere. Traditionally, moral authority in Russian society was under the dominion of the state, but gradually over the course of the nineteenth century, and with spectacular thoroughness during the final Romanov reign of Nicholas II, the state had divested itself of its claim on moral authority. The most important entity that arose to claim that authority and serve as a new guide for Russian society was the intelligentsia. What allows us to give this loosely connected, and often bitterly divisive, sociocultural formation a single name was, primarily, its collective attitude toward power. The intelligentsia spoke on behalf of an ideological alternative (or rather a collection of ideological alternatives) to the continued dominance of its adversary, the state. It premised its claims to intellectual and ethical predominance on both the superiority of its worldview(s) and its repudiation of personal or collective interests. Everything it did, it did for the good of all. Like the state it claimed nothing more than a responsibility to serve the whole of society.

The intelligentsia's frustrated preference for the wholesale transformation of Russian society, in addition to its sense of urgency that change was already long overdue, encouraged extremism in both ideology and practice. Meanwhile, by limiting opportunities for individuals and groups to make meaningful contributions to society, the autocracy encouraged only the turn toward alternative solutions. Because the intelligentsia claimed to speak on behalf of the people as a whole, those among them who espoused a liberal politics similar to liberalism in the West found it difficult to be convincing in the Russian context. They were easily accused of favoring the wealthy over the laboring masses. With the help of Marxist ideology in the late nineteenth century, liberalism would eventually gain greater credence, but at least among the radical intelligentsia a basic, distinguishing characteristic, as one of their chroniclers relates, was a "unanimous, deeply felt and deliberate repudiation of any expression of constitutionalism."[22]

While a substantial part of the intelligentsia had an intellectual aversion to the liberal agenda, the bulk of the population was simply indifferent to the finer points of political principle. Despite rapid urbanization, at the end of the nineteenth century the majority of Russia's population continued to live in the countryside, where it remained difficult to rise above poverty, illiteracy, and disconnection from the world beyond the local community. In the city among the working classes, education and literacy had made significant gains by this time, and even in the face of great hardship workers were beginning to establish some social and political connections with the rest of society. But the late Imperial Russian city was a difficult and deadly place to live, and even in the city it was not easy for urban workers to pass beyond their local communities in order to forge connections with the rest of society. The idea that society could gain influence through the consolidation of public opinion remained largely an objective of the well educated and well heeled. For politically engaged workers various forms of local activism had more appeal. One member of the working class defined liberals as people who "like looking at liberty from windows and doing nothing, and then taking a stroll to the theatres and balls."[23] Not surprisingly in this climate, political violence, and even simple hooliganism, appealed as alternatives to public discourse. Such approaches to the public sphere inevitably served as self-reinforcing mechanisms to keep a politics of compromise and cooperation at bay.

Does the Russian experience prove, then, that a proper civil society can emerge only under conditions dominated by a developed bourgeoisie? It is not difficult to see how a wealthy and influential middle class helps sustain the growth and stability of civil society. Seeking to maintain the kind of steady security in which profits can be made, to ensure that private property is inviolate, and to secure reliable channels of recourse if treated unfairly, Europe's bourgeoisie came to value that combination of the rule of law and access to public opinion essential to political liberalism. But historians of Western Europe have demonstrated repeatedly that this simple connection between bourgeois interests and liberal politics appears much more complicated when one moves away from theory and closer to the ground of lived experience. Russia's case only complicates the matter further. Adele Lindenmeyr's study of Russian charity, for instance, provides an interesting example of the potential disassociation between class origins and political practice. Russian charitable associations not only managed to thrive despite governmentally imposed limits and the absence of a large middle class, but by opening up a space in which individuals and groups could contribute to society they actively helped instill a consciousness of the value of civic culture and the need to expand civil society.[24]

It cannot be denied that Russia's intelligentsia sought and won a central place in the public consciousness: more than any other identifiable social entity, it set the tone and claimed the high ground of moral authority. And yet in spite of the intelligentsia's important and obvious contributions to the growth of civic ideals, scholars interested in the rise of civil society have often opted to bracket out the intelligentsia as an unrelated phenomenon. But such an approach not only produces a false picture of Russian society; it constitutes a tacit acknowledgement of the weakness of civil society in its inability to reach the educated members of the public on whom the intelligentsia had a powerful effect. Like it or not, the intelligentsia was not an alternative to civil society so much as a constituent part of its Russian version.

Still, it is important to keep in mind that the intelligentsia's notoriety has made it far too easy to overlook the wider circles of educated Russian public discourse and activism that emphasized local concerns, gradual progress, and basic rights. A feuilletonist for the newspaper *Golos* voiced the hope in 1874 that with the addition of a national history museum Red Square would become "one of the characteristic squares of Europe."[25] This writer did not hope Russia would surpass Europe so much as become one European country among many. Humble aspirations such as this, alien to the intelligentsia perspective, were pervasive in less-exalted publications such as the widely circulated daily newspapers. They helped propel the increasingly wide-spread but less dramatic everyday work of specialists in the zemstvos, law courts, educational institutions, charities, municipal governments, and so on. Russia's civic culture included both strains. While we must not overlook the continued importance of the "heroism and asceticism" of the Russian intelligentsia, it would be equally mistaken to discount the respect accorded to practitioners of "small deeds." Russia's civil society took its distinct form in a unique combination of the state's simultaneous reluctance and persuasion, the intelligentsia's insistence on radical alternatives, and a more docile and patient lobbying for incremental gains in social autonomy.

Russia's Unique Civic Culture

Having explored the complex and multifaceted nature of this civil society, we may now return to the problems inherent within the terminology we have relied on. The term "civil society" in Russian studies has suffered from the imprecise and dualistic usage described above. Continued problems inherent within the attempt to define an Imperial Russian civil society are eloquently affirmed by the outpouring of linguistic creativity that has accompanied attempts to give a proper name to Russia's civil society. Civil society has been described in recent years as "nascent," "unrealized," "fledgling," and a "dream." Similarly, late-imperial attitudes toward politics have been referred to as "protoliberal."[26] Implicit within all these terms is the teleological assumption that connects civil society and liberal-democratic government. A textbook can unproblematically refer to Imperial Russian civil society by relying on the one definition of the term that is concerned mainly with social autonomy and interaction, while scholars unwilling to acknowledge the existence of a full-fledged civil society draw on the alternative notion that, properly speaking, civil society is civil society only when it eventually leads to liberal government.

Because this quandary stems from the imprecision of the initial concept of civil society, it will not be solved without an essential shift in terminology. A more promising approach to Russia's civil society in the early twenty-first century would involve a shift in focus from longstanding implicit comparison to Western Europe to close examination of its special qualities in Russia. In this respect, Murray Frame's insight that politically powerful civil societies suffer from their own inherent disadvantages would be a good place to start. Frame argues that a society strong and united enough to stand up to state power may also have the capacity in its own right to suppress individual differences and enforce social conformity. According to Frame, "the notion of a unified civil society therefore appears somewhat contradictory, because its very essence, and its unique strength, lie in its resistance to unity, and therefore its resistance to monopoly and manipulation."[27] Frame's point also implies that those societies that do not possess the social or ideological unity to exert considerable political power may instead possess other advantages. If societies united around a powerful middle class can prove restrictive, societies in which a lack of sociopolitical unity provokes more intensive argumentation may possess a dynamism absent from their more settled counterparts. Imperial Russian society failed to "counterbalance" the state, but it did create a sphere of dynamic social interaction and public debate that left an indelible mark on European culture as a whole.

What have been called the more mature civil societies of Western Europe established a network of refined principles within which their "respectable" contributors operated. Perhaps the most important of these was the increasingly careful delineation of the public and private spheres. At the same time, a more extensive delineation of spheres took shape in the various realms of knowledge. Bourgeois society greatly emphasized essential distinctions between different practices: religion, politics, business, science, art, and so on. These realms remained distinct through a tacit acceptance that separate truth claims operated at the basis of each of them. The separation of Church and State, the "freedom" of the market, the "laws" of physics, art for art's sake: such familiar ideas flourished in most realms of endeavor, and the need to keep the spheres separate from one another was considered a basic mechanism assuring the progress of civilization. While radical philosophers from Marx to Nietzsche liked to punch holes in the myths that maintained these distinctions, separate realms of knowledge and practice remained (and remain) a foundational part of the operation of modern, Western societies.

By contrast, the Russian public sphere did not display as well developed a sense of these separations. To be sure, the Russian public had its artists, scientists, entrepreneurs, and specialists of all kinds, but Russian philosophers, writers, social thinkers, and polemicists exhibited a tendency to eschew separation and pursue integration. Truths intrinsic to the sciences might also have relevance to the arts, religious and secular thought were intertwined, and thinkers as diverse as Nikolai Chernyshevsky, Lev Tolstoy, and Vladimir Soloviev made it a central goal to tear down what they considered specious divisions between separate branches of knowledge. Absent a keen appreciation for the maintenance of distinct spheres, Russian public discourse developed the important distinguishing characteristic of envisioning and addressing vast, unsolvable questions, questions in which social, spiritual, and political issues were not taken as fully formed but over and over again needed to be examined at the roots where they intertwined with one another. The whole tenor of Russian thought in the late-imperial period expresses a willingness to reimagine the world from the ground up.

Russia witnessed a political, intellectual and artistic efflorescence in the second half of the nineteenth century that ranks among the most remarkable in European history. From sweeping novels and influential literary criticism, to great art in multiple fields (music, painting, and dance in particular), to spiritual and political philosophy, Russia managed to make a huge contribution to world culture. Even the general strike of 1905 presented to the world a new use of civic structures to effect political change. At the same time, Russia also pioneered a number of innovations that have brought the world far more harm than good, including the invention of systematic political terrorism and the dissemination of virulent anti-Semitism.[28]

Surely the achievement of democracy is not the sole criterion on which we should judge Russia's civil society. Other characteristic features of Russia's public sphere could be mentioned as well: a unique relationship between the public and private spheres, the prominent position of women in some areas, the politicization of the arts, the idealization of the *narod*, the state-inherited emphasis on service, the interpenetration of high and low culture, and so on. Nevertheless it must be acknowledged that the very tendencies that produced Russia's burst of creativity also served as impediments to the attainment of political independence. The tormented energies and contentiousness that characterized Russia's public culture established a dynamic and productive urban sphere, but at the same time they helped prevent the achievement of a politically stable civil society. Born in part of the basic polarizations within Russian society, the desire for totalizing solutions tended to produce further polarization. Late Imperial Russian public discourse inhibited consensus and coalition-building and encouraged radical activism and utopian dreams.

Then again, as Nancy Bermeo has pointed out, civil society is not a moral category: "the associations in civil society can be good or evil or something else."[29] Civil society is not necessarily tolerant and liberal; it is not always non-violent, and it does not necessarily lead to democracy. From this point of view, Russia managed to create its own version of civil society without relying on a substantial middle class and without acquiring a definite political direction. If we accept a more flexible definition of civil society, we will be able to appreciate with greater accuracy the kind of society that did emerge in the waning years of the Russia Empire. In the end, however, despite its unique character and significant contributions, its most notable and memorable feature will always be that it did not last.

Notes

1   I refer here to the widely used text *A History of Russia*. Early editions do not include the term "civil society" in the index, whereas the most recent edition includes an entire section dedicated to the topic. See Riasanovsky, *A History of Russia*, 4th edn., and Riasanovsky and Steinberg, *A History of Russia*, 7th edn, 411–13.
2   Respectively, Porter, *The Zemstvo*, 291, and Laura Engelstein, "The Dream of Civil Society in Tsarist Russia," in Bermeo and Nord, *Civil Society*, 25.
3   Gellner, *Conditions of Liberty*, 5.
4   Locke, *Second Treatise*, 49
5   Forgacs, ed., *Gramsci Reader*, 222–30.
6   For a discussion of such developments in a global context, see Sen, *Identity and Violence*, 49–58.
7   Forgacs, ed., *Gramsci Reader*, 228–9.
8   Pipes, *Russia*, p. xxi.
9   Cited respectively in Lincoln, *Dark Shadow*, 196, and Robbins, *Famine in Russia*, 180.
10 Cited in Blackwell, *Russian Industrialization*, 50–1.
11 Kornilov, *Obshchestvennoe dvizhenie*, 31.
12 See Brooks, *Russia Learned to Read*, and McReynolds, *The News*.
13 Alfred Rieber, "Interest Group Politics in the Era of the Great Reforms," in Eklof et al., eds., *Russia's Great Reforms, 1855–1881*, 59.
14 Naidenov, *Vospominania*, 12.
15 Lindenmeyr, *Poverty*, 216–17.
16 See Joan Neuberger, "Popular Legal Cultures: The St Petersburg *Mirovoi Sud*," in Eklof et al., eds., *Russia's Great Reforms, 1855–1881*, 231–46.
17 Cited in Thomas Porter and William Gleason, "The Zemstvo and the Transformation of Russian Society," in Conroy, ed., *Emerging Democracy*, 64.
18 Ibid., 80–4.
19 Brower, *The Russian City*, 92.
20 See Thurston, *Liberal City*, 187.
21 Bradley, "Subjects into Citizens," 1105.
22 Venturi, *Roots of Revolution*, 485.

23 Shishko, *Kravchinskii*, 38.
24 Lindenmeyr, *Poverty* , 230–1.
25 Anon., *"Moskovskie Zametki,"* *Golos*, Apr. 30, 1874.
26 Joseph Bradley, "Voluntary Associations, Civic Culture and *Obshchestvennost'* in Moscow, " and Samuel Kassow, "Russia's Unrealized Civil Society," in Clowes, Kassow, and West, eds., *Between Tsar and People*, 148 and 367–71. See also Engelstein, "Dream," in Bermeo and Nord, *Civil Society*, 23–41.
27 Murray Frame, "Culture, Patronage and Civil Society: Theatrical Impresarios in Late-Imperial Russia" in Thatcher, ed., *Late Imperial Russia*, 65.
28 On many of these influences, both positive and negative, see Marks, *How Russia Shaped the Modern World*.
29 Nancy Bermeo, "Civil Society after Democracy," in Bermeo and Nord, *Civil Society*, 238.

References

Bermeo, Nancy, and Nord, Philip (2000). *Civil Society before Democracy: Lessons from Nineteenth-Century Europe*. Rowan and Littlefield, New York.

Blackwell, William (1968). *The Beginnings of Russian Industrialization, 1800–1860*. Princeton University Press, Princeton.

Bradley, Joseph (2002). "Subjects into Citizens: Societies, Civil Society, and Autocracy in Russia," *American Historical Review*, 107/3.

Brooks, Geoffrey (1985). *When Russia Learned to Read: Literacy and Popular Literature, 1861–1917*. Princeton University Press, Princeton.

Brower, Daniel (1990). *The Russian City between Tradition and Modernity, 1850–1900*. University of California Press, Berkeley.

Clowes, Edith W., Kassow, Samuel D., and West, James L. (eds.) (1991). *Between Tsar and People: Educated Society and the Quest for Public Identity in Late-Imperial Russia*. Princeton University Press, Princeton.

Conroy, Mary Schaeffer (ed.) (1998). *Emerging Democracy in Late-Imperial Russia*. University Press of Colorado, Niwot, CO.

Eklof, B., Bushnell, J., and Zakharova, L. (eds.) (1994). *Russia's Great Reforms, 1855–1881*. Indiana University Press, Bloomington, IN.

Forgacs, David (ed.) (1988). *An Antonio Gramsci Reader*. Schocken Books, New York.

Gellner, Ernest (1994). *Conditions of Liberty: Civil Society and its Rivals*. Penguin Books, London.

Kornilov, A. A. (1909). *Obshchestvennoe dvizhenie pri Aleksandra II, 1855–1881*. Moscow.

Lincoln, W. Bruce (1983). *In War's Dark Shadow*. Touchstone Books, New York.

Lindenmeyr, Adele (1996). *Poverty Is Not a Vice: Charity, Society and the State in Imperial Russia*. Princeton University Press, Princeton.

Locke, John (1952). *The Second Treatise of Government*. Macmillan, New York.

McReynolds, Louise (1991). *The News under Russia's Old Regime*. Princeton University Press, Princeton.

Marks, Stephen (2003). *How Russia Shaped the Modern World*. Princeton University Press, Princeton.

Naidenov, N. A. (1905). *Vospominania o vedennom, slyshannom i ispytanom*. Moscow.

Pipes, Richard (1990). *Russia under the Old Regime*. Penguin, London.

Porter, Thomas Earl (1991). *The Zemstvo and the Emergence of Civil Society in Late Imperial Russia, 1864–1917*. Mellen Research University Press, San Francisco.

Riasanovsky, Nicholas (1984). *A History of Russia*. 4th edn. Oxford University Press, New York.

Riasanovsky, Nicholas, and Steinberg, Mark (2005). *A History of Russia.* 7th edn. Oxford University Press, New York.

Robbins, Richard (1975). *Famine in Russia, 1891–1892.* Columbia University Press, New York.

Sen, Amartya (2006). *Identity and Violence: The Illusion of Destiny.* Norton, London.

Shishko, L. (1906). *Sergei Mikhailovich Kravchinskii i kruzhok Chaikovtsev.* St Petersburg.

Thatcher, Ian (ed.) (2005). *Late Imperial Russia: Problems and Prospects.* Manchester University Press, Manchester.

Thurston, Robert (1987). *Liberal City, Conservative State: Moscow and Russia's Urban Crisis.* Oxford University Press, New York.

Venturi, Franco (1960). *Roots of Revolution.* University of Chicago Press, Chicago.

Further Reading

Arendt, Hannah (1958). *The Human Condition.* University of Chicago Press, Chicago.

Ascher, Abraham (2001). *P. A. Stolypin: The Search for Stability in Late-Imperial Russia.* Stanford University Press, Stanford, CA.

Balzer, Harley (ed.) (1996). *Russia's Missing Middle Class: The Professions in Russian History.* M. E. Sharpe, Armonk, NY.

Cohen, Jean L., and Arato, Andrew (1992). Civil Society and Political Theory. MIT Press, Cambridge, MA.

Crisp, Olga, and Edmondson, Linda (1989). Civil Rights in Imperial Russia. Oxford University Press, Oxford.

Deakin, Nicholas (2001). *In Search of Civil Society.* Palgrave, New York.

Edwards, Michael (2004). *Civil Society.* Polity Press, Cambridge.

Emmons, Terence (1983). *The Formation of Political Parties and the First National Elections in Russia.* Harvard University Press, Cambridge, MA.

Emmons, Terence, and Vucinich, Wayne (eds.) (1982). *The Zemstvo in Russia: An Experiment in Local Self-Government.* Harvard University Press, Cambridge, MA.

Habermas, Juergen (1991). *The Structural Transformation of the Public Sphere*, trans. Thomas Burger. MIT Press, Cambridge, MA.

Hall, John (ed.) (1995). *Civil Society: Theory, History, Comparison.* Polity Press, Cambridge.

Hamm, Michael (ed.) (1986). *The City in Late-Imperial Russia.* Indiana University Press, Bloomington, IN.

Herlihy, Patricia (2002). *The Alcoholic Empire: Vodka and Politics in Late-Imperial Russia.* Oxford University Press, Oxford.

Lincoln, W. Bruce (1990). *The Great Reforms: Autocracy, Bureaucracy and the Politics of Change in Imperial Russia.* Northern Illinois University Press, DeKalb, IL.

McReynolds, Louise (2003). *Russia at Play: Leisure Activities at the End of the Tsarist Era.* Cornell University Press, Ithaca, NY. and London.

Seligman, Adam (1992). *The Idea of Civil Society.* Free Press, New York.

West, James, and Petrov, Iurii (eds.) (1998). *Merchant Moscow: Images of Russia's Vanished Bourgeoisie.* Princeton University Press, Princeton.

Chapter Fifteen

Russia: Minorities and Empire

Robert Geraci

To undertake a summary of the ethno-national dimension of the Russian Empire in just several thousand words is a task dauntingly similar to ruling such an empire: it requires some combination of colossal genius and colossal foolishness. Not only was the empire geographically one of the largest – if not *the* largest – in history, covering a sixth of the earth's land at its height and nearly every kind of terrain. It was of dizzying demographic diversity, encompassing scores of languages, dozens of religions, and almost every form of economic life. During its roughly 350 years of existence it grew prodigiously, often in ways and degrees that changed its very nature. This lifespan also witnessed remarkable political, economic, social, and cultural changes, yet the way in which the empire reflected them was notoriously uneven. Most of the generalizations one might make about the empire's peoples and their experiences under the tsars, therefore, are complicated by exceptions too numerous to mention. Frustrated by the challenge of finding a formulation that is entirely accurate or reliable, the writer of such an overview must at some point not only feign ignorance of many of these details so as not to confuse readers, but even embrace it so as not to become paralyzed by the task.

After surveying the process of imperial expansion by which Russia acquired its multi-ethnic population, this chapter will describe the main parameters of tsarist policy and attitudes toward the minorities of the empire from its beginning up to the revolutionary era of the early twentieth century. Because the chapter is chiefly concerned with state policies and actions toward minority peoples – a topic relatively easy to summarize and generalize about – it cannot cover the whole range of attitudes and behaviors of individuals and groups outside the imperial government. It also cannot adequately convey – though it does attempt to explain roughly – the subjective experiences of minority peoples. For a fuller understanding of the topic, readers are urged to consult the list of sources for further reading.

Conquest, Expansion, Resistance

The key event in the transformation of the Russian state into a multi-ethnic empire was the Muscovite invasion and conquest of the Chingissid (post-Mongol) khanates of Kazan, Astrakhan, and Siberia between 1552 and 1581. Strictly speaking this was not the first time that the Muscovites had annexed a previously separate state; this had happened in 1380 with the overthrow of the Novgorod Republic. Nor was it the first time they had subjugated culturally distinct peoples – the northern reaches of Muscovy were already populated in part by non-Slavic, non-Christian indigenous peoples. But it was the first time that these two types of conquest coincided. It was also the first conquest of peoples professing another major world religion – Islam, which the Turkic peoples of the Volga–Urals region – known primarily as Tatars and Bashkirs – had first encountered some 500 years earlier. The "gathering of the lands of the Golden Horde," as the conquests were called, was undertaken both as an act of vengeance against the Mongol–Tatars for their previous dominance over Muscovy and as an act of Christian messianism.

Annexation of the Volga–Ural lands cleared the way eastward for Russian fur traders, who traversed all Siberia imposing the tsar's fur tax, or *iasak*, on indigenous communities. When the tribes did not comply, violence was frequently used. Additionally, Orthodox missionaries often accompanied or followed the traders, converting the peoples to Christianity. In the course of the seventeenth century, the fur trade led the Russian state to declare dominion over nearly all of Asia north of China and Mongolia, with the Russian–Chinese border clearly defined in a treaty of 1689. The other most significant expansion of the seventeenth century was Muscovy's annexation of the eastern or "left-bank" (of the Dnieper River) part of Ukraine, including the city of Kiev, the former capital of medieval Rus' founded in the ninth century. Present-day Ukrainian historians regard the annexation as a hostile conquest, and the Cossack leader Ivan Mazeppa, who led an attempt at secession some fifty years later, as a hero. Russian sources usually describe it as a voluntary act on the part of the Ukrainians, who shared a common religion with the Russians as well as a closely related language.

In the first years of the eighteenth century, Peter the Great expanded the borders of Russia to the Baltic Sea through a protracted war with Sweden (1700–21), and built there a new imperial capital, St Petersburg, and a naval port, Kronstadt. The region was inhabited by groups known today as Estonians, Latvians, Lithuanians, and Finns, most of whom were peasants dominated by German- and Swedish-speaking landed elites. Peter's efforts to extend Russia southward to the Black Sea for commercial and naval purposes were solidified only during the reign of Catherine the Great decades later, through two major wars of expansion against the Ottoman Empire. Russia gained control of the north shore of that sea, including the last remaining Tatar khanate, Crimea. Catherine sought to make the fertile and strategically significant southern regions of the empire, which she called New Russia, more productive by settling them with Slavic as well as German, Greek, Armenian, and Jewish immigrants and refugees.

Jews became a significant part of the empire's population as a result of Russia's role in the partitions of Poland in 1772, 1793, and 1795. The partitions provoked a Polish patriotic rebellion, whose failure ended with Russia gaining a densely, diversely populated swathe of territory containing not only parts of Poland but also much of what is present-day Lithuania, Belarus, and western (right-bank) Ukraine. The region was home to millions of Catholics and Jews, and thousands of adherents of the Uniate Church, a hybrid of Catholicism and Orthodoxy created by a sixteenth-century treaty.

In 1815, after victory over Napoleonic France, Russia would also gain the formerly Prussian share of the partitions, which Napoleon had called the Grand Duchy of Warsaw. This followed other territorial gains of the early nineteenth century: after having seized Finland from Sweden in 1809, Russia took Bessarabia (now Moldova) from the Ottomans in the same year. Georgia, which had requested Russian protectorate status in 1783 to defend its Christian population against the Ottoman and Persian empires, was annexed in 1801. Wars with Persia waged by Alexander I brought into the empire Azerbaijan, populated primarily by Shiite Muslims, and the eastern part of Armenia, whose Gregorian Orthodox religion was older than the Russians' and more distinct from it than the Georgian variant.

In the early nineteenth century Russia also annexed large parts of the Caucasus mountain range, including the entire eastern coast of the Black Sea, after continued war against the Turks. From approximately 1818 to 1864, the mountain people of these regions waged a long guerrilla resistance against Russian incursion and annexation. In the east, the imam Shamil united Daghestanis, Chechens, Lezgins, and others under the banner of Islamic holy war, while in the western mountains a separate resistance involved the Circassians, Adygeis, and others. Only when Shamil was captured in 1859 did the Russian army decisively gain the upper hand; in the first half of the 1860s it finished off the job of securing the western Caucasus by slaughtering or expelling across the Turkish border hundreds of thousands of Circassians and neighboring peoples.

The largest influx of Muslim peoples into the Russian fold was also the last major act of tsarist expansion: the conquest of Turkestan (also known as Russian Central Asia), which brought some twenty million new subjects. Some of the Kazakh steppe hordes had been under Russian protection since 1730. But it was the frenzied competition with Great Britain for dominance in Central Asia – the so-called Great Game – that inspired a long series of Russian military campaigns between 1864 and 1885. Some inhabitants of the region – particularly the Turkmens along the Caspian Sea – resisted fiercely and were defeated only with the application of considerable brutality.

Although non-Russian peoples in many regions of the vast Eurasian space tried to resist incorporation into the empire and subsequently rose periodically against Romanov rule and its trappings, none was successful in overthrowing Russian domination until 1917, when the tsarist autocracy collapsed. Although the key events of the 1905 and 1917 revolutions took place largely in the center of the country and involved primarily ethnic Russians, the grievances of minority peoples against tsarist governance – some of which we will address below – played a facilitating role by compounding the government's vulnerability and complicating the challenge of keeping order.

Political and Administrative Integration

Because the Russian government continued to acquire new minority populations in borderland regions until the end of tsarist rule, policies regarding the governance and treatment of these populations never achieved any decisive or stable formulation. Since minority governance was never subject to any overarching conceptualization or reform, there accumulated a hodgepodge of overlapping and often philosophically contradictory regulations.

The earliest imperial conquests, such as the Volga–Urals region and eastern Ukraine, were integrated into the Russian administrative system fairly quickly, and eventually received a substantial number of Russian settlers, so that by the late tsarist era they were not strictly "minority" regions. Most official rhetoric depicted the entire territory of Russia as a future Russian nation state. In general, however, the later an area was annexed, the more the state procrastinated in integrating it politically, so that by 1917 much of the empire's territory was still under military rule. For some regions, most notably Siberia, military rule was understood as a function of low population density, though it also reflected the widespread belief that the largely illiterate indigenous peoples of Siberia were not sufficiently advanced to sustain "civil society." Even the Russian population of Siberia, which had surpassed the native population by the early eighteenth century, lacked the aristocratic elite that in European Russia had become the basis for local and regional administration during the time of Catherine II. For other regions in the east and south – Central Asia, Caucasia, and Transcaucasia – the persistence of military rule stemmed from their history of resistance to Russian domination, geopolitical vulnerability, and their predominantly non-Slavic populations. Additionally, the presence of Islam in all these regions raised questions about whether the populations would ever be truly loyal to Russian authority.

Although the biological concept of race was rarely invoked in the Russian Empire, the state did categorize some of its subjects as inferior to the rest in developmental terms: these so-called *inorodtsy* were deemed insufficiently mature to share normal responsibilities such as military service. Invented in 1822 primarily for the peoples of Siberia, the new juridical estate or *soslovie* category used this colloquial label meaning literally "people of other stock." Many of the peoples included in it conformed to Enlightenment notions about "uncivilized" peoples: they lacked political organization at the time of the Russian conquest, subsisted as hunter-gatherers or nomads rather than agriculturalists, and/or practiced polytheistic religions. Yet others did not, such as the Jews (who uniquely among *inorodtsy* were subject to military conscription) and the sedentary majority of Central Asian Muslims, who joined the category upon the conquest of Turkestan. Increasingly, the term conveyed prejudice and condescension more than it did any ethnographic reality.

On the other hand, some peoples of the empire's western regions were regarded as more advanced than the Russians by virtue of their historical experience under West European powers more liberal than Russia. In recognition of this, both Finland and the formerly Prussian part of Poland were annexed to the empire as autonomous constitutional monarchies – a Grand Duchy and a Kingdom, respectively – with the Russian tsar sharing power with elected parliaments, the Diet and the Sejm. (The parts of former Poland annexed directly during the partitions were known as the "Western provinces" and had some of the same administrative apparatus as the central or "Great Russian" provinces.) Yet both peoples found their governments' putative autonomy suspended or unfulfilled for much of the remaining period of tsarist rule, because of the autocracy's great fear of nationalist separatism – a fear quite justified in the case of the Poles, who participated in serious military uprisings in 1830 and 1863. In the post-Napoleonic era, Alexander I also undertook the emancipation of serfs in the Kingdom of Poland and the Baltic region, even though such a measure could not be discussed in Russia proper. Napoleon's having freed the serfs in neighboring Prussia had made emancipation necessary for the sake of preventing widespread unrest. Finland, on the other hand, under Swedish rule until 1809, had been spared the experience of serfdom.

Following the emancipation of the Russian serfs, the administrative organization of minority-populated regions took on an additional dimension. Beginning in 1864, a reform of rural administration gave all social estate groups (*sosloviia*) representation in new assemblies of provinces and districts called *zemstvos*. Insofar as many minority-populated regions – including all those under military rule – were not yet divided into provinces and districts, the reform never reached them. Indeed, as late as 1917, even some provinces of European Russia remained without the *zemstvos*. Most likely the expectation of *zemstvo* self-administration – which would have to include minorities in the respective *soslovie* groups, and therefore might become a conduit for nationalist and even separatist agitation – compounded the state's reluctance to extend the provincial administrative structure to borderland regions. Even if the Russian state's failure to do so was largely inspired by the presence of minority subjects, such as Muslims, it bears emphasizing that the absence of *zemstvos* deprived ethnic Russian subjects in these regions, even as it did the minorities.[1]

In 1870 town and city governments, analogously, were given representative self-administration in the form of city dumas, although elections to these bodies were divided not by estate membership but by levels of urban property ownership and tax burden. Even some cities in the militarily governed borderlands lacking *zemstvo* institutions (such as Tiflis, Baku, Tashkent, and cities in Siberia) enjoyed duma administration, and had minorities represented. The 1870 statute, however, limited the representation of certain minority groups by prohibiting any duma from having more than one-third non-Christian deputies; in the 1892 revision of the municipal statute, this maximum was lowered to one-fifth.

Social Status and Economic Rights

Through most of Russian history, new subjects of the Russian Empire were usually granted the same social estate (*soslovie*) status that they had enjoyed under previous authority, membership in the same estate institutions as the Russians, and the right to pursue the same livelihood. A Georgian noble owning land and serfs was given a Russian aristocratic title and allowed to keep his land and serfs; a Tatar merchant was entered into one of the Russian merchant guilds and retained trading rights in his city of residence; a Ukrainian serf remained a serf under Russian rule. Historians such as Andreas Kappeler have referred to this general practice as a "pragmatic" approach to empire-building, since it helped ensure the loyalty of new elites, who would in turn keep order in their regions – though use of this label should not be taken to mean that Russian authorities' belief in the primacy of social heredity over national heredity in determining status was either insincere or merely provisional.

By the nineteenth century, the application of this principle over hundreds of years had resulted in an enormous number of "former" Germans, Tatars, Poles, and Ukrainians among the Russian aristocratic and bureaucratic elites of St Petersburg and Moscow. To the historian, the key to the ethnic origins of such elites is often surnames, even if the endings characteristic of some national groups were often replaced by Russian ones. Typically, such families, after moving to the centers of power, had given up their former languages and religions and become thoroughly Russified. Usually such changes were obligatory only if one had great ambitions and left the native region. Occasionally the tsars applied greater pressure, as when Peter I deprived many Volga Tatar aristocrats of their land and serfs, and thus turned them into state peasants, for refusing to convert to Orthodoxy. If one came from a non-Russian religious background, marriage to a Russian Orthodox person required conversion, although Peter I abolished this requirement for adherents of other Christian faiths, as long as the offspring of mixed marriages were to be raised as Orthodox.

So, while talented individuals from minority backgrounds reached the corridors of power fairly frequently, by the time they or their offspring had arrived they were no longer identified as minorities. Baltic Germans were the only group exception: they often retained their ancestral language, religion, and group affiliation, even after generations of service in Petersburg. Their culture was generally treated with deference, occasional slander by the Slavophiles notwithstanding. The German language was known to many Russian aristocrats well into the nineteenth century; Protestantism was rarely stigmatized; and Germans were stereotyped as good managers and administrators, particularly in financial matters (several served as Minister of Finance). Prominent statesmen of other minority groups – such as Adam Czartoryski, a Polish aristocrat who was one of Alexander I's principal advisors; and Mikhail T. Loris-Melikov, an Armenian who served briefly as Minister of the Interior under Alexander II (1880–1) – were quite rare. High-ranking military officers from minority elites were somewhat more common; Prince Petr I. Bagration, a Georgian general in the Napoleonic Wars and hero of 1812, is a particularly prominent example.

In some cases minorities were actively barred from bureaucratic employment. Jews were generally prohibited from working in state service. After the 1863 uprising, Poles could not serve in Poland or the Western provinces, ostensibly for fear that they would introduce separatist propaganda into the region, though they could do so elsewhere in the empire, including St Petersburg. Similar restrictions may have been applied elsewhere, perhaps without being formalized: a mayor of Tiflis recalled that in the late nineteenth and early twentieth centuries Armenians could not be appointed to bureaucratic or professional positions in the Caucasus region because of commonly held stereotypes among the Russian elite of Armenians as political radicals and separatists.[2]

The role of commercially inclined subgroups of certain minority peoples presented a special challenge to officialdom. During the eighteenth century, ambitions for rapid economic and industrial development often led the tsars and their advisors to encourage the activity of minority groups and even foreigners by granting special status in the form of local monopolies and exemptions from taxes, tolls, and licensing fees. The state was aware of the relative inexperience and risk aversion of Russian merchants – as well as their low numbers – and appreciated the convenience of having borderland minorities facilitate trade with neighboring countries. Thus representatives of certain minority communities were able to accumulate both wealth and prestige in spite of disadvantages they might have faced as newcomers and as minorities. By the early nineteenth century, however, this concessionary approach was falling out of favor with the rise of free-trade ideology and Russian nationalism, along with the increasing vilification of Jewish economic activity.

Most Jews were registered legally to the *meshchanstvo*, the lesser of the urban *sosloviia* composed of petty traders and craftspeople. Though they were sometimes allowed to rise into the ranks of the merchantry or to enter professions through education, no Jews could be settled as peasants or serve in the bureaucracy. In the early 1790s, complaints by Russian merchants in Moscow and elsewhere about competition from Jews (and alleged illegal trade practices by them) resulted in the establishment of the Pale of Settlement, an area of fifteen provinces in the western and southwestern region to which most Jewish residency was confined, virtually until the end of the tsarist era. The Pale was largely a Russian reaction to the stereotype of Jews as ruthless and immoral exploiters, yet – as Jewish spokesmen and advocates have frequently pointed out – ironically it did more to reinforce negative behavior than to discourage it. Because of the combined limitations on occupation and residency, Jews were so ubiquitous in trades and commerce within the Pale that in the eyes of Slavic peasants profit-seeking became synonymous with Jewish-ness. And it seems to have been almost impossible to survive in such overpopulated occupations if one did not resort to wiles and deception.

If to mainstream Russia the Jewish question was: "Can the vices of Jews be reformed so as to make their legal emancipation a possibility for the future?", to advocates for the Jews it was essentially the reverse: to the extent that negative stereotypes about Jews may have reflected problematic behavior, was legal emancipation not a necessary *precondition* for its eradication? Since Russian officialdom and folk opinion both tended to regard Jewish insularity and "exploitation" of non-Jews as rooted in religion or national character, for the time being piling restriction on top of restriction seemed necessary to protect the political, economic, and social order – especially the Slavic peasantry. Consequently Jews became subject to more extensive social and economic discrimination than any other ethno-national or religious group in the empire.

State officials sometimes used particular models of the economic organization of the empire as justification for their efforts to curb the influence of non-Russian merchants in particular regions. They might pay lip-service to the ideal of integrating border regions such as Caucasia/Transcaucasia, Turkestan, and Poland into the Russian economy through the activity of Russian commercial personnel. Often they spoke of the importance of trade for engendering loyalty to and identification with the Russian center after times of unrest. But it was not always clear whether integration meant making the border region economically identical to the center, or giving it some distinctive role. These regions, in fact, were sometimes spoken of as "colonies" of Russia, on the Western model, that were to be limited to the roles of providers of raw materials and markets for Russian industrial products. The real beneficiary was not really the nation or empire but the powerful lobby of ethnic Russian industrialists in Moscow. This elite included many Old Believers, a group that by the late nineteenth century had virtually transcended its minority status. For reasons of self-interest, the Muscovites resented native merchants of these regions, who either chose to import foreign goods in lieu of marketing those from Russia, or, even worse, competed head to head with Russian industrialists. In any event, officials found that typically few Russian merchants were interested in getting involved in these border regions. Native commercial elites – Armenians in Transcaucasia, so-called Sart Muslims in Turkestan, Poles and Jews in Poland, and Germans in the Baltic region – continued to dominate, sometimes with grudging support from the government for the financial benefits they brought.[3] On the whole, the nineteenth century saw a gradual decline in the prevalence of differential rights within the commercial and industrial economy, and increased enforcement of equal economic opportunities. In many parts of the empire, commerce and industry proceeded quite harmoniously as inherently multi-ethnic spheres. Earlier concessions and traditions had resulted in the occupation of certain economic niches by specific minority groups, and these seem to have elicited little controversy. Some conflict did emerge in many cities and towns beginning in the 1880s, when it became fashionable for municipal governments to pass laws restricting the hours of trade on Sundays. These laws reflected overlapping motivations, including Christian piety and attention to the demands of commercial employees for leisure time. Jewish and Muslim merchants, shop-owners, and peddlers faced the pressure of having to cease trading on Sunday to satisfy the laws, as well as to rest on their own weekly days of religious observance. Some such communities petitioned for the option of taking their own days off in lieu of Sundays, but, even when local authorities and Christian merchants were willing to forge such a compromise, St Petersburg stood firmly against it. The matter became particularly stressful in many cities after 1906, when the Stolypin government enacted emergency legislation requiring all municipal governments to adopt such laws. Ultimately the measure failed to pass the State Duma.[4]

The tsarist state was particularly reluctant to let economic matters take their own course when it came to the Jews and the Poles, and especially on the question of landownership. From the 1860s onward, both Poles and Jews were barred from acquiring land in the nine Western provinces, though for different reasons. Poles (who in fact already owned a good deal of land in the region, but could not purchase more) were considered a political threat to the region for their possible separatism; Jews were considered to be economic exploiters of the Slavic peasantry. Soon afterward, Jews were prohibited even from working as managers of real estate in the region. Similar land restrictions were issued for Turkestan in the 1880s and 1890s.[5] Barring all non-Christians other than natives of Turkestan from owning land there (and from owning stock in companies that owned land there) limited not only the influence of Jews in the region but also that of Tatars; the argument was that the Tatars sought to exploit the region as a field for "fanatical" Islamic propaganda, especially among Kazakhs, who were supposedly less than whole-hearted adherents of Islam.[6] Ironically, it was ultimately the influence of ethnic Russians and Ukrainians on Kazakh land that helped turn Central Asia into a hotbed of unrest by the eve of the twentieth century. In the 1890s, the state made an aggressive effort to resettle peasants on the steppe in order to alleviate rural poverty in the Russian heartland, granting free parcels of land to each family who settled under official auspices. This program infringed significantly on the grazing lands used by Kazakh nomads, crowding many out and forcing them to become sedentary on small parcels, even without any real knowledge of agriculture. The resulting resentment toward Russians on the part of Turkestan natives was a major factor in the Andijan uprising of 1898 and was also felt in the broader uprising of 1916.[7]

Cultural Status and Russification

Early Russian imperialism, from the sixteenth to the eighteenth centuries, was often characterized by a messianic religious zeal; new subjects were often under considerable pressure to convert to Orthodoxy, although this pressure was limited by pragmatic considerations, including shortage of church personnel. In the late eighteenth century, Catherine II instituted a new policy of religious toleration and administration that would become the basis for the governance of non-Orthodox populations throughout the empire. Catherine's enlightened humanism was offended by the brutality of the Church's treatment of Muslims in the Volga region – which included the destruction of mosques and the kidnapping of Tatar children to place them in monasteries, where they were forcibly converted.

Catherine was not indifferent to the consideration that greater cultural homogeneity might make Russia easier to govern, but she thought it better to wait until the dominant religion, language, and culture were adopted voluntarily, rather than having to be imposed by force. So she brought missionary efforts to a halt, allowed the Tatars to rebuild mosques, and established a sort of Muslim equivalent to the Orthodox Church's Holy Synod, called the Muslim Spiritual Assembly, headed by a cleric called the mufti. The idea was to domesticate the practice of Islam in Russia – making a state institution the authority on matters such as religious schooling, publishing, pilgrimage, places of worship, clerical personnel, marriage and divorce, and religious law – so as to ensure that the religion would enhance moral order and popular loyalty without allowing foreign influence that the state might not be able to control.

Over the next several decades, the same idea was applied to Buddhists, Catholics, Protestants, Jews, and others as well. This arrangement, arguably, even gave religious minorities some advantages over Russian Orthodoxy: unlike the lay administrator of the Orthodox Holy Synod, the head of each minority religious administration was a clergyman; furthermore, while Orthodox priests never received state salaries, within each minority religion a subset of "official" clergy did. This is not, however, to say that adherents of minority religions always felt that they enjoyed full freedom of worship. Frequently the religious boards had new regulations imposed on them from the outside by state administrators, and the state was particularly aggressive where possible religious influence from abroad was concerned.

This system of confessional administration – in which the lives of most imperial subjects were significantly influenced by one or another of these religious boards – remained in place until 1917. Paradoxically, however, it coexisted with nineteenth-century developments that sometimes contradicted the Catherinian respect for diversity by putting pressure on minorities to undergo cultural homogenization. The doctrine of "Official Nationality," which originated in 1833 from a slogan coined by Nicholas I's Minister of Education, named "Orthodoxy, Autocracy, and Nationality," as the three pillars of the Russian Empire. The last term did not amount to a policy, or even a set of policies, but was rather an impulse to privilege the status of the Russian Empire's titular people. One could call it a statement of Russians' putative "cultural sovereignty" in the empire. Unlike political sovereignty, for the lack of which it may have been designed in part to compensate, it offered little beyond greater self-esteem to the Russians and perhaps a demonstration effect to the outside world.

Nicholas himself best expressed a significant dimension of Official Nationality when, in a discussion of the cultural differences preventing a peaceful annexation of Caucasia, he said he looked forward to a day when all people ruled by the tsars would "speak Russian, act Russian, and feel Russian."[8] During this era, many of Russia's historians argued that such an outcome was virtually inevitable, and the evidence was in the eventual Russification of previous generations of minority subjects, through the power of everyday life among the Russian people. Of course, for this ideal of full and organic Russification to make sense, the state had to be accepting of miscegenation between Russians and all minority peoples, and it was. Mixing and intermarriage were not feared and denounced (as was the case in the overseas empires of other European powers), but regarded as a desirable norm for borderland regions, as long as all non-Christian spouses converted to Orthodoxy and Russian culture and identity dominated the lives of mixed generations of offspring.

Though in one sense this myth of organic Russification seemed to make heavy-handed policies unnecessary, seen from a different angle it seemed to provide a justification for them. Since Russification was inevitable anyway, and Russia was therefore not really an empire in the artificial and morally dubious European sense, tsarist statesmen reasoned that pushing assimilation along was not only permissible but admirable. The new pressures, not surprisingly, came down hardest on Poles, who were close Slavic relatives of the Russians but had decisively influenced the turn in imperial ideology through their uprising and war to throw off Russian sovereignty in 1830–1. In the wake of the Russian army's victory, St Petersburg gradually undid most of the autonomous institutions granted to the Kingdom of Poland in 1815. Autonomy remained on the books but was significantly modified by the so-called Organic Statute of 1832 that sought to make Poland a more "organic" part of Russia. Following another rebellion in 1863, even the name Kingdom of Poland fell out of use, replaced by the designation "Vistula region."

Official Polonophobia influenced cultural policies in both the former Kingdom and the Western provinces. The two main carriers of Polish identity were the Catholic Church and the Polish language, and following the rebellions both were suppressed to varying degrees and in various ways, as the state sought to "de-polonize" the region. Polish language ceased to be taught in schools of the Western provinces by the late 1830s. The University of Vil'na was purged of Polish professors and students, as well as the language, and a new Russian-language university was founded in Kiev as a counterweight to Polish intellectual influence.

Catholic worship could hardly be suppressed altogether, but its institutions found themselves under increasing pressure. Priests had to be trained in a special St Petersburg seminary. Church lands were confiscated several times by the state. In 1839 the hybrid Uniate Church dating from the time of the Polish–Lithuanian Commonwealth – liturgically identical to Russian Orthodoxy, but loyal to the papacy – was putatively liquidated by a stroke of the tsar's pen. By the nineteenth century both the Catholic and Orthodox sides had come to suspect each other of co-opting the Uniates to further their respective national causes. Not surprisingly, pockets of underground Uniate worship remained well after 1839. In 1875 the tsarist state attempted to eradicate such survivals in the Kholm diocese. Uniate practices were later relegalized by a tsarist concession in 1905, as the state attempted to halt the spread of revolution.

In the wake of the 1830 rebellions, policies toward the Ukraine region were devised to deny significant cultural differences with the Russians, even though some officials felt that Ukrainian identity had some appeal as a deterrent to possible Polonization. Ukrainians became known officially as "Little Russians" for the rest of the nineteenth century. The words "Ukraine" and "Ukrainian" were shunned, and the language, which had become the medium as well as the substantive focus of a nascent national movement spearheaded in part by the poet Taras Shevchenko, was regarded officially as merely a dialect of Russian used by peasants of the southern region. The patriotic and separatist-minded Society of Sts Cyril and Methodius was forcibly disbanded in 1847–8 and several of its members arrested.

Jews felt assimilatory pressure early in the nineteenth century, through the cantonist system of military conscription of Jewish boys that began in the 1820s and ended only in the 1850s. The arrangement allowed the Jewish communal body (*kahal*) to send boys as young as 12 into service, and was a thinly veiled attempt to force young, vulnerable individuals to convert to Orthodoxy. In 1844, the government issued a comprehensive reform of Jewish life that abolished the *kahal*, which was described as an insular and stifling institution, and introduced a new state-sponsored Jewish school system designed to teach Jewish children to abandon the "useless" or immoral occupations of their parents and become "useful" members of Russian society.

Some Jews took the critique of their culture to heart and embraced a movement of Haskalah or enlightenment, while retaining Jewish religion and cultural identity. Some others converted in order to open the way to a school or profession. Yet eventually, fearing that Jews might be using formal assimilation (whether or not it included baptism) to undermine Russian culture and society while becoming less conspicuous, the state began openly to discourage the Russification and assimilation of Jews. Laws were passed making it difficult or impossible for Jews to change their surnames. Later in the century, restrictions on Jews would begin to refer to "people of Jewish origin" so as to apply equally to converts, suggesting a racial rather than religious or ethnographic definition of Jewish identity. In the eyes of many state officials, the acculturative ideal of Official Nationality simply did not apply to Jews, as it did to virtually all other minorities.

Under Nicholas I, missionary work was recommenced in the Volga region, for the purposes both of converting Tatars to Orthodoxy and of keeping nominal Christians within the Church at a time of increasingly aggressive Muslim propaganda efforts. The Kazan Theological Academy, founded in 1842, was made the laboratory for new approaches to missions that ostensibly would emphasize the sincere religious basis for conversion rather than the use of force and material enticements. Missions, however, were still controversial for the mistrust they aroused among Muslim peasants, and so the tsarist state never committed the resources necessary to wage an all-out Christianization campaign in the churches or schools of the region.

During the era of Great Reforms, in which Russian society and governance underwent so many fundamental changes, the liberal inclinations of tsar Alexander II toward the empire's minorities were manifested but briefly, with the abolition of the canton system of Jewish conscription; permission for greater numbers of Jews to leave the Pale of Settlement; the restoration of Polish autonomy; and permission for some Ukrainian-language publications. For with the Poles' rising expectations came another revolt in 1863, and upon its suppression a broad crackdown on minority populations throughout the empire. Catholic Church lands were seized, monasteries closed, communication with Rome forbidden, and the entire institution placed under the jurisdiction of the Ministry of the Interior. The University of Warsaw was Russianized, and educated Poles were forced to migrate out of Poland and the Western provinces if they wished to serve in the bureaucracy. After 1863, Russian decisively replaced

Polish in all government business. In the Western provinces, Russian officials – though lacking a clear legal mandate for it – attempted to curb even the unofficial use of spoken Polish in public. Even in the former Kingdom of Poland, decrees of 1879 and 1885 limited the use of Polish in schools only to the teaching of Catholicism and of the language itself. The severity of the backlash led many educated Poles to renounce romantic ambitions for independence and to espouse a more pragmatic focus on piecemeal reform and improvement known as "Warsaw positivism."

The prohibition on most publications in Ukrainian returned in a decree of 1863, with Minister of the Interior P. A. Valuev declaring: "There has never been, there is not, and there cannot be an independent Little Russian language. The dialect spoken by the man in the street is Russian, and has merely been corrupted by the influence of Poland."[9] The restrictions were quickly counteracted by the importation of books and periodicals from the neighboring Galician region of the more liberal Austro-Hungarian Empire, and had to be supplemented by an explicit ban on the smuggling in 1876. The southwestern section of the Russian Geographical Society was closed because of its presumed role in bolstering Ukrainian consciousness. The 1870s also saw the growth of the Pan-Slav movement, which championed Russia's tutelage over Slavs from the Habsburg and Ottoman empires and the reconquest of Constantinople for Christianity. And after the conquest of Central Asia it would turn out (as shown in the imperial census of 1897) that Russians could be said to constitute a numerical majority of the empire only if that category included the "Little Russians," making the perceived urgency of this matter understandable.

Now the Lithuanians too fell under the cloak of tsarist policy as it attempted to deprive the Poles of potential allies or pawns. Religiously and historically akin to Poles, the Lithuanians saw the writing and printing of their language officially switched from Latin (often referred to as "Polish letters") to Cyrillic script in the mid-1860s. Through this measure the state was attempting to cut the Lithuanians off from Polish literary influence, to validate and strengthen Lithuanians' separate identity, and facilitate their learning of Russian. The population, however, failed to adopt the Cyrillic publications and compensated by smuggling in traditional Lithuanian-language materials from East Prussia.

In spite of the absence of national separatism in the Volga region, an analogous project was spearheaded there by the lay Orthodox missionary Nikolai I. Il'minskii, a professor in the Kazan Theological Academy who used Cyrillicized Tatar (and eventually Chuvash and other local languages) in religious education within communities Christianized from the sixteenth to eighteenth centuries, in order to make them less vulnerable to the growing Islamic revival movement. Il'minskii was criticized by Russian nationalists for using such minority languages in his schools rather than Russian, but he argued that the use of Cyrillic would at least shield these Christians from the literary influence of Tatars who wrote and published in Arabic letters. Islam by its very nature, then (and probably in light of the only recently ended war in the Caucasus), was viewed as the religious equivalent of Polish separatism. For this reason, until the revolution of 1905 the Turkic peoples endured a form of repression that went beyond even that visited upon the Jews: denial of permission to publish periodicals in their native tongues.[10]

In both the western and eastern regions of the Russian Empire, then, tsarist nationality policies were designed to defend certain favored minority groups against assimilation by larger ones perceived as dangerous, through the bolstering of the smaller people's identities – and even by abetting the creation of separate ethnic consciousness where none or little had existed previously. Because of the wide geographic dispersal and influence of both these minority "villains" – the Poles in the west and the Muslims in the east and south – this motif actually can account for a surprising number of specific policies and events. Occasionally the roles of certain peoples varied according to the time and place. The Armenians are a case in point. During the war against the Caucasus mountaineers, they along with the Georgians were regarded as exemplars of the possibility of Christianization and civilization in the region, and were frequently elevated to positions of regional importance. Yet later in the century, under changed circumstances and new government priorities, the Armenians fell out of favor. Official opinion and behavior now favored the Muslim Azeris and the Georgians, both of whom were perceived as the Armenians' rivals.

Minority Discontent and Revolution

Matters only became worse for minority peoples following the assassination of Alexander II in 1881 by Populist revolutionaries. His son, Alexander III, was firmly convinced (erroneously as it would turn out) that the empire could be safeguarded from the revolutionary movement through the increased repression of non-Russians. First and foremost, court circles believed, was the necessity of curbing the activities of Jews, who were well represented (but by no means dominant) in the Populist movement. Folk opinion in the southwest blamed the Jews specifically for the assassination, leading to a major wave of pogroms in 1881 and 1882. While historians have found no evidence of St Petersburg's hand in provoking the violence, it is generally agreed that the government did far too little to curb it, and its proposed solutions tended to imply that the Jews themselves were to blame. In May of 1882 the so-called May Laws or Temporary Laws (which were to remain in effect until 1905) prohibited Jews from living in rural areas of the Pale. Quotas were placed on the numbers of Jews who could attend secondary schools and universities, though they were not always enforced, especially outside the capitals. An attempt was made to bar Jews from the practice of law, and large cities such as Kiev and Moscow undertook periodic expulsions of large numbers of Jewish residents. The reactions of the Jewish population were various: continued attempts to assimilate through conversion (now a less effective tactic); self-defense through professions such as law and academics; emigration; increased participation in liberal and revolutionary opposition movements; and finally the more distant ambition of Zionism.

Late in the nineteenth century there remained little expectation that Muslims in Russia would convert to Orthodoxy at any point in the near future. In newly conquered Turkestan, for fear of provoking unrest, Governor General Konstantin von Kaufman instituted a policy of more or less ignoring Islam in the region (not even placing its subjects under the jurisdiction of a muftiate). He appears to have hoped that it would fade out on its own at some unspecified future time. In 1870 the Ministry of Education adopted an educational system for Muslim children that sought to foster loyalty and civic participation through the teaching of Russian language while providing Islamic instruction. But these schools made only minor inroads into Central Asia; even in the Volga–Urals region, where the initiative was headquartered, they failed to secure the trust of the Tatar population, which remained largely hostile. The new school system was undermined by more transparently aggressive policies, beginning with an 1874 decree formally transferring all existing Muslim confessional schools to Ministry of Education jurisdiction. That decree, as well as other new laws aimed at restricting the training and authority of Islamic clergy and at isolating Muslims bit by bit from civic life in the Volga–Ural region – many of them promoted by Il'minskii and his ally Konstantin P. Pobedonostsev in the Holy Synod – fostered discontent and made it difficult for Russian Muslims to believe the government's repeated denials that it wished eventually to convert all of them to Christianity.[11]

Just as it had earlier become clear that state officials no longer regarded Jewish assimilation to Russian culture as a truly possible or desirable outcome, in the early twentieth century there developed a similar antipathy to – even fear of – Muslim assimilation. Though few Muslims had any incentive to convert to Orthodoxy, a cultural enlightenment and renewal movement emerged that was in some respects like the earlier Jewish Haskalah. The *jadid* (meaning "new") began as a reform of pedagogy in Arabic but led to a thoroughgoing reappraisal of the role of Islam in Muslim life and the advocacy of a greater engagement with the surrounding Russian society. Muslim schools began to teach Russian voluntarily and eagerly, where previously they had resisted state decrees demanding that they do so. State officials became so fearful of clandestine Muslim activity – in the form of the mostly chimerical Pan-Turkist and Pan-Islamist movements – that in the years after 1905 they reversed their decades-old policy of requiring the teaching of Russian and began to forbid it, instead allying with the conservative mullahs, whom they had previously considered hopelessly reactionary, in a campaign to liquidate the jadid movement.[12]

Increasingly severe restrictions on Jews and Muslims can be attributed to the intensification of older religious and cultural prejudices against them. More novel during the reigns of Alexander III and Nicholas II was the political and cultural repression of minority peoples who had previously been considered fundamentally loyal and more or less left alone. These included the Baltic peoples, the Finns, and the Armenians. In the Baltic region, the government in 1885 imposed Russian as the official language of administration (supplanting the German of the loyal elite there) and took control over all primary schooling. Slightly later it installed Russian in the schools and in the University of Dorpat, which was closed temporarily and reopened as Iur'ev University, now inhabited primarily by Russian faculty and students. In 1889 Russian judicial institutions and language replaced regional ones in the Baltic provinces. The Holy Synod sponsored numerous new Orthodox churches in the region, as it tried to chip away at the influence of Protestantism. As a result, the nascent Estonian, Latvian, and Lithuanian national movements were directed as much against the Russian state as against the traditionally dominant German elite.

Finnish autonomy came under attack in stages, beginning with an 1885 tariff designed to handicap its industries, after which came the abolition of its separate postal system in 1890. On the eve of the twentieth century, under the notorious governor-general Nikolai I. Bobrikov, Finland's army was abolished and its male population conscripted to five years of service in the Russian military. With the supplanting of the Finnish laws by Russian ones in 1899, and the formal suspension of its constitution and the installation of Russian as official language of administration in 1903, Finland lost its autonomy and effectively became a province of Russia.

The Armenians, whose elites had been appreciated for their role in helping to pacify the Caucasus and in the economic development of Transcaucasia, faced increasing vilification by the tsarist state in the 1890s because of their economic dominance in Transcaucasia and their overtures to fellow Armenians in the Ottoman Empire who were experiencing brutal massacres. Under suspicion of separatist ambitions, they saw their religious schools replaced by those of the Ministry of Education in 1896, and in 1903 the Russian state confiscated most of the property of the Armenian Church. Though little specific evidence is available, it was and is widely believed that Azeri pogroms against Armenians in Baku during the chaotic months of 1905 and 1906 were the product of provocation by state officials.[13] Like much of the Finnish population, the Armenians responded to these changes in official treatment by boycotting public institutions and resisting the demands of the Russian state.

In retrospect it is difficult to fathom the tsarist government's lack of awareness that its challenges to the cultural and institutional autonomy of borderland minorities (especially those hitherto considered loyal and unproblematic) might seriously erode its popular support. By the turn of the twentieth century there were few minority populations that did not have significant grievances against the autocracy, and such grievances led them into a variety of oppositional stances and movements. Some of these had resort to violence: Bobrikov was assassinated in Finland in June 1904, and Caucasus Governor-General Grigorii S. Golitsyn nearly met the same fate at the hands of Armenian revolutionaries in October 1903.

Most likely the state had imagined that each of these peoples was unidimensional and thus would be alone in its narrowly nationalist or "tribal" grievances. It failed to see that these subjects, in spite of their various faiths and languages and experiences, would increasingly rally to fundamentally universalistic ideologies (such as liberalism and socialism) to redress them, and that they would find in these ideologies common languages in which to demand change. In most regions, concerns about the general lack of civil rights and economic justice in the empire combined synergistically with such "national" complaints to hasten the collapse of law and order in 1905.

After the massacre of peaceful dissenters in St Petersburg on 9 January 1905 ("Bloody Sunday"), widespread strikes, unrest, and violence ensued in many cities of the empire's borderlands as well as those of Russia proper. The autocratic state, hoping to keep the situation contained geographically, first offered concessions in the realm of ethno-national rights: the religious toleration law of April 17 for Christian minorities; the recognition of Ukrainian as a separate language and reversal of its repression; the restoration of separate Finnish military conscription; and allowance for the increased use of Polish and other minority languages in schooling. Such measures failed to have a calming effect. After the tsar's manifesto of October 17, and the birth of a quasi-constitutional political order, minority representatives to the State Duma were active on many fronts, in addition to those of specific relevance to their communities.

Most of the ethnically defined parties and blocs were loosely affiliated with the moderate left-of-center Constitutional Democrats (Kadets) in the quest for a true rule-of-law state; their ethno-national organization was quite often largely a function of linguistic and/or regional convenience. (Most Russians in the Kadet party, and even some in the more conservative Union of October 17, were committed to the equalization of rights along ethno-national lines.) The chief exceptions were those parties having a basis in ethnic Russian identity. Russian nationalists, knowing that the sociopolitical dominance of their group could continue only with the survival of autocracy, chose a far-right orientation. The most notorious, the virulently anti-Semitic Union of Russian People – responsible for many of the hundreds of pogroms in which some 1,000 Jews were killed during the weeks following the October Manifesto – was increasingly regarded by tsarist authority as a trusted ally in its struggle against liberalism and radicalism. Conservative forces blocked most signifi-cant initiatives for redressing minority grievances.

In its eleven years of existence, the State Duma discussed but failed to pass legisla-tion to enforce and extend the April 17 religious toleration decree, and to reform the legal position of Russia's Jews. A bill providing for universal access to primary education passed the Duma but was blocked by the State Council partly because of its inclusion of a provision allowing minority children to be schooled in their native languages. And such actions by the tsar's bureaucracy as the repression of the jadid movement, the recurrence of attacks on Finnish autonomy, and support of the notori-ous Beilis ritual-murder case provoked fresh outrage in minority communities and among some Russians as well. The redressing of tsarism's crimes against many of its non-Russian peoples would be high on the agendas of leaders of the revolutions of February and October 1917.

Traditionally the discussion of Russia as a multi-ethnic empire was dominated by the metaphor of the "prison of the peoples" coined by Lenin. As this brief summary suggests, to some extent the label is apt, particularly for the Jews – whose historical memories have been the ones most accessible in the Western countries because of the scale of their emigration – and for the last few decades of the tsarist period for a number of other peoples. The empire was at its most oppressive in this last stage when it emphasized conformity to the extent that it seemed to be trying to make itself into a Russian nation state. With regard to the Jews, the empire was often guilty of the opposite offense: of erecting too many barriers to integration. Overall, however, describing the experience of Russia's minorities only in terms of punishment, deprivation, and victimization is to overlook the complexity and diver-sity of the tsarist system and its agents as well as of minority communities themselves. At many times, in many places, and for many of its peoples, the Russian Empire did "work," in the sense that it recognized many of their most important needs and helped to satisfy them. Without being excessively cynical, historians evaluating the experience of Russia's imperial minorities must remember that twenty-first-century conceptions of human rights and standards of living are not always appropriate yard-sticks; it often makes more sense to compare the lot of minorities to their ethnic Russian contemporaries – putatively the empire's best and most privileged people – whose lives, it often emerges, were not much easier. Social status and class determined the quality of individuals' lives much more powerfully than did ethno-national catego-ries. Recent scholarship has transcended simple dichotomies of freedom versus oppression and victimhood versus resistance to describe the variety of experiences within a single minority "group" and the ways in which even the least privileged could often make do by manipulating practices, laws, and institutions to suit their own needs and make their situation more tolerable. Scholars have also become increasingly conscious that the tsarist state was relatively fragmented, weak, inefficient, and risk averse when it came to imposing an agenda on its subjects, minority or otherwise. The "prison of the peoples" metaphor surely helps us to understand the role of minority peoples in the collapse of the Russian Empire, but without the recognition of that label's distortion of history, we would be at a loss to explain why the empire survived as long as it did.

Notes

1   In the late nineteenth century proposals were made to introduce *zemstvos* to the Western provinces by eliminating the ethnic element deemed undesirable: the Polish landowners. The idea was to have only peasants represented in the *zemstvos*, so that the Poles would be disenfranchised. The plan was eventually advanced by Prime Minister Petr D. Stolypin during the Duma period, but was blocked by the State Council.

2   Alexander Khatissian, "The Memoirs of a Mayor," *Armenian Review*, 2/4 (Winter 1949–50), 109. Previously, Armenians had been considered quite loyal and many of them had been employed in the military administration of the Caucasia and Transcaucasia.

3   There is some evidence that in some large industries such as oil, the government's increasingly liberal stance with regard to foreign ownership was a way of limiting the activity of domestic minorities in industrial production. See, e.g., M. Ia. Gefter, ed., *Monopolisticheskii kapital v neftianoi promyshlennosti Rossii, 1883–1914: Dokumenty i materialy* (Moscow–Leningrad, 1961), 116.

4   Robert Geraci, "Sunday Laws and Ethno-Commercial Rivalry in the Russian Empire, 1880s–1914," *National Council on Eurasian and East European Research Working Papers* (Feb. 22, 2006).

5   Thomas C. Owen, *The Corporation under Russian Law, 1800–1917: A Study in Tsarist Economic Policy* (Cambridge University Press, Cambridge and New York, 1991), 118–32. In spite of the concerns used by tsarist officials to justify such restrictions, Owen describes them as arbitrary, based on irrational ethnic hostility more than any real concern for the public interest.

6   Russian State Historical Archive (RGIA), fo. 20, op. 6, d. 219, and fo. 1291, op. 84, 1906 g., d. 90.

7   Daniel R. Brower, *Turkestan and the Fate of the Russian Empire* (Routledge/Curzon, London and New York, 2003), ch. 5.

8   A similar phrase (the mountain peoples had to be made to "speak, think, and feel Russian") has also been attributed to General Aleksei Vel'iaminov, who served Nicholas on the Caucasian front in the 1830s. Quoted in Virginia Martin, *Law and Custom in the Steppe: The Kazakhs of the Middle Horde and Russian Colonialism in the Nineteenth Century* (RouledgeCurzon, London and New York, 2001), 179 n. 8.

9   Quoted in Andreas Kappeler, *The Russian Empire: A Multi-Ethnic History* (Longman, Harlow, 2001), 256.

10 The only exceptions were two newspapers published bilingually in Russian and Turkic, one a jadidist publication from Bakhchisarai (Crimea), and the other an official government newspaper published in Tashkent.

11 Robert Geraci, *Window on the East: National and Imperial identities in Late Tsarist Russia*, Cornell University Press, Ithaca, NY, and London, 2001, chs. 4, 7.

12 Ibid., ch. 8.

13 Tadeusz Swietochowskii, *Russian Azerbaijan, 1905–1920: The Shaping of National Identity in a Muslim Community* (Cambridge University Press, Cambridge, 1985), 40–1; Firouzeh Mostashari, *On the Religious Frontier: Tsarist Russia and Islam in the Caucasus* (I. B. Tauris, London and New York, 2006), 104.

References

Becker, Seymour (1986). "The Muslim East in Nineteenth-Century Russian Popular Historiography," *Central Asian Survey*, 5/3–4: 25–47.

Brower, Daniel (2003). *Turkestan and the Fate of the Russian Empire*. RoutledgeCurzon, New York.

Brower, Daniel, and Lazzerini, Edward (eds.) (1997). *Russia's Orient: Imperial Borderlands and Peoples, 1700–1917*. Indiana University Press, Bloomington, IN.

Geraci, Robert, and Khodarkovsky, Michael (2001). *Of Religion and Empire: Missions, Conversion and Tolerance in Tsarist Russia*. Cornell University Press, Ithica, NY.

Kappeler, Andreas (2001). *Russia: A Multiethnic History*. Longman, Harlow.

Kappeler, Andreas, et al. (eds.) (2003). *Culture, Nation and Identity: The Ukrainian–Russian Encounter (1600–1945)*. Canadian Institute of Ukrainian Studies Press, Edmonton and Toronto.

Klier, John (1986). *Russia Gathers her Jews: The Origins of the Jewish Question in Russia 1772–1825*. Northern Illinois University Press, Dekalb, IL.

Klier, John (1995). *Imperial Russia's Jewish Question, 1855–1881*. Cambridge University Press, Cambridge.

Owen, Thomas (1991). *The Corporation under Russian Law: A Study in Tsarist Economic Policy*. Cambridge University Press, Cambridge.

Rodkiewicz, Witold (1998). *Russian Nationality Policy in the Western Provinces of the Empire (1863–1905)*. Scientific Society of Lublin, Lublin.

Slezkine, Yuri (1994). *Arctic Mirrors: Russia and the Small Peoples of the North*. Cornell University Press, Ithaca, NY, and London.

Weeks, Theodore (1996). *Nation and State in Late Imperial Russia: Nationality and Russification on the Western Frontier, 1863–1914*. Northern Illinois University Press, DeKalb, IL.

Further Reading

Crews, Robert (2006). *For Prophet and Tsar: Islam and Empire in Russia and Central Asia*. Harvard University Press, Cambridge, MA.

Geraci, Robert (2001). *Window on the East: National and Imperial Identities in Late Tsarist Russia*. Cornell University Press, Ithaca, NY, and London.

Hosking, Geoffrey (2006). *Rulers and Victims: The Russians in the Soviet Union*. Harvard University Press, Cambridge, MA.

Jersild, Austin (2002). *Orientalism and Empire: North Caucasus Mountain People and the Georgian Frontier, 1845–1917*. McGill-Queens's Press, Montreal.

Layton, Susan (1994). *Russian Literature and Empire: The Conquest of the Caucasus from Pushkin to Tolstoy*. Cambridge University Press, Cambridge.

Nathans, Benjamin (2002). *Beyond the Pale: The Jewish Encounter with Late Imperial Russia*. University of California Press, Berkeley, and London.

Slezkine, Yuri (2004). *The Jewish Century*. Princeton University Press, Princeton.

Sunderland, Willard (2004). *Taming the Wild Field: Colonization on the Russian Steppe*. Cornell University Press, Ithaca, NY.

CHAPTER SIXTEEN

The Intelligentsia and its Critics

GARY SAUL MORSON

> No class in Russian history has had a more momentous impact on the destinies of that nation or indeed of the modern world.
>
> Martin Malia [1: 4]

The Russian intelligentsia decisively affected the modern world by its very existence as (arguably) the first intelligentsia in the special sense to be discussed below. Under its influence, Russia became the first country in which "terrorist" or "revolutionary" was a recognized career option.[1] In 1917, when a group of *intelligenty* (members of the intelligentsia) led by Lenin seized power, Russia invented the form of government and society we know as totalitarianism.

Malia's statement is also true in a different way. In reaction to the intelligentsia, Russian writers and thinkers – Tolstoy, Dostoevsky, Chekhov, Bakhtin, and others – formulated a series of ideas that may be the most profound Russian contribution to world culture.

What Is the Intelligentsia?

Histories of Russian culture typically devote considerable space to "the intelligentsia." The intelligentsia exercised an influence on society and the autocracy that many believe was as significant as that of the gentry, peasantry, or bourgeoisie. Its behavior, style of thought, and specific ideas constitute, for better or worse, a key Russian contribution to the world. What is often called Russian philosophical fiction is better characterized as anti-philosophical fiction, if by philosophy one means the systematic, all-explaining ideologies professed by *intelligenty*.

But what is the "intelligentsia"? Russian thinkers constantly posed this question, and the number of writings devoted to it are legion. Debates on philosophy, politics, and society often took the form of defining the "true" *intelligent*. It is therefore both important and very difficult to give a definition.

We get the word "intelligentsia" from Russia, where it came into circulation around 1860.[2] The term never had a single fixed meaning and it named overlapping groups. But everyone's definition included one group, which was often known as the "classical" intelligentsia or the intelligentsia in the narrow sense of the word.

In broader senses, the term could refer to people active before the word itself was coined. In this sense, some have regarded the intellectual "circles" of the 1840s as consisting of *intelligenty*, while others have called these people (perhaps with the exception of Bakunin) mere pre-*intelligenty*. Still earlier thinkers, like Alexander Radishchev, Nikolai Novikov, or Peter Chaadaev have also been classed both as *intelligenty* and as pre-*intelligenty*.

In the term's most inclusive meaning, the intelligentsia consisted of anyone broadly literate or anyone whose career demanded education, but such a definition was itself often polemical, an attempt to say that the "true" *intelligent* did not require linea-ments of a "classical" *intelligent*. By the beginning of the twentieth century, the intelligentsia had evolved to the point where the classical intelligentsia seemed to be a distinct minority, essentially passé, until one group of them – the Bolsheviks – seized power. From that point on, the term took on a quite different meaning, inasmuch as one feature of the classical intelligentsia – its opposition to the government – had to change. Soviet usage of the term was closer to "toilers with the mind" than its classical meaning [1; 2].

It is true, as Boris Elkin has suggested, that the classical (or radical) intelligentsia never constituted a majority of the educated [3: 32–3]. But it is no less true that for decades this minority set the agenda and that less committed people sympa-thized with them. Russian novels are replete with figures who, while far from clas-sical *intelligenty* themselves, mouth their clichés. We may speak of the intelligentsia as a series of concentric circles, with the classical intelligentsia as the innermost one and each surrounding circle consisting of fellow travelers to a greater or lesser degree.

For convenience, we may identify three criteria for a classical *intelligent*: (1) a sense of identity *as* an intelligent, (2) a way of life, including special customs and mores, and (3) a set of ideas.

Identity: Herzen and the Pre-Intelligentsia

Members of the intelligentsia identified themselves primarily *as* members of the intel-ligentsia, rather than as members of a given social class or profession who happened to be educated. That is one reason why, as Nicholas Berdyaev put the commonly made point,

> Western people would make a mistake if they identified the Russian intelligentsia with those who in the West are known as "intellectuals." "Intellectuals" are people of intel-lectual work and creativeness, mainly learned people . . . The Russian intelligentsia is an entirely different group: and to it may belong people occupied in no intellectual work, and generally not particularly intellectual. [4,: 19]

An unintellectual or barely educated revolutionary might qualify as a classical *intelli-gent*, but Leo Tolstoy, who used his title of Count, lived on his family estate, and believed in God, did not. The Decembrists may have included educated people, thinkers, and some radicals, but their primary identity remained officers or noblemen, and they were servants of the state [5: 28]. To be an *intelligent* one needed to make the intelligentsia the group with which one identified.

Some thought of *intelligenty* as originally "repentant noblemen," and many were from the nobility, but prototypically and symbolically the *intelligenty* were "raznochintsy" – literally, people of various ranks, and implicitly, people who did not come from one of the major established classes. Some models, like Chernyshevsky, Dobroliubov, or (later) Stalin, were sons of priests or had studied in a Russian Orthodox seminary, and so, strangely enough, by the 1870s to call someone a "seminarian" was something like calling him a red. Seminarians were typically poor but educated, and an easy translation made it possible to convert the messianism of Russian Orthodox theology to secular messianic ideologies.

The classical intelligentsia found its roots in its shared rootlessness. In Pushkin's generation, almost everyone important in Russian high culture belonged to the army or court circles, but by the 1860s *intelligenty* took for granted that officers aided oppression. After the Decembrists, the next generation of gentry idealists made ideas their whole world, and philosophy became a sort of "internal emigration" – or so many felt. In his autobiography, Herzen eloquently evoked the sense of home provided by the "circles" of young thinkers, and circles were to become a constant feature of intelligentsia life [see 6]. The "generation of the forties" took an important step toward becoming the classic intelligentsia by beginning to shift their primary allegiance outside their social class to what would become in effect a new "class."

The world governed by the tsar might be barbarous and backward, but in the world of ideas life might be numinous and meaningful: this idealism of the 1840s served as a bridge to intelligentsia extremism. Herzen describes how these circles demanded "an unthinking acceptance of Hegel's *Phenomenology* and *Logic*" and how the abstractions of German philosophy seemed more real than life itself.

> People who loved each other avoided each other for weeks at a time because they disagreed about the definition of "all-embracing spirit," or had taken as a personal insult an opinion on "the absolute personality and its existence in itself." Everything that in reality was direct, every simple feeling, was exalted into abstract categories and came back from them without a drop of living blood, a pale algebraic shadow . . . The very tear that started to the eye was strictly referred to its proper classification, to Gemüth or "the tragic in the heart." [6: 398–400]

Herzen's evident irony reflects his sense that such idealism was apolitical or conservative, and Herzen reports how Vissarion Belinsky was at first willing even to justify the autocracy because, in Hegel's phrase, "all that is real is rational." Herzen himself plunged into Hegel in order to refute such views, and at last discovered in Hegel's ideas "the algebra of revolution" [6: 403]. After the regime's repression in response to the revolutions of 1848, the internal emigration of ideas soon led to the still starker alienation of exile abroad (Herzen) or imprisonment and exile to remote parts of Russia (Dostoevsky).

Nihilists

He was not a nihilist for nothing!

Turgenev, *Fathers and Children* [7: 46–7]

The generation of the 1860s defined itself by opposition not only to Russian society but also to the generation of the 1840s. Now the iconic figures, who were to be turned into secular saints, came not from the gentry but from the *raznochintsy*. Indeed, it was this predominance of the socially unacceptable *raznochintsy* that contributed to a sense of separate identity [1: 12]. The coinage of the word "intelligentsia" at this time marks the group's increasing self-consciousness as distinct. The Latin origin of the word also reflects its coinage by seminarians – who were obliged to speak Latin in Russian Orthodox academies – whereas the preferred foreign language of the gentry was French. Latin, in fact, became an intelligentsia emblem.

Nikolai Chernyshevsky and Nikolai Dobroliubov became models for the intelligentsia, not least in their choice of profession. They were *zhurnalisty* – not exactly journalists in our sense, but polemical and radical writers for periodicals, for the "thick journals" that themselves became a symbolic intelligentsia institution. Even to fight the nihilists, one needed a periodical, and so Dostoevsky, now no longer a radical, started his own, first *Time*, then *Epoch*, and eventually *The Diary of a Writer*. Professions not concerned with radical activity became mere ways of earning a living while an *intelligent*'s real calling was either revolutionary propaganda or, at least, the cultivation of sympathy for it. That attitude to one's profession underlies the quip that appears in Dostoevsky's *The Possessed*: is it wise to hire an engineer who believes in universal destruction? [8: 94].

Many *intelligenty* were ex-students. Expulsion from the university itself became a sort of graduation conferring what one scholar has called a nihilist's diploma [9: 25]. In a society in which only a very few ever attended university, to be an expelled student indicated both special education and a willingness to endanger it for a cause.

It became commonplace to compare the intelligentsia to a religious order, a group that had separated itself from the world and ordinary forms of life for a transcendent, sacred purpose. Revolution was perceived in apocalyptic terms. Sergei Nechaev called his terrorist document "The Catechism of a Revolutionary" and he evoked enthusiasm with an undisguised millenarian vocabulary:

> The revolutionary is a doomed man. He has no interests, no affairs, no feelings, no habits, no property, not even a name . . . In the very depths of his being, not just in words, but in deed, he has severed every tie with the civil order, with the educated world, and with all laws, conventions, ethics, and generally accepted rules of this world, and if he continues to inhabit it, it is only to destroy it more effectively . . . He is not a revolutionary if he feels compassion for something in this world. If he would pause before carrying out a decision affecting any individual of this world, he must always be aware of the fact that he hates everything equally. He would be in jeopardy if he should have any family, friends, or love relations. [10: 241–4][3]

What is rejected is "this world," an obvious adaptation of the New Testament. Here alienation goes further than it ever did with Herzen, who despised all Puritanism and particularly valued friendship and love relations. In fact, the tension between love and devotion to revolution was to emerge as a common theme in revolutionary thought and in the "terrorist novel."

Way of Life: "Realist Manners"

Berdyaev repeats the commonplace that the intelligentsia had "its own manners and customs and even its own physical appearance, by which it is always possible to recognize a member of the intelligentsia" [4: 16]. The sense of being a small and beleaguered group, combined with a set of antagonistic moral and political ideas, led to a rigorous code of anti-social personal behavior. Adherence to that code served as both a sign of belonging and a proof of moral superiority. Critics, memoirists, and fiction writers from all political persuasions remarked on the distinct customs and manners of the intelligentsia.

In *Fathers and Children*, Turgenev offers an example of a setpiece of mid to late nineteenth-century fiction, the gathering of the *intelligenty*. Turgenev is universally acknowledged to be a highly accurate observer, to the point where his novels are almost ethnographic guides, even when, in this case, his scenes are written with unmistakable satiric intent. Bazarov, Arkady, and the young nihilist Victor Sitnikov visit Kukshina, and from the moment they enter her house they are confronted with "unmistakable signs of the progressive tendencies of the mistress" [7: 51]. They find the disheveled Kukshina in a drawing room resembling a study, with uncut thick journals lying on dusty tables and cigarette butts scattered everywhere.

It soon becomes apparent that Kukshina's carelessness and languid speech are entirely studied and require constant rehearsal. She was brought up with aristocratic manners and has had to study the nihilist alternative the way others acquired the social code of the nobility, a kind of reverse education on which memoirists commented. So intent is Kukshina on getting her bad manners right that, watching her, "one felt impelled to ask her, 'What's the matter, are you hungry? Or bored? Or shy? What are you fidgeting about?'" [7: 52].

Kukshina parades the names of writers, scientists, and journalists – in the course of a page she mentions German chemist Justus Liebig, Fenimore Cooper, George Sand, Emerson, a radical journalist, and the wholly fictitious Kislyakov (roughly, Sourpuss) – and makes everyone aware she knows which figures are just joining the nihilist canon and which are on their way out.

> "They tell me you've begun singing the praises of George Sand again. A retrograde woman, and nothing else! How can people compare her with Emerson? She hasn't any ideas on education, nor physiology, nor anything. I am sure she's never heard of embryology, and in these days – what can be done without that?" (Evdoksya [Kukshina] even threw up her hands.) [7: 53]

It is unclear whether this married woman actually has had liaisons, but she makes a point of suggesting that she has. Because "my lawful spouse, Monsieur Kukshin" lives in Moscow, she announces, she intends to go abroad:

> "To Paris, of course?" queried Bazarov.
> "To Paris and to Heidelberg."
> "Why to Heidelberg?"
> "How can you ask? Why, [the chemist] Bunsen's there!"
> To this Bazarov could find no reply.

"Pierre Sapozhnikov . . . it was he who undertook to escort me. Thank God, I'm free;
  I have no children . . . What was that I said: *thank God!* It's no matter though."
Evdoksya rolled up a cigarette between her fingers, which were brown with tobacco
  stains, passed the edge across her tongue, sucked it, and began smoking. The maid
  came in with a tray. [7: 53–4]

Smoking was almost compulsory for a *nigilistka* (nihilist woman). Consider the story
of how Dostoevsky met his second wife. Dostoevsky wanted a strong, independent
woman, but such tended to be nihilists and atheists. As it happened, he was desperate
to turn in a novel on time. He accepted a suggestion to hire a graduate of the first
Russian stenography school's first graduating class so he could dictate the work
(eventually, *The Gambler*). When the stenographer arrived, he paid her little attention
until she, a non-smoker, refused a cigarette. Dostoevsky asked himself: if she does
not smoke, perhaps she believes in God? In fact, she did, and, not only was she not
a nihilist, but she had been brought up loving Dostoevsky's fiction.[4]

Dirty fingernails also became a nihilist symbol, perhaps because Pushkin's Eugene
Onegin cultivated his aristocratic nails. Indeed, as one contemporary observed,
"everything [one thought and did] – beginning with theoretical peaks, religious
views, the basis of the state, and the organization of society, all the way to quotidian
customs, to clothing, and to hair styles" became subject to intelligentsia dictate [cited
11: 5]. Interestingly enough, *intelligenty* would often reject all codes of behavior as
repressive while ruthlessly enforcing their own. In *The Possessed*, one *intelligent*,
Madame Virginsky, has an affair on principle with a truly loathsome man. At the
novel's gathering of the *intelligenty* on the pretext of celebrating a name day, a
schoolgirl denounces namedays because it is necessary "to disregard conventions,
even the most innocent . . . there are no innocent conventions" [8: 401]. When she
claims it is immoral for people at the meeting to waste time in aimless conversation,
a schoolboy replies: "there's no such thing as moral or immoral" [8: 405], which
does not prevent him from insisting, in the next breath, that the commandment to
honor thy father and mother is immoral, as "every one in Russia knows from
Belinsky" [8: 405].

Amid the hubbub, the revolutionary Pyotr Stepanovich asks the hostess for a pair
of scissors. At first she takes offense:

"What do you want scissors for?" she asked, with wide-open eyes.
  "I've forgotten to cut my nails; I've been meaning to for the last three days," he
observed, scrutinizing his long and dirty nails with unruffled composure.
  Arina Prohorovna crimsoned, but Miss Virginsky seemed pleased . . . Arina Prohorovna
at last grasped that these were realistic manners, and was ashamed of her sensitiveness.
[8: 409]

Everyone is on the alert to detect a lapse into good manners. Elena Shtakenshneider,
the daughter of a court architect, who kept a literary salon, wrote in her diary:

We now have two censorships and, as it were, two governments, and it's hard to say
which is more severe. The Gogolian officials, clean-shaven and wearing medals around
their necks, are fading into the background, while new ones are coming on stage. They
wear sideburns and haven't got medals around their necks, and they, simultaneously,
are the guardians of order and the guardians of disorder. [11: 7]

Way of Life: Chernyshevsky versus Chekhov

Chernyshevsky came by his bad manners honestly. As Turgenev remarked that Chernyshevsky's writing style aroused physical repulsion in him, Tolstoy described him as the gentleman who stinks of bedbugs. But later nihilists made "the imitation of Chernyshevsky" a quasi-religious duty, so that even their debauchery had an almost puritanical air.

Chernyshevsky's utopian novel *What Is To Be Done?* rapidly became a handbook for living, a sort of intelligentsia updating of Peter the Great's Book of Deportment for the Westernizing nobility. Herzen remarked that "young Russians were almost all out of *What Is To Be Done?* after 1862, with the addition of a few of Bazarov's traits" [cited 11: 16]. In part for this reason, this novel became for decades by far the most widely read work of fiction in Russia. One professor remarked that "in my sixteen years at the university I never met a student who had not read the famous novel while he was still in school" [cited 11: 28]. One *intelligent* recollected that "we read the novel practically on bended knee, with the kind of piety . . . with which sacred books are read"; another, describing how people imitated the characters in the novel, observed that "we made the novel into a kind of Koran in which we looked for and found . . . exact instructions on how to act in specific situations" [cited 11: 27]. Even the stranger aspects of the book – fictitious marriage, providing one's wife with lovers, vatic dreams, faked suicide – became part of the intelligentsia panoply of possible behavior.

Intelligentsia morality provoked the hostility not only of conservatives but also of Chekhov, whose nose for falsity and bullying was acutely sensitive. He objected strenuously to *intelligents'* sense of superiority. Asked to join an intelligentsia circle, he refused with a restatement of his fundamental values – honesty and simple acts of kindness for which "you've got to be . . . just a plain human being. Let us be ordinary people, let us adopt the same attitude *toward all*, then an artificially overwrought solidarity will not be needed."[5] No less angrily, Chekhov argued against the intellectual conformity of prescribed beliefs: "Under the banner of science, art, and oppressed free-thinking among us in Russia, such toads and crocodiles will rule in ways not known even at the time of the Inquisition in Spain."[6] Chekhov's famous letter to his brother Nikolai can be read as a counter-statement to intelligentsial morals.

In my opinion [Chekhov wrote,] people of culture must fulfill the following conditions:

1. They respect the human personality and are therefore forbearing, gentle, courteous, and compliant . . .
2. They are sympathetic not only to beggars and cats . . .
3. They respect the property of others and therefore pay their debts.
4. They are pure of heart and fear lying like fire. They don't lie even in small matters . . . They do not pose.
5. They do not play upon the heartstrings in order to excite pity . . . They don't say: "I'm misunderstood!" . . .
6. They are not vain . . .
7. If they have talent, they respect it . . .

8. They develop an aesthetic taste. They cannot bring themselves to fall asleep in
   their clothes, look with unconcern at a crack in the wall with bedbugs in it,
   breathe foul air, walk across a floor that has been spat on . . . Such are cultured
   people . . . What you need is constant work.[7]

Respect property and pay one's debts? Develop an aesthetic sense and worry about
housekeeping? Respect not the collective but the individual personality? Furthermore,
Chekhov omits all reference to ideology, theory, or any kind of politics. It would be
hard to imagine a more anti-intelligentsia set of recommendations.

In his critique of the intelligentsia, the critic Mikhail Gershenzon cites Chekhov's
portraits of the "slovenliness," closed-mindedness, and disrespect for individuality
characteristic of the intelligentsia. For Gershenzon, ordinary good manners, caring
for one's family, and basic human decency matter more than politics and are far
superior to ideologically derived mores:

> What has our intelligentsia's thought been doing for the last half-century? . . . A handful
> of revolutionaries has been going from house to house and knocking on every door:
> "Everyone into the street! It's shameful to stay at home!" And every consciousness, the
> halt, the blind and the armless, poured out into the square; no one stayed home. For
> half a century they have been milling about, wailing, and quarreling. At home there's
> dirt, destitution, disorder, but the master doesn't care. He is out in public, saving the
> people – and that is easier and more entertaining than drudgery at home. [12: 58]

Ideas: Negation

A true intelligent had to subscribe to a set of ideas. In most accounts, those ideas
included materialism, atheism, and the mystique of revolution. While accurate as far
as it goes, this enumeration is too simple. Each of these three terms was understood
in a particular way; the meaning of each evolved over time; and other beliefs were
arguably as important.

Turgenev saw the common thread linking these beliefs as sheer negation – hence
his term nihilism. In the gathering of the nihilists in *Fathers and Children*, Sitnikov
mouths intelligentsia pieties: "Would you believe it, when Evgeny Vasilyich [Bazarov]
said for the first time that it was not right to recognize any authorities, I felt such
enthusiasm, as though my eyes were opened" [7: 50]. The nihilists "discussed at
length whether marriage was a prejudice or a crime" [7: 55], and Sitnikov looks for
opportunities to express his contempt for anyone and anything. "The possibility of
feeling and expressing contempt," Turgenev observes, "was the most agreeable sensa-
tion to Sitnikov" [7: 54]. Bazarov himself denies, among other things, all ideals, love
beyond physiological impulse, and the beauty of nature. "Nature, too, is non-
sense . . . Nature's not a temple, but a workshop" [7: 33]. Bazarov dissects a frog
and avers that people possess nothing but what can be dissected, an observation that
provoked the critic Dmitrii Pisarev to claim that the salvation of Russia of Russia lies
in the dissected frog [11: 17]. Bazarov claims: "Raphael's not worth a brass farthing"
[7: 42]; "Aristocracy, Liberalism, progress, principles . . . if you think of it, what a
lot of useless and foreign words" [7: 38]. In the novel's best-known exchange, Arkady
rejects all the beliefs of his uncle, a liberal of the 1840s:

"I've told you already, uncle, that we don't recognize any authorities," put in Arkady.

"We act by virtue of what we recognize as useful," observed Bazarov. "At the present time, negation is the most useful of all – and we deny –"

"Everything?"

"Everything!"

"What, not only art and poetry . . . but even . . . horrible to say . . ."

"Everything," repeated Bazarov, with indescribable composure . . . [7: 39]

"We decided . . . to confine ourselves to abuse."

"And that is called nihilism?"

"And that is called nihilism," Bazarov repeated, this time with peculiar rudeness . . .

"We shall destroy, because we are a force," observed Arkady. [7: 41]

Sheer negation of this sort had an enormous appeal. Bakunin's most famous aphorism thrilled Herzen and others: "the will to destroy is also a creative will."[8] In *Crime and Punishment*, the *intelligent* Lebeziatnikov intones: "We have gone further [than earlier *intelligents*] in our convictions. We reject more!" [13: 359].

Ideas: The Munchausen Syndrome

Notwithstanding their denial of all ideals, the nihilists insisted on the duty to save the people. They wound up preaching a sort of idealistic materialism. Vladimir Soloviev caught this contradiction in what he called "the intelligentsia syllogism": man is descended from the apes; therefore, love thy neighbor as thyself. Others pointed to the contradiction of maintaining absolute materialist determinism while urging people to action. Sergei Bulgakov observed that "the intelligentsia asserts that the personality is wholly a product of the environment, and at the same time suggests to it that it improve its surroundings, like Baron Munchausen pulling himself out of the swamp by his own hair" [14: 36]. Nevertheless, a peculiar synthesis of nihilism and messianism became a hallmark of the intelligentsia.

The doctrines that tended to appeal most were those that managed to lend themselves to both denial and soteriology. Utilitarianism clearly fit the bill; in Russia, unlike England, it did not underpin liberalism. Anarchism, populism, and Marxism were also readily adaptable.

Supposedly, intelligentsia doctrines derived from science, but this "science" had little to do with the skeptical weighing of evidence. Nihilists and other *intelligenty* characteristically evaluated the truth of ideas not by evidence or logic but by their capacity to promote revolution. Berdyaev lamented "the almost insane tendency to judge philosophical doctrines and truths according to political and utilitarian criteria . . . The intelligentsia's basic moral premise is summed up in the formula: let truth perish, if its death will enable the people to live better and will make men happier; down with truth, if it stands in the way of the sacred cry, 'down with autocracy'" [15: 5–6]. It is only a short step from this understanding of truth to the Soviet doctrine that one can refute a scientific theory not only by scientific evidence but also by demonstrating its incompatibility with Marxism-Leninism, a doctrine used (at one time) to reject genetics and the chemical theory of resonance.[9]

Ideas: Terrorism and "The Russian Aspect of their Teachings"

Dostoevsky shrewdly noted that, when Russians accept foreign thinkers, they typically interpret them in ways those thinkers would not have recognized. Every idea is taken to its extreme, every philosophy becomes an algebra for revolution, and each hypothesis somehow lends itself to universal salvation: this is what Dostoevsky calls "the Russian aspect of their [Western thinkers'] teachings" [16: 288]. A Russian *intelligent* is someone who can read Darwin and promptly decide to become a pickpocket, for the good of the people. "And therein lies the real horror," Dostoevsky observes, "that in Russia one can commit the foulest and most villainous acts without being in the least a villain!" [16: 286].

By villainy, Dostoevsky, above all meant terrorism. Russian terrorism was itself one of the country's decisive contributions to world culture. The constantly romanticized People's Will, which succeeded in assassinating Tsar Alexander II in 1881, was arguably "the first modern terrorist organization in the world" [17: 3]. After a period of calm, terrorism resumed on a much larger scale at the beginning of the twentieth century, when it became an "all pervasive phenomenon" [2: 5]. From October 1905 through the end of 1907, almost 4,500 state officials were killed or injured, along with an approximately equal number of private individuals. From January 1908 through May 1910, authorities chronicled about 20,000 terrorist acts resulting in over 7,500 causalities [17: 21]. As significant as the number was the reaction of non-terrorist liberals, who, by and large, demonstrated sympathy for the terrorists. In *The Possessed*, Dostoevsky foresaw this reaction.

Dostoevsky also perceived what others later did, that terrorism was not only a political but also a psychological and metaphysical act. Like gambling, it was addictive and promised a total change almost overnight, a sort of secular version of the promise in Revelation: "Behold, I make all things new!" It was commonly argued that terrorism doubly affirms the metaphysical freedom of the individual because it implies the effectiveness of both victim and killer. Dostoevsky liked to say that Russians do not become atheists, but rather come to believe devoutly in atheism; by the same token, terrorism itself became a sort of religion, complete with the sacrifice of oneself and others.

Ideas: Grouse and Sturgeon

Like other millenarian sects, the intelligentsia tended to believe in the urgency of the present moment. In *The Possessed*, the *intelligent* Shigalev looks "as though he were expecting the destruction of the world, and not at some indefinite time and in accordance with prophecies, which might never be fulfilled, but quite definitely, as though it were to be the day after tomorrow at twenty-five minutes past ten" [8: 135]. Unsurprisingly, the intelligentsia rejected Boris Chicherin's argument that change must happen gradually so that people could acquire the habits of respecting law rather than arbitrary power.[10] In fact, the intelligentsia and the conservatives shared a hostility to the very notion of law: even Herzen saw Russia's lack of a sense of legality as a sign that the capitalist stage of history could be skipped [see 18: 20]. The Soviet regime was the direct inheritor of such ideas, which still thrive.

To the horror of the intelligentsia's critics, Lenin insisted that the revolution was the supreme law and that anything promoting it is moral. Trotsky contended that the laws of nature and human nature would also come under revolutionary control. Under Party leadership, he wrote, man will come to remake his own psychology and even master subconscious processes. The physical environment will become entirely planned: "Man in Socialist society will command nature in its entirety, with its grouse and sturgeons. He will point out places for mountains and for passes. He will change the course of rivers, and he will lay down rules for the oceans" [19: 252]. Such thinking fed the intelligentsia's most important contribution to world culture, totalitarianism.

Perhaps only one nineteenth-century thinker foresaw totalitarianism. In Dostoevsky's *The Possessed*, the revolutionaries describe it in detail. They intend to cut off "a hundred million heads" and to regulate all culture and the minutest details of everyday life. Pyotr Stepanovich endorses Shigalev's proposals for a system that, like the Chinese cultural revolution and Khmer Rouge Cambodia, institutes universal spying and abolishes high culture as incompatible with absolute equality:

> Cicero will have his tongue cut out, Copernicus will have his eyes put out, Shakespeare will be stoned . . . the thirst for culture is an aristocratic thirst . . . Only the necessary is necessary, that's the motto of the whole world henceforward . . . Absolute submission, absolute loss of individuality . . . [8: 424–5]

But how did Dostoevsky know? The answer is that he seriously asked what would happen if the intelligentsia's ideas were ever put into practice.

Ideas: Raskolnikovism and the People

Dostoevsky also identified a structure common to various intelligentsia ideologies. Whether they adhered to nihilism, populism, anarchism, Marxism, or other systems of thought, *intelligenty* presumed that a vanguard, a group of "critically thinking individuals," must exercise power. The vanguard would of course consist of *intelligenty*: the very word "intelligentsia" implied superior insight (intelligence). In *Crime and Punishment*, Raskolnikov adopts a series of incompatible theories, but always maintains the justice of murder performed by a person with superior insight. He has written an article dividing humanity into two groups: a few "extraordinary people," like Solon or Napoleon, who may "overstep boundaries" and violate moral laws to realize their ideas, and the rest of humanity, who are mere breeders.

Theory explains all and so theoreticians should rule. Berdyaev described how the intelligentsia

> managed to give even the most practical social concerns a philosophical character . . . it saw the agrarian and labor problems as problems of universal salvation, and it gave sociological doctrines an almost theological color . . . The Russian intelligentsia wished to live and to determine its attitude to the most practical and prosaic aspects of social life on the basis of a materialist catechism and metaphysics. [15: 3]

The devil who visits Ivan Karamazov paraphrases the argument that "all is permitted" for the one who truly understands, and then remarks: "That's all very charming; but if you want to swindle why do you want a moral sanction for doing it? But that's our modern Russian [*intelligent*] all over. He can't bring himself to swindle without a moral sanction" [20: 616].

Critically thinking individuals save the people, and so every intelligentsia theory carried with it a corresponding account of "the people." If, for many nihilists of the 1860s, the people were an ignorant mass to be enlightened, for Herzen, the Populists, and many after, the peasants carried in potential a truth that could redeem the world. For the Marxists, the nascent working class represented the true people. In all three cases, the intelligentsia would play the crucial role in salvation, a doctrine that eventually led to the Soviet dictatorship in the name of the people.

Critics of the intelligentsia often regarded intelligentsia accounts of the people as absurd. Dostoevsky, who lived among common people in his prison camp and as a private in the army, never ceased to ridicule the intelligentsia for describing the people as theory said they must be rather than as they really were. In *Anna Karenina*, Koznyshev holds very definite views of the peasantry "deduced . . . chiefly from contrast with other modes of life. He never changed his opinion of the peasantry and his sympathetic attitude toward them" [21: 252]. From every conversation with peasants, Koznyshev "would deduce general conclusions in favor of the peasantry and in confirmation of his understanding them" [21: 251]. Of course, the only way in which *every* encounter could confirm one's opinion is if disconfirmation is foreclosed. In contrast, Levin, who works with the peasants daily, sees them in all their perplexing variety. He therefore "had no definite views of the peasantry . . . For him to say that he knew the peasantry would have been the same as to say he knew men" [21: 252].

Other critics discovered danger in the intelligentsia's condescension. Sergei Bulgakov observed that worship of the people goes hand in hand with "an arrogant view of the people as an object of salvation, as a minor" [14: 42–3] and that the intelligentsia's heroic view of itself "presupposes a passive object of activity, the nation of humanity that is being saved . . . for all its striving for democracy, the intelligentsia is only a special kind of aristocratic class, arrogantly contrasting itself to 'common people'" [14: 29].

Ideas: Time

Critics of the intelligentsia took issue with its attitude towards time: the present moment and the people living in it could be sacrificed for the glorious future. This attitude justified terrorism, murder, indeed anything. In *From the Other Shore*, Herzen pointedly asks:

> If progress is the end, for whom are we working? Who is this Moloch who, as the toilers approach him, instead of rewarding them, only recedes, and as a consolation to the exhausted, doomed multitudes . . . can give back only the mocking answer that after their death all will be beautiful on earth? Do you truly wish to condemn all human beings alive today to the sad role . . . of wretched galley slaves, up to their knees in mud, dragging a barge filled with some mysterious treasure and with the words "progress in the future" inscribed on its bows? . . . This alone should serve as a warning to people: an end that is infinitely remote is not an end, but, if you like, a trap; an end must be nearer – it ought to be, at the very least, the laborer's wage, or pleasure in the work done. [22: 36–7].

Herzen argues that we should care for the living, not just for future generations, and for specific people, not just for humanity in general. We should also recognize in any case that we cannot know the future. "There is no *libretto* . . . In history all i s improvisation, all is will, all is *ex tempore*" [22: 39]. These skeptical assertions contradict the tenets of the intelligentsia but shaped the views of Tolstoy and Dostoevsky.

The Counter-Tradition: *Signposts*

Signposts: A Collection of Essays on the Russian Intelligentsia (1909), probably the most famous book on the intelligentsia, criticized it mercilessly. If ever a work could be called scandalous, this was it.[11] It went through five editions in a year, and the fifth included an appendix listing over two hundred books and articles written in response. Individuals, journals, even political parties published replies, almost all negative. Since most of the contributors were liberals, and one of them (Peter Struve) was a leader of the liberal Kadet Party, they were disappointed that Paul Miliukov, the head of the Kadets, toured Russia to denounce the book's attempt to pry liberals from the revolutionary tradition. Miliukov's response confirmed the contributors' contention that the classical intelligentsia enjoyed dangerous prestige even among those whose political ideas should have made them oppose it.

The *Signposts* contributors distinguished between thinking people and a classical intelligentsia, or, as Berdyaev put the point, between a genuine intelligentsia and a dangerous *intelligentshchina* (roughly, intelligent-itis) [15: 1]. They sought to replace the latter with the former. To do so, they argued that, in addition to the intelligentsia tradition, Russia also had a counter-tradition of thinkers opposed to the intelligentsia. Since the 1860s, the counter-tradition consisted first of all of Russia's best writers, in part because they recognized the impossibility of creating great literature while subscribing to "ready-made" dogmas or while turning art into simple propaganda, as the intelligentsia demanded. Struve identified Chekhov, Tolstoy, Dostoevsky, Tiutchev, and Fet, not Chernyshevsky, Dobroliubov, and Mikhailovsky, as the true heirs of Novikov, Pushkin, Chaadaev, and other pre-intelligentsia thinkers [23: 120]. With only slight exaggeration, Mikhail Gershenzon concluded that, "in Russia, an almost infallible gauge of the strength of an artist's genius is the extent of his hatred for the intelligentsia" [12: 60].

The Counter-Tradition: Surprisingness

We may go further than *Signposts*: the great Russian writers not only criticized intelligentsia ideas but also offered powerful alternatives. I believe that the philosophies of the Russian counter-tradition constitute Russia's greatest contribution to world thought. That counter-tradition also includes Russia's greatest theorist, Mikhail Bakhtin, whose ideas represent a distillation and extension of the writers he so admired, especially Dostoevsky. Here I can only foreground those counter-traditional ideas that can easily be seen as responses to the intelligentsia.

By and large, the members of the counter-tradition shared a sense that no theory would ever be adequate to understanding the complexity of the world or of each individual in it. European thought since the seventeenth century has been obsessed with the idea that what Newton did for astronomy can be done for society – that we are on the verge of a true social science with which we can predict and control social reality. Russian *intelligenty* may have taken the faith in such "moral Newtonianism" to an extreme, but they were far from unique in accepting it. The great novels subject such "theoretism," as Bakhtin called it, to withering critique. They call for an enriched view of what Aristotle called "practical wisdom."

In *War and Peace*, Tolstoy argues that, in the social world, if we trace causes back, things do not simplify, they ramify. We therefore never arrive at anything like Newton's few laws. Whatever laws might exist would be useless because they would be as complex or more complex than the phenomena themselves. "What science can there be," Prince Andrei asks himself, "in a matter in which, as in every practical matter, nothing can be determined and everything depends on innumerable conditions, the significance of which becomes manifest at a particular moment and no one can tell when that moment will come?" [24: 775]. "As in every practical matter": Tolstoy indicates that his skepticism about a science of warfare applies to the entire social world.

There cannot be a social science, because genuine *contingency* reigns. As Aristotle defined the term, a contingent event is one that can either be or not be. Social life does not resemble Newtonian astronomy where the position of Mars can be calculated in advance and the present moment is the automatic result of earlier moments. We can never "foresee all contingencies" [24: 929], as Pierre and General Pfühl imagine. Andrei asks: "What are we facing tomorrow? A hundred million diverse chances, which will be decided on the instant by whether we run or they run, whether this man or that man is killed" [24: 930]. "On the instant": *presentness* matters because more than one thing can happen at any given moment.

Not just contingency but also individual freedom may give the world "surprisingness" (another term of Bakhtin's). Russian novels are renowned for their unmatched psychology, but they are psychological in a special sense. When Dostoevsky (of all people) denied being a psychologist, he meant that no science could ever make human beings predictable [see 25: 60–1]. As Bakhtin paraphrased Dostoevsky's idea, humanness entails "unfinalizability," the "capacity to outgrow . . . from within and to render *untrue* any externalizing and finalizing definition":

> In Dostoevsky's artistic thinking, the genuine life of the personality takes place at the point of noncoincidence between a man and himself, at his point of departure beyond the limits of all he is as a material being, a being that can be spied on, defined, predicted apart from its own will, "at second hand." [25: 59]

> An individual cannot be completely incarnated into the flesh of existing socio-historical categories . . . There always remains an unrealized surplus of humanness. [26: 37]

The Counter-Tradition: Prosaics[12]

Counter-traditional thinkers contended that what makes history happen and what makes lives good or bad is not grand events or extreme situations but the sum total of *ordinary* events. In *War and Peace*, Tolstoy argues at length that a sort of optical illusion makes us credit dramatic events with too much efficacy, as someone viewing a distant hilltop where only treetops were visible might conclude that the region contains nothing but trees. Prosaic events, which conform to no laws, are in their very multiplicity much more important.

The same is true of individual lives. We truly live in the ordinary, not the dramatic, moments. In a famous essay, Tolstoy tells the story of the painter Bryullov, who corrected a pupil's sketch.

> The pupil . . . exclaimed: "Why you only touched it a tiny bit, but it is quite another thing." Bryullov replied: "art begins where the tiny bit begins."
>
> That saying is strikingly true not only of art but of all life. One may say that true life begins where the tiny bit begins – where what seem to us minute and infinitely small alterations take place. True life is not lived where great external changes take place – where people move about, clash, fight, and slay one another – it is lived only where these tiny, tiny infinitesimally small changes occur . . . Tiny, tiny alterations – but on them depend the most immense and terrible consequences. [27: 81–2]

Tolstoy achieves his supreme realism by tracing tiny alterations of consciousness. Chekhov's plays and stories demonstrate that it is not momentous but daily actions that matter most. In *Uncle Vanya*, Elena Andreevma briefly speaks for the author when she observes: "Ivan Petrovich, you are an educated, intelligent man, and I should think that you would see that the world is being destroyed not by crime and fire but . . . by all these petty squabbles" [28: 191].

By the same logic, there can never be a comprehensive *theory* of ethics. On the contrary, ethics is a matter of sensitivity to particular *cases*. In this sense, Tolstoy stands for a revival of casuistry in the original sense of the word. When Levin and Pierre finally find they can make good moral decisions, Tolstoy does not state the principle by which they decide, because there is no principle. Instead, the author lists a page of decisions they make correctly, case by case. Ethical judgment can be improved not by learning some abstraction but by careful observation, empathy, and reflection on particular instances. One reason realist novels are so important is that they give us richer descriptions of complex cases, including people's inner speech, than we ever encounter in daily life, much less in the works of psychologists or philosophers.

Because no theory can guarantee the right decision, we must take responsibility for our actions at each present moment. As Bakhtin liked to say, there is no alibi. He objects to surrendering one's sense of right and wrong to an ideology, a church, the Party, or anything larger than ourselves. Marxism or revolutionism notwithstanding, "there is no person in general, there is me, there is a definite concrete other: my close friend, my contemporary (social humanity), the past and future of real people" [29: 117]. Choice begins with my "singular singularity": "That which can be accomplished by me [right now], cannot be accomplished by anyone else, ever" [29: 112].

Notes

1   See [17] for an account of the movement and its significance.
2   See Malia's note on the derivation of the word [1: 18].
3   Some attribute "The Catechism of a Revolutionary" to Bakunin and Nechaev together –
     e.g. Dmytryshyn [10: 241].

4 On the courtship and its relation to Dostoevsky's novel *The Gambler*, see [30; 151–69; 31].

5 Letter of May 3, 1888 [32: 165].

6 Letter of Aug. 27, 1888 [32: 165].

7 Letter of Mar. ?, 1886 [32: 111–13].

8 Translation amended [from 33: 57].

9 The chemical theory of resonance, a consequence of quantum physics, held that the structural formula of a molecule is obtained by the superposition of all the possible individual structures – their "resonance." This theory was rejected for displaying agnosticism, subjective idealism, and mechanism [see 34: 432–6].

10 On Chicherin and legality, see [18: 25–6; 35; 36; 37].

11 One historian, working on the assumption that virtually every educated person had read *Signposts*, even used its circulation figures as a step in calculating the intelligentsia's size [see 38: 7].

12 "Prosaics" is my own coinage of long standing [see 39; 40; 41].

References

1. Malia, Martin (1961). "What Is the Intelligentsia?" in Richard Pipes, ed., *The Russian Intelligentsia*. Columbia University Press, New York, 1–18.

2. Pipes, Richard (1961). "The Historical Evolution of the Russian Intelligentsia," in Richard Pipes, ed., *The Russian Intelligentsia*. Columbia University Press, New York, 47–62.

3. Elkin, Boris (1961). "The Russian Intelligentsia on the Eve of the Revolution," in Richard Pipes, ed., *The Russian Intelligentsia*. Columbia University Press, New York, 32–46.

4. Berdyaev, Nicolas (1960). *The Origin of Russian Communism*. University of Michigan Press, Ann Arbor.

5. Gleason, Abbott (1980). *Young Russia: The Genesis of Russian Radicalism in the 1860s*. University of Chicago Press, Chicago.

6. Herzen, Alexander (1968). *My Past and Thoughts: The Memoirs of Alexander Herzen*, vol. 2, trans. Constance Garnett. Alfred A. Knopf, New York.

7. Turgenev, Ivan (1966). *Fathers and Sons*, ed. Ralph Matlaw. Norton, New York.

8. Dostoevsky, Fyodor (1963). *The Possessed*, trans. Constance Garnett. Modern Library, New York.

9. Hingley, Ronald (1967). *Nihilists: Russian Radicals and Revolutionaries in the Reign of Alexander II (1855–81)*. Delacorte, New York.

10. Nechaev, Sergei (1967). "The Catechism of a Revolutionary," in Basil Dmytryshyn, ed., *Imperial Russia: A Source Book, 1700–1917*. Holt, Rinehart, New York, 241–6.

11. Paperno, Irina (1988). *Chernyshevsky and the Age of Realism: A Study in the Semiotics of Behavior*. Stanford University Press, Stanford, CA.

12. Gershenzon, Mikhail (1986). "Creative Self-Consciousness," in Marshall S. Shatz and Judith E. Zimmerman, eds., *Signposts: A Collection of Articles on the Russian Intelligentsia*. Charles Schlacks Jr., Irvine, CA. 51–69.

13. Dostoevsky, Fyodor (1950). *Crime and Punishment*, trans. Constance Garnett. Modern Library, New York.

14. Bulgakov, Sergei (1986). "Heroism and Asceticism (Reflections on the Religious Nature of the Russian Intelligentsia)," in Marshall S. Shatz and Judith E. Zimmerman, eds., *Signposts: A Collection of Articles on the Russian Intelligentsia*. Charles Schlacks Jr., Irvine, CA, 17–49.

15. Berdiaev, Nikolai (1986). "Philosophical Verity and Intelligentsia Truth," in Marshall S. Shatz and Judith E. Zimmerman, eds., *Signposts: A Collection of Articles on the Russian Intelligentsia*. Charles Schlacks Jr., Irvine, CA, 1–16.

16. Dostoevsky, Fyodor (1994). *A Writer's Diary*, vol. 1, trans. Kenneth Lantz. Northwestern University Press, Evanston, IL.

17. Geifman, Anna (1993). *Thou Shalt Kill: Revolutionary Terrorism in Russia, 1984–1917.* Princeton University Press, Princeton.

18. Schapiro, Leonard (1961). "The Pre-Revolutionary Russian Intelligentsia and the Legal Order," in Richard Pipes, ed., *The Russian Intelligentsia*. Columbia University Press, New York, 19–31.

19. Trotsky, Leon (1971). *Literature and Revolution*. University of Michigan Press, Ann Arbor.

20. Dostoevsky, Fyodor (1976). *The Brothers Karamazov*, ed. Ralph Matlaw. Norton, New York.

21. Tolstoy, Leo (1965). *Anna Karenina*, trans. Constance Garnett, rev. Leonard J. Kent and Nina Berberova. Modern Library, New York.

22. Herzen, Alexander (1979). *From the Other Shore and The Russian People and Socialism*, trans. Moura Budberg and Richard Wollheim. Oxford University Press, Oxford.

23. Struve, Peter (1986). "The Intelligentsia and Revolution," in Marshall S. Shatz and Judith E. Zimmerman, eds., *Signposts: A Collection of Articles on the Russian Intelligentsia*. Charles Schlacks Jr., Irvine, CA, 115–29.

24. Tolstoy, Leo (1968). *War and Peace*, trans. Ann Dunnigan, Signet, New York.

25. Bakhtin, Mikhail (1984). *Problems of Dostoevsky's Poetics*, trans. Caryl Emerson. University of Minnesota Press, Minneapolis.

26. Bakhtin, Mikhail (1981). *The Dialogic Imagination: Four Essays*, trans. Caryl Emerson and Michael Holquist. University of Texas Press, Austin, TX.

27. Tolstoy, Leo (1961). *Recollections and Essays*, trans. Aylmer Maude. Oxford University Press, London.

28. Chekhov, Anton (1964). *The Major Plays*, trans. Ann Dunnigan. Signet, New York.

29. Bakhtin, Mikhail M. (1986). "K filosofii postupka," in *Filosofiia i sotsiologiia nauki i tekhniki* [for 1984–5]. Academy of Sciences, Moscow, 80–160.

30. Frank, Joseph (1995). *Dostoevsky: The Miraculous Years, 1865–1871*. Robson, London.

31. Morson, Gary Saul (2003). "Introduction: Writing like Roulette," in Fyodor Dostoevsky, *The Gambler*, ed. Gary Saul Morson. Modern Library, New York, pp. xi–xliii.

32. Simmons, Ernest J. (1962). *Chekhov: A Biography*. Little, Brown, Boston.

33. Dolgoff, Sam (ed.) (1971). *Bakunin on Anarchy: Selected Works by the Activist-Founder of World Anarchism*. Vintage, New York.

34. Wetter, Gustav A. (1958). *Dialectical Materialism: A Historical and Systematic Survey of Philosophy in the Soviet Union*, trans. Peter Heath. Praeger, New York.

35. Hamburg, G. M. (ed.) (1998). *Liberty, Equality, and the Market: Essays by B. N. Chicherin*. Yale University Press, New Haven.

36. Morson, Gary Saul (1998). "Foreword: Why Read Chicherin?" in G. M. Hamburg, (ed.) (1998). *Liberty, Equality, and the Market: Essays by B. N. Chicherin*. Yale University Press, New Haven, pp. ix–xxix.

37. Hamburg, G. M. (1998). "An Eccentric Vision: The Political Philosophy of B. N. Chicherin," in G. M. Hamburg, ed., *Liberty, Equality, and the Market: Essays by B. N. Chicherin*. Yale University Press, New Haven, 1–65.

38. Read, Christopher (1979). *Religion, Revelation, and the Russian Intelligentsia, 1900–1912: The "Vekhi" Debate and its Intellectual Background*. Macmillan, London.

39. Morson, Gary Saul (1988). "Prosaics: An Approach to the Humanities," *American Scholar*, 47/4: 515–28.

40. Morson, Gary Saul (1987). *Hidden in Plain View: Narrative and Creative Potentials in "War and Peace."* Stanford University Press, Stanford, CA.

41. Morson, Gary Saul, and Emerson, Caryl (1990). *Mikhail Bakhtin: Creation of a Prosaics.* Stanford University Press, Stanford, CA.

Further Reading

Berdyaev, Nicolas (1947). *The Russian Idea*, trans. R. M. French. Beacon, Boston.

Berlin, Isaiah (1994). *Russian Thinkers.* Penguin, London.

Billington, James H. (1970).*The Icon and the Axe: An Interpretive History of Russian Culture.* Vintage, New York.

Kelly, Aileen M. (1998). *Toward Another Shore: Russian Thinkers between Necessity and Chance.* Yale University Press, New Haven.

Schapiro, Leonard (1987). *Russian Studies*, ed. Ellen Dahrendorf. Viking, New York.

Venturi, Franco (1966). *Roots of Revolution: A History of the Populist and Socialist Movements in Nineteenth Century Russia.* Grossett and Dunlap, New York.

CHAPTER SEVENTEEN

Russian Modernism

ANDREW WACHTEL

In the first decade of the twentieth century a pleiad of young writers, composers, stage directors, and visual artists burst onto the Russian and then the European artistic scene. From the turn of the century until the late 1920s, these figures (including writers Anna Akhmatova, Aleksandr Blok, Osip Mandelstam, Vladimir Mayakovsky, Boris Pasternak, and Marina Tsvetaeva, composers Aleksandr Scriabin, Igor Stravinsky, and Dmitry Shostakovich, theater directors Vsevelod Meyerhold, and Aleksandr Tairov, movie directors Sergei Eisentstein and Dziga Vertov, and visual artists Nataliia Goncharova, Vassily Kandinsky, Kazimir Malevich, and Vladimir Tatlin), almost all born between 1880 and 1900, created works that captured the attention of cultured Europeans. Almost all of them retain enormous power and appeal to this day. Living in a tumultuous period that spanned the apocalyptic expectations of the fin de siècle, the disappointment of the failed Russian Revolution of 1905, the wanton destruction of the First World War, the Revolution of 1917 and the Civil War that followed in its wake, and the consolidation of the Soviet state, these artists, generally grouped under the heading "modernists," were inevitably witnesses to their epoch, even as they struggled to preserve their artistic autonomy.

As was the case with each previous European cultural movement since neoclassicism, modernism did not originate in Russia, but rather entered Russia as an "import product" with a definite time lag. The earliest works of French modernism date to the 1860s and 1870s (Charles Baudelaire, generally acknowledged to be the "father" of modernism, died in 1867), but it is impossible to speak of a Russian modernism before the mid-1890s. However, Russian artists caught up to their European predecessors before the end of the first decade of the twentieth century and, by the 1910s and 1920s, took a dominant "exporter" role in this trans-European movement, which is distinguished less by the similarity of the artistic work produced by various "modernists" than by the broadly shared mindset or world view these disparate artists held.

There is no generally accepted definition of what constitutes modernism, nor which works and artists should be accounted modernist. The confusion is certainly not for lack of effort at definition, as the literature on modernism and its various national incarnations is vast, but rather it results from the enormous variety of work that might be considered modernist and the attempts by critics to classify this work based on many different criteria. In the Russian context, some critics have defined modernism quite narrowly, taking into account only those artists and works that fit into a clearly defined time period and that shared an aesthetic and an undergirding philosophy – at their most strict, such definitions focus on the so-called avant-garde, particularly in approximately the decade after 1909. Other critics, however, prefer to consider a broad group of writers and artists whose work and thought displays "modernist tendencies": in this case one can go back to Tolstoy and Dostoevsky, forward to the 1960s, and include almost everything in between. In this chapter, I will take a middle ground, examining works of writers, artists, composers, film-makers, and theater directors from the mid-1890s until the late 1920s that share key features that distinguish them from the works of their predecessors and successors (as well as from the copious non-modernist work of their contemporaries). Although not every one of these characteristics can be found in each work I call modernist, in broad strokes I would identify the following as key features of Russian modernism.

1. Rather than attempting to reflect or comment on the phenomenal reality of the world as perceived by a "normal" (read bourgeois or aristocratic) viewer, the modernist work focuses on the idiosyncratic perspective of the artist, which is frequently claimed to reflect the world as "it really is" (hidden or noumenal reality). In the most extreme cases, art creates its own universe, divorced from the apparent reality of our world. As a corollary, the modernist work often foregrounds mystical, irrational, or spiritual elements that had rarely been treated (except satirically) in the literature of the second half of the nineteenth century.
2. The modernist work strives for originality, particularly formal originality.
3. The modernist work displays a disdain for traditional "good taste," and is not immediately comprehensible to the uninitiated reader or spectator. Even when certain groups of modernists make use of "popular" or "mass" culture, they refigure this material in ways that make it incomprehensible to the masses. As a result, modernist art takes on a certain hermetic quality and must be explicated if it is to be understood and appreciated. The manifesto therefore takes on central importance in modernist culture, and for many modernists theory becomes inseparable from creative work.
4. Although there were many great individual modernist artists, modernism as a whole displays a strong penchant for collective/collaborative artistic expression expressed in almanacs, journals, exhibitions, manifestos, and theatrical productions.
5. Intermediality was a particular feature of Russian modernism. Many leading writers had tried their hand at visual art or musical composition; rare was the visual artist who did not produce literary or manifesto texts, and so forth.
6. Russian modernism exhibits a strong utopian streak. This is related to its goal of remaking rather than describing the world.
7. The modernist artist often attempts to blur the distinction between art and life. As Irina Paperno puts it:

    the Symbolists [and this tendency can be found in modernism in general] aspired to merge the antitheses of life and art into a unity. Art was proclaimed to be a force capable of, and destined for, the "creation of life" (*tvorchestvo zhizni*), while "life" was viewed as an object of artistic creation or as a creative act. In this sense, art turned into "real life" and "life" turned into art; they became one. For the artist no separation existed between "man" and "poet," between personal life (*zhizn'*) and artistic (creative) activity (*tvorchestvo*).[1]

This was often an uncomfortable mix, responsible for a host of broken lives and suicides; at the same time it created a hothouse environment conducive to artistic creativity.

One way to begin a discussion of how modernism sets itself apart from its immediate predecessors is to contrast statements about "typical" works of art from the realist and modernist periods made by their respective creators. The first is in a letter that Lev Tolstoy wrote to Nikolai Strakhov in 1876 responding to a question about the meaning of *Anna Karenina*. "If I wanted through words to say everything that I wished to express in my novel, then I would have to write the same novel that I wrote from the beginning."[2] The second is by Malevich in his pamphlet "From Cubism and Futurism to Suprematism," a pamphlet that features his notorious Black Square on the cover: "I have transformed myself *in the zero of form* and have fished myself out of the *rubbishy slough of academic art*. I have destroyed the ring of the horizon and got out of the circle of objects, the horizon ring that has imprisoned the artist and the forms of nature."[3]

Tolstoy's statement is, first of all, in a private letter and in response to a genuine query from an actual reader (simultaneously one of Russia's leading critics), one of many thousands who had enjoyed his novel either in serial form or in its final version. Strakhov's interest points to the fact that normal well-educated Russians actually read Tolstoy's work and were curious enough about what he wished to say to ask him. Their fascination with the novel is not surprising. As any reader will recall, the story that Tolstoy tells in *Anna Karenina* is filled with references to and connections with contemporary Russian life and is therefore accessible to a broad spectrum of readers. It is written in a language quite close to the idiom spoken by educated Russians of Tolstoy's day, and it was seen and reviewed by all the major critics. Tolstoy feels no necessity to communicate his understanding of the meaning of his work to an individual reader, at least in part because he can reasonably imagine that readers should be able to figure out for themselves what it means (though naturally they did not understand every nuance that Tolstoy put into his work). In any case, even had Tolstoy wished to explain the novel, he claims to find it impossible to do so because the actual words in which his story is told are the most adequate means to convey his meaning – indeed, he insists that those words are the only way in which his meaning could be conveyed. The fact that Tolstoy wrote and rewrote his novels many times is well known, and this indicates that he had a burning desire to say things precisely, just as he did say them. His willingness to publish the novel was an indication that, whatever difficulties he might have had in expressing his meaning, the search was over and the text could now stand on its own.

By contrast to Tolstoy's novel, Malevich's *Black Square* and other Suprematist works had been seen by relatively few viewers. They were painted in a visual language far removed from that comprehensible to educated Russians in their "normal life," and the meaning of the work was to them completely opaque. Rather than reflecting some realities of Russian life, Malevich's work creates its own reality, which explicitly rejects the possibility of correspondence between the work and the world. More importantly, even from the artist's point of view, the meaning of the work is not seen to be entirely explicable from the work itself. To become legible, it requires explanation in the form of the public manifesto. Finally, the particular work should be seen as part of an ongoing artistic experiment rather than as a finished project. The black square is a kind of artistic ground zero from which Malevich would move to a red square, various geometrical monochrome shapes, and so forth, all in the service and the creation of a new, parallel artistic world.

Malevich's *Black Square* and his commentaries on it come at the culmination of some twenty years of developments in Russian modernism. In order to understand how we get from *Anna Karenina* to the *Black Square* we must move back in time to the beginnings of the Russian modernist movement. In 1894 Valery Briusov published, at his own expense, a series of volumes entitled *Russian Symbolists*. As Joan Grossman puts it: "Bryusov later maintained that the purpose of these volumes was to provide models of various poetic forms. Moreover, by asserting that there *was* a Russian Symbolist school, he hoped to create one and ultimately to win acceptance for the new poetry."[4] As his diary reveals, Briusov's artistic position was directly related to his search for a life role: "Talent, even genius, by honest means earns only gradual success, if that. That's not enough! For me it's not enough. I must choose another way . . . And I see it: Decadence. Yes! Whatever one may say, whether it is false, or ridiculous, it is moving ahead, developing, and the future belongs to it, especially when it finds a worthy leader. And that leader will be I! Yes, I."[5] Note the way that theory has run ahead of artistic practice here; Briusov first comes to the idea of creating modernist work and only then does he actually create it.

For Briusov and the first generation of Russian modernists the key cultural desiderata were to broaden the themes available to literature (most particularly to jettison the broadly held expectation in Russia that literature should fulfill a social function), and to focus on formal issues. Chief among the themes that the Decadents pioneered in Russian literature were the mystical and the erotic. Thus, Briusov's notorious one-line poem "O, zakroi tvoi blednye nogi" (Oh, close up your pale legs) (1894) can be seen as a typical early modernist literary experiment insofar as it lacks any social point and foregrounds the erotic in a way that previous generations of writers would not have accepted.

The aestheticism of the first generation of Russian Symbolists was extended and advertised in a series of brilliant and opulently produced cultural journals that took a leading role in introducing new European cultural developments to Russia as well as providing an outlet for new Russian artistic work and a re-evaluation of earlier cultural production. The first of these journals, *Mir iskusstva* (The World of Art), began publication in 1898 and continued through 1904. It was followed by *Vesy* (The Scales, 1904–9) and *Zolotoe runo* (*The Golden Fleece*, 1906–9). A key feature of all these journals was their inclusion not merely of literary, but also of philosophical and critical texts, as well as original works of visual art. They thus embodied two central principles of modernism – the spirit of collective artistic enterprise and the translatability of various artistic media.

The decadent generation of modernists focused primarily on aesthetic issues and can therefore be seen primarily as a reaction against the prevailing trends of Russian nineteenth-century literature. What they lacked was a philosophical foundation, which was provided by the so-called Symbolists. This group of poets and thinkers, most importantly Andrei Bely, Aleksandr Blok, and Viacheslav Ivanov, further developed the formal and aesthetic program that had animated the work of their immediate predecessors, but they introduced an apocalyptic thematic derived from the thought of the Russian religious philosopher Vladimir Solovev, as well as a strong Nietzschean element. Of particular importance to Russian modernist thought was Solovev's insistence on the dualistic nature of the world (a world of phenomenal appearance hiding one of noumenal reality), his search for universal harmony through the symbol of Sophia (the eternal feminine principle), and his expectation of an imminent apocalypse.

The very titles of some of Bely's essays from the first decade of the twentieth century ("The Forms of Art," "Symbolism as Worldview," "The Apocalypse in Russian Poetry," "The Magic of Words") indicate the spiritual and mystical nature of his artistic search, one that he pursued not merely in theoretical work but also in such important literary texts as his *Four Symphonies* (again, the very title of the work indicates the melding of the arts, in this case musical composition and literature). Ivanov, trained as a classicist, complemented Bely's Solovevian strivings with a Nietzschean-inspired vision of the world as balanced between Dionysian and Apollonian elements. For both Ivanov and Bely, the artist becomes a "theurge," able to mediate between the world of surface forms and that of deeper spiritual reality. As such, the artist's mission is not to reflect the reality of surrounding life but rather to reveal the true meaning of the world that is generally hidden behind that surface reality. The symbol plays an exceptionally important role in this process, for it reveals the correspondences between an object in the world and its transcendental meaning.

Beginning in 1905, Ivanov's St Petersburg apartment became the site of a cultural salon that drew a glittering array of the most talented modernists.

> The legendary Wednesday gatherings, beginning late in the evening and extending far into the night, brought together poets, artists, and philosophers for readings, criticism and philosophical debate . . . The list of visitors to those Wednesday events included virtually every significant poet of the time (not only the Symbolists but also the Acmeists and Futurists, some of whom had their public "debuts" there), as well as a host of leading figures from other areas of Russian culture.[6]

Blok's 1901 poem "Predchustvuiu tebia" (I apprehend you) is a typical example of the poetic work of the Symbolists in the years before the 1905 Revolution:

> *And with longing and love you will shake off*
> *The heavy dream of everyday consciousness.*
> (V. Solovev)

> I apprehend You. The years pass by –
> Yet in constant form, I apprehend You.

> The whole horizon is aflame - impossibly sharp,
> And mute, I wait, – with longing and with love.

> The whole horizon is aflame, and your appearance near.
> And yet I fear that You will change your form,

Give rise to impudent suspicion
By changing Your familiar contours in the end.

Oh, how I'll fall – so low and bitter,
Defeated by my fatal dreams!

How sharp is the horizon! Radiance is near.
And yet I fear that You will change your form.

The poem's epigraph from Solovev both invokes Blok's spiritual inspiration and calls on the reader to slough off the weight of everyday reality in order, presumably, to see beyond it. Blok sets up a sharp contrast between the poetic "I" and the object of his perception (its capitalized, second-person-singular pronoun hinting at a link with the divine). What precisely the poetic "I" sees is nebulous, but a spirit of apocalyptic foreboding hovers above the whole poem. Of cardinal importance is the symbol of the sun ("the whole horizon is aflame"), which was frequently invoked by the Symbolists in connection with the apocalyptic image of the "woman clothed in the sun" (derived from the image in John 12: 1).

In the wake of the failed Russian Revolution of 1905, Symbolism underwent a certain crisis, as its apocalyptic predictions failed to materialize. But, even if some of the ideological expectations of symbolism fell away, its essential aesthetic stance and assumptions remained in place, as could be seen in Blok's "lyric drama" *Balaganchik* (The Puppet Booth) (1906). Like the journal, theatrical production was an exceptionally important locus of Russian modernist artistic practice, because theatre was by nature a collective enterprise in which text, music, sets, and costumes blended into an artistic whole – for the modernists, then, the theatrical production was an ideal *Gesamtkunstwerk* (total work of art), a concept borrowed from the artistic vision (and to some extent practice) of Richard Wagner. As opposed to Wagner, however, who wrote the music and libretto for his operas as well as designed the theatre in which they were ideally to be performed, Russian modernists tended to work in creative teams, producing exceptionally powerful theatrical works.

The text of *The Puppet Booth* can be seen as a sharp satire on the Symbolist movement. It opens with a group of puppet-like figures waiting unsuccessfully for the end of the world, and devolves into a grotesque *commedia dell'arte* derived love triangle. Staged by the exceptionally fertile director Vsevolod Meyerhold (who also played the lead role of Pierrot), with music by Mikhail Kuzmin (an important Symbolist writer as well, and the author of *Kryl'ia* (Wings) (1907), the first openly gay Russian literary work), with costumes and sets by Nikolai Sapunov, the production was notable for Meyerhold's embrace of stylization rather than realist mimesis. An eyewitness commented:

> The entire stage is hung at the sides and rear with blue drapes; this expanse of blue serves as a background as well as reflecting the color of the settings in the little booth erected on the stage. This booth has its own stage, curtain, prompter's box, and proscenium opening. Instead of being masked with the conventional border, the flies, together with all the ropes and wires, are visible to the audience. When the entire set in the booth is hauled aloft, the audience in the actual theatre sees the whole process.[7]

The production caused a scandal, because of its unconventionality, because of its satirical treatment of the Solovevian strivings of Blok's symbolist colleagues, and because the love triangle could be interpreted as a literary recasting of the overheated relationship between Blok, Bely, and Blok's wife, Liubov Mendeleeva. As such it was a dramatic illustration of one of the central tenets of modernism – the belief that art and life, rather than being separate realms of activity, should be merged as much as possible.

Be that as it may, in its aestheticized repudiation of a social role for art or the artist, its resurrection of the stylized theatre of the Italian *commedia*, its blending of verbal, visual, and sonic art, the play and this particular production stand as archetypal examples of Russian modernism. The same basic themes would be reprised a few years later in one of the first major works of Russian modernism to have a successful "export" existence – the ballet *Petrushka*, which was premiered by Diaghilev's celebrated Ballets Russes company in Paris in 1911. Like *The Puppet Booth*, *Petrushka* was a typical Russian *Gesamtkunstwerk* in that it blended the talents of a number of leading Russian modernists, including the young composer Stravinsky, the designer/artist Alexandre Benois, and the choreographer Mikhail Fokine. Insofar as it built on the *commedia* tradition that had already penetrated Russia in the previous decade, *Petrushka* can be seen as a phenomenally successful, but not wholly original step in the development of Russian modernism.

Its successor in the Ballets Russes repertoire, Stravinsky's *Sacre de Printemps* (The Rite of Spring) (1913), was far more original, turning the technique of the *Gesamtkunstwerk* to primitivist material. Primitivism was an important strain of modernism throughout Europe, nowhere more so than in Russia, whose peasants in many respects still lived a fully pre-modern existence. Thus, while West European artists needed to "import" their primitivism from Africa and Asia, Russians could use native traditions that the literature and culture of previous generations had ignored. As Richard Taruskin has shown, Stravinsky's music both in *Petrushka* and in *The Rite of Spring* makes quite a different use of the folk tradition than had his predecessors.[8] While Russian composers since Glinka and through Stravinsky's teacher Rimsky-Korsakov employed folk melodies, they reharmonized them to fit Western musical models and failed to use rhythmic elements alien to the classical tradition. Stravinsky, who had engaged in fieldwork among Russian villagers, made much fuller use of the peasant musical idiom. In *Sacre* his driving, slashing rhythms and unfamiliar harmonies practically caused a riot when the work premiered in Paris. Stravinsky's music was perfectly complemented by the myth-inspired story of human sacrifice, which was given plastic form in the designs of Nikolai Rerikh and the heavy, primitivist choreography of Vaslav Nijinsky.

While the Ballets Russes troupe was successfully exporting one brand of Russian modernism in the immediate prewar years, modernism in Russia itself underwent a two-pronged development. Two main groupings developed out of the crisis of Symbolism at the end of the first decade of the twentieth century – one, the Futurists, emphasized the destruction of earlier literary and cultural forms, while the other, the Acmeists, focused on the continuity of world cultural traditions. Both groupings, however, shared important traits that link them to the general modernist project – these included an unwillingness to create works that were easily accessible to the bourgeois public and a concomitant rejection of the main artistic genres and practices of the nineteenth century, a concern with the texture of language as such, a strong preference for verse over prose, and a predilection for collective undertakings.

The Russian Futurists burst on the scene with a series of manifestos and public events in the years just before the outbreak of the First World War. The most important group of Futurists originally called themselves *budetliane* (from the Slavic future tense of the word "to be") both in order to distinguish themselves from the Italian futurists who had made themselves notorious in Western Europe beginning around 1909 and to emphasize the nativist elements in their program. As was true of many modernists, the leading futurists tended to work in a variety of media, including visual, literary, and what would today be called performance art. Perhaps their most successful artistic form, however, was the manifesto, whose strident tone and public character fit the movement perfectly.

The most famous of these manifestos, *Poshchechina obshchestvennomu vkusu* (The Face of Public Taste) (1912), might be considered the quintessential modernist text. Co-signed by David Burliuk, Aleksandr Kruchenykh, Vladimir Mayakovsky, and Viktor (later Velimir) Khlebnikov, this pithy screed emphasized, and even exaggerated, the Futurists' break with past literary tradition, calling on Russians to "toss Pushkin, Dostoevsky, Tolstoy, etcetera, from the Steamship of modernity."[9] More recent Russian modernist literature was not spared the ire of the young Futurists either, as they attacked the Symbolists with equal gusto, sneering that all they needed was "a dacha on the river" – "the reward of a tailor."

In place of all these predecessors, the Futurists (the oldest of whom, Burliuk, was barely 30) proposed themselves, issuing four demands to the public "from the heights of skyscrapers" (that quintessential image of the modern city):

> We *order* that the poets' *rights* be revered: 1. To enlarge the scope of the poet's vocabulary with arbitrary and created words (word-novelty). 2 To feel an unquenchable hatred for the language existing before their time. 3. To push from their proud brow with horror the laurel wreath of cheap glory that you have fashioned from bathhouse switches. 4. To stand on the rock of the word "we" amidst a sea of catcalls and outrage.

Each of these demands would be developed further in future manifestos and literary work, though the four original signers would eventually develop them in idiosyncratic ways. The *budetliane* were frequently referred to as "cubo-futurists" as well, which emphasized their connection to the "analytic" experiments in art that had been initiated in Paris by Pablo Picasso and Juan Gris. Just as cubists attempted to break down the visual image into its constituent parts, so the cubo-futurist poets tried to break the word into its smallest possible units – hence the fascination, as noted in the "Slap" manifesto, with arbitrary and created words. The former were the primary province of Kruchenykh, whose *zaum* (transsense) language experiments led to the creation of the following poem: "Dyr, bul, shchyl,/ubeshchur/skum/vy so by/r l ez." Though with one exception the poem's words do not exist in Russian, the sound combinations created here "contain more of the Russian national spirit than all of Pushkin's poetry" according to the 1913 Futurist manifesto "The Word as Such."

If Kruchenykh reveled in the arbitrary, Khlebnikov, probably the greatest pure poet of the Futurists, was more concerned with the creative resources of the Russian language, attempting to use its most basic elements to create a new "universal" idiom whose utopian goal was to reverse the misunderstandings among humans that, in the

Judeo-Christian tradition, are seen to stem from God's introduction of various languages as punishment for the attempt to construct the Tower of Babel.

The 1913 Futurist opera *Pobeda nad solntsem* (Victory over the Sun) stands as the central dramatic production of the cubo-futurists. With a text by Kruchenykh (and prologue by Khlebnikov), music by Mikhail Matiushin, and sets and costumes by Kazimir Malevich, the opera tells the story of a group of Futurists who set as their task to overcome the sun and replace it with its futurian equivalent – electric light. The sun, that favorite apocalyptic image for the symbolists, is simultaneously desacralized and deprived of its place at the center of the natural order. From now on, according to the Futurists, it will be man and man alone who will control his destiny, and he will do so using the technical and verbal resources of the modern world. Although the text is by no means a literary masterpiece, it does effectively capture the raw energy of the early Futurists.

Khlebnikov's prologue emphasizes two elements of Russian Futurist thinking – an exceptional verbal creativity and a strong nationalist impulse. Because theatre was imported to Russia in the eighteenth century from France, practically all the theatrical terms in the language are Russified versions of French words. Khlebnikov, however, invites spectators to sit down and enjoy the play in an idiom that uses Slavic word roots and the morphological rules of Russian to build an entire theatrical vocabulary that is simultaneously intensely playful and, after the initial shock, fully comprehensible.

Malevich's brilliant costume and set designs for this production have survived, and they are far more interesting than the text of the play. Highly volumetric and brightly colored, they mark the switch in Malevich's work from cubism to suprematism – indeed, although there is some controversy on this subject, it appears that the famous *Black Square* made its debut in this production, as a curtain design.

On the same bill with "Victory over the Sun" was *Vladimir Mayakovsky: Tragediia* (Vladimir Mayakovsky: A Tragedy), a two-act drama by Russian Futurism's other poet of genius, which, according to the memoirist Benedikt Lifshits, "abolished the boundary between lyric poetry and drama." Though Mayakovsky collaborated in many of the early Futurist activities, his poetic and political work separated him from his erstwhile companions. Though wildly innovative in terms of his rhyming and metaphors, Mayakovsky used neologisms far more sparingly and was generally uninterested in *zaum* and the primitive. On the other hand, he was far more desirous than his colleagues of using literary work to explore the central themes of modern urban life, and he was a more traditional "romantic" in his foregrounding of the poetic "I" (never separated far from his own "I") in all its strivings and appetites. He shared the utopian impulses of his colleagues, but was much more willing and able than they to connect these to the realities of his time, eventually becoming closely linked with the communist state.

Just as the brash futurists were issuing their very public challenge both to classical Russian literature and to their immediate modernist predecessors, another group began to take shape – the Acmeists. As early as 1909 in the literary journal *Apollon* (whose very name hints at a connection to Ivanov's discussions of the Dionysian and Apollonian nature of culture) began to publish texts that can be seen retrospectively as having initiated the movement. Though clearly inspired by the poetic practice of the Symbolists, the future Acmeists were dismayed at the obscure and mystical sides of Symbolism. Taking as his immediate model the sometime symbolist Innokenty Annensky, the young poet Nikolai Gumilov began to formulate what he called an "organic" poetry that would preserve the best of the recent generation of Russian poetry while eliminating its artificiality and mysticism.

The official debut of Acmeism as a literary movement came in the January 1913 issue of *Apollon*. Like the practice of the Futurists, though very different in tone and content, this "Acmeist" number of the journal contained both manifestos (one by Gumilev and another by Sergei Gorodetsky) and poetic works by Gumilev and Gorodetsky as well as by Vladimir Narbut, Anna Akhmatova, and Osip Mandelstam that were billed as illustrations of the "theoretical views" presented in the manifestos. Of these, Mandelstam's poem "Hagia Sophia" is perhaps the best example of the early Acmeist aesthetic. Mandelstam paints a word picture of this church using precise, even technical language to capture architecture in verse. He emphasizes the "madeness" of the building, attempting to recover Emperor Justinian's thoughts as he built the church, and he focuses on the connectivity of the cultural tradition, noting the fact that exactly 107 of the church's columns were taken from the Temple of Diana at Ephesus. He closes with a hymn to the eternal continuity of classical culture:

> And the spherical, wise building
> The ages and the nations will outlive,
> And the angels' plangent weeping
> will not warp the darkened gilt.

The outbreak of the First World War in the summer of 1914 was a seminal event in the development of European history, and naturally had a major effect on the development of Russian modernist art. The war stranded many leading Russian artists in Western Europe – particularly those close to the Diaghilev troupe. Many chose to stay, especially after the upheaval of the February and October revolutions of 1917 had changed Russia's social and political order forever. As a result, the Russian version of the ballet *Gesamtkunstwerk* became fully naturalized in France, and what had originally been a Russian modernist tradition broadened to include the talents not merely of the émigrés, but also those of Picasso, Gris, Matisse, Poulenc, Satie, and Cocteau, all under Diaghilev's mercurial aegis.

Inside Russia, some artists met the beginning of the war with patriotic enthusiasm. Though few modernist practitioners actually participated in the fighting, one can find patriotic and even chauvinistic works by writers from across a broad spectrum of modernist movements (the Symbolist Fedor Sologub, Acmeist Gumilov, and Futurist Vladimir Burliuk, one of the few Russian modernists killed in action during the war). The majority of Russian modernists, however, were unsure as to how to react. As Richard Stites puts it: "Russian high culture writers and artists had difficulty responding to the war because of reservations about the programmatic or 'occasional' use of art and, for some, because of ambivalence about the war itself. The intellectual idiom of nuances, interior rumination, and transcendent vision fit poorly with such a direct and brutal experience as war."[10]

As the war dragged on, Russia became somewhat isolated from cultural developments in Western Europe, a deprivation that was felt all the more strongly because of the transnational character of modernism. Furthermore, the war tended to turn the public's eye away from culture, making it harder for the various modernists to make their voices, collective or individual, heard. Still, in the period 1914–17 many of the leading modernist writers (including Mayakovsky, Khlebnikov, Akhmatova, Mandelstam, Tsvetaeva, and Pasternak) produced fine collections of poetry or individual poems, important collective art exhibitions were held, innovative theatrical productions went up, and journals such as *Apollon* continued to publish.

At least one key cultural development was initiated during the war years – student discussion groups in Moscow and St Petersburg coalesced to form what would become the Russian Formalist School of literary criticism. Literary and cultural criticism had, to be sure, been part of Symbolist practice. As early as 1901–2 Dmitry Merezhkovsky published his *L. Tolstoy and Dostoevsky*, which interpreted the work of these two novelists through a Solovevian lens, and Bely wrote a series of penetrating theoretical essays in the first decade of the twentieth century. Nevertheless, the formalist school was more radical in its methodology and far-reaching in its influence. The Formalists hoped to make the study of literary and cultural texts a science, and hence they focused on the formal qualities of the text itself rather than extra-textual issues such as its presumed ideological content, historical context, or purported authorial intent. Art, in their formulation, "estranges the world," thereby allowing it to be perceived as it is rather than as it seems. The study of literature, they believed, had to focus on the way texts are constructed, an insight that was aided by their ties to the Futurist innovators whose interest lay with the "word as such." Indeed, a number of the original Formalists, including Viktor Shklovsky and Roman Jakobson, were quite closely connected to the Futurists. Like other modernist movements, the Formalists preferred collective to individual action and expressed themselves in the brash language of the manifesto.

The Bolshevik Revolution of 1917 provided a major impetus to developments in literature and the arts in general. Some of the leading modernist artists opposed the communist takeover and joined the approximately one million Russians who fled the country. Most artists, however, were at least somewhat sympathetic with the Bolshevik desires to remake society, and many were active supporters of the communists, at least in the immediate aftermath of the revolution. The Futurists and their avant-garde compatriots were among the most vocal supporters of the new regime. Believing that their revolutionary artistic experiments presaged and paralleled political developments, they proclaimed themselves the appropriate artistic representatives of the new order. Mayakovsky, for example, wrote a series of works supporting the new regime, most publicly his play *Misteria-Buff*. Premiered for the first anniversary of the Bolshevik Revolution under the direction of Meyerhold (also an ardent supporter of the new regime) with designs by Malevich, the work was characterized as a "heroic, epic, and satirical depiction of our age." The characters in the play are divided between the "clean" (satiric portraits of capitalist exploiters) and the "unclean," the international proletariat who eventually destroy the old order and create a utopian, fully mechanized, promised land.

Although many avant-garde artists were appointed to positions of cultural leadership in the immediate aftermath of the revolution, the incomprehensibility of their work to the working class (and to many of the Bolshevik leaders, whose tastes ran to the bourgeois art of the late nineteenth century) blunted their attempts to take command of Soviet culture. Nevertheless, even if the modernists were not able fully to control Soviet artistic activity, modernist art and literature flourished in the immediate aftermath of the revolution. A particularly powerful group of artists, writers, and theorists grouped around the journal *LEF* (Left Front of Art), which began publication in 1922. In accord with the call from the Bolshevik minister of education Anatoly Lunacharsky for "art to give revolution its mouthpiece," *LEF* published a broad spectrum of artists, writers, and thinkers who wished to create art in the service of the revolution. Among the most important contributors to the journal were Mayakovsky, Aleksandr Rodchenko, Isaac Babel, Eisenstein, and Dzhiga Vertov.

Film, which in the prewar era had played primarily an entertainment role, became a central medium of modernist creativity in the 1920s. A number of the Formalists were fascinated by the potential of film to "bare the device" and reveal the world through estrangement. The technique of montage (or the juxtaposition of filmed images through the editing process) was developed brilliantly in the avant-garde directorial work of Vertov (*Man with a Movie Camera*) (1929) and the more conventionally narrative films of Eisenstein (who had begun his career as a student of Meyerhold) such as *The Battleship Potemkin* (1925). Parallel to the activities of the *LEF* artists were those of the so-called Constructivists. Although primarily a movement in visual arts, Constructivism also played an important role in Russian theatre in the early 1920s, playing an organizing role in a number of seminal productions of Meyerhold and Aleksandr Tairov. The Constructivists believed in the need fully to merge art and life, and shared the utopian proclivities of modernist thinking. Their clean geometric compositions were widely influential in Western Europe in the 1920s.

Of particular importance in the early 1920s was prose fiction, which had previously played a relatively minor role in modernist literary production. To be sure, there had been significant novels by Symbolists, most importantly Bely's *Petersburg* (1916). But in the postrevolutionary years modernist-inflected prose became widespread. Sometimes described as examples of "ornamental prose", these works foreground the linguistic element of the text, using traditionally poetic devices of sound patterning, repetition, and word weaving to achieve their effects. Perhaps the most celebrated piece of revolutionary ornamental prose was Boris Pilniak's novel *Golyi god* (*The Naked Year*, written in 1920), which in hypnotic rhythms provides a collage of images describing the experience of the Russian Civil War in a provincial town. Major modernist poets (including Mandelstam, Pasternak, and Tsvetaeva) also produced prose texts distinguished by complex verbal texture, intricate patterning, and unconventional narrative structure during this period.

By the second half of the 1920s, the modernist experiment in Russia had for the most part run its course, and Soviet literature and visual arts evolved slowly toward a more realist idiom. There is a great deal of controversy as to why this happened. The first scholars to consider the issue focused on the role of the Soviet state. There is certainly no question that in the course of the 1920s the Soviet bureaucracy, headed by the increasingly powerful Joseph Stalin, became less willing to allow the types of artistic experimentation that were the modernist stock in trade. And it is also true that Socialist Realism, proclaimed in 1934 the only acceptable method of artistic production in the USSR, was at least on the surface quite traditional in its presentation.

The fate of OBERIU (*Ob"edineniie real'nogo iskusstva*, Association for Real Art), the last important modernist group to arise in the USSR, is illustrative of the view that the demise of modernism was primarily a result of state intervention. OBERIU, whose leading members were Daniil Kharms, Aleksandr Vvedensky, Nikolai Zabolotsky, and Konstantin Vaginov, was active in Leningrad between 1927 and 1930. Like any self-respecting modernist group, OBERIU prepared a manifesto prior to its public debut, a literary evening entitled "Three Left Hours." The manifesto decried increasing state pressure on leading modernist artists, and contained a typical modernist claim that the art of OBERIU would erase the conventional meanings of things and words to uncover their essence. "Three Left Hours" was criticized severely in the Leningrad Press, however, and the members of OBERIU found it practically impossible to publish their experimental work, particularly after a 1930 critical article branded them "class enemies." Both Kharms and Vvedensky perished during the purges, never to see their major work in print. It came to light only in the 1960s, and then only in Samizdat.

More recently, however, though not denying that state intolerance played a role in the decline of modernism in the USSR, scholars have begun to focus on the internal exhaustion of the modernist impulse within the ranks of the modernists themselves, and also to examine the ways in which the Soviet state, and Socialist Realism as its artistic method, co-opted certain core modernist principles even as they silenced many modernist artists.

The modernist impulse always to "make it new" and "throw it away" could not, after all, be sustained indefinitely. Every period of radical experimentation must be followed by some kind of consolidation, and in many cases the best and most lasting Soviet works beginning in the late 1920s can be read as attempts by once-radical modernists to come to terms with the need for sustainability, legibility, and artistic permanence. This pattern can be seen in the later poetic practice of Pasternak, for example, in the prose writings of Andrei Platonov, in the painting of Malevich, the films of Eisenstein, and in at least some of the music of Shostakovich. In each case, we see an artist who was basically sympathetic to the Soviet state voluntarily "tone down" his more overt modernist practices in an attempt to participate in the state's announced goals of remaking Soviet citizens. Even so, much of the work these artists produced was nevertheless rejected by the authorities and remained unpublished, unseen, or unheard for many years.

As an illustration of this shift, one might examine the 1929 production of Mayakovsky's play *The Bedbug*. Staged by Meyerhold with music by Shostakovich and costumes and designs by a trio of artists who called themselves the Kukryniksy and Rodchenko, this production was one of the last major collective endeavors by the once revolutionary avant-garde. The text, however, was far less brash than those Mayakovsky had produced earlier. Written for the most part in a fully accessible idiom, shorn of the extravagant metaphors and loud propaganda of his earlier dramatic work, the play has as its protagonist the former proletarian Ivan Prisypkin. By the mid-1920s, however, Prisypkin, who has changed his name to the more fashionable Pierre Skrypkin, wants nothing more than to trade his union card for the easy life that can be his by marrying the well-to-do daughter of a NEP-era capitalist. Having jilted his true communist girlfriend Zoya Berezkina, Prisypkin/Skrypkin goes ahead with his marriage, only to perish in a fire at his drunken wedding reception. The second half of the play is set fifty years in the future, when perfect communism has apparently been achieved. Zoya Berezkina, now a research assistant in a scientific laboratory, participates in an experiment to unfreeze and revive someone who has been frozen for fifty years. This turns out to be Prisypkin/Skrypkin, who brings all his old habits into the perfect but sterile world of the communist future. Quite quickly, he infects all he meets with the "diseases" of the 1920s such as alcoholism, love, dancing, and individuality. At the end of the play, to protect the perfect world of the future, he is locked in a zoo cage with only one companion from his former days to keep him company – a bedbug.

The play's message is exceptionally ambiguous. There is no doubt that, in the context of 1920s Russia, Skrypkin appears as a selfish villain, and certainly Mayakovsky himself was well known as a staunch opponent of the bourgeoisification of Soviet life in the mid to late 1920s. At the same time, in the context of the "perfect communist future," Skrypkin seems almost attractive, for the future world has been so completely sanitized that its utopian promise takes on strongly dystopian tones. Ultimately, audiences do not know whether to sympathize with the hapless Skrypkin or to castigate him. The sets and costumes set the story off perfectly – in the first half the Kukryniksy created a completely realistic 1920s backdrop, but this return to realism, while justified by the script, is a far cry from the radical constructivist vision that Meyerhold had espoused in the early 1920s. And the "futuristic" sets and costumes of Rodchenko, while again perfectly in keeping with the play, seem faintly menacing in their cold, black and white starkness. Even Shostakovich's music (certainly not his best nor his most extensive score) lacks the sonic modernism that was so powerfully evoked in his earlier opera *The Nose*, for example.

Finally, there is the intriguing claim that the Soviet state, with Stalin as its leader, essentially usurped the modernist impulse. As a number of scholars have noted, Soviet art of the 1930s retains many of the underlying philosophical premises of modernism even as it rejects some of its most characteristic devices. In particular, Soviet art retains a highly utopian character, and the artist, now refigured in Stalin's words as an "engineer of human souls," retains a position of central importance as mediator between what appears to be true on the surface and its underlying meaning. As the statutes of the Soviet Writers Union put it: "Socialist realism . . . demands of the sincere writer a historically concrete presentation of reality in its revolutionary development."

Regardless of which view one accepts regarding the demise of modernism, it is unquestionably true that by the middle to late 1930s the exceptional artistic creativity characteristic of Russian culture in the first third of the twentieth century had been spent. Experimental literature, art, music, and film would not reappear on the Soviet scene until the late 1950s, when Khrushchev's "thaw" allowed a new generation of artists to rediscover the modernist heritage and to create a late Soviet modernism/postmodernism whose parameters go well beyond the scope of this survey.

Notes

1   Irina Paperno, Introduction, in Paperno and Joan Grossman (eds.), *Creating Life: The Aesthetic Utopia of Russian Modernism*. Stanford University Press, Stanford, CA, 1994, 1.
2   L. N. Tolstoi, *Polnoe sobranie socheninenii*. 90 vols. Khudozhestvennaia Literatura, Moscow, 1928–58, vol. 6w, p. 268; translation mine.

3   John E. Bowlt (ed.), *Russian Art of the Avant Garde*, Thames and Hudson, New York, 1988, 118.
4   Joan Grossman, *Valery Bryusov and the Riddle of Russian Decadence*, University of California Press, Berkeley, 1985, 36–7.
5   Quoted in ibid. 35.
6   Michael Wachtel, Introduction, in Viacheslav Ivanov, *Selected Essays*, trans. Robert Bird, ed. Michael Wachtel, Northwestern University Press, Evanston, IL, 2001, ix.
7   Quoted in Edward Braun, *The Theatre of Meyerhold: Revolution on the Stage*. Drama Book Specialists, New York, 69.
8   Richard Taruskin, *Stravinsky and the Russian Traditions: A Biography of the Works through Mavra*. Berkeley: University of California Press, 1996.
9   V. N. Terekhina and A. P. Zimenkov (1999). *Russkii futurizm. Teoriia, praktika, kritika, vospominaniia*. Nasledie, Moscow, 41; translation mine.
10 Aviel Roshwald and Richard Stites (eds.), *European Culture in the Great War: The Arts, Entertainment, and Propaganda, 1914–1918*. Cambridge University Press, Cambridge, 9.

References

Braun, Edward (1979). *The Theatre of Meyerhold: Revolution on the Stage*. Drama Book Specialists, New York.
Bowlt, John E. (ed.) (1988). *Russian Art of the Avant Garde*. Thames and Hudson, New York.
Grossman, Joan (1985). *Valery Bryusov and the Riddle of Russian Decadence*. University of California Press, Berkeley.
Ivanov, Viacheslav (2001). *Selected Essays*, trans. Robert Bird, ed. Michael Wachtel. Northwestern University Press, Evanston, IL.
Paperno, Irina, and Grossman, Joan (eds.). (1994). *Creating Life: The Aesthetic Utopia of Russian Modernism*. Stanford University Press, Stanford, CA.
Roshwald, Aviel, and Stites, Richard (eds.) (1999). *European Culture in the Great War: The Arts, Entertainment, and Propaganda, 1914–1918*. Cambridge University Press, Cambridge.
Taruskin, Richard (1996). *Stravinsky and the Russian Traditions: A Biography of the Works through Mavra*. University of California Press, Berkeley.
Terekhina V. N., and Zimenkov, A. P. (1999). *Russkii futurizm. Teoriia, praktika, kritika, vospominaniia*. Nasledie, Moscow.
Tolstoi, L. N. (1928–58). *Polnoe sobranie socheninenii*. 90 vols. Khudozhestvennaia Literatura, Moscow.

Further Reading

Belyi, Andrei (1978). Petersburg. trans. Robert Maguire and John Malmstad. Indiana University Press, Bloomington, IN.
Erlich, Victor (1994). *Modernism and Revolution: Russian Literature in Transition*. Harvard University Press, Cambridge, MA.
Gasparov, Boris, Hughes, Robert P., and Paperno, Irina (eds.) (1992). *Cultural Mythologies of Russian Modernism: From the Golden Age to the Silver Age*. University of California Press, Berkeley.
Kelly, Catriona, and Lovell, Stephen (eds.) (2000). *Russian Literature, Modernism and the Visual Arts*. Cambridge University Press, Cambridge.

Kutik, Ilya, and Wachtel, Andrew (eds.). *From the Ends to the Beginning: A Bilingual Anthology of Russian Verse.* www.russianpoetry.net. This anthology contains selections of poetry by all the leading modernist poets mentioned in the article. Many of the poems are accompanied by audio recordings in the original Russian, in some cases read by the authors themselves.

Langen, Timothy, and Weir, Justin (2000). *Eight Twentieth-Century Russian Plays.* Northwestern University Press, Evanston, IL.

Painter, Kirsten Blythe (2006). *Flint on a Bright Stone: A Revolution of Precision and Restraint in American, Russian, and German Modernism.* Stanford University Press, Stanford, CA.

Perloff, Marjorie (1986). *The Futurist Moment: Avant-garde, Avant Guerre, and the Language of Rupture.* University of Chicago Press, Chicago.

Rudnitsky, Konstantin (1988). *Russian and Soviet Theater, 1905–1932,* trans. Roxane Permar. *Harry Abrams,* New York.

Striedter, Jurij (1989). *Literary Structure, Evolution, and Value: Russian Formalism and Czech Structuralism Reconsidered.* Harvard University Press, Cambridge, MA.

Wachtel, Andrew (ed.) (1998). *Petrushka: Sources and Contexts.* Northwestern University Press, Evanston.

CHAPTER EIGHTEEN

Russia's Popular Culture in History and Theory

LOUISE MCREYNOLDS

"Popular culture" has long enjoyed a tortuous history because of the ways in which intellectual elites continue to co-opt it. The concept became particularly problematic from the middle of the nineteenth century, when many of the sweeping social and political changes associated with modernity forced both "popular" and "culture" to be distinguished according to scholarly, not just aesthetic, criteria. As a consequence, both components became embedded in debates about sociopolitical hierarchies built along an historical continuum. The elites condemned as "popular" that which in their view aroused an instinctual rather than a cerebral response, and they politicized aesthetics when they argued that it was their obligation to cultivate the undiscriminating masses to bring them up to their own level of sophisticated appreciation. Academics served as handmaidens to politicians in the resultant consensus that relegated the popular as inferior to the elite, and implicitly the West sat at the top of this hierarchy of values.

The politics that had appropriated the popular put Tsarist Russia's intellectual elites in a particular predicament because they considered themselves "Western," an evaluation of the country as a whole that could hardly survive the Bolshevik Revolution. Later, the Second World War and subsequent decolonization exposed some of the moral inferiorities of Western elites, which launched an academic scramble for new answers to old questions. Political scientists supplied one of the first answers, and they did so by constructing another hierarchy, this one based on a division of the world into thirds. The West again sat atop, the communist countries now in second place, which distinguished them from the former colonies who became collectivized pejoratively as the Third World. By the 1960s, in reaction against the value judgments implicit in this division, many scholars had determined to destroy the hierarchical prejudices. They ventured across disciplinary boundaries, spearheading what became the Cultural Studies movement, which aimed to invest non-elitist culture with political as well as aesthetic legitimacy.

Privileging the popular, Cultural Studies upended the hierarchy. This presented a special problem for Russian/Soviet Studies, because the American strategy for fighting the cultural battles of the cold war had depended upon the presumed superiority

of Westernized elites. So, while in some areas "popular culture" had become revital-
ized as a category of analysis, it remained peripheral to the study of Russia, Tsarist
and Soviet, because studies of that country continued to be mired in a historiography
that centered around Russia's relationship to the West. In fact, the pre-Cultural
Studies paradigm provided an important analytical frame because it highlighted sharp
contrasts between Russia and the West. This paradigm originated in the historical
context that transformed "popular culture" into "mass society" and is closely associated with the possibilities for mass consumption that were multiplying at the turn of
the twentieth century; it would have political implications with the explosion of revolution in Russia in 1917.

Before the advent of the industrialization that had precipitated mass society, when
the estate-based population could be sharply differentiated between lord and peasant,
"popular" was employed meaningfully from its Latin root, *popularis*, "of the people."
Combining it with culture evoked Roman poet Juvenal's dismissal of popular ambitions as the instinctual desire for "bread and circuses." The French Revolution, in
contrast, testified that the people could not be politically discounted so easily. One
of the sharpest reactions against this revolution inspired the Romantic movement,
led by literati who blamed French intellectuals of the Enlightenment for their blind
faith in the superiority of reason over the irrational in human nature. These Romantics
anticipated the emergence of anthropology as a scientific discipline when they identified their uneducated, largely peasant populations as the ahistorical repositories of
"authentic" ethnic cultures. Primarily concerned with the uniqueness of each national
identity, Romanticism brought particularly poignant problems to its Russian disciples,
who were struggling to find a shared identity with the massive peasant population.
The relationship of the intellectuals to the people, and the question of which one
would shape the national culture, became especially strained because of the depth of
that divide.

In nineteenth-century Europe, the combined aftershocks of the political revolution
in France and the industrial revolution in England transformed the rural peasantry
into an urban proletariat, one increasingly outspoken in its demands to participate in
public life. In his *Culture and Anarchy* (1869), Matthew Arnold became among the
first to connect politics directly to culture by arguing that the latter could be used
to smooth over the class differences that threatened revolution. Arnold envisioned a
national unity based on a shared culture that he characterized as "the best that has
been thought or known in the world." His definition implicitly favored elite culture,
a value judgment that underscored the connection between aesthetic and political
values. This underscored the West's sense of superiority, and in ways that stimulated
increased identification with Western cultural values by Russian intellectuals who
shared his ambitions.

The most dramatic cultural repercussions of the industrial revolution created new
avenues for mobility, social and political. Once aesthetics could be packaged and made
readily available, they surrendered their status as an identifying marker that distinguished the elite. Industrialization facilitated the mass production of so many items,
from clothing to literature, and the mass distribution of them threatened to overwhelm
many of the commonly accepted boundaries that had differentiated social groups from
each other. A new kind of society was emerging, one based in a commercialization of
culture that allowed "popular" to become a measurement that was registered by

numbers of purchases, by "mass" consumption. Anxieties heightened among those who had the most status to lose, and the cultural elites feared becoming overwhelmed, as had happened to social elites by their nemeses, the bourgeois middle classes.

Taking shape in the middle, this new culture eschewed the pretense that the arts inhabited a space separate from politics. Writing in 1915, American literary critic Van Wyck Brooks entered "middlebrow" into the social lexicon with his search for a "genial middle ground" between "highbrow" and "lowbrow." Like Arnold, Brooks feared the sharp cultural divide that would be politically deleterious. His pseudo-scientific cranial distinctions borrowed from a political vocabulary that charted the ascent of humankind in such a way as to justify the favorable historical position occupied by educated Anglo-Saxons, and therefore his work ultimately exacerbated debates about hierarchy. Middlebrow exuded the same vulgarity as "bourgeois" in matters of taste, and it acquired political meaning through its implied suggestion of leveling. Including middlebrow as a category forced the highbrow to come up with new techniques to maintain his position atop the sociopolitical hierarchy. Lowbrow now referred to the crudest of cultural forms; later assignations of it as "pulp" and "trash" equated form with content in unambiguous terminology.

The commercialization of culture was associated with the purchasing power and tastes of the middlebrow, which contributed to a reformulation of understandings of popular culture. Parallel to commercialization, the nascent discipline of anthropology was applying methodologies from social science to Romanticism's view of popular culture by separating the commercial, or that which had been produced *for* the people, from those cultural artifacts that had been produced *by* them. The efforts to use science rather than aesthetics to critique cultures, articulated most eloquently by Franz Boas, a contemporary of Brooks, were pivotal to undermining the role of hierarchy. Emphasizing the uniqueness of each group, the social sciences made the intrinsic worth of the various cultures relative to each other. This held potential danger for the European elites because it subverted the use of specifically Western aesthetics as the fundamental criteria of value.

Writing against the backdrop of the Bolshevik Revolution and the rise of fascism in the 1920s, Italian Marxist Antonio Gramsci tried to sort through this *mélange* of ideas about mass and popular, commercial and bourgeois, and the displacement of cultural elites from positions of authority. Gramsci became the first to apply these conflated views of culture as a factor in historical analysis when he used them to explain a flaw in Marx's historical trajectory. Trying to understand why the Italian proletariat had not seized political power, Gramsci feared that bourgeois culture was pre-empting the revolutionary potential of the working classes. A Marxist, he accepted class politics as a given, and he connected culture to politics through an understanding of ideology that was more fluid than the social determinists of the nineteenth century had allowed. Invoking the term "hegemony" to describe restraints that were psychological rather than specifically economic, Gramsci showed culture to be a protean sphere in which social and political relations were formed and reified according to ideological values, in this case, capitalistic. Thus did he enter the new thoughts about culture into broader conversations about historical change.

Concurring with Gramsci that culture was ideological, Bolshevik Leon Trotsky argued for the necessity of a proletarian culture to secure the transition to socialism in the emergent Soviet Union. The infant state even set up a short-lived organization to promote this, the Proletkul't. Then, as the Communist Party increasingly asserted itself throughout national life, it replaced Proletkul't with legislation intentionally designed to establish a culture that would propagate an objectified citizen, *homo sovieticus*. In the next few years, fascist Europe made it plain that the communists were not alone in their conviction that culture could be mass produced with the specific objective of transforming popular values. These authoritarian regimes added a new wrinkle to the problem of definition by equating both "mass" or "popular" with "public."

Western democracies, especially the United States, dismissed the popular cultures of Soviet Russia and the fascist European states as mere instruments of political power. Because, as critics saw it, communist and fascist consumers did not enjoy genuine freedom of commercial choice, the state-produced cultures were artificial. As a result, the critics paid serious attention only to the views of those among the intellectual elites who used higher culture to criticize their authoritarian regimes, which ensconced the highbrow atop the hierarchy. Ironically, the commercialized Western cultures could not reap substantive gains by claiming a superiority that derived from freedom of choice. Led by the powerful Frankfurt School, whose members had escaped both communism and fascism, Western cultural observers shared Gramsci's worries about middlebrow culture, if not necessarily his Marxist politics. Their main concern was that the privileging of profits over aesthetics would blunt the critical edge of the elite and render its members ineffectual. Only fellow traveler Walter Benjamin held out hope that mass-produced culture could help to democratize, though only if it were not commercialized.

By the 1950s, the postwar recovery in Europe and the cold war between the United States and the Soviet Union continued the politicization of culture, as historicized by Andrew Ross in *No Respect: Intellectuals and Popular Culture* (1989). "Mass" and "middlebrow" were alternately championed or reviled, depending upon the operative understanding of democracy. Once again it was revisionist Marxists who took the lead. Borrowing Gramsci's notion of the "public intellectual," historians such as E. P. Thompson contributed to the Cultural Studies movement precisely because they wanted to make visible the ties between culture and politics. Primarily concerned with the lower classes, they were eager to demonstrate that these social groupings were "present at their own creation," in Thompson's felicitous phrasing, and not passive pawns, victims of Gramscian-articulated ideologies. Literary critic Raymond Williams moved beyond Gramsci in the extent to which he connected the imaginative to the material in his *Culture and Society* (1958). As Williams argued, the creation of culture was more a social than a purely artistic process, because it reflected a "whole way of life," a complex of relationships informed by shifting socioeconomic structures, values, and tastes.

Across the channel French intellectuals, although less publically oriented than their British counterparts, began to expose the fissures in that bedrock of elite culture, the Enlightenment. Led by Michel Foucault, they blended some Gramscian questions about cultural hegemony with Cultural Studies' recognition that groups participate in the inception of their own cultures. Not specifically intending to do so, Foucault nevertheless suggested a meaningful revision of Gramsci's work when he separated hegemony from a specific social class and wrote instead about "discourses," a much more fluid concept that allowed for various groups to shape the culture that structured their lives. Because Foucault stressed political and socioeconomic structures, his work, like Gramsci's, continued to limit the agency of individuals. Less deterministic than Marxists, he foregrounded historical moments where cultures ruptured in resistance, diverting the linear flow of the status quo. Other theorists in agreement with the contours of Foucauldian thought, especially sociologists Pierre Bourdieu and Michel de Certeau, further refined the substance of Williams's argument that the genesis of the subjective individual is interactive and in constant transition. Significantly, subjectivity was no longer recognized as being formed essentially through the exercise of individual reason, *pace* the Enlightenment. Culture finally achieved autonomy vis-à-vis its socioeconomic base through Bourdieu's recognition that culture could be saved and invested like other forms of capital. Bourdieu bound the material to the imaginative, underscoring the point that the production of culture is a social process.

Another continental theory, structuralism, although born of linguistics, became influential in the deployment of popular culture as an analytic category when adopted by anthropologists. Led by Claude Lévi-Strauss, structural anthropologists added rituals and other behaviors to the totems and other artifacts that could be analyzed symbolically. Influenced by sociologist Max Weber's thoughts on the relationship between culture and community, anthropologist Clifford Geertz evocatively argued "that man is an animal suspended in webs of significance he himself has spun." Academics began deploying Geertz's method of interpretive anthropology, which he characterized as writing "thick descriptions," in innovative ways. Not only did they find a voice for some of those who had been silenced in history, but, moreover, they questioned the historical narrative itself. This application of methodologies from the social sciences resulted in what became the "new" social history, the crucial progenitor to the likewise "new" cultural history of the 1980s. Peasant Studies emerged as a subdiscipline of this social history, and it depended upon the anthropological usage of popular culture as a category of analysis, because its main concern was to illuminate social systems that kept groups together. Research paid close attention to the peasants' collective actions, interested in how they were resisting or adapting to outside forces. The seminal work came from anthropologist of southeast Asia James C. Scott, whose *Moral Economy of the Peasant* (1976) and *Weapons of the Weak* (1985) showed peasants appropriating power on at least a few of their own terms. Scott's work invited a rethinking of what constituted power in political relationships; peasants could no longer be condescended to for their supposedly instinctual desires.

Culture was now understood more democratically. When the Enlightenment no longer offered the safe haven of superiority to an educated elite, the aesthetics associated with it also fell from the perch. Artists now celebrated commerce, as exemplified by Andy Warhol's simple rendition of a can of tomato soup in 1962. Inspired much as Warhol had been by the penetration of mass production and marketing into public life, a group of academics bolted from the traditional disciplines grouped together under American Studies to form the Popular Culture Association in the 1960s. Cleansing the contempt from "commerce," they also began using commercial culture to explore other questions of social and political constructions. Merging critical theory with a new respect for the artifacts of popular culture, they utilized a vast array of texts as primary sources, especially commercial commodities. Moreover, this movement shifted the narrative away from political structures to people-cum-purchasers. Race, class, and gender sprang to the forefront, and academics continued to slip across disciplines as they sought to write about the cultural constructions of subjective experiences. Women's Studies expanded into Gender Studies, for example, and such highly commercial items as harlequin romances and western movies provided valuable sources for analyzing how personal experiences were constructed, and how this played out in the broader arena of society and politics.

In his 1985 novel *White Noise*, American novelist Don DeLillo parodied the uncritical intellectual celebration of these new views of popular culture by designing a fictional college course devoted to the study of a box of cereal. Although this course could have taught much about Western culture, if held next door to a class on Russian or Soviet history, it would have accentuated the degree to which the study of Russia and the Soviet Union remained trapped in a different culture, the political culture of the cold war. Russian Studies employed the most traditional understandings of culture, in both the aesthetic and anthropological applications of the term. Employing such a theoretical anachronism worked because politics drove historiography, and Imperial Russia was studied largely as the prehistory of the Bolshevik Revolution. The success of that revolution had provided the defining moment in Russia's history, and subsequent interpretations began with the politics of that moment. The historical question that dominated research was: did the Soviet government legitimately reflect the concerns of the population? An affirmative response would suggest that the USSR was some form of democracy. Political scientists, led especially by Leonard Schapiro, with his uncompromising rejection of the claims of Soviet democracy, dominated in Western academics with their self-styled science of "kremlinology." Operating within a narrow view of politics, Western academics pored over the texts and actions of leaders, more interested in official agendas than in ordinary people and everyday lives. Because no liberal element had successfully withstood the Bolsheviks, it became commonplace to assume that Russian society lacked a bourgeoisie, and hence a commercial culture. In this scenario, the questions Gramsci had asked did not appear pertinent.

Equally important, Marxism allowed a place of privilege to the highbrow, one that suited a culturally conservative academic agenda. According to Marx's theory of historical materialism, the capitalist bourgeoisie would wrest power from extant feudal institutions before they would be deposed in turn by the proletariat. Tsarist Russia evidenced obvious signs of the perpetuation of feudalism, notably in its autocratic government and estate-based social system, and no middle class had emerged by 1917 to establish an electoral system grounded in private property. Lenin explained this anomaly away by arguing that Russia could essentially skip the capitalist stage, which he conveniently squeezed between revolutions of 1905 and 1917. His argument complemented the Western historiography that had also anticipated the emergence of a middle class as a natural historical development. Thus the liberal "Whig" historians made the same assumptions about society in Tsarist Russia as Lenin and his Soviet heirs did, albeit with fundamentally opposite appreciations of the Bolsheviks' success.

This brushing-aside of commercialization directed scholarly attention to elitist culture, especially that developed by those who opposed the successive Russian and Soviet governments. The Russian intelligentsia themselves had helped to place this imprimatur on the elevated status of their work because they self-consciously used their art as a political platform. The extraordinarily rich highbrow culture in nineteenth-century Russia intensified this attraction, just as the later generations of artists who opposed the communist regime spoke most eloquently about the freedom of the human soul. Thus it was easy to frame studies of Russian and Soviet cultural production around the politics of oppression, the embattled and humanitarian artist against the obscurantist state. Forced to negotiate the boundaries of the permissible with censors rather than with the paying public, Russian artists of all the creative media introduced representations that transcended specifically Russian sensibilities and situations.

In the 1850s, for example, both Russia and the United States were dealing with the morality of maintaining enserfed/enslaved populations. Two novels appeared to challenge the national passivity toward such inhumane treatment of fellow countrymen, Ivan Turgenev's *A Sportsman's Sketches* and Harriet Beecher Stowe's *Uncle Tom's Cabin*. Turgenev is still taught in literature classes, but Stowe's middlebrow melodrama, after being translated for the stage and becoming one of the most widely seen plays in theatrical history, never made it into the canon of classical American literature. Critics can argue that Turgenev wrote in images that raised universal questions of human relationships, whereas Stowe's story was constrained by cliché and sentimentalism, rooted in a historically specific American moment. Yet is that not one of the primary benefits of popular culture, to capture the moment?

In 1966 James Billington published what became the canonical history of Russian culture, *The Icon and the Axe: An Interpretive History of Russian Culture*, the title derived from what he claimed would be found hanging on the wall in every peasant hut. As eclectic as it is lengthy, *The Icon and the Axe* covers the broad sweep of Russian and Soviet history. Despite the title, Billington devotes considerable attention to the culture created by those distanced from the masses and their myths, the intelligentsia who dissented against the sequence of authoritarian regimes. Billington found no historical middlebrow capable of negotiating either the politics or the aesthetics between noble and commoner. *The Icon and the Axe* presented an idea of culture that differentiated sharply between high and low. Peasant culture evolved from superstition and spirituality, and elitist culture primarily from a failed Westernization. *The Icon and the Axe* fitted neatly into an established historiography and provided cultural evidence of why Russia had not joined the consortium of European, Western powers. Sympathetic to the frustrated elites, both Billington and Leonard Schapiro wrote monographs about nineteenth-century intellectuals, populist Nikolai Mikhailovskii and Turgenev, respectively, as if they were holding out hope for an Arnoldian national unity around the culture of the intelligentsia in a post-Soviet state.

Keeping peasant culture in the village offered a political benefit, because it could account for the ignorance that made the peasants the pawns of ideologues. Historians found themselves in a position somewhat analogous to that of the populists of the previous century, facing the daunting task of integrating the recently liberated peasants into the larger culture, yet overpowered by their sheer numbers. The first concerted attempt to introduce the Russian peasant to the English-speaking reader, *The Peasant in Nineteenth-Century Russia* (1968), edited by Wayne Vucinich, made evident that Russia's history could not be understood without a better understanding of its majority population. Peasant Studies took off as a subdiscipline of Russian history, resulting in a wealth of scholarship on the most populous social category in Russia, and a succession of authors demonstrated the vitality of peasant culture in adapting to change, whether it came under the impress of government decree, industrialization, or collectivization. These works consider peasant culture "popular" in the anthropological sense because, produced *by* peasants themselves, it reflected the totality of their systems and values. This body of scholarship includes for the prerevolutionary era: Steven Hoch, *Serfdom and Social Control in Russia* (1986); Ben Eklof, *Russian Peasant Schools* (1986); and Christine Worobec, *Peasant Russia* (1991). Study of the Soviet era also benefited from greater attention to studies of cultural networks. The peasants' use of their social systems and values to struggle against Stalin, whose policy of collectivization probably surpassed even serfdom in its brutality, has been chronicled in Sheila Fitzpatrick's *Stalin's Peasants* (1994) and Lynne Viola's *Peasant Rebels under Stalin* (1996).

Russian Peasant Studies is not simply derivative of Western scholarship, nor in general agreement about popular culture. Stephen Frank, in *Crime, Cultural Conflict, and Justice in Rural Russia, 1856–1914* (1999), Cathy Frierson, in *All Russia is Burning!: A Cultural History of Fire and Arson in Late Imperial Russia* (2002), and Jane Burbank in *Russian Peasants Go to Court* (2004), for example, have explicitly taken up questions posed by Scott and arrived at differing conclusions. The authors included in this chapter diverge chiefly on the degree to which they view peasants appropriating outside forces or resisting them, and on whether the peasants' principal objective was to maintain the status quo or to adapt their extant systems to outside challenges. Analytical differences matter here because they have implications for examining the persistence of authoritarian regimes in Russia, as relevant to post-Soviet historiography as to pre-Soviet. Culture is too protean to ensure that even using a common methodology will result in common conclusions.

Russia's peasants could not escape their alter egos, the proletarians into whom industrialization transformed them. Because the legitimacy of the Bolshevik Revolution depended upon the measure of genuine support extended by Marx's revolutionary class, workers quickly became objects of investigation by the new social historians. Initially, political history had dominated in studies of the working class, directed by the question of whether or not workers were striking for a different political system or simply for better conditions. But studying rural culture had made it clear that a prior question had to be asked – that is, how extensively had workers made the transition from village to city, adapting to the new systems and values. Reginald Zelnik took the initiative in this, moving from his fundamentally social and political history, *Labor and Society in Tsarist Russia* (1971), to a sensitive analysis of the autobiography of Semen Kanatchikov in *Radical Worker in Tsarist Russia* (1986). Kanatchikov articulated his personal transformation from a peasant into a "conscious" worker, which allowed Zelnik to illustrate how a Russian individual functioning in a specific culture, suspended in the working-class "webs of significance that we ourselves have spun," could achieve a distinctive subjectivity.

Social history depends upon the aggregate rather than the individual, and the historiographical demands of evaluating the political actions taken by the lower classes in 1917 continued to influence the ways in which historians approached working-class culture. The basic issue addressed was whether or not workers had lost their identity as peasants and had taken revolutionary political action because they specifically understood and wanted a new type of government; in other words, were Russia's workers consciously present at the creation of socialism, or were they the inchoate dark masses, responding to frustration and oppression with violence rather than reason? From the perspective of cold-war historiography, the legitimacy of the Soviet state rested on the answer to this question. Books that took up this question include Diane Koenker's *Moscow Workers and the 1917 Revolution* (1981), Joseph Bradley's *Muzhik and Muscovite* (1985), and Robert Edelman's *Proletarian Peasants* (1987). The social history of the working class began to take the cultural turn perceptibly in Mark Steinberg's *Moral Communities* (1992) and Joan Neuberger's *Hooliganism: Crime, Culture, and Power in St Petersburg, 1900–1914* (1993), which enlarged the scope of which actions could be considered political.

Collectively, these works were talking about symbolic behavior in ways that derived from a new way of thinking about class politics, but they remained rooted in the Bolshevik Revolution as the event that anchored the master narrative. My point is by no means to underplay the importance of either the revolution or the scholarship. Rather, I seek to underscore how the focus on the events of 1917 as the climax of the narrative prompts a specific set of questions that determined how the sources would be mined for evidence. For example, Soviet historians approached peasants and workers first as political beings. Although some exemplary scholarship resulted, exemplified by V. P. Danilov's works on the peasantry, the authors did not engage their subjects from the perspective of popular culture. The new social history drew largely from the anthropological meaning of popular culture because its goal was to explicate collective behavior rather than to construct the individual subject.

For all its innovations, and the crossing of interdisciplinary boundaries that reinvigorated the study of popular culture, the new social history kept the anthropological "popular" disconnected from the commercial "mass." In Russian studies, this distinction was as much a product of the debated legitimacy of a socialist government as it was the unexplored acceptance of the notion that Tsarist Russia lacked a lively commercial culture, and its concomitant, a middle class. In other area studies, however, especially that of the United States, the Popular Culture Association's reclamation of commercial culture, and its appropriation of "mass" in the process, had revolutionized popular culture as an analytical category. In addition, the association's work depended upon the use of excitingly innovative sources, such as pulp fiction and movies marketed to the masses. The study of political, social, and sexual relationships could be broadened, offering substantively different possibilities for understanding historical changes – or even the lack thereof. The political became personal. But this mattered little to Russianists as long as popular culture referred to peasants, and mass culture to a state plan for the forced transformation of the individual into *homo sovieticus*. It would take a reassessment of the French Revolution to provide an exit strategy.

When François Furet attacked the dominant Marxist paradigm in his *Interpreting the French Revolution* (1981), he opened the door for substantively different ways to evaluate political revolution. Lynn Hunt, professing that she was less interested in the standard approaches that looked for "origins and outcomes," built her *Politics, Culture, and Class in the French Revolution* (1984) upon Furet's critique. Hunt reconceptualized the nature of revolutionary politics by locating it in the symbols and activities found in popular culture rather than in social relationships. Russianists drew from this and expanded politics beyond ideology to include the creation of a distinctive political culture in *Bolshevik Culture: Experiment and Order in the Russian Revolution* (1985), edited by Abbott Gleason, Richard Stites, and Peter Kenez. Because the contributors were driven more by finding different ways to understand Bolshevism than by new theoretical ways of thinking about its subjective influences, it would be premature to say that the discipline had taken the cultural turn.

The Russian Revolution remained ensnared in webs of significance spun by outsiders: the Enlightenment, its French antecedent in 1789, and especially by Karl Marx. Possibilities for rethinking these influences were therefore welcomed. The first step was to constitute the cultural independently from the social, and to separate it then according to the hierarchy of the "brow" in search of the missing middle. Russia's highbrow culture had long been familiar, but considerably less was known about the extent to which a commercial culture had grown successfully in tandem with the rapid industrialization that had followed the Great Reforms of the 1860s. Soviet scholarship had been hampered by the Leninist insistence that Russia lacked a middle class. Despite this restriction by dogmatic theory, several informative monographs appeared – for example, I. V. Nest'ev's entertaining look at prerevolutionary nightclub culture, *Zvezdy russkoi estrady* (Stars of the Russian Estrada) (1970).

In addition, the Soviet government maintained several prestigious Institutes for the Study of Culture that produced path-breaking works even within the theoretical confines of Marxism. Neia Zorkaia, from the Moscow branch, broke the most ground with *Na rubezhe stoletii: U istokov massovogo iskusstva v Rossii 1900–1910 gg.* (At the Turn of the Century: The Sources of the Mass Arts in Russia, 1900–1910) (1976). Zorkaia's subsequent analyses of silent films helped to recover what has become one of the most valuable sources for analyzing popular culture, the silver screen. A. V. Blium, Albin Konechnyi, and Evgenii Dukov were among others who began publishing in these years on culture and entertainments; their work would gain a wider audience in the post-soviet era, when the status of popular culture changed. However, the topic of commercial culture maintained its secondary status as long as an argument for the proliferation of it challenged both Leninist and Whiggish rejection of the presence of a middle class.

The breakthrough came with Jeffrey Brooks's *When Russia Learned to Read: Literacy and Popular Literature, 1861–1917* (1985). Brooks's sweeping survey successfully identified the overlaps in the various notions of "popular," "mass," and "commercial" as applied to Russia's culture. Moreover, he tiered the "brows" and revealed their connectedness to each other, providing the most detailed evidence yet of the extent of a genuine pluralism in prerevolutionary Russian society. Brooks challenged the basis of a historiography that had depended upon the absence of a fundamental commercialism. Perhaps most significantly, he used the commercial literature to test the strength of the values associated with the rise of middle classes in the West when relocated into a different cultural environment. As Brooks argued, the standard Western themes of individualism and the triumph of professionalism and scientific reason associated with capitalism did not play out the same in Russia. Even though he was writing about the reading materials of the lower classes, Brooks's discussion of commercial, cultural values made it no longer feasible to accept the absence of a middlebrow on the basis of another absence, that of representative politics. Brooks successfully established an agenda that placed Russia in a comparative framework, without making claims with respect to the viability of a Western-style political system.

This assertion of the sociopolitical role of commercial culture opened new avenues for research. The mass-circulation press, commercially funded by advertisements, provided evidence of the growth of a public opinion independent of the autocracy in Louise McReynolds's *The News under Russia's Old Regime* (1991). The proliferation of a popular press challenged the intelligentsia as well, thus undermining to some degree their centrality to the historiography. In her *Keys to Happiness: Sex and the Search for Modernity in Fin-de-siècle Russia* (1992), Laura Engelstein negotiated the cultural turn by using a broad swathe of cultural enterprises, from the professional to the commercialized, to discuss their influences on subjective experiences. By emphasizing subjectivity, she brought the new theoretical uses of culture as an analytic category to bear on the study of prerevolutionary Russia. The analogues she found to Western experiences did not reproduce the basis for liberalism in Tsarist Russia, which allowed Engelstein to contravene the cold-war historiography that demanded a paradigm of Westernization.

Locating a commercial culture in Tsarist Russia still could not resolve the issue of Soviet culture, mass produced by the state. The central problem stemmed from the need to overcome the inclination to interpret the artifacts of state culture as something more than propaganda. Vera Dunham's *In Stalin's Time: Middleclass Values in Soviet Fiction* (1976) stands out in its use of cultural values to locate a Soviet bourgeoisie, but, because this book was not informed by Bourdieu's observation that culture functions as a form of capital, it did not invest the Soviet consumers of middlebrow products with the degree of autonomy that they merited. The central problem lay in drawing the interpretive line between producer and consumer. Herein lay the sticking point: the logical contradiction between production by the government and freedom of choice by the consumer.

The Soviet government did indeed greatly restrict the individual liberties of its citizens, compounding as it did the negative force of censorship with its own positive program that prescribed cultural initiatives. The most influential work on the relationship between culture and political power came from Sheila Fitzpatrick, whose pioneering research over two decades on the "cultural revolution" of the 1920s charted the transition to Stalinism, her essays collected in *The Cultural Front: Power and Culture in Revolutionary Russia* (1992). In Fitzpatrick's studies. "culture" lay primarily, although not exclusively, in the educational institutions that had also been mentioned by Gramsci as a source of hegemonic controls. The revolution in culture entailed the rise to power of a generational cohort schooled in a conservative proto-Marxism. These students supplanted their "bourgeois" teachers and forced the old intelligentsia back into opposition, the position that they had occupied under the tsars. The most culturally infamous outcome of this was the decision taken by the Communist Party in 1934 that creative fiction should follow the principles of "socialist realism," an appropriation of the intelligentsia's dictum that art must serve the masses. "Serving" in this case meant facilitating the birth of *homo sovieticus.*

As long as socialist realism was considered an artificial construct, an aesthetic created by ideological imperatives rather than consumers' tastes, it lacked authenticity as a source for understanding the values of those who purchased it. On the other hand, as Katerina Clark argued successfully in *The Soviet Novel: History as Ritual*

(1981), socialist realism borrowed from Russia's literary past and engaged its audiences in more than crude attempts to legitimize the regime. Clark's work was among the first to have been influenced by Mikhail Bakhtin, a Soviet theoretician in disfavor with the regime for developing ideas about language that undermined the monologic system of the Soviet word: we, the government, speak; you, the populace, listen. Like other revisionist Marxists, such as Gramsci and the Frankfurt School, Bakhtin understood the acquisition of culture to be a dynamic process, a form of social interaction, regardless of the political source of the material. Irina Paperno brought this to bear on the biography of an individual member of the nineteenth-century intelligentsia in *Chernyshevsky and the Age of Realism: A Study in the Semiotics of Behavior* (1988). Clark and Paperno used critical theory to analyze materials that would account for an element of subjectivity in *homo sovieticus*, although it was not really until the Soviet Union itself began to evolve more pluralistically that scholarly approaches to Soviet culture shifted decisively.

From the mid-1980s, Mikhail Gorbachev's reformist policies of *glasnost* and *perestroika* cracked open and began restructuring the study of popular culture. Gorbachev's wife, Raisa, famous for her promotion of cultural initiatives, endorsed an official Cultural Fond directed by Dmitri Likhachev, an academician renowned for his work in Old Russian literature. Likhachev's commitment to culture was as visceral as it was cerebral, and before his death in 1999 he had moved actively into politics on a platform maintaining the significance of culture to national identity. Likhachev echoed Arnold with his belief that culture could build a bridge across conflictual interests. Though his concerns about post-Soviet culture did not embrace the explosion of the commercial, the attention that he brought to culture helped to sharpen the analysis of non-statist, mass-oriented culture.

Cultural Studies came to Russia as an organized, multidisciplinary project with Nancy Condee and Vladimir Padunov, who administered the "Working Group on Contemporary Russian Culture (1990–93)"; coincidentally, this project oversaw the collapse of communism and the first stages of post-Soviet culture. The group itself was cross-cultural, an originative example of the sort of cross-fertilization of ideas among Western and Soviet/Russian scholars that would soon become standard practice. Contributors determined at the outset that the tensions between official and unofficial culture would affect any autonomous cultural model that they could hope to come up with. Shying away from the standard case for Russian exceptionalism, they emphasized the viability of applying critical theories familiar in analyses of the West to Russian culture. The group's first batch of working papers, *Russian Culture in Transition* (1993), employed culture as the source from which to illustrate another transition, away from a focus on the strictly political and toward the exploration of subjective experience in daily life. The early Bolshevik ideal of *homo sovieticus* was gendered, nationalized, and individualized, and he or she was found to be a complex entity, not an automaton.

Further groundwork had to be laid, fundamental information provided, and the highbrow viewpoint of the intelligentsia relativized. Richard Stites's textbook *Russian Popular Culture: Entertainment and Society since 1900* (1992) supplied the basic introduction to mass culture, especially in the Soviet Union, introducing movie stars and hit tunes, spotlighting their consumption rather than their production. Another text introduced specifically Russian Cultural Studies: Catriona Kelly and David

Shepherd, eds., *Constructing Russian Culture in the Age of Revolution, 1881–1940* (1998). *Imperial Russia: New Histories for the Empire* (1998), edited by Jane Burbank and David Ransel, grew out of a conference whose participants were exploring the "anthropological turn," and suggested ways to rethink the historiography of the tsarist era. Richard Wortman, with a nod to Geertz, even pushed the autocracy around the cultural turn in his two-volume *Scenarios of Power: Myth and Ceremony in Russian Monarchy* (1995, 2000). And, in *Magnetic Mountain: Stalinism as Civilization* (1995), Stephen Kotkin changed the terms of the debate about Stalinism by shifting attention away from the individual tyrant and toward the individuals who had grown up and lived in the social and cultural system that Stalin's politics had created. An interdisciplinary collection of essays edited by Laura Engelstein and Stephanie Sandler, *Self and Story in Russian History* (2000), foregrounded the centrality of subjective, individual experience in Russia and the Soviet Union.

The collapse of the Soviet Union has meant that the state can no longer exercise so determining an influence over either mass-produced culture or the scholarship that analyzes it. Both tsarist and Soviet censorships restricted options and stifled voices, but state controls could tell only part of the story. As Abbott Gleason has effectively demonstrated in *Totalitarianism: The Inner History of the Cold War* (1997), the images of the mightiness of the Soviet state were themselves the product of a distinctive political culture, the same one that had kept political scientists deliberating the legitimacy of the regime and literary scholars focused on the dissidence in the arts. The fall of the Communist Party brought the paradigm down with it, freeing scholars up to start raising questions about the personal experiences of lives lived. The return of "Russia" from its incarnation as the Soviet Union has generated meaningful dialogue across intellectual and cultural traditions, reduced the competition to find the most satisfying political explanation for the USSR, and has given credibility to cultural products previously undervalued as propaganda. Raymond Williams's position that creating culture is fundamentally a social process has become relevant to Russia.

The scholarly outpouring since the fall of the Soviet Union in 1991 has resulted in new ways to pose old questions, as well as the necessity of formulating new ones. Once again, anthropologists have played a leading role, in large measure because the nature of their research, fieldwork, puts them in direct conversation with many who are experiencing the changes first hand. Bruce Grant's *In the Soviet House of Culture: A Century of Perestroikas* (1995) and Nancy Ries's *Russian Talk: Culture and Conversation during Perestroika* (1997) are exemplary of this endeavor. Anthropologists began replacing political scientists in the drawing-up of new paradigms, because they offer a demonstrable methodology that has the benefit of being distanced from the failure of kremlinology to anticipate the collapse of the Soviet Union. Heirs to Boas, they accepted the relativism inherent in culture, and they endowed quotidian Soviet life with the legitimacy that politics had refused it. As "globalization" now casts its shadow over structures of analysis, from the economic to the historical, it is necessary to rethink Russia, Eastern Europe, and the rest of the Soviet empire as postsocialist countries in a world being reconstituted accordingly. Katherine Verdery's work has made anthropology central, because of how she uses culture to explain contemporary social and political attitudes. Her observation that socialism "provided a cognitive map for those who lived it" affirms the cultural influence of the system without imposing value judgments on it.

Russian scholars liberated by the dissolution of Communist Party controls have contributed enormously to the revolution in popular culture. Not only could they open their work to critical theories, reshaping some of them in the process; they were also able to cross opened borders and participate in academic life as students as well as teachers, exchanging ideas and enjoying the right of return. Svetlana Boym's *Common Places: Mythologies of Everyday Life in Russia* (1994) began a trend that has extended considerably from this rather withering look at Soviet mass culture. Alexander Prokhorov and Elena Prokhorova, who studied under Condee and Padunov, are exemplary of the new generation of Russian scholars writing with theoretical insights into the mass culture they enjoyed as children. An anthropologist by training, Serguei Oushakine has reversed traditional research strategy and looks at cultural practices in the Soviet era to find the ruptures in the political system, thereby seeing the culture rather than the politics functioning as the agent of change. Taking a cue from the Popular Culture Association, they are successfully blending the notions of "mass" and "popular" and discussing how movies, singers, and television serials reflected upon society, and what this might have meant to politics.

Equally important is how cultural analysis can help to fill in the blanks left by social and political histories. The "woman question," for example, has expanded beyond the fundamentals of equality to address femininity as well as feminism, exemplified by Helena Goscilo and Beth Holmgren, eds., *Russia, Women, Culture* (1998). Additionally, in *Russian Masculinities in History and Culture* (2002), edited by Barbara Clements, Rebecca Friedman, and Dan Healey, the Russian male found his gendered identity used to explore aspects of political behavior rather than his political pronouncements. Homosexuality becomes less a taboo and more a personal choice in Laurie Essig's *Queer in Russia : A Story of Sex, Self, and the Other* (1999). Research does not always stop abruptly in 1917, but often addresses Russian/Soviet history along a continuum. Cultural categories themselves have fruitfully crossed the 1917 divide, as in Louise McReynolds and Joan Neuberger, eds., *Imitations of Life: Two Centuries of Melodrama in Russia* (2002).

In addition to the expansion of theoretical options for analysis, the growth of the source base, seemingly exponential in places, has made this research possible. Increasing amounts of primary sources of popular culture have been translated into other languages. Technology has revolutionized the accessibility of all media. The British Film Institute, for example, put together twenty-eight prerevolutionary films on ten cassettes, released by Milestone Film and Video (1992); Yuri Tsivian has complemented this with several analyses of the silent cinema, including *Early Cinema in Russia and its Cultural Reception* (1994). Soviet movies and television programs, especially contemporary serials, are sold inexpensively on DVDs, often available for purchase online. In 2005 the Research Centre for East European Studies in Bremen launched *kultura*, a monthly Internet review covering current events and trends in Russian culture.

Recent works synthesize various aspects of popular culture, going beyond the narratives and focusing instead upon how it can shed light on social and other historical changes. Among the more significant are: Robert Edelman, *Serious Fun: A History of Spectator Sports in the USSR* (1993); Adele Barker, ed., *Consuming Russia: Popular Culture, Sex, and Society since Gorbachev* (1999); Evgenii Dukov, ed., *Razvlekatel'naia kul'tura Rossii XVIII-XIX vv.: ocherki istorii i teorii* (The Culture of Entertainment in Russia, 18th–19th Centuries. Essays in History and Theory) (2001); Louise McReynolds, *Russia at Play: Leisure Activities at the End of the Tsarist Era* (2003); and Richard Stites, *Serfdom, Society, and the Arts in Imperial Russia: The Pleasure and the Power* (2005). This list, by no means exhaustive, anchors that controversial "mass culture," the one dreaded by the Frankfurt School but embraced by the Popular Culture Association, into Russian historiography. These new monographs make plain the importance of quotidian experience to unraveling larger historical questions. They must be joined on the shelf by others that investigate contemporary mass culture's connections to its Soviet past. Of equal significance, elite culture must be interrogated as it has been in Western critical theory, and not just continue to be accepted at its anti-authoritarian face value.

If the Cultural Studies project has taught anything, it is the futility of applying master narratives: because the contexts in which they are consumed are inevitably culturally contingent, every storyline has embedded in it a disruptive, alternative way of reading it. Therefore, it is often more productive to listen for Delillo's "white noise" in the texts, possibilities for reading between the lines of wisdom dispensed to see the different ways in which the story could have been received. In his *Culture as History* (1984), Warren Susman famously argued that to understand the 1930s in the United States it would be more profitable to study the cartoon character Mickey Mouse than President Roosevelt. Perhaps the same could hold true for the comic Cheburashka, an illustrated animal of indeterminate species beloved among generations of Soviet children and who survived 1991. In the Soviet era, Cheburashka inhabited the confined spaces of a telephone booth. In a post-Soviet adventure, however, he purchased an apartment in Moscow. And, fittingly, *Homo Sovieticus* is now a heavy metal rock band.

References

Alexander, Jeffrey C., and Seidman, Steven (eds.) (1990). *Culture and Society: Contemporary Debates.* Cambridge University Press, Cambridge.

Barker, Adele (ed.)(1999). *Consuming Russia: Popular Culture, Sex, and Society since Gorbachev.* Duke University Press, Durham, NC.

Bradley, Joseph (1985). *Muzhik and Muscovite: Urbanization in Late Imperial Russia.* University of California Press, Berkeley.

Burbank, Jane (2004). *Russian Peasants Go to Court: Legal Culture in the Countryside, 1905–1917.* Indiana University Press, Bloomington.

Edelman, Robert (1993). *Serious Fun: A History of Spectator Sports in the USSR.* Oxford University Press, New York.

Eklof, Ben (1986). *Russian Peasant Schools: Officialdom, Village Culture, and Popular Pedagogy, 1864–1914.* University of California Press, Berkeley.

Frank, Stephen (1999). *Crime, Cultural Conflict, and Justice in Rural Russia, 1856–1914.* University of California Press, Berkeley.

Frierson, Cathy (2002). *All Russia is Burning! A Cultural History of Fire and Arson in Late Imperial Russia.* University of Washington Press, Seattle.

Gramsci, Antonio (1971). *Selections from the Prison Notebooks.* International Publishers, New York.

Hoch, Stephen (1986). *Serfdom and Social Control in Russia: Petrovskoe, a village in Tambov.* University of Chicago Press, Chicago.

Jay, Martin (1996). *The Dialectical Imagination: A History of the Frankfurt School and the Institute of Social Research, 1923–1950.* University of California Press, Berkeley.

Kelly, Catriona, and Shepherd, David (eds.) (1998). *Constructing Russian Culture in the Age of Revolution, 1881–1940.* Oxford University Press, New York.

Koenker, Diane (1981). *Moscow Workers and the 1917 Revolution.* Princeton University Press, Princeton.

Kotsonis, Yanni (1999). *Making Peasants Backward: Agricultural Cooperatives and the Agrarian Question in Russia, 1861-1914.* Macmillan Press, Basingstoke, Hampshire.

Kuznetsov, Evgenii (1958). *Iz proshlogo russkoi estrady. Istoricheski ocherki.* Iskusstvo, Mosocw.

Neuberger, Joan (1993). *Hooliganism: Crime, Culture, and Power in St. Petersburg, 1900–1914.* University of California Press, Berkeley.

Paperno, Irina (1988). *Chernyshevsky and the Age of Realism: A Study in the Semiotics of Behavior.* Stanford University Press, Stanford, CA.

Savchenko, B. A. (1992). *Kumiry russkoi estrady.* Znanie, Moscow.

Steinberg, Mark (1992). *Moral Communities: The Culture of Class Relations in the Russian Printing Industry, 1867–1907.* University of California Press, Berkeley.

Trotsky, Leon (2005). *Literature and Revolution.* Haymarket Books, San Fransisco.

Verdery, Katherine (1996). *What was Socialism, and What Comes Next?* Princeton University Press, Princeton.

Von Geldern, James, and McReynolds, Louise (eds.) (1998). *Entertaining Tsarist Russia: Tales, Songs, Plays, Movies, Jokes, Ads, and Images from Russian Urban Life, 1779–1917.* Indiana University Press, Bloomington, IN.

Worobec, Christine (1991). *Peasant Russia: Family and Community in the Post-Emancipation Period.* Princeton University Press, Princeton.

Further Reading

Alexander, Jeffrey C. (2005). *The Meanings of Social Life: A Cultural Sociology.* Oxford University Press, New York.

Dirks, Nicholas B., Eley, Geoff, and Ortner, Sherry B. (eds.) (1993). *Culture/Power/History.* Princeton University Press, Princeton.

Dukov, Evgenii (ed.) (2001). *Razvlekatel'naia kul'tura Rossii XVIII–XIX vv.: ocherki istorii i teorii.* Dmitrii Bulanin, St Petersburg.

Hall, Stuart (1997). *Representation: Cultural Representations and Signifying Practices.* Sage, Newcastle.

McReynolds, Louise (2003). *Russia at Play: Leisure Activities at the End of the Tsarist Era* (2003). Cornell University Press, Ithaca, NY.

Steinberg, Mark (2002). *Proletarian Imagination: Self, modernity, and the sacred in Russia, 1910–1925.* Cornell University Press, Ithaca, NY.

Stites, Richard (2005). *Serfdom, Society, and the Arts in Imperial Russia: The Pleasure and the Power.* Yale University Press, New Haven.

Storey, John (2003). *Cultural Studies and the Study of Popular Culture: Theories and Methods.* University of Georgia Press, Athens, GA.

Strinati, Dominic (1995). *An Introduction to Theories of Popular Culture.* Routledge. New York.

Zorkaia, Neia (2000). *Khudozhestvennaia zhizn' Rossii 1970-kh: issledovaniia, materialy, dokumenty.* Gos. Institut Iskusstvoznaniia, Moscow.

CHAPTER NINETEEN

The Russian Experience of the First World War

MELISSA STOCKDALE

Scholars commonly regard the First World War as one of the most formative events of the twentieth century. It is also one of the most studied events, at least for every major combatant except Russia. That country's under-representation in the enormous literature on the war is not really surprising – for decades, the revolution completely overshadowed study of Russia's experience of the Great War. Western scholars debated the degree to which the war impeded or hastened the onset of revolution, but for some seventy years only a handful studied the war period as a subject in its own right. For Soviet scholars, the discontents of workers, soldiers, and peasants during 1914–17, and the political bankruptcy of all parties but the Bolsheviks, were practically the only suitable topics for a war Russia had lost and Vladimir Lenin had condemned as "imperialist."[1]

But the demise of the Soviet Union, and the resultant opening of archives and the lifting of taboos, are transforming study of the late tsarist period. Historians have rediscovered what Russians refer to as their "unknown" or "forgotten" war and are rethinking approaches to its study.[2] This chapter will offer an account of the war, its conduct, and its costs, situating these, where possible, in their broader European context. It will explore the most critical debates concerning Russia's policies and their consequences, including the nature and impact of national mobilization, and why it was that Russia alone, of the major powers, could not sustain the fight to the end. It will also consider problems of periodization, a freighted issue in the case of Russia, in part because there the conclusion of peace did not mark the end of armed conflict.

Decisions for War

Who was primarily responsible for starting the First World War is one of the most voluminously treated questions within the voluminous literature on the war. In declaring war on July 19, 1914 (old style), the German authorities put the blame on Russia, which had ordered a general mobilization of its army on July 18 despite Germany's warning that it would view such mobilization as an act of war. This effort

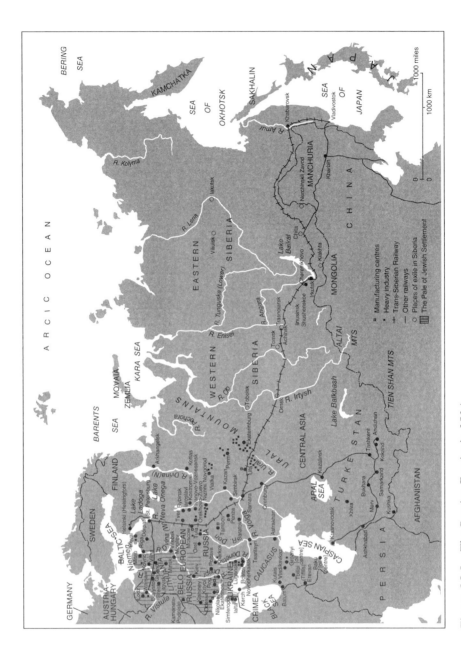

Figure 19.1 The Russian Empire in 1914
Source: Hans Rogger, *Russia in the Age of Modernisation and Revolution 1881-1917* (Longman, 1983)

to deflect blame was popularly accepted by the German public at the time, and has found some scholarly supporters since. However, most scholars today assign the major portion of guilt for the war to Germany, whose leaders were prepared to try to achieve their far-reaching economic and territorial objectives by means of war when other methods had failed.

More interesting is why the tsarist government allowed itself to be drawn into a major war, when there were so many reasons strenuously to avoid one. Among the latter was the problem of preparedness: the ambitious program of military rebuilding and reform embarked on after Russia's defeat by Japan in 1905 was not scheduled to be completed until 1917. Russia was not fully ready to wage a European war (a circumstance that figured very much in German thinking.) Secondly, working-class discontent had increased markedly over the previous two years, and in July 1914, as the European diplomatic crisis was unfolding, Russia's capital was in the throes of industrial strikes involving more than a million people; there was reason to worry that a declaration of war could trigger disorders and mass rioting throughout the country. Even should the outbreak of war find popular acceptance, political risks were high: in 1905, military failures had fueled revolution, suggesting the strong possibility that failure in a new war could do the same. In fact, political police chief P. N. Durnovo warned the tsar in February 1914 that in the case of defeat "social revolution will inevitably manifest itself in its most extreme form," predicting that the army would prove to be "too demoralized to act as a bulwark of law and order" and that Russia would be plunged into hopeless anarchy, "the end of which cannot even be foreseen."[3]

Why, then, did Nicholas order the general mobilization that risked continental war? His generals pointed out that, were he to follow his inclination and order a partial mobilization directed against Austria–Hungary, and then have to respond to the potential German threat with a more general one, Russia's complex mobilization process would be thrown into disarray and the country left vulnerable. Considerations of international status were also at work. Many ministers feared that failing again to respond to Austria's extension of its power in the Balkans, as a weakened Russia had been forced to do in 1908, would irrevocably drop it from the ranks of the Great Powers. Pressure from educated public opinion tended to reinforce such concerns. The rise of Russian nationalism among educated elites, following the country's humiliation in the Russo-Japanese War, meant that much of the elite and the press were loudly insisting that Russia must stand up for its Slavic "brother" Serbia – and itself – in the face of Teutonic bullying. Further, Russia assumed, as did virtually every other European state at the time, that the war would be a short one. When cabinet ministers assured the tsar that the post-1905 reforms had made Russia economically and militarily prepared to wage war if it must, they had in mind a conflict that would last months, not years.

Finally, since imperialist desiderata loomed so large in the critique of the war by radical Social Democrats like Vladimir Lenin, it is worth noting that territorial and economic objectives were later additions to Russian war aims. Positive ambitions, such as the longstanding desire for acquisition of Constantinople and control over the Dardanelles Straits, played almost no causal role in going to war. Rather, these began to feature in Russian thinking as circumstances altered – the prime example being Turkey's joining the hostilities on the side of the central powers in October 1914 –

and the costs of the war mounted. As was the case for most belligerent countries in the First World War, Russia's positive war aims (which many experts feel were never particularly coherent) changed and aggrandized as the "short war" dragged on.[4]

The War's First Ten Months

While there is no standard periodization of Russia's war experience, there has been a strong tendency in Western scholarly literature to characterize Russia, war effort as more or less doomed to fail by the late summer of 1915. One could offer quite different periodizations of the Russian war effort, however, depending upon whether one is analyzing the purely military side, economic mobilization, or mood and morale. This being said, a good case can be made for treating as a distinct period the first ten months of Russia's war experience, when expectations of victory in a relatively short war and social cohesion both remained fairly strong.

In Russia, as in France and elsewhere in Europe, the outbreak of war initially evoked a "sacred union" (*sviatoe edinenie*) – an outpouring of national unity and resolve in the face of external threat. In St Petersburg, the massive industrial strikes peacefully dissolved. The patriotic behavior of a crowd of nearly 200,000 people, who gathered before the Winter Palace on July 20 and spontaneously began singing the national anthem when the tsar appeared before them on a balcony, made a huge impression. Also of symbolic importance was the special one-day session on July 26 of the lower house of the Russian legislature, the State Duma. There, deputies from across the political spectrum, as well as those representing many of the empire's ethnic minorities, affirmed their united support of the war effort, burying – at least temporarily – their deep differences with each other and with the monarchic regime. In the countryside, the response to the declaration of war appeared to be more resigned than uplifted, but that was true of rural areas in France and Germany as well. Mobilization of the army went far more smoothly than had been the case during the Russo-Japanese War. Although draft riots occurred in 16 provinces, some 3.9 million men were called up according to schedule. Meanwhile, in 1914 expression of anti-war sentiment was small scale and rare, confined largely to groups in the revolutionary parties. Russian elites were thrilled (if somewhat surprised) by the way love of the fatherland had apparently transcended the empire's social, ethnic, and confessional divides.[5]

The war on the eastern front differed in several ways from that on the better-known western front. In the west, mobility disappeared early. By October 1914, opposing armies were dug into trenches along a densely manned, 400-mile-long front that was not to change by more than a few miles until 1918. In contrast, on much of the 1,000-mile long eastern front – which was consequently much more thinly manned – the potential for mobility remained, and great swathes of territory could change hands. For Russia, there were in fact three enemies to be faced: Germany, along the northern portion of the front; Austria–Hungary, on the southwest portion; and Turkey, from October 1914, on the Caucasus front. The variety of foes, and the enormous length of the front, contributed to Russia's difficulties in deciding upon coherent strategies, coordinating the efforts of its armies, and maintaining effective communications.[6]

Russia and France had anticipated an early German thrust into France, which was exactly what Germany's Schlieffen Plan called for. Russia had therefore promised it would relieve the pressure of that blow by an incursion into East Prussia no later than the fifteenth day of mobilization – far earlier than the Germans would have expected. It duly did so, causing Germany to peel five divisions off from its invasion of France and rush them eastward. At the resulting battle of Tannenberg, August 15–18, the German Eighth Army smashed Russia's larger Second Army, which lost approximately 140,000 men. Tannenberg would be Germany's greatest victory of the entire war. Russian leaders chose to regard this costly defeat as a heroic act of self-sacrifice for the Allied cause – one they increasingly came to feel that the French did not fully appreciate. Germany dealt Russia further defeats in 1914, and in October seemed likely to take Warsaw, one of the empire's most important urban and industrial centers. Offsetting these poor showings against German armies, the Russian armies acquitted themselves much better on their southeastern front. The campaign against Austria–Hungary gave Russia control of all eastern Galicia by September, a region whose "restoration" to Russia ultra-nationalists had long desired.

Despite the terrible casualties of 1914, and the fact that the fighting was lasting longer than expected, support for the war held quite strong into late spring 1915. The oft-repeated assertion that initial public support "quickly evaporated" does not stand up to scrutiny. And, though many members of the educated classes were angered by the continued influence of reactionary ministers, and appalled by early evidence of poor planning – a prime example being the gross mismanagement of medical services for the troops – the domestic political truce held. In January, when the Duma was allowed a brief special session to approve the budget and reiterate its united support of the war effort, deputies chose not to make their criticisms public.

There were a number of reasons for this continued support. Economic dislocations and material hardships were not yet as severe as they would become. Hardship was also mitigated by new stipends the treasury paid to the families of mobilized soldiers, a provision of the military reforms of 1912. Though not large, the state stipends were nonetheless more generous and much more widely distributed than was the case in other belligerent countries (illustrating that Russia was by no means always lagging behind more economically developed states in its provisions for conducting war.)[7] Favorable military and diplomatic developments were also important in shaping public perceptions of the war. In February 1915, after a long siege, the major Austrian fortress of Przemysl fell to the Russians, opening the way for a major offensive in the Carpathians. This victory, along with the public announcement in early May that Italy had entered the war on the side of the Entente allies, was jubilantly received by a Russian public that saw in them harbingers of a speedy end to the war.

Ignorance of their losses also fed Russian expectations of victory. Strict censorship laws, especially in the extensive parts of the empire placed under military rather than civil administration as of July 1914, meant the public was not fully aware of the extent of casualties, population displacements, or other problems with the war effort. Publications that transgressed against the censorship rules faced fines or worse; in 1914–15, the authorities summarily closed some sixty-four newspapers and journals. Nor could more active dissent easily be manifested. At the very outbreak of war, the police prophylactically arrested dozens of prominent Socialist Revolutionaries, Bolsheviks, and Mensheviks, on the assumption that they would be harmful to the war effort. The authorities also sent a deliberately intimidating message in November 1914 by illegally stripping of their parliamentary immunity the five Bolshevik Duma deputies who had *not* voted to approve the war and then trying them on charges of treason.[8]

Crises and Mobilization (May 1915–September 1916)

As far as the public could tell, Russia's military fortunes changed disastrously in mid-May. Successes against Austria–Hungary had induced that empire to appeal urgently for help to Germany. The German High Command, with its armies locked in bloody stalemate on the western front and confronted by the need to shift large numbers of men east to save its ally, decided to rethink its strategy: it would now concentrate on Russia. In late April a series of German offensives began that would lead to five months of reverses for Russia, the so-called Great Retreat. The Germans and Austrians enjoyed only slight numerical advantage, but a great advantage in heavy artillery, rifles, shells, and other ordnance: the Russian army was now revealed to be tragically under-equipped. Whole units were wiped out, retreats turned into routs, hundreds of thousands of Russian soldiers – some without rifles or bullets for rifles – surrendered. Galicia was lost in the spring, Warsaw fell on July 22, and the remainder of Poland by mid-August. In late August it appeared that Riga might be taken. Millions of refugees – many starving or sick – were driven into the rear, complicating the military retreat and constituting a humanitarian crisis of frightening proportions.

Military crisis on this scale created profound ruptures in the "sacred union," both politically and socially, but also galvanized a national mobilization of the home front in an effort to avert catastrophe. Into the spring of 1915, the Russian economy and home front were still largely unmobilized. Some organization of human resources had occurred, primarily on behalf of soldiers and their families. Within the first weeks of the outbreak of war, the tsar had allowed the the formation of a Union of Zemstvos and Union of Cities to organize medical services for sick and wounded soldiers – the sort of all-Russian civic organization long desired by the educated public and long resisted by the authorities as a potential encroachment on autocratic and bureaucratic privilege. These efforts were energetic and effective, winning military approval and public acclaim; there were other large-scale relief efforts as well. But, in general, Russia lagged behind most of the belligerent countries in coming to understand the nature of this war, and that winning it would necessitate mobilization, not just of industry, but of virtually every human and material resource.

In May 1915 Nicholas swallowed his reluctance to permit more extensive public and business involvement in the war effort by authorizing organization of five special councils (*osobye soveshchaniia*) for organizing defense production, food supply, fuel, transport, and refugees. Unusually for Russia, they included representatives of industry and public organizations, not just government officials. The special councils were quickly followed by creation of the so-called War Industries Committees (WIC), intended to stimulate and coordinate industrial production outside Petrograd; these included representatives of labor, another novelty. The effort to mobilize industry for wartime production paid off – in artillery, rifles, cars and trucks, and essential supplies ranging from bandages to barbed wire. Monthly production of 3-inch shell, for example, rose from 440,000 in May 1915 to 1,740,000 in May 1916 to 2,900,000 by that September. Much of the credit for these successes was claimed by the new public entities, including *Zemgor* (the Union of Cities and Union of Zemstvos' Committee for Supply of the Army.) Since the 1970s, however, scholars have questioned the contributions some of these organizations made, also remarking on pernicious side effects, such as a redundancy of efforts, and the increasing lack of coordination in the economy.[9]

The far-reaching economic mobilization was only part of a larger national-cultural mobilization that gained momentum in 1915. Both governmental and public efforts sought to sustain popular morale through education, propaganda, and material assistance. From the very start of the conflict, publishers, entertainers, and film-makers had profitably disseminated patriotic images and themes to a mass market. Schools, clubs, and libraries in most parts of the empire hosted discussions of the war and its significance for Russia. The Russian Orthodox Church instituted a weekly prayer service for fallen soldiers, set up hospitals and sanatoria in church-owned buildings, and organized rural aid efforts through parish councils. Professionally based organizations, like the Society of Russian Teachers, undertook war relief activities throughout the country; big relief organizations headed by members of the imperial family, such as the Tatiana Committee for Refugees, had a similarly national reach. Hundreds of smaller aid organizations were sponsored by local businesses and societies. A good example of joint state and public efforts are the war loan campaigns of 1916: newspapers donated thousands of column inches to publicizing the loan, societies and clubs conducted ambitious subscription drives, and colorful posters depicting stalwart workers and soldiers proclaimed "All for the war," "The fatherland needs your help," and "Doing your bit for the loan is a patriotic duty!"[10]

The political crisis of summer 1915 is far better known than the public mobilization. It would be hard to exaggerate the shock and anger among elites over munitions shortages, stinging defeats, and unpreparedness for dealing with refugees. These generated concern about the competence of the high command and the authorities to conduct the war. Many urged convocation of the Duma, which was finally permitted to open on July 19, the anniversary of the outbreak of war. Almost immediately, a majority of parties in the Duma formed a coalition (something unthinkable in prewar days); this "Progressive Bloc" worked out a compromise program of social and political reforms intended to assuage public opinion and rebuild national unity. It also called for replacement of the sitting Council of Ministers with a new, less conservative ministry enjoying "public confidence." Most of the Council of Ministers guardedly supported this plan – they, too, believed that concessions and new leadership were required at a moment when the country teetered on the brink of disaster. Instead, they were horrified to learn that the deeply patriotic tsar had decided to quit the capital and assume personal command of the army, a step that would saddle him with personal responsibility for any future defeats. Nicholas, incensed when they offered resignations in an attempt to dissuade him, ignored their advice as well as the proposals of the Progressive Bloc.

The immediate military crisis that evoked all these developments ended in mid-September, as the overstretched German offensive ground to a halt after taking Vilnius and the Russians began rolling back Austro-Hungarian forces further south. Nonetheless, many scholars date the effective end to Russia's hopes for winning the war from this time. Some do so primarily on the grounds that, by the end of the

Great Retreat, casualties and economic dislocations had been so enormous, and popular disillusionment with the war so profound, that no real recovery was possible. Others have grounded the argument more politically, seeing in Nicholas's rejection of social and political conciliation, and his assumption of command, a fateful turning point. It was not merely that the regime had lost a golden opportunity to regain the confidence of the educated elite and portions of the common people. The monarch's relocation to military headquarters created a power vacuum in the rear, which the reactionary Empress Alexandra would try herself to fill, with disastrous results for the reputation and legitimacy of the ruling house.[11]

However, few Russians at the time regarded their cause as already lost, and it is possible to see the next twelve months as a transitional period that might have gone either way. It was a time of improving military fortunes, worsening economic conditions, renewed repression, and lost opportunities.

From mid-September 1915, with the front line stabilized and outright defeat averted, Nicholas felt empowered to tackle political issues. In addition to closing the Duma for nearly five months, and replacing the ministers who had attempted to resign with more reactionary – and often poorly qualified – individuals, he pursued a broader agenda. Censorship became stricter and surveillance of the population heightened. The police began aggressively rounding up not just members of revolutionary parties, but moderate socialists and pacifists as well. In trying to address material hardships and labor discontents, the regime also opted for the non-conciliatory route. Thus, when the tsar's Chief of Staff, General M. V. Alekseev, recommended granting concessions to frustrated workers in the summer of 1916, Nicholas ignored his advice. And, while the official rhetoric of national unity was not abandoned, in practice new Minister of the Interior A. N. Khvostov – a conservative nationalist appointed in late September 1915 – included Russian citizens of German descent in his strident campaign against "German dominance." Evangelical congregations were persecuted or shut down. Government subsidies increased to right-wing, ultra-nationalist monarchic organizations and publications that spewed hatred towards Jews, Poles, and other ethnically non-Russian citizens of the empire.[12]

Yet these attempted shows of strength, in contrast to Soviet authorities' policies during the Second World War, were not sufficiently strong or consistent to accomplish their ends. The imperial government alienated the public organizations and the Duma, but was unwilling to risk the consequences of closing them entirely. Censorship was stricter, but not strict enough to stifle an increasingly outspoken press. A "temporary dictatorship" established in summer 1916 to deal with the worsening food supply – a move that some scholars believe might have been more effective than the democratization desired by progressive public opinion – proved not very dictatorial and solved nothing. Meanwhile, firings and reshufflings of cabinet ministers assumed dizzying proportions. With four different prime ministers and five ministers of the interior in just nineteen months, pursuing coherent policy was virtually precluded.

For much of 1916, however, continued hopes that a decisive military victory would soon end the war kept popular and elite discontents from assuming dangerous proportions. The national economic mobilization begun in 1915 was correcting the worst shortages in materiel; the troops were also better fed and clothed. In February 1916, Russia achieved a major victory against the Turks by capturing the fortress complex of Erzerum. Military censors now characterized the mood of the troops as "cheerful, confident, calm." A further boost to morale came from the stunning initial success of General Aleksei A. Brusilov's offensive, which opened on May 22, 1916 and punched 60 miles through Austrian lines, taking half a million prisoners. Heartened by Russian successes, Romania finally entered the war in August on the Entente side; many hoped – quite wrongly – that this addition would decisively affect the eastern front.[13]

Dysfunction, Revolution, Peace (September 1916–March 1918)

The turning point in the public mood – and arguably in Russia's ability to win the war – came in the autumn of 1916. After its brilliant start, the Brusilov offensive concluded indecisively, having cost nearly a million casualties. Romania's offensive turned almost immediately into debacle. By September, as the Russian army dug into new positions for the winter, soldiers lost hope that victory was in sight. Pervasive food shortages, the soaring cost of living, and spy mania dominated the pages of the press. Increasingly, the population believed the war effort was being subverted from within. Many doubted the loyalty to Russia of the German-born empress and her favorites – such as Prime Minister Boris Sturmer, a Russian citizen of German descent, and the peasant "holy man" Grigorii Rasputin. In October, the head of the Union of Zemstvos warned Duma president M. V. Rodzianko about the widespread belief that "an enemy hand secretly influences the direction of our state affairs." These dangerous, delegitimizing suspicions burst into the open on November 1, 1916, when liberal party leader Pavel N. Miliukov gave a speech in the Duma listing the many disasters characterized the government's conduct of the war and paused repeatedly to ask: "Is this stupidity or is this treason?" Illicit copies of this speech rapidly circulated all over Russia, reinforcing concern about traitors at the regime's very core.[14]

This was the background against which food riots in Petrograd in February 1917 turned into an anti-war protest, mass political protest, and then revolution. When Nicholas appealed to his generals for loyal troops to put down the disorders in the capital, they concluded that it was already too late to resort to force. Instead, they advised that he abdicate in order to avoid triggering internecine struggle that would enable Germany to defeat Russia. This consideration was decisive. Nicholas decided to abdicate in favor of his brother Michael, who declined to take the throne.

The end of monarchical rule on March 2, 1917 did not end Russia's involvement in the war. The new Provisional Government resolved to honor Russia's commitment to its allies and continue the fight until victory. The Petrograd Soviet, though more insistent on renouncing annexations and indemnities and more open to the possibility of a negotiated peace, was similarly committed to defending "free Russia" from German militarism. The soldier-citizen, whose expanded political and civil rights were enshrined in the March "Declaration of Soldiers' Rights," was now proclaimed to be defending freedom *and* the fatherland.[15] Initially, the great majority of the population shared this commitment to a defensive war. This point is worth stressing, since the war weariness of much of the empire's population by early 1917 is too often viewed outside its broader European context and taken as equivalent to rejection of the war effort *in toto*. Now well into its third year, the First World War was increasingly unpopular with the common people in most countries, which is why governments everywhere in 1917 made unprecedented efforts to remobilize their citizens' energies.[16] But in Russia, which lacked a legitimate governmental authority and with the economic situation continuing to unravel, national unity faced especially severe challenges. There, working people's willingness to continue a war that seemed endless, and disproportionately costly to them, eroded with shocking speed.

The Provisional Government and Petrograd Soviet, with the help of numerous civic organizations, sought to propagandize the war and offer more material rewards to soldiers and their families. There was also an effort, inspired by the example of the French Revolution, to raise a revolutionary volunteer army to bolster the sagging spirits of the regular troops at the front. Appeals went out to "All to whom the fate of the Motherland is dear, to whom the idea of the brotherhood of peoples is dear – workers, soldiers, women, cadets, students, officers, civil servants – come to us under the red banner of the volunteer battalions!" Some 50,000 men and 5,000 women volunteered for these shock units and "battalions of death," but they could not restore the fighting spirit of the regular army. The ill-advised offensive launched in June 1917, an undertaking Imperial Russia had promised the Allies and which the Provisional Government chose to honor, quickly collapsed. Discipline in front-line and reserve units broke down, fraternization increased, and more and more troops simply deserted.[17]

Not surprisingly, a number of factors – new and cumulative – contributed to the imperial army's collapse. These included inadequate provisioning as transport broke down, letters to soldiers from loved ones detailing worsening material conditions at home, and the inordinately heavy casualties sustained by field-level officers over the course of the war. These high casualties meant that by early 1917 some 90 percent of field officers were inexperienced replacements, and thus less able to wield authority over their men. Revolutionaries' anti-war or defeatist agitation at the front also played a part, although their influence on soldiers was exaggerated by opponents at the time. There were contemporaries who believed that draconian discipline could still have pulled the disintegrating army together: that was the conviction of most members of the middle and upper classes and career military men, and what General Lavr G. Kornilov tried to apply once he was appointed Supreme Commander in late July. However, others at the time, and a majority of scholars since, have concluded that by then it was already too late to save the Russian army as a fighting force.[18]

These developments help explain the growing popularity of the Bolshevik message, from July 1917, that it was possible quickly to conclude a just peace. The Bolsheviks insisted that only they were prepared to do so, in contrast to representatives of other classes and parties who did not genuinely desire to end the war. They seized power on October 26, and one of the first decrees of their new government, the Soviet of Peoples' Commissars, was the "Decree on Peace." It called for an immediate three months' armistice on all fronts in order to conduct negotiations for a democratic peace without annexations or indemnities. The decree also announced the intention to publish the tsarist government's wartime secret treaties – a move intended to sow discord amongst member states of both alliances as well as to incite popular revulsion against continuing an imperialist war for booty.

However, the Allied governments' refusal to recognize either the new Soviet government or its peace proposal, and the accelerated disintegration of the Russian

Army, forced the Soviet government to sign an armistice with Germany and its allies on December 2, 1917. The Bolshevik leadership tried to drag out the negotiations at Brest-Litovsk, hoping that the example of revolution in Russia would spark war-weary European populations to revolt and thus make conclusion of a separate peace unnecessary. But the weak Russian position became weaker still when Germany and Austria–Hungary signed a separate peace on February 9, 1918, with representatives of the Central Rada – the body claiming governmental authority in a free Ukraine – thereby legitimizing Ukraine's claim to be a sovereign state independent of Russia. The Russian delegation, now headed by Lev Trotsky, tried to stall by declaring that Soviet Russia would make "neither war nor peace" and decamping for Petrograd; the exasperated German Supreme Command resumed the offensive. By the time Lenin managed to browbeat the party leadership and Congress of Soviets into accepting terms, on the pragmatic grounds that only peace could save the revolution, German forces had advanced 150 miles deeper into Russian territory and German demands had escalated.[19]

The Treaty of Brest-Litovsk, signed March 3, 1918, between Russia and the Quadruple Alliance, was one of the harshest in modern history. Soviet Russia lost 34 percent of the population of the former Russian Empire, 54 percent of its industrial capacity, and invaluable natural resources. Territorial losses – including lands ceded directly to Germany and Turkey as well as lands included within the borders of new sovereign states carved out of imperial territory – amounted to 1.3 million square miles. Russia also agreed to demobilize its army and navy. The treaty lasted only eight months, being nullified by the armistice Germany signed with the remaining Entente powers on November 11. But, though the Soviet government eventually regained most of the territories ceded by its terms, in the short run its punitive provisions and the act of concluding a separate peace had serious repercussions. The ignominious treaty was hugely unpopular within Russia, alienating most of the Bolsheviks' few remaining socialist allies and helping transform armed opposition to Bolshevik power into full-blown civil war.[20]

Russia's participation in the First World War had catastrophic results: terrible loss of life, the destruction of the Imperial regime, a bloody civil war. But historians do not agree as to why Russia's war experience proved so disastrous, or even the exact scale of the devastation. They disagree as well over which factors to privilege in explaining the problems with Russia's war, particularly the material and economic ones and the contested issue of what might be termed national–cultural "underdevelopment." We will now take up some of those issues.

Military and Production

To what degree were Russia's setbacks on the battlefield due to the organization and caliber of its armed forces? Historians writing on the Russian military have noted numerous inadequacies in the army's high command, organization, and political culture – including insufficient numbers of officers and NCOs, and the gap separating officers from the rank and file. Problems in the reserve system, along with high casualties (including men captured), meant that by early 1915 the army was experiencing a general crisis of manpower, though contemporaries imagined that the Russian Army was a giant "steamroller" with an almost inexhaustible supply of men. The desperate need for men prompted unpopular changes to the conscription laws and an ill-advised labor conscription of Central Asian ethnic groups exempt from the draft; the latter helped trigger massive rioting across the Asian steppe, resulting in thousands of deaths, in the summer and fall of 1916.

Poor generalship played a role in military failures, especially in the first year. Some of the high command's problems were unique, such as its management of the Russian territories under military control (discussed below.) Organizationally, *stavka* (general headquarters) simply did not have sufficient control over individual commanders to force execution of a coherent policy. However, for any student of the First World War in general, many of the charges leveled against the Russian command will look quite familiar. Aloofness from the front, unimaginative tactics, the profligate waste of men, and a slow learning curve – none of these deficiencies was unique to the Russian command.[21]

Munitions shortages were the principal reason adduced for Russian military failures by many generals and members of the public at the time. The quantity of shell – both heavy and shrapnel – was already insufficient in September 1914. Every belligerent country was experiencing alarming shortages of shell by the spring of 1915, but Russia's shortfalls were deeper than others. They made for much higher casualties and deprived it of the defensive advantage usually enjoyed during this war. For example, when Germany made its major breakthrough in Galicia at Gorlice-Tarnow on May 2, 1915, the Russian Army was limited to firing four rounds of artillery per day. One in four soldiers at the front did not even have rifles; famously, and horribly, instructions were issued that unarmed soldiers should pick up the weapons dropped by their slain comrades.

Some scholars have viewed these shortfalls more broadly as a crisis of economic backwardness: the First World War was the first "total war" of the modern era, and Russia, an industrializing but largely agrarian country, was simply not sufficiently developed to sustain a modern industrialized war over the long haul. Norman Stone disputed this in his highly influential 1976 study of the eastern front. In his view, the admittedly deep shortages of 1915 became a convenient excuse for military ineptitude and failure; although most of the shortages were corrected by 1916, military performance did not, for the most part, greatly improve. Rather, he contended, the war accelerated processes of economic modernization that predated the war and reshaped the country socially and economically – so extensively, in fact, that they introduced intolerable strains that finally destroyed the existing order. In this reading, Russia's wartime crisis was ultimately one of modernization rather than backwardness.[22]

Even so, current scholarship tends to see Russia's economic underdevelopment as a critical weakness of its war effort. Besides deficiencies in defense industries per se, there were other undeveloped sectors of the economy, such as chemical industries and machine tools, that were critical to defense production. Russia had been heavily dependent on imports in these areas – another sign of relative economic underdevelopment – and, since its two most important warm-water ports, on the Baltic and Black Seas, were blockaded by Germany and Turkey, importing goods necessary to create domestic war industries was impeded. Transport was one of the worst problems associated with underdevelopment. European Russia's rail network was far less dense than Germany's or even Austria–Hungary's. This insufficiency of rail had several implications. Militarily, as William Fuller has pointed out, it meant Russia could not swiftly move reserves up to the front, or move units at the front from one sector to another, so that operations had to be planned on a massive scale and command had less ability to respond to changing circumstances. On the home front, lack of rail complicated delivery of fuel and raw materials for industrial production, contributing to terrible bottlenecks. Over the course of the war, as the rate of breakdown of locomotives and rolling stock far outstripped their replacement, there began to be serious problems with supplying both the army and the major urban areas with necessary supplies.[23] The recurrent food shortages that fueled the February 1917 rioting in Petrograd, which led to revolution, had less to do with the shortfalls in agricultural production than with the inability of the rail network to supply the active army, industry, *and* the urban population.

The Home Front and the War

The burdens of the war were unevenly distributed, a circumstance that would be critical to the war's outcome. In regional terms, those hardest hit lived in the areas that were theaters of war or immediately adjacent to them – that is, Russia's western borderlands, especially tsarist Poland, eastern Galicia, and the Baltic region. In one sense, the damage wrought in the borderlands, by both contending armies and foreign occupation, parallels the better-known experience in northern France and Flanders: infrastructure and industrial capacity were destroyed, movable resources looted, civilians killed, uprooted, or subjected to requisitioning and forced labor.[24] But the situation on Russia's front was more complex, more singular, and, ultimately, more terrible for civilians, than that on the Western Front, in part because of Russia's own actions and policies rather than the behavior of the enemy.

A unique characteristic of the Russian war zone was the law that gave the military total power – even civil and legal – in areas near the front; when this power was misused, the central government itself was virtually powerless to check the abuses. The military reversals of 1915, lack of planning for mass civilian evacuations during retreat, and suspicions concerning the true loyalties of ethnically non-Russian border populations combined to produce terrible results. The Russian military conducted scorched-earth policies as it retreated, took thousands of hostages from the empire's own subjects, and prophylactically deported hundreds of thousands more into the interior to avert their possible collaboration with the advancing enemy. Peter Gatrell has explored the mass scale of population displacement, estimating nearly six million refugees by 1917. In the borderlands that comprised much of the war zone, the non-Russians tended to suffer even more than the rest of the population. Poles, Lithuanians, Russian Germans, and above all Jews could become scapegoats for military debacle, while locals sometimes took advantage of the chaos and disruption of existing social and economic hierarchies to wreak havoc on groups who differed confessionally or ethnically.[25]

Outside the war zones, as a general rule the war affected urban populations much more adversely than rural people. Food and fuel shortages, an increasing problem from late summer 1915, were an urban phenomenon. As the cost of living soared – prices on commodities rose over 45 percent during the first eighteen months of the war, and a frightening 94 percent in 1916 – those on fixed incomes or receiving low wages were hardest hit. The expanded demand for labor could also create opportunities, of course; women gained more and better paying jobs in the factory workforce, as well as jobs in areas previously closed to them, such as transport. But the influx of people for factory work and, often, of refugee populations, put an intolerable strain on housing supply and city services. Local authorities were not always successful in their struggle to prevent outbreaks of epidemics in filthy, overcrowded cities, with health facilities stretched to the breaking point by war.

The unprecedented scale and pace of all these changes to living and working conditions in the cities undermined social cohesion and stability. Strikes resumed in Russia in 1915, after a near total cessation in the first six months of the war. More than 539,000 individuals participated in strikes in 1915 and over 878,000 in 1916. While some strikes were non-economic in nature (over 100,000 workers in three major cities struck in September 1915 to protest the closing of the Duma), the most protracted were reactions to the steeply rising cost of living.[26] Strikes were not the only form of urban unrest. Bad news from the front could spark disorders, the worst being the anti-German riots that engulfed Moscow for three days in late May 1915, resulting in over 70 million rubles' worth of destruction. Protests related to shortages or high prices for basic necessities probably accounted for the most widespread disorder; food riots, often accompanied by the smashing and looting of shops, grew in frequency in 1916. This kind of disturbance was particularly hard to bring under control, thanks in part to the large numbers of women, many of them soldiers' wives, taking part. In several cases, as in the Urals cities of Cheliabinsk and Orenburg, troops deployed against food rioters refused to obey orders to fire on the crowd, an ominous foretaste of what was to happen in Petrograd.[27]

Less research has been done on the experience of the war in the countryside, and particularly its regional variations, but overall one can say that material conditions there tended to be less difficult than in urban areas. In regions removed from the war zones, peasant families often saw their material situation improve. The treasury stipends paid to families of mobilized soldiers – and most soldiers were peasants – provided a new, steady source of cash, while higher prices for farm products could also translate into higher peasant income. Lack of labor posed a problem in the late summer of 1914, when mobilization of the army seriously complicated getting in the harvest. Thereafter, labor shortages tended to be manageable on peasant farms, where women, children, and the elderly shouldered the field work. (Big estates and commercial farms, which depended on hired labor, were much harder hit.) But, even with unaccustomed cash to spend, rural people discovered that the precipitous drop in production of consumer goods meant there was precious little to buy. Lacking incentives to produce for market, many peasants basically stopped doing so, thereby contributing to the provisioning crisis in the army and cities that developed by 1917.[28]

In every combatant country, as the war dragged into its third year and the hardships mounted, resentment over inequality of sacrifice mounted, too. In Russia, families wrote petitions complaining that their men folk were being drafted while others got deferments; low-income urban dwellers, struggling to find and afford food for their families, complained of shopkeepers' price-gouging; nearly all the humble members of society resented manufacturers' wartime profits and the apparent lack of hardship among more privileged layers of society. Perceived inequality of sacrifice for the war effort did not run strictly along class lines – frontline soldiers were often outraged, for example, when workers already making far more than they struck for higher wages. But a general conviction on the part of poorer members of society that they were being made to suffer disproportionally for the "common cause" became more pronounced and more bitter over the course of 1916.

Thus, huge casualties sustained over too long a time; too many defeats and too little discernible progress towards victory; inflation, shortages, and the unequal distribution of hardship, fueling class and ethnic tensions – all these took an enormous toll on the population's ability and resolve to continue fighting. It is true that other countries nonetheless managed to weather equally severe economic hardships, as in the case of blockaded Germany in 1916–17 after the failure of the potato harvest. But Germany was, throughout the war, an occupier rather than a country that was occupied – it had victories and their fruits to sustain hope in final victory.

Many contemporary critics had such comparisons in mind: the governments of France, Germany, and Britain, they believed, made effective use of human and material resources and kept their people united. In Russia, by contrast, resources were wasted and problems exacerbated by inept policies, incompetent implementation, and the refusal to empower the public to craft solutions. Had the Progressive Bloc organized in the Duma in summer 1915 been given more control over policy, had the public organizations been given a bigger role in mobilizing the economy, things might have turned out differently. In recent decades, many scholars have tended to dismiss these views as wishful thinking or even a different kind of scapegoating, one that fingered the reactionary tsarist government as the root cause of Russia's wartime failure. In such views, the progressive public was not so competent, the authorities not so clueless, or the problems not so amenable to solution, as the "liberal narrative" assumes.[29]

It may be that Russia was, in fact, simply too underdeveloped to sustain total, industrialized war. But an updated argument can also be made for the importance of the political factor, insofar as the credibility and legitimacy of the regime are concerned. This is not to say that, if Nicholas had been more willing to conciliate public opinion in summer 1915, the country's manifold problems could have been swiftly corrected. But, in refusing to democratize and share decision-making in the war effort, the tsarist government also deprived itself of the possibility of sharing blame. It remained, in effect, "sole owner" of continuing losses and worsening economic conditions. The circumstance that internal enemies were popularly blamed for many of the problems only worsened the government's reputation, since its apparent failure to thwart these enemies suggested either incompetence or connivance. As the war dragged into its third year with no external achievements or internal concessions to mollify the population, amid the spectacle of governmental incompetence and scandal – with ministers hired and fired at the whim of a "German" empress and the sexually promiscuous peasant reputed to be her lover – the ruling house was utterly discredited. By the fall of 1916, as the secret police anxiously reported, growing parts of the population and the active army had concluded that the war could not be won by the present government, whether it be due to "stupidity or treason."

The regime had lost both its credibility *and* its legitimacy, something that did not happen in any other combatant country until the final month of the allied advance against Germany in 1918. So long as a regime retains legitimacy in the eyes of much of its population, it may be forgiven many blunders and hardships in wartime. Thus, it is entirely possible that, had the political situation been different in Russia in February 1917, even if there had still been shortages causing food riots to break out in the capital, the military and civil elite could have dealt with them. The symbolic figure of the tsar, the embodiment of traditional authority and the object of the Russian soldier's oath of loyalty, would still have been available as a source of legitimacy. Russia might then have been able to do what an exhausted France, facing mutinies in its army, was able to do after April 1917: forego offensives for the time being, hold the line, and wait for the arrival in Europe of sufficient numbers of American soldiers and supplies to tip the balance in the Entente's favor.

Costs and Consequences

The chaotic state of statistical records for the period 1914–18 make calculating Russia's demographic losses hard to do with certainty. Estimates of Russia's total fatalities for the army, based on Soviet calculations of the 1920s, put them at approximately 1.66 million (killed in battle, died from wounds or disease, MIA, and died in captivity), with total military casualties ranging from 7.2 to 8.5 million. This rate is considerably lower than those sustained by several other combatant countries. However, more recent scholarship makes Russian casualties higher. A. D. Stepanov has calculated a possible range of figures for deaths in the military, from a low of approximately 1.7 million to a high of over 3.37 million. Adding in non-fatal casualties, he arrives at an approximate figure of 11.4 million military casualties out of a total of 17.6 million mobilized men (navy included), for a casualty rate of 60.6 percent. By this reckoning, Russia's military casualties in the war were actually the highest of any power. Austria–Hungary, for example, suffered casualties of 58.8 per cent; France, 57.3 per cent; and Germany, 56.3 per cent.[30]

If we include civilian deaths, for which figures are even more problematic, estimates on total war-related deaths for Russia range from approximately 2.3 million to Stepanov's estimated maximum possible of 4,447,405. In Russia's Great War, however, civilian suffering more often took the form of severe economic hardship and/or forced population displacement – and the resultant impoverishment and health crises – rather than outright death. Thus, in thinking of the human toll of the war, we need to consider also the huge refugee population of perhaps six million persons. Though these figures would be dwarfed by the catastrophic losses and dislocations soon to follow from Russia's Civil War, they are sufficiently terrible in their own right. We can only guess at the number of soldiers' whose postwar lives were made miserable or cut short by the effects of gassing, shellshock, wounds, tuberculosis, or other diseases incurred while in service.

The economic impact of the war is also difficult to tease out from those of revolution and civil war, a problem compounded by destruction of many financial records. Blockade of Russia's principal ports and other disruption to trade cost tens of billions of rubles. Heavy fighting in, and enemy occupation of, broad swathes of the western borderlands deprived the country of natural resources, as well as causing incalculable damage to infrastructure and industry. (After the war Russia, unlike Belgium and France, would receive no reparations to aid in rebuilding regions ravaged by occupation.) Revenues were also curtailed by wartime prohibition, an idealistic measure that cost the state some 24 percent of prewar annual revenues garnered through its liquor monopoly. Like most states in the First World War, Russia did not rely on taxation to finance its colossal wartime expenditures (approximately 38.65 billion rubles by September 1, 1917.) Instead, it depended heavily on loans, both foreign and domestic, creating enormous debt. The state also resorted to printing money – 31 percent of war expenditure was covered by issuing paper notes – feeding inflation that assumed runaway proportions by 1917. Overall, we can also note a serious decline in income and consumption. Though figures for wartime trends in economic activity are patchy, and some kinds of large-scale industrial production rose impressively, it is clear that the general trend was negative. A recent estimate of Russian national income for the years 1913–17, taking income for 1913 as 100, shows an overall decline in 1917 to 67.7 per cent of the 1913 level. The declining output of commodities meant that consumption dropped even more, to perhaps less than half its 1913 level.[31]

Domestically, issues such as the war's impact on democratization, citizenship rights, and women's rights – all of which figure in scholarship on the war experience of the other combatant countries – are hard to determine, since in the case of Russia we cannot disentangle war-produced outcomes from what the revolution consolidated or gave. For example, it is clear that in Britain and the United States women's contributions to the war effort helped tip the balance in favor of their gaining the franchise after the war's conclusion. In Russia, women's warwork might have played a role in their gaining the vote, but women's suffrage was granted in July 1917 by the Provisional Government as part of a larger universal suffrage law that fulfilled one of the promises of the revolution. However, we can suppose that in Russia, as in the other combatant countries, there would in any event have been some postwar broadening of access to education and opportunities, some restructuring of social relationships. The wartime mobilization of the home front had simply shaken things up too much; it had also created expectations of postwar rights and rewards that would be reinforced by the revolutionary rhetoric of rights, equality, and opportunity. For example, soldiers and their families had been told that their wartime service and sacrifice entitled them to material aid from the state, and there is evidence that by 1917 many had internalized such ideas.[32]

One effect of the First World War in virtually every combatant state was further to nationalize populations. For some peoples of the Russian Empire, such as the Ukrainians, the war experience indeed served as a crucible for forging national consciousness. But the degree to which the war affected the idea of Russian nationhood remains disputed. Many scholars doubt that Russian national consciousness was a mass sensibility in the Great War, also questioning the existence of the state patriotism that would stem from it. Some characterize patriotism and national consciousness as mainly urban phenomena. I. Iu. Porshneva, for example, believes that the ambitious wartime efforts to disseminate modern, "state-minded" views came too late to be internalized by the majority of peasants. However, other scholars believe the war furthered creation of a modern, Russian national consciousness. Eric Lohr charts the wartime explosion of economic nationalism in Russia, a phenomenon that built on resentment of decades of German economic dominance and transcended class boundaries. One of its consequences was an unprecedented program of state-directed sequestration of the property and resources of "enemy aliens," broadly defined.

Joshua Sanborn suggests that mass conscription and the experience of service in a self-consciously "national" military helped build national consciousness.[33]

The putative underdevelopment of a national idea or state consciousness among the mass of the population has important implications for explaining Russia's defeat. It shifts emphasis from Russia being too economically undeveloped to wage a modern, industrialized war to its insufficient cultural–national development. In a total war of nations in arms, only countries able to mobilize the entire nation behind their war effort could sustain the ordeal to the end. In this line of thinking, multinational imperial Russia – much like the Ottoman Empire but unlike more nationally minded European belligerents – could not mobilize a "nation."

Two other common phenomena of this totalizing war were increased state power and states' resort to techniques of mass mobilization. To what degree did these occur in Russia as well? Newer research modifies or complicates an older picture of a more unique Russian experience, one in which a strong, centralized imperial state increasingly *lost* power and control during the war, and was too reactionary or wary of its people to attempt its mobilization. On the one hand, the imperial government was weakened by ceding control over part of the country to the military authorities, by the emergence of public organizations that overlapped or even competed with it for management of war production and food supply, and by the internal disorganization of the central bureaucracy from late 1915 on. On the other hand, the state also stepped up surveillance and censorship of its population; increased its intervention in the economy; and did more than has been realized to propagandize the population's support for a national war effort.

In general, recent scholarship has shown greater appreciation for the war's profound impact on Russia, and the interconnectedness of the war and revolution. For example, Peter Holquist has made an influential case for how the general wartime phenomena of increased state power and mobilization combined, in Russia, with a pre-existing belief in the state's transformative capacities, and the outbreak of revolution, to shape a new Soviet society. "In Russia, the revolution wove together an ethos of violence merging out of the First World War with an insistent demand for remaking Russian society . . . Total war and total revolution thus acted upon each other in a reciprocal way." In this view, many of the practices we have customarily seen as innovations of the revolution or the Bolsheviks – generalized surveillance, propaganda and mobilization techniques, and prophylactic use of violence against suspect population groups – might be better understood as developments of wartime practices and values. Similarly, a number of scholars now conceptualize Russia's war, revolution, and civil war as constituting a distinct whole, a "seven years' war" or "continuum of crisis" with long-term effects on the fledgling Soviet state.[34]

Conclusion

Whatever the debates over periodization, human costs, and factors in defeat, the more we learn of Russia's "unknown war," the more significant it appears. The war mobilized, and displaced, masses of the population on an unprecedented scale: for combat, for industry, as refugees. It affected the role and practices of the state, the organization of the economy, national identities. The scale of its losses and privations stoked popular anger, social tensions, and narratives about internal enemies and treason that would outlive the war itself. Russia's experience of the First World War was both catalyst and crucible of the revolution.

Notes

1 The classic treatment in English of Russia's war experience is Michael T. Florinsky, *The End of the Russian Empire* (New Haven: Yale University Press, 1931); a detailed and readable narrative is W. Bruce Lincoln, *Passage through Armageddon: The Russians in War and Revolution* (New York: Simon and Schuster, 1986). An example of the political orthodoxy required of Soviet scholarship on the war experience is the well-researched study by V. S. Diakin, *Russkaia burzhuaziia i tsarizm v pervoi mirovoi voiny (1914–1917)* (Leningrad: Izd. "Nauka," 1967).

2 On the effacement of the memory of the war in Soviet Russia, see Catherine Merridale, *Night of Stone: Death and Memory in Twentieth-Century Russia* (New York: Penguin, 2001), 96–101, and Aaron J. Cohen, "Oh, That! Myth, Memory, and World War I in the Russian Emigration and the Soviet Union," *Slavic Review*, 62/1 (Spring 2003), 69–86.

3 An excerpt of Durnovo's famous memo can be found in Ronald Kowalski, ed., *The Russian Revolution, 1917–1921* (Routledge: London and New York, 1997), 18–19.

4 On Russian deliberations in the weeks leading up to the war, see D. C. B. Lieven, *Russia and the Origins of the First World War* (London: St Martin's Press, 1983); Keith Neilson, "Russia," in Keith Wilson, ed., *Decisions for War 1914* (New York: St Martin's Press, 1995), 97–121; and David McLaren McDonald, *United Government and Foreign Policy in Russia, 1900–1914* (Cambridge, MA: Harvard University Press, 1992), 199–207.

5 The most detailed analysis of the military mobilization is Josh Sanborn, "The Mobilization of 1914 and the Question of the Russian Nation: A Reexamination," *Slavic Review*, 59/2 (Summer 2000), 267–89.

6 An influential English language work is Norman Stone, *The Eastern Front, 1914–1917* (London: Penguin Books, 1998; first published 1975). An excellent short analysis of Russia's military conduct of the war – differing from Stone on the competence of the high command and several other issues – is William C. Fuller, Jr., "The Eastern Front," in Jay Winter, Geoffrey Parker, and Mary R. Habeck, eds., *The Great War and the Twentieth Century* (New Haven: Yale University Press, 2000), 30–61.

7 See Emily E. Pyle, "Village Social Relations and the Reception of Soldiers' Family Aid Policies in Russia, 1912–1921," Ph.D. Diss., University of Chicago, 1997.

8 As early as November 1914, the war split the Socialist Revolutionary Party (PSR) into a "defensist" group that supported the Russian war effort and internationalist or "defeatist" groups that opposed it; Michael Melancon, *The Socialist Revolutionaries and the Russian Anti-War Movement, 1914–1917* (Columbus, OH: Ohio State University Press, 1990), 20–40. Religiously motivated pacifists also had trouble with the authorities: see D. Khaints, "Adventisty Sed'mogo Dnia i otkaz ot uchastiia v voennykh deistviiakh," in T. A. Pavlova, ed., *Dolgii put' rossiiskogo patsifizma* (Moscow: Institut vseobshchei istorii RAN, 1997), 173–4.

9 See Lewis H. Siegelbaum, *The Politics of Industrial Mobilization: A Study of the War Industries Committees* (New York: St Martin's Press, 1983), and Stone, *Eastern Front*, 209–11.

10 On commercial patriotic undertakings, see Hubertus F. Jahn, *Patriotic Culture in Russia during World War I* (Ithaca, NY: Cornell University Press, 1995); a case study of efforts to inform peasants about the war is Scott J. Seregny, "Zemstvos, Peasants and Citizenship: The Russian Adult Education Movement and World War I,' *Slavic Review*, 59/4 (Summer 2000), 290–315. On loans, see Paul N. Apostol, "Credit Operations," in Alexander M.

Michelson et al., *Russian Public Finance during the War* (New Haven: Yale University Press, 1928), 249–52, 263–77; posters are in N. I. Baburina, *Russkii plakat pervoi mirovoi voiny* (Moscow: Isskustvo i kul'tura, 1992), 64–84.

11 For the fateful implications of Nicholas's assumption of personal command, see, e.g., Richard Pipes, *The Russian Revolution* (New York: Alfred A. Knopf, 1990), 224–8.

12 On the police, see Jonathan Daly, *The Watchful State: Security Police and Opposition in Russia, 1906–1917* (DeKalb, IL: University of Northern Illinois Press, 2004), 159–214. The fullest study of the press is A. F. Berezhnoi, *Russkaia legal'naia pechat' v gody pervoi mirovoi voiny* (Leningrad: "Nauka," 1975).

13 Military censorship report of April 1916 for the Southwestern Armies and Kiev Military district, Rossiiskii Gosudarstvennyi Voenno-Istoricheskii Arkhiv (RGVIA), fo. 2003, op. 1, d. 1486, ll. 63–4.

14 Report of the gendarmerie of Moscow Province in GARF, fo. 58, op. 5, d. 399, l. 187. An absorbing study of the implications of spy mania is William C. Fuller, Jr., *The Foe Within: Fantasies of Treason and the End of Imperial Russia* (Ithaca, NY: Cornell University Press, 2006), esp. 150–84, 258–64.

15 On citizenship in 1917, see Orlando Figes and Boris Kolonitskii, *Interpreting the Russian Revolution: The Language and Symbols of 1917* (New Haven: Yale University Press, 1999), 104–26, and S. A. Smith, "Citizenship and the Russian Nation during World War I: A Comment," *Slavic Review*, 59/40 (Summer 2000), 316–29.

16 On the national remobilizations in Europe, see the influential collection edited by John Horne, *State, Society and Mobilization in Europe during the First World War* (Cambridge: Cambridge University Press, 1997), and especially his introduction, pp. 1–17.

17 *Rech'* (June, 18, 1917), 5. On the women volunteers, see Melissa K. Stockdale, "My Death for the Motherland is Happiness: Women, Patriotism, and Soldiering in Russia's Great War, 1914–1917," *American Historical Review*, 109 (Feb. 2004), 78–116; and Laurie Stoff, *They Fought for the Motherland: Russia's Women Soldiers in World War I and the Revolution* (Lawrence, KS: University of Kansas Press, 2006).

18 The most comprehensive treatment in any language of the collapse of the imperial army is Allan K. Wildman, *The End of the Russian Imperial Army*. Vol. 1. *The Old Army and the Soldiers' Revolt*. Vol 2. *The Road to Soviet Power and Peace* (Princeton: Princeton University Press, 1980, 1987).

19 John W. Wheeler Bennett, *The Forgotten Peace. Brest Litovsk, March 1918* (New York: William and Morrow Co., 1939), 66–95. On peace efforts and the "defensist" line, see Rex A. Wade, *The Russian Search for Peace: February–October 1917* (Stanford, CA: Stanford University Press, 1969). On Ukraine, see Stephan M. Horak, *The First Treaty of World War I: Ukraine's Treaty with the Central Powers of February, 1918* (Boulder, CO: East European Monographs, 1988).

20 Wheeler-Bennett, *The Forgotten Peace*, 266–73, 344–46, 362, and 403–08, which includes the text of the treaty. For the Soviet state's reconquest or reincorporation of most of the lands lost in 1918, see Richard Pipes, *The Formation of the Soviet Union: Communism and Nationalism, 1917–1923* (Cambridge, MA.: Harvard University Press, 1964).

21 David R. Jones, "Russia," in Robin Higham, ed., with Dennis F. Showalter, *Researching World War I: A Handbook* (Westport, CT: Greenwood Press, 2003); Joshua Sanborn, *Drafting the Russian Nation: Military Conscription, Total War, and Mass Politics, 1905–1925* (Dekalb, IL: Northern Illinois University Press, 2003), 29–38; Wildman, *End of the Russian Imperial Army*, vol. 1, pp. 65–105. Some scholars see in the large numbers of Russians taken prisoner – a million in 1915 alone – evidence that the Russian peasant soldier lacked the attitude of his German, French, and British equivalents; e.g. John Keegan, *The First World War* (New York: Alfred Knopf, 1999), 342–3.

22   Stone, *The Eastern Front*, 194–211.

23   Fuller, "Eastern Front," 41, also notes that, even with soaring output, Russia remained short of rifles, large-caliber artillery, and machine guns.

24   Until fairly recently, scholarship neglected the violence inflicted upon civilian populations in the First World War; a good introduction is Stephane Audoin-Rouzeau and Annette Becker, *14–18. Understanding the Great War*, trans. Catherine Temerson (New York: Hill and Wang, 2002), 45–90.

25   Recent work on population displacements and the war experience in the borderlands includes Peter Gatrell, *A Whole Empire Walking: Refugees in Russia during World War I* (Bloomington, IN: Indiana University Press, 1999); A. Iu. Bakhturina, *Okrainy rossiiskii imperii: gosudarstvennoe upravlenie i natsional'naia politika v gody pervoi mirovoi voiny (1914–1917 gg.)* (Moscow: Rosspen, 2004); Eric Lohr, 'The Russian Army and the Jews: Mass Deportation, Hostages, and Violence during World War I," *Russian Review*, 60/3 (July 2001), 404–19; Alexander Victor Prusin, *Nationalizing a Borderland: War, Ethnicity, and Anti-Jewish Violence in East Galicia, 1914–1920* (Tuscaloosa, AL: University of Alabama Press, 2005); and, from the German perspective, Vejas Gabriel Liulevicius, *War Land on the Eastern Front: Culture, National Identity, and German Occupation in World War I* (Cambridge: Cambridge University Press, 2000).

26   On urban working people in the war, see Peter Gatrell, *Russia's First World War: A Social and Economic History* (Harlow: Pearson Education, 2005), 68–71, and Iu. V. Kirianov, "Rabochie Rossii i voina: novye podkhodky i analizu problemy," in V. I. Malkov, ed., *Pervaia mirovaia voina. Prolog XX veka* (Moscow: "Nauka," 1998), 432–46; Kirianov believes that Soviet-era scholarship greatly exaggerated the anti-war nature of strikes. On women, see Alfred G. Meyer, "The Impact of World War I on Russian Women's Lives," in Barbara Evans Clements et al., *Russia's Women: Accommodation, Resistance, Transformation* (Berkeley, 1991), 208–24. On workers in wartime Petrograd, see Robert B. McKean, *St Petersburg between the Revolutions: Workers and Revolutionaries, June 1907–February 1917* (New Haven: Yale University Press, 1990), 318–49, 406–29. For the European context, see Leopold Haimson and G. Sapelli, eds., *Strikes, Social Conflict, and the First World War: An International Perspective* (Milan: Feltrinelli, 1992).

27   O. S. Porshneva, "Problemy voiny i mira v obshchestvennoi bor'be na urale. 1914–1918," in Malkov, *Pervaia mirovaia voina*, 466–7; Barbara Alpern Engel, "Not by Bread Alone: Subsistence Riots in Russia during World War I," *Journal of Modern History*, 69/4 (Dec. 1997), 721, and Mark Baker, "Rampaging *Soldatki*, Cowering Police, Bazaar Riots and Moral Economy: The Social Impact of the Great War in Kharkiv Province," *Canadian–American Slavic Studies*, 35 (2001), 137–55. For the Moscow riots, see Eric Lohr, *Nationalizing the Russian Empire: The Campaign against Enemy Aliens during World War I* (Cambridge, MA: Harvard University Press, 2003), 31–54.

28   Far more has been written on grain production and the bread crisis than on rural experience of the war *per se*; for the former, see Lars T. Lih, *Bread and Authority in Russia, 1914–1921* (Berkeley: University of California Press, 1990). Still the fullest work on the village in the war is A. M. Anfimov, *Rossiiskaia derevnia v gody pervoi mirovoi voiny (1914–fev. 1917)* (Moscow: Sotsekgiz, 1962); see also Gatrell, *Russia's First World War*, 72–6, and O. S. Porshneva, *Krest"iane, rabochie i soldaty Rossii nakanune i v gody pervoi mirovoi voiny* (Moscow: ROSSPEN, 2004), 68–116.

29   e.g., Raymond Pearson, *The Russian Moderates and the Crisis of Tsarism 1914–1917* (London: MacMillan Press, 1977), who concludes that in 1917 the magnitude of the problems and the inadequacies of Russian moderates meant their last chance to exercise power "could only be another chance to fail" (p. 181).

30   Commonly used figures come from *Rossiia v mirovoi voine 1914–1918 gg v tsifrakh* (Moscow: Tsentral'noe statisticheskoe upravlenie, 1925), and Stanislas Kohn, "The Vital

Statistics of European Russia during the World War, 1914–1917," in Kohn and Alexander F. Meyendorff, *The Cost of the War to Russia* (New Haven: Yale University Press, 1932), 37–9. Both sources admit their figures are probably too low. The higher estimates are found in A. I. Stepanov, "Obshchie demograficheskie poteri naseleniia Rossii v pervoi mirovoi voiny," in Malkov, *Pervaia mirovaia voina*, 478–80; Stepanov's figures for number of men mobilized are also higher.

31 Alexander M. Michelin et al., *Russian Public Finance during the* War (New Haven: Yale University Press, 1928), 215–20; Gatrell, *Russia's First World War*, 248–9.

32 On the extension of citizenship rights, see, e.g., Nicoletta F. Gullace, *"The Blood of Our Sons": Men, Women, and the Renegotiation of British Citizenship during the Great War* (New York: Palgrave, 2002). For wartime views on rights and rewards owed to soldiers, see Melissa K. Stockdale, "United in Gratitude: Honoring Soldiers and Defining the Nation in Russia's Great War," *Kritika. Explorations in Russian and Eurasian History*, 7/3 (Summer 2006), 459–85.

33 For non-Russians, see Mark von Hagen, "The Great War and the Mobilization of Ethnicity in the Russian Empire," in Barnett Rubin and Jack Snyder, eds., *Post-Soviet Political Order* (London: Routledge, 1998), 34–57. On Russian national consciousness, see, e.g., Jahn, *Patriotic Culture*, 172–7; Porshneva, *Krest'iane, rabochie i soldaty*, 86–91, 260–62; Lohr, *Nationalizing the Russian Empire*, 166–73; Sanborn, *Drafting the Russian Nation*, 13–19.

34 Peter Holquist, *Making War, Forging Revolution: Russia's Continuum of Crisis, 1914–1921* (Cambridge, MA: Harvard University Press, 2002), esp. 206–240, 284–86; Igor Narskii, *Zhizn' v katastrofe. Budni naseleniia Urala v 1917–1922 gg.* (Moscow: ROSSPEN, 2001), 23–4; for debate over conceptualizing this period as Russia's "long first world war," see N. N. Smirnov et al, *Rossiia i pervaia mirovaia voina. (Materialy mezhdunarodnogo nauchnogo kollokviuma)* (St Peterburg: Izd. "Dmitrii Bulanin," 1999), especially 541–52.

References

Brusilov, A. (1930). *A Soldier's Notebook, 1914–1918*. Macmillan and Co., London.

Florinsky, M. (1931). *The End of the Russian Empire*. Yale University Press, New Haven.

Fuller, W. (2006). *The Foes Within: Fantasies of Treason and the End of Imperial Russia*. Cornell University Press, Ithaca, NY.

Fuller, W. (2000). "The Eastern Front," in J. Winter, G. Parker, and M. Habeck (eds.), *The Great War and the Twentieth Century*. Yale University Press, New Haven, 30–68.

Gatrell, P. (1999). *A Whole Empire Walking. Refugees in Russia during World War I*. Indiana University Press, Bloomington, IN.

Gatrell, P. (2005). *Russia's First World War: A Social and Economic History*. Pearson Education Ltd, Harlow.

Holquist, P. (2002). *Making War, Forging Revolution: Russia's Continuum of Crisis, 1914–1921*. Harvard University Press, Cambridge, MA.

Jahn, H. (1995). *Patriotic Culture in Russia during World War I*. Cornell University Press, Ithaca, NY.

Kohn, S., and Meyendorff, A. (1932). *The Cost of the War to Russia*. Yale University Press, London.

Lieven, D. (1983). *Russia and the Origins of the First World War*. St Martin's Press, London.

Lih, L. (1990). *Bread and Authority in Russia, 1914–1921*. University of California Press, Berkeley.

Lincoln, W. B. (1986). *Passage through Armageddon: The Russians in War and Revolution*. Simon and Schuster, New York.

Lohr, E. (2003). *Nationalizing the Russian Empire: The Campaign against Enemy Aliens during World War I*. Harvard University Press, Cambridge, MA.

Merridale, C. (2001). *Night of Stone: Death and Memory in Twentieth-Century Russia*. Penguin, New York.

Meyer, A. (1991). "The Impact of World War I on Russian Women's Lives," in B. Clements et al., *Russia's Women: Accomodation, Resistance, Transformation*, University of California Press, Berkeley, 208–24.

Pearson, R. (1977). *The Russian Moderates and the Crisis of Tsardom 1914–1917*. Macmillan Press Ltd., London.

Porshneva, O. (2004). *Krest"iane, rabochie i soldaty Rossii nakanune i v gody pervoi mirovoi voiny*. ROSSPEN, Moscow.

Sanborn, J. (2000). "The Mobilization of 1914 and the Question of the Russian Nation: A Reexamination," *Slavic Review*, 59/2: 290–315.

Sanborn, J. (2003). *Drafting the Russian Nation. Military Conscription, Total War and Mass Politics, 1905–1925*, Northern Illinois Press, DeKalb, IL.

Seregny, S. (2000). "Zemstvos, Peasants and Citizenship: The Russian Adult Education Movement and World War I," *Slavic Review*, 59/2: 290–315.

Smirnov, N., et al. (1999). *Rossiia i pervaia mirovaia voina. (Materialy mezhdunarodnogo nauchnogo kollokviuma)*. Izd. "Dmitrii Bulanin," St Petersburg.

Smith, S. (2000). "Citizenship and the Russian Nation during World War I: A Comment," in *Slavic Review*, 59/2: 316–29.

Malkov, V. (ed.) (1994). *Pervaia mirovaia voina Prolog XX veka*. "Nauka," Moscow.

Stockdale, M. (2004). "My Death for the Motherland is Happiness: Women, Patriotism and Soldiering in Russia's Great War, 1914–1917," *American Historical Review*, 109/1: 78–116.

Stone, N. (1998, 1975). *The Eastern Front, 1914–1917*. Penguin Books, London.

Von Hagen, M. (1998). *The Great War and the Mobilization of Ethnicity in the Russian Empire*, in B. Rubin and J. Snyder (eds.), *Post Soviet Political Order*. Routledge, London, 34–57.

Wade, R. (1969). *The Russian Search for Peace: February–October 1917*. Stanford University Press, Stanford, CO.

Wheeler-Bennett, J. (1939). *The Forgotten Peace. Brest Litovsk, March, 1918*. William Morrow Co., New York.

Wildman, A. (1980, 1987). *The End of the Russian Imperial Army*. Vol. 1. *The Old Army and the Soldiers' Revolt*. Vol. 2. *The Road to Soviet Power and Peace*. Princeton University Press, Princeton.

Further Reading

Brusilov, A. (1930). *A Soldier's Notebook, 1914–1918*. Macmillan, London. Accessible memoir by most celebrated Russian general of the war.

Baburina, N. I. (1992). *Russkii plakat pervoi mirovoi voiny* [The Russian Poster in the First World War]. Isskustvo i kul'tura, Moscow. Excellent collection of First World War posters, with text in English as well as Russian.

Florinsky, M. T. (1931). *The End of the Russian Empire*. Yale University Press, New Haven. Classic English-language history of the war, part of the important 8-volume "Russian Series" of the Carnegie Endowment's Economic and Social History of the World War.

Fuller, W. C., Jr. (2006). *The Foe Within: Fantasies of Treason and the End of Imperial Russia*. Cornell University Press, Ithaca, NY. Absorbing exploration of spy mania and its consequences.

Gatrell, P. (1999). *A Whole Empire Walking: Refugees in Russia during World War One.* Indiana University Press, Bloomington, IN. Innovative examination of population displacement and its repercussions.

Gatrell, P. (2005). *Russia's First World War: A Social and Economic History.* Pearson Education Ltd, Harlow. Brief, up-to-date overview by a leading scholar.

Golovin, N. (1931). *The Russian Army in the World War.* Yale University Press, New Haven. Influential account by a Russian general, emphasizing munitions shortages and lack of popular patriotism as factors in defeat.

Holquist, P. (2002). *Making War, Forging Revolution. Russia's Continuum of Crisis, 1914–1921.* Harvard University Press, Cambridge, MA. Explores total war's impact on the revolution and Soviet state practices.

Jahn, H. (1995). *Patriotic Culture in Russia during World War I.* Cornell University Press, Ithaca, NY. Well-illustrated discussion of prints, performance, and film in the war's first year.

Lohr, E. (2003). *Nationalizing the Russian Empire. The Campaign against Enemy Aliens during World War I.* Harvard University Press, Cambridge, MA. Important study of economic nationalism and ethnic cleansing.

Sanborn, J. (2003). Drafting the Russian Nation. Military Conscription, Total War, and Mass Politics, 1905–1925. Northern Illinois University Press, Dekalb, IL. Excellent, theoretically informed study of the nationalizing effects of mass military service.

Siegelbaum, L. (1983). *The Politics of Industrial Mobilization: A Study of the War Industries Committees.* St Martin's Press, New York. Detailed, critical study of committees' actual contribution to war effort.

Smirnov, N., et al. (1999). *Rossiia i pervaia mirovaia voina. (Materialy mezhdunarodnogo nauchnogo kollokviuma)* [Russia and the First World War: Materials from an International Scholarly Colloquium]. Izd. "Dmitrii Bulanin," St Petersburg. Sophisticated collection of papers covering diverse aspects of the war, plus participants' debates over theoretical approaches.

Stone, N. (1998). *The Eastern Front, 1914–1917.* Penguin, London. First published 1975. Pioneering study of the eastern front, dismisses munitions shortages as explanation for Russia's defeats.

Wildman, A. (1980, 1987). *The End of the Russian Imperial Army.* Vol. 1. *The Old Army and the Soldiers' Revolt.* Vol 2. *The Road to Soviet Power and Peace.* Princeton University Press, Princeton. Exhaustive study of the army's internal dynamics in 1917–18, sympathetic to the soldiers' revolt.

PART IV

The Soviet Union

CHAPTER TWENTY

From the First World War to Civil War, 1914–1923

MARK VON HAGEN

The Civil War that erupted on the territory of the former Russian Empire has been generally dated as 1917/18–21, whereas the First World War is traditionally dated 1914–1918. Despite the brief formal chronological overlap, historians of Russia who have explored either of these wars have generally treated them as distinct periods marked by a fundamental caesura in 1917. Since the late 1960s more historians have written about the Civil War in Russia than they have about the First World War there, both inside the Soviet Union but also outside it. They have generally treated that set of conflicts that culminated in the establishment of Bolshevik rule over most – but not all – of the territory of the former Romanov Empire as part of Soviet history and firmly rooted in the struggles unleashed during 1917, particularly the seizure of power in Petrograd by a minority party, the Bolsheviks, who were determined to overthrow the old order and establish a dictatorship of the proletariat.[1]

One of the unintended consequences of this periodization has been the delimiting of the territory and populations under consideration to those that eventually found themselves within the boundaries of the Soviet Union,[2] thereby also narrowing the range of alternative outcomes described and granting the emergence of the USSR a decided air of Whiggish inevitability.[3] Another important consequence has been to look for the roots of Stalinism and its authoritarian political culture in the Civil War period.[4] Such a quest for Stalinist roots often implicitly presumed that the Bolsheviks had a fresh start in late 1917, and that their slide toward authoritarianism was either the result of their militant ideology or the circumstances of the Civil War, or some complicated combination of the two.

The few historians who have treated Russia's involvement in the First World War wrote about those campaigns, by contrast, as the final chapters of the Old Regime, even bringing their stories to an end in late 1917, despite the war's continuation until November 1918 (and only if we ignore the earlier treaties signed at Brest-Litovsk).[5] The war – and the attendant collapse of Imperial Russia – was seen as resulting from the sins of the Old Regime and either its stubborn unwillingness or structural incapacity to make the transition to a modern nation state and prosperous market economy within the confines of dynastic autocracy. The collapse of the Old Regime is described as virtually total, again conditioning us to think of 1917 as a – perhaps the – fundamental rupture in Russian history.

Contemporaries, however, saw less of a caesura than subsequent historians; for many who lived through these years, the First World War, revolution, and civil war fused in one traumatic "time of troubles" that recalled an earlier period of foreign invasion and internecine violence after the death of Ivan the Terrible. Recently, historians have begun to revisit the period 1914–21/23 with a sense of its greater continuities.[6] The struggle of the old politics with the new, symbolized at the beginning of 1917 in the rivalry of the Provisional Government and the Petrograd Soviet, the so-called dual power, did not come to an abrupt end in November 1917, certainly not outside Bolshevik-held Russia, and not even in the capitals of Petrograd and Moscow. In Kiev, Omsk, Samara, Tiflis, Helsinki, and Tashkent, the political elites and ideas of late Imperial Russia continued to do battle with their emerging rivals and eventual successors, who chose radically new visions of state and nation. But, in invoking again the radical changes, perhaps we presume too much that the old politics was only supplanted by the new, when the alternate periodization suggested above provides much evidence that the old politics also shaped the new in fundamental ways. As one example, one could trace the origins of the dual-power regime – usually seen as emerging in 1917 – to the first months of the war, when the army command had virtually a free hand in vast front-line zones and later in the occupied territories and when the authorities in Petrograd – the State Council and the civilian ministries – issued orders in vain to the front-line commanders and the commander-in-chief.[7] Furthermore, state-sponsored or state-led campaigns of radical change had many of their roots in the First World War, itself a set of processes that produced profound social, organizational, and political change – much of it unintentional or at least not anticipated by its unleashers – across the Eurasian landmass. The army presided over extralegal redistributions of property and pre-emptive deportations of ethnic communities, especially Poles, Germans, Jews, and other minority nationalities.

The First World War is described as the first global total war, in which boundaries between fighting armies and civilian populations dissolved, while international borders were violently redrawn time and again. The "Russian Civil War," however, is treated primarily as a conflict between Reds and Whites, despite frequently dismissive discussion (though in the case of Soviet scholarship a ritual insistence on the centrality) of the "foreign intervention" and the broader international contexts. Vladimir Lenin appears to have persuaded subsequent historians when he pronounced in 1918 that there was no choice between Red and White, no middle ground for Russian political development, because of the threat of foreign imperialist designs on the new Bolshevik state. It is as if the cold-war isolation and autarky of the Soviet state, and its putatively unique and special features, had their origins in the "capitalist encirclement" of these early years. Instead, we can begin to see – once we look across the great divide of 1917 – that the First World War left the new Bolshevik order with definite building blocks in the form of transformed ideas, institutions, and communities. Neither 1917 nor 1921 could be a return to the status quo ante 1914. The war that started in 1914 forced modernity onto Russia and Russia onto modernity in ways that resonated throughout the subsequent century.

The Military and Political History of the "Time of Troubles"

Russia entered the war against Germany and Austria-Hungary on August 2, 1914. Following on prewar commitments, Russia fought as an ally of Britain and France. Soon the Ottoman Empire entered on the side of the Central Powers, thereby making the western and southern fronts (known as the eastern front from the pan-European perspective) the crucial ones for most of the war. The initial months of the war were marked by German victories over Russia in East Prussia, while Russian armies defeated the imperial and royal forces of the Habsburg monarchy and occupied Galicia and Bukovyna until the summer of 1915.

The hasty and chaotic retreat of the Russian forces in June 1915 was accompanied by a large-scale evacuation and the sudden emergence of a refugee problem for the imperial authorities, who were ill-equipped to deal with the challenge.[8] The retreat also provoked vocal criticism of the government from the parliamentary opposition. Emperor Nicholas II dismissed his uncle as Supreme Commander-in-Chief and assumed that position himself; he also dismissed Grand Duke Nicholas' chief of staff, Nikolai Ianushkevich. Public organizations stepped in to help with a growing list of problems, from refugee resettlement and aid to care for the wounded soldiers and provisioning the army.

The tsar reluctantly granted temporary powers to the War Industries Committees and the Union of Zemstvos and Towns (Zemgor).[9] Still, the opposition grew increasingly frustrated and sufficiently emboldened to criticize the autocracy and demand ministers responsible to the Duma. The Progressive bloc, a loose coalition of moderate and conservative parties, demanded still more political reforms in the name of patriotism and better prosecution of the war.[10] These measures collectively achieved some success, when a Russian offensive led by General Alexei Brusilov recaptured the territories lost in the prior year. The political situation in the capitals, however, and the frequent ministerial replacements sharply eroded elite confidence in the imperial family. Conspiracies began to take shape around the assassination of the Empress' favorite, the Siberian "holy man," Grigorii Rasputin, and for the removal of the imperial couple themselves. In December 1916, conservative nobles and right-wing politicians murdered Rasputin in a desperate attempt to remove his influence at court.

Earlier in 1916 the Russian state, this time with the sanction of the Duma, ordered the call-up of reservists and single-breadwinners to compensate for the tremendous manpower losses during the first year and a half of the fighting; these new conscripts were reluctant to serve and became the carriers of discontent that spread rapidly through the ranks. Also in 1916 a labor mobilization ordered for Russian Turkestan (today's Central Asia) provoked a bloody uprising of mostly Turko-Muslim natives against Russian and Ukrainian settlers in the region that resembled the brutal colonial wars of the British and French empires. Order was restored only at great cost in lives on both sides and with the flight of hundreds of thousands of natives across the border to imperial China (Xinjiang).

In March 1917, a delegation of high-ranking military officers persuaded Nicholas to abdicate the throne in favor of his brother after strikes and a bread riot in the capital; but the emperor's brother, Mikhail, immediately refused the throne, thereby bringing the 300-year-old Romanov dynasty to an end. The Provisional Government was formed from a committee of the Duma to assume authority over Russia until the convening of the Constituent Assembly; very quickly, that government was challenged by the spokesmen of workers, soldiers, and peasants, who coalesced in the Petrograd Soviet of Workers' and Soldiers' Deputies. The two powers entered a period of uneasy coexistence known as the "dual authority."

Outside the capital, similarly improvised authorities were taking shape. For example, in Kiev, the public organizations united in an Executive Committee of the Council of Public Organizations, which was recognized by the Provisional Government as the legitimate authority in the city and adjacent region. A Kiev Soviet of Workers' Deputies formed to challenge that authority, as did an institution characteristic of much of the imperial borderlands, the Ukrainian Central Rada, which formed to defend and promote the interests of the Ukrainian nation in the name of autonomy and a federalist restructuring of the empire. The dual-authority regime, which quickly became more accurately a "poly-authority" regime, underwent several political crises, primarily over foreign policy (war aims, more specifically, and the character of the future peace) and national autonomy for the minorities, but also over land and labor issues.

In May socialist ministers from the Soviet entered the Provisional Government for the first coalition of Kadets, Octobrists, Mensheviks, Social Revolutionaries, and others. Also in May the Commander-in-Chief, General Mikhail Alexeev, was replaced by the hero of the 1916 offensive, Alexei Brusilov, and Army Minister Alexander Guchkov, an Octobrist, was replaced by Alexander Kerensky, a Trudovik (member of the Labor Group of the State Duma) closely allied to the Social Revolutionaries; a July offensive intended to reverse the alarming deterioration of the Russian Army failed against a stubborn German counterattack. The death penalty was reinstated to combat the rising tide of soldier disobedience and desertion, but produced the opposite effect: further demoralization, desertion, and widespread lynching of unpopular officers.[11]

Meanwhile in July another crisis, this time over the demands of the Ukrainian Central Rada for recognition of Ukraine's autonomy, confronted the coalition government with serious difficulties, leading to the resignation of all but the socialist ministers. Alexander Kerensky took over as prime minister from Prince Georgii Lvov.

The political crisis in the capital, combined with the economic breakdown and widespread shortages, the rising antiwar sentiment, and the general radicalization of opposition politics opened considerable space for the most extreme left-wing party, the Bolsheviks, led by Vladimir Lenin/Ulianov.

After an abortive set of risings against the dual-authority regime in July, the Bolshevik leaders were arrested or went into hiding. Now Kerensky, heading a moderate socialist coalition government, appealed to the bourgeoisie and the centrist parties by calling an All Russian Conference in Moscow, but the government immediately faced a new challenge from the Commander-in-Chief, General Lavr Kornilov, who had become the hero of the Moscow conference and who in August marched on the capital to restore order and remove Kerensky's government. A desperate Kerensky armed the city's workers and appealed to them to defend his regime; he also formed yet another coalition government, this one even more short-lived than its predecessors. Kornilov's attempted putsch and its defeat delivered to the Bolsheviks an unanticipated victory and set the stage for their uprisings in Petrograd and Moscow the following month.

With majorities in the Petrograd and Moscow soviets (as well as large representations in other major cities of the empire), the Bolsheviks seized power in the capitals at the end of 1917, but were soon pressured to invite the Left SR faction into a short-lived coalition. The new government issued decrees on land reform and peace, sent a delegation to Brest-Litovsk to begin negotiations with the Central Powers, and encouraged the workers, peasants, and soldiers to remake the political and social orders. Opposition began forming almost immediately around the country, but internal opposition within the Bolshevik movement erupted over the terms of the Brest Treaty. Left Socialist Revolutionaries protested against the "imperialist peace" and called for revolutionary war against the Germans.[12]

In May 1918 a mutiny of Czech prisoners of war, who had been organized into the so-called Czechoslovak Legion and were on their way across Siberia to return to the western front in Europe, ignited a revolt against the young Bolshevik dictatorship and opened up a space for governments to form from moderate socialists and liberal nationalists, in large measure the coalition that had made up the last several Provisional Governments. A rival government was set up in Samara that had its counterparts elsewhere in the empire; for example, the Siberian Duma declared its sovereignty and refused to recognize the new Bolshevik authorities in Petrograd. In the south, military officers began organizing the Volunteer Army, the core of what would become known as the White movement and which brought together a very uneasy coalition of military men, conservatives, and moderate socialists. In Siberia Admiral Alexander Kolchak ousted the moderates and installed himself as supreme leader of Russia in a brutal military dictatorship; Generals Petr Vrangel and Anton Denikin built an army to reconquer Russia, while General Nikolai Iudenich launched a similar effort to the north.

During 1918 the Bolsheviks suffered a series of reverses and their control was reduced to the territory around Moscow. In 1919 the Whites achieved their greatest victories over the Red forces, but were divided among themselves and operating from bases on the periphery of the former empire, where their Russian nationalism alienated non-Russian movements for autonomy and independence as much as their conservative social policies turned away workers, peasants, and other democratic forces. The Bolsheviks enjoyed the further advantage of controlling the former imperial heartland, with its strategic railroad connections and arms plants. The Russian Civil War was exacerbated and prolonged by the support of the Allies for the White forces and of the Germans (and Turks) for the Ukrainian, Baltic, Caucasian, and Finnish breakaway states.

Just as the Red Army was beginning to turn back the tide of the White challenge, a newly independent and irredentist Polish Republic under Josef Pilsudski invaded Ukraine and thereby provoked a counteroffensive from the Soviet state during 1920. By late November the Soviet–Ukrainian–Polish war had come to an end, with the Treaty of Riga repartitioning Ukraine between Poland and the Soviet Union. The end of hostilities with Poland allowed the Red Army to return its attention to defeating the remnants of the White forces in Crimea, expelling the armies of General Vrangel, who had succeeded the fallen Denikin. The Baltic states, Finland, and Poland remained independent after the peace treaties of the postwar period. But the

Red Army succeeded in regathering much of the former Russian Empire, notably in Ukraine, Siberia, Transcaucasia, and Central Asia (formerly Turkestan). The end of the war left the new Soviet state with an army of some five million, a highly militarized political economy, and suffering from general devastation and exhaustion.[13]

Challenges to the International Order and National Liberation

Among the causes and consequences of the First World War War were rival imperial projects of "national liberation," which over the course of the war involved the great powers in ever more ambitious promises of self-rule and even independence. Out of the Habsburg, Hohenzollern, Romanov, and Ottoman empires emerged a new political geography of East Central Europe and the Middle East. The new states were the results of decades of political activism by national awakeners – those intellectuals, clergy, and others – who raised native language and ethnicity as the most important markers of identity in the modern world. Once the empires went to war with one another, they all sponsored organizations and publishing activities of various expatriate nationalists, among whom the most prominent were the Poles, Finns, Balts, Ukrainians, and Caucasians.

An important legacy of the First World War was this internationalizing of ethnic and social conflicts that had marked it almost from the beginning. Both the Central Powers and the Entente cast the war as the struggle of international coalitions of clashing civilizations, and especially Germany sponsored national and social revolutionary movements to bring down their rival Russian and British empires. Lenin and American President Woodrow Wilson proclaimed separate versions of national self-determination in 1917 and thereby raised expectations of international intervention for oppressed minorities still higher. Those expectations, however much they were to be frustrated, nonetheless came to be institutionalized in the League of Nations and the Communist International.[14]

Indeed, every major contending party on the territory of the Eurasian land mass, expected to be "saved" from defeat by outside intervention – from the Bolsheviks' expectations of international proletarian revolution to the Whites' and democratic counterrevolutions' hopes for aid from the Entente powers, to Poland's and Finland's hopes for international recognition at the Versailles conference. Outside the territory of the former Russian Empire, national and social movements looked for other forms of outside help – Bela Kun's Hungarian revolution hoping for Soviet aid in 1919, together with the Asian and Middle Eastern revolutionaries who gathered in Baku that year at the Congress of Peoples of the East.

The Germans, Austrians, and Turks occupied much of the Russian Empire's western and southern borderlands – from Finland to the Caucasus – until late November 1918; the plans of the German High Command evolved rapidly in the conditions of wartime occupation and homeland devastation into visions of colonization and settlement in the vast eastern realm (Ostraum) inhabited by the borderland peoples (Randvoelker) of the Russian Empire.[15] (After the signing of the armistice in November 1918, the British and French were able to overcome their wartime hostility to the Germans and asked them to remain as a protectorate against the Bolsheviks for at least another few years in the Baltic states and Caucasus. The Japanese left the Far East and Siberia only in 1922.)

Josef Pilsudski's vision of federalism for East Central Europe, albeit dominated by a resurrected Poland, also endorsed the principle of a band of buffer states between Russia and Europe that was to be constituted by detaching the nations of Russia's western borderlands from Muscovy.[16] Poland, too, made appeals to both Central and Entente governments during and after the First World War. During its war with Soviet Russia, fought largely on Ukrainian territory, Poland relied on help from France and Britain. In short, the postwar Eurasian geopolitical arrangement was up for grabs long before November 1918 and for several years following the armistice. When considered against this experience, the Bolshevik reconquista and occupation did not initially seem much different from any number of previous occupation regimes. Their reliance on local collaborators, usually representing minority communities or speaking in the name of still emergent classes or nations, is clear from the histories of the various incarnations of Soviet Ukraine, Red Finland, Litbel (a joint revolutionary government for Lithuania and Belarus), and other "authoritative" and "representative" proto-regimes.[17]

Clearly those parts of the former Russian Empire that were occupied by the Central Powers had the most direct constraints placed on their actions and their policies shaped more powerfully by their "protectors." But even for those regimes that were not occupied by a foreign power, especially the Whites and the Soviet state, Russia's (and the Entente's) war with Germany and the Central Powers remained at the center of their political lives and ideologies. The Whites, despite their frustrations with the Entente powers and their representatives in Russia and despite the efforts of several conservative and monarchist advisors to reorient the White leadership toward Germany, never signed a treaty with the Central Powers and held it against both Lenin's Sovnarkom and Ukraine's succession of governments that they did sign a traitorous peace at Brest-Litovsk. The White campaigns of the Civil War were also cast as reconquista of "a great Russia, one and indivisible."

The Bolshevik leadership (and membership more broadly) divided sharply over peace with Russia's wartime enemies, especially at the cost of signing away at least one-third of the empire's territory and resources; Leon Trotsky, Commisar for Foreign Affairs, even made halting and temporary overtures to the Allies after the renewal of the German offensive in early 1918. The split over war and peace within the Bolshevik Party mirrored similar splits in the other most significant rival socialist parties, the SRs and the Mensheviks. The politics of "revolutionary defensism" and "revolutionary war" had allowed the Left to capture the anti-German patriotism of the Russian working class during 1917; this important wedding of nationalist and socialist appeals helped the Bolsheviks make the transition from insurrectionary movement to state-holding institution. Internationalism was not abandoned, but rather insisted upon fiercely, at the same time that the preservation of the first revolutionary Russian state was being accommodated in the new regime's self-identity.

Even if, as most scholars have concluded, allied (and German) aid proved to be inadequate to turn the tide in the battle between Reds and Whites (or even Reds and Poles), the expectation of intervention and support was an important part of the planning of nearly every major contender for authority in the region. The aid did prolong the Civil War for longer than it would have otherwise lasted. The Bolsheviks' determination to raise the oppressed and injured of the world against their imperialist and capitalist overlords had its analogue in the radical vision of international revolution pursued since 1914 by the German Emperor Wilhelm II and several members of his entourage, and possibly even the national-liberation propaganda of the Russian state in its pitting of the Slavic peoples against the barbaric Teutonic world. In sum, the states and elites of the region had come to expect unprecedented levels of international intervention in their affairs to set borders, protect from would-be invaders and conquerors, and uphold their claims to national sovereignty.

Mobilization, War and Revolution

The 1917 revolutions and the civil wars that followed have been described by social historians as a period of mobilization of large sectors of the population in defense of their visions of a just future and often of their very physical survival. Peasants, workers, soldiers, national minority communities, women, youth, and other groups rallied around slogans of revolutionary change and learned to demonstrate, barricade, strike, mutiny, and otherwise make new claims on authority after the abdication of the Romanov tsar.[18] The origins of this new type of social mobilization can also be found in the early years of the war, when "public organizations" made up of liberal and leftist professionals took shape to provide desperately needed support for the war effort in the face of the colossal mismanagement and incompetence of the tsarist bureaucracy. These organizations included the Union of Towns and Zemstvos (Zemgor, activists in local self-government) and later the War Industries Committees (with representatives from industry, the bureaucracy, and labor); they provided relief to wounded and sick soldiers and to refugees, organized food and other supplies for the army, and generally came quickly to rival the autocracy for authority over the Russian Empire.

With every defeat of the Russian army, the liberals and moderate leftists were emboldened to represent themselves as the voice of the Russian people against a discredited dynasty and its political order. Peter Holquist has described these efforts at societal mobilization as "a parastatal complex," in effect already exercising power together with the army and often against the actual civilian bureaucracy, even if not constitutionally recognized as sharing in the state's authority. It was the elites of this parastatal complex who began to articulate a form of national patriotism based on winning the war and Russia's great-power status; indeed, the liberals and conservatives in the opposition argued that they could prosecute the war much better than the autocracy.

The Provisional Government that seized power from the autocracy in February 1917 was nothing less than the executive organ of this parastatal complex. Prince Georgii Lvov, the first prime minister, had been chairman of the Zemgor; the minister of defense, Alexander Guchkov, was chair of the War Industries Committee; this pattern was replicated at the provincial and municipal level as well, where representatives of the public organizations became governors, commissars, and mayors. The Petrograd Soviet, in turn, was led by moderate socialists, Mensheviks, and Social Revolutionaries, who had also entered into the politics of the parastatal complex through the war industries committees and who shared a mostly patriotic orientation to the war, now that the autocracy was overthrown. This politics was known as "revolutionary defensism" and served to realign a formerly antiwar Left with the new "revolutionary regime" in Petrograd.[19]

But, just as the representatives of educated society had mobilized to support the war effort and thereby to claim authority in the eyes of the people, so too those new elites soon found themselves challenged by even newer mobilized communities who also claimed to understand the needs of the revolution. Workers, peasants, Cossacks, soldiers, and others also took over crucial roles of local self-defense and provisioning as central power was dismantled without new guarantees of law and order firmly in place. Memoirists refer to this phenomenon as komitetchina, a proliferation of committees that organized meetings, passed resolutions, demanded changes, and often threatened to take matters into their own hands if their demands were not satisfied by the dual-authority regime. As the imperial economy collapsed under the weight of the war and the enemy blockade, a politics of desperation pitted vulnerable communities against those who claimed to be the new state authorities. This politics, too, had its origins in the refugee and evacuee communities of the first years of the war. Refugees, for example, found themselves thrown into alien environments with little or no resources to support them, even when the local population had the will to do so; predictably, the war years were marked by pogroms against the unwelcome guests, who were themselves torn out of their traditional communal organizations and authority structures. Such uprooted and vulnerable populations were particularly receptive to the radical politics of the extreme left and right.

The important role of the expanding parastatal complex not only blurred the boundaries between public and private spheres, but also between civilian and military ones, as the war contributed to the militarization of the population, economy, and culture of the Russian Empire and its successor states. Militarization was an important aspect of the total war that Europe unleashed on itself during 1914–18. If we consider the management of multinational armies, the belligerent powers on the eastern front all engaged in various experiments involving the "nationalization" of their armies and thereby militarized national identities; for Austria–Hungary such national military units were not unusual, but for Germany and Russia they marked a departure from the tradition of extraterritorial deployment of multiethnic units. These experimental units were called national guards or legions and were formed from expatriate volunteers and later from among prisoners of war: the Czechoslovak, Finnish, and Polish Legions, the Latvian and Ukrainian Sharpshooters, eventually even Jewish self-defense detachments and formations.

The war also contributed to the militarization of social or class identities, especially during 1917, most notably in the varieties of class-based local defense units that were formed. Red Guards putatively united proletarians, or at least factory workers, in armed bands to defend factories and their working-class families;[20] peasant armed bands of varying degrees of organizational complexity and longevity also formed in the countryside with similar motivations of defending peasant communities from marauding armies and, not infrequently, other peasant bands.[21] The territory between Russia and Poland, especially Ukraine, was a particularly fertile ground for these improvisations; among the most notable were the anarchist "armies" of Nestor Makhno.

In this general culture of militarization, the Cossacks played particularly significant roles in supporting one regime or another against their enemies. The Cossacks represented a longer tradition of militarization of peasant farmers in Russian, Polish, and Ukrainian history. They fought for and against the Reds, the Whites, the Greens, but their temporary allies were generally quick to learn the lesson that Cossack loyalties diminished as the battles stretched farther from their traditional Cossack homelands.[22] One of the defining features of Ukraine's and Siberia's sociopolitical and military organization during these years was summed up by detractors of various political persuasions as *atamanshchina*, or *otomanshchyna*, after the atamans who claimed charismatic authority over their followers/troops; this evoked the era of Cossack rule over the area in the early modern period. A frequent English-language translation of this term was warlordism, meant to convey both the breakdown of traditional military organizations, the imperial army above all, but also the Whites and other successors, and the "democratization" of the military calling – or at least armed self-defense – against the myriad and rival armed detachments that preyed upon large swathes of territory.

The socialist parties, too, particularly the Bolsheviks and the Socialist Revolutionaries, underwent a militarization during the war as they rebuilt their underground fighting (or combat) organizations that had been so devastated by Prime Minister Petr Stolypin's suppression of the revolutions of 1905–07. The fighting organizations (*boevye otriady*) proved very useful as mobilizational vehicles in 1917 and were at the core of many Red Guard and later Red Army units. A good part of the socialist intelligentsia had seen actual military service at the front and were elected by their soldiers' committees in 1917 to positions as spokesmen.[23] This experience gave these socialists preparation for the next phase of their militarization, the organization of partisan units, either for or against the Reds or Whites; during the Civil War the SRs and Bolsheviks/Communists frequently resorted to calls to arms from party leaders.[24] In Ukraine the Ukrainian SRs likewise organized peasant fighting detachments and so did nationalist–socialist intellectuals in their fight for survival in the devastated and vulnerable Ukrainian lands.[25] And, just as the slogans of "revolutionary defensism" and "revolutionary war" accommodated a still inchoate nationalism to the ideology of socialist internationalism, so too did they allow for a dramatic about-face in the socialist movement, which had so long identified the army, officers, and militarism as the enemies of democracy and socialism. War fought in the name of the socialist fatherland or Russian revolutionary democracy was a noble cause. Many in the socialist parties, however, felt that their ideals had been too compromised by the exigencies of wartime and referred pejoratively to the Civil War period as "military" or "war" communism.[26]

It is not surprising, then, that the militarizing and nationalizing effects of the First World War shaped the revolution and Civil War in multiple yet profound ways. It was not only the Bolsheviks who were perceived as having militarized socialism; militarization affected the postwar political orders in the region on the right (and center) as well. One sign of the transformation was the rise to state power of military men in newly independent states in East Central Europe in the course of and aftermath of the First World War. Pavlo Skoropadskyi, Hetman of Ukraine for little more than half a year in 1918,[27] Gustav Mannerheim, founder of independent Finland's armed forces and briefly regent for the new state (and later President of Finland, 1944–6),[28] and Josef Pilsudski, erstwhile revolutionary terrorist, founder of the Polish Legions, and first head of the independent Polish republic,[29] are only three of the postwar East Central Europe heads of state to have emerged from the military forces of the empires that preceded those states. Other examples include King

Alexander of Yugoslavia, who had served in the Russian army's elite Corps of Pages (and even married into the Russian nobility; his sister and her husband Prince Ivan Romanov, were killed by the Bolsheviks in 1918); Alexander ruled over the united kingdom of South Slavs from its founding in 1918 to his assassination in 1934. In Hungary Admiral Nicholas Horthy de Nagybanya defeated a communist revolution led by Bela Kun to become regent and head of newly independent Hungary until 1944. In defeated postwar Germany, the wartime high command continued to exercise considerable power in the Weimar government; Field Marshall Paul von Hindenburg won election as president in 1925 and eventually appointed Adolf Hitler as chancellor. Kemal Atatürk certainly deserves inclusion in this group, as a Young Turk and military hero who rose to power as modern Turkey's first president and dictator. Moreover, all these men can be compared to the Russian White generals who led the anti-Bolshevik struggle during the Civil War from the former empire's borderlands.

Total war and the end of monarchies in the region shaped the conditions that made rule by military men attractive and acceptable transitional stages from empire to nation and from monarchy to republic, including the Soviet variant of that form of rule. Those same wars and the attendant collapse of the Old Regime empires had many other lasting consequences as well. The "time of troubles" that extended from 1914 to 1923 brought in its wake an unprecedented brutalization of society and the inuring to violence of large segments of the most active sectors of the population, particularly young and middle-aged males. The losses in human lives and injuries, loss of limbs, epidemics, and famines diminished labor productivity for at least a decade across the entire region. These catastrophes were compounded by the forced relocation of millions of people from their prewar homelands, the breakup of families and resultant rise of child homelessness and orphan populations. The years of fighting disrupted the prewar economies and left much of the physical plant in shambles, especially in those borderlands where the combat was at its most intense.

The world war and civil war that brought the Old Regime empires crashing down also gave rise to new forms of politics and new social structures. Especially in the former Russian Empire, the dominance of the imperial aristocracy, merchantry, and clergy was violently supplanted by a new plebeian order and a new set of elites that claimed to rule in the name of the previously disfranchised classes, especially the peasantry and working class. The politics of social mobilization that had been pursued by the wartime mass political parties persisted as an important tool of the new governments, even when, as in the case of the Soviet state, a single-party dictatorship eventually displaced the pluralism of the prewar and wartime political cultures. Finally, in the wake of the collapse of traditional loyalties to empire and monarch/emperor, identities were reorganized along ethnonational lines, with several rising national elites having had a brief experience of statehood from Georgia to Ukraine and in Central Asia. The postwar regime of national minority supervised by the League of Nations and the Leninist nationality policy of the USSR consolidated trends that had their roots in the wartime rhetoric and practice of "national liberation." Even the authoritarian Soviet Union of Lenin and Joseph Stalin was organized into national republics in a variant of federalism that the prewar Bolshevik Party would have found anathema.

Notes

1 The most important studies in this scholarship include those by Alexander Rabinowitch – *Prelude to Revolution* (Bloomington, IN: Indiana University Press, 1991); and *The Bolsheviks Come to Power* (New York: W. W. Norton, 1976) – and his students and colleagues – notably Donald Raleigh, Rex Wade, William Rosenberg, Diane Koenker, R. Grigor Suny, and others; see also Suny's historiographical essays on the links between 1917 and the Civil War,: "Toward a Social History of the October Revolution," *American Historical Review*, 88/1 (1983), 31–52; and his "Revision and Retreat in the Historiography of 1917: Social History and its Critics," *Russian Review*, 53/2 (Apr. 1994), 165–82. See also the conference volume edited by Ron Suny, William Rosenberg, and Alexander Rabinowitch, *Party, State, and Society in the Russian Civil War* (Bloomington, IN: Indiana University Press, 1989).

2 Most of the literature mentioned in n. 1 covered developments in the European Russian parts of the Soviet Union (Suny's early work on Baku stands as an exception and Evan Mawdsley's *The Russian Civil War* (Boston: Allen & Unwin, 1987) as the best overall recent synthesis), while even the most comprehensive treatment of the non-Russians and the national question during this period, that of Richard Pipes (*Formation of the Soviet Union: Communism and National Liberation, 1917–1923* (Cambridge, MA: Harvard University Press, 1954)) still omits discussion of Finland, Poland, and the Baltic states because they fell outside the borders of the Soviet state (at least until 1939).

3 The historian perhaps most identified with this "Whiggish" acceptance of the Soviet state's emergence was E. H. Carr in his multi-volume history of the Bolshevik revolution and early Soviet state. See especially *The Bolshevik Revolution, 1917–1923*, 3 vols. (New York: W. W. Norton, 1966).

4 I argued for a militarization of socialism during the Civil War years in *Soldiers in the Proletarian Dictatorship: The Red Army and the Soviet Socialist State, 1917–1930* (Ithaca, NY: Cornell University Press, 1990); see also the articles by Suny cited in n. 1 for some of the polemics around the origins of Stalinism. For some classic statements of the thesis of Civil War origins, see Robert C. Tucker, "Leszek Kolakowski," in Tucker, ed., *Stalinism: Essays in Historical Interpretation* (New York: Norton, 1977).

5 This is true of the best study of Russia's involvement in the First World War until recently, Norman Stone, *The Eastern Front: 1914–1917* (New York: Scribner, 1975).

6 Many memoirists describe the period as the "time of troubles," evoking the sixteenth-century collapse of state and society. See Iu. V. Got'e, *Time of Troubles, the Diary of Iurii Vladimirovich Got'e*, trans., ed., and intro. Terence Emmons (Princeton: Princeton University Press, 1988); Anton Denikin, *Ocherki russkoi smuty*, 5 vols. (Paris: J. Povolozky & Cie., 1921–6). See also Peter Holquist, *Making War, Forging Revolution* (Cambridge, MA: Harvard University Press, 2002); Orlando Figes, *People's Tragedy: The Russian Revolution, 1891–1924* (New York: Viking, 1997); and earlier statements of this periodization in Lars Lih, *Bread and Authority in Russia, 1914–1921* (Berkeley: University of California Press, 1990) and Roger Pethybridge, *The Social Prelude to Stalinism* (New York: St Martin's Press, 1974).

7 See a description of the martial-law regime in Daniel Graf, "The Reign of the Generals: Military Government in Western Russia, 1914–1915," Ph.D. diss., University of Nebraska, 1972.

8 Peter Gattrell, *A Whole Empire Walking: Refugees in Russia during World War I* (Bloomington, IN: Indiana University Press, 1999).

9 See William Ewing Gleason, "The All-Russian Union of Towns and the All-Russian Union of Zemstvos in World War I: 1914–1917," Ph.D. diss., Indiana University, 1972; and two volumes of *Economic and Social History of the World War: Russian Series*, vol. 4

entitled *The War and the Russian Government: The Central Government*, covering the municipal government and the All-Russian Union of Towns by Paul P. Gronsky and Nicholas J. Astrov (New Haven: Yale University Press, 1929); and T. J. Polner's collaboration with Vladimir Obolensky and Sergius P. Turin in the same series, entitled *Russian Local Government during the War and the Union of Zemstvos* (New Haven: Yale University Press, 1930); on war-industries committees, see Lewis Siegelbaum, *The Politics of Industrial Mobilization, 1914–1917: A Study of the War-Industries Committees* (New York: St Martin's Press, 1983).

10   See Raymond Pearson, *The Russian Moderates and the Crisis of Tsarism, 1914–1917* (New York: Barnes and Noble, 1977).

11   On soldiers' politics during 1917, see two volumes by Allan K. Wildman, *The End of the Russian Imperial Army* (Princeton: Princeton University Press, 1980, 1987).

12   See John W. Wheeler-Bennett, *Brest-Litovsk, The Forgotten Peace: March 1918* (New York: William Morrow & Company, 1939).

13   On the Russian Civil War, see Mawdsley, *The Russian Civil War*.

14   Arno Mayer, *Wilson vs. Lenin: Political Origins of the New Diplomacy, 1917–1918* (Cleveland, OH: World Publishing Co., 1964).

15   Fritz Fischer, *Germany's Aims in the First World War* (New York: W. W. Norton, 1967); and those scholars who responded to his work. See also Peter Borowsky, *Deutsche Ukrainepolitik 1918: Unter besonderer Berücksichtigung der Wirtschaftsfragen* (Lübeck and Hamburg: Matthiesen, 1970).

16   M. K. Dziewanowski, *Joseph Pilsudski: A European Federalist, 1918–1922* (Stanford, CA: Hoover Institution Press, 1969).

17   Richard Pipes, *Formation*.

18   John L. H. Keep, *The Russian Revolution: A Study in Mass Mobilization* (New York: Norton, 1976).

19   Ziva Galili y Garcia, "Origins of Revolutionary Defensism: I. G. Tseretelli and the 'Siberian Zimmerwaldists'," *Slavic Review*, 41 (Sept. 1982), 454–76; George Katkov, *Russia 1917: The February Revolution* (New York: Harper and Row, 1967), 23–37.

20   See Rex Wade, *Red Guards and Workers' Militias in the Russian Revolution* (Stanford, CA: Stanford University Press, 1984).

21   Orlando Figes, *Peasant Russia, Civil War: The Volga Countryside in Revolution (1917–1921)* (New York: Oxford University Press, 1989).

22   The Cossacks as historical memory and organizational model were enshrined in not only the emergent Ukrainian national movement, but in the separatist and autonomist movements of Siberia, the Don, the Kuban, and elsewhere.

23   For the role of the socialist intelligentsia in the army, see Wildman, *The End of the Russian Imperial Army*.

24   See the memoirs of Paul Dotsenko, a Siberian SR after his exile from Novorossiisk under Nicholas II, on his career in organizing socialist partisans for resistance against the Reds and later the Whites as well: *The Struggle for Democracy in Siberia* (Stanford, CA: Hoover Institution Press, 1983).

25   On the Ukrainian revolution, see John S. Reshetar, *The Ukrainian Revolution: A Study in Nationalism* (Princeton: Princeton University Press, 1952).

26   Such critiques came from the European left, notably Rosa Luxemburg and Karl Kautsky, but also from within the Russian socialist movement. On war communism as pejorative, see Stephen Cohen, *Bukharin and the Bolshevik Revolution: A Political Biography* (New York: A. A. Knopf, 1973).

27   See Taras Hunczak, "The Ukraine under Hetman Pavlo Skoropadskyi," in Taras Hunczak, ed., *The Ukraine, 1917–1921: A Study in Revolution* (Cambridge, MA: Harvard Ukrainian Research Institute, 1977), 61–81; and Mark von Hagen, "'I Love Russia, and/but I

Want Ukraine,' or How a Russian General Became Hetman of the Ukrainian State, 1917–1918," in Frank Sysyn and Serhii Plokhii, eds., *Synopsis: A Collection of Essays in Honor of Zenon E. Kohut* (Edmonton and Toronto: Canadian Institute of Ukrainian Studies Press, 2005).

28 See Tancred Borenius, *Field-Marshal Mannerheim* (London and Melbourne: Hutchinson & Co., 1940).

29 The best study of Pilsudski remains Joseph Rothschild, *Pilsudski's Coup d'état* (New York and London: Columbia University Press, 1966).

References

Borenius, Tancred (1940). *Field-Marshal Mannerheim.* Hutchinson & Co., London and Melbourne.

Borowsky, Peter (1970). *Deutsche Ukrainepolitik 1918: Unter besonderer Berücksichtigung der Wirtschaftsfragen.* Matthiesen, Lübeck and Hamburg.

Carr. E. H. (1966). *The Bolshevik Revolution, 1917–1923.* 3 vols. W. W. Norton, New York.

Cohen, Stephen (1973). *Bukharin and the Bolshevik Revolution: A Political Biography.* A. A. Knopf, New York.

Denikin, Anton (1921–6). *Ocherki russkoi smuty.* 5 vols. J. Povolozky & Cie., Paris.

Dotsenko, Paul (1983). *The Struggle for Democracy in Siberia.* Hoover Institution Press, Stanford, CA.

Dziewanowski, M. K. (1969). *Joseph Pilsudski: A European Federalist, 1918–1922.* Hoover Institution Press, Stanford, CA.

Figes, Orlando (1989). *Peasant Russia, Civil War: The Volga Countryside in Revolution (1917–1921).* Oxford University Press, New York.

Figes, Orlando (1997). *People's Tragedy: The Russian Revolution, 1891–1924.* Viking, New York

Fischer, Fritz (1967). *Germany's Aims in the First World War.* W. W. Norton, New York.

Galili y Garcia, Ziva (1982). "Origins of Revolutionary Defensism: I. G. Tseretelli and the 'Siberian Zimmerwaldists'," *Slavic Review*, 41 (Sept)., 454–76.

Gattrell, Peter (1999). *A Whole Empire Walking: Refuges in Russia during World War I.* Indiana University Press, Bloomington, IN.

Gleason, William Ewing (1972). "The All-Russian Union of Towns and the All-Russian Union of Zemstvos in World War I: 1914–1917," Ph.D. diss., Indiana University.

Got'e, Iu. V. (1988). *Time of Troubles, the Diary of Iurii Vladimirovich Got'e*, trans., ed., and intro. Terence Emmons. Princeton University Press, Princeton.

Graf, Daniel (1972). "The Reign of the Generals: Military Government in Western Russia, 1914–1915," Ph.D. diss., University of Nebraska.

Gronsky, Paul P., and Astrov, Nicholas J. (1929). *Economic and Social History of the World War: Russian Series*, vol. 4: *The War and the Russian Government: The Central Government*, Yale University Press, New Haven.

Holquist, Peter (2002). *Making War, Forging Revolution.* Harvard University Press, Cambridge, MA.

Hunczak, Taras (1977). "The Ukraine under Hetman Pavlo Skoropadskyi," in Taras Hunczak (ed.), *The Ukraine, 1917–1921: A Study in Revolution.* Harvard Ukrainian Research Institute, Cambridge, MA, 61–81.

Katkov, George (1967). *Russia 1917: The February Revolution.* Harper and Row, New York.

Keep, John L. H. (1976). *The Russian Revolution: A Study in Mass Mobilization.* Norton, New York.

Lih, Lars (1990). *Bread and Authority in Russia, 1914–1921.* University of California Press, Berkeley.

Mawdsley, Evan (1987). *The Russian Civil War*. Allen & Unwin, Boston.

Mayer, Arno (1964). *Wilson vs. Lenin: Political Origins of the New Diplomacy, 1917–1918*. World Publishing Co., Cleveland, OH.

Pearson, Raymond (1977). *The Russian Moderates and the Crisis of Tsarism, 1914–1917*. Barnes and Noble, New York.

Pethybridge, Roger (1974). *The Social Prelude to Stalinism*. St Martin's Press, New York.

Pipes, Richard (1954). *Formation of the Soviet Union: Communism and National Liberation, 1917–1923*. Harvard University Press, Cambridge, MA.

Polner, T. J. (1930). *Russian Local Government during the War and the Union of Zemstvos* . Yale University Press, New Haven.

Rabinowitch, Alexander (1991). *Prelude to Revolution*. Indiana University Press, Bloomington, IN.

Rabinowitch, Alexander (1976). *The Bolsheviks Come to Power*. W. W. Norton, New York.

Reshetar, John S. (1952). *The Ukrainian Revolution: A Study in Nationalism*. Princeton University Press, Princeton.

Rothschild, Joseph (1966). *Pilsudski's Coup d'état*. Columbia University Press, New York and London.

Siegelbaum, Lewis (1983). *The Politics of Industrial Mobilization, 1914–1917: A Study of the War-Industries Committees*. St Martin's Press, New York.

Stone, Norman (1975). *The Eastern Front: 1914–1917*. Scribner, New York.

Suny, R. Grigor (1983). "Toward a Social History of the October Revolution," *American Historical Review*, 88/1: 31–52.

Suny, R. Grigor (1994). "Revision and Retreat in the Historiography of 1917: Social History and its Critics," *Russian Review*, 53/2: 165–82.

Suny, R. Grigor, Rosenberg, William, and Rabinowitch, Alexander (1989). *Party, State, and Society in the Russian Civil War*. Indiana University Press, Bloomington, IN.

Tucker, Robert C. (ed.) (1977). *Stalinism: Essays in Historical Interpretation*. Norton, New York.

Von Hagen, Mark (1990). *Soldiers in the Proletarian Dictatorship: The Red Army and the Soviet Socialist State, 1917–1930*. Cornell University Press, Ithaca, NY.

Von Hagen, Mark (2005). " 'I Love Russia, and/but I Want Ukraine,' or How a Russian General Became Hetman of the Ukrainian State, 1917–1918, " in Frank Sysyn and Serhii Plokhii, eds., *Synopsis: A Collection of Essays in Honor of Zenon E. Kohut*. Canadian Institute of Ukrainian Studies Press, Edmonton and Toronto.

Wade, Rex (1984). *Red Guards and Workers' Militias in the Russian Revolution*. Stanford University Press, Stanford, CA.

Wheeler-Bennett, John W. (1939). *Brest-Litovsk, The Forgotten Peace: March 1918*. William Morrow & Company, New York.

Wildman, Allan K. (1980, 1987). *The End of the Russian Imperial Army*. Princeton University Press, Princeton.

Further Reading

Carr, E. H. (1966). *The Bolshevik Revolution, 1917–1923*. 3 vols. W. W. Norton, New York.

Chamberlin, William H. (1935*). The Russian Revolution, 1917–1921*. 2 vols. Macmillan, New York.

Figes, Orlando (1997). *People's Tragedy: The Russian Revolution, 1891–1924*. Viking, New York.

Holquist, Peter (2002). *Making War, Forging Revolution*. Harvard University Press, Cambridge, MA.

Lincoln, W. Bruce (1986). *Passage through Armageddon: The Russians in War and Revolution, 1914–1918.* Simon and Schuster, New York.

Mawdsley, Evan (1987). The Russian Civil War. Allen & Unwin, Boston.

Pipes, Richard (1954). *The Formation of the Soviet Union.* Harvard University Press, Cambridge, MA.

Pipes, Richard (1990). *The Russian Revolution.* Knopf, New York.

Pipes, Richard (1993). *Russia under the Bolshevik Regime.* Knopf, New York.

Stone, Norman (1975). *The Eastern Front: 1914–1917.* Scribner, New York.

CHAPTER TWENTY-ONE

The Woman Question in Russia: Contradictions and Ambivalence

ELIZABETH A. WOOD

The "woman question" in nineteenth- and early twentieth-century Russia focused principally on the position of women in the family and society. It was one of the so-called burning social issues that occupied the Russian intelligentsia in the second half of the nineteenth century, questions such as the emancipation of the peasants and the Jews, and the rise of national consciousness.

Yet it was perhaps the least straightforward of the burning questions, the one most burdened by contradictions and ambivalence. It was, for one thing, very much a question about the place of men and masculinity under autocracy. Although it ostensibly addressed notions of how to improve women's lot, it also contained within it and even perpetuated deeply misogynist notions of women's backwardness. The early woman question was also often a code phrase for authors seeking to evade the strict censorship under Tsar Nicholas I (1825–55); they wrote about women as a way of talking about revolution and radical social change. Contemporaries perceived the woman question as a native development that had organic Russian roots. Yet in actuality it came to Russia as an import, borrowing many Western ideas, yet melding them with Russian intellectual and moral traditions in a new synthesis.

Historians and literature scholars debate the timing and nature of the earliest appearances of the woman question. Most general discussions date it from the time of discussions of the emancipation of the peasantry – that is, the late 1850s and early 1860s. Yet it is easy to see the roots in changes under Peter the Great and Catherine the Great, as well as in the 1830s–40s [1–4].

Historians have posited a number of factors contributing to the discussion of women's position in society and the possible ways to change that position through education and work: Enlightenment prioritization of education as a vehicle for social change; Catherine the Great's commitment to creating rational citizens; the alternative gender models contained in the memoirs of Princess Dashkova and the so-called Cavalry Maid, Nadezhda Durova; the rise of a new ideal of companionate marriage; the eroding of women's subject position after the Russian defeat in the Crimean War, and the need for many so-called superfluous women of the nobility (that is, those who had not married) to find gainful employment once the serfs were freed and the nobility lost much of their income.

Scholarship about the woman question in Russian history has expanded greatly since the 1990s. Most recently, scholars in the field of Russian literature have generated a raft of monographs and articles exploring women's own writings and the ways in which they contributed to gender understandings in the nineteenth and early twentieth centuries [5–7]. The older scholarship (my own included) tended to emphasize the ways in which the woman question, as expressed in the thick journals of the 1850s–70s, tended to be written principally by and for men [1, 2, 8–10]. As Nikolai Shelgunov wrote so vividly in 1870: "Who among our women writers – and we have many of them – has studied the woman question and written about it? Not one" [11: 11]. While it is true that discussion of the woman question in the thick journals was dominated by men, women writers were addressing similar issues, albeit in fictionalized form, in their belles-lettres. Here they focused on loveless arranged marriages, on the restrictions of the family, on women's choices between motherhood and independence [12–15].

The earliest history of the woman question in Russia is intimately linked with new ideas of "upbringing" (*vospitanie*) dating from the 1770s and ideas of "personality" (*lichnost'*) from the 1830s. In medieval Russia and up to the early eighteenth century elite women had been cloistered, leading lives segregated from their male family members, with minimal education and contact with the outside world. It was only under Peter the Great that new decrees allowed Russian subjects, male and female, to make their own choices in marriage (rather than having those dictated by parents or other relatives). Peter also actively required women to attend his grand social assemblies.

Catherine the Great brought in Enlightenment ideas from France and Germany particularly concerning education and citizenship. Catherine's unofficial minister of education, Ivan Betskoi, sought to transform what the historian Vasily Kliuchevsky once called "the raw material" of childhood, through upbringing, so as to make proper male and female adult citizens [16: 431–2]. While Catherine's overall goal was to create "a new race of people," she viewed women's status as particularly crucial in their roles as mothers of the next generation. Upbringing, especially in the sense of the moral training of both female and male children, she saw as "the root of all evil and good" [17: 312 n. 2; 18].

Women's education was still limited, however, to their roles as wives and mothers. Graduates of the Smol'nyi Institute were to be "good Russian wives, caring mothers, and zealous homemakers" [1: 306]. From the time of Catherine's son Paul I onward, one goal of formalized education for young Russian girls was in fact to make sure that they did not receive too much education.

The quintessential "good wives," historically speaking, were, of course, the so-called Decembrist wives – that is, those wives (and two French mistresses) who followed their husbands into exile after their failed uprising in December 1825. Historians have debated whether they contributed to the later emergence of the woman question. Some have claimed they were nothing more than sentimental creatures who upheld patriarchal notions by following their husbands, while others have held that their choice to endure the hardships of Siberia with their husbands made a political statement, which later inspired women activists and changed notions of women's possible roles [1: 8].

The Decembrist wives represented an important link in the chain of ideas leading up to the celebrated woman question of the 1860s precisely because they demonstrated the importance of nineteenth-century men's *ideals* for women. The core notion associated with the Decembrist wives was one of self-sacrifice, an ideal aspired to by both men and women in the generation of repentant noblemen (the 1830s and 1840s). Egotism in the woman question – that is, trying to emancipate women for their own sake – was considered unacceptable, but women taking actions that would benefit the larger collective were lauded, especially when they were perceived as martyrs.

The ideas that played a key part in fomenting the Decembrist revolution – equality, liberty, fraternity, citizenship, Masonic revivals of early Christian values – all these had not been sufficiently strong to persuade the men of the Decembrist movement to include women in their revolutionary societies. Women in their view could only have an auxiliary role organizing philanthropic and private societies.

These Enlightenment and Masonic ideas did, however, combine with German idealism to create notions of the Beautiful Woman, the ideal relationship that would help to restore the wholeness of the alienated, superfluous man emerging at the time [19]. Nikolai Nekrasov and others wrote sentimental poems and stories of women peasants being violated by their male owners. Noblemen began to feel guilty not only toward their peasants but also toward Russian women, both noble and serf. They began as well to bemoan the lot of so-called fallen women.

A whole genre of writing, produced by both male and female authors, beginning in the 1830s, was devoted to the hardships of women's lot [1: 101–9, 20]. The initial way out, discussed by early members of the intelligentsia, including men like Vissarion Belinsky, focused on making women "human." This corresponded to the Hegelian notion of needing to foster true individuality [21: 313–34; 22: 131–6].

Nonetheless, even the most ardent male proponents of the woman question tended to describe women's emancipation primarily as it related to men. Women were to be viewed in terms of their "elevated spiritual harmony," wrote Belinsky in 1835: "Woman is the guardian angel of man in all the steps of his life." She was to be "the radiant guiding star of his life, his support, his source of strength, which does not let his soul chill, grow hard, and weaken" [23: 29–30].

The setting for producing many of the ideas that went into these writings was the salons of the 1830s–1850s [24, 25]. Here women played an important role as hostesses, encouraging lively discussion among individuals of all social estates. Avdotia Panaeva and other salonnières also provided the financial backing for some of the thick journals for which this period is famous, including the journal the *Contemporary* (*Sovremennik*) where many of the articles about women's education and employment were published [26, 27]. Because Russian upper-class women could maintain property independently from men, they were particularly valued as a source of funds for both legal and later illegal revolutionary movements.

In the 1830s and 1840s George Sand's novels caused a firestorm among the Russian intelligentsia. In her novel *Jacques* (1834), Sand told the story of a young male hero who committed suicide in order to free the woman he loved so she could marry the man of her dreams. A number of Russian novels now took up this theme, among them Aleksandr Druzhinin, *Polinka Saks* (1847); Alexander Herzen, *Who is to Blame?* (1845–7); and, most famously, Nikolai Chernyshevskii, *What is to be Done?*

(1863). In all these novels male authors tend to focus on the actions of the male protagonists, particularly their dramatic rescue of the young women. The male characters are known by their last names and/or by their full name and patronymic, whereas the females are known by their first names in diminutive form (e.g., Polinka, Verinka in Druzhinin's novellas) [28, 29].

Freedom in marriage became the rallying cry of much of the intelligentsia. In salons and thick journals they now began to discuss the injustices of arranged marriages and marriages undertaken for convenience, the social costs of the illegality of divorce, the despotism of the patriarchal noble family, and women's legal inferiority in inheritance and property. One effect of this idealism of the people of the 1840s was an intertwining of the public and the private, the attachment of intense political and moral significance to social arrangements.

When Russia lost the Crimean War in 1856, both government and society became even more obsessed with the country's apparent backwardness. Many of the markers of that backwardness were linked to the female sex: high illiteracy (which theoretically could be fixed if mothers had higher reading skills so they could help their children); high infant mortality (which was blamed on women's poor mothering skills, their alienation from society); high rates of venereal disease (which could be blamed on prostitution and on the low numbers of trained medical personnel in the country) [22].

Nikolai Pirogov, one of the leading reformers of the late 1950s and early 1860s, now argued in his "Questions of Life" that women should be allowed to serve in professional capacities as nurses. With higher education and professional attainments they would cease to be mere "dolls" in society and prove useful to the nation. Other negative female stereotypes predominated in the discussion as well, especially stereotypes of society ladies who thought only about the marriages their parents were arranging for them; of more middle-class ladies trapped in the conservative sway of their merchant families who could be saved by marriages only with radical students from the university [1, 8, 30]. Even Alexander II's Minister of Education, Avraam Norov, wrote to the tsar in 1856, begging for more education for girls and young women, claiming that it would help foster improvements in "family morals" and in "citizenship," since those were areas "on which the woman has such a powerful influence" [31: 297].

Education for women became a particular focus of agitation for a number of reasons. One was the perception that young people (both male and female) needed to educate themselves first before they could be "useful" to the silent masses of Russia. Another was the direct influence of John Stuart Mill, who claimed that, if women were held back in their intellectual and spiritual development, then men could not advance either. As the emancipation began to be noisily discussed and then implemented, gentry women became increasingly aware that they could no longer afford to be the *lishniaia* (extra one), living in their brothers' homes if they never married.

Professionally, women also now had more choices, as Tsar Alexander II's reforms created whole new professions (for example, pharmaceutical work) and encouraged others in which women's work was considered acceptable, especially journalism, medicine, and law [32–35]. Maria Vernadskaia (1831–60), Russia's first woman economist, declaimed insistently that women must stand on their own two feet and learn to work if they were to have independence [6: 263–323; 8: 35–7; 36]. Other radicals, such as Petr Zaichnevsky and Mikhail Bakunin, advocated full equality between women and men, the abolition of church and civil marriage, and the public education of children [8: 117, 124].

The woman question, as it developed in the 1860s, also had a performative aspect. Male radicals played the parts of knights rescuing women, while women often dressed and acted as nihilists, who violated the norms of high society. They cut their hair short, wore black dresses, smoked cigarettes, used coarse language, addressed everyone as equals (using *ty*, the familiar form), lived in communal apartments. Scholars have often interpreted this latter behavior as part of the rise of the people of mixed rank (*raznochintsy*) in Russia in this period [6: 215–22, 29:17–20]. While this is an important part of the story, it also had a lot to do with a wholesale rejection of "civility," "high society," and "femininity" (*zhenstvennost'*), which was perceived as being linked to the alienation of the superfluous man. Women wanted to have their own autonomy, their own "personality" [37, 38].

Conservatives and radicals now waged battles royal over what they referred to as "female types" (*zhenskie tipy*) and women's "destiny" (*naznachenie*). They wrote articles on women's "upbringing and significance in the family and society," and on their "foreordained position" (*prednaznachenie*) in society [10]. For both conservatives and radicals what mattered most was what women could do for the nation (and/or for the revolution), whether by shoring up positive traditional values or by undermining harmful old ones and allowing new ones to take root.

Arranged marriages were one of the most frequent targets of both male and female writers in the 1860s. Following in the footsteps of Sand's *Jacques*, many famous male writers became involved in so-called love triangles, where the protagonists had to sort out all their feelings, while striving to suppress all feelings of jealousy. Jealousy would demean the males experiencing it and imprison the females who were its object [8, 28].

The challenge of the woman question was that it was often patronizing toward real flesh-and-blood women. The anarchist (and former prince) Peter Kropotkin unconsciously demonstrated this attitude in his memoirs:

> With some severity the [male] nihilist would repulse the "lady" who chattered trivia and boasted of her "femininity" in her manners and the refinement of her toilette. He would say directly to her: "How can you not be ashamed to chatter such inanities and wear a chignon of false hair?" The nihilist wanted, above all, to see in a woman a comrade, a person, not a doll or a "bread-and-butter miss." A nihilist would never give up his seat for a woman entering the room if he saw she wasn't tired and there were other seats in the room. He treated her like a comrade. But if a girl, even one he didn't know at all, showed an interest in learning something, he would give her lessons and was ready to go halfway across the city to help her. [39: 269]

This passage provides an excellent example of what Arja Rosenholm has perceptively called the "hierarchical asymmetry" in the "topography" of gender relations in the woman question [6: 11–17]. It is the man who decides whether a given woman is worthy of his attention, censuring those whom he finds wanting. And it is the man who strives to help the young lady (whom he now refers to as a "girl") through private lessons so she will join him as a "comrade" and a "person." The woman in this account is portrayed as passive, while he is active, seeking her out, walking across town, teaching her.

A common metaphor in the early woman question that underlined the gender asymmetry was that of women's awakening and then educating the next generation. The lead editorial in the journal *Rassvet* (the Dawn) (1859–62) sounded the clarion call: "Finally, at the dawn of a new day for Russia, the spirit flies down to the sleeping Russian woman and it awakens her, pointing out the path she must travel in order to make herself a citizen and prepare herself for her high duty – to be the educator of the new generation now being born" [40: 78].

The most famous exposition of the idea of so-called "new people" was Nikolai Chernyshevsky's novel *What is to be Done?* Here too one can see an extended example of the intelligentsia's ambivalence toward women. On the one hand, *What is to be Done?* is usually understood as a *Bildungsroman* of the heroine Vera Pavlovna: she is rescued from her family; she founds a sewing cooperative; she is allowed to have freedom in her romantic relations.

Yet within the novel there are three competing "tales about new people," all important for analyzing the woman question. One is the tale of two men, Lopukhov and Kirsanov, who bond with each other, almost to the exclusion of the heroine; one is the tale of Vera Pavlovna, who is the object of male solicitousness; and one is the tale of a third, unrelated man (Rakhmetov), who spurns all women.

In the first subplot Lopukhov and Kirsanov spend hours deciding who and what is best for Vera Pavlovna. They come to the conclusion (without asking her) that, even though she does not realize it yet, she has fallen in love with Kirsanov, despite her marriage to Lopukhov. Following the example of George Sand's *Jacques*, Lopukhov, unbeknownst to Vera, fakes a suicide and escapes to America. The discussion *between the men* takes center stage.

The bond between man and woman, especially that of Lopukhov and Vera, follows what Irina Paperno has called "the teacher scheme." On the literal level Lopukhov enters Vera's natal family's household to work as a tutor for her brother. But he also has fantasies of teaching Vera, helping to liberate her from the darkness of her family of origin. Chernyshevsky himself had had fantasies of teaching his bride: "I will become her teacher. I will explain my notions to her and open the encyclopedia of civilization to her" [29: 98]. In real life Chernyshevsky's bride, Olga Sokratovna, apparently laughed at him when he made such a proposal. But Vera Pavlovna does not. Although she later becomes quite active in establishing her cooperatives, she is principally portrayed as following the advice of the men.

The third story – the one most often cited, and the one that Vladimir Lenin most identified with in his own essay called "What is to be Done?" – is that of the professional revolutionary Rakhmetov, who appears out of nowhere. He has no first name at all. Described as "belonging to a different breed" and as "the rigorist," he has taught himself to base his life entirely on certain principles, including the principle not to have anything to do with women.

Nominally the novel focuses directly on Vera's emancipation. She becomes independent under Lopukhov's and later Kirsanov's tutelage. Nonetheless, the long dialogues between Lophukhov and Kirsanov tend to emphasize their superior ability to recognize what Vera is experiencing. Rakhmetov also stresses that he, as an "extraordinary man," can overcome his feelings whereas women (and ordinary men) cannot.

And Chernyshevksy's narrator makes frequent references to the differences between the "perspicacious" reader, on the one hand, who will understand everything, and "female" and "common" readers, on the other, who will need assistance or who will not understand the novel at all.

In the 1860s and 1870s thousands of young people began a movement "to the people" in which they hoped to bring the peasantry education and exposure to modern ideas. Some hoped that the long, slow process of learning and exposure to new ideas would prepare the peasantry for a new society. Others hoped that exposure to such ideas would light a spark that would ignite a revolution in the countryside. In many of these populist movements women were considered to hold a special place as "the strong," "the pure," "a test of the males' moral regeneration" [41: 150]. Petr Lavrov, one of the leaders of the new populist movement, later described the women of the famous Chaikovsky circle in the 1860s and 1870s as "the purest embodiment of the ideal, limitlessly devoted and self-sacrificing women who have so often inspired our poets and novelists" [38: 125; 42–45].

Reading the memoirs of some of these populist women, one cannot help noticing how they strove constantly to prove their dedication, loyalty, and self-sacrifice. They pleaded to be transferred to the most dangerous assignments. On the one hand, these activities had traditionally been coded as "male." Yet at the same time they showed a dedication to the "family" of revolutionaries that perpetuated female stereotypes.

This was not, I would argue, because women were inherently more "moral" [38]. Rather, whether consciously or unconsciously, they were trying not to appear stereotypically female while at the same time not threatening the dominant group (men). They had to show they were active, not passive (the female stereotype), while at the same time showing that they were dedicated, not self-serving and excessively independent. They had to be careful as well of the tsarist police, lest they be labeled "loose women" and arrested for prostitution [8: 121–2; 44–45].

At this time there were many women and men who were deeply ambivalent about the woman question, even opposed to it. Among male writers, from the beginning there predominated an assumption that women's *difference* from men was the main cause of their subordination to and inequality with men. Many subscribed to the view expressed by M. L. Mikhailov, one of the first authors on the woman question: "There should be nothing feminine in women except their sex. All other traits should be neither masculine nor feminine, but purely human" [8: 46].

Women in the populist and revolutionary movements of the 1870s also expressed ambivalence about the woman question.. Many of them joined women-only discussion groups, but only for brief periods of time. They hoped that in so doing they would learn to reason for themselves, becoming in the process less shy, less prone to let the men dominate discussions [38, 42, 45].

In the 1860s reformist women also began concretely working to solve the twin challenges of the woman question: education (since women were excluded from the universities) and work (since women had little training). Using their high-society connections with ministers (including Dmitri Miliutin, whose wife sympathized with their cause), they lobbied extensively during balls and other social events to persuade the government to permit higher-education courses for women and also courses for "learned midwives." Women students also pressured the government by going abroad to study, so exasperating government officials that they finally issued a decree in 1873 requiring all women students abroad to come home on pain of losing the right to teach in the villages and practice medicine (which was their goal in going abroad to study in the first place). Even once higher-education courses were established, however, women graduates still could not work in government service or obtain ranks that would lead to their ennoblement separate from their fathers' and husbands' positions [32, 46–47].

In the area of employment, feminist reformers (especially the famous trio of Anna Filosofova, Nadezhda Stasova, and Mariia Trubnikova) organized sewing cooperatives, publishing cooperatives, and living cooperatives, such as the Society to Provide Cheap Lodgings. Later, in the 1880s and 1890s, Filosofova and Stasova worked with others to found the Russian Women's Mutual Philanthropic Society, which was modeled on US women's clubs that combined self-help and social advocacy [8, 48].

In the 1880s and 1890s, as Marxism began to penetrate into Russia, the new theorists tended to take primarily an instrumental view of the woman question and women's position in society. If the overthrow of autocracy was to be accomplished, everyone – women as well as men – needed to join the revolutionary movement. That meant women would need to be emancipated from their "patriarchal isolation" and the "stultifying world of housework" [49: 548; 50: 202]. Yet at the same time Social Democratic writings consistently express enormous anxieties about women. If they were not mobilized and carefully coached, they would doubtless prove to be "passive," "indifferent," "a bulwark for counterrevolutionary and anti-Soviet agitation" [51: 9]. They were "the most backward and immobile element," one that had served as "a brake in all previous revolutions" [52: 169; 53: 521].

In 1909 Alexandra Kollontai published *The Social Bases of the Woman Question*, a 400-page treatise designed to show that the question of women's emancipation could not be separated from the larger social struggles of the day. Only when the entire economic order was restructured would women become truly free and equal. She insisted that women could never view men as their enemies; rather they must always see them as their comrades. Nonetheless, she did take up some of the classic issues of the woman question: the double morality in which women had to choose between what Kollontai saw as the "bondage of marriage" and the slavery of prostitution, as well as the problems of education, work, maternity, and childcare. Kollontai and other Social Democrats consistently assumed that the revolution would solve these problems. Moreover, after the revolution, the state would take over many of the tasks currently fulfilled by women within the family (childcare, cooking, and laundry, to name a few). By implication, gender relations between the sexes would not have to be changed, as the state would simply step in to liberate women from all the extra labor of care for cooking, the house, and children [54: 58–73].

Kollontai and her Social Democratic comrades had good reason to be threatened by the feminists. In the years between 1900 and 1917 they were organizing en masse and promising to reach out to women of all estates. In 1904 Maria Pokrovskaia founded a new journal, the *Women's Messenger* (*Zhenskii Vestnik*), specifically devoted to a renewed focus on the woman question and to advocating for women's equal rights. The Union of Equal Rights for Women, founded in spring 1905, had 8,000 members by 1906. Soon thereafter, the Women's Progressive Party was founded, one of the first women's political parties in the world. By 1907 a second feminist journal had begun publishing, the *Union of Women* (*Soiuz Zhenshchin*) [55–58].

As Rochelle Ruthchild and Linda Edmondson have pointed out, the demand for female suffrage (a key part of Western notions of feminism) did not develop in Russia as early as in Western Europe, principally because of men's and women's "equal rightlessness," as contemporaries put it. Even feminists in this period were hampered by their ambivalence about women's equality. As Mariia Chekhova, a prominent liberal feminist, wrote: "We are far from that naive and nearsighted feminism which dreams about resolving the women question outside of ties with general political and social questions, equalizing women's rights with men independent of general rights and social equality" [57: 180].

Feminists now openly called themselves "equal-righters" (*ravnopravki*). In 1905 men of the Russian Empire obtained the vote, while women still had not, and many groups, including the male leadership of the liberal Constitutional Democrats, were deeply ambivalent about whether the vote should be extended to them. The woman question had now evolved from a general concern about "women's destiny" and issues of education and employment, to legal grievances about rights that women did not have and unfair restrictions that they faced. Some of the key issues being hotly debated in Russia, both within the feminist community and within the larger liberal and socialist intelligentsia, included women's property and inheritance rights, their right to their own passports, the restrictions facing schoolteachers who married, and the registration and surveillance of prostitutes [36, 59].

While feminists mostly agreed about the need for suffrage, they disagreed vehemently over the issue of separatism – that is, whether women's organizations should be separate from those of men or should, on the contrary, be fighting within the context of the overall political struggle. Further splits emerged between so-called liberal and socialist feminists – that is, those supporting a moderate constitutional outcome and those hoping for a full-fledged revolution. The League for Women's Equal Rights (1907–17), for example, tried to combine philanthropy, education, and mutual aid, on the one hand, with political demands, on the other, while remaining on the whole fairly moderate and legally registered with the authorities. The Union of Women's Equal Rights (1905–8), by contrast, never attained legal status and focused primarily on lobbying for female suffrage and equal rights. Militant and implacable, its members marched in demonstrations and even staffed the barricades during the 1905 uprisings. However, they let men join as members, and one (N. V. Chekhov) even served on their Central Board. The Women's Progressive Party (1905–17), by contrast, was militantly separatist, not allowing any men to join, but otherwise not quite as politically militant as the Union [60].

The women's movements were harassed constantly by the tsarist authorities and periodically by the liberal and socialist parties. The Social Democrats branded them as "bourgeois feminists" and claimed, untruthfully, that they had no interest in working women [61]. The right-wing Octobrists criticized them for their empty chatter. By 1908 the authorities had made it virtually impossible for the suffragists to get their word out through meetings and petitions [8: 213–15].

The feminists held one last general conference, the First All Russian Women's Congress, in December 1908, with over 1,000 women in attendance. Unfortunately, the groups in attendance were so disparate they could not find a common language. Women workers and peasants claimed they were not being heard. Upper-class women claimed that working women were interrupting them and that socialist groups were not supporting women's suffrage [8, 55]. In 1910 feminists met doctors, bureaucrats, and members of the intelligentsia to hold the All Russian Congress for the Struggle against the Trade in Women and its Causes. Here, too, class conflicts and differing ideas of how to solve women's issues disrupted the proceedings [62: 219–30].

In February 1917 on International Women's Day feminists combined forces with factory women to demand both bread and suffrage. The story usually told is that the beginning of the February Revolution was marked by women workers taking to the streets protesting about the lack of food in the stores. Yet Rochelle Ruthchild has been able to show that the banners women carried into the streets were indeed suffrage banners. Some 40,000 women rallied, calling to the men to join them. Two days later, Prince L'vov, head of the Provisional Government, promised to include women in the suffrage; on July 20 the Provisional Government extended the vote to women.

When the Bolshevik government came to power in October 1917, it created a special women's section of the party (*zhenotdel*), as a place to discuss and resolve the "women question" once and for all. As Nadezhda Krupskaia had explained in 1913: "The 'woman question' for male and female workers is a question of how to draw the backward masses of women workers into organization, how best to explain to them their interests, how best to make them into comrades in the general struggle" [63: 37].

Krupskaia was adamant that the way to solve the woman question had to be solidarity among female and male workers, especially their joint commitment to a common cause, common goals, and a common path. But, where a separate organization was needed, she and her comrades in the women's section agreed, it was to serve a remedial purpose that would bring women "up to" the standards of men, that would make them "human" instead of female, comrades instead of backwards women who knew only the path from the threshold to the stove (as the Russian proverb said).

It was easy for the top party leadership to declare by fiat in 1930 that the woman question had been "solved." Henceforth, only small women's sectors (*zhensektory*) were permitted to continue functioning, and then only in Central Asia [64–66].

Central Asia had, in fact, long been the site of a specific version of the woman question: the quest for what Gregory Massell once called a "surrogate proletariat." Since there was no discernible local proletariat through whom revolution could be fomented, the central authorities in Moscow, after trying several other solutions, settled on women's liberation as an excuse for becoming involved in "liberating" the whole region. By 1927 this campaign had been named a *hujum*, or assault against the "moldy old ways" of female seclusion and inequality. Once again, male authorities demonstrated that they knew best how women should be emancipated [67–68].

Limited discussion of the woman question re-emerged under Nikita Khrushchev and Leonid Brezhnev in a public airing of women's difficulties in carrying the "double burden" of work and childcare (or, as some noted, the triple burden of those two plus housework). During the Khrushchev years official women's organizations were revived, now called *zhensovety*, and once again designed to mobilize women into the workplace and the party. During the Brezhnev years new topics in economics and demography were added to the traditional woman question as social scientists became concerned about the declining state of the Soviet economy. These were still principally instrumental concerns (how would women serve the state?); yet they did show a renewed interest in investigating women's actual position in society [66].

In the Gorbachev and Yeltsin years the woman question emerged with new vigor as scholars and activists began examining *patriarkhal'nost'*, the patriarchal nature of society [69–73]. *"Feminizm"* (that is, feminism in the Western sense) was still a taboo topic in the general media despite the general love of foreign words in politics, as Linda Edmondson has noted in the context of the early twentieth century [74: 197].

In addition to the urgent problems of health and demographics (continued from the Brezhnev years), gender researchers now began asking questions about women's legal and social rights, their involvement in the business world, female unemployment, labor discrimination against women, domestic violence, poverty among single mothers, contraception, and pornography. New research centers were created such as the Moscow Center for Gender Studies (established in April 1990), and similar ones in St Petersburg, Ivanovo, Kharkov, and Minsk. In 1998 there were some 150 such centers in Central and Eastern Europe, the former Soviet Union, and Mongolia, and some 600 non-governmental organizations had registered with the Russian Ministry of Justice [75–77].

Since the fall of the Soviet Union, scholars of gender relations in Russia have criticized the Soviet-era woman question for its role in obscuring rather than clarifying women's issues. Olga Voronina has called it "one of the most refined social mystifications" of that era [78: 37]. Anastasiya Posadskaya, one of today's leading feminists, has argued that Russia today is in the grip of a "patriarchal renaissance" [79: 4]. Despite reservations about the old woman question, new questions of women's and gender studies continue to nurture fruitful discussions and advances in scholarship.

References

1. Tishkin, G. A. (1984). *Zhenskii vopros v Rossii 50–60 gg. XIX v. Izd.* Leningradskogo universiteta, Leningrad.
2. Wood, E. A. (1997). *Baba and Comrade: Gender and Politics in Revolutionary Russia.* Indiana University Press, Bloomington, IN.
3. "Introduction" (2002). In R. Bisha, J. M. Gheith, C. Holden, and W. G. Wagner (eds.) *Russian Women, 1698–1917: Experience and Expression: An Anthology of Sources.* Indiana University Press, Bloomington, IN.
4. Meehan-Waters, B. (1975). "Catherine the Great and the Problem of Female Rule". *Russian Review*, 34/3: 293–307.
5. Costlow, J. T. (1994). "Love, Work, and the Woman Question in Mid Nineteenth-Century Women's Writing," in T. W. Clyman and D. Greene (eds.), *Women Writers in Russian Literature.* Praeger, Westport, CT, 61–75.
6. Rosenholm, A. (1999). *Gendering Awakening: Femininity and the Russian Woman Question of the 1860s.* Kikimora Publications, Helsinki.
7. Rosenholm, A. (1996). "The Woman Question of the 1860s, and the Ambiguity of the 'Learned Woman,'" in R. Marsh (ed.), *Gender and Russian Literature: New Perspectives.* Cambridge University Press, Cambridge, 112–28.
8. Stites, R. (1978). *The Women's Liberation Movement in Russia: Feminism, Nihilism, and Bolshevism, 1860–1930.* Princeton University Press, Princeton.

9. Pushkareva, N. (1997). *Women in Russian History from the Tenth to the Twentieth Century.* M. E. Sharpe, Armonk, NY.

10. Uspenskaia, V. (ed.) (2005). *Muzhskie otvety na zhenskii vopros v Rossii. Vtoraia polovina XIX v.- pervaia tret' XX v.: antologiia.* 2 vols. Feminist-Press, Tver.

11. Shelgunov, N. (1870). "Zhenskoe bezdushie," *Delo*, 9.

12. Kelly, C. (1994). *A History of Russian Women's Writing, 1820–1992.* Clarendon Press, Oxford.

13. Marsh, R. (ed.) (1996). *Gender and Russian Literature: New Perspectives.* Cambridge University Press, Cambridge.

14. Clyman, T. W., and Greene, D. (eds.) (1994). *Women Writers in Russian Literature.* Praeger, Westport, CT.

15. Barker, A. M., and Gheith, J. M. (eds.) (2002). *A History of Women's Writing in Russia.* Cambridge University Press, Cambridge.

16. Okenfuss, M. J. (1977). "V. O. Kliuchevskii on Childhood and Education in Early Modern Russia," *History of Education Quarterly*, 17/4: 417–47.

17. Nash, C. S. (1981). "Educating New Mothers: Women and the Enlightenment in Russia," *History of Education Quarterly*, 21/3: 301–16.

18. Ransel, D. (1980). "Ivan Betskoi and the Institutionalization of Enlightenment in Russia," *Canadian–American Slavic Studies*, 14/3: 327–38.

19. Dunham, V. S. (1960). "The Strong-Woman Motif," in Cyril E. Black, ed., *The Transformation of Russian Society.* Harvard University Press, Cambridge, MA, 459–83.

20. Durova, N. (1989). *The Calvalry Maiden: Journals of a Russian Officer in the Napoleonic War*, trans. and notes M. F. Zirin. Indiana University Press, Bloomington, IN.

21. Malia, M. (1961). *Alexander Herzen and the Birth of Russian Socialism.* Harvard University Press, Cambridge, MA.

22. Wood, E. A. (2005). *Performing Justice: Agitation Trials in Soviet Russia.* Cornell University Press, Ithaca, NY.

23. Belinskii, V. (1835). "Review of a Victim," in Robin Bisha et al., eds., *Russian Women, 1698–1917.* Indiana University Press, Bloomington, IN.

24. Gheith, J. M. (2002). "Women of the 1830s and 1850s," in Barker and Gheith (eds.), *A History of Women's Writing*, 85–99.

25. Bernstein, L. (1996). "Women on the Verge of a New Language: Russian Salon Hostesses in the First Half of the Nineteenth Century," in H. Goscilo and B. Holmgren (eds.), *Russia–Women–Culture.* Indiana University Press, Bloomington, IN, 209–24.

26. Ledkovsky, M. (1974). "Avdotya Panaeva: Her Salon and her Life," *Russian Literature Triquarterly*, 9.

27. Gregg, R. (1975). "A Brackish Hippocrene: Nekrasov, Panaeva, and the 'Prose in Love,'" *Slavic Review*, 34/4: 731–51.

28. Eidelman, D. D. (1994). *George Sand and the Nineteenth-Century Russian Love-Triangle Novels.* Bucknell University Press, Lewisburg, PA.

29. Paperno, I. (1988). *Chernyshevsky and the Age of Realism: A Study in the Semiotics of Behavior.* Stanford University Press, Stanford, CA.

30. Pirogov, "Voprosy zhizni" (1856). excerpted in Bisha et al., eds., *Russian Women*, 33–4.

31. Tyrkova, A. V. (ed.) (1915). *Sbornik Pamiati Anny Pavlovny Filosofovoi.* P. Golike i A. Vil'borg, Petrograd, vol. 2.

32. Likhacheva, E. (1901). *Materialy dlia istorii zhenskago obrazovaniia v Rossii (1858–1880).* tip. M.M. Stasiulevicha, St Petersburg.

33. Conroy, M. S. (1994). *In Health and in Sickness: Pharmacy, Pharmacists and the Pharmaceutical Industry in Late Imperial, Early Soviet Russia.* East European Monographs, Boulder, CO.

34. Norton, B. T., and Gheith, J. M. (eds.) (2001). *An Improper Profession: Women, Gender, and Journalism in Imperial Russia.* Duke University Press, Durham, NC.

35. Ruane, C. (1994). *Gender, Class, and the Professionalization of Russian City Teachers, 1860–1914.* University of Pittsburgh Press, Pittsburgh.

36. Vernadskaia, M. (1862). "Naznachenie zhenshchiny," excerpted in Bisha et al. (eds.), *Russian Women,* 34–42.

37. Pavlova, K. (1978). *A Double Life,* trans. and intro. B. H. Monter. Ardis, Ann Arbor.

38. Engel, B. A. (1983). *Mothers and Daughters: Women of the Intelligentsia in Nineteenth-Century Russia.* Cambridge University Press, Cambridge.

39. Kropotkin, P. A. (1966). *Zapiski revoliutsionnera.* Mysl', Moscow.

40. Heldt Monter, B. (1977). "Rassvet (1859–1862) and the Woman Question," *Slavic Review* 36/1: 76–85.

41. McNeal, R. H. (1971–2). "Women in the Russian Radical Movement," *Journal of Social History,* 5/2: 143–63.

42. Knight, A. (1975). "The Fritschi: A Study of Female Radicals in the Russian Populist Movement," *Canadian–American Slavic Studies,* 9/1: 1–17.

43. Kelly, A. (1975). "Revolutionary Women," *New York Review of Books,* 17: 20–2.

44. Faure, C. (1979). "Une violence paradoxale: Aux sources d'un défi, des femmes terroristes dans les années 1880," in Christiane Dufrancatel et al. (eds.), L'Histoire sans qualités. Galillee, Paris.

45. Kelly, A. (1987). "Self-Censorship and the Russian Intelligentsia," *Slavic Review,* 46/2: 193–213.

46. Dudgeon, R. A. (1975). "Women and Higher Education in Russia, 1855–1905." Ph.D. dissertation, George Washington University.

47. Johanson, C. (1987). *Women's Struggle for Higher Education in Russia, 1855–1900.* McGill-Queen's University Press, Kingston, Ont.

48. Ruthchild, R. (2001). "Filosofova," "Russian Women's Mutual Philanthropic Society," and "Stasova," in N. C. Noonan and C. Nechemias (eds.) (2001), *Encyclopedia of Russian Women's Movements.* Greenwood Press, Westport, CT, 22–4, 61–4, 83–6.

49. Lenin, V. I. (1899). "Razvitie kapitalizma v Rossii," in *Polnoe sobranie sochinenii* (hereinafter *PSS*). 5th edn. Moscow, 1958–65, v. 3.

50. Lenin, V. I. (1919)., "O zadachakh zhenskogo rabochego dvizheniia v Rossii," *PSS,* vol. 39.

51. Kollontai, A. (1919) "Kak i dlia chego sozvan byl pervyi Vserossiiskii s"ezd rabotnits," in *Kommunisticheskaia Partiia i organizatsiia rabotnits.* Moscow.

52. Lenin, V. I. (1919). "Doklad o partinoi programme", *PSS,* vol. 38.

53. V. I. Lenin. (1919). "Rech' na kursakh agitatorov otdela okhrany materinstva i mladenchestva NKSO," in *PSS,* vol. 37.

54. Kollontai, A. (1977). *Selected Writings,* trans. with an intro. and commentaries Alix Holt. W. W. Norton, New York.

55. Edmondson, L. (1984). *Feminism in Russia, 1900–1917.* Stanford University Press, Stanford, CA.

56. Edmondson, L. (2001). "Mariia Pokrovskaia and Zhenskii vestnik: Feminist Separatism in Theory and Practice," in Norton and Gheith (eds.) *Improper Profession,* 196–21.

57. Ruthchild, R. G. (2001). "Writing for the Rights: Four Feminist Journalists: Mariia Chekhova, Liubov' Gurevich, Mariia Pokrovskaia, and Ariadna Tyrkova," in Norton and Gheith (eds.), *Improper Profession,* 167–95.

58. Bobroff, A. (1974). "The Bolsheviks and Working Women, 1905–20," *Soviet Studies,* 26/4: 540–67.

59. Wagner, W. G. (1989). "The Trojan Mare: Women's Rights and Civil Rights in Late Imperial Russia," in Olga Crisp and Linda Edmondson (eds.), *Civil Rights in Imperial Russia*. Clarendon Press, Oxford.

60. Ruthchild, R. G. (2001). "Liga ravnopraviia zhenshchin," in Noonan and Nechemias (eds.) *Encyclopedia of Russian Women's Movements*, 38–41.

61. Ruthchild, R. G. (2006). "'Bourgeois' Feminism: Gender, Class, and the Women's Equal Rights Union in Russia, 1905–1908." Paper presented at the European Social Science History Conference, Amsterdam.

62. Bernstein, L. (1995). *Sonia's Daughters: Prostitutes and their Regulation in Imperial Russia*. University of California Press, Berkeley.

63. Bessonova, A. F. (1955). "K istorii izdaniia zhurnala 'Rabotnitsa,'" *Istoricheskii arkhiv*, 4.

64. Hayden, C. E. (1976). "Zhenotdel and the Bolshevik Party," *Russian History*, 3/2: 150–73.

65. Goldman, W. Z. (1996). "Industrial Politics, Peasant Rebellion and the Death of the Proletarian Women's Movement in the USSR," *Slavic Review*, 55/1: 46–77.

66. Buckley, M. (1989). *Women and Ideology in the Soviet Union*. University of Michigan Press, Ann Arbor.

67. Massell, G. J. (1974). *Surrogate Proletariat: Moslem Women and Revolutionary Strategies in Soviet Central Asia, 1919–1929*. Princeton University Press, Princeton.

68. Northrop, D. (2004). *Veiled Empire: Gender and Power in Stalinist Central Asia*. Cornell University Press, Ithaca, NY.

69. Lipovskaya, O. (1990). "Why Men Have Not Been Overcome: Or, 'the Costs of Emancipation,'" *Russia and the World*, 18: 29–32.

70. Goscilo, H. (1993). "Domostroika or Perestroika: The Construction of Womanhood in Culture under Glasnost," in T. Lahusen and G. Kuperman (eds.), *Late Soviet Culture: From Perestroika to Novostroika*. Duke University Press, Durham, NC, 233–55.

71. Khotkina, Z. (2002). "Ten Years of Gender Studies in Russia," *Russian Social Science Review* (July–Aug.), 4–12.

72. Konstantinova, V. (1994). "No Longer Totalitarianism, But Not Yet Democracy: The Emergence of an Independent Women's Movement in Russia," in A. Posadskaya (ed.), *Women in Russia: A New Era of Russian Feminism*, trans. Kate Clark. Verso, London, 57–73.

73. Rimashevskaia, N. (1992). "The New Women's Studies," in M. Buckley (ed.). *Perestroika and Soviet Women*. Cambridge University Press, Cambridge.

74. Bartlett R., Edmondson L., with Kelly, C. and Smith, S. (1998). "Collapse and Creation: Issues of Identity and the Russian Fin de Siècle," in C. Kelly and D. Shepherd (eds.), *Constructing Russian Culture in the Age of Revolution, 1881–1940*. Oxford University Press, Oxford, 165–216.

75. Gender Studies and Women's Studies Directory (1998). *Resources in the Countries of Central & Eastern Europe, the former Soviet Union & Mongolia*. The Open Society Institute Program, Budapest.

76. Abubikirova, N. I., Klimenkova, T. A., Kochkina, E. V., Regentova, M. A., and Troinova, T. G. (1998). *Zhenskie npravitel'stvennye organizatsii Rossii i SNG*. Izd. Eslan, Moscow.

77. Sperling, V. (1999). *Organizing Women in Contemporary Russia: Engendering Transition*. Cambridge University Press, Cambridge.

78. Voronina, O. (1994). "The Mythology of Women's Emancipation in the USSR as the Foundation for a Policy of Discrimination," in A. Posadskaya (ed.), *Women in Russia: A New Era in Feminism*. Verso, London.

79. Posadskaya, A. (1994) "Introduction," in Posadskaya (ed.), *Women in Russia*.

Further Reading

Atkinson, D., Dallin, A., and Lapidus, G. W. (eds.) (1977). *Women in Russia*. Stanford University Press, Stanford, CA.

Buckley, M. (ed.) (1992). *Perestroika and Soviet Women*. Cambridge University Press, Cambridge.

Chatterjee, C. (2002). *Celebrating Women: Gender, Festival Culture, and Bolshevik Ideology, 1910–1939*. University of Pittsburgh Press, Pittsburgh.

Chirkov, P. M. (1978). *Reshenie zhenskogo voprosa v SSSR (1917–1937 gg.)*. Mysl', Moscow.

Clements, B., Engel, B. A., and Worobec, C. D. (eds.) (1991). *Russia's Women: Accomodation, Resistance, Transformation*. University of California Press, Berkeley.

Costlow, J. T., Sandler, S., and Vowles, J. (eds.) (1993). Sexuality *and the Body in Russian Culture*. Stanford University Press, Stanford, CA.

Edmondson, L. (ed.) (1992). *Women and Society in Russia and the Soviet Union*. Cambridge University Press, Cambridge.

Engel, B. A. (2004). *Women in Russia, 1700–2000*. Cambridge University Press, Cambridge.

Gheith, J. M. (2004). *Finding the Middle Ground: Krestovskii, Tur, and the Power of Ambivalence in Nineteenth-Century Russian Women's Prose*. Northwestern University Press, Evanston, IL.

Goldman, W. Z. (1993). *Women, the State and Revolution: Soviet Family Policy and Social Life, 1917–1936*. Cambridge University Press, Cambridge.

Goscilo, H., and Holmgren, B. (eds.) (1996). *Russia–Women–Culture*. Indiana University Press, Bloomington, IN.

Heldt, B. (1987). *Terrible Perfection: Women and Russian Literature*. Indiana University Press, Bloomington, IN.

Lapidus, G. W. (1978). *Women in Soviet Society: Equality, Development, and Social Change*. University of California Press, Berkeley, IN.

McDermid, J. (1988). "The Influence of Western Ideas on the Development of the Woman Question in Nineteenth-Century Russian Thought," *Irish Slavonic Studies*, 9: 21–36.

Racioppi, L., and See, K. O. (1995). "Organizing Women before and after the Fall: Women's Politics in the Soviet Union and Post-Soviet Russia," *Signs*, 20/4: 818–50.

Rai, S., Pilkington, H., and Phizacklea, A. (eds.) (1992). *Women in the Face of Change: The Soviet Union, Eastern Europe, and China*. Routledge, New York.

Rimashevskaia, N. M. (1991). *Zhenshchiny v obshchestve; Realii, problemy, prognozy*. Nauka, Moscow.

CHAPTER TWENTY-TWO

Stalinism and the 1930s

LYNNE VIOLA

What is Stalinism? This term received its scholarly imprimatur in 1975 when Robert C. Tucker convened a conference under the auspices of the Rockefeller Foundation in Bellagio, Italy, entitled "Stalinism and Communist Political Culture."[1] The historiographical contribution of the conference was to differentiate Stalin and his rule (focused primarily on the 1930s) from Lenin, from the Russian Revolution of October 1917, and indeed from a monolithic definition of socialism. In so doing, the conference participants distanced themselves from the reigning cold-war paradigm of totalitarianism that posited a static model of Soviet socialism.[2] In Tucker's definition, Stalinism represented a specific political culture made up of a leader cult dependent on Stalin's personality, the revolutionary–civil-war heritage of the Communist Party, and the inheritance of statist elements from the tsarist past.[3] Stephen F. Cohen, who here and elsewhere maintained that there was a programmatic alternative to Stalinism in the form of the New Economic Policy of the 1920s, described Stalinism quite simply as "excess."[4] Moshe Lewin added a social component, arguing that the enormous social flux let loose by revolution, civil war, and the First Five Year Plan, resulted in the collapse of coherent class forces, thus allowing for the rise of a "Leviathan state" embodied in the person of Stalin.[5]

In these definitions, Stalinism is a kind of syndrome – that is, an amalgamation of characteristics (symptoms) rather than a definition of the -ism in and of itself. The term is therefore descriptive rather than explanatory. *Webster's New World Dictionary* defines an -ism as "the act, practice, or result" of its accompanying noun. A secondary definition is "the doctrine, school, theory, or principle" associated with its noun. A tertiary definition is "an abnormal condition caused by" the noun in question.[6] In the case of Stalinism, Stalin is at the center of the -ism, whether as causal factor, as leader of school or theory, or as root of the abnormality of his reign. The -ism collapses in the absence of Stalin, *ipso facto* offering more of a "great-man" interpretation than an actual and broadly applicable -ism. At the same time, the term suggests an exceptionalist view of the USSR under Stalin, feeding back into cold-war assumptions of the *sui generis* nature of Soviet Communism.

It is necessary to de-center and contextualize Stalin within the conundrum known as Stalinism. For, whatever the phenomenon connoted by Stalinism, it was far more complex than a "great-man" approach to history suggests. At the same time that it was more complex, it was also far more insidious and not quite as *sui generis* as the traditional definitions of Stalinism imply. The great twentieth-century Russian poet Marina Tsvetaeva once wrote: "There are people of a particular epoch and there are epochs incarnated in people."[7] Stalin was as much an embodiment of his times and country as he was deus ex machina.

Stalinism

Stalinism represented first and foremost the concept of "socialism in one country" in practice. Defying the odds against a Marxian "proletarian" revolution taking place in an underdeveloped agrarian nation, Lenin and his Bolshevik Party had seized power in 1917 based on the prospect of a European-wide social revolution that would come to the assistance of "backward" Soviet Russia. When the European revolution failed to materialize, it became clear that Soviet Russia would have to go it alone, with hope for a wider revolution postponed to the indefinite future.

Socialism in one country became a method for "building socialism" – that is, for modernizing the country in order to raise it to the requisite economic and social level to support socialism. Under Stalin, socialism in one country became an autarkic alternative to capitalist modernization based on a combination of state-led industrialization and a "tribute" from the peasantry.

At the July 1928 Central Committee plenum of the Communist Party, Stalin spelled out his recipe for the socialist modernization of peasant Russia. He said:

> In capitalist countries industrialization was usually based not only on internal accumulation but also on the plundering of other countries, the plundering of colonies or vanquished countries, or on substantial loans from abroad. You know that for hundreds of years England used to drain all its colonies, from every continent, and in this way injected additional investments into its industry . . . Our country differs from the capitalist countries, by the way, in that it cannot and must not engage in the plundering of colonies or in the plundering of other countries in general. Therefore this path is closed to us. But our country doesn't have loans from abroad either. Consequently, this path is closed to us as well. In that case what is left for us? One choice is left: to develop industry, to industrialize the country on the basis of internal accumulation . . . But where are the sources of this accumulation? As I said, there are two such sources: first, the working class, which creates valuable output and moves industry forward; and second, the peasantry.
>
> The situation in our country with regard to the peasantry in this case is the following: it pays the state not only ordinary taxes, direct and indirect, but it also pays relatively high prices for goods from industry – that is first of all – and it doesn't receive the full value of the prices of agricultural products – that is second of all. This is an additional tax on the peasantry in the interests of developing industry, which serves the whole country, including the peasantry. This is something like a "tribute," something like a surtax, where we are forced to take temporarily in order to sustain and further develop the current rate of industrial growth . . . This situation, needless to say, is unpleasant. But we would not be bolsheviks if we papered over this fact and closed our eyes to the

fact that, unfortunately, our industry and our country cannot manage without this additional tax on the peasantry . . .[8]

The peasantry would serve as the primary resource for the country's modernization. The "extraction" of capital for industrialization would, in fact, largely determine the form and contours of Stalin's rule in the 1930s.

The First Five Year Plan (1928–32) represented, in essence, Stalin's solution to the problem of Russian backwardness. Its twin planks were rapid industrialization and the forced collectivization of agriculture. Collectivization was intended to transform a peasant agriculture based largely on communal land tenure into a modern, socialized agriculture based on collective labor and ownership of the "means of production." The *kolkhoz*, or collective farm, would replace the traditional Russian peasant commune. Soviet agriculture would be large scale and modern, facilitating the pumping-over of resources from agriculture to industry.

Stalin famously described collectivization as a "revolution from above."[9] The decision to proceed, or better to forge ahead, in this direction did not emerge in a vacuum of either sheer power or ideological hubris.[10] In the broadest terms, the economic policy alternative to revolution from above was a more organic and balanced approach to industrialization, based in part on the further development of textiles and light industry as well as on Nikolai Bukharin's politically self-destructive call for the peasants "to enrich themselves." This approach to economic development put forth by the Right Opposition to Stalin would have allowed, in theory and over time, the expansion of a domestic market, the growth of light industry, and a gradual rollover of capital resources into heavy industry. This was "socialism at a snail's pace," to borrow another of the less than felicitous phrases associated with the Right Opposition.[11]

The Stalinist alternative was a rapid state-generated industrialization drive, focused on heavy industry and based on the forced accumulation of internal resources for capital funding. Stalin and his allies in the Communist Party aimed for the creation of an autarkic industrialized polity with the full capability to shore up its defenses within the context of "capitalist encirclement" and what was perceived as the inevitable war with the capitalist powers of the West.

The two alternatives, set out in crude and overly generalized terms here, had parallels in prerevolutionary economic development.[12] And, as in the past, the choice was determined less by economic factors than by political considerations, particularly those tied to the needs of state and defense. In addition and significantly, the choice represented in the Stalin revolution emerged from a context of profound and destabilizing crisis.

The context of the Stalin revolution determined its contour. Collectivization grew out of the crisis of the New Economic Policy (NEP) of the 1920s, a crisis that developed as a result of a combination of structural and economic problems, partly of the party's own making; ideological factors and party infighting; and a tense and threatening (though undoubtedly exaggerated) international situation. The war scare of 1927 was of major importance as the backdrop for the Stalin revolution – both because it allowed the Stalinist leadership levers of political manipulation and because it set off a chain of reactions that would almost inevitably lead to a radical solution to the industrialization debate.

The crisis of NEP consisted of a series of interrelated crises: the war scare; the grain-requisitioning crisis and resultant upswing in rural violence; an element, the dimensions of which are still undefined, of urban instability sparked by rising food prices, queues, and rationing; and the struggle within the party featuring a series of well-informed critiques of grain-requisitioning practices. Stalin and company's perception, real and manipulated, of the limits of NEP, the peasantry "sabotage" of industrialization through the withholding of grain from the market, and the interplay of domestic and international enemies radicalized the atmosphere. And, even before the "great turn," the OGPU (the secret police) had launched a series of mass operations leading to the arrests of thousands of traders, merchants, and NEP men as well as enabling a kind of *de facto* dekulakization through the growing use of administrative fines and exile.[13]

The crisis atmosphere gave birth to the Stalin revolution, defining its form and parameters. The state implemented collectivization as an act of virtual war. Violence was assumed as a necessary corollary to the revolution and as an "inevitable" result of the class war with the kulak (or prosperous peasant). Although the actual military was minimally employed in the countryside – largely for political reasons and fears of instability amidst the army's peasant base – the implementation of collectivization featured the use of military practices and, to a certain extent, assumed the scale of a war. The state deployed the urban party and thousands of industrial workers in a series of mass mobilizations. Plenipotentiary rule was meant to override and overcome what was viewed as the inertia or resistance of a weak local government. Headquarters were set up on the district level to conduct operations. And the deportation of the kulaks was nothing if not a vast exercise in troop mobilization, substituting families for soldiers but following the basic transport and housing rules for rapid troop deployment. Collectivization would be conducted as a *campaign* in the full meaning of the term. Violence, arbitrariness, and "excesses" would be everywhere, reaching nightmare proportions and sparking massive peasant resistance.[14]

In the meantime, industrialization was underway at the same frantic pace. The First Five Year Plan was, in fact, declared fulfilled in four years, thanks to "shock work," "socialist competition," and "Bolshevik tempos." Although far from all planned targets were fulfilled and there were significant shortfalls in agriculture and light industry, the gains in heavy industry were impressive. The Communist Party had begun to lay the infrastructure for a mighty industrial monolith.[15]

But it was a monolith built on the back of the peasantry. The peasantry's "tribute," to use Stalin's terminology, fueled Soviet modernization with both labor and capital, even though the costs of collectivization proved immense in the short term (1928–32).[16] The peasantry did not, however, accept collectivization passively. In 1930 alone, at the height of collectivization, there were close to 14,000 mass disturbances with over 2.5 million participants. At the same time, there were over 1,000 murders of rural officials and activists and over 6,000 cases of arson. The violence of the collectivization campaign also resulted in a veritable exodus of peasant labor from the countryside – close to two million peasants labeled as kulaks were deported for forced labor in the gulag's special settlements and another ten million fled the countryside for the cities in the course of the First Five Year Plan.[17]

The immediate social consequences of the First Five Year Plan were drastic. Famine in the countryside and social instability in the cities followed in the wake of the First

Five Year Plan. The famine was devastating, resulting in the death of somewhere between five and six million people, mainly rural inhabitants.[18] The institution of an internal passport system in late 1932 was an attempt to control what had become a massive and unprecedented migratory flow, begun during the First Five Year Plan and made worse by the famine. Periodic police round-ups of those who fell outside the passport system – declassed elements, criminals, runaway kulaks – became a standard method of attempting to control the skyrocketing urban population.[19]

The First Five Year Plan set in motion a chain of events that would reverberate through the course of the 1930s. The polity that emerged, itself a product of the crisis of NEP, was characterized by despotism; emergency rule featuring campaigns, extra-judicial administration by plenipotentiary forces, and the widespread use of the secret police; and militarized approaches to policy implementation. Repression assumed a massive scale. The secret police expanded in size and power, approaching a state within the state and presiding over a vast economic empire of forced labor, first populated by deported kulaks, that came to be known as the gulag.

Stalin's personality cult also emerged at this time, in part as a result of Stalin's own vanity, in part as a result of the need to bolster authority amidst a largely traditional country in the throes of upheaval and instability.[20] Despite muted criticism within the Communist Party and unrest outside it, Stalin's authority was uncontested in practice. And his voice was decisive in setting the course of the major policies of the day, from collectivization to the great terror of 1937–8.[21]

Under Stalin, the USSR became an extraction state based on a total and almost continuous mobilization of people and resources for the purpose of "building socialism," a process that became the goal in itself. Once Stalin had made the decision to transform peasant Russia into a military–industrial behemoth, as it were overnight, extreme centralization and the instrumental use of repression became virtually the primary method of governance. The sheer size of the nation, its underdeveloped transportation and communication networks, climatic extremes, and undergovernment reinforced Stalin's own despotic tendencies, leading to hyper-centralization, emergency rule, and the use of the secret police as a kind of supra-agency allowing Stalin to override or attempt to override the provincial outposts of Soviet power with their vested local interests and inbred inclinations to either inertia or extremes.[22] The use of repression to control and mobilize people and resources became a substitute for more routine methods of administration and governance.

Building socialism under Stalin, however, was more than simply economic and social modernization. It extended to state building, as the center endeavored to control its vast expanses. The increasing use of repression against party and government elites, culminating in the Moscow show trials and the Great Terror of 1937–8, was based not simply on Stalin's paranoia – though that undoubtedly played a huge role – but on the need to shore up the center's control in a country that had been torn apart by years of revolution, civil war, and the chaos of the First Five Year Plan. In the course of the First Five Year Plan, the provincial party committees had acquired enormous powers and resources, especially those in industrial areas. From the time of the 1934 Central Committee "Congress of Victors," when Stalin ominously decried the "bigwigs" in the party, Moscow sought to undermine the provincial elites, using them additionally as scapegoats for the social and economic chaos generated by Moscow's radical policies.[23]

The elite purge was accompanied by a mass purge of ordinary men and women, in a series of campaigns whose dimensions became known only after the fall of the Soviet Union. The infamous "anti-kulak campaign" (order 00447) was the largest and bloodiest in a series of police campaigns through the 1930s that sought to stem the tide of social chaos set off by the First Five Year plan. Order 00447 was aimed against "former kulaks, criminals and other anti-social elements," with quotas set at over 75,000 for subjects fated to arrest or execution, and 193,000 for those destined for forced labor in the gulag. The total numbers of repressed in the campaign reached over 268,000 people. Other mass campaigns, aimed at specific "ethnic" groups, accompanied the anti-kulak campaign, resulting in mass arrests of a large series of individuals representing diaspora populations in the Soviet Union. According to official statistics, in 1937 and 1938 alone, the NKVD arrested 1,575,259 people, leading to 1,344,923 convictions and 681,692 executions; by early 1939, well over two million people were imprisoned within the labor camps, colonies, and prisons of the gulag.[24]

Like the elite purges, the mass campaigns were repressive exercises in attempting to regain control – in this case, of a population both feared and geographically mobile. The regime also carried out at this time a series of repressive actions aimed at shoring up its borders – the forced population movements of suspect border populations and their replacement by ostensibly loyal subjects (often demobilized Red Army soldiers and their families). Both the elite purges and the mass campaigns were implemented within an atmosphere of mass paranoia and omnipresent conspiracy theories. Russia's leading historian of the Stalin era, Oleg Khlevniuk, has suggested that Stalin was additionally motivated in the terror by the need to eliminate a possible (and surely mythical) "fifth column" that could rear its head in the face of what was viewed as the inevitability of war.[25]

The great terror thus was a continuation of the Stalin Revolution of the First Five Year Plan. That "revolution" had set in motion a chain of consequences to which the state would be forced to react through the course of the decade: (1) center– periphery power conflicts; (2) demographic chaos; (3) a population viewed as "suspect" and "alien" and not yet entirely "pacified"; and (4) an economy based on heavy industry and in need of continual "extractions," which, in turn, had the effect of constantly reinforcing the mobilizational and repressive momentum of the First Five Year Plan through unending levies of forced labor, "tribute" from the country-side, and exploitation of the USSR's vast natural and mineral resources.

The 1930s as a whole made up the "Stalin revolution." Stalinism was, by the very nature of the policies set in motion from the late 1920s, reactive and contingent rather than the brainchild of either one man or some sort of ideological blueprint. This is not to minimize either Stalin's personal role or the role of ideological factors, but rather to contextualize each within forces greater than both. Stalin's despotism operated in tandem with the times, both enhancing the use of repression and being reinforced by it. And the ideological principles of a Stalinized Marxism provided rationale and, perhaps, ultimate goals.

The irony of Stalinism, however, is that, in spite of the immense and almost unparalleled repressive powers of the regime and of Stalin, the USSR was a weak state founded upon governance through force rather than through routine administrative channels, never mind laws, and erected upon an agrarian base too weak to support the emerging industrial and military superpower except through ever-expanding centralization and force. Stalinism, in a very real sense, was a postrevolutionary settlement, a recentralization and reintegration of the empire after its dissolution in the 1917 Revolution and subsequent Civil War. It became a recipe for the forced transition of an agrarian nation into a modernized entity built nonetheless on contradictions that could never be erased and that ultimately eroded the USSR from within in the decades after Stalin's death.

Interpretations

The -ism is more complex than the noun. Stalinism was, above all, a recipe for the forced modernization, along "socialist" lines, of a "backward" agrarian nation. Stalinist modernization was based on the brutal exploitation of the peasantry, its transformation, to paraphrase Stalin, into an internal colony to finance and provide labor for industrialization. Given the minority status of the supposed "dictatorship of the proletariat," the peasantry's "transformation" could be achieved only with the massive use of force. The Stalinist state thus became an *extraction state* based on emergency mobilizations of urban cadres with plenipotentiary powers to implement policies in a series of continual ad hoc campaigns. Police rule augmented campaign rule as a constant and seemingly omnipotent presence in state–society interactions. Power and governance were centralized to an extreme degree, and at the top of the edifice was the leader cult combining both the symbolic glorification of the communist deity and the very real despotic powers of Stalin.

This was the essence of Stalinism. Its basic components were further shaped by an atmosphere of almost continual crisis that dominated perception and reality throughout the decade. The crisis atmosphere was conditioned and replenished by Stalin's own paranoia, all-pervasive conspiracy theories featuring enemies within and enemies without, and the *idée fixe* of capitalist encirclement and the inevitable war with the West. Given this context, joined with the First Five Year Plan's enormous impact, Stalinist policies were consistently shortsighted, reactive, and shaped by contingency. There was no "blueprint" for Stalinism and the bloody contours that the postrevolutionary settlement assumed.

Within this general picture, Stalin is decentered from the -ism, although by no means excluded. He is neither absolved from responsibility, nor are his very real role in decision-making or his arbitrary powers slighted. They are, rather, contextualized within the constraints of both time and country and the consequences resulting from the chaotic implementation of the First Five Year Plan.

Given these constraints, what role did ideology play in shaping Stalin's Soviet Union? The issue of ideology cannot be negated in attempts to understand Stalinism; nor can it be taken at face value. During the cold war, scholars often granted ideology a paramount role in interpretations of Soviet history. It was assumed that a "Leninist blueprint" led directly to the Stalinist dictatorship. The ideological basis of the socialist economy along with supposed aspirations for world revolution (and domination) were taken for granted.[26]

Revisionist scholars in the 1980s and 1990s were often accused of slighting ideology. It is more accurate to say that they looked beyond ideology in search of a theoretical actuality without in fact denying ideology. They asked different questions.

Unlike traditional scholars whose basic question was "why," revisionist scholars were more interested in "how" – how policy was actually implemented, how policy was received by society, and so on. Given this understanding and approach, the idea of an ideological blueprint was simply not realistic.[27]

With the fall of the Soviet Union, a new generation of scholars, in part influenced by the conservative thinking of Martin Malia, returned to the issue of ideology.[28] Although their works were by no means reductionist or monocausal, ideology again became a central defining feature of Soviet history, linking Lenin and the revolution to Stalin by way of basic policy constants such as the socialist economy and certain enduring socialist principles.[29]

Like the Stalin in Stalinism, however, ideology must be contextualized. The why and how of traditional and revisionist scholars must be combined. While there is no doubt that Stalin's version of Marxist-Leninism played an important role in establishing ultimate policy goals, it is essential to stress that this version of ideology was neither static nor did it represent some sort of cohesive program. Instead, it changed over time, contingent on circumstance and the needs of state and dictator.

Perhaps ideology's most important role was the way in which its most general precepts became a part of Soviet sensibilities, informing the everyday behavior and actions of officials, activists, and ordinary citizens. Ideology in this way was transformed into praxis and had a greater impact than any supposed blueprint. It laid the basis for crude ideological prejudices against targeted enemies, paranoid certainties of the inevitability of war, and a readiness to sacrifice the individual for the sake of an imagined collective. This transference of ideas into action helped create the actuality of Stalinism, the end results of policy implementation.

Ideology was additionally important in providing rationalizations and scapegoats for the consequences of the monstrous policies of the 1930s. It established a universe of Manichean dimensions with a cast of friends and foes that would dominate what might be called the Stalinist mindset. Ideology also played a key role in setting the end goals of the revolution, the dream of what became an ever-receding radiant future toward which struggle must never – and would never – cease. In this respect, it became an important "weapon" in the building of socialism – that is, in modernization, state building, and the unending mobilizations of the population necessary to support this goal.

The "Soviet experiment" did not occur in a vacuum. Ideological hubris does not adequately or entirely "explain" Stalinism. Some scholars have extended their interpretations outward, seeking to understand Soviet developments within the context of comparative history. This emphasis has a long tradition in the Western historiography. Its earliest manifestation was in the totalitarian and modernization models.[30] The totalitarian model arose as an attempt to understand the largely political similarities among Communist and fascist states in the prewar period and then developed into a veritable American ideology of foreign policy.[31] The modernization model, though clearly biased toward the West as the universal, focused on industrialization and agrarian revolution as fundamental aspects of modernization, inserting the Soviet Union into a larger comparative framework of development.

Comparative approaches have returned to the study of Soviet history in recent years. While such approaches continue to be largely centered on the West, they are far more expansive in their understanding. The "modernity school" focuses on the role of the interventionist state in the twentieth century and its attempts to "mold" its polity and society according to rational "Enlightenment" ideals.[32] A less Western-oriented variant, derived from James Scott's work on "high modernism," places Russia within a larger context of largely failed experiments in *creating* the modern.[33]

The modernity school is associated with a cohort of scholars trained at Columbia University in the 1990s. Their focus is largely on the state. They view the modern state as a child of the Enlightenment, bent primarily toward molding and sculpting society according to supposedly rational aims of (a very subjective) betterment. Policies as diverse as social welfare, universal education, dekulakization, and the Nazi "final solution" can all be subsumed into this paradigm. Adherents distinguish between the liberal and illiberal state, as well as on a series of particularist factors (primarily ideology) in order to understand the scale of repression that occurred in the Soviet Union and Nazi Germany, but still see a common denominator in the activity and ethos of the modern state.[34]

Following the work of Zygmunt Bauman on the Holocaust, the shorthand of the "gardening state" has served as a useful metaphor for the activities of the modern state and especially the modern "illiberal" state.[35] Both the Soviet Union and Nazi Germany were avid, as well as omnipotent, "gardeners," weeding out what they viewed as alien, enemy, or subhuman, and cultivating (or attempting to cultivate) a new "man." This kind of gardening then can be used to explain the forced population movements, police activities, and repression of the Stalin years.

While the modernity school bases its comparisons primarily within a Western context, James Scott expands the field of comparison beyond the Western world. At the same time, his focus is broader, in that his analysis includes both state intentions (the focus of the modernity school) and the reality on the ground – that is, how state policies were put into practice, received, and altered. Scott uses the term "high modernism" to describe the state's desire for "mastery of nature (including human nature), and, above all, the rational design of social order commensurate with the scientific understanding of natural laws."[36] In the context of Soviet history, high modernism, in combination with an authoritarian state, transformed modern techniques in social engineering into societal disaster. In the case of collectivization, for example, the policy was implemented from the outside on a subject population in a void of local knowledge and within the context of an illiberal polity.[37]

Modernity and high modernism, clearly thematically closely related, provide useful tools for understanding Stalinism. It may be that Scott provides the more useful comparison for understanding the Soviet state, given that he does not limit his focus to the West. The Soviet Union, after all, still remained a largely agrarian nation with a traditional peasantry and a relatively small industrial proletariat *circa* 1930. The modernity school does not factor in the underlying impact of socioeconomic structures, thereby missing a key point related to both why the state looms so large over society and why there was such a huge disjuncture between the visions of state actors and the reality in the field, one of the most persistent and often ignored themes of Soviet (Russian) history.[38]

It is also important to note a series of factors that may not fit so seamlessly within the modernity approach. First of all, the Soviet Union, unlike Nazi Germany, for example, cannot be characterized as a "strong state." Administration came from the center; policy was not implemented through routine channels of government, because there were no routine channels of government. Rather, policy erupted, campaign style, through plenipotentiary rule and local sweeps, after which inertia reigned. The state was not strong nor was it effective in the sense of being able to achieve the results of its vision. As a result, the center governed largely *by means of* repression. Repression became not a manifestation of state strength, but an expression of state weakness and a substitute for routine channels of government.[39]

The state, moreover, did not act in a vacuum. It confronted not a quicksand or an atomized society, but a fairly strong and complex society made up of cohesive communities with their own traditions and identities, able and willing at least to attempt to defend themselves.[40] The garden was not so malleable, and this too affected the outcome. The general economic context was also quite different. In comparison with the West, it is debatable if Russia, with its huge peasantry and backward economy, could be categorized as "modern." And here arises the greatest disjuncture of all: the intentions and visions of the center may have been "modern" (or at least modernizing), but the capacity for realizing them, the process, and the results were not.[41]

In this respect, the comparisons between Nazi Germany and the Soviet Union that dominate among the adherents of the totalitarian model as well as among some members of the modernity school may not be the most salient. As Mark Mazower has written, the Holocaust may not be the most useful "historical benchmark for modern mass violence." "Most other states," he writes, "that have perpetuated acts of mass violence over the past century were less efficient, differently organized, and motivated by different sets of beliefs and strategies."[42]

Nonetheless, a broader, comparative perspective illuminates important features of Stalinism by placing them within the context of the modern state. Such a perspective also serves to highlight the peculiarities of the *Russian* twentieth century, which in turn can help us understand the tragedy of the Soviet experiment.

An understanding of *Russian* peculiarities is essential, for Stalinism was never entirely free of the weight of the past. Despite revolution, despite Soviet claims of a new world, Stalinism cannot be understood in the absence of the legacy of the Russian Empire. Needless to say, this proposition has a venerable historiographical tradition in the West.[43]

The Russian Revolution of 1917 did not alter the basic themes of Russian history. The imperative of geography, soil, and climate; the role of the state and state centralization; expansion; modernization; and the primacy of defense needs did not disappear in the wake of the revolution. To a certain extent, one could argue that these themes were if anything accentuated as central power disintegrated with the revolution and was reconstituted through the various political and economic processes associated with Stalinism.

The most important series of continuities between patterns of prerevolutionary and postrevolutionary historical development revolve around the role and nature of the state. It is a truism of Russian history that the state served as the primary agent of historical change. Its defining role is explained variously by reference to the sheer size of the country; the dependent nature of social estates, especially the gentry; the proverbial missing middle class or weak civil society; and agrarian backwardness and rural undergovernment, to offer a far from exhaustive list. Whichever one of these factors one cares to highlight, it is incontestable that the Russian state was an "interventionist" state, and long before the advent of "modernity."[44]

The history of the Muscovite and imperial periods is to a great extent a history of state building from the center out. The Muscovite princes "gathered" the lands (and the revenues); the imperial monarchs extended their reign in an almost continuous process of geographical expansion and (often failed) administrative reform. State building emanated from the center; power was centrifugal. Defensive needs and the absence of natural geographical boundaries pushed state building and expansion. New territories were peopled by a continuous process of migration and Russian colonization, voluntary and involuntary, and the borders were shored up by the strategic placement of service gentry (through gifts of land) on the new frontiers.

In the imperial period, state building and expansion often came as a response to the West (meaning, in fact, England, France, Austria, and Prussia). The problem of Russian "backwardness" was both real and constructed. The reality lies in Russia's comparative position to the West: Russian was continually playing "catch up" with its economy. Its constructed nature is apparent both in the sense that the West may not have been the best yardstick with which to measure Russian development[45] and in the sense that the problematization (fetish?) of backwardness became a key to Russian economic development and intelligentsia thinking about Russia's future.

The state was the key player in economic modernization during the periods of greatest momentum. Economic development in turn bolstered state building, as the state strengthened its powers and existing might in conjunction with economic progress. Economic development also reinforced expansion, as the state sought outlets to ports and access to natural resources; migration and colonization then followed in the wake of expansion.

Russian state building, economic modernization, and expansion depended upon the extreme centralization of resources. The Russian state was always an extraction state, dependent upon the lands, the villages for its revenues, all the more so given the slow and weak development of urbanization and the largely agrarian basis of the country. Both state and towns developed in an exploitative symbiosis with the countryside. Taxes, grain, labor, and cannon fodder were siphoned from the countryside as the Russian state developed. The countryside – and particularly the peasantry – found itself in a subordinate economic position.

As cultural Westernization came to accompany economic Westernization, especially in the late eighteenth and nineteenth centuries, the countryside fell further behind and there appeared the proverbial cultural gulf between town and countryside so emphasized in the classic historiography of prerevolutionary Russia. The peasantry soon came to represent an entirely other culture, whether signified by its Russianness, its primitivism, its "inherent revolutionary" state, or the supposed inevitability of its disappearance with the advent of a modern industrial society. For the state, though, the peasantry remained first and foremost an economic resource upon which to base development, whether organically through the development of an internal market (as under Bunge) or more forcefully and artificially as a revenue base for financing industry (as under Vishnegradskii and Witte).

Russian development occurred in spurts, interrupted by long periods of inertia and stagnation. So when comparisons are made between the Stalin revolution and earlier period of Russian history, historians generally look to Peter the Great, the Great

Reform era, or Witte's industrial efforts. Although some such comparisons amount to little more than history by analogy, what is important to note is that the fundamentals of Russian state and economic development came together during these periods as responses to a persistent condition, persistent structures, persistent problems – for example, geography, defense, centralization, backwardness.

Russian history has been simplified in order to demonstrate the *Russian* features of Stalinism. In concrete terms, these features were most apparent in the collectivization of Soviet agriculture. Collectivization was in part just a more extreme effort at state building and economic extraction. It was state initiated, controlled by a center seemingly forever hampered by weak provincial and rural government. It was an extreme exercise in state building, an attempt to extend political, economic, and cultural controls over the countryside. It was a massive exercise in the expropriation of the peasantry's resources, reducing state–rural relations to sheer force. Collectivization also worked as an agent in expansion and colonization, as the social and political detritus of collectivization (that is, the "kulak") was siphoned off in dekulakization to "colonize" the north and east and to serve as a forced labor army for the exploitation of the country's vast natural resources. Cultural imperialism continued to animate Bolshevik policy, as the peasantry came to be viewed as a class destined to disappear with industrialization, in need of "proletarian" tutelage (*shefstvo*) in order to disappear, and "socially dangerous" in its politics and therefore in need of the eyes and ears of the secret police. Finally, defensive needs, real and perceived, played a key role in the entire assembly of policies that together formed the Stalin revolution.

Is this then an argument for *Russian* exceptionalism? It is decidedly not. The fiercely autarkic nature of Soviet development under Stalin, its anti-Western and anti-capitalist character, surely set it apart from Russian tradition. The scale of repression necessary to implement policy also set it apart. And, of course, Marxist–Leninist–Stalinist ideology was essential to the situation and certainly cast cultural imperialism in a new light.

It is, instead, an argument for broadening the parameters of our understanding of Stalinism and Soviet historical development. An understanding of Russian patterns of development based on structural determinants and longstanding problems must be combined with the new insights from comparisons with other twentieth-century states and a clear sense of the role of ideology in order to begin to understand the nature of Stalinism. This combination, along with the features outlined in the first part of this chapter, flesh out the phenomenon in a way that offers a deeper contextualization for understanding Stalin's despotic rule.

Conclusion

E. H. Carr once wrote that "those who insist so fervently on the moral condemnation of the individual sometimes unconsciously provide an alibi for whole groups and societies." They may also unconsciously or otherwise erect blinders to the very complexities of a historical phenomenon.

The phenomenon known as Stalinism was one such complex historical phenomenon. It cannot and should not be "normalized." Stalin, the person, cannot be removed from the equation nor can his responsibility be reduced. However, at the same time, a broader understanding and contextualization of Stalinism are essential in order to go beyond the facile cold-war interpretations that continue to dominate thinking inside and outside the field of Russian history.

Stalinism remains a useful concept. It defines a concrete period, although this discussion is confined to the 1930s with a recognition that the Stalinism of the war and postwar period evolved. It differentiates the Stalin era from what preceded and what followed without, however, dismissing the realities of continuities from the revolutionary and prerevolutionary periods. And it recognizes the singularity of the atrocities associated with Stalin's name.

Stalinism as a concept, however, can be useful only if it goes beyond a "great-man" understanding of history. Stalinism was first and foremost a recipe for a non-capitalist modernization (with some decidedly non-modern characteristics) based on a nationalized economy. The agrarian context of Stalinism is of central importance. The peasantry is too often the missing element in analyses of these times, given historiographical biases toward urban and political history. Its status as "internal colony" supporting the infrastructure of modernization turned the Stalinist state into an extraction state based on the use of force. Stalinism, to use Moshe Lewin's characteristic, was a form of agrarian despotism.[46] It shared features of the modern state as well as certain features of Russian historical development based on a continuation of similar patterns, structures, and problems. The ideology of a Stalinized Marxism set both desiderata and the general tenor of those brutalized times.

If Stalinism is contextualized, the term becomes explanatory as well as descriptive, thus advancing beyond the descriptions offered at the Bellagio conference. One might ask if it is worth maintaining the -ism, given the broadened parameters of this definition. Is Stalinism as a concept applicable elsewhere? Defined strictly as a non-capitalist path of modernization, the term might be useful in understandings of other twentieth-century agrarian nations that chose Marxist alternatives to capitalist development. But by and large the term is rooted in a particular time and country with a particular leader who, not without reason, provides the -ism with its noun.

Notes

1 The conference papers were published in Tucker, ed., *Stalinism*.
2 On the history of totalitarianism as a scholarly model, see Gleason, *Totalitarianism*.
3 Tucker, "Stalinism as Revolution from Above," in Tucker, ed., *Stalinism*, 77–108.
4 Cohen, "Bolshevism and Stalinism," in ibid. 3–29.
5 Lewin, "The Social Background of Stalinism," in ibid. 111–36.
6 *Webster's New World Dictionary of the American Language*, 2nd college edn. (New York: Simon and Schuster, 1982), 747.
7 Tsvetaeva, *Earthly Signs*, 136.
8 Viola et al., eds., *The War against the Peasantry*, 98–9.
9 *History of the Communist Party of the Soviet Union (Bolsheviks). Short Course*, 305.
10 It is beyond the scope of this essay to delve into this debate; it should be noted, however, that a fuller exploration of the debate is finally possible with the publication of the five-volume *Kak lomali NEP*, transcripts of the Central Committee plena of the late 1920s, and the five-volume *Tragediia Sovetskoi derevni*, the first volume of which sheds important new light on the issues at stake. Iakovlev., ed., *Kak lomali NEP*; and Danilov, Manning, and Viola, eds., *Tragediia Sovetskoi derevni*.

11   On Bukharin and the Right Opposition, see the classic work by Cohen, *Bukharin and the Bolshevik Revolution*.

12   See von Laue, *Sergei Witte and the Industrialization of Russia*; and id., *Why Lenin? Why Stalin? Why Gorbachev*.

13   For an excellent summary of this period, see Osokina, *Our Daily Bread*, esp. ch. 2–3. For a discussion and documentation of the crisis, see Danilov et al., eds., *Tragediia Sovetskoi derevni*, vol. 1, Introduction.

14   On collectivization, see Davies, *The Socialist Offensive*; Lewin, *Russian Peasants and Soviet Power*; and Viola, *The Unknown Gulag*.

15   Plan targets for industry are compared to actual results in Nove, *An Economic History of the USSR*, 194–7.

16   On the costs of collectivization and its contribution to industry within the context of the First Five Year Plan period, see the debate between Millar and Nove, "A Debate on Collectivization: Was Stalin Really Necessary,". 49–62.

17   Viola, *Peasant Rebels under Stalin*, 118, 140; id., *The Unknown Gulag*; and Fitzpatrick, *The Russian Revolution*, 140.

18   See the discussion in Davies and Wheatcroft, *The Industrialisation of Soviet Russia: The Years of Hunger*, 412–15.

19   On the role of the police in the periodic urban purges, see Shearer, "Crime and Social Disorder in Stalin's Russia;" id., "Social Disorder, Mass Repression, and the NKVD during the 1930s," in McLoughlin and McDermott, eds., *Stalin's Terror*; and Paul M. Hagenloh, " 'Socially Harmful Elements' and the Great Terror," in Fitzpatrick, ed., *Stalinism*. On worker unrest, see Rossman, *Worker Resistance under Stalin*.

20   David Brandenberger, "Stalin as Symbol: A Case Study of the Personality Cult and its Construction," in Davies and Harris, eds., *Stalin*, 249–70.

21   On Stalin's central role in decision-making, see Viola et al., eds., *The War against the Peasantry*, esp. ch. 4; Davies, Khlevniuk, and Rees, eds., *The Stalin–Kaganovich Correspondence*, introduction; and Oleg Khlevniuk, "The Objectives of the Great Terror, 1937–1938," in Hoffman, ed., *Stalinism*, 87–104.

22   On the power of the periphery, see Harris, *The Great Urals*.

23   See, e.g., Getty, *The Origins of the Great Purges*.

24   Viola, *The Unknown Gulag*, ch. 8.

25   Khlevniuk, "The Objectives of the Great Terror," in Hoffmann, ed., *Stalinism*.

26   For discussion and a bibliography of these sources, see Cohen, "Bolshevism and Stalinism," in Tucker, ed., *Stalinism*, 6–7.

27   A classic statement of this tendency is Fitzpatrick, *The Russian Revolution*. See also Getty, *The Origins of the Great Purges*, and Viola, *The Best Sons of the Fatherland*.

28   For example, Martin Malia wrote: "it is ideology that explains both the total scope and the inordinate cost of Stalin's Revolution." See Martin Malia, "The Soviet Tragedy: A History of Socialism in Russia," in Hoffmann, ed., *Stalinism*, 72.

29   A good example is Kotkin, *Magnetic Mountain*.

30   On the history of the concept of totalitarianism, see Gleason, *Totalitarianism*; for a classic example of the genre, see Friedrich and Brzezinski, *Totalitarian Dictatorship and Autocracy*. The most sophisticated and intellectually challenging account remains, of course, Arendt, *The Origins of Totalitarianism*. For a summary description of the modernization approach, see Black, *The Dynamics of Modernization*.

31   See, e.g., Spiro and Barber, "Counter-Ideological Uses of 'Totalitarianism'."

32   The founding work is Kotkin, *Magnetic Mountain*.

33   Scott, *Seeing like a State*.

34   The best of these works have the advantage (over the totalitarian model) of spanning the revolutionary divide. See, in particular, Peter Holquist, "State Violence as Technique,"

in Weiner, ed., *Landscaping the Human Garden*, 19–45; and id., "To Count, to Extract, to Exterminate," 111–44.

35 Bauman, *Modernity and the Holocaust*. For a brilliant application of this concept to Soviet history, see Weiner, "Nature, Nurture, and Memory in a Socialist Utopia," 1114–55.

36 Scott, *Seeing like a State*, 4.

37 See, e.g., Viola, "The Aesthetic of Stalinist Planning," 101–28.

38 Ibid.

39 Ibid.; and id., "The Campaign to Eliminate the Kulak as a Class," 503–24.

40 See Viola, ed., *Contending with Stalinism* – especially chapters by Viola, Rossman, and Northrop.

41 This disjucture may have something in common with another trend in the historiography, labeled "neo-traditionalism." This trend is often counterposed to the modernity school; I think, in fact, that the trends are compatible. For an illuminating article, see Terry Martin, "Modernization or Neo-Traditionalism? Ascribed Nationality and Soviet Primordialism," in Fitzpatrick, ed., *Stalinism*, 348–67.

42 Mark Mazower, "Violence and the State in the Twentieth Century," 1160.

43 e.g., Berdyaev, *The Origins of Russian Communism*; von Laue, *Sergei Witte and the Industrialization of Russia*; id., *Why Lenin? Why Stalin? Why Gorbachev?*; Pipes, *Russia under the Old Regime*; Timasheff, *The Great Retreat*; Tucker, "Stalinism as Revolution from Above," in Tucker, ed., *Stalinism*, 77–108; id., *Stalin in Power*.

44 See, e.g., Raeff, *The Well-Ordered Police State*.

45 On this point, see the interesting collection edited by Chirot, *The Origins of Backwardness in Eastern Europe*.

46 Lewin, *The Soviet Century*.

References

Arendt, Hannah (1973). *The Origins of Totalitarianism*. Harvest, New York.

Bauman, Zygmunt (1989). *Modernity and the Holocaust*. Cornell University Press, Ithaca, NY.

Berdyaev, Nicolas (1972). *The Origins of Russian Communism*. University of Michigan Press, Ann Arbor, MI.

Black, C. E. (1967). *The Dynamics of Modernization: A Study in Comparative History*. Harper, New York.

Chirot, Daniel (1989). *The Origins of Backwardness in Eastern Europe: Economics and Politics from the Middle Ages until the Early Twentieth Century*. University of California Press, Berkeley.

Cohen, Stephen F. (1980). *Bukharin and the Bolshevik Revolution: A Political Biography, 1888–1938*. Rev. edn. Oxford University Press, New York.

Danilov, V. P., Manning, R. T., and Viola, L. (eds.) (1999–2006). *Tragediia Sovetskoi derevni: Kollektivizatsiia i raskulachivanie. Dokumenty i materialy v 5-kh tomakh. 1927–1939*. 5 vols. Rosspen, Moscow.

Davies, R. W. (1980). *The Socialist Offensive. The Collectivisation of Soviet Agriculture, 1929–1930*. Harvard University Press, Cambridge, MA.

Davies, R. W., and Wheatcroft, Stephen G. (2004). *The Industrialisation of Soviet Russia: The Years of Hunger. Soviet Agriculture, 1931–1933*. Palgrave, New York.

Davies, R. W., Khlevniuk, Oleg V., and Rees, E. A. (eds.) (2003). *The Stalin–Kaganovich Correspondence, 1931–36*, trans. Steven Shabad. Yale University Press, New Haven.

Davies, Sarah, and Harris, James (eds.) (2005). *Stalin: A New History*. Cambridge University Press, Cambridge.

Fitzpatrick, Sheila (1994). *The Russian Revolution*. 2nd edn. Oxford University Press, New York and Oxford.

Fitzpatrick, Sheila (ed.) (2000). *Stalinism: New Directions*. Routledge, London and New York.

Friedrich, Carl J., and Brzezinski, Zbigniew (1965). *Totalitarian Dictatorship and Autocracy*. Praeger, New York.

Getty, J. Arch. (1985). *The Origins of the Great Purges*. Cambridge University Press, Cambridge and New York.

Gleason, Abbott (1995). *Totalitarianism: The Inner History of the Cold War*. Oxford University Press, New York.

Harris, James R. (1999). *The Great Urals: Regionalism and the Evolution of the Soviet System*. Cornell University Press, Ithaca, NY.

History of the Communist Party of the Soviet Union (Bolsheviks). Short Course (1976), 1939 edn. Proletarian Publishers, San Francisco.

Hoffmann, David L. (ed.) (2003). *Stalinism*. Blackwell, Oxford.

Holquist, Peter (2001). "To Count, to Extract, to Exterminate: Population Statistics and Population Politics in Late Imperial Russia and Soviet Russia," in Ronald Grigor Suny and Terry Martin (eds.), *A State of Nations: Empire and Nation-Making in the Age of Lenin and Stalin*. Oxford University Press, Ithaca, NY.

Iakovlev, A. N. (ed.) (2000). *Kak lomali NEP: Stenogrammy plenumov TsK VKP (b), 1928–1929 gg*. 5 vols. Materik, Moscow.

Kotkin, Stephen (1997). *Magnetic Mountain: Stalinism as a Civilization*. University of California Press, Berkeley.

Lewin, M. (1975). *Russian Peasants and Soviet Power: A Study of Collectivization*, trans. Irene Nove. Norton, New York.

Lewin, Moshe (2005). *The Soviet Century*. Verso, London.

Mazower, Mark (2002). "Violence and the State in the Twentieth Century," *American Historical Review*, 107/4. 4.

McLoughlin, Barry, and McDermott, Kevin (eds.) (2002). *Stalin's Terror*. Palgrave, London.

Millar, James R., and Nove, Alec (1976). "A Debate on Collectivization: Was Stalin Really Necessary?" *Problems of Communism*, 25.

Nove, Alec (1992). *An Economic History of the USSR, 1917–1991*. Penguin, London.

Osokina, Elena (2001). *Our Daily Bread: Socialist Distribution and the Art of Survival in Stalin's Russia, 1927–1941*, trans. Kate Transchel. M. E. Sharpe, Armonk, NY.

Pipes, Richard (2005). *Russia under the Old Regime*. Scribner, New York.

Raeff, Marc (1983). *The Well-Ordered Police State: Social and Institutional Change through Law in the Germanies and Russia, 1600–1800*. Yale University Press, New Haven.

Rossman, Jeffrey J. (2005). *Worker Resistance under Stalin: Class and Revolution on the Shop Floor*. Harvard University Press, Cambridge, MA.

Scott, James C. (1998). *Seeing like a State: How Certain Schemes to Improve the Human Condition have Failed*. Yale University Press, New Haven.

Shearer, David (1998). "Crime and Social Disorder in Stalin's Russia: A Reassessment of the Great Retreat and the Origins of Mass Repression." *Cahiers du monde russe*, 39/1–2.

Spiro, Herbert J., and Barber, Benjamin R. (1970). "Counter-Ideological Uses of 'Totalitarianism'." *Politics and Society*, 1/1.

Timasheff, Nicholas S. (1946). *The Great Retreat: The Growth and Decline of Communism in Russia*. Dutton, New York.

Tsvetaeva, Marina (2002). *Earthly Signs: Moscow Diaries, 1917–1922*, ed. and trans. James Gambrell. Yale University Press, New Haven.

Tucker, Robert C. (1990). *Stalin in Power: The Revolution from Above, 1928–1941*. Norton, New York.

Tucker, Robert C. (ed.) (1977). *Stalinism: Essays in Historical Interpretation*. Norton, New York.

Viola, Lynne (2003). "The Aesthetic of Stalinist Planning and the World of the Special Villages." *Kritika*, 4/1.

Viola, Lynne (1987). *The Best Sons of the Fatherland*. Oxford University Press, New York.

Viola, Lynne (1986). "The Campaign to Eliminate the Kulak as a Class, Winter 1929–1930: A Reevaluation of the Legislation." *Slavic Review*, 45/3.

Viola, Lynne (ed.) (2002). *Contending with Stalinism: Soviet Power and Popular Resistance in the 1930s*. Cornell University Press, Ithaca, NY.

Viola, Lynne (1996). *Peasant Rebels under Stalin: Collectivization and the Culture of Peasant Resistance*. Oxford University Press, New York.

Viola, Lynne (2007). *The Unknown Gulag: The Lost World of Stalin's Special Settlements*. Oxford University Press, New York.

Viola, Lynne, Danilov, V. P., Ivnitskii, N. A., and Kozlov, Denis (eds.) (2005). *The War against the Peasantry, 1927–1930*, trans. Steven Shabad. Yale University Press, New Haven.

Von Laue, Theodore H. (1974). *Sergei Witte and the Industrialization of Russia*. Atheneum, New York.

Von Laue, Theodore H. (1993). *Why Lenin? Why Stalin? Why Gorbachev? The Rise and Fall of the Soviet System*. 3rd edn. Harper Collins, New York.

Weiner, Amir (ed.) (2003). *Landscaping the Human Garden: Twentieth-Century Population Management in a Comparative Framework*. Stanford University Press, Stanford, CA.

Weiner, Amir (1999). "Nature, Nurture, and Memory in a Socialist Utopia: Delineating the Soviet Socio-Ethnic Body in the Age of Socialism." *American Historical Review*, 104/4.

Further Reading

The literature on the Stalinist 1930s is voluminous. A good introduction to the historiography is Chris Ward, *Stalin's Russia*, 2nd ed. (London: Arnold, 1999).Giuseppe Boffa's *The Stalin Phenomenon*, tr. Nicholas Fersen (Ithaca, NY: Cornell University Press, 1992), though slightly dated, presents a very readable general introduction to the traditional literature. Among the many biographies of Stalin, Robert Service's *Stalin: A Biography* (London: Macmillan, 2004); Robert Tucker's *Stalin in Power: The Revolution from Above, 1928–1941* (New York: Norton, 1990); and Dmitri Volkogonov's *Stalin: Triumph and Tragedy*, tr. Harold Shukman (New York: Grove Weidenfeld, 1991) can be singled out as solid scholarly works. R. W. Davies' *Industrialisation of Soviet Russia* series (vol. 1–3 published by Harvard University Press, 1980–88; vols. 4–5 by Palgrave, 1996, 2004 (with Stephen G. Wheatcroft) and a forthcoming volume with Oleg V. Khlevniuk) is the classic history of the economy in the 1930s, presenting the most thorough empirical survey of the decade as a whole. Merle Fainsod's *Smolensk Under Soviet Rule* (Cambridge, Mass.: Harvard University Press, 1958) and Sheila Fitzpatrick's *Everyday Stalinism* (New York: Oxford University Press, 1999) best capture the realities of state and society in the 1930s. Alexander I. Solzhenitsyn, *The Gulag Archipelago*, tr. Thomas P. Whitney and Harry

Willetts, 3 vols. (New York: Harper and Row, 1973) remains the standard history of the gulag.

Since the fall of the Soviet Union, scholars have published a large variety of archival document collections. The most notable in English are from the Yale University Press Annals of Communism series and (for the 1930s) include: J. Arch Getty and Oleg V. Naumov, eds. *The Road to Terror* (1999); Oleg V. Khlevniuk, ed., *The History of the Gulag* (2004); Louis Siegelbaum and Andrei Sokolov, eds., *Stalinism as a Way of Life* (2000); and Lynne Viola et al., ed., *The War Against the Peasantry* (2005).

CHAPTER TWENTY-THREE

The Soviet Union in the Second World War

NIKITA LOMAGIN
(translated by Melissa Stockdale and Abbott Gleason)

The Second World War played a huge role in Soviet and world history. If the First World War laid the foundations of the history of communism, the Second World War turned communism into a genuinely global system and provided the basis for its influential half-century long career.[1] When the war began, the USSR was one of seven world powers, but by mid-1945 it had emerged as one of only two superpowers. Prior to the war it did not have friends and dependable allies, being in international affairs essentially a pariah state. After the war the Soviet Union became the leader of the bloc of socialist countries opposing the countries of the capitalist world, headed by the United States. Before the war, the probability that the Soviet system would be long-lived was not rated very highly, because of the serious crisis evoked by purges and the Great Terror. After the war this system began to look like a genuine alternative to the capitalist model, since it had managed to prevail against Nazi Germany and its allies.

Thus, the Second World War shifted the center of gravity of Soviet history. It marked the end of a period of activity commencing in October 1917 and leading to the Stalinist consolidation of the new order on the eve of the war. Henceforth, the Soviet undertaking reoriented itself toward the international arena. In the words of Martin Malia, "the era of the experiment was over; the era of the empire was about to begin."

At the same time, the war was a test of the solidity of the Soviet system. In 1939 the core question was whether the socialism engineered in the Soviet Union would prove more successful than tsarism in defending the state. The Soviet Union managed not only to win the war, but also to broaden substantially its influence in the world. So it is no coincidence that in the following decades Soviet leaders ascribed this victory to the merits of the system and asserted that there was no need for fundamental changes. Nonetheless, the question as to how successful this system proved to be in the war years will continue to interest historians, since the Soviet Union very nearly lost the war before it began to win it.[2]

The Second World War, and especially the setbacks of the first two years of the Soviet Union's war with Germany and the *Wehrmacht*'s protracted occupation of

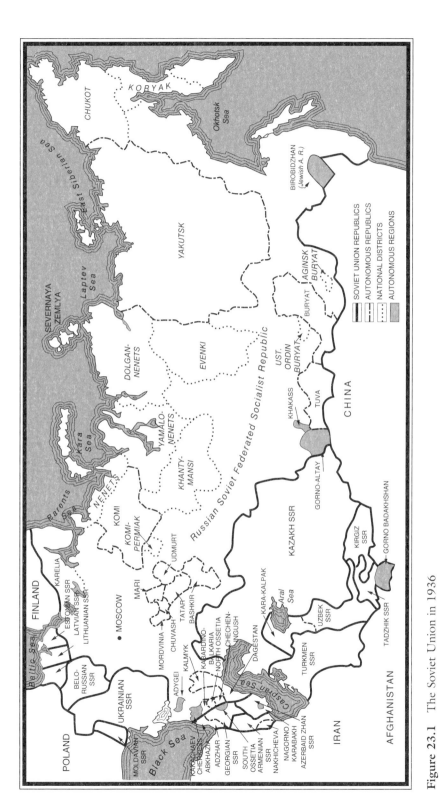

Figure 23.1 The Soviet Union in 1936
Source: Ian Grey, *The Horizon history of Russia* (American Heritage Publishing Co., Inc., 1970)

the country, planted doubts in the people about the viability of the Soviet regime. They also evoked significant and large-scale protests against Stalinism, some of which took the form of armed struggle. Investigations based on materials in the party and NKVD archives, opened in the 1990s, show that expectations of profound changes in the economic and political realm were widely diffused among the civilian population and armed forces. After the victory over Nazism, people experienced something very like the "Decembrism" that followed Russia's defeat of Napoleon. This was a powerful force that subsequently predetermined the movement of society toward greater freedom and the Khrushchev thaw.

In this chapter we will look at the most important disputed issues in the history of the Soviet Union during the Second World War. These include the Soviet Union's path toward war, showing the reasons that drove Stalin into alliance with Nazi Germany and an expansionist policy after the infamous Molotov–Ribbentrop pact. Of great interest is a set of questions connected with the functioning of the machinery of state, which, in contrast to the tsarist regime in the First World War, and in spite of serious military defeats in the campaigns of 1941–2, was able to secure the relative reliability of the rear. Equally important are the relations of the authorities and the people during the war, including the entire spectrum of moods in society. We are presently witnessing a genuine explosion of interest in the "human dimension" of the war. This is due in part to radical changes in Russian society, which have influenced the social sciences in rejecting dogmatism and ideological constraints, as well as to the powerful influence on Russia's historians of new tendencies in world historical science, including the strengthening of genres focusing on human experience, such as social history.[3] Finally, the issues of collaboration and the partisan movement are essential to understanding the people's attitude to the regime.

The USSR at the Beginning of the Second World War: Strengthening Geostrategic Positions?

Until recently, the extensive Western historiography on Soviet foreign policy, and especially on Soviet–German relations in the period 1939–41, scarcely examined the question of the Soviet Union's entrance into the Second World War, since it was considered completely clear. As a rule, there was discussion of the partnership and cooperation between the USSR and the Third Reich, of the Soviet Union's support of Germany, and even of their continuing relationship after the start of the Second World War.[4] As of 2009, one can observe a completely different picture in Russia's own historical writing. The traditional orientation of the Russian historiography of the USSR's foreign policy, since it cannot entirely ignore recently published documents, tries to accommodate the new evidence within the old framework. For example, it puts the main emphasis on the legal correctness of the Soviet invasion of Poland and the historic legitimacy of the reunification with the USSR of Western Ukraine and Belorussia, which had earlier been part of Tsarist Russia.[5]

The traditional orientation in contemporary Russian historiography (which happily is no longer the sole orientation) enjoys the support of official circles, as is seen in the declaration of the Russian Ministry of Foreign Affairs in connection with the sixtieth anniversary of September 17, 1939. It says, in part:

Without justifying the actions of the Stalin regime in the international arena, it is at the same time impossible not to see that they were dictated less by an aspiration to seize foreign territory than by the necessity of guaranteeing the security of the country. The assertions of official Warsaw, and also of several of its representatives abroad, that "aggression by the former USSR against Poland" was carried out on September 17 is not corroborated in international-legal documents.[6]

From the beginning of the Second World War, in his plans and actions Stalin proceeded less from a set of understandings with Nazi Germany, connected with the non-aggression pact of August 23, 1939, than from the actual unfolding of events. The most important factors influencing subsequent decisions of the Soviet leadership were the *Wehrmacht*'s swift destruction of the Polish army and the so-called phony war in the West, instead of the active armed conflict that had been expected.

Stalin had counted on getting a sufficiently long breathing space for raising the battle readiness of the Red Army, a necessity if he was to bargain from a position of strength at the anticipated peace negotiations. His policy was not determined by ideological predilections. It was directed exclusively at maintaining the state interests of the Soviet Union. At its basis lay the concept of "spheres of influence," a concept detrimental to the sovereignty of neighboring states. The idea of creating a buffer zone along the entire length of the western frontier was a legacy of the Russian tsars, who considered free access to the Black Sea in the south and to the Baltic Sea in the north a necessary condition for Russia's establishment as a great European power and for defense of its vulnerable borders. The small states all along the buffer zone between the Soviet Union and Germany, from Finland in the north to Turkey in the south, would have to accommodate their policies to the geopolitical interests of their two powerful neighbors.

After Germany had unleashed war against Poland, the Soviet leadership was not confident that the *Wehrmacht* would necessarily stop at the line of division of Poland agreed upon in the secret protocol of the non-aggression pact. Two questions moved to the forefront: how to introduce Soviet troops onto the territory of Poland, and how to justify this troop movement to the Soviet people and the entire world. A Soviet note delivered to the Polish ambassador in Moscow September 17, 1939 stated: "Poland has been turned into a convenient arena for military accidents and surprises that could create a threat to the USSR. Therefore the Soviet government, which has been neutral until now, can no longer remain neutral when confronted by these facts."

Simultaneously, the USSR declared to the ambassadors of twenty-four countries with which it had diplomatic relations that it was continuing to preserve neutrality in the war. Poland's government and chief command, having evaluated the situation, affirmed that Poland was not in a state of war with the Soviet Union. The Polish population was hostile to the Red Army, but a majority of the population of western Ukraine and western Belorussia met the Red Army men as liberators. During the Polish campaign Soviet troops interned more than 230,000 Polish soldiers and officers who were on the territory of the western districts of Belorussia and Ukraine. The majority of them subsequently fought in Polish formations together with the Red Army or with the troops of the Allies. But 14,700 Polish officers, civil servants, police, and intelligence operatives were arrested and shot by the organs of the NKVD in

1940. The Soviets acknowledged the shooting of the Polish officers only in 1990; though it has still not been fully investigated, the Russian General Procurator closed the criminal case on the shootings in 2005.

On September 24, 1939 Germany and the USSR signed a new "Treaty on Friendship and Borders" in Moscow. By its provisions, the border between the Soviet Union and Germany was drawn roughly along the so-called Curzon Line, acknowledged in 1919 by the Supreme Council of the Entente. Stalin's proposal to draw the border not along the Vistula but according to the internationally acknowledged Curzon Line reflected his effort to avoid everything that in future might cause friction between Germany and the Soviet Union.[7]

The "Treaty on Friendship and Borders" signified a further rapprochement of the Soviet Union with the German Reich, even as the security interests of the USSR demanded that it remain neutral and not bind itself tightly to Germany. At the same time, the new treaty with the Reich made Soviet–German relations more defined. Western Belorussia and Western Ukraine were brought into the USSR. Moscow obtained freedom of action in the Baltic region and could set about realizing the secret protocol of August 23, 1939 concerning Finland, Estonia, Latvia, and Lithuania.

International conditions at the end of September 1939 also dictated the concrete policies on the Baltic states, so that the Soviet leadership did not immediately undertake the political and territorial reconstruction of the republics provided for in the secret protocols with Germany. The Soviet Union was interested in the stationing of its troops and naval bases in the Baltic, in order to prevent transformation of these territories into a bridgehead for a German attack on the USSR. The governments of Lithuania, Latvia, and Estonia were forced to accept the Soviet proposal – essentially an ultimatum – on concluding an agreement about mutual aid, including military assistance. In the fall of 1939, then, the Soviet government, acting within the parameters set by the secret protocols, sought at the same time to observe the external norms of international law. Illustrative of this are the choice of timing for introducing Soviet troops into Poland (after the Polish government had left the country), the forms of treaties with the Baltic republics, and observance of the conditions of these treaties up to the summer of 1940, when the *Wehrmacht*'s successes in France sharply changed strategic circumstances.

Considerations of a military–strategic nature prompted the Stalin leadership to enter negotiations with Finland to settle a series of territorial questions. Initially, the Soviet Union tried to attain from Finland treaties analogous to those concluded with the Baltic states. Having received a negative answer, the Soviet Union came out with proposals for moving the border on the Karelian isthmus by several dozen kilometers and for safeguarding Leningrad, a vital political, military, and economic center. The USSR also requested transfer to it of several islands in the Gulf of Finland, part of the territory of the Rybachii and Srednyii peninsulas in the Barents Sea, in exchange for twice the territory in Soviet Karelia. It also proposed leasing the Khanko peninsula for construction of a naval base. After Finnish rejection of the Soviet proposals and the termination of negotiations November 13, 1939, both sides began to prepare for a military solution to the problem.

Following the border incident of November 26, a circumstance that the Soviet side refused to investigate jointly with Finland, the government of the USSR declared its withdrawal from its non-aggression pact. On November 30, without a declaration of war, the Red Army crossed the border. The Soviet–Finnish war had begun.

Sustaining huge losses at the front, and experiencing serious pressure from influential allies of Finland, Stalin was compelled to renounce plans for the sovietization of Finland and signed a peace treaty on March 12, 1940. The Soviet Union improved its strategic position in the north and northwest. It created the precondition for guaranteeing the security of Leningrad by the Murmansk railroad, along which a large stream of trucks would subsequently flow into the USSR within the framework of Lend Lease. The USSR also obtained the Karelian Isthmus and several other territories, and the Khanko peninsula was transferred to it on lease.

At the same time, the war had a number of extremely negative consequences for the Soviet Union. Soviet troop losses were 87,507 killed, 39,369 missing in action, and more than 5,000 captured. Losses on the Finnish side were less half these figures. Numerous deficiencies in the Red Army's organization, tactics, arms, and management of troops were revealed in the course of military operations. Perceptions of the weakness of the Red Army in the West, and above all in Germany, were heightened. The Soviet–Finnish war also stirred up anti-Soviet forces in Western Europe and the USA.

The swift development of military operations in the summer of 1940 in Western Europe, the concentration of *Wehrmacht* forces in Eastern Prussia, and the possibility of the transfer of German troops to the east gave Stalin grounds for fearing a German invasion of the Baltic region. An abundance of intelligence on the growth within the ruling circles of the Baltic states of hostility toward the USSR, and on their connections with Germany, nudged the Soviet leadership into taking action. The Soviet government directed a note to the leadership of Lithuania (June 14) and Latvia and Estonia (June 16) saying it considered it absolutely necessary and urgent that they form governments able to guarantee the "honorable implementation" of the treaties of mutual assistance with the USSR. It also demanded an increase in the number of Soviet troops on the territory of the Baltic region.

Elections to the legislative bodies were held in Latvia, Lithuania, and Estonia on July 14–15; these bodies speedily proclaimed Soviet power and voted for unification with the USSR, which took place in August 1940. Aiming to ensure profound sovietization of the Baltic republics, the Stalin leadership employed traditional methods: mass repressions and deportations of opponents of the Soviet regime and "socially alien elements" in the summer of 1940. The victims constituted a great part of the national elite of the newly incorporated republics.

The international community regarded the incorporation of the Baltic republics into the USSR as annexation, a manifestation of the imperial ambitions of a communist totalitarian state. There was a sharp deterioration in the Soviet Union's relations with England and the United States – that is, with those countries that were its potential allies at a time when the conflicts between the USSR and Nazi Germany were becoming ever clearer.[8] Stalin's step was a major political mistake, with far-reaching consequences as well for the attitudes of the peoples of the incorporated republics. The negative consequences of the violent sovietization of the Baltic region are still making themselves felt in Russia's relations with Estonia, Latvia, and Lithuania in our own day.

With Germany's help, in the summer of 1940 the Soviet Union also resolved the so-called Bessarabian question. Throughout 1940, Stalin was agitated not only by

German military successes but also by the problem of British naval supremacy in the Mediterranean. Recalling the experience of the Crimean War and the allied intervention in the Russian Civil War, Stalin feared that Turkey could serve as a beachhead for a new attack on the Soviet Union. In his view only complete control over the Black Sea coast and the mouth of the Danube could give final form to the security achieved by the Molotov–Ribbentrop pact. Expansion to the mouth of the Danube did not have as its primary goal the acquisition of land, but gave Stalin control over the river and served as a springboard for further advancement toward the Straits. Stalin considered securing a land bridge to the Turkish Straits an important condition for achieving any new settlement of the Straits question.[9]

Toward the end of June 1940 a declaration was made to the Romanian government on the necessity of restoring historic fairness and speedily resolving the question of returning Bessarabia to the Soviet Union. Although the Romanian government agreed only to open negotiations, the Soviet Union demanded that Romanian forces be cleared from the territory of Bessarabia and the northern part of Bukovina. The Red Army entered Bessarabia and northern Bukovina on June 28, 1940. On August 2 the Moldavian SSSR was fashioned from a large part of Bessarabia and the Moldavian Autonomous Republic (in existence since 1924); northern Bukovina and the southern regions of Bessarabia became part of Soviet Ukraine.

For the most part, the population of the USSR supported Stalin's foreign policy. People were completely in thrall to official propaganda, approving the "liberating" and "noble" mission of the Red Army in giving fraternal help to the Ukrainians and Belorussians in Poland, and believing in the necessity of replacing Litvinov's foreign-policy team. They took on faith Soviet propaganda declarations concerning the perfidy of the "White Finns" and the necessity of helping to create a people's government in Finland. They were similarly convinced of their right to strong measures in deciding the fate of the "potato republics," and so on. However, there were also those who did not agree with this aggressive foreign-policy course, expressing doubts about the durability of the alliance with Germany and breaking relations with the democratic states.

In sum, Soviet foreign policy in 1939–41 led to a situation that not only did not strengthen the geostrategic position of the Soviet Union, but in fact weakened it. In the first place, as a result of dividing Poland with Germany, the USSR deprived itself of a buffer zone that had earlier made a sudden attack by Germany impossible. Secondly, by concluding a non-aggression pact with Germany, Stalin secured Hitler against the possibility of a war on two fronts. In essence, this untied Germany's hands for the subjugation of Europe, whose resources were then placed in the service of the *Wehrmacht*. In the third place, Stalin's agreement in August 1939 to supply Germany with oil, non-ferrous metals, and food stuffs promoted the success of the Nazis in the West. As a result, in June 1941 Germany was a much more threatening opponent than it had been in 1939. At the same time, the breathing space granted the Soviet Union by the non-aggression pact did not bring about the expected dividends. Territorial acquisitions did not give greater security. On the contrary, the fortifications on the old border were demolished before fortified installations had been built on the new one. The forcible sovietization of the Baltic region alienated the overwhelming majority of the population, causing them to welcome the Germans as liberators when Germany attacked the Soviet Union. The Winter War of 1939–40, unleashed by Stalin against Finland, revealed serious shortcomings in the areas of military leadership and the supply of troops and pushed Hitler toward accelerating preparations for war against the USSR.

The USSR on the Eve of the Second World War

In domestic politics under the conditions prevailing at the beginning of the Second World War, the Soviet leadership paid particular attention to increasing its military potential in the event of a struggle with potential opponents of the regime who might stab the Soviet Union in the back, should it find itself in a major war. Political control is the most important function of any state, and as such was a general European phenomenon – the "contemporary form of politics," which had appeared long before Bolshevism.[10] But under communism it had become the alpha and omega of the new regime.

The tasks of political control were formulated on the basis of the authorities' expectations of the actions of the probable opponent and the behavior of the population under conditions prevailing at the time, and with respect to circumstances resulting from the introduction of various measures. The adoption of preventive measures was necessitated by three important factors. In the first place, the leadership of the Communist Party and the organs of internal security based their work on the assumption of a sharpening of the class struggle as "socialist construction" proceeded. This alone was sufficient cause for a far-reaching strengthening of measures against real and imagined enemies of the Soviet regime, above all against anyone belonging to non-communist organizations. All "former people," which meant those who had held any sort of government post in pre-Revolutionary Russia or owned property, were considered such potentially dangerous opponents of the regime. Secondly, the powers had a sufficiently accurate idea of the mood of the population, which scarcely conformed to the slogan about moral and political unity and universal support for the politics of the party and government. On the basis of numerous special communications and reports from NKVD organs and party informers, the political leadership concluded that, in case of war, sporadic spasms of discontent might lead to some more serious consequences than the isolated instances of disloyalty that had been comparatively frequent in the prewar years. Thirdly, the security organs of the army and navy – and those of the Soviet Union as a whole – clearly understood what a powerful weapon the propaganda that Germany had successfully employed from the beginning of the Second World War would be in the hands of their adversary.[11] Nor did they fail to consider precisely those questions raised by the anti-Soviet content of German literature. The abundance of anti-Stalinist material contained in it, the systematic critique of the internal and external politics of the Soviet Union left no doubt whatever about the fundamental direction of the adversary's propaganda in the coming war.

Here one must emphasize that Lev Trotsky, living in exile in Mexico City, was the last of the cohort of leaders of the Russian Revolution, who to the end of his life remained the most resolute opponent of Stalin and Stalinism. Between 1938 and 1940 he published a host of articles in the foreign press about Stalin and his foreign policy. Intelligence agents brought them to the Kremlin, and they had an influence on the choice of priorities in the sphere of political control on the eve of the war.

However, the most fundamental dangers for the regime lay less in former political opponents of Stalin than in the broad political discontent building in the country. Thomas Rigby, in his research on the "dark culture" in the Soviet Union, asserts that the political hypocrisy of the authorities was a ticking time bomb. The collapse of the Soviet Union in the end was facilitated by the existence of an official rhetoric about democracy and constitutional rights, which could be exploited by those who were striving for real democracy.[12] Material from Soviet archives confirms this assertion. On the eve of the war with Germany, the campaign to choose deputies for soviets at various levels, but also measures taken by the authorities to strengthen discipline and defense capacity, were repeatedly understood with reference to the violation of political rights and civil liberties.[13]

Unhealthy attitudes, in conjunction with the contracting of a loan in order to increase defense capacity on the eve of a war with Germany, took possession of the most diverse categories of the working population – from those made answerable according to the decree of June 20, 1940 criminalizing lateness and absenteeism, to shock workers, including members of the KOMSOMOL (the Soviet Youth Organization) and the Communist Party. Workers explained their reluctance to subscribe to the loan in significant amounts with reference to onerous living conditions, high prices, and the general resort by the state to coercive means. Workers were unhappy with its compulsory nature. "Anti-Soviet and unhealthy" moods were recorded in many Leningrad concerns; workers said that "the government is behaving like Hitler"; "Soviet power skins the worker"; "Soviet loans are worse than the tsarist ones"; "no kind of improvement in life is apparent, I go around without boots and breeches," and so on.[14]

Analogous moods among the people were recorded in connection with the transition to an eight-hour work day and to a seven-day work week; the prohibition against workers and employees quitting a position without authorization; the government's decree introducing tuition fees for advanced secondary, technical, and higher education, and so on. Workers criticized the authorities' measures as backtracking from the gains of the revolution and constitutional norms. "We old Bolsheviks have taken a great moral blow," said one of the regime's critics, for "our achievements, the achievements of the revolution, have all come to nothing."

Workers characterized the new labor legislation as the introduction of serfdom into the USSR. In September 1940 workers at large factories declared that "in Germany the unemployed live better," that "the Baltic republics will soon understand what Soviet power is really like," that "in the event of war in the USSR there will be a big change, since everyone's dissatisfied with the existing laws, but for now they're just waiting for the chance," and, finally, "that's not what was expected from revolution."

In this way, as the Second World War began, the social, economic, and political situation in the country developed in directions that were very undesirable to the authorities. Party informants and organs of the NKVD noted the growth of political protest, including overtly political declarations, the dissemination of leaflets, rumors, and calls for strikes. Workers discussed the topic of revolution as never before. Leaflets and graffiti declared "Soon we'll strike" and "Down with the government of oppression, poverty and prisons." Rumors circulated about strikes in the city's factories. Workers talked about a "second revolution," about a rebellion against the government.

According to Sarah Davies: "It was felt that the people's patience was exhausted, that only a small shove was needed to push them over the edge, and that 1940 or 1941 would witness the end of Soviet power."[15]

The population's attitude toward the future enemy, Nazi Germany, was varied and complex. Conclusion of the 1939 non-aggression pact and a subsequent series of economic and political agreements produced a fundamental change in Soviet internal propaganda. But it was very hard to overcome the public's mistrust of Germany. Documents of the organs of state security and party informants testify to the painful perception of the rapprochement with the Nazis on the part of practically all sectors of society. Agents of the NKVD noted that many people were struck by the suddenness of the change of course in Soviet foreign policy and expressed doubts about the durability of the treaty. Moreover, individuals from virtually every part of the population expressed mistrust of the German government, which "will continue its aggressive policy" directed first against France, England, and Poland, but then toward the USSR as well.

Some felt the reason that "everything happened so quickly" was the similarity of the political regimes of the USSR and Germany. Citing the pronouncement of one critic of the pact, an NKVD report remarked that

> it was simple for the two dictatorships to reach an agreement – no opposition leaders, no parliaments . . . How will our historians be feeling now, you know they were shouting about the teutonic knights, about the Ice Battle, Alexander Nevsky and so on and now they'll have to shout about a century or even centuries of friendship. Everyone knows if they'd talked about that two years ago, they'd either have been put in prison or just shot.[16]

The Polish campaign substantially influenced the mood of Soviet people, especially military personnel. It "accumulated the aggressive potential . . . of the public," strengthening the "romantic excitement of war." The quick and easy victory consolidated the Red Army's image of invincibility, promoting the revival of imperial sentiments. Even in the course of the Winter War with Finland this "romantic excitement of war" didn't disappear entirely. "Veterans of the 'liberationist' campaign who had served in the western regions continued to think in such categories as 'a new type of war' and met June 1941 conditioned by the Polish-inspired psychological readiness for war."[17]

The Soviet Regime in the War with Germany: Over-Centralization, Political Control, and the Art of Compromise

During the wartime months of 1941 the Soviet Union found itself at the edge of an abyss. Indeed, until the battle of Stalingrad the likelihood of defeat remained very high. Although the war was a disaster for the peoples of the Soviet Union for its entire duration, the first year and a half proved to be the most difficult. The shattering defeats of this period gave rise to questions about Stalin's responsibility for this catastrophe and about the role played by the structural deficiencies of the Soviet system. None of Stalin's other actions evoked so many pointed discussions in the former Soviet Union as did his leadership in the war, since literally everyone was affected by the nearly total ruination of the country and the death of tens of millions of people.

In the scholarly literature four reasons are usually advanced to explain the colossal failures of the initial period of the war with Germany. The unsuccessful wager on the appeasement of aggression, which found expression in the non-aggression pact with Germany, is particularly emphasized among Stalin's mistakes. A second reason is the extremely low quality of Stalin's military leadership. Stalin did not take into account information from Soviet intelligence on the imminent attack, or warnings from the English and US governments about German military preparations. Without bearing in mind the speed of the German advance deep into Soviet territory, Stalin ordered troops only to attack or to hold their positions. The sole result of this was that approximately 3.9 million Soviet servicemen were taken prisoner during the first seven months of the war, a figure greater than the number of troops the Germans had thrown against the Soviet Union. The third reason for failures was the cumbersome, overcentralized system of administration of the armies, which destroyed local initiative at every level of the chain of command: those commanding armies and divisions were afraid to make independent decisions even when extreme situations arose. Finally, a number of historians have suggested that a fundamental reason for the defeats in the early period of the war was the unwillingness of the people (and above all, Red Army men) to defend Soviet power. In support of this thesis they adduce data on the huge number of Soviet prisoners of war and the friendly attitude toward the Germans on the part of the civilian population in territories that the *Wehrmacht* occupied. Also mentioned is the regime's clearly expressed lack of confidence in the loyalty of Soviet prisoners of war, who over the course of the entire war were denied the right to defense.

In the Soviet Union the concept of a Soviet prisoner of war, with an acknowledged legal status, did not exist. In the opinion of a number of historians, there is no more eloquent testimony to the regime's lack of confidence in the viability of its own handiwork than such an attitude toward Soviet citizens who had fallen into captivity.[18]

Following this logic, some historians are inclined to see Hitler's inability to exploit the favorable situation and use the dissatisfaction of the Soviet people as one source of Stalin's eventual success, along with Stalin's highly effective policy, which was able to use Russian patriotism and simultaneously depend on the mighty repressive apparatus.

The role of the Soviet system in securing victory was very significant, for the simple reason that it constituted a political–military model for organizing society that was now functioning in its native element. Immediately after the start of Nazi aggression the entire country was subordinated to the State Committee on Defense (GKO), with Stalin at its head. The most trustworthy individuals from his inner circle entered the GKO, and it was the GKO that directed the activities of the party, security organs, the army, and commissariats of the economic bloc devoted to carrying out urgent military tasks. During the war years the GKO put into effect roughly 10,000 different directives and decrees (7–8 per day, on average), about two-thirds of which were related in some way to economic questions and the organization of war production.

One of the main achievements of the State Committee on Defense in the first months of the war was the evacuation of approximately 1,500 factories eastward, to

Central Asia, the Volga, the Urals, and Siberia. Over the course of the war some ten million people were relocated in this way. By the end of the war more than half the metal smelted in the USSR was produced in the eastern part of the country, while before the war less than 20 per cent was smelted there. In 1943 this unique resettlement of industry allowed the Soviet Union to far outstrip Germany in production of airplanes, tanks, and artillery.

Similarly, through the joint efforts of the party, security organs, and army the center accomplished the organization of the partisan movement on territories occupied by the *Wehrmacht*. In May 1942 the Central Staff of the partisan movement was created under General Headquarters (*stavka*) of the Supreme Command. Simultaneously, partisan movement staffs were formed under the military soviets of the fronts.

However, the vigorous partisan movement did not come into being immediately. During the first year and a half of the war, in a large part of the occupied territories the population did not actively oppose the occupiers. For example, until the middle of 1943 in the occupied territory of Leningrad region, according to data already published during the Soviet era, the number of active abettors of the occupiers destroyed by state security organs exceeded the number of partisan units formed there. Nonetheless, the ability of the regime to ignite the fire of resistance, its determination to mobilize and concentrate enormous human and industrial resources on strategic orientations, in conditions of crisis, played an important role in the achievement of victory.

The organs of state security assumed exceptional significance with the onset of war. In contrast to the First World War, the authorities did not hesitate in dealing with potential and real opponents of the regime. What is more, in war conditions a redistribution of the functions of power took place that favored the military-repressive organs. Their wartime work unfolded on the mighty foundation laid in the preceding years. There was talk of optimizing the model for organizing society, which came together as a whole in the USSR in the 1930s.

Already at the very start of the war there began revision of categories of registration, which were filled not only on an ethnic basis, with representatives of the peoples of the countries fighting the USSR, but also with special wartime categories: deserters, those with self-inflicted wounds, refugees, individuals who had resided in the occupied territories, and "defeatists." It turned out that the majority of these individuals were not inscribed in the traditional categories of registration according to this or that political "orientation." Thanks to this circumstance, the organs of state security were in a complicated situation: they continued to conduct agent-operative work among the groups customarily subject to registration at the same time as there developed, unattended by agents of the secret police, a stratum of anti-Soviet feeling among people previously loyal to the regime.

The NKVD carried out arrests of the politically suspect, to which number related not only individuals who were on the operational registration of the organs of the NKVD, but also ordinary Soviet citizens. The principle of collective responsibility for the dissemination of rumors that caused alarm among the population was introduced. In large cities jamming services were created with the goal of neutralizing the enemy's radio propaganda.

The system also took upon itself new repressive functions. One of these was the revision of the ethnic map of the Soviet Union through the deportation of entire peoples in the interests of state security. The Volga Germans were the first ethnic group subjected to resettlement. Despite having lived in Russia for nearly two centuries and being for the most part absolutely loyal to the regime, they were subjected to deportation in the summer of 1941 shortly after the war began. The same fate befell ethnic Germans, Finns, and representatives of other "unreliable" peoples living in various large cities, including Moscow and Leningrad. "Ethnic cleansings" were also carried out in the army: the so-called westerners – those who'd been conscripted into the Red Army from territories brought into the Soviet Union after the Molotov–Ribbentrop pact – were removed from their units. In 1944, after the northern Caucasus and Crimea had been liberated from German forces, Chechens, Ingush, Crimean Tatars, and a number of other small peoples were subjected to deportation for "complicity with the enemy." Although only an insignificant part of these peoples cooperated with the occupying forces, one and all were deported, at the earliest possible date and under inhuman conditions. The goal of the deportations was creation of an ethnically homogeneous population on strategically important territories and liquidation of potential sources of disloyalty to the Soviet regime.

Despite the strengthening of the organs of internal affairs, in the sphere of political control in most cases local organs of the NKVD were not allowed absolute arbitrary rule. The central apparatus of the NKVD, the leadership of local party organizations, the military procuracy, and the military tribunals, through their combined efforts and their separate actions, ensured that, on the whole, despite the gravity of the situation in the rear and at the front in the fall and winter of 1941–2, the organs of political control acted within the limits of the laws of wartime.

Alongside the intensification of administrative–repressive functions, in the interests of consolidating society the Soviet regime demonstrated a capacity for some flexibility. Initial slogans calling people to join battle for socialism were discarded. Stalin began instead to appeal to feelings of Russian patriotism, reviving memories in the people of warrior heroes of the past, from the time of Alexander Nevsky to the war of 1812. What is more, the Soviet regime began to call the conflict with Nazi Germany not an "anti-imperialist" but a fatherland war, in the image of the war of 1812. The introduction of new symbols, including replacement of the national anthem; a return to historic names of streets and squares in big cities; the dissolution of the Comintern; and a series of other measures demonstrated a departure from orthodox communism. Stalin's new religious policy, expressed in allowing the selection of a new Orthodox patriarch in 1943, was determined less by the growth of religious feelings in society and by the patriotic position of the majority of the Orthodox clergy, than by a desire to use the Church to provide a moral basis for the just war that the Soviet Union was conducting. As Stalin openly acknowledged in a conversation with one Western diplomat: "The population would not fight for us communists, but it will fight for Mother Russia."[19]

One of the most substantial changes in the country's political life in the war period, which was reflected in the mood of the population, was the state's rapprochement with the Russian Orthodox Church. As one worker from Leningrad remarked in conversation with a co-worker: "If the Bolsheviks always related to the church like they do now, the whole people would make much of them and idolize them. The Russian people don't need much. Just preserve their customs for them and for this they'll give their life for you." Despite Soviet power's god-bashing in the prewar period, the religious faith of huge numbers of people remained intact. According to a census of the population that included a question on religion, about half those responding considered themselves believers.[20]

Indeed, after Nazi Germany's attack on the USSR the Soviet state changed its former religious policy in order to mobilize the entire population for the struggle with the enemy. Already in the initial period of the war, further attack on the official church had been rejected, arrests of Orthodox clergy and service people had practically ceased, and anti-religious work had been curtailed. However, this did not mean an end to the work of operatives of the organs of state security among believers and the clergy.[21]

Under wartime conditions, part of the population of the USSR became convinced that communism and religion could get along with each other quite well, that "soon the time will come when even communists will be able to go to church." What is more, even some members of the Communist Party accepted the changes in Soviet state policy on the question of relations with the Church, "seriously and for a long time," in so far as "the clergy has become different, 'revolutionary,' in distinction to 1918–20, when they were reactionary." Believers welcomed with "satisfaction" the decision to allow religious processions and evening services for the celebration of Easter. They thanked the authorities and above all Stalin.

However the growth of religiosity, quite natural in a period of war, and likewise the increase in the clergy's activities, evoked an extremely negative reaction at NKVD headquarters in the Lubianka. The reasons for this were not only many years' experience in rooting out nonconformity of any sort, but also the existence of unverified evidence of collaboration with the enemy by a significant part of Orthodox clergy in the occupied territory. With the conclusion of the war and the disappearance of the need to exploit the Orthodox Church as a powerful mobilizing factor, the authorities felt the time for forced compromise with the Church had ended, and increasingly reverted to their accustomed methods of work.

The propaganda of patriotism in the USSR was conducted from the beginning of the war on an unprecedented scale. However, the single-minded "consciousness raising" did not always produce the desired consequences. The search in wartime for a new identity for the entire country pushed individuals from diverse social groups toward the idea that Russia as a national state "had ceased to exist, thanks to the Bolsheviks," even raising xenophobia in some. The new trend in the way that national history was covered stirred up the most varied ideas in connection with the nationality question, including discussion of the need to create a Russian national state, and the predominance of non-Russians, and especially Jews, in the organs of power. The latter was expressed in direct criticism of a series of representatives of the highest echelons of power, including Stalin himself and his closest circle. According to the evidence of party informants, anti-Semitism began to develop in the big cities; this was an important element in the population's mood in 1941–2.

In addition to indulgences of an ideological nature, concessions were also made that improved material living conditions. In order to resolve the provisioning problem at least partially, it was decided to increase the size of peasants' personal plots at the expense of collective farm fields and even to create kitchen gardens in the cities. The population thus received a new space for taking personal initiative that could, from a long-term perspective, pose a threat to the very nature of the system.

In February 1945 Soviet ambassador to France A. E. Bogomolov gave a presentation before a group of Russian émigrés laying out the official point of view on Soviet society's trajectory of development during the war and its connection with Russian history. Bogomolov noted that the Soviet people respected the reforms of Peter the Great and the actions of those Russian governments that were for the good of Russia. However, in the opinion of the Soviet diplomat one could not see in this some sort of move to the right or return to the past. As he put it, one cannot make the past come back, neither the monarchy nor the order that "flashed by between February and October." He recommended taking the same view of the government's change in attitude toward the Orthodox Church.[22]

The Life Experience and Moods of the Population during the Second World War

The war with Germany brought a great deal of grief to the Soviet people. For all practical purposes every family lost someone – either at the front, under occupation, or on the home front. The Soviet quality of life declined dramatically. In towns and worker settlements basic supplies and industrial goods were dispensed using ration cards, with various norms for different levels of society. Workers in defense plants and in the fuel industry enjoyed preferential rights to bread, in the top category. The entire population was divided into four categories for purposes of supply: workers and those of equivalent status, service personnel, dependents, and all children under 12.

Wartime levels of per capita consumption declined significantly, above all for such products as flour, meat, and sugar. The situation was particularly serious near the front and in liberated territory. There was simply not enough to eat. People died from hunger and famine-related illnesses. In Leningrad alone, blockaded by German and Finnish troops, more than 800,000 people died of starvation.

Many workers and engineering–technical personnel in urban areas were given higher norms. At the end of 1944, for example, more than 60 percent of all workers and engineers in towns received bread norms of between 600 and 1,000 grams, and norms of 500 grams went to fewer than 40 percent. Aside from the general rationing of bread and certain industrial products, there were seven additional centrally controlled supply norms. Membership on a special list entitled some to particularly high levels: the city of Moscow, peat-producing enterprises, and so on. The authorities were able to use rationed supplies to stimulate high labor productivity in industry, in scientific research institutes, in engineering bureaux. In addition, there was a system of preferences and privileges for the party and bureaucratic apparatus.

The growth of patriotic sentiment among the majority of the population meant that coercive measures to achieve the fulfillment of labor obligations were not necessary. But some extraordinary measures were adopted: the upgrading of institutions for the training of worker and service personnel for non-stop work, labor mobilization, and so on. Unauthorized departure from military factories was punished by incarceration for five to eight years. Some 276,000 people were sentenced for this offense in 1944. One widespread practice was the massive resort to overtime and holiday labor. It often happened that 14- and 15-year-old adolescents worked as long hours as adults, for weeks at a time, but were also required to put in overtime and work nightshifts. Similar measures, undertaken to raise labor intensity, were enacted in the countryside. Work norms for collective farmers were significantly increased. For the first time, minimal work norms for adolescents were introduced. Collective farmers who could not produce an acceptable excuse for failure to fulfill work norms could be taken to court and sentenced to collective labor for up to six months. Ration books were not given out in rural areas, but the distribution of funds and products declined sharply. From the national economy the collective farmer began to receive less than 200 grams of wheat and about 100 grams of potatoes a day – that is, a glass of wheat and one little potato. Meat, butter, and milk were in practice not given out. As earlier, the rural community's own livestock and fowl were their only secure source of meat, milk, and eggs. Life in the Soviet countryside was very hard.

In wartime many families, having lost the breadwinner to the front, lived on the earnings of women. Women who toiled behind the lines acquired new professions, some of them "male", and worked overtime for the sake of their children. It was the same in the countryside. In practice, women simply took over the work of men who had gone to the front.

In the war years the state provided help to the families of front fighters. A peculiarity of this aid was that the determination of the real needs of these families was made not by the designated social institutions, but by the territorial organs of the NKVD. Pensions for orphans were small; in the towns the amount was between 100 and 250 rubles, depending on the number of family members who could not work. For example, one kilogram of beef cost about 240 rubles. In addition to pensions and grants, there were privileges respecting taxes, rent, and so on, but the life of a front soldier's family was even more complicated than an orphan's.

Support for those wounded in the war was also quite limited – a mere 150 rubles a month. The wounded also had privileges with respect to the acquisition of shelter and the right to a free education in technical schools and universities and preference in hiring. In all there were more than 2,500,000 wounded officers and ordinary soldiers. In the Russian Federation alone more than 300 special homes were opened. In these homes donations and gifts from the Red Cross were distributed. But, despite all these measures, many led a very hard life. Along with the grants and privileges given to the families of front fighters, we should also remember the relatives of soldiers, officers, and political workers who were captured by the enemy and considered traitors.

The losses inflicted on the Soviet Union by Germany constituted approximately 30 percent of its national wealth. An enormous number of houses in towns and villages were annihilated or destroyed. Soviet people lived in extraordinarily cramped and uncomfortable circumstances. The average living space per person in a Russian town in 1945 amounted to 4.5 square meters, and less in some towns, especially along the Volga, in the Urals, and in those districts that had been under occupation.

However, the years of the war are remembered not only for destruction and loss, hunger and cold. They were a period of steadfastness and self-sacrifice for the sake of victory. For the overwhelming majority of the Soviet people the wartime slogan "Everything for the front! Everything for victory!" became a call to action. At the beginning of the war the overwhelming majority of the population shared in the patriotic mood. Many were convinced there would be a quick victory. People supposed that it would be a "little conflict that would be settled soon." They thought it might last only three or four months.

The patriotic outburst found its expression in the fact that the mass mobilization of those under military obligation, born between 1905 and 1918, was over in a week. Moreover, the military recruitment offices were inundated by thousands of offers to volunteer for the front. At the same time, however, enormous lines appeared in stores. People bought up sugar, salt, matches, trying to create food reserves. Savings banks were mobbed. People tried to sell their obligations on state loans and get hold of their savings.

Over the first several days of the war, the military news was sad and confusing to people. The patriotic mood and confidence of victory that had united the overwhelming majority in the first weeks of the war quickly weakened, giving way to that broad spectrum of feelings and thoughts that had characterized the prewar period. In conditions of growing military crisis these heterogeneous moods developed extraordinarily rapidly, evident not only in prodigies of heroism and stoicism but also in incidents of anti-Semitism, and also in the passive expectation of denunciations that "everybody took for granted."

The readiness of Western countries to help the Soviet Union in the war against Germany was regarded skeptically early in the war. Largely out of habit, people were also doubtful about the agreement with the British to take common action in the war against Germany. The rapprochement of the Soviet Union with England and the United States in the first weeks of the war was regarded with great caution by the population and does not appear to have been an essential factor in the development of the public mood. The war with Germany was regarded as a kind of duel, in which "the democracies" would play at most the role of honest seconds.[23]

The feelings of uncertainty evident in the first two or three weeks of the war grew steadily. The worsening situation at the front, the introduction of rationing in mid-July 1941, the absence of trustworthy information about the situation at the front and in the country as a whole – all this spread doubts about the ability of the regime to defend the country.

The well-known Soviet writer and critic Olga Freudenberg[24] remarked in the first months of the war, when the army was suffering defeat after defeat, that information was becoming scarcer and scarcer. "The Bureau of Information has begun to present to the starving soul of the Soviet citizen," she wrote, "formulas, phrases of an almost Homeric type, which leave a taste of grief and repulsion in the mouth. Rumors have begun to do their work . . . A special system has been created to draw a veil over bad news, but there is also a system to understand and draw this veil aside . . . formulaic news reports have led to a lack of interest in the news."[25]

In August 1941, when the German army was swiftly approaching the vitally important centers of the USSR, the negative popular mood became ever more widespread. In various versions it was ever more widely alleged among the workers that Jews and communists were the malefactors in all the ills crashing down upon the country, that peasant soldiers resented Soviet power for forced collectivization, that military leaders were guilty of treachery and sabotage.

In these first months some of the population reacted positively to the stream of social demagogy being spread by the Nazis through various channels. The lack of clear understanding by a part of the population as to what Nazi Germany wanted out of the war and the defeats at the front led to popular moods of a pro-Nazi, defeatist, and, in a number of cases, even a pro-German kind. Their number constantly grew and, according to the military censor, reached a high water mark of 20 percent in blockaded Leningrad in January 1942.

After the success of the Red Army at Moscow in December 1941 and especially after Stalingrad in February 1943, the mood in the army and in the rear underwent a fundamental change. The successes of the Red Army partially restored the lost confidence in the leadership. However, the expectation of change became, for all practical purposes, general – change in the direction of economic and political liberalization. A rejection of the collective farms, a return to NEP (Lenin's New Economic Program), freedom of religion, the realization of constitutional rights and liberties – all this seemed not only conceivable but possible. Although the population was exhausted by the war and waited with impatience for any signs of its end, pro-German and defeatist points of view completely disappeared. Hopes for the evolution of the regime were distinctly widespread, stemming, in the opinion of many, from the influence of the allies.

In the final two years of the war the popular mood was defined by the position at the front, the great intensity of foreign political events, and a significant growth in sympathy toward religion, which in many cases took on the character of politically nonconformist activities. There was also the return from evacuation and formerly occupied districts of the people who had lived in them before the war. Those who returned from the ranks of the partisans reported that "on our rations you live hungry," but "in the German rear it was better." Such opinions were supported by the relatives of people who had found themselves in occupied territory or in the ranks of the partisans. The testimony of eyewitnesses to the effect that "not all Germans are like they're described in the newspapers" was found in letters from previously occupied territory. This quarrel about whether life was better under the Germans or under Soviet rule continued throughout 1944.

The westward movement of the Red Army and relations with the countries of Central and Eastern Europe inevitably called forth a multitude of conversations and discussions. The taboo on discussion of domestic politics meant that foreign political questions evoked the greatest interest. No one did time in prison or camp for relating critically to foreign policy. Workers were interested not only in Finnish affairs and the second front, but also in "faraway" countries – Bulgaria, Rumania, France, Turkey, and China.

With the succession of victories, people began to forget their earlier resentment of the authorities. The old belief in the future and great power consciousness quickly re-established itself among the people; as a result, their conception of Stalin, the ideal representative of Soviet power, also changed. Conversations surfaced about the future, about postwar reconstruction of the world and the new role of the Soviet Union in world politics. In response to Stalin's speech on the occasion of the twenty-seventh anniversary of the October Revolution he was called "the most brilliant figure of the present era."

So the situation at the end of 1944 was quite striking. Although wartime tasks still commanded the most attention, more and more attention was being bestowed on postwar structuring of the world. Successes at the front led to a situation in which the intelligentsia (and, incidentally, a large number of other folks) no longer opposed themselves to the authorities. The great contradiction between the powers that be and the people was wiped away in the face of victory, and the division between "us" and "them" ceased to exist. "We won"; "they have to reckon with us"; "our point of view was victorious" – the widespread currency of expressions like these symbolized the unity of the people and the authorities in the final stages of the war.

The news of the victory over Nazi Germany had an enormous influence on the mood of the whole people. Patriotic utterance was the order of the day. Even those who had been discontented with the regime could not remain indifferent. The services of Stalin were praised to the skies; the contribution of the people themselves to victory was lessened.

The success of the Soviet delegation at the Potsdam conference further strengthened the authority of Stalin, enabled the revival of his cult, and drove those who had counted on change in the Soviet Union through the influence of the allies to despair. The allies (chiefly the United States) needed the support of Stalin and yielded to his pressure. But the great thing was the establishment of the long-awaited world of tomorrow. The military censor noticed that people congratulated each other, their near and dear, their relatives, with a celebration of the great victory, expressing the hope that now, finally, "family happiness will return, real life will return." The messianism of the Russian people, its particular destiny to be in the vanguard of the historical process, and also the pre-eminence of the Soviet system – these were the predominant themes at the time of victory.

In sum, the mood of the people in wartime was truly contradictory. Condemnation of certain actions or aspects of the regime coexisted comfortably with support for other of its actions, as is characteristic of authoritarian societies. The staying power of Stalinism as a political system consisted not only in a mighty apparatus of political control, but also in the presence of a broad base of support among various groups for which Stalinism continued to be regarded as progressive.

Life in Occupied Territory: Questions of Collaborationism

A peculiarity of the war was that an enormous expanse of Soviet territory with a population of eighty million people was occupied by the enemy, and for significant portions of the USSR the occupation lasted for more than two years. It is no coincidence that the problem of collaborationism with the occupier was a really painful one for the Soviet regime. Russian historians began to discuss it only after "restructuring" (perestroika) had begun in the latter 1980s. In the Stalinist period, collaboration was defined extraordinarily broadly. Collaborators included those who had surrendered and members of their families, people who had joined the German army and police informers, and also Soviet citizens who had worked in factories and enterprises run by the occupational authorities.

Academician Iu. A. Poliakov hazarded the really bold judgment that, "in comparison with other countries, the rather significant number of collaborators in occupied territory testifies to the separatist tendencies among more than one nationality and also about the strength of the social-political opposition."[26] In occupied territories anti-Soviet and pro-German views, signifying collaboration with the occupiers, were expressed openly. In the remainder of the country such views could naturally not be so expressed; they would be punished according to the laws of war.

Authors of the four-volume study of *The Great Fatherland War* (the eastern front of the Second World War in Soviet-Russian parlance) justly stress that in the mass consciousness of the Soviet people "state patriotism prevailed" but indicated nevertheless that

> it would not be right to be silent about the fact that, as has been frequently mentioned, there were other views of the war, which were variously expressed. For example, on occupied territory anti-Soviet and pro-German views often resulted in complicity and cooperation with the enemy . . . There were even those who did not openly oppose participation in the war of liberation, but at that very time made every effort to remain in the rear and if, against their will, they were forced to put on the uniform, deserted at some opportune moment.

Nationalistic elements, refugees from the pre-revolutionary ruling classes, and social groups were among their number, as were a significant part of the population of the republics incorporated into the USSR on the eve of the war, and victims of collectivization and the repression of the 1930s.[27]

For the most part the collaboration of ordinary citizens bore an involuntary character, as in the case of Soviet citizens, especially in urban areas, who had no other way of ensuring the survival of their families. According to the majority of Russian historians, there is no serious reason to include all Soviet prisoners of war among the traitors, since the majority of them found themselves in captivity only as a result of circumstances beyond their control: being wounded, surrounded, or losing contact with their units, and so forth. By way of evidence for this thesis it is customary to observe that, out of more than twenty million who participated in the military during the war, about 200,000 were involved in various "volunteer" formations, of whom fewer than 100,000 took part directly in military action against the Red Army.[28]

The clearest and most open kind of collaborationism involved service in the German military and police units. Russian units in the German army can be divided into four categories: "eastern, volunteer" formations; units of the Russian Army of Liberation (ROA); construction battalions of the Organization of Death; and defectors, the so-called *Khivi* or *Hiwi* (short for *Hilfswilliger* in German). According to Russian historians, something on the order of 540,000–550,000 people were involved.

Recruitment to these eastern military organizations proceeded along national lines. According to German sources, more than 180 such formations were created: 75 were Russian; 42 were drawn from Cossacks of the Don, Kuban, and Terek regions; 11 were Georgian; there were 12 from the people of the northern Caucasus; 13 from Azerbaizhan; 8 from Armenia. Some too were reunited with Lithuanian, Latvian, and Estonian partisans. The eastern forces were used for the defense of objectives behind the lines, railroads, and the struggle against partisans. The combat ability of the volunteer formations varied. But for the struggle against the partisans the German command considered them fully prepared.

At the beginning of 1943, the Germans undertook to create some units of the so-called Russian Army of Liberation under the command of General A. A. Vlasov, who sincerely, if extremely naively, believed in the possibility of some kind of "third way" for Russia, the creation of a truly free Russia, without the Bolsheviks, based temporarily on the support of German forces.[29] However, among the ROA "volunteers," many were not really anti-Soviet, and the ROA did not achieve any serious successes on the battlefield. Prisoners of war flocked to Vlasov, hoping to avoid death by starvation in German captivity – and fled at the first opportunity. This is clear from the mass desertion of ROA soldiers to the side of the partisans from the second half of 1943. The German command was forced in several places at the front to dismantle the volunteer formations and dispatch individuals to POW camps. ROA units existed until the end of hostilities, but the top officers, with Vlasov at the head, were executed after the war.

Among the various categories of Soviet people who served in the German army were the Khivi (*Hilfswilliger*), defectors who were thrown together from prisoners of war and inhabitants of the occupied territories. They served in the rear of the actual German military forces, in kitchens and workshops, as drivers, farriers, and so on. In ordinary German infantry divisions something like 10 percent were this sort of "volunteer"; in transport columns they were as many as 50 percent. Around the beginning of 1943 there were as many as 400,000 such auxiliaries in the *Wehrmacht*.

An important place in the creation and maintenance of the "new order" was occupied by the so-called organs of local self-government. Unlike Ukraine, Belorussia, and the Baltic republics, on the occupied territory of Russia there was no unified system of control in the urban and rural districts. Basing themselves on the anti-Soviet points of view of those working in the apparatus of the occupation administration, the Germans tried to attract the local population to the implementation of their political, economic, and military measures.

A certain number of Soviet citizens from the civilian population of the occupied districts and prisoners of war found themselves in service with the auxiliary police, which was created in the majority of population centers and typically consisted of three to five people working under each village elder in the region. The obligations of the auxiliary police included keeping an eye on the implementation of bureaucratic work at German command headquarters and the maintenance of order there; registering the local inhabitants; rendering assistance to the security organs in their exposure of communists, partisans, and those cooperating with Soviet authorities; bringing the population into useful economic labor; ensuring the timely implementation of the economic needs of the occupation, and so forth. These local police significantly lightened the German work load in the occupied territory and were understood by the German authorities to be an essential factor in the pacification of the country.

Service in the police was really popular with the inhabitants, as practically speaking the police and their families did not experience the burdens of the occupation. First of all, as a rule police in the towns and villages received the customary German rations for those serving behind the lines, as well as tobacco, vodka, sweets, and other items given to German soldiers. The possibility of receiving a place to live and land also stimulated people's desire to work in the police. From the summer of 1942, the best apartments were given to the police, and, even more important, land. All servants of the police were given a home and livestock. Thirdly, all relatives of the police were excused from conscripted labor, requisitions, taxes, but chiefly from the threat of being sent to Germany. Finally, auxiliary police also received monetary compensation of between 20 and 600 rubles a month, depending on where they were serving and their responsibilities. According to German sources, there were more than 60,000 Soviet citizens on the German rolls in December of 1941.[30]

Analysis of the documents of the German military command undertaken by American intelligence soon after the war's end shows that, in the first weeks of the war, the majority of the *Wehrmacht* reports about the situation in the occupied territories mentions the pro-German mood of the population and its readiness to cooperate with the Germans. These reports suggest the deep unpopularity of the communist regime and indicate that many people expressed the hope that the Red Army had already been defeated. The rapid disappearance of the representatives of the old regime and the stunning successes of the German army strengthened the conviction among the population that the new authorities were to be taken seriously and were in place for the long haul. Such popular beliefs were strengthened by measures that the Soviet government itself took after the German attack: the destruction and abandonment of factories and institutions, the destruction of crops and residual stores of foodstuffs. The sum total of these circumstances raised great hopes and expectations among those electing to stay with the Germans; the population of the occupied districts supposed that the arrival of the Germans would lead to an improvement in their standard of living, the annihilation of the collective farms, and the restoration of religious life.

Nevertheless, individual terroristic acts directed against active collaborators (mayors, police drawn from the local population) indicate that Soviet power in the districts occupied by the Germans had its supporters, and that the Germans, despite their victory, were not able to eliminate them. These supporters were watching the population and awaiting their hour. Information thus reached people about the activities of the Red Army in the districts liberated from the Germans, where accomplices of the occupiers were savagely eliminated.

On the other side, murders committed by the partisans (and they killed German soldiers and officers) called forth a corresponding repression from the German side and gradually created an equivalent distrust and detestation among the local population. In villages where German troops were garrisoned, the soldiers as a rule behaved peacefully, often giving away leftovers from their rations to the poor. German military doctors provided medical help to the local population (often because they feared the outbreak of epidemics). The provisioning and supply of the German army was still normal.

The positive attitude of the local population toward the Germans began to deteriorate in the spring of 1942 when they began to requisition food, seize cattle, and appear all over the countryside, even as information was spreading about horrors that had taken place over the winter in prisoner-of-war camps.

The material dimensions of the German occupation made themselves felt much more sharply in urban than in rural areas. In the first place, in towns and cities, there was the German civilian administration, headed by Nazis, alongside the military authorities. All the decrees and directives of the Nazi Party were fulfilled extraordinarily strictly and literally in the towns. But in the countryside, especially near the front where there was military rule, these regulations often remained on paper and for various reasons (chiefly having to do with the security forces) were not enforced. Secondly, in the cities, a great part of the population was forced by the Germans to abandon its work and engage in unaccustomed manual labor, of a sort that essentially could not ensure their survival. Thirdly, the Germans completely failed to provide food and fuel for the cities, whose inhabitants received ration cards, whose dimensions depended on local authorities and their relationship to the countryside. In any event, the ration could keep one alive only for a few days. In the majority of urban areas the Germans provided electricity, water, and so on only to those homes and those inhabitants in whose work they had an interest – the population on the whole remained without light, and so on. Hospitals, shelters, schools, and the like almost never received any kind of support from the local government, which really had no resources to provide. As a result of all this, from the first months of the occupation the most improbable examples of speculation and the black market developed in cities, with the Germans themselves taking part, despite severe deterrent measures. Finally, the public executions and mass shootings of Jews provoked great indignation in the cities. Local inhabitants refused to buy or even simply to take possessions of the murdered Jews and refused to attend executions, despite being ordered to do so, and often loudly expressed their opposition to these measures.[31]

Hardliners in the German occupation authorities, always the majority, requisitioned products for the *Wehrmacht*, sent raw materials to Germany, and sent cultural treasures back to Germany or destroyed them. In addition, the German authorities recruited labor to be sent to Germany and dispatched to Germany even the very youngest who were capable of work. Under the cruelest German supervision, hundreds of thousands of people took part in the construction of military installations and railroads, not to speak of snow removal.

The so-called agrarian reform of 1942 on occupied Soviet territory was the very most important action in the German "eastern" policy. Its significance consisted not only in the acquisition of "living space," but also in the attempt to neutralize the allied blockade by resurrecting the earlier role of Russia as the most important supplier of foodstuffs to Europe. This policy fitted perfectly with Hitler's views on the future of Soviet cities and the possibility of using hunger to deurbanize and deindustrialize the Soviet Union. However, under wartime conditions, these plans could be realized only with the preservation of collectivized agriculture.

The New Agricultural Law of 15 February, 1942, foresaw the transition to small-producer agriculture through a series of transitional stages: communal agriculture (in fact collective farms) and agricultural collaboratives. Through this mechanism, however, individual ownership of small pieces of land, adjoining the peasant's home, would be introduced, and also the individual ownership of livestock would become possible. The land was divided between peasants, but norms for delivery remained collective. The creation of independent family farming was envisaged as the final stage of the agrarian reform. But this right was to be given only to those who demonstrated their reliability, provided the obligatory deliveries, and possessed technical equipment or cattle.

The agrarian reform, begun in the spring of 1942, for all its limitations and timidity, found support among the peasants. It attracted peasant sympathy to the German side and until the middle of 1943 deprived the Soviet leadership of the hope of any broad popular movement of opposition to the occupying forces. All this got the attention of the NKVD, which recognized the presence of a significant number of collaborators in the territory under German occupation.

However, from the early fall of 1942, discontent with the Germans among the population of the occupied districts began to grow. There were general causes for this discontent and popular hostility to the Germans, but also specific causes, conditioned by the different positions of the rural and urban populations. In the cities, for example, the more developed population recognized the essentially racist character of German policy more quickly. The public execution of people suspected of sympathy with Bolshevism and of diverse hostages, the wholesale liquidation of Jews and gypsies – all this weighed most heavily on the population.

For the first two years of the war the population was able to convince itself that the occupation authorities were not yet strong enough to dislodge the Soviet presence, however fragmentary, even deep behind the German lines. Such opinions strengthened around December 1941–January 1942, when the *Wehrmacht* not only failed to take Moscow, but had to retreat. Successes around Moscow and the continuing defense of Leningrad showed that the Red Army had succeeded in coming back from its failures and that the outcome of the war was not yet decided. After Stalingrad the population naturally subordinated itself to a regime that could crush the *Wehrmacht* in the enormous battle on the Volga. Nevertheless, the memory of the division of collective farm land and the *relatively* free economic activity of 1942 lingered in the minds of the peasants. The weakening of the ideological Soviet press, the activity of "new" schools, and the rebirth in many districts of religious life posed complex tasks for Soviet power during the immediate postwar years.

The Results of the Second World War

The most important result of the war was the destruction of Nazism and Japanese militarism. Pre-eminent in force, the broad economic potential of the anti-Hitler coalition enabled a convincing victory over the states of the fascist bloc. The Soviet Union made an extremely significant contribution to that victory. Its armies annihilated 607 enemy divisions on the Soviet–German front, disabled 72 percent of their personnel and 75 percent of their military technology. But the price paid for the war by the Soviet Union was uniquely great. The Soviet Union suffered more than other states: overall more than twenty-seven million people were lost. Of these, some 8.6 million soldiers and sailors were killed on the front lines, and around 5.3 million were captured and imprisoned. Of these latter, only 1.8 million returned. The majority of the fallen perished in 1941–2. More than a million Soviet servicemen died in battles in Eastern and Central Europe, in the Balkans, in China, and in Korea. Of these, 600,000 died in Poland, 140,000 in Czechoslovakia, the same number in Hungary, and more than 100,000 in Germany.[32] Millions of Soviet citizens died as a result of forced deportations to Germany or were destroyed by the invaders on occupied Soviet territory. The rough overall total was 13.7 million men and women.[33]

The war dealt an enormous blow to the Soviet economy. Twenty-five million people remained without shelter. Some 1,710 towns and settlements were destroyed, and more than 70,000 villages. Six million buildings were gone and 32,000 factories; 41,000 electric power stations were wrecked, along with around 63,000 kilometers of power lines and almost 2,000 bridges and other structures for electric power. The country was bled white, but at the same time the Soviet Union possessed what was in all probability the mightiest land army in the world, and its forces occupied enormous territories in Europe and Asia. The moral authority of the Soviet Union was also revived. European and Asian people on the Left during the struggle against Nazism saw the USSR as a force – together with the USA and Great Britain – capable of supporting and accelerating democratic transformation in the world. It seemed to many that the allied conferences at Teheran, Yalta, and Potsdam laid the foundations for an agreement among the great powers that would assure the peaceful and democratic future of humanity. The so-called Yalta system, created by the allies, would allow for peaceful cooperation and the avoidance of major war for half a century. The fundamental experience of the times would also support many new international organizations, among them the United Nations.

But in the course of the war contradictions came to the fore and matured between the Soviet Union and the Western allies about the postwar reconstruction of the world. In the absence of a unifying threat after the war was over, the former allies in the anti-Hitler coalition became opponents in a new war – a cold one.

Notes

1   Martin Malia, *The Soviet Tragedy. The History of Socialism in Russia, 1917–1991*, New York: Free Press, 1994, 273, 291; Amir Weiner, *Making Sense of War: The Second World War and the Fate of the Bolshevik Revolution*, Princeton: Princeton University Press, 2001, 365.

2   Malia, *Soviet Tragedy*, 274.

3   e.g. E. S. Seniavskaia, *1941–1945: Frontovoe pokolenie* (1941–1945: The Frontline Generation), Institute of Russian History RAN, Moscow, 1995.

4   e.g. Banka Pietrow-Ennker, *Stalinismus-Sicherheit-Offensive: Das dritte Reich in der Konzeption der sowjetischen Aussenpolitik 1933 bis 1941*, Schwartz Verlag, Melsungen, 1983; B. Stegemann, "Politik und Kriegfuhrung in der ersten Phase der deutschen Initiative," in *Das deutsche Reich und der Zweite Weltkrieg*. Bd2/Hrsg. Vom Militargeschichte Forschungsamts, Deutsche Verlags-Anstalt, Stuttgart, 1979; G. L. Weinberg, *A World at Arms*, Cambridge: Cambridge University Press, 1995.

5   O. Rzheshevskii, "Zhestokii urok istorii. Nachalo Vtoroi mirovoi voiny bylo predopredeleno eshche v noiabre 1918-go," *Voennoe obozrenie. Ezhenedelnoe prilozhenie k Nezavisimoi gazete* ("The Harsh Lesson of History. The Beginning of the Second World War was already Predestined in November 1918," Military review. A Weekly supplement to *Nezavisimaia gazeta*), 33 (1999), 5.

6   Press communiqué of Sept. 14, 1999. Published on the official website of the Ministry of Internal Affairs of the Russian Federation (MID RF): www.mid.ru.

7   *Oglasheniiu podlezhit. SSSR–Germanii. 1939–1941* (Unclassified. USSR–Germany. 1939–1941), Moscow, 1991, 114.

8   A. S. Orlov, "Nakanune: raschety i proschety" ("On the Eve: Estimates and Reckonings"), in G. N. Sevost'ianov, ed., *Voina i obshchestvo, 1941–1945*, 2 vols. Moscow: Nauka, 2004, vol. 1, pp. 29–31.

9   Gabriel Gorodetsky, *Grand Delusion. Stalin and the German Invasion of Russia*, New Haven: Yale University Press, 1999, 28–33.

10 Peter Holquist, " 'Information is the Alpha and Omega of Our Work': Bolshevik Surveillance in its Pan-European Context," *Journal of Modern History*, 69 (Sept. 1997), 416–18.

11 M. Burtsev, *Prozrenie* (Recovery of Sight), Moscow, Voennoe izdatel'stvo Ministerstva Oborony, 1981, 24. Information on the activities of the propaganda companies of the

Wehrmacht Main Administration of Political Propaganda (RKKA) was obtained from the Intelligence Administration of the General Staff: TsAMO RF, fo. 32, op. 11306, d. 8, ll. 712–32.

12   Thomas Rigby, "Reconceptualising the Soviet System," in S. White, A. Pravda, and Z. Gitelman, eds., *Developments in Soviet and Post-Soviet Politics*, 2nd edn., Durham, NC, and London, Duke University Press, 1992, 313–14.

13   N. Lomagin, *Leningrad v blokade* (Leningrad during the Blockade), Eksto: Iauza, Moscow, 2005, 128

14   Ibid. 132.

15   Sarah Davies, *Popular Opinion in Stalin's Russia. Terror, Propaganda, and Dissent, 1934–1941*, Cambridge: Cambridge University Press, 1997, 45.

16   V. S. Gusev, N. A. Lomagin, O. N. Stepanov, et al., *Mezhdunarodnoe polozhenie glazami leningradtsev, 1941–1945. Iz Arkhiva Upravleniia Federal'noi Sluzhby Bezopasnosti no n. Sankt-Peterburgu i Leningradskoi oblasti* (The International Situation through Leningraders' Eyes, 1941–1945. From the Archive of the Administration of the Federal Security Service for St Petersburg and Leningrad Oblast), St Petersburg: Evropeiskii dom, 1996, 10.

17   V. A. Tokarev, "Sovetskoe obshchestvo i pol'skaia kampaniia 1939 g.: 'Romanticheskoe oshchushchenie voiny'" ("Soviet Society and the Polish Campaign, 1939: 'The Romantic Excitement of War'"), in I. V. Narskii and O. Iu. Nikonov, eds., *Chelovek i voina. Voina kak iavlenie kul'tury* (Humanity and War. War as Phenomenon of Culture), Moscow, 2001, 410–13.

18   I. Gofman, *Stalinskaia voina na unichtozhenie: planirovanie, osushchestvlenie, dokumenty* (Perevod s nemetskogo), Moscow, 2006, 111–30. Joachim Hoffmann, *Stalins Vernichtungskrieg 1941–1945*, Herbig, Munich, 1990.

19   Malia, *Soviet Tragedy*, 288.

20   M. V. Shkarovskii, *Russkaia pravoslavnaia tserkov' i Sovetskoe gosudarstvo v 1943–1964 godakh: ot "peremiriia" k novoi voine* (The Russian Orthodox Church and the Soviet State, 1943–1964: From "Armistice" to War), St Petersburg, 1995, 9.

21   From September 1943 the newly created Soviet for Russian Orthodox Church Affairs, under Sovnarkom, was headed by Colonel of State Security G. Karpov, who was simultaneously head of the "church" section of the Fifth directorate of the NKVD.

22   E. M. Primakov et al., *Chemu svideteli my byli . . . Perepiska byvshikh tsarskikh diplomatov 1934–1940. Sbornik dokumentov v dvukh knigakh* (What we were Witnesses to . . . Correspondence of Former Tsarist Diplomats, 1934–1940. A Collection of Documents in Two Volumes), Moscow, 1998, 588–9.

23   Lomagin, *Leningrad v blokade*, 210.

24   Olga Mikhailovna Freudenberg (1890–1955), the cousin of Boris Pasternak, many-sided scholar of historical poetics, folklore theory, mythological-ritual forms, and the literature of Antiquity. She was the author of *The Poetics of Subject and Genre* (Poetika siuzheta i zhanra) (1936), *The Myth and Literature of Antiquity* (Mif i literatura drevnosti), 1978, and many articles.

25   Freudenberg, *Osada cheloveka* (Humanity Besieged), 10.

26   Iu. A. Poliakov, "O massovom soznanii v gody voiny," *Istoricheskaia nauka: liudi i problemy* ("On Mass Consciousness in Wartime," in Historical Science: People and Problems), Moscow, 1999, 176.

27   *Velikaia Otechestvennaia voina 1941–1945, Voenno-istoricheskie ocherki. Kniga chetvertaia. Narod i voina* (The Great Fatherland War 1941–1945. Military-Historical Essays. Book Four. The People and the War), Moscow, 1999, 11–12; see also I. A. Giliakov, *Kollaboratsionistskoe dvizhenie sredi tiurko-musul'manskikh voennoplennikh i emigrantov v gody Vtoroi mirovoi voiny* (Movements of Collaboration among Turko-Muslim Prisoners

of War and Emigrants in the Years of the Second World War), doctoral dissertation, University of Kazan, 2003. See also A. V. Okorokov, *Antisovetskie voiskie formirovaniia v gody Vtoroi mirovoi voiny* (Anti-Soviet Military Formations in the Years of the Second World War), doctoral dissertation, Military University Ministry of Defense, Russian Federation, 2003; A. I. Volkhin, *Deiatel'nost' organov gosudarstvennoi bezopasnosti Urala i Zapadnoi Sibiri v gody Velikoi Otechestvennoi voiny* (The Activities of the Organs of State Security in the Urals and Western Siberia during the Great Fatherland War), doctoral dissertation at Ural State University, 2003.

28   M. A. Gareev, "O mifakh starykh i novykh" (On Old and New Myths), *Voenno-istoricheskii zhurnal*, 4 (1991), 49; V. A. Perezhogin, "Voprosy kollaboratsionizma" (Questions of Collaborationism), *Voina i obshchestvo, 1941–1945*, vol. 2, bk. 2, Moscow, 2004, 293.

29   Among the commanding officers of the Russian Liberation Army (ROA) were more than a few people who had occupied significant posts in the Red Army before being captured and had been awarded important military decorations. Between the fall of 1944 and the spring of 1945, a lieutenant general in the Red Army, six major generals, one brigade commissar, one brigade commander, forty-two colonels, one captain first rank, twenty-one lieutenant colonels, two battalion commissars, forty-nine majors, etc., served in the ROA. The Chief of Staff of the Vlasov units was a former professor at the General Staff Academy and then Deputy Chief of Staff of the northwest front, Major General F. I. Trukhin. The Vlasov fighter squadron commander was Red Army Senior Lieutenant, Hero of the Soviet Union, and Order of Lenin recipient B. Antilevskii; the chief of night-time bombing was Captain S. Bychkov, also a recipient of the Order of Lenin and a Hero of the Soviet Union. The chief of the operations division of the ROA staff was Colonel A. Nerianin, whom the chief of the Red Army General Staff, Marshall Boris Shaposhnikov, had once described as "the most brilliant officer in the Red Army." He was the only graduate of the General Staff Academy in 1940 who was described as "excellent" in all subjects.

30   *Das deutsche Reich und der Zweite Weltkrieg* (The German Empire and the Second World War), vol. 4, Stuttgart, 1983, 1061.

31   Lydia Ossipova Diary, Lydia Osipova Collection, Hoover Institution on War, Revolution and Peace, quoted in Lomagin, *Neizvestnaia blokada* (2nd edn.), bk. 2, Neva, OLMA-PRESS, St Petersburg, 2004, 441–75; see also Columbia University, Bakhmetiev Archive, Box 20 (D. Karov, "Nemetskaja kontrrazvedka v okkupirovannych Oblastiach SSSR v voinu 1941–45 gg.," 23–4,), quoted in Lomagin, *Neizvestnaia blokada* (2nd edn.), bk 1, p. 462.

32   G. F. Krivosheev, ed., *Rossiia i SSSR v voinakh XX veka: Poteri vooruzhennykh sil: Statisticheskoe issledovanie* (Russia and the Soviet Union in the Wars of the Twentieth Century: Military Losses: Statistical Research), Moscow, 2001, 229, 236, 463; *Velikaia Otechestvennaia voina: Tsifry I fakty* (The Great Fatherland War: Numbers and Facts), Moscow, 1995, 101.

33   E. H. Kul'kov, gen. ed., *Mirovie voiny XX veka. V chetirekh knigakh. Kn. 3. Vtoraia mirovaia voina Istoricheskii ocherk* (World Wars of the Twentieth Century. In four volumes. Vol. 3. The Second World War. Historical Essay), Moscow, 2002, 548.

References

Deist, W., et al. (1998–1999). *Das Deutsche Reich und der Zweite Weltkrieg*. Vols. 1–9. Deutsche Verlags-Anstalt, Munich.

Gorodetsky, G. (1999). *Grand Delusion: Stalin and the German Invasion of Russia*. Yale University Press, New Haven and London.

Lomagin, N. (2005). *Leningrad v blokade* (Leningrad in the Blockade). Eksto: Iauza. Moscow.

Malia, M. (1994). *The Soviet Tragedy: The History of Socialism in Russia, 1917–1991*. Free Press, New York.

Pietrow-Ennker, B. (1983). *Stalinismus – Sicherheit Offensive. Das Dritte Reich in der Konzeption der sowietische Aussenpolitik 1933 bis 1941*. Schwartz Verlag, Melsungen.

Weiner A. (2001). *Making Sense of War: The Second World War and the Fate of the Bolshevik Revolution*. Princeton University Press, Princeton.

Zolotarev, V. A., et al. (1998–1999). *Velikaia otechestvennaia voina 1941–1945* (The Great Fatherland War). Vols. 1–4. "Nauka", Moscow.

Further Reading

Erickson, J. (1984). The Road to Stalingrad: Stalin's War with Germany. Westview, Boulder, CO.

Erickson, J. (2002). "The Great Patriotic War: Barbarossa to Stalingrad," in R. Higham and F. Kagan,, eds., *The Military History of the Soviet Union*. Palgrave, New York.

Gorodetsky, G. (1999). *Grand Delusion: Stalin and the German Invasion of Russia*. Yale University Press, New Haven and London.

Merridale, C. (2006). *Ivan's War: Life and Death in the Red Army, 1939–1945*. Metropolitan Books, Henry Holt, New York.

Nekrich, A. M. (1978). *The Punished Peoples*. W. W. Norton, New York.

Salisbury, H. (1969). *The 900 Days. The Siege of Leningrad*. Harper & Row, New York.

Tumarkin N. (1994). *The Living and the Dead*. Basic Books, Harper-Collins, New York.

Weiner, Amir (2001). *Making Sense of War: The Second World War and the Bolshevik Revolution*. Princeton University Press, Princeton.

Werth, Alexander (1964). *Russia at War 1941–1945*. E. P. Dutton, New York.

CHAPTER TWENTY-FOUR

The Cold War

DAVID C. ENGERMAN

While American–Soviet antagonisms began with the Bolshevik Revolution of 1917, the cold war itself started only in the aftermath of the Second World War – on the heels, ironically enough, of the wartime alliance between the two future antagonists. The turn from world war to cold war was neither immediate nor predetermined; it happened incrementally over the late 1940s. The wartime experience had a profound impact on both future superpowers and on the international system in which they operated. In economic terms, the impact of the war on the allies-turned-enemies could not have been more different. American wartime production, starting even before its entry into the Second World War in late 1941, pulled its economy out of a depression that had lasted for most of the preceding decade. For the Soviets, the impact of the war was almost the reverse: the 1930s marked a period of crash industrialization, highly disruptive and destructive (with further disruptions from waves of purges) but ultimately turning the USSR into an industrial power. The Nazi army's rapid and devastating path through the Soviet Union left the country near economic ruin. In human terms, the war was costlier still; scholars now estimate that twenty-seven million Soviet citizens died during the war – roughly one sixth of the prewar population. These differences would shape American and Soviet policies in the postwar world, with the United States seeking to integrate a world economy with free flows of goods and resources, while in the USSR internal reconstruction was the top priority.

Other wartime events also shaped the rise of American–Soviet antagonisms afterwards. Western delays in opening a second front against Nazi Germany – D-Day in 1944 occurred years after Stalin's first request – left the Red Army with more casualties but also with military control over most of eastern and southeastern Europe. Similarly, the prominence of radicals (including many Communists) in local anti-Nazi partisan movements added luster to radical causes after the Nazi defeat. Finally, American use of atomic bombs against Japan in August 1945 cast a shadow over the cold war. The weapons were a closely held secret until they destroyed Hiroshima and Nagasaki – though Soviet espionage had already provided Stalin with ample information about American atomic research. Postwar debates over the future of atomic weapons began with mutual distrust over sharing technologies; this distrust multi-plied after Western authorities uncovered Soviet atomic espionage rings in 1950.

Origins, 1945–1949

Looking backward it is easy to see these issues – the disparate economic impacts, the disposition of forces in Europe, and the use of atomic bombs – as precursors of American–Soviet conflict, and surely they did not augur well for the continuation of the Grand Alliance after the war. At the same time, though, there were definite moments of optimism in 1945 and even afterwards. The meeting of the Big Three (Winston Churchill, Franklin Delano Roosevelt, and Joseph Stalin) in Yalta in February 1945 marked a high point of optimism and cooperation. Soviet and American troops were rapidly advancing on Germany, whose defeat seemed imminent. The Allies agreed in principle to a four-power occupation of Germany. Roosevelt called attention to the enormous sacrifices of the Soviet Union and its hard-won successes against Germany. He agreed to Stalin's proposed changes in Soviet territory, includ-ing the shift of the Soviet boundary westward, even beyond the farthest reaches of the tsarist empire, as well as Soviet control of the Kurile islands and southern Sakhalin in the Pacific. In exchange, the Soviets agreed to join the battle against Japan within three months of Germany's formal defeat. And, in the most controversial act of all, Roosevelt and Churchill recognized the pro-Soviet government in Poland over a Western-oriented government-in-exile in London; Stalin promised that this govern-ment would hold elections – which it would do eventually, but in name only.

By the time representatives of the Grand Alliance met again at Potsdam in summer 1945, much had changed. Allied forces had jointly accepted the surrender of the Nazi regime in May. Roosevelt had died in April, replaced by Harry Truman, who as vice president had known little about his boss's wartime diplomacy. And in Britain, Clement Attlee had ridden a Labour groundswell into office, replacing Winston Churchill while the conference was still in session. Gone, too, was the spirit of col-laboration that had infused the Yalta gathering. Even on topics that built on Yalta agreements, rifts between the Western allies and the Soviet Union grew. The allies agreed on the four-way division of Germany and Austria and on Soviet entry in the war on Japan. The differing economic circumstances loomed large in the disputes over reparations. The Soviet Union sought $10 billion from Germany (to be taken from all zones) in order to rebuild its own economy. But the United States, hoping to rebuild Germany and reintegrate it into the European economy, opposed the Soviet Union's reparation plans. And, acting on their promises at Yalta, the United States and Britain withdrew support for the London Poles, recognizing a provisional "unity" government that was in fact firmly under Soviet control. After Truman received word in Potsdam of the first successful atomic test, the tone further worsened [1].

In spite of these disputes, however, the world war had not yet given rise to a cold war. Much of the postwar settlement remained to be determined. Eastern Europe would be under Soviet influence – but the exact meaning of influence was up for debate. The years from 1945 to 1947 marked the era of "People's Democracies" in Eastern Europe. The Soviet Union insisted upon governments kindly disposed to it – to provide a buffer between it and oft-hostile European powers – but not necessarily Soviet puppets. Indeed, in many parts of the region, Communist parties were major political forces for reasons having little to do with the USSR; flush from the heroics of various partisan movements, endorsing a political platform that appealed to substantial portions of the population, local communist parties had respectable showings in Albania, Bulgaria, Czechoslovakia, and Yugoslavia [2]. A similar phenomenon in Western Europe was of grave concern to American policy-makers; radical parties were potent factors in the postwar domestic politics of France and Italy [3]. In both Eastern and Western Europe, American officials saw the rise of radicalism as the fruits of Moscow's machinations, not a reflection of local circumstances.

Meanwhile relations between the onetime Allies continued to fray. The year 1946 saw numerous declarations of the cold war, some public and some secret. That February, Stalin gave a widely publicized "campaign speech" in the Stalin District of Moscow (how could he lose in a district named after him?) in which he announced the Soviet intention to prepare for war – not in the immediate future, when the country would be focused on rebuilding, but in the long run. Like any good incumbent, Stalin stressed the Soviet achievements in recent years, most notably the industrial might and collective sacrifice that had allowed the USSR to defeat Nazism. The American response to the speech was extreme; one Washington politico called it "the declaration of World War Three." Later that month, American diplomat George Frost Kennan offered a long response to a brief enquiry about Soviet behavior, providing a historical and political explanation for the Stalin speech and acts of Soviet obstreperousness. Kennan's so-called Long Telegram offered a thorough analysis of Soviet policies, warning that Stalin had already concluded that there could be no "permanent *modus vivendi*" with the capitalist world and its undisputed leader, the United States. Yet the Soviet Union was not set on immediate world conquest; it would be "neither schematic nor adventuristic." Instead, it would seek advantage only where it would not face "unnecessary risks." To meet the Soviet threat, Kennan indicated, the United States must have "sufficient force" and demonstrate a "readiness to use it." Avant la lettre, Kennan was proposing containment – not rolling back Soviet power in the short term, but preventing its further spread. As Kennan's telegram gained attention and adherents in Washington that winter, it found public reinforcement from Winston Churchill. Churchill declared that an "Iron Curtain" had descended across Europe – and that the Soviet Union would not be satisfied with control of Europe east of that curtain (from Stettin on the Baltic to Trieste on the Adriatic). It sought, warned Churchill in dire tones, to extend its influence as far as possible, making it a "menace to world civilization" comparable to Hitler's Germany. A year later, President Truman announced his Doctrine, declaring American willingness to support any fight for freedom against totalitarianism; American policy, in other words, made containment of the Soviet Union into official policy on a global scale – further reinforced by Kennan's famous 1947 article "The Sources of Soviet Conduct," which belatedly coined the term for what had already become American policy [4].

Long unknown to scholars, the Soviet Union had its own version of a Long Telegram, written by the Soviet ambassador in Washington, N. V. Novikov, in September 1946. Like Kennan's earlier dispatch (of which the author had no direct knowledge), Novikov attributed to the other side an unceasing plan for world conquest. American foreign policy, Novikov warned, would seek "world domination" through both economic and military means: the "penetration of American capital" and the establishment of American military outposts around the world. Because the USSR stood in the way of such policies, the United States would aim at "limiting or dislodging the influence of the Soviet Union," not just in Eastern Europe but around the world. Both telegrams saw American–Soviet conflict as inevitable and as global – and blamed the tensions on the global aspirations of the other side [5].

Germany in particular provided fuel for the escalating conflict. At Yalta, the Big Three agreed that Germany should eventually be unified, but this left open a variety of possibilities, from an economically neutered and politically neutral Germany to one closely aligned with one side or the other. All agreed, however, on the temporary division of Germany, under joint occupation of the United States, the Soviet Union, Britain, and France, with the capital, Berlin, similarly divided into occupation zones. The flux of events in Germany, however, quickly turned a temporary division into a seemingly permanent one [6]. Soviet reparations policy denuded the Soviet zone (east of the Elbe, more of an agricultural region than an industrial one) of industrial equipment, transferring whole factories onto eastward-bound trains. The Soviet military authorities were well aware of the population's opposition to the dismantling of German industry, recording in their files a sarcastic philippic from 1947:

> Welcome, liberators! . . .
> You liberate us from everything, from cars and machines.
> You take along with you train cars and rail installations.
> From all of this rubbish – you've liberated us!
> We cry for joy.
> How good you are to us.

Nor was the harshness of Soviet occupation limited to the economic sphere. Violent rampages by Red Army soldiers were a dreadful commonplace in the early years of the occupation. Soldiers in the occupation, having imbibed years of anti-German propaganda and large quantities of alcohol, acted out revenge against the German population. Assaults and rapes left the population fearful of the occupiers; few German families or neighborhoods were untouched by the fact or the threat of personal violence. When German Communists raised the issue with Stalin, he accused them of insulting the good name of the Red Army. The practices, as well as the policies, of the Soviet occupation quickly squandered popular support, hastening both the emigration of Germans from the Soviet zone to the west and the tightening of political controls. In 1946, Stalin rejected the economic reforms that he had previously endorsed at Potsdam [7]. As the Western powers joined together in a bloc, they furthered their aims of rebuilding the German economy – and reintegrating it into the West European economy.

The major American move to rebuild Europe came the following year, as Secretary of State George Marshall gave what must be one of the most expensive commencement addresses in American history; following up on his promise cost the US government at least $13 billion over the next four years. Citing the continued economic crisis in Western Europe – slowly rebuilding from the wartime devastation, only to face harsh winters and in some countries political turmoil – Marshall proposed a massive aid program. The US government quickly established the European Recovery

Program, universally known as the "Marshall Plan." Technically open to all countries affected by wartime destruction and disruption, the plan called for European nations to determine collectively their needs, and to present each other (and eventually the United States) with internal data about current conditions and problems. This proviso ensured Soviet rejection of the aid, as Kennan, working as Marshall's chief advisor, intended [8].

The initial meeting of potential Marshall Plan recipients took place in Paris in July 1947. Soviet leaders had decided not to participate in the plan, as expected – but also barred their East European allies from getting involved. Shortly before the Paris meeting began, a group of senior Czech officials, including foreign minister Jan Masaryk, were called to Moscow for consultations. They found instead an ultimatum: reject the Marshall Plan (which they had generally favored) or face "serious conse-quences." Upon returning to Prague, Masaryk told an aide: "I left for Moscow as the minister of a free state and I am returning as Stalin's slave." Shattered by the experience, and by the rapid loss of Czech independence from Moscow, Masaryk was found dead months later – officially a suicide but most likely an assassination. When Soviet foreign minister Viacheslav Molotov arrived in Paris, he flung accusations of American imperialism and stormed out, trailing behind him the representatives of the USSR's once-independent East European allies. Though economic historians differ about the precise impact of the Marshall Plan on the European economy, there is little doubt about its political impact. It wove together the West European nations in an integrated economic system, with increasingly close political ties to the United States – and left Eastern Europe firmly under Soviet control [9].

The Marshall Plan, furthermore, shaped German affairs, as the western zones quickly expanded economic ties with their western neighbors. As part of the effort at simultaneous reconstruction and reintegration in Germany, the United States, Britain and France announced, in the spring of 1948, that they would undertake a joint currency reform with or without Soviet approval (and with or without the Soviet zone of occupation). The Deutschmark would replace the all-German Reichsmark in the western zones – and, more provocatively, in western Berlin. The Soviet response marked one of the key moments in the early cold war: citing unspecified (that is, nonexistent) technical reasons, the Soviets closed the approved ground access routes between Berlin and the western zones of Germany. This left western Berlin an island in a Red Sea – and ended any lingering hopes that Germany would be reunited in the foreseeable future. The Berlin blockade demonstrated, furthermore, the willingness of the Soviet Union to subordinate local interests and international agreements to geopolitical conflict. British and American authorities immediately undertook a massive airlift to supply the western zones of Berlin. Soviet forces did little to prevent this airborne supply route; any efforts to do so could easily have brought the armies of the onetime allies into direct conflict. The airlift established definitively that the United States would defend its European allies against Soviet military and political threats. By the time the technical problems with land access to Berlin mysteriously disappeared in the summer of 1949, the political boundaries of Europe had been set. The western zones of Germany (and with them, the western areas of Berlin) would join France, Italy, Britain, the Netherlands, and the rest of Western Europe (with the exception of neutral Switzerland and Francisco Franco's Spain) in an alliance with the United States that encompassed economic integration and political cooperation. The creation of the North Atlantic Treaty Organization (NATO) in spring 1949 added a military component to the alliance. In Eastern Europe, meanwhile, Sovietization continued apace. Only Yugoslavia and Albania, run by Communists who owed little to Stalin, kept some distance from the ever-tightening grip of Soviet friendship – and doing so was both hard fought and tenuous. While Europe contained two spheres of influence, they were hardly identical. The West was, in the apt phrase of one historian, an "empire by invitation," whereas Soviet power had been "invited" only rarely in Eastern Europe – and even there had long overstayed its welcome [4].

Globalization, 1949–1962

With the map of Europe redrawn into its postwar political boundaries, the field of the cold war moved quickly to Asia, where the remarkable ability of geopolitics to trump local context was even more evident. China, for instance, was facing its third decade of political instability, wracked by civil war and a long involvement in the Second World War. By 1949, though, it was clear that Mao Zedong's Chinese Communist Party was on the verge of final military victory; the Nationalist forces of Jiang Jieshi (Chiang Kai-shek) were on the run. Mao's victory owed little to the Soviet Union, which had for a time actively supported the Nationalists. Yet in the West, and especially in the United States, the coming Communist victory was seen as further proof of Stalin's design for world conquest. Americans interpreted creation of the People's Republic of China in the fall of 1949 as a sign that Stalin would not be content with Eastern Europe but sought to bring Asia under his control too. The notion that Mao's victory was rooted in Chinese circumstances was absent from official policy discourse in 1949 [10].

This trend continued the following year in Korea. For much of the twentieth century, Korea had been a Japanese colony; with the defeat of Japan in 1945, Korea, too, was occupied jointly by the United States and the Soviet Union, with a dividing line at the 38th parallel. North and South alike had leaders installed by the occupiers. Neither Kim Il Sung (who arrived in Korea in a Red Army uniform) in the North nor Syngman Rhee in the South had a significant local following or a commitment to an honest referendum over the newly independent nation's future. North and South quickly established standalone regimes, but each claimed to be the sole rulers of a unified Korea. Each sought support from its sponsors for reunification by military means. Kim, by playing Mao against Stalin, got a reluctant commitment from the Soviet leader to support an attack on his southern neighbor. When this attack took place in June 1950, American leaders saw it as Stalin's continued expansion by force through Asia. With a confidence unconfirmed by documentary evidence (which, of course, was unavailable to American policy-makers at the time), one Assistant Secretary of State declared that the relationship between the USSR and North Korea was the same as "that between Walt Disney and Donald Duck" – that Stalin had not just guided or ordered but literally created Kim Il Sung and the Korean War [11].

Elements of the Korean scenario would reappear frequently, with each superpower accusing the other of seeking world domination, and blaming it for unrest or political difficulty anywhere in the world. The result was a downward spiral, as each side intervened in a local dispute in order to protect it from the other. While leaders in

1946–7 feared a third world war, what arose in the 1950s was a Third World war, as the sphere of American–Soviet antagonism moved well beyond Europe. The range of instruments employed by the superpowers changed little, with each side offering a combination of political alliance, military support, and economic aid in an effort to woo countries to its own camp.

The cold war in the Third World was a battle to win friends and influence nations, especially those attaining independence after being ruled as colonies of various West European empires. The Soviet Union had a number of important advantages in winning such friends. Its extraordinary economic growth in the preceding two decades provided a model for those nations seeking rapid industrialization – particularly if nationalist leaders ignored the huge financial and human costs of Soviet-style industrialization. By Western estimates, let alone Soviet exaggerations, the USSR boasted a growth rate about twice that of the United States. Secondly, the United States had been – not incorrectly – associated with European colonizers, often favoring colonizers' interests over those of colonies in the reconstruction of Western Europe. Finally, the Soviet Union reoriented its policy toward the developing world after 1953; it offered support for national-liberation movements in former colonies irrespective of formal party affiliation. American officials, in contrast, tended to write off as Communist (or Communist dupes) any nation that refused to join the growing network of American-centered military alliances in Asia, Latin America, and the Middle East [12]. When Muhammad Mosaddeq in Iran threatened to nationalize that country's oil resources (until then available to the British through a long-term and exploitative contract), Western authorities actively worked against him. Even as Mosaddeq called for Western help against Iran's pro-Soviet Tudeh Party, American and British officials organized a coup, carried out in August 1953 [13]. Similarly, a left-leaning government in Guatemala ended up purchasing Czechoslovak arms after being refused Western supplies; CIA officials took this as a sign that the prime minister, Jacobo Arbenz, was a Communist – and promptly organized a coup d'état to replace him with a more reliably pro-Western leader [14]. In both these cases, Kennan's prediction about Soviet opportunism seemed to be holding true; Soviet leaders were quick to seek advantage in Third World conflicts, in Iran by supporting the Tudeh Party and in Guatemala taking advantage of Arbenz's request. Yet the Soviets declined to get directly involved after American actions.

Not all crises between East and West were initiated by one or another superpower. The Taiwan Straits crisis of 1958 demonstrates the complexity of bipolar conflict – and, indeed, also suggests the move away from a cold war with only two antagonists/ protagonists. Since the success of Mao Zedong in 1949, the People's Republic of China ruled the mainland, while the US-supported Nationalists established a Republic of China on the island of Taiwan. The existence of Taiwan was a sign that Mao's victory was not complete, and he frequently sought to enlist Khrushchev in ending the *de facto* division of China. Mao had discussed with Soviet officials his desire to start a military operation against the Nationalists, but met a distinct lack of Soviet enthusiasm. Khrushchev was seeking ways to reduce superpower tensions, to establish some kind of *modus operandi* for the cold war. Mao's interest in escalating the crisis was, on the one hand, related to a desire to solve a lingering local problem. But the Straits crisis, over ten tiny islands, revealed the revolutionary fervor of Mao's China compared to Khrushchev's less confrontational attitude. The years after the Straits crisis saw increasing Sino-Soviet tensions: the end of Soviet assistance in 1960 and even occasional border skirmishes. Ideological exhortations from China exerted a radicalizing pressure on Soviet foreign policy, especially in the early 1960s. This ideological pressure was evident in the Third World, especially in the two regions that would define the cold war in the 1960s: Cuba and Indochina [15].

Nations long independent of European empires faced similar pressures. Thus Fidel Castro's 26th of July Movement in Cuba rejected categorization as Communist. Only after the disastrous American attempt to overthrow Fidel in 1961 – the failed amphibious assault on the Bay of Pigs – did he declare himself a Communist and accept significant support from the Soviet Union. Given Kennedy's fierce rhetoric over Cuba, not to mention the bipartisan Bay of Pigs invasion (planned under Eisenhower, approved by Kennedy), it is easy to understand Castro's desire for protection from an American invasion. This protection began with Soviet political and military support for Cuba, but quickly (and secretly) escalated to include the stationing of Soviet medium-range nuclear missiles and long-range bombers on Cuban territory [16]. This decision reflected the superpower's race for friends and allies in the Third World as well as the logic of nuclear competition: placing weapons so close to the United States allowed the USSR to boost its nuclear threat against the United States on the cheap; in many ways it paralleled the NATO installation of Jupiter missiles in Turkey, also across a small body of water from its intended targets.

As the Third World became a site of increasing tensions, the original site of cold-war conflict, Europe, receded from the center of the cold-war competition. The boundaries of the American and Soviet spheres had been more or less settled. In the aftermath of the Berlin Blockade/airlift, the western zones of Germany became West Germany, a sovereign if attenuated nation firmly in the Western camp. Events in Eastern Europe only reconfirmed the European settlement, and underscored the emptiness of the American rhetoric of "rolling back" Soviet power. American policy would not directly challenge the Soviet sphere of influence, but would seek to contain its expansion – much as Kennan had recommended. Shortly after Stalin's death in March 1953, East German workers took to the streets to protest against new economic policies there, which would have raised expenses of staple items while reinstating the widely reviled piecework system of worker pay. American propagandists celebrated the protests, but offered only rhetorical support for the strikers – and mounted only rhetorical objections when the uprisings ended in the face of Soviet tanks. In 1955 NATO expanded to include West Germany; the creation of the Warsaw Pact in response added a military dimension to the economic and political integration of the two spheres that had already taken place. The pattern in East Germany was repeated three years later, most dramatically in Budapest. Inspired by Soviet leader Nikita Khrushchev's "Secret Speech" in February 1956, which denounced Stalin's excesses and called for a new era of international relations, termed "peaceful coexistence," Hungarian leaders established some distance from the Soviet Union. Intellectuals and political figures, including many leading Communists, overturned some of the most egregious aspects of Sovietization and sought to find a Hungarian road to socialism. While American information agencies, especially those in Europe, celebrated the resistance against the Soviets, in Washington the policy was quite clear: the CIA director said that Hungary was not worth the risk of a new world war. In spite of public rhetoric to the contrary, both cold-war superpowers had accepted the European situation.

The only exception, and this was a partial one, was Berlin. With the anomaly of a western "free city" situated entirely within the east bloc, Berlin symbolized the failure to create a unified Germany acceptable to each side – and, more broadly, the inability to complete the tasks of the Grand Alliance. Between 1958 and 1961 Khrushchev announced a firm ultimatum, but then repeatedly changed its content and timing. He called for a final settlement for Germany that would render Berlin a demilitarized and neutral city. Khrushchev threatened that the ground access to Berlin could once again be discontinued, but he never came close to acting on this threat. The resolution of the Berlin crisis came in 1961, when the East Germans erected, with Soviet approval, a wall between East and West Berlin. (Up until 1961, there was relatively free flow from one zone of Berlin to the other, with heavy traffic from east to west and little going in the other direction.) While President Kennedy reacted strongly to the Wall, he quickly reined in the generals who proposed military responses ranging from saber-rattling to land invasion. Unlike the Berlin crisis of 1948, which threatened to redraw the map of Europe, the crisis of 1961 added barbed wire and then cement to political lines that were already well established [17].

Nuclearization, 1949–1962

Both Kennedy and Khrushchev were acutely aware of the risks of going to war over Berlin, especially given the size and destructive power of their nuclear arsenals. The arms race of the 1950s created a staggering power to destroy the world many times over – and in the process provided incentives for both sides to keep away from direct armed conflict. The first step in nuclearization came when the USSR became the second atomic power by exploding an atomic bomb in August 1949. (No Soviet officials announced the explosion, which American intelligence revealed a few weeks later.) Only two months earlier, the director of the CIA had reiterated his analysts' prediction that the Soviet bomb was at least one – and most likely three – years in the future. Instead, the Soviet bomb project had taken roughly as long as the American one, a fact that was due to the sophistication of Soviet physicists, the urgency of their task, and the fruits of Soviet espionage [18].

The nuclear arms race accelerated as both sides turned from fission weapons (like those exploded in the 1940s) to far more powerful fusion bombs. The American decision came in the wake of the first Soviet test in 1949; the first successful test took place in 1952. The Soviets followed a year later. As President Dwight Eisenhower took office in January 1953, he initiated a national-security review that significantly increased the American reliance on its nuclear arsenal. His logic was rooted in both military competition and domestic politics. Afraid of turning cold-war America into a garrison state, Eisenhower looked to meet America's global security needs without maintaining a massive standing army that would amount to a society permanently at war. Eisenhower wanted nuclear weapons because they provided "more bang for the buck" – that is, they could use the technological advances to replace infantry. He and his secretary of state, John Foster Dulles, endorsed a posture of "massive retaliation," which threatened the use of nuclear weapons in large numbers in response to any global threat. This defense posture had two important implications. First, it severely limited the possibility of American response to localized threats; how could the United States respond to threats that did not rise to the level of a nuclear response? Secondly, investments in technology may prevent a standing army, but they provided their own distortions to American society, as Eisenhower conceded in his 1961 farewell address bemoaning the rise of a "military–industrial complex." Competition over military technology was quickly assimilated into the Soviet Union, already on more of a war footing [19].

As both Soviet and American scientists worked to increase the destructive power of their weapons, the arms race also came to encompass delivery mechanisms: first bombers that could fly higher, faster, and farther; then unmanned missiles that could deliver their cargos with increased range and precision. Both sides devoted brain-power and resources to improving ballistic technologies, with the Soviets scoring a major victory in the first stage of the space race by launching its "Sputnik" satellite in late 1957. In the Soviet Union, technological successes came with high opportunity cost; its military expenditures lagged only slightly behind those of the Americans, yet its overall economy was much smaller. For Khrushchev as for Eisenhower, nuclear weapons offered a way, in theory, to get superpower defense on the cheap. Yet the spiraling arms race ended up increasing the costs for both sides in the 1950s and indeed until the end of the cold war.

The globalization and nuclearization of American–Soviet conflict came to a head in 1962, when American intelligence discovered the Soviet missile installations in Cuba. The Cuban Missile Crisis of October 1962 would be the closest that the cold war came to becoming a hot one. The staunch American position that the USSR should not have missiles 90 miles from American territory ultimately prevailed, but only after both sides engaged in various forms of brinksmanship. The United States announced a "quarantine" that was indistinguishable from a blockade (which is an act of war in international law), while the Soviet Union sent ships right up to the quarantine line to test American resolve. Publicly, the crisis amounted to a major American victory: the Soviets withdrew missile equipment from the island in exchange for a no-invasion pledge from the United States. Secretly, President Kennedy agreed to remove the Jupiter missiles from Turkey. Kennedy was lauded for his crisis man-agement. Critics of Nikita Khrushchev cited Cuba in their efforts to depose him, which they did in 1964 under the leadership of the staid and stable Leonid Brezhnev. Most importantly, though, the Cuban crisis began a slow process of containing cold-war conflict, of finding mechanisms that would prevent a similar crisis moment – at which Armageddon seemed a distinct possibility [16].

Containment, 1962–1975

In the immediate aftermath of the Cuban crisis came a number of stopgap measures to provide a means to de-escalate conflicts that threatened to become nuclear. Kennedy and Khrushchev agreed to establish a "hot-line" teletype between the White House and the Kremlin. The crisis of October 1962 also provided a spur for arms control; absent for the first dozen years of the cold qar, American–Soviet negotiations over the limitation and eventually the reduction of nuclear weapons would become a constant aspect of international politics for the remainder of the cold war. The USA and USSR, along with Great Britain, signed the Limited Test Ban Treaty, banning atmospheric tests, in 1963, after efforts for a comprehensive ban ran aground over inspection and enforcement. (Non-signatories China and France soon conducted atmospheric tests.) Under United Nations auspices, the two superpowers spearheaded talks on nuclear non-proliferation, ultimately yielding a treaty signed in 1968. The first effort to limit superpower weapons stocks came in 1971, with the Strategic Arms Limitation Talks (SALT, known as SALT I after talks continued beyond the initial agreement).

Efforts to regularize cold-war conflict and prevent crises emerged not just in Moscow and Washington. Indeed, a steady flow of proposals to increase contacts across the "Iron Curtain" emerged from the capitals of Western Europe. French and German officials were particularly inclined to establish stronger working relationships – including cultural and economic ties – with east-bloc nations. Charles de Gaulle in France started the process with a visit to Moscow in 1966, in which he called for a reconstruction of world politics. By 1970 West German officials had established much closer ties not only with its eastern neighbor but with the Soviet Union, with which it signed a complex agreement to provide technology and credits for a Soviet natural gas pipeline to Germany. While the United States reluctantly accepted these over-tures, the Soviet attitude toward Eastern Europe was much less tolerant. The efforts to create "socialism with a human face" – without Soviet support – in Czechoslovakia in 1968 were quickly met with the Brezhnev Doctrine, which declared the USSR's right to maintain the socialist bloc against internal and external threats – by interven-tion if necessary. Soviet troops led fraternal Warsaw Pact troops to restore order in restive Czechoslovakia; to ensure that such order would not be fleeting, the Red Army left four divisions in Czechoslovakia. The pursuit of détente in Europe would happen west-to-east – and required Soviet involvement; east-bloc nations had little room to maneuver.

At the same time as East–West contacts grew, however, the cold-war super-powers became increasingly committed to support for their allies (or at least their enemy's enemies) – an institutionalization of the Third World war that had begun in the 1950s. For the United States, the principal arena for conflict was Indochina, ruled as a French colony until the collapse of its army in 1954. For the next decade, the United States offered extensive political, economic, and military support for the anti-Communist forces in South Vietnam. Sending few of its own troops (and those only as advisors), American policy-makers under presidents Eisenhower and Kennedy sought to contain the advance of Communism in this slender and conflict-ridden country in southeast Asia. As the Indochina wars became increasingly international in the 1950s, Soviet officials deferred to China; North Vietnamese Communist leader Ho Chi Minh found his aid redirected from Moscow to Beijing – which generally took care of Ho's military needs. With the growing Sino-Soviet rift and President Kennedy's determination to win the Third World war in the 1960s, international involvement in Indochina became more direct. Soviet diplomats sought to manage local conflicts in the region, while Chinese leaders bolstered their com-mitments to supporting North Vietnamese forces. In 1964 President Johnson faced a deteriorating position for America's South Vietnamese allies, and decided to convert what had been primarily a war-by-proxy into an American war. There were fewer than 1,000 American soldiers in Vietnam when Eisenhower left office, roughly 16,000 when Kennedy was shot – and more than 500,000 when Johnson stepped down in 1969. Though America's Vietnam War had its origins in the cold war – fighting against Communism in Asia – it quickly took on a logic (or an illogic) of its own [20].

Soviet foreign policy, even after the demise of Khrushchev's assertiveness, took full advantage of America's increasingly deep submersion in the Vietnam quagmire [21]. At the same time, though, the Soviet Union found itself wooing increasingly marginal forces – marginal both in terms of economic and political power and in terms of the domestic support for Communism within each of the countries. Soviet opportunism was most successful in the Middle East, thanks more to the availability of opportunities than to Soviet ingenuity. After the Arab–Israeli war of 1967, Arab nations went on an arms-shopping binge, and the Soviet Union was more than happy to oblige. Syria and Egypt became major arms customers, but even they were reluctant allies; Syria refused to sign a friendship pact, despite repeated Soviet invitations. The Egyptian relationship was much closer, but faltered in the 1970s, once the USA had become a major player in the Middle East peace process [22].

Given the increasing ambitions and frustrations in the Third World, it was perhaps not a surprise that American and Soviet leaders sought to contain the cold-war conflict. Here again the impetus came from the West, as Republican Richard Nixon campaigned for president in 1968 on the basis of a secret plan to end the war in Vietnam. There was no secret plan (a leading indicator of Nixon's duplicity), but Nixon and his national security advisor Henry Kissinger approached the Vietnam War from a new, superpower-oriented, perspective. Broadly speaking, they aimed to take advantage of Sino-Soviet antagonisms to reduce international tensions – or, in diplomatic lingo, to establish a détente among the major powers. Emphasizing secret diplomacy and backchannels, Kissinger wooed Brezhnev with promises of treaties to regularize longstanding cold-war issues (like the status of West Berlin), arms control agreements that would help maintain the USSR's hard-won strategic parity with the United States, and, most importantly, increased American and western trade. This latter element would help the struggling Soviet economy, though it could not, in the end, bring it out of its Brezhnev-era stagnation. From the American perspective, stronger relationships with the Communist powers would give it leverage to end American involvement in Vietnam. The strategy would prove successful in its own, limited aims: with the so-called Vietnamization of the war, battles continued, but with less support from former sponsors – and with few if any American troops remaining in Vietnam [23].

Resolution, 1975–1989

Détente marked, in some ways, a reversal of cold-war trends. While the conflict's early stages saw competition in the Third World heighten tensions between the superpowers – Korea, the Taiwan Straits, and Indochina – détente sought to solve Third World problems by reducing bilateral tensions. The high point of détente, the Helsinki accords of 1975, showed just how far the antagonists would go to search for common ground. The agreements were signed by all the nations in Eastern and Western Europe (except for holdout Albania), as well as Canada, the United States, and the Soviet Union. It established common values of human rights and promoted increased cultural contacts and trade.

Détente's impact on the cold war was, ultimately, a deep and deeply ironic one. Though it marked a reduction in American–Soviet tensions, détente at the same time nurtured many of the seeds of the ultimate demise of the Soviet Union and the resulting end of the cold war. East–west commercial and financial ties expanded dramatically in the 1970s, building on European efforts of the 1960s, but culminating in American–Soviet agreements in the early 1970s, as well as the Helsinki pact. These transactions helped turn the travails of the Soviet economy into an international issue. Soviet authorities relied on Western loans to bridge the gap between its own falling contributions and East European economic needs. By the early 1980s, east-bloc debts to Western banks neared $60 billion. At the same time, the Helsinki process offered dissenters within the eastern bloc a new platform and language for their efforts to win political, cultural, and economic freedom there. Intellectuals in Czechoslovakia and Poland led the charge with Charter 77, but Soviet dissidents also used the Helsinki accords and resultant Commission for Security and Cooperation in Europe to win publicity and sometimes even protection for their efforts. The Polish trade unions that became Solidarnosc (Solidarity) in 1980 also came into being in the late 1970s; inspired by local causes, the unions' leaders applied the language of Helsinki in their statements, especially their Charter of Workers' Rights in 1979. By 1980 Solidarnosc had ten million members and many more supporters in Poland. Its calls for economic and political reform marked the largest sustained opposition to Communist rule in Eastern Europe – though it, too, like previous protest movements, was suppressed. European events, combined with local activism, contributed to chronic problems (and eventually crises) of both economy and legitimacy in the eastern bloc [24]. Not even Western aid could resolve the crisis of legitimacy engendered by the Soviet gerontocracy; Brezhnev's death in 1982 was followed by the quick deaths of his next two successors; the age and ill health of the Politburo served as a powerful symbol of the Soviet Union itself, a decrepit industrial behemoth in a post-industrial age [25].

Superpower conflict in the Third World similarly worked against the Soviet Union. Soviet commitments of arms and soldiers multiplied in the 1970s, but in places less and less likely to reap any strategic, economic, or political rewards. Soviet military aid (and arms sales) in Africa increased dramatically in the 1970s, but went primarily to resource-poor areas that offered more varieties of conflict (civil war, ethnic conflict, and geopolitical competition) than they did any direct advantage to the Soviet Union. Soviet aid, furthermore, tended to support individual leaders rather than broader political movements, ultimately placing Soviet bets on increasingly despotic rulers with tenuous holds on power – such as Siad Barre in Somalia and Mengistu Haile Mariam in Ethiopia. Closer to home, Soviet involvement in Afghanistan's long-running civil conflict helped escalate it into both a civil war and a site of cold-war confrontation. Secret American support for the anti-Soviet *mujhadeen* provoked direct Soviet intervention, which quickly became a quagmire [22]. Economic and military commitments in Eastern Europe and the Third World were symptoms of imperial overstretch of the USSR. Its stagnating and even shrinking economy was incapable of maintaining the international position of a superpower. A group of conservative Americans aptly termed the Soviet Union of the 1980s an "impoverished superpower"; a biting joke of unknown origin made the same point: the Soviet Union had become "Upper Volta plus missiles" [26]. As capitalist nations in Europe, North

America, and East Asia showed steady economic growth, the Soviet economy was heading towards the level of the Third World.

Upon assuming the American presidency in 1981, Ronald Reagan promoted a return to harder-line anti-Sovietism – but by this point it is hard to imagine any American policy that would have prolonged the cold war much longer. Reagan initiated an extraordinary buildup of conventional and nuclear weapons, one that the Soviet Union lacked the resources to match. Reagan's Strategic Defense Initiative (SDI, commonly known as Star Wars), further escalated the technological competition well beyond what the Soviet Union could produce without even more distortions to its economy or society [24].

The circumstances that Gorbachev inherited in 1985 were the results of the cold war as well as Soviet domestic policies over the preceding four decades. Ongoing antagonisms with the United States added significant economic, political, and military pressures to a system that was poorly structured to handle them. The Soviet aim to become a global power came at a great cost; the economy was oriented toward guns – for export as well as for home use – rather than butter or even barley. Employing Soviet troops to maintain domestic order was costly enough, but troops in Eastern Europe (not to mention economic subsidies there) further drained the chronically depleted Soviet coffers. Engineers who might have produced significant and enriching innovations found work primarily in military industry – and, unlike the situation in the West, there was minimal civilian spin-off potential from military innovation. By 1985 the structural conditions for Soviet cold-war defeat were well established. But these conditions were not obvious then. Nor did they end the conflict.

The cold war owed its origins to the decisions of Soviet and American leaders in the 1940s – and its end, too, would come about through human actions. The ebb and flow of cold-war conflict had a role to play here as well. When Mikhail Gorbachev took the Soviet helm in 1985, he quickly recognized his country's dire circumstances. To solve them, he turned to a new group of Soviet intellectuals and political figures, many far from the seats of power, who embodied the so-called new thinking in the Soviet Union. While it would be an exaggeration to say that these new thinkers imported their ideas from the West, it is certainly the case that many of them formed their opinions in relation to Western ideas and Western intellectuals [27]. Two decades of cultural and academic engagement were coming to fruition – what had been long criticized by hardline Westerners as being too friendly to the Soviet Union (cultural exchanges, economic relations, détente, and so on) would, in its own way, contribute to the end of the cold war and ultimately to the demise of the Soviet Union [28].

References

1. Leffler, M. P. (1992). *A Preponderance of Power*. Stanford University Press, Stanford, CA.
2. Brzezinski, Z. (1960). *The Soviet Bloc*. Harvard University Press, Cambridge, MA.
3. Judt, T. (2005). *Postwar*. Penguin, London.
4. Gaddis, J. L. (1997). *We Now Know*. Clarendon Press, Oxford.
5. Jensen, K. M. (ed.) (1991). *Origins of the Cold War*. US Institute of Peace, Washington.
6. Eisenberg, C. (1996). *Drawing the Line*. Cambridge University Press, New York.

7. Naimark, N. M. (1995). *The Russians in Germany*. Belknap, Cambridge, MA.
8. Hogan, M. J. (1987). *The Marshall Plan*. Cambridge University Press, New York.
9. Zubok, V. M., and Pleshakov, C. (1996). *Inside the Kremlin's Cold War*. Harvard University Press, Cambridge, MA.
10. Westad, O. A. (ed.) (1998). *Brothers in Arms*. Stanford University Press, Stanford, CA.
11. Cumings, B. (1981, 1990). *The Origins of the Korean War*. Princeton University Press, Princeton.
12. Engerman, D. C. (2004). "The Romance of Economic Development and New Histories of the Cold War." *Diplomatic History*, 28: 23–54.
13. Gasiorowski, M. J., and Byrne, M. (eds.) (2004). *Mohammad Mosaddeq and the 1954 Coup in Iran*. Syracuse University Press, Syracuse, NY.
14. Gliejses, P. (1991). *Shattered Hope*. Princeton University Press, Princeton.
15. Taubman, W. (2003). *Khrushchev*. Norton, New York.
16. Fursenko, A. V., and Naftali, T. (1997). *One Hell of a Gamble*. W. W. Norton, New York.
17. Trachtenberg, M. (1999). *A Constructed Peace*. Princeton University Press, Princeton.
18. Holloway, D. (1994). *Stalin and the Bomb*. Yale University Press, New Haven.
19. Friedberg, A. L. (2000). *In the Shadow of the Garrison State*. Princeton University Press, Princeton.
20. Schulzinger, R. D. (1997). *A Time for War*. Oxford University Press, New York.
21. Gaiduk, I. V. (1996). *The Soviet Union and the Vietnam War*. I. R. Dee, Chicago.
22. Westad, O. A. (2005). *The Global Cold War*. Cambridge University Press, Cambridge.
23. Garthoff, R. L. (1994). *Détente and Confrontation*. 2nd edn. Brookings Institution, Washington.
24. Garthoff, R. L. (1994). *The Great Transition*. Brookings Institution, Washington.
25. Kotkin, S. (2001). *Armageddon Averted*. Oxford University Press, New York.
26. Rowen, H. S., and Wolf, C. (eds.) (1990). *The Impoverished Superpower*. ICS Press, Lanham, MD.
27. Evangelista, M. (1999). *Unarmed Forces*. Cornell University Press, Ithaca, NY.
28. English, R. D. (2000). *Russia and the Idea of the West*. Columbia University Press, New York.

Further Reading

Gaddis, J. L. (1997). *We Now Know*. Clarendon Press, Oxford.

Garthoff, R. L. (1994). *Détente and Confrontation*. 2nd edn. Brookings Institution, Washington.

Garthoff, R. L. (1994). *The Great Transition*. Brookings Institution, Washington.

Kotkin, S. (2001). *Armageddon Averted*. Oxford University Press, New York.

Mastny, V. (1996). *The Cold War and Soviet Insecurity*. Oxford University Press, New York.

Westad, O. A. (2005). *The Global Cold War*. Cambridge University Press, Cambridge.

Zubok, V. M., and Pleshakov, C. (1996). *Inside the Kremlin's Cold War*. Harvard University Press, Cambridge, MA.

CHAPTER TWENTY-FIVE

Old Thinking and New: Khrushchev and Gorbachev

ROBERT ENGLISH

Introduction: Russia and the West through History

At the time of this writing, early in the twenty-first century, independent Russia is more than a decade into a period of growing estrangement from the West and increasing domination of its ex-Soviet neighbors. Following a late-twentieth-century effort at rapprochement with the West and integration with liberal-democratic Europe – and the renunciation of both universalist pretensions and imperial ambitions – this departure poses interpretative as well as policy challenges.

Is it the result of Russia's encirclement by a rising China to the East, a threatening "arc of instability" across its vast southern frontier, and an expanding military bloc to the West – in other words, the traditional response to Russia's seemingly eternal, geographically determined insecurity? Or is this turn better explained by the continuities in Russian culture, a set of deeply ingrained values and beliefs that have, as in the past, strongly resisted the rapid import of Western liberal-democratic, free-market, individualistic practices in favor of authoritarian, collectivist, imperial traditions? Others see more contingent causes for Russia's latest anti-Western departure – not only in the mistakes and misdeeds of the West but also in those of Russia's political elite – chiefly, the failure of hasty and poorly planned liberalizing reforms, both before and especially after communism's collapse. And still others point to the idiosyncrasies of leadership – the ideas, beliefs, motivations and resultant policy choices of key individuals – and so contrast the liberal-democratic-integrationist "new thinking" of Mikhail Gorbachev with the illiberal-authoritarian-imperial instincts of Vladimir Putin.

The repetition of apparently cyclical patterns in national development is a phenomenon that has long intrigued those who study large-scale historical change. Are such cycles "real"? Does this framework obscure dynamic changes even while it illuminates essential continuities? Certainly the history of Russia would seem to support the "cyclical paradigm," with its recurrence of two long-term patterns that are closely intertwined: that of state-building, collapse, and renewed state-building/ expansion, together with repeated swings between integration, alienation, and renewed integration with the West.[1] The "European" Kievan Russian state was succeeded, after over two centuries of Mongol occupation, by the rise of "Asiatic" Muscovy; then, following another state collapse in the "Time of Troubles," Russia forged a powerful new autocracy; at the beginning of the eighteenth century, Peter, the great "Westernizer," crowned his growing empire with his eponymous new capital, Russia's "window on Europe." Catherine continued Peter's work, but together with a mighty European state their legacy also included a backward society and an emergent intelligentsia torn between rival "Westernizer" and "Slavophile" currents. The paradoxical product of Marxist internationalism, implanted in Russia over an epoch of war, revolution, state collapse, and rebuilding, was Stalinist "national Bolshevism," arguably the most anti-Western, xenophobic, and repressive autocracy in Russia's troubled history. So remarkable has been this pattern that Russia's relation to the West was dubbed its "eternal question" long before its reappearance in the late twentieth century. And yet, as also suggested above, Russia's current anti-Western turn can be explained as well by a range of contingent factors (leadership, ideas, specific policy choices) as by more deterministic ones (culture, geography, economic endowments).

As vital as the current debate is, Russia's early twenty-first-century estrangement from the West is too recent, and evidence about its causes insufficiently clear, to permit definitive conclusions about its main causes or historic significance. But we do have both clear evidence and sufficient perspective on the late-twentieth-century rapprochement that preceded it; indeed, it is precisely a broader appreciation of the "new thinking's" origins that is needed to understand its apparent demise. Those origins are the focus of this chapter, and its main argument is on the critical role of ideas and leadership. Most political scientists emphasize the *material* (economic and geopolitical) pressures that drive liberalizing reforms, and many historians stress *culture* (ingrained patterns of belief, behavior, and authority) in explaining resistance to them. By contrast, this chapter will emphasize the more contingent, idiosyncratic factors of *elite intellectual change* and *political leadership* under Nikita Khrushchev in the late 1950s and early 1960s and Mikhail Gorbachev in the 1980s in analyzing the liberalizing, humanizing, cold-war-ending rapprochement known as "new thinking." This perspective also suggests that the prevailing pessimism over Russia's current and future relations with the West may be excessive.

The Rise of Stalinism and the Education of Nikita Khrushchev

Nikita Khrushchev, Joseph Stalin's eventual successor, was in many respects a typical product of the Bolshevik–Stalinist period in Soviet history. Of impoverished, working-class origins, he was naturally attracted to both the ideology of proletarian empowerment and the opportunity the new regime offered for career advancement. Coming of age in an era of revolution and civil war, Khrushchev knew next to nothing of the outside world except the looming danger of "hostile capitalist encirclement," the fledgling workers' state's struggle for survival amid domestic chaos and foreign intervention. His education, like that of his fellow young Communist Party members, was essentially practical; they studied mining and agronomy, construction and industry, with a heavy dose of "political literacy" (*politgramota*, or ideological indoctrination) of crudely simplified Marxism.

Khrushchev and his contemporaries learned little of Russia's long European traditions – the country's most prominent remaining pre-revolutionary intelligentsia were expelled in the early 1920s – while even pro-Bolshevik or Marxist figures such as Maxim Gorky, Vladimir Mayakovsky, and Mikhail Pokrovsky were eventually silenced. Their sin was to have voiced doubt about the Russian national, anti-European turn the revolution had taken. For Khrushchev and others, the siege mentality of *The ABC of Communism* (the new "bible") in the 1920s married seamlessly with the chauvinistic nationalism of the 1930s (hailing once-vilified state-building autocrats such as Ivan the Terrible and Peter the Great). Thus, like other *vydvizhentsy* – those "moving up" rapidly, whose numbers now dwarfed the Bolshevik Party's European-intellectual founders – Khrushchev supported Stalin for careerist reasons (Stalin was the patron of this massive cohort) as well as ideological ones. Stalin's warning of counterrevolutionary plots and impending war resonated strongly with their civil-war-era militancy, never comfortable with the cultural diversity and capitalist revival of the mid-1920s.

These "Genghis Khans with telephones" were not only primed to accept Stalin's call to arms about the threats confronting the Soviet state. They were also steeped in a larger "culture of combat" in which all politics was mortal struggle, in which to doubt the party line was to embrace heresy, and in which dissent was tantamount to treason.[2] This is why even potential opposition had to be ruthlessly crushed, and this was how they rationalized the enormous human costs of Stalin's industrialization and agricultural collectivization (even the man-made famine that Khrushchev witnessed in Ukraine) as unavoidable. And, when Stalin launched the "Great Terror" of 1937–9, the false accusations, fabricated evidence, forced confessions, and staged "show trials" that condemned millions of innocents to execution or labor camps (which itself was often tantamount to a death sentence), they cooperated enthusiastically. Altogether, as Khrushchev's wife Nina (a *politgramota* instructor) later recalled, the 1930s were the best and "most active" years of political and social life.[3]

As for impressions of the West during the searing experience of the Great Terror – even if the "guilty" were overwhelmingly Soviet citizens, and most prominently members of the Communist Party – the entire saga was predicated on foreign enemies plotting counterrevolution and the restoration of capitalism in Russia. The 1930s also saw Stalin eliminate most remaining vestiges of Russia's pre-revolutionary European traditions and Western intellectual heritage: from the near-total isolation of Soviet science and culture from foreign influence, and the purge that crushed a "Westernized" diplomatic corps, to the promulgation at decade's end of the *Short Course* textbook on party history that took demonization of the West – and lionization of Stalin himself – to dizzying new heights. For Khrushchev and the multitudes of his generation of party officials, the Stalinist worldview successfully promulgated over the 1930s was most succinctly and pungently summarized in the infamous "no more beatings" speech that Stalin gave at the beginning of the decade:

> To reduce the tempo is to lag behind. And laggards are beaten. No, we don't want that! The history of old Russia consisted, among other things, in continual beatings for her backwardness. She was beaten by the Mongolian khans. Beaten by the Turkish beys. Beaten by the Swedish feudal lords. Beaten by the Polish–Lithuanian nobles. Beaten by

the Anglo-French capitalists. Beaten by the Japanese barons. Beaten by them all – for her backwardness.[4]

Sure enough, another attempted "beating" came soon, in 1941. Never mind that it was fascist Germany and not the Anglo-American imperialists who attacked. And never mind that Stalin had placed his trust in a pact with Hitler, and that he ignored numerous warnings of impending attack from those same Anglo-Americans, or that Stalin had continued to send vital supplies to Germany even as the Wehrmacht ravaged the continent and the Luftwaffe bombarded England in 1940 and early 1941. Stalin's propaganda machine, and the informational iron curtain that he had built, insured that the massive invasion of Russia launched on June 22, 1941 was instead widely understood as confirmation of his decade-old warnings about mortal enemies from the West. But, even without Stalin's control over information and the interpretation of events, the country's life-or-death struggle in a vicious war that took a staggering twenty-seven million lives was bound to suppress doubts, generate a surge of patriotism, and unite the country around the party and its wartime Generalissimo. *With* that control of information and interpretation, and of course with the USSR's ultimate triumph, the essential correctness of the party line and the genius of Stalin himself were emphatically confirmed.

Not that there weren't new doubts as well. Khrushchev himself, as a front-line commissar, lamented Stalin's stubbornness in the face of the Nazi juggernaut that, in the first years of the way, caused much unnecessary loss of life and the capture of millions of prisoners of war. And millions of other Soviet soldiers in the subsequent march to Germany saw with their own eyes the relative prosperity of European towns and farms that raised doubts about the superiority of the "socialist" system they had sacrificed most of a generation to build. But a combination of renewed repression (including a ruthless "filtering" to muzzle those who had seen too much of the West), redoubled propaganda (the few permitted positive images of the West as anti-fascist allies quickly vanished), and the overwhelming flush of victory effectively silenced most. A future dissident aptly summarized the postwar outlook:

> For a long time I remained an incorrigible "Red Imperialist." In my consciousness ripened a symbiosis, highly typical for the period, of Soviet patriotism and Russian nationalism. Perhaps the main proof of Stalin's genius for me were his annexations. After all, we got back everything we had lost of the former great Russia, and had added more. We stretched from the Elbe River to the China Sea. They were all real victories, and victors are not judged.[5]

Stalin's final years in power, and the onset of the cold war, renewed the anti-Westernism of the Great Terror. From campaigns against "kowtowing before the West" and "cosmopolitanism" (all things foreign, and especially Jewish), to the suppression of writers, scholars, or diplomats inclined to view their erstwhile allies in any but the most negative light – culminating in the launch of another militarized Five Year industrial plan and even preparations for a new round of terror – the xenophobia and isolation of the 1930s were, if anything, intensified. Disappointed hopes for a better and more open postwar life, instead of a return to "barracks socialism," were overwhelmed by the broadly successful cultivation of a "true war psychology."

Khrushchev, De-Stalinization, and the "Thaw"

It was not only Stalinism's ignorance and paranoia about the West, but Stalin's auto-cratic leadership that reduced even Politburo members like Khrushchev to lackeys, that left his successors so frightful upon his death in 1953. "When I'm gone, the imperialist powers will wring your necks like chickens," he had warned. Khrushchev, who would soon win the struggle to succeed Stalin, initially joined in a collective leadership and deferred foreign policy to those hard-line comrades – Andrei Vyshinsky, the purge-trial prosecutor, and Vyacheslav Molotov, Stalin's longtime minister – who had already dealt with the capitalist adversary. And at this time, before accumulating international experience of his own, he largely shared their Stalinist outlook:

> We persisted in believing the delusion perpetrated by Stalin that we were surrounded by enemies, that we had to do battle against them . . . You must realize that for many, many years it was drilled into us that we should not make the slightest concession to the West . . . We looked at things a bit suspiciously . . . we continued to see the world through [Stalin's] eyes and do things according to his style and way of thinking.[6]

Yet the perils of the cold war were too great, and the dangers of unresolved conflicts ringing the Soviet Union too intense, simply to continue the status quo. Accordingly, steps were taken to settle disputes over Iran and Turkey, end the Korean War, repair relations that Stalin had spoiled with Tito, and end the occupation of Austria that had necessarily brought Khrushchev and other members of the Soviet leadership onto the world stage for the first time. And Khrushchev, at least, was encouraged, "real-izing that our enemies feared us as much as we feared them."

The similar intractability of the domestic status quo – a severely lagging postwar recovery, hampered by a terrorized yet restive population with much of its scientific and creative talent muzzled or incarcerated – was part of the motivation for Khrushchev's decision to launch the campaign of de-Stalinization begun with his momentous "secret speech" at the Twentieth Party Congress in 1956. There were other reasons too, including the political goal of tarring rivals who had been more closely associated with Stalin's purges, and even pangs of conscience as he learned the full extent of Stalin's orchestration of the terror. Whatever its motivations, the impact of the "secret speech" (which did not remain secret for long) was tremendous. Beyond the profound psychological shock of knocking the godlike tyrant from his longtime pedestal, the exposure of even part of Stalin's crimes and misdeeds (includ-ing some of his wartime bungling) dealt a blow to the foundations of Communist Party rule from which it would never fully recover. "How could this have happened under the party of Lenin? Where were the other members of the leadership? What guarantee is there that such abuses will not happen again?" were some of the ques-tions that, privately at first, people began asking.

It was similar doubts and accusations that shook communist rule in Eastern Europe, helping provoke rebellions in Poland and Hungary where Soviet de-Stalinization directly undermined the authority of the "little Stalins" who so closely emulated their cruel mentor's policies in their own countries. Communism weathered the storm in Poland, and with the help of Soviet tanks ultimately suppressed armed insurrection in Hungary, but these crises so frightened Khrushchev and the

Soviet leadership that they temporarily halted the obviously delicate policy of de-Stalinization and the full flowering of the "thaw" epoch in the USSR (1956–64). Such international repercussions of Khrushchev's "secret speech" have been thoroughly analyzed. What is less well appreciated is the indirect, subtle, but ultimately powerfully corrosive effect it had on the Stalinist worldview. If Stalin had scripted the show trials, and the convicted had in fact been innocent of joining Anglo-American imperialists in plotting counterrevolution, then did that not mean that the West had *not* been conspiring to undermine the USSR? And, if the entire pretext of the terror had been a sham, then what was the actual nature of the West and its stance toward the USSR?

Such questions too could not be posed openly. But what *was* now officially discussed was the new doctrine of "peaceful coexistence" that Khrushchev had also unveiled at the Twentieth Party Congress. This renounced another Stalinist thesis, that of inevitable (and likely near-term) war with the capitalist West. On the one hand, the new doctrine suggested the possibility of rapprochement and even long-term cooperation; on the other, it retained the principle of an irrevocably class-divided world and could be seen as simply shifting the rivalry from direct to indirect confrontation (as in the Third World). In this sense, the contradictions of "peaceful coexistence" reflected the inconsistencies of Khrushchev-era foreign policy more generally – a partial but not complete break with Stalinist thinking, and deep, enduring ambivalence about the West.

The high and low points of Khrushchev-era foreign policy are well known, from the hopes of the "spirit of Geneva," early disarmament talks, and the general warming of US–Soviet relations even as Moscow's ties with Beijing worsened, to disappointment at American intransigence, renewed confrontation over Berlin, and then the erection of the Berlin Wall (in 1961). Khrushchev was particularly ambivalent about the USA. On the one hand, his unprecedented, month-long visit in 1959 revealed much that he admired: America's vast wealth, agricultural bounty, energy and openness. On the other hand, the conspiratorial-Stalinist outlook led him to imagine insult and duplicity at numerous turns – from the awarding of the Nobel Literature Prize to the "anti-Soviet" writer Boris Pasternak, to the denial of permission to visit Disneyland.

Khrushchev repeatedly fended off his neo-Stalinist colleagues' demand for an end to his tentative détente with the West. But he shared hopes for the rapid worldwide expansion of communism – particularly with the spread of decolonization in the Third World. Socialist-leaning movements from Africa to the Middle East were encouraging, but it was the Cuban revolution that prompted something close to euphoria. Khrushchev and his colleagues were smitten with Fidel Castro: "This is a real revolution," gushed the normally staid Anastas Mikoyan, "I feel as if I've returned to my youth!"[7] And it was this revolutionary enthusiasm and sense that socialism's triumph in the global rivalry with capitalism was imminent that, together with the obvious strategic aims, fueled the disastrous 1962 decision to place nuclear missiles in Cuba.

And yet Khrushchev was statesman enough to back down from the brink of Armageddon. What is more, he drew the same conclusions from the ramifying experience as did US President John Kennedy, and together, over 1963, they worked toward significant improvement in US–Soviet relations with such steps as the Limited

Test Ban Treaty and, on the Soviet side, deep and unilateral cuts in their massive conventional forces. These decisions were not popular in the Politburo, to say the least, and contributed to his colleagues' decision to oust him in 1964.

There is little doubt that Khrushchev's singular leadership was mainly responsible for de-Stalinization and crucial thaw-era progress in Soviet–Western relations. The differences between him and most others in the post-Soviet leadership were great, and at key junctures Khrushchev was the key initiator or supporter of change. All the same, notwithstanding the enormous distance he traveled, the great "de-Stalinizer" was still much hampered by the dictator's political and psychological legacies. As Khrushchev himself observed in the twilight of his leadership: "There's a Stalinist in each of you, there's even some Stalin in me."[8]

The Rebirth of a Russian Intelligentsia

But, if Khrushchev could not break decisively with the Stalinist outlook, he could create the conditions for the rise of a very different worldview in a post-Stalin generation. He did that, first, by ending the terror as well as the atmosphere of fear and impending war that had frozen social and intellectual life in a "besieged fortress." With the return of camp survivors and prisoners of war, and the end of the campaign against "kowtowing to the West" and "cosmopolitanism," there ensued a revival of private intellectual life that saw intense debate on virtually all political issues – domestic and international. Public squares saw impromptu poetry readings, sports clubs, or school lectures. Most often the discussion went on in private *kompanii*, groups that served as

> publishing houses, speakers bureaus . . . seminars in literature, history, philosophy, lin-
> guistics, economics, genetics, physics, music and art . . . Just about every evening, I
> would walk through the dark corridor of some communal flat and open the door of a
> crowded, smoky room . . . Old *politzeki* [political prisoners] would be shouting some-
> thing at young philologists, middle-aged physicists would be locked in hot debates with
> young poets.[9]

The second impetus to rethinking the West came with the admission that Stalin's purge-terror process had all been based on lies – that millions had in fact been innocent of involvement with foreign-backed plots against the USSR – which undermined a central pillar of "hostile capitalist encirclement" for those who reflected on the great national trauma of the 1930s. Together with the enunciation of "peaceful coexistence," this encouraged a far broader rethinking of Russia and the West than Khrushchev had intended. And, with the re-emergence of some notable intellectuals – philosophers, economists, writers, and others, a lucky few who had survived the massacre of the prerevolutionary and pre-Stalin intelligentsia – venues from private salons to university lecturers began re-examining long-suppressed questions about Russian culture, Russia and Europe, and Russia's development in the currents of world civilization. As one Moscow State University student recalled: "One tear after another appeared in the iron curtain. It split and started to slide apart. Truthful information gave birth to questions . . . Society was undergoing a tumultuous reassessment of values."[10]

This re-examination was furthered by the nascent opening of the country to the outside world. Media coverage of Soviet delegations abroad, growing numbers of foreign visitors to Russia, the spread of television, music, Western radio broadcasts, and even some Western consumer goods all brought tangible new images of the world beyond. Official cultural exchanges with the West were begun. Moscow hosted a semi-annual International Film Festival. Soviet students traveled to the International Youth Festival (or welcomed it in Moscow). Literary life made a vital contribution as well; pre-Stalin masters such as Bulgakov, Tsvetaeva, and Mandelstam were now published, and young writers emulated Proust, Joyce, and T. S. Eliot as, in cultural terms, the country began "making an exit from Asia, attaching itself to Europe."[11] Crucially, many once-forbidden foreign authors (from Hemingway and Brecht to Freud) were now published in Russian editions, Western works appeared in such journals as *Novy Mir* (New World), and there was even begun a new journal – *Inostrannaia Literatura* (Foreign Literature) – which quickly gained one of the largest circulations in the country. *Novy Mir* editor Konstantin Simonov, once a Stalin-era favorite, later denounced Stalinist xenophobia and pointedly contrasted legitimate national pride with "superficial patriotism, kvas-bottle patriotism . . . self-glorification and the rejection of all things foreign simply because they are foreign."[12]

A third and equally vital Khrushchev-era contribution to this early new thinking came with far-reaching changes in professional life – in the conditions of work, of research, analysis, discussion, and publication – for specialists concerned with various aspects of international affairs. Young and old, humanists and scientists, from university classes and writers' clubs to private salons, gathered everywhere. Especially in the main urban centers of Moscow and Leningrad, however, new centers of "radicalism, zeal, and creativity"quickly arose.[13] At Moscow State University, the re-emergence of such pre-Stalin, Europe-oriented Marxist historian-philosophers as Bonifatsy Kedrov, Valentin Asmus, and Teodor Oizerman stimulated younger anti-dogmatic scholars such as Yuri Karyakin, Boris Grushin, and Merab Mamardashvili. Other students were fascinated by Yugoslavia's reforms, and some even mobilized – circulating leaflets and forming "solidarity committees" – in support of Hungary's freedom. At the Institute of History, Mikhail Gefter criticized scholarly isolation, questioned national-chauvinist dogmas about an exclusive Soviet path of development, and called for creation of a "worldwide historical canvas." Answering this methodological challenge came such pathbreaking works as Alexander Nekrich's *June 22, 1941* (which drew on Western as well as Soviet sources to detail Stalin's bungling on the eve of the Second World War) and Ivan Maisky's *Memoirs of a Soviet Ambassador*, which faulted Stalinist paranoia for delay in forming anti-fascist alliances with the West. Physicist Peter Kapitsa – who had incurred Stalin's wrath for refusing weapons-related research – criticized academic isolation, branded Soviet social sciences "scholastic and dogmatic," and pushed for international scientific cooperation. Similarly, his colleague Igor Tamm denounced Soviet chauvinism, declared science "universal . . . a vital part of the world's cultural heritage,"[14] and regularly briefed his staff on Western radio broadcasts. Economist Abel Aganbegyan did likewise, supplementing his institute's academic freedoms with regular visits from avant-garde poets, singers, and critical political lectures.

This rethinking of the West received a critical boost with the establishment (or revival) of a number of specialized institutes for the study of international relations.

For decades, such study had withered as world politics was reduced to the simplistic formula of a class-divided world outlined in Lenin's *Imperialism: The Highest Stage of Capitalism*, and was still further constrained by the dogmatism of Stalin's *Short Course* and its logic of "hostile capitalist encirclement" and looming war. Sociology, with its implicit critique of social issues, was essentially shut down in the 1920s; international economics, transformed abroad by depression, war, and the postwar liberal trade system, was scorned in a USSR pursuing central planning and autarky; and the formal study of international relations, another burgeoning field in the West, never even got off the ground. Scholars interested in international issues retreated to historical or cultural studies, to "safe" subjects of the prerevolutionary past, and could touch critically on contemporary issues only by careful allusion or distant analogy.

But in the decade after Khrushchev's "secret speech" – as the country's opening soon highlighted its ignorance of processes underway in the outside world – this neglect was quickly reversed. The former Institute of World Economy and World Politics, closed by Stalin in 1949 for its too-positive view of postwar capitalism's prospects, reopened in 1956 as the Institute of World Economy and International Relations (IMEMO) and quickly became a leading center of original foreign-affairs thought. This was soon followed by others under the aegis of the Soviet Academy of Sciences: the Institute of the Economy of the World Socialist System (to make sense of the growing diversity in Eastern Europe), Institutes of Africa, Latin America, and the Far East, and the Institute of the USA (later renamed the Institute of the USA and Canada, or ISKAN). The latter would rival IMEMO as a center for reappraisal of Soviet policy toward the West, just as the new Novosibirsk Institute of Economics and Industrial Management would become the boldest center of reformist economic–sociological studies.

In all these institutes, notwithstanding an official line that foresaw "growing capitalist contradictions" and a rapid shift toward socialism in the "worldwide correlation of forces," analysts encountered two critical prerequisites for the searching reappraisal of such dogmas: greatly increased access to information on the West, and greatly expanded academic freedoms. Long-closed archives were opened, long-suppressed data were published, and access to Western books, journals, and mass media grew dramatically. As one thaw-era student recalled:

> My second education was conducted in the special section of the library where Western newspapers, magazines and books were kept . . . What I read there began to give me a better understanding of the world [and raised] doubts about the validity of many things I had been taught . . . My understanding of recent history took a quantum leap.[15]

This recollection of a student at the Moscow State Institute of International Relations, the now-invigorated Soviet diplomatic academy, highlights the changes in this vital sphere of international-relations study and practice. New departments were formed, dogmas eased, and even some foreign students now welcomed. Equally critical, for serving diplomats, their conditions of work and life eased tremendously. They ceased to be terrorized servitors in isolated compounds on enemy territory; the activization of Soviet diplomacy meant new freedoms to travel, interact, read, and study foreign countries.

> We in London (like our colleagues in other foreign capitals, I suppose) had a rare opportunity to read *samizdat* [self-published] and émigré publications . . . hardly anybody withstood the temptation of the forbidden fruit. [I myself collected] an entire library . . . the Bible, the Koran, Pasternak, Solzhenitsyn, Okujava, Daniel, Sinyavsky, Alliluyeva, and much else.[16]

Hundreds, and eventually thousands, of other young *mezhdunarodniki* (foreign-affairs specialists) would also gain direct – even if limited – access to the outside world as well. Some accompanied cultural delegations or attended academic conferences in the West, while others undertook research visits to Hungary or Poland (where access to Western literature was vast) or reveled in the diversity of reformist Yugoslavia.

> I was deeply impressed by Yugoslavia's economic reforms, above all by decentralization, rejection of rigid planning, and by their firms' emphasis on the domestic market with free access to foreign markets . . . Food shops resembled those in the West, and their industrial products . . . were already approaching world standards . . . The country's spirit was ruled by "modernism," a striving for everything contemporary and new.[17]

Eastern Europe was also the venue of one of the most influential of these new "oases of critical thought" – namely, the Prague-based editorial staff of the new journal *Problemy Mira i Sotsializma* [Issues of Peace and Socialism]. Founded to supplant the now-defunct Comintern as the center of world socialism – to replace Stalinist *diktat* with a diversity of socialist views under one Soviet-led umbrella – the journal published viewpoints ranging from neo-Stalinist to reformist-social democratic. Perhaps more importantly, under the leadership of the pre-Stalin vintage academic Alexander Rumyantsev, the private (still-unpublishable) debates, the long discussions with French, English, and Italian party colleagues, and the broad personal liberties of life in Prague made it "a cosmopolitan paradise compared to Moscow." Another thaw-era staffer recalled:

> It was a totally non-Soviet environment . . . We were exposed to a huge amount of information on the outside world. And from all that, the idea of imperialist aggression, that the West posed a real threat to the Soviet Union, it instantly disappeared. In Prague people simply found themselves in totally different surroundings, we could take off our ideological blinders. And we turned out to be normal people who could look at the world and our own country normally.[18]

This quotation from Anatoly Chernyaev, one of the most influential perestroika-era "new thinkers," well summarizes the experience of numerous contemporaries.[19] These intellectuals of such diverse background and specialization all engaged in essentially the same radical rethinking of Stalinist (and Leninist) dogmas about a Russia sharply divided from the main currents of European–Western civilization. They debated the same bold articles appearing in *Novy Mir*, patronized the same avant-garde poets and theaters, and read the same illicit copies of Orwell's *Nineteen Eighty-Four*, Djilas's *The New Class*, and Gramsci's *Prison Notebooks* (the latter being a European Marxist's scathing critique of Stalin's national chauvinism). Economists and physicists too devoured Jean-Paul Sartre, alongside pre-revolutionary critics of

Bolshevism such as Semyon Frank and Nikolai Berdyaev, while philosophers and historians pondered works from Evgeny Gnedin's underground memoir of Stalin's purge of pro-Western diplomats in the late-1930s to a report on the CIA's pessimistic analysis of the Soviet economy in the mid-1960s.

Often referred to as "Children of the Twentieth Congress" (the landmark party conclave where de-Stalinization began), these scholar-scientist-analysts may more appropriately be called a new Russian intelligentsia. For it is not only that many critically minded, anti-isolationist, reformist young specialists were now joining research institutes, university faculties, and even party advisory groups, where they would gradually supplant legions of Stalin-trained, half-educated, pseudo-intellectual servitors. It is that they represented a true *intelligentsia* in the fullest sense of the term: "a social group of great intellectual and practical strength, unorganized but numerous and fairly united in spirit."[20] They were still not nearly so numerous as the majority of conservative, careerist bureaucrats. But this liberal minority – whom we might also call "neo-Westernizers" – were acutely conscious about Russian history and their social-political duty as intellectuals. This not only meant a strength of commitment that would prove crucial to the launch of reforms in the 1980s; it also meant a unity across diversity that would preserve a critical mass of liberal through the difficult years between the thaw and perestroika.

New Thinking in the Era of Stagnation

This vital unity was seen in some of the first major political battles of the post-Khrushchev years – later to be dubbed the "era of stagnation." This was not how it appeared at the outset, however, for even many liberals had tired of Khrushchev's erratic leadership and held great hopes for more consistent progress under new leader Leonid Brezhnev. So, when neo-Stalinists in the party (many in the military, but from economic, administrative, and educational-ideological bodies as well) sought to turn back the clock instead, this new intelligentsia rallied to the reformist cause. When conservatives began pushing to rehabilitate Stalin, for example, a large number of prominent scientists and writers joined other intellectuals in protesting directly to the top – and won.[21] When Nekrich's controversial *June 22, 1941* came under attack, his defenders ranged from former *Problemy Mira i Sotsializma* editor Rumyantsev and the veteran diplomat-author Maisky to the young Central Committee staffer Chernyaev. Some of the most outspoken liberals were nevertheless fired from research or journalistic positions (and Nekrich's book was ultimately recalled), but many found "shelter" in the new institutional havens and their more outwardly orthodox (but quietly reformist) directors.[22]

The first years of Brezhnev's rule (1964–82) still seemed a time of reformist promise, and there was a sense of a battle being fought "for Brezhnev's soul." The re-Stalinizers had (at least temporarily) been stopped, *Novy Mir* continued to win important battles with the censors, and Brezhnev himself criticized those who would limit Soviet social sciences to an exclusively "propagandistic" role. Then came the launch of the decentralizing "Kosygin reforms" in apparent response to the liberals' critique of Soviet economic woes. These reforms would ultimately languish – doomed by half-hearted implementation in the face of bureaucratic–ministerial resistance – but what came next raised liberals' hopes even higher. This was the "Prague Spring," the party-initiated Czechoslovak reform movement that many saw as a model for their own country.

> The political and economic system [they] were trying to transform had been created as the mirror image of ours. Therefore, Czechoslovakia's experience [was] transferable to our country. My best-case scenario went something like this. After reforms, Czechoslovakia's workers would be given incentives . . . factory managers would see value in innovation, writers would be allowed to publish. As labor, management and the intelligentsia united, economic indicators would shoot up. Impressed by the Czech economic miracle, Soviet leaders would attempt similar reforms.[23]

The Prague Spring completely captivated Soviet reformers in 1967–8. As already seen, interest in East European reforms had grown since the late 1950s, and the writings of Yugoslav, Hungarian, and Czech reformers (particularly economists such as Janos Kornai and Ota Sik, the latter to become the chief Czech economic theorist) were well known to their Soviet counterparts. Veterans of *Problemy Mira i Sotsialisma* were particularly entranced, given their close ties to the Czechoslovak reformers (and their love of Prague). Developments were monitored closely, and, when the Soviet press turned hostile, some relied on foreign broadcasts and some even learned Czech to keep up with the news via the "fraternal" papers *Literarni Listy* and *Rude Pravo*. One sympathetic observer recalled that "the entire Moscow liberal intelligentsia was preoccupied with the Prague Spring."[24] Alexander Solzhenitsyn's "Open Letter" to the Congress of Czech Writers was "one of the brightest and hottest sparks" of Soviet reformism, while Andrei Sakharov's widely read 1968 *samizdat* memorandum *Reflections on Progress, Coexistence, and Intellectual Freedom* owed much of its inspiration to events in the Czech capital.

Given such hopes, the crushing of the Prague Spring in August 1968 was a major blow to Soviet reformers. Diplomats, historians, foreign-affairs experts, and many others recalled the burning shame they felt that their country was responsible for extinguishing the reformist flame. Chernyaev wrote: 'I suffered terribly over Prague. I condemned it in my soul, to my friends, and told my little schoolgirl daughter 'Remember this – a great country has covered itself with shame and won't be forgiven.'[25]

Others said it openly. Solzhenitsyn, and folk singer Alexander Galich, both stridently compared the Soviet action to Russian nineteenth-century imperialism. *Izvestiia* correspondents Vladlen Krivosheyev and Boris Orlov not only refused to report the official version of events, but dissented directly to the Soviet leadership – for which they were demoted, as was the outspoken *Problemy Mira i Sotsializma* member Vladimir Lukin. Central Committee staffer Alexander Bovin, as well as avant-garde poet Yevgeny Yevtushenko, protested directly to Brezhnev. Historian Gefter defied a party-mandated resolution endorsing the crackdown – as did many other liberals – and was soon fired. So was the editor of *Zhurnalist* (Journalist) Yegor Yakovlev, for provocatively publishing the text of the liberal Czech press law. Altogether, dozens of other liberals lost their jobs at this time or soon thereafter in a larger crackdown on dissent and openly critical thought.

Yet three positives should be noted as well. One was, again, the solidarity of the reformist intelligentsia as certain liberal officials – including Academy of Sciences Vice

President and former editor Rumyantsev, ISKAN director Arbatov, and Central Committee staffer Alexander Yakovlev – managed to "rescue" their fired colleagues and find them new jobs. The second was that, perhaps paradoxically, the episode showed that sweeping reforms of the communist system were indeed possible; the Prague Spring was a party-led movement, after all, and had succeeded until its halting by "big brother" in Moscow – consequently, should a similar movement find high-level sponsorship in the USSR, there would be nothing to stop it! And so, flowing directly from this realization, the third positive outcome of the Prague Spring was an impetus to a subsequent decade of serious reform preparations – less idealistic, more liberal or social democratic than socialist, and far more detailed and thorough-going than the vague, often romantic ideas of the 1960s. Thus, contrary to views of the 1970s–early 1980s as an "era of stagnation," for liberal Westernizing intellectuals it was a period of regrouping, consolidation, and quiet but serious preparation for the next reform epoch.

One current of this nascent new thinking grappled with the larger questions of global development and civilizational challenges as the entire planet – and not just the Soviet Union – approached the late twentieth century. Building on the thaw-era foundations of those historians and philosophers who questioned their country's isolation from global processes, these analysts raised a set of new issues that further challenged dogmas about Soviet exclusivity. Fedor Burlatsky and Georgy Shakhnazarov – as well as the now-openly dissident Sakharov – dispensed with class analysis and cited foreign experience to highlight common problems of administration bureaucracy and to place decentralization democratization on the Soviet agenda. Sociologists such as Boris Grushin, Yuri Levada, and Igor Kon raised issues of labor, youth, and sex common to East and West and pioneered public opinion research on matters of domestic and even foreign affairs. And many young scholars, again inspired by Western research, raised issues from environmental degradation to overpopulation. On the latter, Gerasimov even dared compare Stalinist policies to those of Hitler for encouraging high birth rates under a "supremacist" ideology. By the mid-1970s, such concerns merged into a general critique of *obshchechelovecheskie* (all-human) problems and values more than a decade before that term would enter the mainstream under perestroika. Economists, physicists, philosophers, and cyberneticists joined in a series of debates organized by Prague veteran Frolov in the journal *Voprosy Filosofii* (Philosophical Issues). The "star" contributor was Kapitsa, who stressed the "global nature" of economic, social, and ecological problems, ridiculed those who saw separate "socialist" and "bourgeois" approaches to them, and argued that they could be solved only by the combined efforts of all humanity.[26]

A second stagnation-era reformist current addressed economic problems directly. The failure of Khrushchev's ambitious promise to overtake the United States within a generation was now manifest, as were the systemic woes of the Stalinist-era "command-administrative" system. Among numerous proposals, two stand out: one was to marketize the economy, and the other was to integrate it into the "international division of labor." Young scholars were less entranced by Yugoslav "self-management" or the vague economic goals of the Prague Spring; they were less *political* economists than rigorously, mathematically trained students of Samuelson, Keynes, and Friedman. Hazy thaw-era notions about "the socialist market" were replaced by strongly Western-influenced analyses that emphasized "market social-ism," or simply *the market*.

Aganbegyan had, since the founding of the Novosibirsk Institute, tried the party's patience with his stinging critiques of Soviet socioeconomic woes. Now analysts at ISKAN and IMEMO wrote, mainly for classified or limited-circulation use, reports on an alarming lag in the gathering "scientific-technological revolution." Nikolai Fedorenko and Stanislav Shatalin, of the Central Economic-Mathematical Institute, authored studies whose prognoses were so dire, and whose marketizing proposals so bold, that they left party-ministerial audiences stunned. Perhaps the most notable reforms were proposed by Nikolai Shmelyev, who, in a series of mid-1970s reports, argued that Soviet autarky was crippling the country, that the state monopoly on foreign trade must yield to individual firms' right to contract directly with foreign buyers and sellers, and that joint ventures and foreign investment should be encour-aged, then currency convertibility achieved, leading to Soviet membership in such capitalist international organizations as GATT, the World Bank, and the International Monetary Fund. When they were taken together, the thrust of Shmelyev's proposals was clear: the end of state control over prices, exchange rates, and foreign trade would make most central planning impossible and lead to the broad marketization as well as internationalization of the Soviet economy. Of course, these recommendations were ignored, and elsewhere Shmelyev presciently warned:

> The USSR lags behind [Eastern Europe] and even some developing countries in the use of promising international economic cooperation . . . The biggest growth [has been in] grain imports made possible by Western credits. So now we have a trade deficit with the West. In 1973–74 another factor emerged [namely] a rise in world prices of raw materials and oil which led to a sharp rise in hard currency earnings . . . But this situation is tem-porary, unlikely to last beyond the 1980s.[27]

The third main stagnation-era new-thinking current was that directly concerned with foreign policy and East–West relations. Here, too, the fruits of thaw-era changes were bountiful, as many *mezhdunarodniki* pushed beyond détente's partial rap-prochement, for truly meaningful cooperation with the West. By now a large corps of diplomats with Western experience – tellingly, they called themselves *zapadniki* or "Westernizers" – had developed "great admiration for the West, for the United States . . . respect for the country, its strengths, its people . . . [We grew] strongly dedicated to arms control and improving Soviet–American relations."[28] Academics as well as diplomats now focused on arms talks, some so bold as to claim that it was a growing *Soviet* arsenal that threatened to upset the balance; Arbatov argued that further accumulation of nuclear weapons had lost any purpose, his son Alexei (an IMEMO analyst) contradicted the official line in noting that Moscow's build-up provoked legitimate American worries about a Soviet attack, and ISKAN staffer (and former Prague protestor) Lukin found the same was true of conventional forces, with growing Soviet armies confronting static or shrinking US and Chinese forces.

A key contribution came from the ranks of Soviet scientists – from many econo-mists and other social scientists, to be sure, but more importantly from physicists, chemists, and other natural scientists. Some had been drawn into the Pugwash or Dartmouth conferences beginning in the thaw era, forums where weapons designers grappled with the consequences of their handiwork – and their Western colleagues – in annual, no-holds-barred meetings. Chemist Vitaly Goldansky recalled his first Pugwash meeting as "highly impressive . . . the foreign participants had such command of the scientific and political issues. I learned about non-proliferation, testing, and other matters . . . It broadened my horizons in every way."[29] Theoretical physicist Evgeny Velikhov, future Space Research Institute Director Roald Sagdeyev, and a host of other scientists followed the path blazed by thaw-era exchange pioneer Lev Artsimovich. And parallel, eye-opening experiences came to many others, ranging from rocket designer Boris Raushenbakh (in the mid-1970s joint Apollo–Soyuz spaceflight) to cardiologist Yevgeny Chazov (international physicians' gatherings). They all reveled in the possibilities of further scientific–cultural cooperation, but also worried that the Brezhnev leadership remained untrusting and secretive. As Arbatov publicly warned:

> extreme secrecy leads to deadlock in relations with the USA [and permits] their military–industrial complex to take the arms race to yet another level while weakening the position of those [American] forces in favor of lowering the level of military confrontation and defense outlays. A lack of clarity and openness regarding the intentions of one side always fuels suspicion and fear, encourages worst-case scenarios, and complicates the chances for agreement.[30]

Mikhail Gorbachev: New Leadership for New Thinking

All the liberal *mezhdunarodniki* anguished over détente's demise, the late-1970s return to confrontation that culminated in the 1979 Afghan invasion, the collapse of arms talks, even the onset of a new cold war. Some, showing their principled commitment to new thinking (rather than just opportunism, which many foreign observers saw in their détente-era reformism), risked censure and even their careers in an effort to halt the slide. Bogomolov wrote directly to the Central Committee just after the invasion, arguing that détente's demise had actually begun much earlier, with the worldwide Soviet military buildup: with "Afghanistan our policy went beyond admissible bounds" and Moscow now faced "a protracted war . . . In extremely unfavorable circumstances." Further:

> [our] influence on the non-aligned movement, especially on the Muslim world, has suffered considerably . . . Détente has been blocked and political prerequisites for limiting the arms race have been eliminated . . . Economic and technological pressure on the Soviet Union has grown sharply . . . [There is] growing distrust of Soviet policy and departure from it on the part of Yugoslavia, Romania, North Korea. Even the Hungarian and Polish press reveal open [dissatisfaction] with Soviet action . . . curtailment of our military activity in the Third World could contribute to a gradual return to détente . . . if crisis situations do not spread to other regions, especially to Eastern Europe.[31]

Crisis did soon spread to Eastern Europe, and liberal analysts were no less strident in blaming Soviet policy for the Solidarity debacle in Poland. Meanwhile, in 1980–4, reformist experts spoke up in some open journals, more often in specialized, limited-circulation publications, and in policy memos to the party leadership, on the entire range of foreign concerns. IMEMO and ISKAN analysts criticized Soviet military policy, Soviet policy in Asia and the Third World, and Soviet international economic policy as well. Further, the institute directors appealed directly to the party leadership to halt the deployment of more nuclear weapons in Europe.

Other analysts pushed the broader new-thinking agenda – faulting the hyper-centralization and lack of democracy that stifled Soviet socioeconomic life, sounding the alarm over neglected global, all-human problems, and pleading for renewed East–West economic, scientific, and military–security cooperation. But now, as conservatives (even neo-Stalinists) dominated in a time of weak, transitional leadership, the modest tolerance once shown the liberals ended in a harsh crackdown. Even modestly critical thought was censored, and outspoken liberals were threatened, censured, or driven from their jobs. As Soviet propaganda returned to Stalinesque, pre-war themes – and as some conservatives actually sought again to rehabilitate Stalin – reformers from Arbatov and Shatalin to scores of less-well-known analysts were effectively silenced. Without high-level sponsorship, the new thinking stood no chance.

But that sponsorship was on the horizon, in the person of an energetic young Politburo member named Mikhail Gorbachev. Foreign observers had little inkling of the radical reformer he would soon become, generally emphasizing – like the Politburo members who had elected him party leader – that he was a loyal product of the Soviet system who had been chosen to make it more effective and to address economic problems through modest changes. Yet in background, education, and outlook Gorbachev was already something radically new. He was, for one thing, the first truly post-Stalin leader, shaped not by an epoch of war, terror and "hostile capitalist encirclement" but in an era of thaw, experimentation, and international opening. Not only was his a humanities education – in contrast to the technical-administrative training of all his rivals for power; it came during the Khrushchev years at Moscow State, the country's most diverse, challenging, and liberal institution of higher learning. As a law student, Gorbachev (together with his wife Raisa, a philosophy student and his lifelong political advisor and partner) was exposed to the same eye-opening lectures, the same unsanctioned readings and no-holds-barred debates, as so many future "new thinkers." It was also at university that he formed a lasting friendship with the Czech exchange student Zdenek Mlynar, a future architect of the Prague Spring.

Gorbachev's rise in provincial party administration, outwardly orthodox, was characterized by unusual energy, ambition, intolerance of corruption, and thirst for progress. Less visible at the time were other preparations for the future "leader of new thinking," including several eye-opening visits to both West and East Europe (on party business, but including some independent, "touristic," travel as well). One turning point came with a post-Prague Spring visit to Czechoslovakia, where Gorbachev was stunned by the intensity of popular resentment and now realized that, instead of acting to save socialism, the USSR had for geopolitical reasons crushed a movement "that had ripened within [Czech] society itself."[32] Other travel was similarly broadening, from fostering appreciation of Western liberty and diversity that undermined the "enemy image," to astonishment at the nationwide outpouring of grief and solidarity at the funeral of "heretical" Italian communist leader Enrico Berlinguer, who had criticized Moscow's foreign policy and embodied the social-democratic "deviation" of the Italian Communist Party. Probably equally critical in

Gorbachev's own budding social-democratic orientation was his private reading of everything from Gramsci to Brandt and Mitterrand (in translations prepared for the Soviet elite, but ignored by most anti-academic, careerist Brezhnev-era officials), as well as his wife Raisa's ties to some liberal, "semi-dissident" Moscow scholars.

Upon his 1978 summons to Moscow, Gorbachev continued to seek out the most creative minds for inspiration and advice. He was soon hosting a series of "seminars" with liberal specialists in numerous fields – at first, primarily the economy – who included some recently censured for their too-critical views. They included Aganbegyan, agricultural expert Vladimir Tikhonov, and sociologist Tatyana Zaslavskaya, who recalled discussing "a perestroika of the entire economic system." Perhaps inevitably, Gorbachev's circle expanded to include foreign-policy experts as well. Physicist and arms-control expert Velikhov recalled how their early focus on the use of computers to improve planning quickly turned to ideas for breaking the nuclear stalemate. Soon a "Gorbachev team" of unofficial advisors emerged, led by Velikhov and Arbatov but including IMEMO director Nikolai Inozemtsev, his deputy Yevgeny Primakov, and other consultants (such as Shakhnazarov, Chernyaev, and Frolov).

This activity raised the suspicions of some conservatives; Chernyaev described the anger of Central Committee International Department boss Boris Ponomarev at "this upstart, who's supposed to be working on agriculture, sticking his nose where it doesn't belong."[33] As a rising member of the leadership Gorbachev undertook duties that included more trips abroad, which only expanded his exposure to a larger world. Perhaps most significant was his 1983 trip to Canada, where he quickly established a bond with Soviet ambassador Alexander Yakovlev, a 1970s liberal "exiled" to Ottawa for his frank criticism of Brezhnev-era Russian national chauvinism. Upon his return to Moscow, and at the strong recommendation of Arbatov, Yakovlev replaced the recently deceased Inozemtsev (literally hounded to his death by reactionaries) as director of IMEMO. Yakovlev, later known as "the father of glasnost," quickly revived the institute and became perhaps Gorbachev's most trusted advisor.

The skeptical "materialist" interpretation of Gorbachev's accession in 1985 takes no account of all this preparatory activity, emphasizing instead that he was chosen by his Politburo colleagues to implement changes that would arrest Soviet economic decline and flagging global influence. And so he was, but the radical steps he would soon take – against the preferences of a majority of his Politburo colleagues, none of whom had anything like either his reformist ambitions or his concrete preparations[34] – flowed directly from the advice of his now-numerous new-thinking supporters. Change was likely in, in any event. But under any other sponsorship it would probably have gone in a very modest, domestically focused direction, or perhaps even taken a neo-Stalinist turn, as a number of senior hardliners were encouraging by the mid-1980s.

Instead, after his March 1985 election Gorbachev launched a series of initiatives under which foreign-policy change quickly outstripped domestic. Within months he had replaced the old Stalinist foreign minister Andrei Gromyko with Eduard Shevardnadze, the Georgian party boss who had no foreign-policy experience whatsoever but whom Gorbachev knew and respected as a non-dogmatic innovator. Against hardliners' wishes, he pushed for an immediate summit with the conservative US president Ronald Reagan, and overruled skeptics' gloating at its failure to press instead even harder for arms control. In January 1986 he unveiled a sweeping disarmament proposal – derided by skeptics, but one that essentially outlined the weapons cuts and nuclear build-down that would be enshrined in treaties just a few years later. He also replaced a Brezhnev-era holdover as chief international affairs aide with the liberal Chernyaev, followed by an almost wholesale reliance on longtime "new-thinking" analysts and scholars for foreign-policy advice. Conservative concern turned to outrage – "Just how is he deciding defense issues?" fumed General Staff Chief Sergei Akhromeyev – as Gorbachev increasingly ignored the old councils, committees, and advisory groups that had long shaped a status quo, anti-Western foreign policy.

As domestic bureaucratic–ministerial resistance stymied his efforts at economic reform, Gorbachev turned quickly to *glasnost*, unleashing public opinion to add pressure from below for changes blocked from above. Gorbachev and Yakovlev did not limit the new openness to domestic affairs, but encouraged its extension to the most sensitive foreign-policy issues as well. After he had been in office for less than three years, the USSR was in the midst of a radical transformation. Again, skeptics argue that the boldest foreign-policy changes came only later: the landmark Intermediate Range Nuclear Forces Treaty in 1987; deep and unilateral conventional-force cuts a year later; the breaching of the Berlin Wall in 1989; German reunification and the Strategic Arms Reductions Treaty in 1990. And they attribute these breakthroughs to a rapidly declining Soviet economy that supposedly necessitated these sweeping foreign-policy concessions and a broad "global retreat." The bold new debates over global issues, the broad reappraisal of past and present foreign-policy verities, the attack on stubborn anti-Western dogmas – in other words, the public proliferation of new thinking – are largely irrelevant in this interpretation. Making a virtue of necessity, Gorbachev essentially did what any other Soviet leader would have done in his place.

This materialist perspective on the cold war's end fails on several counts. The economic factor is emphasized to the exclusion of ideas and leadership, the real political process is oversimplified to the point of caricature, and the actual alternatives that existed at various junctures simply disappear. Consider the economic downturn that indeed occurred after 1987–8, and that is sometimes credited with inducing Gorbachev's foreign-policy concessions. That downturn was manifestly not the result of pre-1985 trends but instead *the product of Gorbachev's own* attempted reforms; a different leader, pursuing more modest or state-directed "Chinese-style" reforms, together with more modest foreign-policy changes, would surely not have faced anything like the crisis that confronted Gorbachev for at least another ten years. This is an analytic failure, but the materialist-determinist argument suffers from empirical shortcomings as well. The evidence is overwhelming that Gorbachev had "fallen under the new thinkers' spell" very early on and, by 1986–7 at the latest, was already working toward both broad domestic liberalization and international integration of the USSR – to join, as he put it, "the common stream of human civilization."[35] The intense discussions with his "team" of longtime liberal intellectuals, the rejection of "old-thinking" ideas and individuals, together with proclaimed "de-ideologization" of foreign policy, and the preparation of "new-thinking" foreign-policy principles, security doctrine, and concrete negotiating proposals *all preceded* the economic downturn of the late 1980s. Of course, they could not be implemented immediately – the domestic as well as international obstacles were many – but even a superficial examination of the domestic politics of Gorbachev's new thinking reveals that the materialist-determinists have their chronology reversed.

Among the many underappreciated events in the turbulent domestic politics of perestroika, one deserving special attention is the 1986 Chernobyl disaster, the massive explosion and fire at a Ukrainian nuclear-power plant. Many materialist-realist analyses completely omit this episode; those that include it emphasize only the economic impact of Chernobyl as yet another budgetary burden. This neglect is puzzling, for even cursory examination reveals that Chernobyl's impact was primarily political-ideological, not material. The tragedy required a mobilization of an intensity not seen since the Second World War. Even conservatives had to grasp the inadmissibility of even small-scale conflict. The spread of contamination west across the "iron curtain," as well as the eventual outpouring of Western aid to the East, confirmed the "oneness" of the modern world and the necessity of tackling global problems in unity. Gorbachev's intimates recall Chernobyl as a final, powerful push across the new-thinking Rubicon. It transpired in April; in May Gorbachev delivered a withering critique of Soviet foreign policy at a closed meeting of the Foreign Ministry; soon after he also ordered concessions on openness inspections that broke a negotiating deadlock and led to a July agreement on confidence-building measures in Europe. That summer he also demanded a broad revision in Soviet positions in nuclear-arms talks, which led directly to the Reykjavik summit in October that nearly succeeded in achieving a ban on all nuclear weapons; and in November Gorbachev pushed the old-thinking precepts aside with his declaration that "the interests of societal development and all-human values take precedence over the interests of any particular class."[36]

New thinking was much more than a rationalization for an economically mandated global retreat, nor was it merely an innovation in foreign-policy doctrine aimed at easing East–West confrontation. These it may have been at various points for certain individuals, but for its innovators and implementers – Gorbachev and the liberal, pro-Western intelligentsia – it was both the overcoming of deeply ingrained Stalinist precepts about a "hostile capitalist encirclement" and the broad rejection of even earlier beliefs about a culturally or class-based divide between Western and Russian civilizations. It could not triumph under Khrushchev, so powerful were both the ideological and institutional resistance to it. But, thanks to the process he began, the seeds were planted for the gradual emergence of a significant new-thinking intelligentsia that bore fruit under Gorbachev. They were both essential – without a remarkably open-minded and innovative leader, the new thinking would have continued to languish in an essentially conservative society and ossified political system; but without the powerful ideas and persuasive proposals of a new-thinking intelligentsia, Gorbachev would probably have pursued a far more timid foreign policy. The symbiosis of ideas and leadership at a critical historical juncture – and not mere economic–geopolitical pressure – is what brought the cold war to a swift and peaceful end.

Conclusion: The End of New Thinking?

Yet economic forces would apparently assume primary importance in the decade that followed. After the USSR's largely peaceful dissolution, the ensuing decade-long failure of Russia under Boris Yeltsin to achieve stability and prosperity soured many if not most Russians on the new thinking. Was this the inevitable result of cultural forces – a popular psychology that rejected both the individualism-entrepreneurship necessary for a free-market democracy, and the sociopolitical concessions required for a post-imperial Russia's integration with the West? Or was this a more direct response to economic chaos, as well as the growing fragmentation of Russia itself, that grew so severe as to present another historic crisis of state collapse and so encouraged the traditional response of authoritarian state-rebuilding under Putin? If so, was this economic and geopolitical crisis preordained, or instead due to policy and leadership failures – both that of Yeltsin in bungling the post-communist transition, and that of the West for encouraging flawed policies while exploiting Russia's geopolitical weakness?

As argued at the outset, even at the end of the first decade of the twenty-first century, it is still too soon to determine which sort of explanation, and what factors in which measure, have been chiefly responsible for Russia's current alienation from the West. In historic context, however, it is a comparatively mild alienation. Russia's political ties to the West, its global economic integration as well as its relative political openness, and the persistently admiring opinion of the West (if not of all Western states, or their policies) all justify long-term optimism. Still, at the time of this writing, Western (especially American) commentators generally hold that Russia's attempted "Westernization" under Gorbachev–Yeltsin utterly failed and the new thinking is dead. Certainly the setbacks have been many and the disappointment severe. Yet this pessimism may be an overreaction to short-term problems, as well as romantic and unrealizable hopes on both sides of a Russia swiftly transformed in the American image. Putin's "anti-Western" Russia may ultimately prove to be a developmental phase that, far from another prolonged and embittering isolationist era, is instead one of consolidation and rebuilding for ultimately more successful and enduring international, even "new-thinking," partnership and integration. As before, leadership on both sides will be as important as other factors in shaping the outcome.

Notes

1 Robert C. Tucker, "What Time is it in Russia's History?", AAASS presidential address.

2 On this mentality see Stephen Kotkin, "Coercion and Identity: Workers' Lives in Stalin's Showcase City," in Lewis H. Siegelbaum and Ronald Grigor Suny, eds., *Making Workers Soviet: Power, Class, and Identity*, Ithaca, NY: Cornell University Press, 1994, and Gabor Rittersporn, "The Omnipresent Conspiracy: On Soviet Imagery of Politics and Social Relations in the 1930s," in J. Arch Getty and Roberta T. Manning, eds., *Stalinist Terror: New Perspectives*, New York: Cambridge University Press, 1993.

3 The brief memoir of Nina Khrushcheva appears in Aleksei Adzhubei, *Te Desiat' Let*, Moscow, Sovetskaia Rossia, 1989 (citation from p. 45).

4 I. V. Stalin, "O zadachakh khoziastvennikov (rech' fevraliia 1931 g.)" in Stalin, *Sochinennia*, vol. 13, Moscow: Politicheskoi Literatury, 1951, 38.

5 Lev Kopelev, *Ease My Sorrows*, New York: Random House, 1983, 14.

6 Nikita Khrushchev, *Khrushchev Remembers*, Boston: Little, Brown, 1970, 343.

7 Cited in N. S. Leonov, *Likholet' e. Sekretnye missii*, Moscow: Mezhdunarodnye Otnosheniia, 1995, 55.

8 Cited in Stephen F. Cohen, *Rethinking the Soviet Experience: Politics and History Since 1917*, New York, Oxford University Press, 1971, 111.

9 Lyudmila Alexeyeva and Paul Goldberg, *The Thaw Generation: Coming of Age in the Post-Stalin Era*, Boston: Little, Brown, 1990, 83–4.

10 Raisa Orlova, *Memoirs*, New York: Random House, 1983, 227.

11 Mihajlo Mihajlov, *Moscow Summer*, New York: Farrar, Straus & Giroux, 1965, 168.

12 Konstantin Simonov, *Glazami cheloveka moego pokoleniia. Razmyshleniia o I. V. Staline*, Moscow: Novosti, 1990, 124.

13 R. M. Gorbacheva, *Ia nadieius'*, Moscow: Novosti, 1991, 77.

14 Andrei Sakharov, *Memoirs*, New York: Vintage Books, 1990, 127.

15 Arkady Shevchenko, *Breaking with Moscow*, New York: Knopf, 1985, 71.

16 Victor Karyagin, "Recollections of London," *International Affairs* (Moscow), 7 (1992), 83.

17 Fedor Burlatskii, *Vozhdi i Sovetniki. O Khrushcheve, Andropove, i, ne tol'ko o nihk*, Moscow: Politizdat, 1990, 148.

18 Cited in Robert English, *Russia and the Idea of the West: Gorbachev, Intellectuals, and the End of the Cold War*, New York: Columbia University Press, 2000, 72.

19 Chernyaev, who would become Gorbachev's chief foreign-policy aide in 1986, served in Prague in the 1960s alongside many other future new-thinking luminaries: Georgy Arbatov, Oleg Bogomolov , Ivan Frolov, Gennady Gerasimov, Merab Mamardashvili, Georgy Shakhnazarov and Vadim Zagladin.

20 Alexander Yakovlev, *The Fate of Marxism in Russia*,: Yale University Press, 1993, 111.

21 Along with prominent writers Ilya Ehrenburg, Vladimir Dudintsev, and Viktor Nekrasov were the signatures of physics luminaries Igor Tamm, Peter Kapitsa, Lev Artsimovich, and Andrei Sakharov (the "father of the Soviet hydrogen bomb").

22 ISKAN director Arbatov, for example, took in a dozen or so such "disgraced" scholars.

23 Alexeyeva and Goldberg, *The Thaw Generation*, 210.

24 Ibid. 210.

25 A. S. Cherniaev, *Shest' let s Gorbachevym: Po dnevnikovym zapisiam*, Moscow: Progress-Kultura, 1993, 411.

26 English, *Russia and the Idea of the West*, 131–3.

27 Nikolai Shmelev, *Problemy ekonomicheskogo rosta*, Moscow: Nauka, 1970, 75–7. For detail on Shmelev's and others' economic reform proposals, see English, *Russia and the Idea of the West*,. 141–7.

28 Alexander Bessmertnykh, cited in English, *Russia and the Idea of the West*, 150.

29 Vitaly Goldansky, cited in ibid. 150–1.

30 This is cited from an unpublished ISKAN memo of 1969 obtained by the author.

31 *Some Considerations of the Foreign Policy Results of the 1970s*, Jan. 20, 1980, cited in "Afghanistan: As Seen in 1980," *Moscow News*, 30 (1989), 9.

32 Mikhail Gorbachev and Zdenek Mlynar, "Dialog o perestroike, 'Prazhskoi vesne,' i o sotsializme," unpublished MS, fos. 31, 36.

33 Chernaiav, *Shest' let s Gorbachevym*, 9.

34 As Gaidar Aliev, one of the Politburo's centrist members, later recalled: "He didn't turn out to be the man we'd voted for."

35 Mikhail Gorbachev, *The Crimea Article*.

36 Cited in *Literaturnaia Gazeta*, Nov. 5, 1986.

References

Agursky, M. (1987). *The Third Rome: National Bolshevism in the USSR*. Westview Press, Boulder, CO.

Alexeyeva, L., and Goldberg, P. (1990).*The Thaw Generation: Coming of Age in the Post-Stalin Era*. Little, Brown, Boston.

Arbatov, G. (1992). *The System: An Insider's Life in Soviet Politics*. New York Times Books, New York.

Brown, A. (1996). *The Gorbachev Factor*. Oxford University Press, Oxford.

Chernyaev, A. (2000). *My Six Years with Gorbachev*, trans. and ed. Robert English and Elizabeth Tucker. Pennsylvania State University Press, University Park, PA.

Cohen, S. F. (ed). (1984). *An End to Silence: Uncensored Opinion in the Soviet Union, from Roy Medvedev's Underground Magazine Political Diary*. W. W. Norton, New York.

Cohen, S. F. and van den Heuvel, K. (eds.) (1989). *Voices of Glasnost: Interviews with Gorbachev's Reformers*. W.W. Norton, New York.

English, R. (2000). *Russia and the Idea of the West: Gorbachev, Intellectuals, and the End of the Cold War*. Columbia University Press, New York.

Evangelista, M. (1999). *Unarmed Forces: The Transnational Movement to End the Cold War*. Cornell University Press, Ithaca, NY.

Gorbachev, M. (1996). *Memoirs*. Doubleday, New York.

Kagarlitsky, B. (1988). *The Thinking Reed: Intellectuals and the Soviet State From 1917 to the Present*. Verso, London.

Khrushchev, N. (1970). *Khrushchev Remembers*. Little, Brown, Boston.

Palazchenko, P. (1997). *My Six Years with Gorbachev and Shevardnadze: The Memoir of a Soviet Interpreter*. Pennsylvania State University Press, University Park, PA.

Sagdeyev, R. (1995). *The Making of a Soviet Scientist: My Adventures in Nuclear Fusion and Space from Stalin to Star Wars*. John Wiley & Sons, New York.

Shlapentokh, V. (1990). *Soviet Intellectuals and Political Power: The Post-Stalin Era*. Tauris, London.

Wohlforth, W. (ed.) (1996). *Witnesses to the End of the Cold War*. Johns Hopkins University Press, Baltimore.

Zubkova, E. (1998). *Russia after the War: Hopes, Illusions, and Disappointments, 1945–1957*, trans. and ed. Hugh Ragsdale: M. E. Sharpe, Armonk, NY.

Zubok, V. and Pleshakov, C. (1996). *Inside the Kremlin's Cold War: From Stalin to Khrushchev*. Harvard University Press, Cambridge, MA.

Further Reading

Brown, A. (2007). *Seven Years that Changed the World: Perestroika in Perspective*. Oxford University Press, London.

Cohen, S. (1986). *Rethinking the Soviet Experience: Politics and History since 1917*. Oxford University Press, New York.

Gaddis, J. L. (2005). *The Cold War: A New History*. Penguin, New York.

Garthoff, R. (1994). *The Great Transition: American–Soviet Relations and the End of the Cold War*. Brookings Institution, Washington.

Herrmann, R. K. and Lebow, R.N. (eds.) (2004). *Ending the Cold War: Interpretations, Causation, and the Study of International Relations*. Palgrave, Macmillan, New York.

Leffler, M. (2007). *For the Soul of Mankind: The United States, the Soviet Union, and the Cold War*. Hill and Wang, New York.

Matlock, J. F. (1995). *Autopsy on an Empire: The American Ambassador's Account of the Collapse of the Soviet Union*. Random House, New York.

Matlock, J. F. (2004). *Reagan and Gorbachev: How the Cold War Ended*. Random House, New York.

Taubman, W. (2003). *Khrushchev: The Man and his Era*. W. W. Norton, New York.

Yakovlev, A. (1993). *The Fate of Marxism in Russia*. Yale University Press, New Haven.

Zubok, V. (2007). *A Failed Empire: The Soviet Union in the Cold War from Stalin to Gorbachev*. University of North Carolina Press, Chapel Hill, NC.

CHAPTER TWENTY-SIX

The End of the Soviet Union

ROBERT V. DANIELS

The collapse of Communist Party rule in the Soviet Union in 1991, along with dissolution of the bonds among the fifteen Soviet Republics, was clearly one of the epochal moments defining the history of the twentieth century worldwide. It was an event of the same magnitude as the Revolution of 1917, bringing closure to the Soviet era in Russian history. For many participants and observers it was in fact a new revolution; for others, the final stage of a revolution that had been going on ever since 1917. For some, including Librarian of Congress James Billington, it presaged the beginning of a new Time of Troubles, by analogy with Russia's political crisis back at the beginning of the seventeenth century.[1]

In one important respect the Soviet collapse was unprecedented among regime changes of this order. Such a drastic shift in a country's course, such a profound overturn in a country's institutions, has almost always been the result either of a bloody revolt or of military defeat. In the Soviet case, the old regime passed away quite peacefully, more through fatigue, it would seem, than by force. This circumstance makes it especially hard to understand how the end of the Soviet Union came about, and deepens expert disagreement in explaining this extraordinary development. American Ambassador Jack Matlock, privileged to enjoy a ringside seat at the unfolding of perestroika under Mikhail Gorbachev, confessed that he could not understand the demise of such a formidable regime: "How could such a state simply have destroyed itself?"[2]

* * *

At the outset some clarification is in order. The end of the Soviet Union was not a single event but a cascading sequence of developments, involving four distinct transformations, or processes, one might say, all of them quite profound.[3] One such process was the rejection of Communist Party rule together with the sway of the party's official Marxist-Leninist ideology. A second process, intertwined with the first, was the dismantling of the socialist command economy. Third, and most palpable of these processes on the world stage, was Moscow's surrender of its rule over the

non-Russian Union Republics of the USSR, following its relinquishment of hegemony over the nominally independent satellite states in East–Central Europe.
Consequent on the internal crisis in these three areas was Russia's precipitous fall
from the status of a geopolitical superpower that it had enjoyed in the guise of the
Soviet Union.

Each of these processes of transformation proceeded for its own reasons and with
its own chronology, and these distinctive features must be understood in order to
grasp arguments that have come forth to interpret these developments. Nevertheless,
"the Soviet collapse" is reasonable shorthand to embrace all these interconnected
events. Taken together, the changes that put an end to the Soviet Union and its
ruling system extended in time at least from the advent of Mikhail Gorbachev to
power in 1985 through the turmoil of 1991 and on to Boris Yeltsin's suppression of
the old Russian constitution and Supreme Soviet in 1993.

*　*　*

Communist Party rule was not overthrown in the literal sense, nor did it end abruptly.
Its demise began with Gorbachev's installation as Secretary General of the party in
March 1985, with ideas of reform that were still nebulous.[4] He proceeded rapidly to
restaff the upper bureaucracy with younger officials, but he did not immediately
undertake to overhaul the system as such. The following year, however, frustrated
by bureaucratic resistance to his efforts at economic efficiency and shocked by the
officialdom's sluggish response to the Chernobyl nuclear disaster, he determined to
unleash the intelligentsia and the media as a counterweight to the party apparatus,
and launched his campaigns of glasnost (openness) and perestroika (restructuring).[5]

From this point on, political change unfolded rapidly, often beyond the control
of the General Secretary. When Gorbachev undertook early in 1987 to democratize
the selection of officials within the party organization, he was resisted by Communist
conservatives inspired by his own second-in-command, Second Secretary Yegor
Ligachev.[6] Thereupon, to shore up his reform program and his own leadership,
Gorbachev decided to develop a new power base in the civil government.[7] Breathing
new life, as it were, into the long moribund hierarchy of local and central Soviets,
he had himself elected chairman of the Supreme Soviet. At the same time, he removed
the party apparatus at all levels from direct administrative control of economic and
social functions.[8] Some placards appeared on the streets saying, in a clever appeal to
the spirit of 1917, "All power to the soviets!"

In March 1989, pursuant to constitutional changes that Gorbachev persuaded the
party to approve at its special Nineteenth Conference, elections were held to form a
new "Congress of People's Deputies," along with a smaller Supreme Soviet that the
Congress was to choose from among its own members.[9] This was Russia's first at least
partially democratic ballot since the election of the short-lived Constituent Assembly
in November 1917. Next, in February 1990, Gorbachev prevailed on the Central
Committee of the party to surrender its constitutional monopoly of political power.

Meanwhile a democratic movement crystallized both inside and outside the party
under the leadership of Yeltsin, formerly party chief of the city of Moscow until he
fell out with Gorbachev after failing to be promoted to the Politburo in June 1987,
as he might have expected.[10] Following new, more fully democratic elections in

March 1990 in the union republics, Yeltsin became chairman of the Supreme Soviet of the Russian Republic and used this base to challenge Gorbachev's leadership. Nevertheless, Gorbachev forged ahead and had himself installed by the Union Supreme Soviet in the newly created office of president. In July 1990, at the Twenty-Eighth (and last) Party Congress, he effectively decapitated the party by turning the Politburo into a council of union republic chiefs. Yeltsin nevertheless quit the party on the same occasion, in a demonstrative walkout.

Not long afterwards, squeezed between the reformists and the orthodox Communists, and faced with growing troubles in the economy and in relations with the minority republics, Gorbachev temporarily pulled back. In December 1990 he installed Communist conservatives as vice president (Gennady Yanaev), prime minister (Valentin Pavlov), and minister of defense (Dmitri Yazov). However, in the spring and summer of 1991 Gorbachev swung toward reform once again, negotiating a "Union Treaty" with the newly elected leaders of most of the republics and getting the Central Committee of the party (at its last meeting) to adopt a new, expansively democratic program.[11] Yeltsin meanwhile firmed up his own position in June 1991 by getting himself elected to the new post of president of the Russian Federation by popular ballot, a step that Gorbachev did not venture to take in assuming his Union presidency. In the confrontation between the Union and Russian Federation authorities, Moscow became witness to something like the "dual power" of the Provisional Government and the Petrograd Soviet in 1917.[12]

All this was too much for the Communist conservatives (including Gorbachev's recent appointees), who put in motion their infamous "August Putsch," ostensibly to save the USSR.[13] (So completely had the hold of Marxist ideology dissolved, however, that in their manifesto the plotters never mentioned "communism" or even "socialism.") In failing, the conservatives achieved the opposite of their aims, fatally wounding not only Gorbachev but the party's own power and the Union itself. Yeltsin, politically triumphant, banned the Communist Party on the territory of the Russian Republic, and prepared to take control of the Kremlin for himself.[14] Thus, in the course of six years, did the Communist dictatorship commit gradual suicide, though the death throes of the old order did not subside for two years more.

By the time of their takeover, Yeltsin and his supporters had committed themselves to dismantling not only the USSR but the entire Soviet system, economic as well as political. Their moves quickly put them at odds with the legislative branch of the Russian government, the same Supreme Soviet elected in March 1990 that had made Yeltsin its chairman in May of that year and let its building (the "White House") serve as the base for resistance to the August coup. Matters reached the point by early 1993 where the Supreme Soviet actually attempted to impeach the Russian president, but Yeltsin adroitly saved himself by holding and winning a popular referendum, an advisory ballot without legal force but politically compelling nonetheless.[15] Then he struck back at the Supreme Soviet in September by ordering it to be dissolved, though again the move lacked constitutional foundation. The ironic upshot was the siege, shelling, and capture of the same "White House," by military and police forces who readily overcame the resistance of the revived Communists and other diehards supporting the Supreme Soviet's defiance.

Once Yeltsin had prevailed in the "October Days" of 1993, it proved easy for him to dispose of the remnants of the Soviet political system. Preparing a new constitution with a strong presidency, he ordered a referendum on its adoption and the election of a new parliament with the prerevolutionary name "Duma," illogically chosen pursuant to the new constitution, which was only confirmed in the same vote in December 1993. But to compound the irony, the Communists under Gennady Ziuganov and the ultra-nationalists in the self-styled "Liberal Democratic" party of Vladimir Zhirinovsky did so well electorally that they made no issue of the new legal order. Thus did Russia go all the way back to the politics of the post-1905 period, with a personalistic executive and a chaotic legislature, no good augury for a successful "transition to democracy."

*   *   *

What truly did "collapse," not in 1991 but in its wake, were the economies of Russia and most of the other former Soviet republics. Like Moscow's control over the national minorities of the Soviet Union, the socialist command economy had long depended on the force and discipline of the Communist Party apparatus. Dating in its essentials from the Stalin Revolution of the early 1930s, the command economy had been under strain from the outset, as it endeavored to meet simultaneous demands for industrial investment and military prowess, while consumers suffered the constraints of the bureaucratized trade and service sectors. Growth never kept up with needs, and finally this tension prompted Gorbachev and his reformist advisors to reject the "command-administrative system" in favor of decentralizing the economy.

In 1987–8 Gorbachev's government started to move toward the NEP model of "market socialism," relaxing price and wage controls, legalizing small private enterprise (in the guise of "cooperatives"), and freeing state enterprises to finance themselves with their own profits. But demand outpaced supply, shortages mounted, and the state budget fell sharply into deficit. Inflation loomed. Incentives to management failed to offset the loosening of central planning and party authority, and by 1989 economic growth had yielded to actual decline. Radical reformers, including Yeltsin, opted for the free-market solution embodied in the "five hundred days plan" of 1990, while conservatives called for a return to command economics, and Gorbachev vacillated between them.[16] Thus the Soviet Union was "killed . . . by politics, not by economics."[17] But the effect was reciprocal: by the time of the political crisis of 1991 the deterioration of the economy had fatally undermined Gorbachev's popularity.

The momentum of free-market reform helped Yeltsin sweep Gorbachev aside at the end of 1991, and dominated the economic policy of the Russian Republic as it emerged from the dissolution of the Union. In 1992, under the guidance of Yeltsin's deputy Yegor Gaidar, the Russian government abolished central planning and decontrolled almost all prices, only to unleash rapid inflation. Unfortunately, this "shock therapy" proved to be more shock than therapy, many writers assert, even as callous and stupid as Stalin's collectivization of the peasantry, according to Esther Kingston-Mann.[18] Small state enterprises were allowed to be privatized by their managers (and apartments by their tenants), while schemes were undertaken to privatize large enterprises by issuing stock vouchers to their employees. But, in practice, former state assets became concentrated in the hands of a few successful entrepreneurs, the new "oligarchs," while living standards for most of the population collapsed. Only after the financial crisis of 1998 did the economy in its new capitalist form begin to improve.

*   *   *

The patchwork of nationalities that made up the Soviet Union, where Russians constituted only half of the whole population, was of course not a Communist creation, but the legacy of centuries of Russian imperial expansion. The Union was a reincarnation of the Empire, on lines of fictitious federalism in the framework of the Communist dictatorship, and its real ideology (underscored in the manifesto of the August putchists) was Russian imperialism.[19] Conflicts between national separatism and central repression went back to the beginning of the Soviet regime, but were sharpest in the minority areas annexed by Moscow in the course of the Second World War (the Baltic States, independent between the wars, and the Western Ukraine, historically under Poland or Austria and never previously part of Russia). With the advent of political democratization under Gorbachev, national feeling among the minorities was bound to lead to demands for autonomy and independence.[20]

An exciting opportunity for the minorities was the elections of 1989 and 1990, when "popular fronts" defeated the Communist Party candidates in many regions. New governments in the Baltic States and the Transcaucasian republics proclaimed "sovereignty" and, with the encouragement of Yeltsin's government in the Russian Republic, challenged Moscow over their prerogatives. Violent clashes between nationalist demonstrators and the forces of order in many republics poisoned the atmosphere, and Lithuania went so far in the spring of 1990 as to declare its independence. These threats to the integrity of the Union were one of the main reasons for Gorbachev's temporary turn back to the Communist conservatives in the winter of 1990–1. A particularly bad episode was the violent crackdown on nationalist demonstrators in the Lithuanian capital of Vilnius in January 1991, though Gorbachev claimed he had never authorized the action.[21] When he proposed the new Union Treaty in the spring of 1991, it came too late to appease the Baltics and Transcaucasia, but at the same time it was too much for the Communist conservatives.

The August coup erased all real central authority over the minority republics, despite Gorbachev's efforts to save the Union Treaty.[22] The actual dissolution of the Union government came as an anti-climax, when Yeltsin and the new presidents of Ukraine and Belarus (Leonid Kravchuk and Stanislav Shushkevich, respectively) met at Belovezhsk in Belarus in December 1991 to proclaim the USSR at an end, in favor of the nebulous "Commonwealth of Independent States." Gorbachev, having already surrendered most financial and military controls to appease the republics, was rendered powerless, and had no choice but to resign. Yeltsin's Russian government inherited the Kremlin and the central ministries of the Soviet government, as well as the Soviet Union's diplomatic missions and its UN Security Council seat.

While the Yeltsin government maintained that it had won "independence" from the Soviet Union, the Russian state was clearly the successor to the sovereignty of the Union on the territory of the Russian Federation and in international relations. Strictly speaking, the Union did not "collapse." What really took place was the voluntary decolonization of the Russian Empire, resembling Charles de Gaulle's grant of independence to France's African colonies in the 1960s. As Moscow's authority shriveled in the course of Gorbachev's democratizing reforms, the dummy federalism of the USSR came alive, so to speak, on the basis of the existing union republics.[23] By December 1991 some of these had already declared independence, while the rest were automatically left standing when the Union government was dissolved. Boundaries between the republics remained as they had been arbitrarily drawn by the Soviet regime, leaving large numbers of Russians and others as minorities outside their titular republics.

In their internal politics the newly independent republics went in diverse ways. Most democratic were the Baltic states, breathing life into their Soviet-era parliamentary systems, though they were plagued by the problem of absorbing or rejecting the large Russian minorities in their midst. Ukraine maintained a shaky democracy, as did Moldova and Armenia, though along the way it abandoned its hero of 1991, President Kravchuk. The same happened to President Shushkevich of Belarus, though his successor Alexander Lukashenko proved to be a nostalgic Stalinist. Georgia, with its own complex problem of national minorities, saw the most severe turmoil of any republic. Finally, the Muslim republics, Azerbaijan and the Central Asians, remained in the grip of their former Communist bosses, now turned nationalist and relieved of the constraints of a democratizing center. Learning little from the post-1985 Soviet experience, each of the republics reverted to centralism in its approach to its own national minorities, exemplified most harshly by Moscow's forcible efforts to suppress separatism in the region of Chechnya. At the same time, the economic decline affecting all the republics was exacerbated by the rupture of interdependency within what had been the single economic space of the Soviet Union.

*   *   *

As with the internal crises in the Soviet Union after 1985, the collapse of the country's status in international politics was latent in long-standing weaknesses of the Soviet system and even of tsarist Russia before that. Russia had always aspired to an international role greater than its internal resources could support without the discipline of an authoritarian state to sustain its military efforts. Only on this basis had the Soviet Union together with its bloc of satellite governments in Eastern Europe managed up to 1985 to maintain rough parity with the United States and its NATO allies in the global balance of power.

Since the 1970s this parity had been implicitly acknowledged by the United States in accepting détente between the superpowers on the basis of equivalence in nuclear and conventional forces (as codified in 1972 in the Strategic Arms Limitation Treaty (SALT I) and the Anti-Ballistic Missile (ABM) treaty). However, for the Soviet Union military equivalence came at the price of a relatively much greater strain on a less bountiful economy.[24] That stress underlay Gorbachev's push for both political and economic reform, as well as his initiation of steps to temper cold-war superpower competition, moves that were for the most part welcomed and reciprocated by the United States government. Gorbachev formalized his new approach in the doctrine of "The New Thinking," essentially calling off the Marxist-Leninist doctrine of international class struggle.[25] To this extent there is merit in the argument that American firmness and rearmament during President Ronald Reagan's first term pushed the

Soviet Union into initiating reform, though the ultimate Soviet collapse was unanticipated on all sides.

Between 1987 and 1989 two key elements of Soviet international power started to dissolve as a result of Gorbachev's assault on Communist Party discipline and Marxist-Leninist ideological legitimation. One wavering force was the Soviet military establishment, frustrated in Afghanistan, crimped financially, and progressively demoralized.[26] The other slippage was the Soviet hold on Eastern Europe, weakened both by Gorbachev's interest in reformist governments, including Poland and Hungary, and by his unwillingness to use force to prop up the hardline governments in East Germany and Czechoslovakia. The die was cast in November 1989 when the East German government found it had no choice but to open the Berlin Wall and let the process of German reunification begin.[27] Western assurances that Gorbachev thought he had, not to encroach militarily on the former Soviet sphere or to expand the territory of NATO eastward, turned out to be for naught: Soviet power and influence had suffered an irreparable loss.[28]

An even more serious setback to Moscow's position in the world was the loss of all the Union Republics in 1991. Overnight the Russian Empire was shorn of a third of the territory and half the population that had made up its inner power base, setting the country territorially all the way back to its limits before Peter the Great 300 years before. The ephemeral "Commonwealth of Independent States" that Yeltsin and his collaborators proclaimed to take the place of the liquidated Soviet Union proved to be no meaningful substitute; most of the republics could hardly wait for an opportunity to join what was in their minds the Western alliance against Russia (as the Baltic states actually did in 2004).

Russia, in its Soviet guise or not, has never had any real friends in the world. Coercion has been the only instrument that Russian governments have really understood for advancing their interests. Nor did the Yeltsin regime improve matters; its steps to privatize Russia's economy and natural resources abruptly deprived the state of its oil revenues and the ability to sustain its armed forces. With its military deteriorating as the repeated Russian debacles in Chechnya demonstrated, the threat of force even in the "near abroad" of the former Soviet republics would no longer avail. Russia was confined to what Stephen Sestanovich called "the diplomacy of decline."[29]

To sum up, the three policy sectors of government, the economy, and nationality relations, together with the geopolitical status of the USSR, all manifested a similar sequence in the dismantlement of the old Soviet power. At first, in each area, the process was gradual, with the advent of Gorbachev's perestroika and "New Thinking" in 1985–7. Then trouble accelerated, following the democratizing steps of 1989 together with the East European revolutions. Finally came crisis, with the outright rejection of Soviet pretensions and institutions in 1991. But decolonization of the Union Republics and abandonment of the Soviet sphere of influence in Eastern Europe were matters of separation, not collapse. And political reform did not spin out of control until its effects on the nationalities and in the economy caused Gorbachev to start wavering. True collapse came only in the economic sector, and that was after the end of Communist rule.

* * *

For Russian intellectuals in the nineteenth century there were two "accursed questions": "Who is to blame?" and "What is to be done?" Two "accursed questions" about the end of the Soviet Union are: was the Soviet Union "reformable," and why was its end not "predicted."

There is a scholastic ring to the debate over whether the Soviet Union was "reformable." What is meant by "reform"? At what point did the incremental, quantitative change of "reform" turn into the dramatic, qualitative change of "overthrow" or "collapse"?

Everyone agrees, naturally, that Russia before 1985 was a difficult country to reform, and everyone recognizes that by 1991 or 1993 the political face of the country had been totally transformed. The argument reduces to whether intervening events constituted significant reform or mere "tinkering." Skeptics about Russia's reformability, prior to 1991, were sure that real change was impossible; after that date they insisted that the collapse of the Soviet system proved it could not have been reformed. These arguments, says Stephen Cohen, usually assume what they are trying to prove. Cohen is one of those who take the Gorbachev era at its face value, as a successful transformation in Russia's institutions, political, economic, and nationality relations, until the events of 1990–1 and attacks by both Communist conservatives and impatient reformers fatally undermined Gorbachev and his government.[30]

The contention that the Soviet system was inherently unreformable is closely connected with the totalitarian school of interpreting Soviet history as a whole, following from the definition of totalitarianism as a political order that could not be changed except by violent overthrow from within or, more likely, from without.[31] By this reasoning, Gorbachev's attempt to reform and modernize the Soviet order was only a futile effort to save the old system. His fall and the concomitant breakup of the Union are taken as evidence that the system would yield not to gradual change but only to a catastrophic collapse.

It could be maintained, to be sure, that attempts to tinker with the totalitarian system and to soften its rigor would inevitably get out of hand and culminate in the breakdown of the regime. That implies that the totalitarian order was so brittle that it could not withstand the least perturbation. Such a proposition contradicts the original assumption about the regime's might, and is confounded besides by the history of shocks that the Communist dictatorship survived, from the Stalin Revolution through the Second World War and on to the post-Stalin succession and Khrushchev's experiments. What truly did get out of hand under Gorbachev was, first of all, the national minorities' response to democratization, and, second, the economy bereft of party command. Democratization itself did not get out of control but was undermined by nationality fissures and economic distress.

Whether the Soviet collapse was "predicted" or not depends, naturally, on one's understanding of "prediction." No one in the Soviet Union or outside, not even the political actors involved, anticipated the actual course of events in 1991. But no such dramatic event in history has ever been foreseen in all its particulars. On the other hand, the forces pressing for some kind of fundamental change in the Soviet order had long been recognized in Western scholarship, above all the contradiction in the Soviet economy between administrative overcentralization and the complex needs of modern society.[32] Nationality tensions were well understood, above all by specialists in that area.[33] What was not foreseen – or foreseeable – was Gorbachev's attempt to democratize politics, a matter of the historical accidents of personality and events. Similarly the August coup, its failure, and its fateful outcome.

* * *

When they are faced with such a momentous event as the end of the Soviet Union, it is perhaps natural for people to gravitate toward some kind of quick and simple explanation – a single factor – or at least to try to make sense of events in the frame of one primary reason. Such are the schools of thought attributing the Soviets' demise to outside pressure or to the disintegration of their ideological armor. Other approaches, stressing either systemic contradictions or the interplay of dominant personalities, tend to be more nuanced in their recognition of the multiplicity of factors at play.

For Americans, both officials and academics, exhilarated by the triumphalism of "winning" the cold war, it was tempting to see the end of the Soviet Union as a collapse brought on by American military competition.[34] The argument was that the burden on the Soviet economy of the accelerated arms race initiated by the Reagan Administration in the early 1980s drove the Soviet government into experiments in reform leading to the disintegration of the regime. Such reasoning supported the conviction of the totalitarianism school that a system of the Soviet type could be genuinely changed only by foreign pressure. But military competition was not a new challenge for the Soviet economy. Much more severe stresses had been weathered, above all in the war of 1941–5, which Stalin took as the ultimate validation of his system. Even before the war the Soviet regime had become thoroughly militarized in its outlook and priorities, and throughout the cold war it managed to keep up with the West militarily, even though this was at the expense of the civilian sector.

Outside pressure lends itself to the conspiracy thinking common in Russia. Many among the Communists still think the end of the Soviet Union was simply an American plot, engineered by the CIA in league with Gorbachev or, alternatively, with Yeltsin. More serious is the thesis articulated by Stephen Cohen holding that Russia's post-Soviet economic collapse was driven by American example, advice, and inducements for a misplaced free-market ideal.[35]

The ideological interpretation of the Soviet system's demise has been expounded by some Western academics and by the most anti-Communist Russians.[36] In this view, the Soviet Union was driven by a doctrinal Marxist imperative to try to construct a communist utopia, by whatever means necessary, though this quest ran counter to human nature and was bound to fail sooner or later. Marxism-Leninism presumably supplied the *élan vital* for the regime, and, once belief in the doctrine began to erode, therefore, the Soviet order was thought to be doomed. The problem here is that from the early years of the regime Soviet reality began to diverge from Marxist-Leninist ideology. Reinterpreted by political authority, doctrine became more of an excuse than a guide.[37] Once Gorbachev opened the door with glasnost, there was neither the authority nor the reality to sustain belief.

A more materialistic explanation of the system's crisis is based on the theory of modernization, argued notably by Moshe Lewin. In his view, modernization was pushed in Russia with pre-modern methods by a government of "bureaucratic absolutism," an "agrarian despotism."[38] This "developmental state," more like tsarism than socialism aside from its "permanent hypocrisy" of ideology, undermined its own basis, as success corrupted its bureaucratic ruling class and turned them into self-seeking cynics. Thus the Soviet regime sowed the seeds of its own destruction, so to speak. Nevertheless, Lewin thinks, the system did not suffer "incurable pathology," and could have been cleaned up by a man like Andropov, thereby putting Russia on the Chinese path of authoritarian reform.

The impact of modernization was reflected in the demography of the Communist Party leadership. Stalin's purge of the party apparatus in the late 1930s threw guidance of the Soviet ship of state almost entirely to a generation of youthful officials who were under the age of 35 when they first rose to fill the shoes of the purge victims. This cohort of leaders, conservative bureaucrats by experience and outlook, dominated the Soviet system while as a group it grew old in office over the next forty years. Finally, by the 1980s, death and debility opened the way for reform impulses and more modern thinking, such as Gorbachev came to represent.[39]

A variant of the modernization approach is the notion of "transitions to market democracy," or, as it has been debated by political scientists, "transitology" and "consolidology," postulating a natural if not inevitable movement from authoritarian regimes to liberal ones. Developed mainly by Latin Americanists, the theory brackets Soviet developments with the overthrow of right-wing dictatorships in Greece, the Iberian peninsula, and Latin America in the 1970s.[40] Samuel Huntington, in particular, inspired application of the idea to Russian and Eastern Europe, in his book *The Third Wave* (that is, the third wave of democratization after the first wave in northwest Europe and America in the nineteenth century, and the second wave in Central Europe in the aftermath of the Second World War).[41] "The movement toward democracy," Huntington wrote, "seemed to take on the character of an almost irresistible global tide," which ultimately "engulfed the Communist world . . . and decimated dictatorship in the Soviet bloc." Later on in the book, to be sure, he qualified this enthusiasm for the inevitable with admiration for Gorbachev as one of the necessary "political leaders willing to take the risk." Nevertheless, the notion of a natural wave of democratization has something teleological about it, assuming a sort of cosmic pull toward democratic forms of government, and it is burdened, moreover, by the vast difference in historical circumstances between the Soviet Union and its rightist counterparts.[42] This exception is cited by yet another school of writers as a manifestation of Russian "path dependency," tracing the peculiarities of Russia's post-Communist transformation back to certain determining historical turning points, even to the Muscovite autocracy of Ivan the Great in the fifteenth century.[43]

Did the Soviet collapse actually amount to a new Russian revolution? The Russian sociologist Tatiana Zaslavskaya called Gorbachev's reforms a "second socialist revolution," aiming to overthrow the stagnant neo-Stalinist bureaucracy.[44] Russian political scientist Andrei Melville concurred: the aim of this non-violent revolution was "to build an entirely different model of socialism."[45] Reforms accumulating quantitatively turned into the qualitative change of a revolution, as Thomas Remington put it in Hegelian terms.[46]

Gorbachev himself sometimes referred to perestroika as a revolution,[47] and Leon Aron dates the revolution specifically within the Gorbachev era, between 1987 and 1991.[48] The revolution was a war against the bureaucracy, according to Martin

McCauley and Elizabeth Teague,[49] though one would have to say, ironically, that the bureaucracy won, as it converted the socialist patrimony into personal property.[50] Other writers have embraced Yeltsin's breakup of the Soviet regime as the new revolution, sometimes when their commitment to the totalitarian model required them to make this claim because it ruled out any mere "reform" of the old system.[51]

Jerry Hough puts all these events into a connected revolutionary process, starting when the "moderate" Gorbachev broke the organizational and ideological discipline of the old party apparatus and unintentionally paved the way for the "Robespierrist" Yeltsin.[52] The outcome was a sort of "bourgeois" revolution in reverse, driven by the bureaucratic *nomenklatura* as they sought personal enrichment by appropriating state assets. In effect, the Soviet system was overthrown by its own ruling class, even before Yeltsin officially commenced privatizing the Russian economy.[53] That helps explain why this new Russian revolution, if it really was a revolution, was largely non-violent.[54]

The same revolutionary process extended to the nationalists of the Union Republics, mostly Communist officials, who took advantage of Gorbachev's democratizing reforms to assert their *de facto* independence well beforeYeltsin dissolved the Union.[55] The working class, betrayed by the new revolution, would have been better served by Gorbachev's course toward social democracy, the only alternative, in the view of Paul Christensen, to "Russian Peronism."[56]

A variant of the theory of the revolutionary process carries it all the way back to 1917, or even to the Revolution of 1905. In this view, the classic surge from moderate to extremist revolution ended in the Thermidorean reaction of 1921 and a protracted postrevolutionary dictatorship from Stalin's time to Brezhnev's. Ultimately, like England in the Glorious Revolution of 1688, France in the July Revolution of 1830, and Germany with the replacement of the defeated Nazis by the Federal Republic, the exhausted Communist despotism in Russia yielded to reformist efforts to return to the spirit of the original, moderate phase of the revolution.[57] To be sure, this renovation was inordinately delayed by the longevity of the youthful officialdom that Stalin had installed after the purges – the demographic factor – but it was nevertheless predictable in some form.[58]

In the actual event, this "moderate revolutionary revival" was complicated by political struggles among the revivers, distinguished by how far back in the beginnings of the revolution they went to find their reference points. To accept more of the revolution was, so to speak, a Left variant of the moderate revolutionary revival; to go further back, to a less revolutionary starting point, was the Right variant. Thus, Gorbachev rejected the totalitarian economy of Stalinism and then the one-party politics of Leninism, while he clung to the "socialist choice" of the October Revolution, putting him somewhere between the Mensheviks of 1917 and the early Bolsheviks before they suppressed the Constituent Assembly. Yeltsin, by contrast, rejected everything associated with "socialism," jumped back over the Provisional Government and the February Revolution, and landed his time machine in 1906 with the tsarist Duma and Prime Minister Stolypin. Disagreements over Russia's reformability reflect contrasting sympathies for one or the other of these postrevolutionary variants. Gorbachev's innovations seem to validate the reformability view, whereas Yeltsin's triumph in 1991 seems to prove that the old system could not survive so much surgery.

∗   ∗   ∗

As Tolstoy observed in his philosophical epilogue to *War and Peace*, the further one is removed from events, the easier it is to discern (or imagine) in them the operation of higher historical laws. Conversely, the more closely one follows the details of a historic event, the more clearly emerge the role of individual leaders, their clever or mistaken decisions, and sheer historical accident. In the Soviet collapse, the key personages, obviously, were Mikhail Gorbachev, in the first instance, and secondly Boris Yeltsin, though assessments of their respective impacts differ widely. Paradoxically, it was the centralized and authoritarian character of the Soviet system that made the rule of certain individuals decisive, transmitting their will throughout the country's institutional structure. Thus it was that the reformist Gorbachev could have such a quick and compelling impact, and by the same token that the radical Yeltsin could so suddenly break up that same structure.

Gorbachev, by most accounts, was sincere in his aim to reform the Soviet Union, vague though he may have been in the vision that guided him. Ambassador Matlock and many other writers, including Gorbachev himself in his exhaustive memoirs, show that the program of perestroika unfolded largely as Gorbachev responded to the unanticipated situations that his actions precipitated.[59] To begin with, Gorbachev's elevation to the general secretaryship over a bevy of more senior colleagues was a very close decision, although there is some confusion over the exact circumstances of his selection.[60] Had he held more closely to the approach of his mentor Andropov, as some like Stephen Kotkin speculate, he would have minimized the disruption that his reform efforts caused to the Soviet control structure and thereby set the country on the Chinese path of progress,[61] or in Russian terms on the path of a new NEP (and the original NEP was indeed pursued under a firm Communist dictatorship). But in the actual event, Gorbachev's escalating steps to democratize the party apparatus and then to marginalize it broke the key institution that had held the Soviet Union together and made its economy function.

But this weakness might not have been fatal. Archie Brown, the pre-eminent British Sovietologist, contends that Gorbachev was driven by conviction and experience to push political reform, and did so successfully until his efforts were undercut by other individuals with different agendas, the Communist conservatives and putchists on the one hand, and Yeltsin in alliance with the most radical reformers and minority separatists on the other.[62] "Gorbachev . . . was an evolutionary rather than revolutionary by conviction . . . with an extraordinary capacity for learning and adjusting."

Had it not been for Yeltsin's inordinate power drive and his personal feud with Gorbachev, Brown believes, the two working together could have saved the Union and spared the Soviet peoples the catastrophic economic collapse that actually followed the breakup. But Yeltsin was a "demagogue," on a par with Lenin, in the view of Lilia Shevtsova,[63] or "a typical Bolshevik . . . a human engine without brakes," as the writer Vladimir Bukovsky thought on first seeing Yeltsin on television.[64] There is no doubt that, by inflaming the Communist conservatives, Yeltsin's bumptious moralism as boss of the city of Moscow from 1985 to 1987 energized opposition to Gorbachev and contributed indirectly to the 1991 coup attempt. Yeltsin was, according to Dmitri Simes, a man of "arrogant capriciousness," who was "devoid of any meaningful purpose beyond his own political fortunes."[65] Asked why he had not taken more forceful action to deal with Yeltsin, Gorbachev responded: "I should have listened to those who begged me to send Yeltsin as an ambassador to Africa. But I wanted to give a signal of change, to show that even in our country dissenters could stay in politics. With Yeltsin I ended up as a victim of my own principles."[66]

Yeltsin, for his part, has not lacked for defenders, beginning with his own memoir and his quite objective biographer John Morrison.[67] A preponderance of Western, especially Anglo-American, writers supported Yeltsin from the time his break with Gorbachev became known in the fall of 1987, and carried this sympathy forward into the post-Soviet years, though less so after the violent crisis of October 1993.[68] But, in whatever light he is viewed, Yeltsin has to be recognized as a decisive player on a par with Gorbachev.

Other actors have their place as well. Yegor Ligachev sparked conservative resistance to Gorbachev's reforms, though he shrank from the conspiracy of August 1991. KGB chief Vladimir Kriuchkov made bold to engineer that inadvertently fatal blow to the Soviet system. Economic advisors and national minority leaders played decisive roles in their respective realms to push dissolution of the Soviet system. But, as Mark Beissinger observes: "The critical actors who brought about the demise of the Soviet state were themselves transformed by the broader tide of nationalism that swept through Soviet society during these years."[69]

All in all, when the course of events between 1985 and 1993 is tracked closely, the interaction of factors, political, economic, and nationality, as well as the personal element, is hard to dismiss. Political change was initiated by individual leaders, above all Gorbachev and Yeltsin. It was driven faster and faster by the personal animosity between these two. In turn, political changes had a quick impact on the economy and on nationality relations. Unanticipated consequences in these sectors further destabilized the political realm, up to the crisis of 1993. To be sure, recognizing the role of powerful individuals and accidental events injects an element of indeterminacy into history that is often difficult for the human mind to accept. Nevertheless, it is impossible to imagine the outcome in Russia if any of these elements is removed from the equation.

*   *   *

Any writer on such a gripping event as the end of the Soviet Union naturally sees it from his or her personal viewpoint, not to say bias. This makes it all the more difficult, if not impossible, to sum up the pertinent explanations in some sort of overarching synthesis. Perhaps the best that can be done is to extract the main lines of interpretation and consider how they may be reconciled.

The clearest division among explanations is between the appeal to impersonal historical forces, on the one hand, and the far more concrete description of leaders' actions and chance occurrences. In more philosophical terms, this dichotomy exemplifies the familiar historiographical tension between the nomothetic and ideographic methods.[70] What ought to prevail in historical explanation: the elucidation of law-governed forces and sequences of events, or the narrative description of the ungoverned and often accidental interplay of individual actors? The choice naturally reflects the temperament of each historian, with overtones of the eternal theological debate over predestination and free will.

Impersonal forces at work in the Soviet collapse could be classified into two sorts. One type would be the universal circumstances or processes that happened to bear on the Soviet situation, including the forces of modernization and nationalism and the phenomenon of revolution. The other kind of situational explanation references the specific character of the Soviet system and its inherent weaknesses, whether they be seen as ideological or economic or imperial. Ideographic determinants naturally center on key individuals, made all the more decisive by the centralized character of the Soviet system.

In any case, a multi-factor appraisal is ultimately inescapable. Systemic approaches and personalistic approaches must somehow be reconciled, which is not so difficult as it may seem. Between one form of the Soviet-system approach and one version of the role-of-the-individual explanation there is a compelling congruence. This is the contention that the system, intact on the outside while fatally ill internally, required the push of a strategically placed individual – Gorbachev with his reform endeavors – to start it crumbling into ruins. Jack Matlock neatly synthesizes the two philosophies: "Impersonal social and economic trends may have molded the environment in which decisions were made, but it was the decisions made by political leaders that determined the timing and character of events" (Matlock 1995).

*   *   *

The end of the Soviet Union was nearly the ultimate event in explanatory complexity. From the simple accounts of ideological implosion or "defeat" in a metaphorical "cold war," the Soviet collapse came as a concatenation of diverse actions and processes that defies even the most sophisticated causative analysis. It will long be seen not only as a defining point in Russian history but as a lingering challenge for historical interpretation.

As more time elapses after Russia's transformational experience in the years that led up to 1991 and followed it, that upheaval will no doubt continue to be viewed in many different perspectives. Along the lines of Tolstoy's philosophy, the longer-term movements affecting the country, particularly in economics and in the relationships of international power, will probably draw greater attention, while the personal ambitions and conflicts among individual leaders recede from prominence. Yet future historians will still have to wrestle with the intertwining of diverse and distinct processes that all contributed to an extraordinary outcome.

Notes

1   James H. Billington, *Russia Transformed: Breakthrough to Hope* (New York: Free Press, 1992).

2   Jack F. Matlock, Jr., *Autopsy on an Empire: The American Ambassador's Account of the Collapse of the Soviet Union* (New York: Random House, 1995).

3   A comprehensive collection of articles covering the whole Gorbachev era and addressing each of these processes is Alexander Dallin and Gail W. Lapidus, eds., *The Soviet System from Crisis to Collapse* (rev. edn., Boulder, Colo.: Westview Press, 1995).

4   See, e.g., Michael Dobbs, *Down with Big Brother: The Fall of the Soviet Empire* (New York: Knopf, 1997).

5 Robert V. Daniels, "Gorbachev and the Revolution," *New Leader*, Oct. 19, 1987, repr. in Daniels, *Russia's Transformation: Snapshots of a Crumbling System* (Lanham, MD: Rowman & Littlefield, 1998); Walter Laqueur, *The Long Road to Freedom: Russia and Glasnost* (New York: Scribner's, 1989).

6 Yegor Ligachev, *Inside Gorbachev's Kremlin: The Memoirs of Yegor Ligachev* (New York: Pantheon Books, 1993).

7 Stephen White, *Gorbachev and After* (Cambridge: Cambridge University Press, 1991); Robert Sharlet, *Soviet Constitutional Crisis: From De-Stalinization to Disintegration* (Armonk, NY: M. E. Sharpe, 1992).

8 John Miller, *Mikhail Gorbachev and the End of Soviet Power* (New York: St Martin's Press, 1993); Robert J. Osborn, "Phasing out the Party Apparat as Economic Manager," in Alfred J. Rieber and Alvin Z. Rubinstein, eds., *Perestroika at the Crossroads* (Armonk, NY: M. E. Sharpe, 1991).

9 Michael E. Urban, *More Power to the Soviets: The Democratic Revolution in the USSR* (Aldershot and Brookfield, VT: Edward Elgar Publishing, 1990); Giulietto Chiesa with Douglas T. Northrup, *Transition to Democracy: Political Change in the Soviet Union, 1987–1991* (Hanover, NH: University Press of New England, 1993).

10 Robert V. Daniels, "The End of the Revolution?" *New Leader*, Dec. 30, 1991, repr. in Daniels, *Russia's Transformation*.

11 Draft of the Program published in *Pravda*, Aug. 8, 1991; excerpts translated in Robert V. Daniels, ed., *Soviet Communism from Reform to Collapse* (Lexington, MA: D. C. Heath, 1995).

12 Robert V. Daniels, *The End of the Communist Revolution* (London and New York: Routledge, 1993).

13 Martin Sixsmith, *Moscow Coup: The Death of the Soviet System* (New York: Simon & Schuster, 1991).

14 Andrei S. Grachev, *Final Days: The Inside Story of the Collapse of the Soviet Union* (Boulder, CO: Westview Press, 1995); J. L. Black, *Into the Dustbin of History: The USSR from Coup to Commonwealth, August–December 1991* (Gulf Breeze, FL: Academic International Press, 1993).

15 This effect reflected Russians' regard for "legitimacy" ahead of "legality," according to one Russian historian. Vitalii Nilov, personal communication, Nov. 1993.

16 Anders Åslund, *Gorbachev's Struggle for Economic Reform* (Ithaca, NY: Cornell University Press, 1991); Stanislav Shatalin et al., "Man, Freedom, and the Market (Outline of the Program for Changing over to the Market)," *Izvestiya*, Sept. 4, 1990, translated in *The Current Digest of the Soviet Press*, 42: 35.

17 Michael Ellman and Vladimir Kantorovich, eds., *The Destruction of the Soviet Economic System: An Insiders' History* (Armonk, N.Y.: M. E. Sharpe, 1998).

18 Esther Kingston-Mann, *In Search of the True West: Culture, Economics, and Problems of Russian Development* (Princeton: Princeton University Press, 1999).

19 Yitzhak Brudny, *Reinventing Russia: Russian Nationalism and the Soviet State, 1953–1991* (Cambridge, MA: Harvard University Press, 1998).

20 Mark R. Beissinger, *Nationalist Mobilization and the Collapse of the Soviet State* (Cambridge: Cambridge University Press, 2002).

21 Mikhail Gorbachev, *Memoirs* (New York: Doubleday, 1995).

22 Hélène Carrère D'Encausse, *The End of the Soviet Union: The Triumph of the Nations* (New York: HarperCollins, 1993).

23 Robert V. Daniels, "The Limits of Federalism and the Collapse of the USSR," in James E. Hickey, Jr., and Alexej Ugrinsky, eds., *Government Structures in the USA and the Sovereign States of the Former USSR: Power Allocation among Central, Regional, and Local Governments* (Westport, CO.: Greenwood Press, 1996).

24 Johann P. Arnason, *The Future that Failed: Origins and Destinies of the Soviet Model* (New York: Routledge, 1993).

25 M. S. Gorbachev, *Perestroika: New Thinking for our Country and the World* (New York: Harper & Row, 1987).

26 William E. Odom, *The Collapse of the Soviet Military* (New Haven: Yale University Press, 1998).

27 Gale Stokes, *The Walls Came Tumbling Down: The Collapse of Communism in Eastern Europe* (New York and Oxford: Oxford University Press, 1993).

28 Philip Zelikow and Condoleeza Rice, *Germany Unified and Europe Transformed: A Study in Statecraft* (Cambridge, MA: Harvard University Press, 1995; Zelikow, "NATO Expansion Wasn't Ruled Out," *International Herald Tribune*, Aug. 10, 1995. Cf. Matlock, *Autopsy on an Empire*.

29 Quoted in White, *Gorbachev and After*. See Stephen Sestanovich, ed., *Rethinking Russia's National Interests* (Washington: Center for Strategic and International Studies, 1994).

30 Stephen F. Cohen, "Was the Soviet System Reformable?" *Slavic Review*, 63/3 (Fall 2004).

31 Carl J. Friedrich and Zbigniew Brzezinski, *Totalitarian Dictatorship and Autocracy* (Cambridge, MA: Harvard University Press, 1956). A more critical view is Abbott Gleason, *Totalitarianism: The Inner History of the Cold War* (New York: Oxford University Press, 1995).

32 Michael Cox, ed., *Rethinking the Soviet Collapse: Sovietology, the Death of Communism, and the New Russia* (London and New York: Pinter, 1998); Moshe Lewin, *Russia – USSR – Russia: The Drive and Drift of a Superstate* (New York: New Press, 1995).

33 See, e.g., Paul Goble, "Imperial Endgame: Nationality Problems and the Soviet Future," in Harley D. Balzer, ed., *Five Years that Shook the World: Gorbachev's Unfinished Revolution* (Boulder, CO: Westview Press, 1991).

34 See, e.g., Peter Schweitzer, *Victory: The Reagan Administration's Secret Strategy that Hastened the Collapse of the Soviet Union* (New York: Atlantic Monthly Press, 1994).

35 Stephen F. Cohen, *Failed Crusade: America and the Tragedy of Post-Communist Russia* (New York: Norton, 2000).

36 Martin F. Malia, *The Soviet Tragedy* (New York: Free Press, 1994); Walter Laqueur, *The Dream that Failed: Reflections on the Soviet Union* (New York: Oxford University Press, 1994); Alexander Yakovlev, *The Fate of Marxism in Russia* (New Haven: Yale University Press, 1993); Dmitri Volkogonov, *Autopsy for an Empire: The Seven Leaders Who Built the Soviet Regime* (New York: Free Press, 1998).

37 See Robert V. Daniels, "Stalinist Ideology as False Consciousness," in Marcello Flores and Francesca Gori, eds., *Il mito dell'Urss: La cultura occidentale e l'Unione Sovietica* (Milan: Franco Angeli, 1990), repr. in Daniels, *Trotsky, Stalin, and Socialism* (Boulder, CO: Westview Press, 1991).

38 Lewin, *Russia – USSR – Russia*.

39 Robert V. Daniels, "Political Processes and Generational Change," in Archie Brown, ed., *Political Leadership in the Soviet Union* (London: Macmillan, 1989). The generational factor in stagnation and reformability was anticipated by Severyn Bialer in *Stalin's Successors: Leadership, Stability, and Change in the Soviet Union* (Cambridge: Cambridge University Press, 1980), and by Jerry Hough in *Soviet Leadership in Transition* (Washington: Brookings Institution, 1980).

40 Adam Przeworski, *Democracy and the Market: Political and Economic Reforms in Eastern Europe and Latin America* (Cambridge and New York: Cambridge University Press, 1991),

41 Samuel Huntington, *The Third Wave: Democratization in the Late Twentieth Century* (Norman, OK: University of Oklahoma Press, 1991).

42 Philippe C. Schmitter and Terry Karl, "The Conceptual Travels of Transitologists and Consolidologists: How Far East Should They Attempt to Go?" *Slavic Review*, 53/1 (Spring 1994).

43 Stefan Hedlund, *Russian Path Dependence* (London and New York: Routledge, 2005).

44 Tatiana Zaslavskaya, *The Second Socialist Revolution: An Alternative Soviet Strategy* (Bloomington, IN: Indiana University Press, 1990).

45 Andrei Melville and Gail Lapidus, eds., *The Glasnost Papers: Voices on Reform from Moscow* (Boulder, CO: Westview Press, 1990).

46 Thomas Remington, "Reform, Revolution, and Regime Transition," in Gilbert Rozman, ed., *Dismantling Communism: Common Causes and Regional Variation* (Washington: Woodrow Wilson Center Press, 1992).

47 e.g., *Pravda*, Aug. 2, 1986.

48 Leon Aron, *Russia's Revolution: Essays 1989–2006* (Washington: AEI Press, 2007).

49 In Martin McCauley, ed., *Gorbachev and Perestroika* (New York: St Martin's, 1990).

50 Jerry F. Hough, *Democratization and Revolution in the USSR, 1985–1991* (Washington: Brookings Institution, 1997); Steven L. Solnick, *Stealing the State: Control and Collapse in Soviet Institutions* (Cambridge, MA: Harvard University Press, 1998).

51 See, e.g., M. Steven Fish, *Democracy from Scratch: Opposition and Regime in the New Russian Revolution* (Princeton: Princeton University Press, 1995).

52 Jerry F. Hough, *The Logic of Economic Reform in Russia* (Washington: Brookings Institution, 2001).

53 David M. Kotz with Fred Weir, *Revolution from Above: The Demise of the Soviet System* (London and New York: Routledge, 1997).

54 Cf. Stephen Kotkin, *Armageddon Averted: The Soviet Collapse, 1970–2000* (New York: Oxford University Press, 2001).

55 Beissinger, *Nationalist Mobilization*.

56 Paul Christensen, *Russian Workers in Transition: Labor, Management, and the State under Gorbachev and Yeltsin* (De Kalb: Northern Illinois University Press, 1999). See also Elizabeth Teague, "Manual Workers and the Workplace," in David Lane, ed., *Russia in Flux: The Political and Social Consequences of Reform* (Aldershot and Brookfield, VT: Edward Elgar Publishing, 1992).

57 I have advanced this notion in several places, including *The Nature of Communism* (New York: Random House, 1962); "Il risveglio del rivoluzionario russo," *Rinascita* (Rome), Feb. 14. 1987 (English version, "The Revolutionary Legacy," in Robert V. Daniels, *Is Russia Reformable? Change and Resistance from Stalin to Gorbachev*, Boulder, CO: Westview Press, 1988); *The End of the Communist Revolution* (London: Routledge, 1993); and "The Revolutionary Process, the Moderate Revolutionary Revival, and Post-Communist Russia," in Martine Godet, ed., *De Russia et d'ailleurs: Feux croisés sur l'histoire* (Paris: Institut d'Études Slaves, 1995).

58 See Robert V. Daniels, *Russia: The Roots of Confrontation* (Cambridge, MA: Harvard University Press, 1985).

59 Gorbachev, *Memoirs*.

60 See Archie Brown, *The Gorbachev Factor* (Oxford and New York: Oxford University Press, 1997); Daniels, *End of the Communist Revolution*.

61 Kotkin, *Armageddon Averted*; Hough, *Logic of Economic Reform*.

62 Brown, *Gorbachev Factor*.

63 Lilia Shevtsova, *Yeltsin's Russia: Myths and Realities* (Washington: Carnegie Endowment for International Peace, 1999).

64 Quoted in John Morrison, *Boris Yeltsin: From Bolshevik to Democrat* (New York: Dutton, 1991).

65   Dmitri Simes, *After the Collapse: Russia Seeks its Place as a Great Power* (New York: Simon & Schuster, 1999).
66   Interview on Italian television, Mar. 3, 1995, reported in *La Repubblica*, Mar. 4, 1995; recounted in Robert V. Daniels, "Democracy and Federalism in the Former Soviet Union and the Russian Federation," in Peter J. Stavrakis, Joan DeBardeleben, and Larry Black, eds., *Beyond the Monolith: The Emergence of Regionalism in Post-Soviet Russia* (Washington: Woodrow Wilson Center Press, and Baltimore: Johns Hopkins University Press, 1997).
67   Boris Yeltsin, *The Struggle for Russia* (New York: Times Books, 1994); Morrison, *Boris Yeltsin*.
68   See, e.g., Leon Aron, *Yeltsin: A Revolutionary Life* (New York: St Martin's Press, 2000).
69   Beissinger, *Nationalist Mobilization*.
70   See Ernst Cassirer, *The Logic of the Cultural Sciences* (New Haven: Yale University Press, 2000).

References

Åslund, Anders (1991). *Gorbachev's Struggle for Economic Reform*. Cornell University Press, Ithaca, NY.

Beissinger, Mark R. (2002). *Nationalist Mobilization and the Collapse of the Soviet State*. Cambridge University Press, Cambridge.

Billington, James H. (1992). *Russia Transformed: Breakthrough to Hope*. Free Press, New York.

Brown, Archie (1997). *The Gorbachev Factor*. Oxford University Press, Oxford and New York.

Chiesa, Giulietto, with Northrup, Douglas T. (1993). *Transition to Democracy: Political Change in the Soviet Union, 1987–1991*. University Press of New England, Hanover, NH.

Cohen, Stephen F. (2004). "Was the Soviet System Reformable?" *Slavic Review*, 63/3.

Cox, Michael (ed.) (1998). *Rethinking the Soviet Collapse: Sovietology, the Death of Communism, and the New Russia*. Pinter, London and New York.

Dallin, Alexander, and Lapidus, Gail W. (eds.) (1995). Rev. edn. *The Soviet System from Crisis to Collapse*. Westview Press, Boulder, CO.

Daniels, Robert V. (1993). *The End of the Communist Revolution*. Routledge, London and New York.

Daniels, Robert V. (1998). *Russia's Transformation: Snapshots of a Crumbling System*. Rowman & Littlefield, Lanham, M\d.

Daniels, Robert V. (ed.) (1995). *Soviet Communism from Reform to Collapse*. D. C. Heath, Lexington, MA.

Ellman, Michael, and Kantorovich, Vladimir (eds.) (1998). *The Destruction of the Soviet Economic System: An Insiders' History*. M. E. Sharpe, Armonk, NY.

Gorbachev, Mikhail (1995). *Memoirs*. Doubleday, New York.

Gorbachev, M. S. (1987). *Perestroika: New Thinking for our Country and the World*. Harper & Row, New York.

Hough, Jerry F. (1997). *Democratization and Revolution in the USSR, 1985–1991*. Brookings Institution, Washington.

Kotkin, Steven (2001). *Armageddon Averted: The Soviet Collapse, 1970–2000*. Oxford University Press, New York.

Kotz, David M., with Weir, Fred (1997). *Revolution from Above: The Demise of the Soviet System*. Routledge, London and New York.

Lewin, Moshe. (1995). *Russia – USSR – Russia: The Drive and Drift of a Superstate*. New Press, New York.

Matlock, Jack F., Jr. (1995). *Autopsy on an Empire: The American Ambassador's Account of the Collapse of the Soviet Union*. Random House, New York.

Miller, John (1993). *Mikhail Gorbachev and the End of Soviet Power*. St Martin's Press, New York.

Morrison, John (1991). *Boris Yeltsin: From Bolshevik to Democrat*. Dutton, New York.

Odom, William E. (1998). *The Collapse of the Soviet Military*. Yale University Press, New Haven.

Sixsmith, Martin (1991). *Moscow Coup: The Death of the Soviet System*. Simon & Schuster, New York.

Urban, Michael E. (1990). *More Power to the Soviets: The Democratic Revolution in the USSR*. Edward Elgar Publishing, Aldershot and Brookfield, VT.

White, Stephen (1991). *Gorbachev and After*. Cambridge University Press, Cambridge.

Yeltsin, Boris (1994). *The Struggle for Russia*. Times Books, New York.

Further Reading

Beissinger, Mark R. (2002). *Nationalist Mobilization and the Collapse of the Soviet State*. Cambridge University Press, Cambridge.

Brown, Archie (1997). *The Gorbachev Factor*. Oxford University Press, Oxford and New York.

Cohen, Stephen F. (2004). "Was the Soviet System Reformable?" *Slavic Review*, 63/3.

Cox, Michael (ed.) (1998). *Rethinking the Soviet Collapse: Sovietology, the Death of Communism, and the New Russia*. Pinter, London and New York.

Dallin, Alexander, and Lapidus, Gail W. (eds.) (1995). Rev. edn. *The Soviet System from Crisis to Collapse*. Westview Press, Boulder, CO.

Daniels, Robert V. (1993). *The End of the Communist Revolution*. Routledge, London and New York.

Daniels, Robert V. (ed.) (1995). *Soviet Communism from Reform to Collapse*. D. C. Heath, Lexington, MA.

Ellman, Michael, and Kantorovich, Vladimir (eds.) (1992). *The Disintegration of the Soviet Economic System*. Routledge, London and New York.

Goldman, Marshall I. (1991). *What Went Wrong with Perestroika*. Norton, New York.

Gorbachev, Mikhail (1995). *Memoirs*. New York: Doubleday, 1995.

Hough, Jerry F. (1997). *Democratization and Revolution in the USSR, 1985–1991*. Brookings Institution, Washington.

Kotkin, Stephen (2001). *Armageddon Averted: The Soviet Collapse, 1970–2000*. Oxford University Press, New York.

Kotz, David M., with Weir, Fred (1997). *Revolution from Above: The Demise of the Soviet System*. Routledge, London and New York.

Lewin, Moshe (1995). *Russia – USSR – Russia: The Drive and Drift of a Superstate*. New Press, New York.

Matlock, Jack F., Jr. (1995). *Autopsy on an Empire: The American Ambassador's Account of the Collapse of the Soviet Union*. Random House, New York.

Morrison, John (1991). *Boris Yeltsin: From Bolshevik to Democrat*. Dutton, New York.

White, Stephen (1993). *Gorbachev and After*. Cambridge University Press, Cambridge.

PART V

Whither Russia?

CHAPTER TWENTY-SEVEN

Russia's Post-Soviet Upheaval

BRUCE PARROTT

Since 1991, observers have characterized the upheaval in post-Soviet Russia in many different ways. Some have viewed it as a dramatic breakthrough to democracy and free-market capitalism. Others have regarded it as a chaotic prologue to the reassertion of autocratic power and economic domination by the state. Still others have regarded the direction of change as a variable that would be shaped decisively by the choices of the major actors in Russia's unfolding political drama. Influenced by these diverse outlooks, historically minded observers have drawn parallels with contrasting reformist or autocratic strands of the tsarist and Soviet past.

Given the circumstances, this diversity of views is no surprise. The period since the collapse of the USSR has been one of tremendous political and economic turmoil. Although the same can be said of several other eras in Russian history, writing about such an upheaval while it is still under way poses special intellectual difficulties. For scholars, simply chronicling the torrent of post-Soviet events has been a daunting task. Moreover, because the long-term consequences of the upheaval are still uncertain, scholars cannot be sure which of its contradictory features to put at the center of their accounts. In addition, scholarly interchanges about Russia have commonly occurred against a backdrop of intense public debates over government policy, and the spillover from these policy debates has sometimes shaped the interpretation of scholarly views by laypersons and specialists alike.

Underlying the numerous disagreements about post-Soviet Russia is the perennial theme of historical continuity versus discontinuity. Should the tidal wave of events since the late 1980s be called a revolution, a transition, or a counterrevolution? Which elements of the Soviet past have survived the dissolution of the USSR, and which have not? More specifically, to what extent have attempted changes in governmental and economic institutions altered the behavior of political and social actors? To what degree have groups established during the Soviet era – especially privileged groups – survived, and how has their conduct affected the operation of these new institutions? Not least important, to what extent have past cultural ideas and expectations persisted and shaped the recent behavior of elites and ordinary citizens? This chapter aims to shed some light on these questions, though certainly not to resolve them.

Russian President Boris Yeltsin and many of his backers took power with the avowed objective of transforming Soviet Russia along liberal Western lines. As explained in the sections below, success in this monumental undertaking required a series of fundamental changes: the consolidation of a new Russian state in the geographical heart of the former USSR; the creation of democratic political institutions; the development of a capitalist economy; the construction of an effective system of public administration; and the active political involvement of the citizenry. This huge political agenda was bound to generate many political conflicts and many unanticipated consequences. It opened the latest chapter in the recurring Russian struggle over whether Russia should be Westernized or follow its own distinctive path of development.

Key Turning Points

Before discussing the types of changes mentioned above, a few important turning points in post-Soviet Russia's first fifteen years should be mentioned. Perhaps the most significant was the rapid disintegration of the USSR in 1990–1. Untouched by the destructive turbulence of mass violence or civil war, the Soviet Union's seemingly mighty state structure quickly collapsed. The speed of the collapse generated a widespread sense that Russia had entered a period of historical malleability that would allow new political and economic institutions to be put into place with little reference to those of the Soviet past. In the independent Russian state that emerged under Boris Yeltsin's leadership, the Communist Party was temporarily banned, and a program of radical economic reform known as "shock therapy" was enacted.

The violent clash between Yeltsin and his critics in the Russian parliament in the autumn of 1993 was another turning point. Locked in an increasingly hostile deadlock with the critics, Yeltsin finally dissolved the parliament and used the army to crush those who resisted. One consequence of this confrontation was the adoption of a new Russian constitution that assigned a wide array of government prerogatives to the presidency at the expense of the legislature. The new constitution also relegated the Constitutional Court to a subordinate political role. This constitutional dispensation created a potential for the concentration of autocratic power in the presidency.

The presidential election of 1996 marked a third turning point. By the end of 1995 the severe economic hardships resulting from shock therapy made it seem certain that Yeltsin would be defeated in the impending ballot, possibly by the leader of the refurbished Communist Party of the Russian Federation (CPRF). Yeltsin seriously considered postponing the election, but in the end a group of new business magnates who had acquired great wealth from the first phase of economic reform rallied behind him, enabling him to mount an effective campaign and win a second presidential term. The election was arguably the apogee of the post-Soviet struggle for democratization.

The presidential succession in 1999–2000 was a fourth turning-point. At the end of 1999 Yeltsin unexpectedly resigned a few months before the end of his term to smooth the way for Vladimir Putin, the politically inexperienced prime minister who had spent most of his career in the Soviet security service, to become his successor.

Feverish maneuvering before the election allowed the Kremlin to boost Putin's public popularity and frighten off some better-known candidates who might have prosecuted Yeltsin and his close associates for corruption. Exploiting the public atmosphere of emergency triggered by terrorist bombings inside Russia, Putin easily defeated the candidates who remained in the presidential race.

Yet another turning point was the Kremlin assault on Mikhail Khodorkovsky and his Yukos Corporation in 2003–5. Foreshadowed by Putin's earlier moves against other politically assertive tycoons, the government's systematic destruction of Yukos, Russia's biggest and best-run oil company, recast the relationship between wealth and power. It signified the ascendancy of government officials determined to re-establish the dominance of the Russian state, and it foreshadowed further reductions of electoral competition and freedom in the political arena. These changes were manifested in Putin's preordained re-election in 2004.

National Identity and the Legacy of State Disintegration

The dynamics of the USSR's disintegration shaped the struggles over reform in post-Soviet Russia. Generally speaking, major disagreements about the essential characteristics of a nation severely complicate attempts to democratize its political institutions. Disagreements about who belongs to the nation cannot be resolved through democratic procedures invoked in the name of self-determination, because the procedures themselves require prior agreement about which persons are entitled to participate in democratic decision-making by virtue of their membership in the national community. Rather than issue from formal procedures, a durable consensus on national identity emerges from historical processes of political struggle and cultural contention that typically span decades or centuries.

The breakup of the USSR raised unsettling questions about Russia's national identity, territorial boundaries, and political structure. The aura of uncertainty was lessened somewhat by the fact that Russia had been the largest constituent republic of the Soviet Union. Provisional Russian administrative boundaries and a set of rudimentary political institutions already existed, and Yeltsin and his allies used these institutions as levers to expand their power on the eve of the Soviet collapse. Still, independent Russia's emergence from a larger state hampered the construction of a new political order.

One key problem was whether to "unmix" the populations of the post-Soviet states – and if so, how. A large number of ethnic Russians lived in other former Soviet republics, and a considerable number of non-ethnic Russians now linked by ethnicity to their "own" independent homeland-states (such as Ukraine or Georgia) lived in Russia. Should all these people be made citizens of their nominal homeland-state and "return" to it, even if they had always lived elsewhere? Like most other former republics, Russia dealt with this problem by offering citizenship to all its residents (as well as to the residents of other republics who requested it). However, Latvia and Estonia, two former Soviet republics that strongly distrusted Moscow, refused to follow suit by giving citizenship to all their ethnic Russian inhabitants. Instead, they established stringent criteria for naturalization to emphasize that they had been forcibly incorporated into the USSR under Stalin and to fend off any new efforts by Moscow to control them through the local ethnic Russian population. This helped make the treatment of the Russian diaspora in neighboring countries a neuralgic issue in Russian political life.

The political and ethnic dynamics of the Soviet breakup also generated powerful centrifugal forces inside Russia. A good deal of the profound public disorder that plagued the country during the 1990s may have been unavoidable. But it was undoubtedly intensified by the all-out political duel between Gorbachev and Yeltsin during the Soviet Union's final eighteen months. Just as Yeltsin attempted to split Gorbachev's political base by backing the constitutional claims of other constituent republics against the Soviet central government, Gorbachev attempted to fracture Yeltsin's political base by backing the demands of regional governments inside Russia against the government of the Russian republic. On a legislative level, this political warfare produced a wave of contradictory federal and Russian legislation commonly known as the "war of laws." Moreover, Yeltsin heightened the disorder inside the Russian republic by striving to make it economically ungovernable for Gorbachev's central government.

The centrifugal effects of the bitter rivalry between Gorbachev and Yeltsin were especially troubling because of Russia's internal political structure. Russia itself was a federation consisting partly of regional units that were the nominal homelands of ethnic minorities such as the Tatars, and, in the wake of the Soviet breakup, many Russians feared that it might disintegrate, just as the USSR had done. The fear of disintegration helps explain why Moscow waged two highly destructive local wars to prevent Chechnya, a small territory in Russia's southwest populated primarily by the Chechen ethnic minority, from becoming independent. The sustained brutality of Moscow's security forces in Chechnya was paralleled by numerous acts of terrorism committed by Chechen insurgents in southern Russia and in Moscow.

Constitutional Powers and Political Practices

Constructing reliable political institutions on these shifting national-territorial foundations proved difficult. Although Gorbachev introduced media freedoms and contested elections as part of his campaign to democratize the Soviet system, the battle over reform produced a tangle of governmental structures that lacked a solid constitutional basis, and Russia's achievement of independence sharpened the contradictions among its own government bodies. According to Russia's Soviet-era constitution, its government was parliamentary in form. However, as part of his battle against Gorbachev, Yeltsin had established a new Russian presidency and had won the ensuing popular vote. When the USSR broke up shortly afterward, independent Russia emerged as a clumsy political hybrid. The parliamentary powers ordained by the constitution conflicted with the powers wielded by the president. Constitutional inconsistencies that had been inconsequential during the Soviet era became far more significant after the collapse of the Soviet state.

During the brief surge of national enthusiasm following the failed conservative coup and Russia's achievement of independence, the parliament authorized Yeltsin to make a wide range of decisions by presidential decree, but tensions quickly escalated as he and his parliamentary critics clashed over drafts of a new constitution and the mounting human cost of shock therapy. Convinced that Yeltsin was destroying the economy, these critics resorted to increasingly confrontational tactics, including a serious threat to impeach the president. Yeltsin finally acted to dissolve the parliament; many of his parliamentary opponents barricaded themselves inside the parliament building and designated their own national president and minister of defense. Yeltsin ended the stand-off by ordering the military to shell the building and arrest the occupants. Although he later reversed his promise to hold early presidential elections as part of a crisis settlement, suspicions that he harbored dictatorial ambitions were somewhat allayed by his decision to conduct early balloting for a new parliament and ratification of his proposed constitution.

Scholars agree that the 1993 crisis had a major impact on Russia's short-term political development, but they differ over how deleterious the longer-term effects turned out to be. Viewing the crisis as the decisive moment in post-Soviet history, some have argued that Russia's first eighteen months of independence represented a lost democratic opportunity whose violent termination set the country firmly on the path toward authoritarian rule [1]. Recognizing the crisis as a major setback, others have argued that it did not negate the possibility of further democratic development [2].

In any case, the constitutional system that emerged from Yeltsin's victory over parliament gave excessive power to the president. Under the new constitution, the parliament lacked the authority to approve the president's selection of ministers for the government cabinet; it could reject his nominee for prime minister, but if it did so three times consecutively he could dismiss the parliament and call new elections. This situation made it very difficult for the legislature to exercise effective supervision over government agencies, since the prime minister and cabinet members were beholden for their posts to the president rather than to the parliament. With one brief exception, none of the prime ministers Yeltsin appointed during his eight years as president came from the party with the largest representation in the parliament.

Creating a judicial branch that could apply the laws fairly proved equally difficult. After the 1993 crisis, the Constitutional Court, although not indifferent to the legal rights of citizens, generally refrained from attempting to resolve jurisdictional conflicts between the presidency and the parliament or between the central and regional governments. Courts at the lower levels of the system were still imbued with the dismissive Soviet attitude toward the rights of individuals and were susceptible to pressures from government prosecutors. Well positioned to block the appointment of judges they regarded as unfriendly, many prosecutors were accustomed to ignoring statutory safeguards and exempting law-breakers who had political clout.

Although Russia held national parliamentary and presidential elections at regular intervals after 1993, the conduct of these elections frequently fell short of being certifiably democratic. For the most part, the inadequate provisions for cumulating and checking vote totals made the electoral process opaque and gave rise to doubts that could not be resolved. In a number of instances, however, evidence of systematic electoral fraud came to light. Such fraudulent conduct occurred not only in regional elections but also in national elections for the parliament and the presidency [3: 31–2].

Strong political cross-currents were visible in the presidential election of 1996. On the eve of the campaign, Yeltsin's rock-bottom public-approval ratings seemed to guarantee that he would lose, probably to the head of the CPRF. Confronted with this prospect, Yeltsin prepared to declare a state of emergency and postpone the election, and some oligarchs signaled that they would back this step. Significantly, Yeltsin's presidential campaign committee included the head of the Federal Security Service (FSB), the main institutional successor of the Soviet Committee for State Security (KGB), and the chief of the Presidential Security Service, which also possessed substantial coercive and intelligence-gathering capabilities [4: 14–16]. The chief of the presidential service, a long-time Yeltsin confidant, insisted that the election be postponed, and only after he had lost a struggle with other campaign advisors did Yeltsin decide to hold it on time.

Judged in terms of one key standard, the election marked the democratic high point of Russia's long political history. The intensity of contestation among the candidates and the closeness of the vote totals were unprecedented [5]. But the electoral process from which Yeltsin emerged victorious also exhibited serious flaws. The media, dominated by a handful of new business magnates single-mindedly committed to the president's re-election and journalists with a strong aversion to communism, devoted disproportionately large coverage to the Yeltsin campaign and very little to that of his Communist opponent. Moreover, the media failed to reveal that between the two rounds of voting Yeltsin suffered a heart attack that raised fundamental questions about his capacity to carry out the duties of the presidency.

Four years later the transfer of presidential power from Yeltsin to Putin was marred by much more serious political machinations. In parliamentary elections held shortly before the presidential ballot was slated to occur, government-owned media outlets launched vicious personal attacks on the two prospective presidential candidates who had the best chances of winning the office. Deterred by their shrinking public-approval ratings, these two candidates ultimately decided not to run, although the CPRF candidate and a few other nationally known politicians remained in the race. Yeltsin then resigned several months early, paving the way for Prime Minister Putin, the political newcomer he had chosen as his successor, to become acting president and defeat this less threatening field of opponents in early balloting. During the abbreviated electoral contest Putin did not deign to offer a campaign platform; his victory was already virtually assured. After taking office, his first public act was to issue a decree granting Yeltsin, as a former president, immunity from arrest, prosecution, and interrogation.

The presidential ballot of 2004 marked the post-Soviet low for elections to the office. Because of the Kremlin's tight control over the major media, Putin's high public-approval ratings, and the possibility of incurring personal retaliation, no national politician with a significant political following was willing to enter the race. Instead, Putin faced a small group of second-rank candidates who lacked any chance of defeating him. He won in a landslide, racking up more than 70 percent of the vote.

In addition to fair elections, democratization required a system of political parties that would enable the electorate to hold government leaders responsible for the government's conduct. Russian parties, however, made little contribution to this objective. For the first dozen post-communist years they were weak and, with a few exceptions, transitory. The most important exception was the CPRF, which inherited the diehard adherents who had remained members of the Communist Party of the Soviet Union (CPSU) until it was banned. Many other parties sprang up or disappeared, dividing and combining with new political factions, making it nearly impossible for voters to hold party politicians responsible for government actions. Except for the CPRF, most parties remained centered in Moscow and lacked solid regional roots [6]. In the 2003 parliamentary election, United Russia, a new umbrella party, parlayed slightly less than two-fifths of the party-list vote into control of more than two-thirds of the seats in the lower house. This outcome greatly strengthened Putin's control of the legislature, and it sharpened the appetite of senior officials within the presidential administration to make United Russia a permanent ruling party. During this period, however, party links between the top of the political system and politics at the regional and grass-roots levels actually became weaker [7: 90]. Most presidential candidates, including Yeltsin and Putin, did not run on a party ticket, and powerful interests often found lobbying or bribing bureaucrats and the media more effective than working through legislative parties. At the local level, party formation was hampered by a general public aversion to organizational membership owing to unpleasant past experiences with the intrusiveness of local CPSU activists.

Building Capitalism through Shock Therapy

Because the government had controlled all enterprises as part of a centrally administered command economy, building capitalism required that reformers carry out three broad types of change: market liberalization (paring back government intervention in activities like price-setting and distribution); financial stabilization (cutting government budgets and limiting the money supply to prevent hyperinflation); and privatization (transferring most state-owned enterprises to private owners). Spurred by a sense of crisis, the Yeltsin government tried to introduce all these reforms in a single "big bang."

The attempt to introduce shock therapy generated fierce debates inside Russia and equally intense debates among Western observers and advisors. Advocates believed that political democratization gave reformers a brief window of opportunity to introduce sweeping reforms, that market-friendly institutions would crystallize once the reform program had been enacted, and that drastic change in the economic system would actually reduce the burden on society over the medium and long terms [8]. Opponents argued that shock therapy was a type of radical social engineering akin to what the Bolsheviks had attempted decades before, that it would impose unacceptable human costs, and that enacting it without widespread social involvement would trigger an authoritarian popular backlash against democratization as well as economic reform [9].

The actual outcome fell midway between these forecasts. Economically, attempts to implement shock therapy turned out to be far more difficult and painful than the proponents had anticipated. Politically, the short-term effects were less damaging to electoral democratization than many opponents had feared. Nonetheless, shock therapy did badly damage Russia's long-term prospects for democratization in ways that became clearer over time.

Some reformers tried to ensure that privatization would give ordinary Russians a stake in economic change, but with little effect. The volume of lucrative economic resources waiting to be privatized was vast, and there was no tested body of law and administrative procedure to regulate the scramble for ownership. With economic stakes like these on the block, Russia's shaky governmental structures came under tremendous pressure. To capture these large new sources of wealth, ambitious individuals had compelling motives to manipulate the loose government privatization guidelines and subvert existing legal processes. The result was an enormous increase of economic inequality. By 2005 Russia ranked fourth worldwide in the number of billionaires, all of them created in no more than a decade and a half.

The Russian elite that emerged during the 1990s was an amalgam of the old and the new. Members of the *nomenklatura*, the group of highly placed officials in the communist era, used their inside connections to obtain new governmental posts and the lion's share of many economic resources [10]. Perhaps the best example is Viktor Chernomyrdin, a former Soviet oil and gas official who accumulated enormous wealth for himself and his family while serving as prime minister during the 1990s. On the other hand, the *nomenklatura* did not survive completely unscathed or unchallenged. Having gone soft in the final Soviet decades, some of its members failed to adapt to the fierce new forms of political and economic struggle and experienced downward social mobility. Moreover, the ranks of the new rich included other ambitious individuals who had risen from positions on the fringes of Soviet society. In a pattern somewhat reminiscent of the tsarist era, this latter group of "upstart" oligarchs contained a disproportionate number of persons from non-ethnic Russian backgrounds [11: 123–5].

The struggle to acquire new sources of wealth was vicious and sometimes deadly. Criminal gangs quickly entered the arena, and disputes over money and property often ended in violence. In the "mob war" of the early 1990s, dozens of bankers were murdered, primarily in Moscow [12: 21, 31–2]. Even the long-term winners in this struggle were at risk. In 1993 Boris Berezovsky, whose ruthlessness and ties with organized crime later enabled him to become extremely powerful, fled to Israel for several months to escape physical threats; and, after his return to Russia, he was nearly killed by a car bomb detonated by his rivals for control of the bourgeoning automobile market.

Faced with such dangers, the oligarchs sought to protect themselves by creating their own security forces. The Yeltsin government's continuing fiscal crisis led to drastic reductions in the budgets of the military and the security police and to large layoffs of personnel. The oligarchs exploited this situation, using their new wealth to hire individuals talented in the arts of intelligence gathering and physical coercion. An especially striking example was the holding company founded by Vladimir Gusinsky, a rising media magnate during the early Yeltsin years. To protect its interests and enforce its business agreements, Gusinsky's company set up a 1,000-man private security force headed by Filip Bobkov, a former deputy chairman of the KGB who had directed the KGB department charged with monitoring and persecuting dissenters critical of the Soviet regime. Many free-standing private security companies were founded by former government officials with similar backgrounds [13: 77, 133].

During the Yeltsin era security was much easier for tycoons to buy than for entrepreneurs of modest means. In the first two or three years of economic reform many new businesses were begun from scratch. Soon, however, the reported growth in the number of small businesses flattened out. One explanation was a surge in the activities of organized crime, which viewed small businesses as inviting targets for the extortion of "protection" payments. Perhaps even more important was the spread of predatory behavior among government officials, who used their positions to squeeze bribes out of small business owners in exchange for allowing them to operate. To reduce such harassment, many small entrepreneurs switched their activities to the underground economy, but much of the reported slowdown in creating new businesses was undoubtedly real.

The obstacles to the growth of small business had political as well as economic implications. In most countries, small-business owners are an economic mainstay of the middle class. In post-Soviet Russia, the middle class grew, but it contained disproportionately large numbers of white-collar workers employed at various levels of government. Some evidence suggests that, in Russia, small enterprise owners were the business group most favorably disposed toward the election of political leaders and the rule of law [14]. By contrast, white-collar government employees lacked independent sources of legitimate income but had plentiful opportunities for graft that predisposed them against reform. The thwarted development of the small business sector therefore narrowed the social foundation for the growth of democracy.

Western scholars differed over the implications of these trends for the future. Some close observers believed that the forces of economic competition and elite self-interest would gradually lead to a less predatory type of capitalism, much as these factors had gradually transformed the nineteenth-century American robber barons into a more responsible capitalist class [15, 13]. Viewed from this angle, privatization was a discrete stage in Russia's development, and the richest businesspeople and a late-developing middle class would ultimately join forces to curb state power and protect their property rights. By contrast, other observers believed that "crony capitalism" had struck deep roots that made the stabilization of private property rights unlikely. In this view, the long-standing political and economic hegemony of the Russian state made a shift to temperate politics and a clear demarcation between the state and the economy improbable [16: 1–10].

Under Putin the forms of elite competition over property changed significantly. By comparison with the mid-1990s, the use of physical violence to settle business disputes declined. However, this did not signify that Russian business practices were converging with those of the advanced capitalist countries. By undermining some oligarchs, the severe financial crisis of 1998 opened a new round of struggle in which aggressive new entrants manipulated bankruptcy laws and local "pocket" jurisdictions to seize holdings from their financially depleted competitors. In other words, a harsh struggle among business magnates continued even after a large volume of property had been transferred from the state into private hands. This raised fundamental questions. Rather than simply whet the tycoons' appetites for amassing assets, could privatization awaken their interest in productive entrepreneurship? And could government reformers facilitate such a shift by strengthening the curbs on illicit economic activities? Although the answers remained unclear, in 2006 the gangland-style murder of the deputy chairman of the Russian Central Bank, who had campaigned to reduce corruption in commercial banking, reinforced doubts that reformers could tame the all-out struggle for economic advantage.

Federalism and Public Administration

Successful democratization and marketization both depended on basic changes in the operation of Russian government agencies. To make a transition to capitalist democracy, these agencies had to sacrifice many previous powers associated with the centralized control of society while taking on many new tasks associated with the operation of a market economy. Russian bureaucrats frequently had a strong incentive to cling to their old prerogatives, especially when these could be used to extract bribes. Moreover, they often lacked the capacity to fulfill their new responsibilities because of a shortage of necessary technical skills or guidance from up-to-date laws. The struggle to reconstruct the territorial state compounded the difficulty of ensuring effective public administration.

The Russian government's attempts to collect taxes and balance the state budget are a case in point. During the final stage of Yeltsin's duel with Gorbachev, the government of the Russian republic conducted economic warfare against the Soviet central government for control of fiscal resources and industrial enterprises. The goal was to paralyze the central government by persuading Russian banks and regional administrations to refuse to make their regular tax payments into the federal budget while continuing to draw their regular federal subsidies from the budget. In addition, the Yeltsin camp attacked the central government's control over enterprises situated in Russia by offering the enterprise directors lower tax rates and bigger subsidies if they would switch their allegiance to Yeltsin. One effect of this gambit was to teach regional administrators and economic managers that they could avoid or reduce tax burdens by negotiating with higher-level overseers and playing them off against each other [17: 64–6]. This lesson later contributed to the plunge in the Russian government's own tax receipts, which dropped from about one-sixth of GDP in 1992 to less than one-tenth of GDP in 1996.

Russia's problems with public administration were intensified by the challenge of building an effective federal system that could govern the country's far-flung regions. Like the USSR, Soviet Russia had been a federation in name but a unitary state in fact. Even without the rest of the USSR, the territory of the Russian Federation still encompassed eleven time zones, and Moscow was accustomed to dealing with this vast domain through centralized means. During the 1990s, however, the political free-for-all at the center allowed for a large dispersion of political and economic authority that benefited many of the regions. Playing on divisions and disorganization inside the central government, the most assertive and well-endowed regions managed to wrest a great deal of power from Moscow and often ignored its wishes.

Although some regions still relied on budget subsidies from Moscow, the Yeltsin government was equally in need of active support from the regions. Above all, it needed regional governments to use their so-called administrative resources to mobilize and channel the pro-Yeltsin vote during the hard-fought presidential race of 1996. This factor shaped the reallocation of power between the central and regional governments. The specific distribution of power between Moscow and individual regions was decided through log-rolling and bilateral deals whose terms were usually not divulged. As a result, Russia lacked a coherent national pattern of center–region relations worked out through public discussion and legislative action – one of the main features of a genuine federation [18]. These circumstances spawned many legal and policy conflicts between the federal and regional governments. Near the close of Yeltsin's presidency one analysis found that roughly a quarter of regional laws and regulations were incompatible with the federal constitution [19].

Putin worked hard to eliminate such inconsistencies and claw back power for the central government. His steady consolidation of power in the presidency made it harder for the regions to win concessions from Moscow by playing political contenders off against each other, especially during elections. Shortly after taking office, he established seven administrative "super regions" headed by presidential appointees. The leader of each super region was supposed to oversee about a dozen regional governments and ensure that their policies meshed with those promulgated in Moscow. Putin also attempted to promote civil-service reform and streamline the central government bureaucracy.

Although these steps reduced the contradictions between regional and federal laws, the numerous inconsistencies persisted, and dysfunctional behavior by government bureaucracies remained widespread. This is probably one reason why in 2004–5 Putin pushed through federal legislation replacing the popular election of regional executives with appointment by the president. Rationalized as a response to Chechen terrorists' bloody school seizure at Beslan, the measure was actually an additional attempt to increase federal leverage in regional affairs. It also had the convenient side effect of removing regional governorships as an electoral springboard from which aspiring politicians could challenge the incumbents in Moscow. The measure further undermined the elements of federalism in Russia, and it increased the risk that excessive power would be concentrated in the presidency.

Civil Society and Political Culture

The idea of civil society played an important role in the demise of Soviet communism. Fostered by Soviet dissenters, the notion helped erode the ideological claims of the party–state regime by challenging the tenet that the interests of the state were superior to those of any individual or social group. Public optimism and popular involvement in civil-society groups peaked during the campaign for glasnost and perestroika set in motion by Gorbachev [20]. After this high point, however, Russian society underwent a marked political demobilization, and the civil-society ideal was never embodied in an extensive network of associations with proven organizational structures and secure economic resources.

A major cause of society's political demobilization was shock therapy. The decision to free many prices caused a huge spike in inflation that wiped out savings and drove down the standard of living for many Russians. Russia's GDP fell by between one-third and one-half in the first three years of independence and continued to shrink for most of the decade. Many white-collar employees and skilled workers became impoverished. They also suffered from mounting wage arrears, as cash-starved government agencies and businesses sought to cover financial shortfalls by holding back wages owed to their employees [21]. The economic crisis reinforced the lingering societal effects of decades of regimentation by the Soviet regime.

Society also experienced a demographic crisis. In the dozen years after independence, Russia's reported population declined by about 4 percent, and life expectancy dropped by more than two years. Although the origins of the crisis could be traced back to the final three or four decades of Soviet power, shock therapy did nothing to ease it, and the rate of population loss appeared likely to accelerate under the influence of high levels of environmental pollution and grave public health problems, including AIDS [22–3]. Some observers predicted that the economy would soon be hobbled by a severe shortage of workers and that the declining number of able-bodied men of draft age could shrink the military to less than half its current size. As in many industrial states, the demand for new workers contributed to high levels of immigration (much of it illegal) from Third World regions such as Central Asia, and the influx of these non-Slavic immigrants sparked vigorous controversy between nationalists who opposed immigration and businesspeople who favored it.

Under Putin, the country's ethnic diversity increasingly became a source of social tensions. Ethnic Russians made up about four-fifths of the population. Although this was a much higher level of ethnic homogeneity than the USSR had possessed, some parts of Russia, such as the Northern Caucasus and the middle Volga region, were home to large concentrations of ethnic minorities. The marked increase in frictions between ethnic Russians and ethnic groups from the Northern Caucasus was reflected in a growing Russian tendency to view all persons from the Caucasus as members of a single racial category of untrustworthy "blacks." During Putin's presidency hate crimes against minorities received widespread publicity, and popular sentiment favoring "Russia for the Russians" gained ground. This outlook received support from several ultraconservative Russian Orthodox clerics who maintained that only individuals with Orthodox backgrounds were authentic Russians – a narrow view that relegated the members of non-Orthodox minorities to a position of inferiority.

These trends raised the question of whether Russia was becoming a civil society or an "uncivil" one. In any society, the uncivil and civil sectors both consist of active voluntary associations, and both are autonomous from the state. The essential difference is that uncivil groups deny that other social groups have legitimate interests, and they deal with other groups by illicit means that may include blackmail and violence. Although even solidly democratic countries are home to some uncivil groups, the key issue is the social balance between civil and uncivil associations.

In post-Soviet Russia the balance shifted in an unfavorable direction. The level of citizen membership in voluntary associations remained very low by international standards, and the professional and entrepreneurial elements of society took few steps to organize themselves and promote their interests as groups [24–6]. Much as in the Soviet era, trust remained vitally important to ordinary Russians, but they placed their trust in individuals with whom they had longstanding personal ties, not in impersonal civic organizations [27]. Although numerous non-governmental organizations (NGOs) were created, most lacked broad-based support and relied heavily on foreign donors for funding. Meanwhile, uncivil social elements grew and thrived. These elements included organized crime, networks of corruption, and terrorist cells. During Putin's time in office the level of criminal activity remained high, and substantial evidence indicated that government corruption continued to spread.

The spread of opinion polling after 1991 enabled scholars to examine the longstanding notion that Russian culture was intrinsically authoritarian [28]. Research in the early 2000s showed that Russians valued the new personal freedoms gained since the Soviet era. Most respondents also disliked the idea of any major changes of political structure that would amount to a formal repudiation of democratic principles. Strikingly, they regarded the current government as being just as unresponsive to public opinion as the Soviet government had been, and they believed the current government was less likely to treat them fairly, in part because they saw it as far more corrupt [29]. Despite their widespread endorsement of democratic values, respondents were much less ready to favor resistance to certain arbitrary official acts, including violations of human rights and press freedoms, which citizens in most democratic countries would regard as undemocratic [30]. A significant minority of respondents, young as well as old, also had ambivalent or positive feelings about Stalin as a leader [31].These findings indicated that Russian political culture included a very substantial democratic component that had survived the turmoil of the 1990s. But they also suggested that ordinary Russians had retained little taste for the sort of civic action that might influence the evolution of the political system.

The New Quest for a "Strong State"

When Putin became president, most Russians greeted him as a welcome change from the ailing and erratic Yeltsin. Methodical and low-key, Putin spoke frankly about the country's problems and seemed determined to address them. He put a special emphasis on establishing order in Russian public life and strengthening the faltering economy. Putin promised to establish the "dictatorship of law" by requiring consistent compliance from the oligarchs as well as ordinary citizens and by making the laws and administrative decisions of various state organs consistent with one another.

Among Putin's early achievements were the introduction of simplified tax laws that boosted government revenues, a new macroeconomic discipline that helped Russia pay down its foreign debts, and an impressive economic revival sustained in large measure by a steep rise in the price of Russian oil on global markets. Between 2000 and 2005 the average real income of Russians increased by about 75 percent, reducing the number of people below the official poverty line by half. Thanks partly to these positive economic trends, Putin's public-approval ratings consistently ranked above 70 percent.

Although Putin regularly paid lip-service to the idea of furthering democratization as well as economic liberalization, his acts increasingly belied his words. One straw in the wind was his heavy reliance on personnel with security-service backgrounds to fill governmental posts having nothing to do with security issues. Putin had been plucked from political obscurity in the late 1990s and lacked a wide circle of politicians he could trust. A belief that this narrow political base would limit his freedom of maneuver may have been Yeltsin's main motive for choosing him to become the next president. Putin coped with this shortage of tested political acquaintances by turning to individuals from the security police and the armed forces – the so-called *siloviki* or "force wielders." Individuals with these backgrounds made up about a third of the ministers and deputy ministers appointed in Putin's early years as president, plus about 70 percent of the staffs of the new super regions [32–3]. Within this pool, former members of the security services were politically more significant than ex-military men, because the security services had traditionally penetrated all sectors of Russian society and possessed an array of manipulative tools that extended well beyond the threat or use of violence. Although the *siloviki* were far from being a unified bloc, their growing reach had deeply negative implications for the nature of political life and any future prospect of political liberalization.

These appointments reinforced the tendency of the state to play an assertive role. The initial targets of state pressure were Berezovsky and Gusinsky, the two oligarchs who had acquired dominant positions in the media and had used their media power to advance their own narrow objectives. Under Kremlin-orchestrated harassment from the tax police, compliant creditors such as the giant Gazprom energy corporation, and the courts, the two were stripped of their media empires and driven into foreign exile.

The biggest watershed in the Kremlin's relations with the oligarchs was the Khodorkovsky affair of 2003–5. Mikhail Khodorkovsky, head of Yukos, the richest and most efficient Russian oil company, ignored oblique signals from the government that he should follow Gusinsky and Berezovsky into exile. Instead he waded more deeply into politics and began to finance opposition parties in the run-up to the 2003 parliamentary elections. He also worked to reduce the taxation of energy companies – taxation that was needed to maintain Russia's new-found fiscal health – and challenged the government monopoly on the transportation of energy for export.

Political motives underlay the trial and imprisonment of Khodorkovsky on charges of embezzlement and tax evasion. In the course of privatization the defendant had unquestionably engaged in many illegal and corrupt acts, but so had other tycoons who were not brought to trial. Moreover, Khodorkovsky had recently set his company on a new course, improving its transparency and corporate governance in order to attract foreign investment. His real offense was to challenge the Kremlin's increasing political dominance. The arrest was artfully timed to appeal to Russian voters, who had bitter memories of the injustices of privatization and would soon have an opportunity to vote in the parliamentary and presidential elections. One survey showed that nearly 80 percent of the respondents endorsed reviewing or revoking the results of the privatization process and that almost 60 percent favored initiating criminal investigations of the rich [34].

Putin's policy toward civil society was more energetic and restrictive than Yeltsin's. Harassment of civil-society activists by the police and tax authorities intensified, and the government began to sponsor its own "in-house" organizations to compete against genuinely autonomous associations [25]. The Kremlin also gave business groups cues about which compliant civic organizations to support and which organizations to avoid. Suspended above this assortment of sponsored associations was a new, quasi-autonomous "Public Chamber." Ostensibly the government created it to facilitate consultations with society, but its main purpose was to siphon off authentic grass-roots energy and initiatives. These measures bore a significant resemblance to the Soviet approach to society after Stalin's death. Although far less comprehensive and repressive than the Soviet approach, Putin's policy revealed a similar distrust of self-directed social activity and the unregulated articulation of social interests.

Conclusion: Scholarship and Policy

In the first decade and a half after the USSR's collapse, systematic scholarly research on contemporary Russia was much easier to conduct than during the Soviet era. Nonetheless, one important intellectual continuity linked the two periods: the tendency for scholarly debates and disputes about government policy to become intertwined. In the late 1980s and early 1990s the urgent task of adapting US diplomacy to the enormous changes in the region triggered vigorous controversies over American policy. In the world of scholarship, the tone was sometimes set by broader US polemics over who had been wrong about the impending Soviet collapse and who had been right. For the next dozen years or so, US academic and policy debates revolved around such issues as the prospects for Russian democracy and Russian capitalism, as well as the relationship between trends in Russia and general processes of globalization. The academic debates had a significant generational dimension: social scientists who had built up their expertise on the region during the Soviet era struggled to relate their knowledge to the new situation, while many younger social scientists chose to focus their research on post-Soviet developments rather than the Soviet years.

In the scholarly debates, most specialists on Russian politics were skeptical of the feasibility of a Russian transition to democracy and treated it as only a contingent possibility [35]. However, the terms of the concurrent US disputes over government policy sometimes led to public misunderstandings of these scholarly views, as well as to occasional misunderstandings among scholars themselves. The public misunderstandings stemmed partly from laypersons' reasonable assumption that scholarly references to a transition in Russia meant that the implied destination would ultimately be reached. In addition, the confusion about Russian trends resulted from scholars' occasional tendency to set up a straw-man interpretation of "transitology" in order to make their own research appear more innovative or more credible. Carried over from the cold-war era, these political habits and academic practices clouded discussions of the strengths and weaknesses of scholarship on Russia's post-Soviet development.

As Putin approached his second presidential term, scholarly opinions began to shift. Some experts started to treat the post-Soviet years not as a historical rupture but as a period having important continuities with the tsarist and Soviet eras [1, 36]. Others suggested that, instead of following a linear path toward a liberal political and economic outcome, recent events in Russia reflected a cyclical pattern in which comparatively liberal stages alternated with authoritarian ones [37]. Guided by a certain view of the balance between historical determinants and individual agency, some analysts maintained that the impact of the tsarist and Soviet legacies on post-Soviet developments had proven decisive. Viewing events from a different angle, other analysts saw those legacies as malleable and as less significant than present-day socioeconomic circumstances and political decisions [38; 3: 92–113].

Today it is impossible to know which interpretation will seem most accurate to future historians who look back on this epic national upheaval. However, the prevailing trends in Russia are likely to become clearer after another change of presidential leadership. This will be true especially if the change of leadership coincides with a major deterioration in Russia's economic situation because of a sharp drop in revenues from global energy sales. In that case, the transfer of presidential power and a buildup of economic pressure will test the durability of the political order that has crystallized in recent years.

References

1. Reddaway, P., and Glinski, D. (2001). *The Tragedy of Russia's Reforms: Market Bolshevism against Democracy.* United States Institute of Peace Press, Washington.
2. McFaul, M. (2001). *Russia's Unfinished Revolution: Political Change from Gorbachev to Putin.* Cornell University Press, Ithaca, NY.

3. Fish, M. S. (2005). *Democracy Derailed in Russia*. Cambridge University Press, New York.
4. Knight, A. (1999). *The Security Services and the Decline of Democracy in Russia*. Donald W. Treadgold Papers, No. 23. University of Washington Press, Seattle.
5. Colton, T. J. (2005). "Putin and the Attenuation of Russian Democracy," in A. Pravda, ed., *Leading Russia – Putin in Perspective: Essays in Honour of Archie Brown*. Oxford University Press, New York, 103–18.
6. Rose, R. (2001). "How Floating Parties Frustrate Democratic Accountability: A Supply-Side View of Russia's Elections," in A. Brown, ed., *Contemporary Russian Politics: A Reader*. Oxford University Press, New York, 215–23.
7. White, S. (2005). "The Political Parties," in S. White, Z. Gitelman, and R. Sakwa, eds., *Developments in Russian Politics*. 6th edn. Duke University Press, Durham, NC, 80–95.
8. Aslund, A. (1995). *How Russia Became a Market Economy*. Brookings Institution, Washington.
9. Ickes, B., Murrell, P., and Ryterman, R. (1997). "End of the Tunnel? The Effects of Financial Stabilization in Russia," *Post-Soviet Affairs*, 13/2 (Apr.–June), 105–33.
10. Kryshtanovskaya, O., and White, S. (1996). "From Soviet nomenklatura to Russian elite," *Europe-Asia Studies*, 48/5: 711–33.
11. Goldman, M. (2003). *The Piratization of Russia: Russian Reform Goes Awry*. Routledge, New York.
12. Klebnikov, P. (2000). *Godfather of the Kremlin: Boris Berezovsky and the Looting of Russia*. Harcourt, Brace, New York.
13. Volkov, V. (2002). *Violent Entrepreneurs: The Use of Force in the Making of Russian Capitalism*. Cornell University Press, Ithaca, NY.
14. Frye. T. (2003). "Markets, Democracy, and New Private Business in Russia," *Post-Soviet Affairs*, 19/1 (Jan.–Mar.), 24–45.
15. Aslund, A. (2002). *Building Capitalism: The Transformation of the Former Soviet Bloc*. Cambridge University Press, New York.
16. Barnes, A. (2006). *Owning Russia: The Struggle over Factories, Farms, and Power*. Cornell University Press, Ithaca, NY.
17. Nagy, P. M. (2000). *The Meltdown of the Russian State: The Deformation and Collapse of the State in Russia*. Edward Elgar, Northampton, MA.
18. Stepan, A. (2000). "Russian Federalism in Comparative Perspective," *Post-Soviet Affairs*, 16/2 (Apr.–June), 133–76.
19. Ross, C. (2004). "Putin's Federal Reforms," in C. Ross (ed.), *Russian Politics under Putin*. Manchester University Press, New York.
20. Hosking, G., Aves, J., and Duncan, P. (1992). *The Road to Post-Communism: Independent Political Movements in the Soviet Union, 1985–1991*. Pinter, London and New York.
21. Javeline, D. (2003). *Protest and the Politics of Blame: The Russian Response to Unpaid Wages*. University of Michigan Press, Ann Arbor, MI.
22. Feshbach, M. (2001). "Russia's Population Meltdown," *Wilson Quarterly*, 5/1: 12–21.
23. Eberstadt, N. (2002). "The Future of AIDS: Grim Toll in Russia, China, and India." *Foreign Affairs*, 81/6: 22–45.
24. Howard, M. (2003). *The Weakness of Civil Society in Post-Communist Europe*. Cambridge University Press, New York.
25. McFaul, M., and Treyger, E. (2004). "Civil Society," in M. McFaul, N. Petrov, and A. Ryabov (eds.), *Between Dictatorship and Democracy: Russian Post-Communist Political Reform*. Carnegie Endowment for International Peace, Washington, 135–73.
26. Balzer, H. (2003). "Routinization of the new Russians?" *Russian Review*, 62/1 (Jan.), 15–36.

27. Ledeneva, A. (1998). *Russia's Economy of Favours: Blat, Networking and Informal Exchange*. Cambridge University Press, Cambridge.
28. Bahry, D. (1999). "Comrades into Citizens? Russian Political Culture and Public Support for the Transition," *Slavic Review*, 58/4: 841–53.
29. White, S. (2004). "Russia's Disempowered Electorate," in C. Ross (ed.), *Russian Politics under Putin*. Manchester University Press, Manchester, 76–94.
30. Petukhov, V., and Ryabov, A. (2004). "Public Attitudes about Democracy," in M. McFaul, N. Petrov, and A. Ryabov (eds.), *Between Dictatorship and Democracy: Russian Post-Communist Political Reform*. Carnegie Endowment for International Peace, Washington, 268–91.
31. Mendelson, S., and Gerber, T. (2005). "Soviet Nostalgia: An Impediment to Russian Democratization," *Washington Quarterly*, 29/1: 83–96.
32. Anderson, J. (2006). "The Chekist Takeover of the Russian State," *International Journal of Intelligence and Counterintelligence*, 19/2: 237–88.
33. Kryshtanovskaya, O., and White, S. (2003). "Putin's Militocracy," *Post-Soviet Affairs*, 19/4 (Oct.–Dec.), 289–306.
34. Guriev, S., and Rachinsky, A. (2005). "The Role of Oligarchs in Russian Capitalism," *Economic Perspectives*, 19/1: 131–50.
35. Gans-Morse, J. (2004). "Searching for Transitologists: Contemporary Theories of Post-Communist Transitions and the Myth of a Dominant Paradigm," *Post-Soviet Affairs* (Oct.–Dec.), 20/4: 320–49.
36. Hedlund, S. (2006). "Vladimir the Great, Grand Prince of Muscovy: Resurrecting the Russian Service State," *Europe–Asia Studies*, 58/5: 775–801.
37. Hale, H. (2005). "Regime Cycles: Democracy, Autocracy, and Revolution in Post-Soviet Eurasia," *World Politics*, 58/1 (Oct.), 133–65.
38. Shleifer, A. (2005). *A Normal Country: Russia after Communism*. Harvard University Press, Cambridge, MA.

Further Reading

Breslauer, G. (2002). *Gorbachev and Yeltsin as Leaders*. Cambridge University Press, New York.

Evans, A., Henry, L. A., and Sundstrom, L. M. (2005). *Russian Civil Society: A Critical Assessment*. M. E. Sharpe, Armonk, NY.

Hale, H. (2006). *Why Not Parties in Russia? Democracy, Federalism, and the State*. Cambridge University Press, New York.

Hedlund, S. (2005). *Russian Path Dependence*. Routledge, New York.

Herspring, D. (2006). *Putin's Russia: Past Imperfect, Future Uncertain*. 3rd edn. Rowman & Littlefield, Lanham, MD.

Hoffman, D. E. (2001). *The Oligarchs: Wealth and Power in the New Russia*. Public Affairs, New York.

March, L. (2002). *The Communist Party in Post-Soviet Russia*. Manchester University Press, Manchester.

McFaul, M., and Colton T. (2002). "Are Russians Undemocratic?" *Post-Soviet Affairs*, 18/2:, 91–132.

Reddaway, P., and Orttung, R. (eds.) (2004–5), *Dynamics of Russian Politics: Putin's Reform of Federal–Regional Relations*. 2 vols. Rowman & Littlefield, Lanham, MD.

Shevtsova L. F. (2005). *Putin's Russia*. Rev. edn. Carnegie Endowment for International Peace, Washington.

CHAPTER TWENTY-EIGHT

Russian History and the Future of Russia

WILLIAM E. ODOM

The State of the Debate

Several futures are open to any country in principle, but in the centuries-old debates over "whither Russia," the anticipated ones have commonly been reduced to two, either "Westernization" or Russia's "special way." Russian Westernizers today (2009) and in the past have had the predominant regime types extant in Western Europe as concrete models on which to base their thinking. Russian Slavophiles and the contemporary anti-Westernizers – Eurasianists are the best known [1] – do not. They offer only cloudy alternatives, involving mixes of authoritarianism and communalism based on xenophobia, neo-nazism, or spiritualism, too vaguely defined to support concrete programs. Western thinking has also been generally confined to this dichotomous view of Russia's prospective futures.

After the Soviet Union collapsed, most Western observers were remarkably optimistic about the prospects for liberal democracy. By the mid-1990s, they were proclaiming that Russia had "turned the corner" to democracy, ignoring the "liberal" part, and that its "polarized politics" had ended [2, 3]. After about a decade, optimism yielded to pessimism, as many observers began lamenting that Russia was backsliding from democracy [4]. Actually, it was not. Elections were being held regularly. As for the "liberal" part, key civil rights were indeed being restricted, but the state had defended them only selectively in the 1990s. Most important, private property rights were never stabilized. Thus little changed beyond a turnover of elites – Putin's "silovki" (Putin's political cadres) took over from Yeltsin's "family" (Yeltin's close supporters).

Parallel to Russia's democratization has been its "marketization," shifting from a state-owned and directed economy to a market system. Here, too, Western pessimism has followed initial optimism. As the Putin government methodically took away the property of several of Russia's new multi-billionaires, the so-called oligarchs, fears arose that Russia was restoring state control of its economy. This was true in some respects, but transition to a market had not gone far in the first place. Again, the "liberal" part, institutions for managing a competitive market economy, had largely remained formal laws on paper.

The political transition to elections was easy. The economic transition to an effective market was proving impossible. No major state in modern history had more central control of its economy than the Soviet Union. Introducing a market involved shifting vast wealth – the whole of the country's land and capital – from state to private hands. It was unprecedented. And if it was to succeed, new liberal political institutions also had to be created, the existence of which Western economists tend to take for granted in their theorizing. Thus Western economic advisors took one set of messages to Russia while Western political scientists took another set, largely disconnected from one another. Meanwhile, historians mostly stood aside, commenting but voicing no consensus.

In the aftermath, much acrimony has been exchanged among all parties to the "whither Russia" debate. In fact, none was or is very convincing, because the key challenge, creating liberal institutions, was largely ignored until later. Without such institutions firmly established, the redistribution of wealth was bound to be chaotic, unfair, and periodically violent; fraught with fraud, corruption, and conspiracies; and viewed by the public as grossly unjust. The unavoidable result has been a highly ineffective market coexisting with several anti-market institutions, legacies from Soviet and earlier times.

The critics of so-called shock-therapy policy, allegedly to blame for this mess, insisted that there were gradualist alternatives that would have avoided it. Although such alternatives have yet to be defined beyond rhetorical assertions, a gradualist approach would probably have bogged down, producing an indefinite stalemate [5, 6]. Actually, that is what happened, because genuine "shock therapy" was never tried, only parts of it [7: ch. 6]. Most of the discussion about post-Soviet Russia's development, therefore, has been disconnected from Russia's realities in important ways, more so in the West than in Russia, but even there fantasies are invoked as often as facts.

To have a better view of Russia's future, we need to leave the traditional dichotomous debate. The first step out is a better understanding of what path Russia has been on. That requires a brief review of Russian history and an introduction to the concept of "path dependence" applied to political and economic institutional development. At that point, it should be clear that the issue is not a choice between a Western and special Russian path. It is whether or not Russia can escape its path dependence. If it can, then several futures become possible. Next we must examine objective conditions that either favor or reduce Russia's prospects for becoming a liberal democracy. In the process, we will discover that there are more than two courses open to Russia, some more probable than others.

This line of analysis leads to the conclusion that Russia is neither Europeanizing nor Russianizing. Instead, it appears to be breaking with its past in significant ways that could push it onto any of several other paths, including variants of Latin Americanizing, Africanizing, and Asianizing. Its best prospect, although highly improbable, would be Turkeyization.

What Path Has Russia Been Following?

Since the time of at least Peter the Great, both Russians and foreign observers have believed that Russia was Westernizing. Yet the outcome has never been what was expected. Initially Westernization meant technological change but also included a commitment to Western culture. Catherine the Great brought liberal political ideas to Russia but soon abandoned them. Her grandson, Alexander I, toyed with liberal political institutions, initiated significant ministerial reforms, but then abandoned his liberal impulses. Nicholas I, although known as a reactionary, actually considered emancipation of the serfs but met greater resistance among the nobility than he wanted to confront. Alexander II's Great Reforms in the 1860s and 1870s opened the way for genuine liberal developments – local government reforms, military reforms, adoption of European code law, and the beginnings of a modern market economy. Although they were slowed down by the reaction after Alexander's assassination by revolutionaries, they yielded more effective state administration and the beginnings of industrialization in the last half of the nineteenth century. Liberal trends had one more chance after the 1905 Revolution. Nicholas II reluctantly signed the October Manifesto, permitting political parties, elections, and the creation of the State Duma, but he refused to subordinate the monarchy to the rule of law.

The First World War opened the door to revolution in 1917, ending liberal change entirely. Although the subsequent Soviet regime was judged to be a radical break with Russia's past, it turned out to be a throwback to Petrine Russia. The Bolsheviks largely dressed up traditional Russian institutions in new ideological rhetoric. The empire was restored as a socialist union. Serfdom was reincarnated in the collective farm system. Alexander II's promising legal reform was abolished, and the Communist Party assumed the unlimited powers the tsars had had. State control of the economy became more complete than ever before. And the military and secret police were the mainstays of the regime, as in tsarist days.

We see in this brief review that a stubborn institutional continuity has survived throughout Russian history, notwithstanding repeated upheavals and continuous Western influences. They changed Russia but did not undermine the basic character of Russian institutions. To use Samuel Huntington's distinction, Russia "modernized," but it did not "westernize" [8]. It did not throw off its "predatory state" (an exploitative regime that tries to maximize the ruler's revenues) and install a "contract state" (a constitutional regime dependent on a Western-type legal system).

"Liberal" democracy is impossible without this binary change – from "the rule of the one" to the rule-based "rule of the few," which normally leads to "participation by the many." And it has shown no more promise of occurring since 1991 than it did after 1905. In fact, the pattern of elections and political parties in contemporary Russia is remarkably analogous to the one between 1906 and 1914. Both started with several parties representing a broad range of interests. Nicholas II narrowed the parties to those he found tolerable. His fourth and last Duma had only four. Putin reduced the number of parties to four in the fourth Duma, elected in 2003 [9]. Of the four, three support the Kremlin.

If we are to anticipate Russia's future development, therefore, we must explain the source of this remarkable continuity. Is there a deeper determinism at work in Russia? There is, and it can be explained by the idea of institutional "path dependence."

Path Dependence

If we use this concept, we can go beyond the vague language of Russia's special path and special mission better better to understand why Russia behaved as it has. To do so, we need a more technical understanding of it, and that takes us to advances in economic analysis.

Economists have come to realize that their neoclassical theory of markets cannot account for the failure of firms to adopt the newer and more efficient solutions in technology and organizational design. Firms make investments and sustain organizational designs that block corrective feedback from the market place. Private and organizational incentives soon create a "lock-in" to an "institutional path" that becomes extremely costly to escape. An oft-cited example is Paul David's account of why the typewriter keyboard layout, or "QWERTY," has not been replaced by one that would allow much faster typing speeds [10]. Having made large investments in equipment and training, firms refused to pay the costs of change to a more efficient path. Other such cases have been identified and explained, considerably advancing our understanding of path dependence [11].

The same analysis can be applied to political systems [12]. It must, of course, be adapted. "Institutions" must be divided into "formal" (for example, the laws or regulations defining the state and its responsibilities and operations) and "informal" (for example, the beliefs, attitudes, degree of social trust, and so on, that make up the popular mindset of the society). Formal institutions are relatively easy to change on paper, although not in practice. They both adapt to and shape informal institutions, bringing congruence between the two over time. Informal institutions – that is, the "political culture" or the "national character" – are far more resistant to change. They reflect a "lock-in" embedded in the public psyche. Political culture and national character are old categories, long used in political science and history, but they are difficult to pin down empirically and have tended to be neglected [13, 14]. Of late, however, political culture has enjoyed a revival [15]. In dealing with the Russian case, we have long known national character and political culture play a large role determining Russia's developmental path. Now we can be more specific about how and why.

Although a number of scholars have applied "path dependence" to political institutions, Nobelist Douglass C. North has been a leader in making it applicable to any country [16]. He begins with a theory of the state as a "predatory" entity, "acting as a discriminating monopolist, separating each group of constituents and devising property rights for each so as to maximize state income" [16: 21–4]. Concerned primarily with his own "private rate of return," the ruler inexorably, although not necessarily intentionally, introduces inefficient allocations of property rights, which result in high transaction costs in the economy. The ruler's laws and regulations, dictating those allocations, are the "formal institutions." To account for a state's "informal institution," North then adds a "theory of ideology" that is equivalent to "political culture" – that is, entrenched beliefs about what to expect of political leaders and what is just and unjust in social and economic relations.

In countries that have been able to replace predatory rulers with a "contract state" – that is, one that acts as a "third-party enforcer," an entity that assures stable property rights and mediates contract disputes according to laws – transaction costs have declined, permitting much larger gains from trade and commerce. "Third-party enforcement" is achieved by a constitutional order, a deal in which a country's elites agree to abide by rules. Thus they have become "contract states." Only contract states have sustained economic growth over long periods in modern times. Central to this conclusion, it should be emphasized, is the role of "transaction costs" – that is, the costs above and beyond production costs required to move products to market and sell them. Reducing them is the key to economic growth.

Puzzled as to why countries with poorly performing economies fail to borrow the policies of successful countries, North found the answer in "path dependence" [17]. Their lock-in to predatory institutions, formal and informal, with high "transaction costs," prevents reforms that would institute "third-party enforcement" of property rights and contracts – that is, a constitutional order. As he put it: "Third-party enforcement means the development of the state as a coercive force able to monitor property rights and enforce contracts effectively, *but no one at this stage of our knowledge knows how to create such an entity*" (emphasis added) [17: 59]. This should come as sobering news to those Westerners who lecture Russia and other countries as if they actually know how. It undercuts almost all the contemporary theories of democratic and economic transitions.

The Russian Case

Russian rulers have consistently pursued predatory revenue practices and have never acknowledged private property rights as inviolable. The price has been consistently high transaction costs for the economy. Nor has Russia managed to achieve an enduring constitutional order. The suggestive power of North's theories for their case is strong indeed.

Stefan Hedlund, a Swedish economist, has, to our advantage, devoted an entire book to Russian path dependence [18]. According to his analysis, there have been only a few opportunities for breaking Russia's institutional "lock-in" since the time of Kievan Rus' to the present. One was missed in Novgorod, followed by a lock-in under Muscovite rulers, who were heavily endowed with Mongol secular institutions. The Muscovy system reached its peak under Peter the Great but began to erode in the course of the next two centuries. From the time of Catherine the Great through to the end of the nineteenth century, a number of possibilities emerged, but all were lost. Catherine made gestures toward stabilizing property rights with the Charter of the Nobility (1785) but did not carry through because that would have tied her own hands in dealing with the nobility. Had Alexander I not abandoned his inclination to install a constitutional system, especially after the defeat of Napoleon, Russia might have been set on a new path. By far the best prospects for breaking the lock-in came with Alexander II's Great Reforms, but his assassination by radicals allowed reactionaries in the government to reinforce the lock-in. Finally, the October Manifesto after the 1905 Revolution and the Stolypin land reform laws might have produced a constitutional order, but the First World War foreclosed that hope. With the arrival of Soviet rule, the Muscovy lock-in was reasserted.

According to Hedlund, central to Russia's path dependence is the Muscovy view of property rights. It did not make the distinction found in Roman law between property as *dominum* and as *imperium* [18: 318]. Individuals had the former right, the state had the latter. And the state recognized and protected the *dominum* property rights of the individual, asserting only its right to *imperium* and taxation. Moscow adopted the Mongol view of property: only the khan owned property, not his subjects, and they used it at his sufferance. In this tradition, the tsars considered the whole of Russia as their private patrimony; likewise, the Bolsheviks took control of all property for the "working and toiling classes," which, they insisted, were embodied in the Communist Party.

The Russian regime, therefore, became an extreme example of a "predatory" state very early and never yielded to efforts to subordinate it to a constitutional order. Not surprisingly, Russian economic performance has always remained poor. True, as Alexander Gerschenkron has pointed out, spurts of state-driven growth have occurred, soon exhausting the population, followed by long periods of stagnation [19]. Now we can add to Gerschenkron's analysis a deeper explanation of the slowdown and exhaustion. The perverse allocation of property rights, the army of rent-seeking state officials, the absence of rule of law for contract enforcement, and rampant corruption strangled each of these occasional bursts of economic development after a few decades.

It is not difficult to begin to see how Russian political culture was highly resistant to social trust that could keep transaction costs low. Russian literature, from the late eighteenth century right down through Pushkin, Gogol, Chekhov, Zoshchenko, Voinovich, and dozens of others, provides a highly textured picture of that culture. If we view it from the position of the monarchy, we can see that the ruler faced an unresponsive state apparatus populated by duplicitous and scheming subjects. It should occasion little surprise, therefore, that no Russian ruler dared submit the monarchy to the rule of law. No one would abide by law without compulsion, and all would use their creative skills to twist the law to cheat the state and obstruct their fellow subjects. Creating an honest state apparatus to provide compulsion and collect revenues efficiently was also impossible. The only way the ruler could maintain power was through arbitrary use of his own discretion in allocating resources and justice to buy the responsiveness of his agents or to punish them.

Admittedly, many state employees behave precisely this way in Western constitutional regimes, but the degree has always been far greater in Russia. At some point "quantitative" factors make a "qualitative" difference. When the ratio of mistrust to trust in social relations is not only greater than one, but often several times greater, the transaction costs of formal rule enforcement simply become too high for any state to maintain. Thus the ruler is forced to resort to techniques of governing that accord more with the informal institutions. In nineteenth-century Russia, for example, entrepreneurs were denied easy permission to form "limited liability corporations," a legal device that was facilitating larger investment globally. The tsar held on tightly to the approval process, often denying it to the most competent entrepreneurs in Russia because of their ethnicity [20].

Path-dependence theory can make contemporary Russian political culture understandable in a new way. Yeltsin's privatization process, intended to introduce an effective market system, and his process for establishing a constitution immediately ran into the deeply rooted informal institutions. The state agents implementing reforms may have had good intentions, but to move forward, they were soon following age-old behavior patterns that insured high transaction costs in the newly privatized firms, the courts' use of newly drafted laws, banking, and state fiscal policy.

Putin's policies for establishing a strong state and overcoming the chaos of the 1990s can be seen the same way. His agents, mostly recruited from the security services and the military, brought deeply ingrained anti-liberal informal institutions to their work. For example, the fates of several new business "oligarchs" reveal their disregard for private property rights.

The last thing to expect from either Yeltsin's rule or Putin's was adherence to a constitutional order. They could no more risk taking that road than could Catherine the Great and her successors. When Gorbachev risked implementing liberalization policies, it should have been obvious that the Soviet Union would collapse if he persisted [21: 28]. A smooth transition to any version of a stable liberal Soviet regime would have been unprecedented. Not only were the informal institutions of Soviet society a staggering obstacle, but there are no examples of liberal constitutional states embracing a dozen or more national minority component territories. Even two or three such minorities occasionally threaten the stability of mature liberal democracies – for example, Canada, Belgium, and the United Kingdom. The breakup of the multinational Soviet state, therefore, was a sine qua non for a successful shift to a constitutional order. Unlike all his predecessors, therefore, Gorbachev apparently did not appreciate the probable consequences of his own policy decisions [22: 397–401].

We should now better understand the peculiar nature of Russia's path dependence. The Russian Federation has retained several of the age-old predatory practices in one way or another. Property rights are kept unstable because the state manipulates them as it sees fit to maximize its "private rate of return." Courts are not allowed to play the "third-party enforcement" role in dealing with contract disputes if they seriously threaten to limit the state's discretion. Thousands of officials are left to engage in rent-seeking for their livelihood. Businessmen must follow discriminating monopoly and resource-stripping strategies rather than strategies based on lower production costs of more competitive products. Employees must resort to informal networking and scamming at the expense of employers.

What Next?

"Path dependence" strongly biases our expectations toward "determinism," and with some justification. The historical record vindicates it statistically, making it the best basis for prediction. Of the 191 members of the United Nations General Assembly, only about two dozen have broken their institutional lock-ins to create and sustain genuine constitutional orders for a generation or more [23]. To be a weak predatory state with a poor economy, therefore, is normal. To be a stable liberal state with a thriving economy is exceptional.

Still, countries have achieved constitutional orders, becoming exceptional. It is possible. We must, therefore, examine more rigorously Russia's prospects for joining this liberal minority. How best to do that?

Two viewpoints must be employed. First, are Russia's structural conditions such that a break of the lock-in is conceivable any time soon? These are sometimes called "the social requisites" for liberal democracy [24]. Secondly, because leaders' choices also count in bringing political and economic change, we must consider the quality of Russian political leaders, especially their attitudes toward liberal reforms leading to a contract state.

The Requisites

Because the literature on social requisites is long, we will be highly selective. To that end, let us use Robert Dahl's framework for "polyarchy" (his term for liberal democracy). Dahl subsumes most of the requisites in seven categories, or "conditions," that favor or discourage a successful liberal democratic development [25: 202–7]. They are (1) historical sequences; (2) the socioeconomic order; (3) level of economic development; (4) equalities and inequalities; (5) subcultural pluralism; (6) domination by a foreign power; and (7) beliefs of political activists. In the interest of brevity, and since (2), (3), and (4) concern aspects of economic conditions, we shall treat them as one and reduce the number to five. Also, (7) allows us to introduce the second viewpoint, political voluntarism and the role of leaders.

1. *Historical sequence.* Dahl observes that the United States and other older "polyarchies" first liberalized – that is, instituted constitutional restraints on the state – and then expanded participation. The attainment of an effective constitutional order preceded wide inclusion for electoral participation. The record of the other course, moving straight to universal suffrage and then liberalizing, is poor. The result has been "illiberal democracy" that almost never becomes a genuine constitutional order – that is, it may have a constitution on paper, but in practice the state violates it when it sees fit. Therefore, the Russian historical sequence, the rapid expansion of participation before achieving a constitutional breakthrough, is unfavorable to liberalization later on.

Barrington Moore, Jr., studying historical sequences, emphasized that peasantries disappeared in countries that became the advanced liberal democracies [26]. Where they did not, dictatorship was the outcome. The Russian peasantry made up over 80 percent of the population in 1917. In the early twenty-first century, the agrarian population is about one-third of the total, a major change. But are those remaining on "collective farms" truly "farmers"? Or are they still peasants? They are mostly literate, which farmers normally are. But they are still landless, which farmers normally are not. Thus Russia's peasant problem has not entirely vanished, but it has been greatly reduced in size, as both a political and an economic factor. It should not, therefore, block a regime that is determined to install a stable constitutional order, as it has in the past.

Moore is also famous for his maxim "no bourgeoisie, no democracy" [26]. Is Russia's urban white-collar class really a "bourgeoisie"? Many Western scholars say yes, but classical liberals and Karl Marx would say no. To be bourgeois, one must own property. That kind of class is tiny in Russia today (2009) and insecure about its property. Again, historical sequence has not favored Russia.

2. *Economic conditions.* By Third World standards, Soviet economic levels were moderately favorable to liberal democracy. Equality was considerable, and "relative deprivation" was not as great as in many countries. These conditions were probably sufficient, although not highly favorable, for liberal democracy.

Dahl emphasizes that, the more wealth is diffused in a society, the better the prospects for liberal democracy. The large class of "free farmers" in predominantly rural America permitted its creation of a "polyarchy" before it urbanized. Even after

Yelstin's economic reforms, centralization of Russia's economy remained great, highly unfavorable to liberal democracy. The continuing "statist" character of Russia's economy trumps the other two favorable conditions – relatively advanced economic development and greater income equality – because it continues to impose many of the huge transaction costs that leveled Soviet growth the mid-1950s and produced enduring stagnation. Putin's reassertion of state control has made the prospects for a liberal outcome all the more unfavorable.

3. *Subcultural pluralism.*   Here we confront not only Russia's "nationality question," but also the growing fissures along sectarian lines – Orthodoxy, Islam, and other denominations of Christianity.

Of all changes resulting from the collapse of the Soviet Union, the large reduction in national minorities is arguably the most important. Since Muscovy's absorption of non-Russians within the empire, they have exerted centrifugal political forces, requiring large Russian military and police establishments to contain them. That has justified large military expenditures as well as encouraged a statist economic policy and an inefficient taxation system [27].

The arrival of modern nationalism in the nineteenth century strengthened these centrifugal forces. Reducing their number reduces the demands for both military power and central control of the economy.

The critical nature of the nationality factor as we approach 2010 is best understood in the context of a vicious circle in Russian development, one caused by three inter-related, structural problems: (1) the old peasant question – that is, lagging economic development, (2) the nationality question, and (3) the military question [22]. The key to breaking this circle is removing the nationality problem. At no time in modern Russian history has the number of minority nationalities been smaller than it is in 2009, falling from about 100 in the Soviet Union to 23 in the Russian Federation. With the significant exception of Chechnya, the national republics have essentially accommodated to Moscow's rule.

This greatly reduces the military and police requirements for domestic political stability as well as lessens the external threat. In the past, most countries on Russia's borders appeared threatening, when in fact they were reacting to fears of Russian expansion. Though it may seem inconceivable to its leaders today, no other country wants to invade Russia. Accordingly, they no longer have a genuine requirement for a large military establishment. This is a radical break with the past.

The war in Chechnya risks reversing this favorable change. Not only does it sharpen national minority fissures in the North Caucasus but it also exacerbates the issue of sectarian Islam more broadly in the Russian Federation.

In sum, cultural fragmentation remains an obstacle to liberal democracy, but it has been reduced dramatically.

4. *Foreign domination.*   In modern times, Russia has experienced only two brief occupations, Napoleon's 1812 invasion, and Hitler's 1941 invasion. The French inspired liberal aspirations in Russia military circles, leading to the Decembrist uprising. Because Hitler's political institutions were remarkably similar to most of Stalin's, there was not much to borrow. Neither, however, was a critical influence.

Mongol rule for about two centuries had a profound effect, seldom appreciated properly in modern times, Donald Ostrowski's research being a notable exception [28]. Methods of administration and tax collection, and particularly the Mongol view of property rights, took root in Muscovy and survive into the contemporary era, as Hedlund has pointed out [18: ch. 11]. On balance, the legacies of foreign domination are adverse.

5. *Beliefs of political activists.*   By this Dahl means "political culture," but especially among political elites. That, of course, shifts our viewpoint to political voluntarism and the role of leaders. One might expect promise in this area. After all, the Soviet Union did produce Gorbachev and Yeltsin. Many of their close aides had cast off key political beliefs acquired in their early socialization. Under Yeltsin, the outlook remained positive in the early 1990s but began to decline. Thereafter, Putin and his team have methodically squeezed out those officials with liberal political attitudes.

Andrei Illarionov's resignation as Putin's personal advisor on economic policy is indicative [29]. A strong proponent of a market economy, he finally wrote off Putin's policies as hopelessly flawed. In the legislature, the decline of the liberal political parties in the 2003 Duma elections marked the effective elimination of liberal reformers. Trends in political attitudes in the broad public are no more encouraging. Since 1991, public support for civil rights has declined steadily [30].

Does this mean that we can ignore all the changes wrought by the Soviet collapse, economic adjustments, and the much greater access ordinary Russians have to foreign media? Certainly not. Political culture, however, changes most slowly. Yet it shows signs of being in flux in Russia. The much larger portion of the population being urban and literate today (2009) than in 1917 makes it more porous to new ideas and changing outlooks. The change, however, need not be liberal. Germany and Japan in the 1930s had more educated societies than most in the world and rejected liberalism aggressively. Russia's disastrous public-health conditions and demographic trends are bound to affect political culture, but one cannot say how. Fairly large numbers of Russians, and not just the rich, are traveling abroad. They do not return to the impervious peasantry and officialdom in Russia of the 1800s, as the peripatetic Russian intelligentsia did. They might, therefore, have more success in introducing foreign institutions. But they could just as easily bring home xenophobic reactions. Finally, the nature of international business interactions as we approach the second decade of the twenty-first century could prove more invasive than in past, becoming an important source of change.

What will emerge from this *mélange* of social upheavals is impossible to assess. Its mix of hope, nostalgia, envy, fear, uncertainly, inferiority feelings, and ambivalence about the Soviet and Russian past will surely alter Russian political culture, but core features – high levels of social mistrust, disregard for human life, and anger at the outside world – could survive, precluding a liberal political outcome.

Politics, Economics, and History

Using both the path-dependency view and Dahl's "conditions" for assessing Russia's future allows us to overcome the boundaries separating the way political scientists, economists, and historians have looked at that question. Dahl takes history into account, linking it causally with political development. His considerations of economics are enlightening but tend to be more correlations than causal explanations. North's use of path dependency links all three – politics, economics, and history – identifying interrelated casual connections.

In regard to the politics–economics connection, it must also be noted that path dependence helps maintain political stability and differences in economic performance. In his classic study *Political Order in Changing Societies*, Huntington asserts that political order is a function of the degree of institutionalization in a society [31]. Both the Soviet Union and the United States, he observes, were highly stable because both were highly institutionalized. But he left open the question of causal connection between the type of regime and economic performance. Huntington and most other political scientists have long noticed a strong correlation between democracy and level of economic development but have differed about the causal connection. North's use of path dependence implicitly confirms Huntington's view of the source of political stability; at the same time, it identifies the causal connection. Liberalism, not democracy as widely assumed, explains economic effectiveness. The Soviet Union was institutionalized and stable but at the price of huge transaction costs for its economy. The United States remains stable with radically smaller transaction costs for its economy. Most studies of the Russian Federation have conflated liberalism and democracy, thereby missing the most critical variable for economic development.

If Not Liberal Democracy, Then What?

At this point, one is left with a strong sense of determinism about Russia's future. Yielding to it is tempting, but we know that things do change and that historical determinism has its limits, even in Russia. Suppose Moscow fails to acquire the lost Soviet territories. And suppose Chechnya is either expelled or eventually integrated into the federation. Then the longer run for Russia begins to look different. The disruption of the old "vicious circle" in Russian historical development could become permanent. The implication can be better understood through some historical reflection.

In 1917, Lenin's strategy for breaking the Russian monarchy aimed directly at the vicious circle's three structural features. His slogan, "Bread, Peace, and Land," told the peasants to desert from the army and to take the land as their own. That dealt with the economic and military questions in a radically new way. It destroyed the army and diffused economic power. "National Self-Determination" encouraged the national minorities to dismember the empire. With the army dissolving, national separatists were able to throw off Russian rule, a radical resolution to the nationality question. Lenin must have understood the old "vicious circle" quite clearly, not only because his 1917 slogans support that inference, but also because he knew precisely how to restore the empire once he held the power.

Gorbachev apparently did not understand the interrelationship of these three questions. He saw how the military burden blocked economic improvement, so he tried to reduce it through arms-control agreements and unilateral force reductions. At the same time, his glasnost policy facilitated popular resistance to military

conscription. Opponents of military conscription soon merged with national independence movements, first in the Baltic region, then in the Caucasus, and finally in
Ukraine [22: chs. 12, 13]. Thereafter, the Soviet Union was doomed.

If Gorbachev had first let the national minorities go their own way, that would
have made it easier to weaken the military and decentralize the economy. Whether
this sequence was feasible is another question; it probably was not. In fact, Gorbachev
never contemplated letting the national republics secede. When his aides, Chernyaev
and Shakhnazarov, advised him to let the Baltic states go, he replied, "that will be
without me" [2: 343]. When Boris Yeltsin, Leonid Kravchuk, and Stanislav
Shushkevich signed the agreement to dissolve the Soviet Union in December 1991,
they merely made *de jure* what was already *de facto*.

If Putin was to restore a Russian empire, then he had first restore the military,
something he claimed to be doing but without notable success. As long as the empire
is not restored, then political forces for a more decentralized economy and stable
private property rights at least have a chance. If those forces began to succeed, the
end of the empire could soon become irreversible. That would mark a major break
with the Muscovy lock-in. New economic incentives, over a couple of decades, could
begin to erode the old political culture.

Such a development path, of course, depends on several things. The European
Union's expansion, the consolidation of NATO enlargement, and peace in the rest
of Eastern Europe must continue. Other things must change, especially leadership
attitudes and beliefs about the wisdom of stabilizing property rights and making the
state an effective "third-party enforcer." Finally, still others must not: Russia must
not rebuild a large military and restore the empire.

The chances of all these things working out properly are not great. In the second
decade of the twenty-first century, therefore, a liberal regime with an effective
economy is most unlikely. Does this mean, then, that the Eurasianists will take power
and guide Russia? Probably not.

As suggested at the beginning of this chapter, we need to think of Russia as having
not just two possible futures. To fail to Westernize would be to fail to Europeanize.
Europe, however, is neither the only new path for Russia nor the most likely one.
Several countries, such as Brazil, Mexico, Nigeria, Indonesia, Iran, and India, were
called "countries of the future" many decades ago, expected to succeed in emulating
the pattern of European and American development. Decades later they are still
"countries of the future." They are locked into inefficient institutions. Most are
variants of the "weak-state" syndrome so cogently defined by Joel Migdal [32].
Whether praetorian dictatorships or illiberal democracies, they are without the
administrative capacity to penetrate and govern directly all the social subgroups
controlled by local strong men, and they are poor at taxation. They may appear
strong formally, but they are trapped in conditions where leadership survival, not
effective reform, has to be their primary goal. Cutting deals with local strong men,
not bringing them under central control and administrative authority, is the price of
survival.

Some of them have suffered the fate of oil wealth. Large inflows of capital from
oil and gas exports have been destructive for both political institutions and the
economies of Nigeria, Venezuela, Peru, Mexico, and others. Russia is becoming seriously infected with the oil and gas export disease, sometimes called the "Dutch

disease" [33]. Barring a radical drop in oil and gas prices, this path is the most prob-able one for Russia to follow over the next decade and perhaps longer. Many also suffer major public health and environmental crises and adverse demographic trends, as does Russia [34].

Thus we could be witnessing a major break in Russian history. The loss of the larger national republics dramatically changes the context for Russian politics, and, in turn, greatly reduces its military requirements. That should break the "vicious circle" in Russian history, and it might also break what Hedlund calls the "Muscovy lock-in": that is, a patrimonial state where property rights can be arbitrarily reallocated by the ruler, where law is designed to regiment society, not to limit the state and protect individual rights, where the ruler and his clique seek to maximize their income with little regard for overall economic product. Russia's new direction, however, will soon not be toward Europe, but it will have some distinctive Russian features, although not those expected by its contemporary anti-Westernizers. Nor is it likely to be toward East Asia, on the paths that China and Vietnam are traveling. Rather Russia is more likely to become a "normal country" in the sense that most of the countries in the world are normal – weak states with inefficient and unstable alloca-tions of property rights, a considerable degree of authoritarianism, and poorly per-forming economies.

Perhaps Russia will escape that fate, but the chances decline as time passes, allow-ing a new lock-in to changed, but still ineffective, institutions. Still, outside Europe there is a model that Russia could follow that leads to a promising outcome: Turkey. Kemal Mustafa Ataturk saw Turkey's loss of the Ottoman Empire as a chance for radical change in Turkish political institutions. Although ruling as a dictator and waving the banner of Turkish nationalism, he skillfully isolated one and then another set of opponents, stealthily moving the regime toward a liberal constitution order. His Kemalist successors have carried through but have failed to make permanent the binary shift from "the rule of the one" to the "rule of the many." Two factors have caused the periodic reversals, Kurdish nationalism and residual legacies of Islamic political culture. Still, Turkey has avoided a permanent relapse.

The parallels with Russia are striking. If Putin's successor, Dmitry Medvedev, were to adopt a Kemalist strategy, he would pretend to be anti-Western while actually installing the basic components of liberal order in Russia. He would have to reject efforts to regain lost Soviet territories, and eventually he would have to confront several reactionary groups, neutralize or defeat them, and bring all major political factions to accept a constitutional deal. Even then, making it stick long enough to become permanent would be a challenge but not insurmountable.

Structural factors count heavily in determining Russia's future, but, finally, leaders will decide it, albeit within the narrow limits of what structural realities make possible. Loss of empire, economic upheaval, and military weakness are the most significant consequences of the collapse of the Soviet Union, potentially disrupting Russia's long-enduring path dependence. They greatly widen limits of the possible in Russia today, as the twentieth anniversary of the end of the Soviet Union approaches. For the first time in their history, Russian leaders with exceptional vision and very good fortune could then put their country on a liberal path. The odds, however, do not favor this outcome, and the window of opportunity will not remain open for long.

References

1. Shenfield, S. (2001). *Russian Fascism: Traditions, Tendencies, Movements*. M. E. Sharpe, Armonk, NY.
2. Sestanovich, S. (1994). "Russia Turns the Corner," *Foreign Affairs*, 73/1: 83–98.
3. McFaul, M. (1997). *Russia's 1996 Election: The End of Polarized Politics*. Hoover Institution Press, Stanford, CA.
4. Edwards, J., and Kemp, Jack (chairmen) (2006). "Russia's Wrong Direction: What the United States Can and Should Do." Task Force Report, Council on Foreign Relations, New York.
5. Cohen, S. F. (2001). *Failed Crusade: America and the Tragedy of Post-Communist Russia*. W. W. Norton, New York.
6. Reddaway, P., and Glinski, D. (2001). *The Tragedy of Market Reforms: Market Bolshevism against Democracy*. US Institute of Peace, Washington.
7. Fish, M. S. (2005). *Democracy Derailed in Russia. The Failure of Open Politics*. Cambridge University Press, New York.
8. Huntington, S. P. (1999). T*he Clash of Civilizations and the Remaking of World Order*. Simon & Schuster, New York.
9. Makarov, Nikolai (Dec. 19, 2003). Russian Information Agency (RIA), Moscow.
10. David, Paul (1985). "Clio and the Economics of QWERTY," *American Economic Review*, 75/2: 332–37.
11. Arthur, W. B. (1988). "Self-Reinforcing Mechanisms," in P. Anderson, K. Arrow, and D. Pines (eds.), *The Economy as an Evolving Complex System*. University of Michigan Press, Ann Arbor, MI, 9–14.
12. Pierson, P. (2000). "Increasing Returns, Path Dependence, and the Study of Politics," *American Political Science Review*, 94/2: 251–67.
13. Kohn, H. (1944). *The Idea of Nationalism: A Study of its Origins and its Background*. Macmillan, New York.
14. Pye, L. W., and Verba, S. (eds.) (1965). *Political Culture and Political Development*. Princeton University Press, Princeton.
15. Harrison, L. (2006). *The Central Liberal Truth: How Politics Can Change a Culture and Save Itself*. Oxford University Press, New York.
16. North, D. C. (1981). *Structure and Change in Economic History*. W. W. Norton, New York.
17. North, D. C. (1990). *Institutions, Institutional Change, and Economic Performance*. Cambridge University Press, New York.
18. Hedlund, Stefan (2005). *Russian Path Dependence*. Routledge, London.
19. Gerschenkron, A. (1970). *Europe in the Russian Mirror*. Cambridge University Press, Cambridge.
20. Owen, T. C. (1991). *The Corporation under Russian Law, 1800–1917: A Study in Tsarist Economic Policy*. Cambridge University Press, New York.
21. Odom, W. E. (1987). "How Far Can Soviet Reform Go?" *Problems of Communism*, 36/6: 18–34.
22. Odom, W. E. (1998). *The Collapse of the Soviet Military*. Yale University Press, New Haven.
23. Odom, W. E., and Dujarric, R. (2004). *America's Inadvertent Empire*. Yale University Press, New Haven.
24. Lipset, S. (1994). "The Social Requisites of Democracy," *American Sociological Review*, 59/1: 1–22.
25. Dahl, R. A. (1971). *Polyarchy: Participation and Opposition*. Yale University Press, New Haven.

26. Moore, Barrington, Jr. (1966). *Social Origins of Dictatorship and Democracy: Lord and Peasant in the Making of the Modern World*. Beacon Press, Boston.
27. Levi, M. (1988). *Of Rule and Revenue*. University of California Press, Berkeley.
28. Ostrowski, D. (1999). *Muscovy and the Mongols: Cross-Cultural Influences on the Steppe Frontier, 1303–1589*. Cambridge University Press, New York.
29. Meyer, H. (December 27, 2005). Associated Press, Moscow.
30. Gurin, C. (2005). "Poll Indicates Weak Support for Many Democratic Rights," *Eurasian Daily Monitor* (Oct. 29). Jamestown Foundation, Washington.
31. Huntington, S. P. (1968). *Political Order in Changing Societies*. Yale University Press, New Haven.
32. Migdal, J. (1987). *Strong Societies and Weak States: State–Society Relations and State Capabilities in the Third World*. Princeton University Press, Princeton.
33. Ellman, M. (ed.) (2006). *Russian Oil: Bonanza or Curse?* Anthem Press, New York.
34. Eberstadt, N. (1999). "Russia: Too Sick to Matter," *Policy Review* (June–July), 3–24.

Further Reading

Fish, Steven M. (2005). *Democracy Derailed in Russia: The Failure of Open Politics*. Cambridge University Press, New York. A rather technical but accessible analysis that gives both a grass-roots and a top-level view of Russia under Putin. The author remains cautiously optimistic about the future of democracy in Russia.

Gaddy, Clifford, and Hill, Fiona (2003). *Siberian Curse: How Communist Planners Left Russia out in the Cold*. Brookings Institution, Washington. On environmental, demographic, and economic legacies that significantly affect Russia's future.

Hedlund, Stefan (2006). *Russian Path Dependency*. Routledge, London. A path-breaking study using "path-dependence" theory to interpret Russian history and to speculate on Russia's future.

Hoffman, David (2003). *The Oligarchs: Wealth and Power in the New Russia*, Public Affairs, New York. Very accessible account of the privatization process and the emergence of a few multi-billionaires.

McDaniel, Tim (1996). *Agony of the Russia Idea*. Princeton University Press, Princeton. Useful for understanding Russian "political culture" and how it impedes liberal reforms.

Reddaway, Peter, and Orttung, Robert W. (eds.) (2004 and 2005). *The Dynamics of Russian Politics: Putin's Reform of Federal–Regional Relations*. 2 vols. Rowan and Littlefield, Lanham, MD. Collections of essays by both Western and Russian scholars that provide a textured assessment of local politics and the regions' relationship with Moscow.

Index